International Studies of the
Committee on International Relations
University of Notre Dame

The Volunteer Army and

Allied Intervention

in South Russia, 1917-1921

THE VOLUNTEER ARMY
and

A Study in the Politics and Diplomacy
of the Russian Civil War

ALLIED INTERVENTION

IN SOUTH RUSSIA,
1917-1921

By George A. Brinkley

UNIVERSITY OF NOTRE DAME PRESS · 1966

Library of Congress Catalog Card Number: 66-15501

Manufactured in the United States

TO ANN

rge A. Brinkley, assistant professor of
rnment and international studies at
University of Notre Dame, received
Ph.D. from Columbia University. The
ent work is enriched by a year of re-
ch in the USSR.

PREFACE

The Russian civil war and the accompanying Allied intervention from 1917 to 1921 have long been recognized as major events in the great upheaval which was unleashed by World War I. Yet today, almost half a century after these events, they remain less than fully analyzed or even chronicled. One of the reasons for this situation lies in the extreme complexity of the international struggle which took place on the territory of the former Russian Empire. Armies, political parties, and ideological issues proliferated rapidly in the virulent breeding ground created by the collapse of both political order and established value systems in Russia. Moreover, the international problems of the first World War in history served to complicate further any question thrown up by the general catastrophe.

War, civil war, and foreign intervention were not new phenomena in world history in 1917, of course. Not even their simultaneous appearance at the same focal point of international politics was unprecedented. But now this combination of international crisis patterns took place in the context of a revolutionary transition affecting the traditional structure of diplomacy and international law and putting radically opposed ideologies at the center of political action. The resulting confusion, imposed on Europe by the breakdown of the old order, put into question many of the legal and moral foundations of the existing state system. Governments had for the first time been obliged to marshal all of the resources of the nation in a massive effort which, with it all, led not to quick victory but to virtual collapse for all of the belligerents.

It was in this state of stress that Russia experienced a military and political paralysis, and her allies, Britain and France, were faced with the prospect of losing a partner considered essential to victory. The deterioration of Russian power before the March Revolution of 1917 was a serious blow to the Entente in the war against Germany. It became a crisis of major proportions when the Bolsheviks seized control of the state in November 1917 and immediately issued a call for peace to be brought about by popular revolution in all of the belligerent countries. By November 1918, when World War I ended, Russia was in the throes of an all-embracing civil war, and the Allies were committed to a variety of forces which had remained loyal to the Entente and now sought a continuation of aid to overthrow the Bolshevik regime.

With the Armistice in November 1918, some Allied spokesmen argued that all reason for continuing the intervention had ended, while others pointed to an obligation to stand by those forces in Russia to whom commitments had already been made and stressed the importance of the anti-Bolshevik war as a necessary part of the struggle to restore peace and order to Europe. Choice between these two points of view was extremely difficult for the Allied governments. The intervention, undertaken initially simply as a means to continue the war against Germany, would require a much broader range of policy decisions after November 1918, but such decisions were made only haphazardly, if at all. The Allies, trying to treat the Russian problem as merely a final battle of World War I, tended to evade the responsibility which inevitably accompanied the continuation of the intervention in a revolutionary situation. They thus neither conspired to make an all-out military effort nor consistently pursued the opportunities for peacemaking.

Meanwhile the Russian civil war grew into a major conflict. The first important resistance to the Bolshevik regime had come chiefly from two elements: from a variety of socialist parties which rejected Bolshevik policies and from the non-Russian borderlands which demanded autonomy. The most important of the latter, the Ukraine and Transcaucasia, were initially also led by socialists, although the Cossack areas, which also resisted Bolshevik encroachment, tended toward more conservative leadership. The first real turning point for the major groups in both of these elements of opposition was the dis-

missal of the Constituent Assembly in January 1918. Once this demo-
cratically elected body, intended as the determiner of Russia's future
structure and policies, had been forcibly disbanded by the Bolsheviks, both the popular Socialist Revolutionaries and the non-Russian
borderlands separated themselves from the Soviet power center and
took up positions of active resistance and independence.

This stage of the civil war was quickly superseded, however, by the
emergence in the autumn of 1918 of more conservative forces, both
in Siberia and in South Russia, which proved themselves considerably
more capable of military action by virtue of their attraction of the
largest number of professional army officers. Significant political elements, particularly the Constitutional Democrats (Kadets), who had
been the major party in the establishment of the first Provisional
government in March 1917, also attached themselves to these military forces, but the most important change which occurred at this
stage of the war was the assertion of leadership by the military. While
many of the top military leaders were moderate in their political
views, a notable effect of this shift was the imposition of a kind of
moratorium on political debate and democratic organization within
the major anti-Bolshevik Russian forces for the sake of military victory.

In South Russia the chief force which rose to the challenge in this
second stage, after a long period of organization, was the Volunteer
Army. Founded by two former commanders-in-chief of the Russian
army, Generals Alekseev and Kornilov, and subsequently led for two
years by General Denikin and at the end by General Wrangel, this
army relied heavily on Cossack support, stood for a temporary military
dictatorship and the reincorporation of the borderland nationalities
which had separated themselves from Russia. It also called for delay-
ing any major decisions on such matters as agrarian reform and reorganization of the state structure until victory over the Bolsheviks had
been won and a new constituent assembly could be elected. For these
reasons, the Volunteer Army clashed both with the anti-Bolshevik
socialists who had the broadest popular following and with the non-
Russian borderland governments which controlled large sections of
the South.

The Volunteers did attract Allied attention and obtained extensive
support, especially from the British, but relations with the Allies were
not smooth or always cordial. Volunteer relations with the French in
fact reached a point of open hostility in the spring and summer of
1919 at the very moment when Allied aid was most essential. The

policies and actions of the Volunteers were easily, if not always fairly, subjected to charges of reaction and tsarist restoration, a reputation that helped to alienate potential allies both in Russia and abroad despite efforts by General Denikin to correct this situation. For these and other reasons the Volunteers failed, just as others, to oust the Bolsheviks from power.

This study of the Volunteer Army and its relations with the Allied Powers and the borderland states proceeds on the assumption that neither the domestic arena in which the Russian struggle occurred nor the international setting and meaning of these events can be properly understood in isolation from each other. Both must be treated simultaneously, and this of course imposes a problem with regard to the judicious selection of relevant material and events with which to deal. It would be foolish for anyone to claim infallibility in making such a selection, but it is important to stress the point here that in view of the special significance attached to the interrelationship between domestic upheaval and foreign involvement nothing less than the requisite treatment of both aspects could serve the purpose at hand.

While treating two different manifestations of the general question at the same time, however, this study does not presume to cover all aspects of the civil war or of the intervention therein. On the contrary, it is deliberately limited to that part of the general upheaval which took place in South Russia. The focus throughout is on the political, and even more accurately on the international political, aspects of the struggle in South Russia. The tide of military battle, for example, is not treated in detail since it must be regarded as secondary to the battle of political issues and foreign entanglement. The same point must be made with regard to the policies and actions of the Allied Powers. While their domestic conditions, their diplomacy in the World War and at the Paris Peace Conference, and their own party struggles are all a part of the general environment of the events in question, they are discussed only in so far as they impinge directly on the intervention and more particularly on the intervention in South Russia. Of major concern here, therefore, is the intervention as it operated in the field, as it appeared in the confused and often contradictory relations between Allied agents and forces, on the one hand, and, on the other hand, the Russian elements which they sought in one manner or another to aid.

Finally, this study is focused on the Volunteer Army both because it was the major anti-Bolshevik force in South Russia and because in this area it was the chief recipient of Allied aid and attention during the civil war period. Indeed, after mid-1919 Allied assistance was primarily directed to the Volunteer Army as the one real prospect for victory over the Bolsheviks. Even where British and French intervention forces were directly involved with non-Russian borderland nationalities and governments in the South, relations with the Volunteers constituted a decisive consideration for all concerned. In dealing with the Allied intervention in these areas this study thus puts relations with the Volunteer Army at the center of attention.

While these restrictions on the scope of this study are necessary, it should also be noted that the part of the civil war and intervention which took place in South Russia was indeed probably the most meaningful of all. In the first place it was in the South where the most notable formations of both military and political forces arose in opposition to the Bolshevik regime. It was in South Russia that the clearest confrontations developed between socialism and Bolshevism, between liberalism and conservatism, between Great Russian chauvinism and non-Russian nationalism, and between different Allied policies. The South, in short, demonstrated in microcosm all of the problems raised by the civil war and the intervention.

For these reasons South Russia may be regarded as the most significant, and the most complex, of all the areas of the war. It is, therefore, of notable importance that it is this area which has been given the least attention by scholars dealing with the intervention. Although studies of the activities and fate of the non-Russian nationalities in the South, of the formation and operation of the Red Army, and of the decision-making of the Allied Powers at the Peace Conference in Paris are all available, the major anti-Bolshevik force and the intervention in South Russia have received far less attention. The object of this study is, therefore, to focus research on the interrelations between the intervening Powers and the Volunteer Army. Its major purpose is to analyze the tortuous course of Allied-Volunteer relations and the causes for the conflicts within the anti-Bolshevik camp in the South in order to reach conclusions on their failure.

The fulfillment of this purpose, of course, required the availability of primary sources. No researcher in the field of international affairs and Russian history is likely to be satisfied with the materials available, and this author admits to numerous frustrations in his efforts to gain access to collections which might have added more detail. However, the situation with regard to research in the history of the Russian revolution and civil war and the Allied intervention has substantially improved in recent years. Significant glimpses into German, French, and British materials have been allowed to scholars, the Soviet Union has published useful documentary collections, and, most importantly here, several archives in the United States have been opened. This work relies especially heavily on primary materials found in the Columbia University Russian Archive and the Hoover Library, many of which were not accessible a few years ago. While these sources allow a detailed study of a sort impossible in the past, it is also important to note that there is a wealth of memoir material in this field, both published and unpublished, much of which has not been fully exploited. Finally, in the matter of sources the author has attempted throughout to cite both published and unpublished sources and, where it seemed useful, to note English translations as well, although this has naturally resulted in rather lengthy notes. It is hoped that this will add a value to the work which a more simplified system of notation would preclude.

Winston Churchill once wrote that the Volunteer Army should be made the subject of "an historical monograph to be read with gratitude by all their comrades in the British Empire, in France, in Italy and in the United States" (*The World Crisis: The Aftermath*, p. 87). The author (who incidentally does not anticipate such gratitude) accepted this suggestion while engaged in work at the Russian Institute of Columbia University and owes a special acknowledgement of thanks for assistance and advice in the preparation of this study to Professors Philip E. Mosely and Henry L. Roberts, whose wise counsel was largely responsible for the successful conversion of the idea into its written form. He also wishes to express his special gratitude to the Ford Foundation and the University of Notre Dame, which provided financial support; to the Inter-University Committee on Travel Grants, which made it possible to do a part of the research in the Soviet Union; to Professor S. D. Kertesz of Notre Dame's Program of Soviet and East European Studies for his encouragement and generous assistance; to the Curator of the Columbia University Russian Archive, Mr. L. F. Magerovsky, and the then Curator of Slavic materials at the Hoover Library, Mr. Witold S. Sworakowski, both of whom provided invaluable guidance through the vast storehouses of papers and documents over which they preside; to Mrs. Xenia Denikin and Baroness Olga Wrangel, who graciously extended permission to use materials in their care; to the staff of the Foreign Affairs Section of the United States National Archives for their valuable aid; and to the readers of the manuscript who offered invaluable suggestions for improving it, Professors John Thompson of Indiana University, Richard Ullman of Princeton University, and John Bradley of Manchester University. Of course, any deficiencies which remain in this work are attributable to no one but the author himself.

To my wife, who contributed so much to its preparation, this book is dedicated.

December, 1965   GEORGE BRINKLEY

CONTENTS

xvii

PART I

RUSSIA AND THE WORLD WAR

1: THE DISINTEGRATION OF RUSSIA

In that fateful first week of November 1917, in the midst of World War I, five of Russia's top generals were languishing in a converted monastery prison in the unimportant village of Bykhov. One month earlier they had constituted the high command of the Russian army and its best front commanders. One month later they would be engaged in a crusade to liberate their country as the leaders of a new Volunteer Army hastily formed in the southern provinces. But in November, at the time of the Bolshevik Revolution, they—Generals L. G. Kornilov, A. I. Denikin, A. S. Lukomskii, I. P. Romanovskii, and S. L. Markov, together with a number of junior officers—were under arrest, charged with treason against the Russian Republic. Their incarceration had been ordered by Alexander Kerenskii, prime minister and war minister of the Provisional government. Since the armed guard stationed at the prison was in fact a detachment of soldiers loyal to the "prisoners," particularly to the chief among them, Kornilov, these generals could have fled their cells at any time. They had, however, chosen to submit their case to public trial and would not leave Bykhov so long as the promise of open confrontation with their accuser, Kerenskii, was assured.[1]

The fate of these five generals would have been of some importance for Russia in any circumstances, but it was of particular significance in the autumn of 1917. The Kornilov-Kerenskii conflict marked the culmination of an ominous trend toward disintegration which had scarred the much heralded democratic revolution in Russia from its beginning in March 1917.[2] Instead of bringing unity and a reinvigoration of the war effort, as Russia's allies, Britain and France, had hoped and the Provisional government's first foreign minister, Paul Miliukov, had promised, the revolution had brought into the open that long-festering antagonism between socialist and conservative elements

3

which prevented the establishment of stable authority and frustrated efforts to restore order and discipline among the troops.[3] The Constitutional Democratic (Kadet) party which had assumed leadership in the new government established by the Duma on March 15 seemed, of all Russian parties, the most admirably suited to converting Russia from autocracy to a moderate constitutional regime in the image of West European governments. As a leading spokesman for the Kadets and then for the Provisional government, Miliukov had earned great respect both in Russia and abroad for his sharp criticism of the old regime's inadequacies and his call for the closest union with the Western democracies. Yet when it came to the realities of power, none of Russia's parties was prepared to meet the crisis, perhaps least of all the moderate Kadets whose westernized platform and intellectual character separated them from the masses and made them the easy target of both Left and Right.

The Left, composed predominantly of Socialist Revolutionaries and Social Democrats representing the peasants and workers respectively in the increasingly powerful soviets, saw its duty to lie in continuous pressure on the government for domestic reforms and if not an end to the World War, then at least a revision of its aims to repudiate the policy of secret diplomacy and territorial acquisitions of the fallen tsarist regime.[4] The Right, whose strength lay in centuries of Russian tradition, in the existing bureaucracy, and in the inclination of the military to see salvation only in firm authority and discipline, demanded a postponement of reforms and loyal adherence to the wartime alliance and its secret agreements, which, among other things, promised control of the Turkish Straits to Russia as a reward for victory. The growing power of the soviets, particularly in the armed forces, was viewed as a threat to the very foundations of political order and military effectiveness.[5] Caught between these two points of view, the Provisional government had found itself challenged both for its modest attempts to compromise with the soviets and for its efforts to keep Russia in the war. Neither the prospect of a popularly elected Constituent Assembly, for which elections had to be postponed until November, nor attempts to put a better face, a "democratic" interpretation, on the wartime agreements with Britain and France could resolve the problems of political and economic collapse or inspire a people fed up with fighting and tempted by slogans of peace and social revolution.[6]

Under the circumstances existing in Russia, popular emotions were easily aroused; what might have been simply a debate over war aims and methods of reform had become instead a prolonged crisis in which the government steadily lost both its support and its ability to act. During May uncontrollable street demonstrations had brought the government to the brink of collapse. General Kornilov, then commander of the Petrograd military district and responsible for keeping order in the capital, had found his troops joining the mobs rather than curbing them.[7] Miliukov's resignation, forced because of his persistent refusal to renounce the principle of territorial acquisitions, and the bringing of more socialists into the government had temporarily saved the day, but it had also set a precedent for future crises.[8] Kerenskii, initially the only member of the Petrograd soviet in the government, took over the post of war minister in the new cabinet and began a campaign both to "democratize" the army and to raise morale by a new offensive. But his success in the former had only further undermined the authority of the officers, while his failure with the latter had led General Kornilov to wire him angrily from the front that his policies were creating havoc while the country was perishing.[9] A British observer of the ill-fated July offensive, Major General Sir Alfred Knox, had reported to London that the Russian army was "irretrievably ruined as a fighting organisation."[10] Nor was the trouble only at the front. The "July Days" in the capital had created a new crisis which resulted in the resignation of most of the Kadets still in the government.

Kerenskii, who then became prime minister, was no radical revolutionary, nor were the leaders of the soviets at this stage, for the majority control in the soviets was still composed chiefly of moderate Social Democrats (Mensheviks) and Socialist Revolutionaries dedicated to the principles of democratic government and gradual reform.[11] However, the instability of the government, the fear on the Left in general of a return of the reactionaries, and the complete exhaustion of the country in its efforts to continue the war had all contributed to a situation which offered opportunities for the extremists, notably the Bolshevik Social Democrats, to discredit the moderates and, even when driven underground, to win increasing support in both the soviets and in the population at large. By September a Bolshevik-Left Socialist Revolutionary coalition had become predominant on the Left, and on the Right conservative elements had gravitated toward support for a military coup.

It was in these circumstances that the conflict had erupted between

Kerenskii and General Kornilov, now the commander-in-chief and the favorite of the advocates of repressive action against the Left. During September a misunderstanding, brought about largely by rumors and the activities of self-styled mediaries, had led Kerenskii to interpret new demands on the restoration of strong government and military discipline from Kornilov as an ultimatum to be backed by military action against the soviets and followed by the establishment of a military dictatorship. He had responded by ordering Kornilov's arrest and calling on the Left to support him. Kornilov in turn had denounced Kerenskii and called for public backing to install a new government. Kornilov, who had been provoked into his "treason" by what he thought was a betrayal by Kerenskii, was to a large extent—just as Kerenskii—a victim of circumstances. He was only partially aware of the plots to overthrow the government being hatched by others, including some of his own advisers, who hoped to use him to establish a dictatorship. However, he was one of many now convinced that the Bolsheviks were preparing a repeat of the July demonstrations and an attempt to seize power. While not reactionary in his views[12]—in fact he still had no political program as such—Kornilov was certain in his own mind that the Bolsheviks, and indeed many other socialists, were traitors to Russia and would make her easy prey for Germany.

Moreover, despite their earlier differences, he and Kerenskii had agreed on the need to send reliable troops to Petrograd, and he had been led to believe by his talks on September 5 with Boris Savinkov, Kerenskii's deputy in the war ministry, that Kerenskii was now prepared to take a stand against the extreme Left and strengthen the government's position by declaring martial law in the capital. Shortly thereafter the self-appointed intermediary, V. N. L'vov, even appeared to bring from Kerenskii an oblique offer to resign in Kornilov's favor. Although in fact Kerenskii had made no such suggestion, Kornilov naively assumed that he was being invited to replace the prime minister or at least to join him in a shared exercise of the highest authority in a reorganized government. Just as Kornilov was initiating action based on these mistaken assumptions, Kerenskii's worst fears had been aroused by a warning on September 8 from the same V. N. L'vov, who now reported that Kornilov was demanding the immediate resignation of the government and the delegation of full power to himself.

Believing that Kornilov was going to use the troops headed for Petrograd to carry out a military coup and might even be planning his assassination, Kerenskii panicked and dramatically shifted his position. Responding instinctively and ignoring the advice of others, among them Savinkov, he called upon the Petrograd soviet, including the Bolsheviks, to save the government from the expected counterrevolution. Upon receiving Kerenskii's order for his removal on September 9, Kornilov in turn mistakenly concluded that he had been betrayed by Kerenskii (who now declared himself commander-in-chief) and by Savinkov (who was named military governor of Petrograd to prepare its defense) in a scheme to oust him as commander of the army. Partly because of his impetuous character and partly because of his convictions, Kornilov then plunged headlong into the showdown with Kerenskii. Seeing himself as the savior of his country, he had vowed to carry out the very seizure of power which he had been accused of plotting.[13]

As a capable commander and patriot who wanted to see Russia strong and able to continue the war, Kornilov had received encouragement both before and after the open break with Kerenskii from liberal as well as conservative political circles, from the officer corps, and, not least in importance, from the Allied military representatives in Petrograd and at headquarters who were in close contact with him and sympathetic to his cause.[14] Although the Allied ambassadors maintained a policy of official noninvolvement and rejected requests from Kornilov's backers for open support, the coincidental presence of a British armored car brigade among the troops being moved toward the capital by Kornilov lent weight to Bolshevik charges that the Allies were behind a plot to overthrow the government.[15] Kerenskii himself charged that a British agent delivered large sums of money to Kornilov and categorically rejected the appeal of the Allied governments that he "come to terms with General Kornilov, not only in the interests of Russia herself, but in that of the Allies."[16]

While Kerenskii had rejected the offer of mediation by the Allied ambassadors, he had not, on the other hand, rejected the offer of the retired army commander-in-chief, General M. V. Alekseev, to intercede in the dispute. Kornilov, who soon realized the futility and danger of a violent conflict when his troops were easily halted by the forces hastily mobilized by the soviet, had also agreed to Alekseev's mediation and on September 14 had submitted to arrest on the understanding that Kerenskii would act to restore normal command relations in the army and allow a fair and open trial for him and his associates.[17] The commander of the southwestern front, General A. I. Denikin, and his staff had been arrested by their "political com-

missar" in Berdychev and moved to Bykhov, where this impressive
gathering of Russia's military leadership then awaited further developments.[18] General Alekseev had temporarily assumed the post of
chief of staff (Kerenskii himself took over as commander-in-chief)
until the appointment of General N. N. Dukhonin.

Meanwhile, the fiasco of the "Kornilov affair" had, more than anything else, given the Bolsheviks new hopes for seizing power for themselves. Kerenskii, who had in effect turned over the defense of the
capital to the Petrograd soviet, now under the influence of Bolshevik
leadership, could not despite his vigorous efforts work the miracle
required to put the government back in control of events. Consequently, on the night of November 6–7 the Bolsheviks succeeded in
carrying out a coup, using the armed guard of the soviet, which ousted
the government with startling ease. A small band of Cossacks under
General P. N. Krasnov, which Kerenskii finally rallied to his defense,
proved totally inadequate to the task; Krasnov was captured and held
for a time by the Bolsheviks, and Kerenskii fled abroad.[19] As the head
of the new government, or Council of People's Commissars, V. I.
Lenin (Ulianov) declared to the assembled Congress of Soviets on
November 8 that the Soviet government would take Russia out of the
hated war, renounce annexations and indemnities, and at last give
peace, food, and the land to the people. A new era had begun.

                              *   *   *   *   *   *

In the course of more than a decade of polemical struggle within
the Russian Social Democratic party prior to 1917, Lenin had emerged
as the undisputed leader of its radical, revolutionary wing. He had,
indeed, largely created this revolutionary Left wing of the party and
had cleverly, if inaccurately, dubbed it the Bolshevik (majority) faction after instigating a split with the larger "minority" (Menshevik)
element at the party's second congress in 1903. From that time on the
Bolshevik faction had distinguished itself from the more moderate
Mensheviks by two main facets of its credo, which constituted the
essence of Lenin's revision of Marxism: (1) the insistence that a small,
tightly disciplined, conspiratorial organization was essential to the
seizure of power, the immediate goal, and (2) the conviction that this
party must unconditionally dedicate itself to bringing about a world-
wide revolution, which would ultimately overthrow all existing governments, beginning with the European capitalist regimes, and
establish an international socialist system.[20]

In his refuge in Switzerland during the war years, Lenin had gradually formulated the basic outlines of the Bolshevik tactics designed to bring the party to power and instigate revolution throughout Europe. Proceeding from the conviction that all of the belligerent Powers were "ripe" for revolution, Lenin had sought successfully to win control of the soviets, as the spontaneously developed instrument of popular opposition to the "imperialist" war, and then to use the soviets to win control of the country.[21] Once in power, the task, in Lenin's view, was to appeal directly to the "oppressed masses" of Europe, especially of Germany, to overthrow their governments and join with Russia in a truly "just" and "lasting" peace on the basis of the Bolshevik program. His famous slogan of "peace" was, therefore, closely bound up with his plan of revolution. Believing that a "democratic" peace could be achieved only through a conversion of the existing war into a civil war of the masses against all of the belligerent governments, he had formulated his "foreign policy" in the following terms as early as 1915:

> We would propose peace to all the belligerents on the condition of the liberation of colonies and all dependent and oppressed nations which are denied full rights. Neither Germany nor England and France would accept this condition under their present governments. Then we would have to prepare and conduct a revolutionary war; that is, we would not only introduce by the most decisive measures our whole minimum program [in Russia], but also begin systematically to raise revolts by all peoples presently oppressed by the Great Russians, all colonies and dependent countries of Asia (India, China, Persia, and others) and also—and first of all—we would rouse the socialist proletariat of Europe to a revolt against its governments, in spite of its social-chauvinists.[22]

Lenin thus expected that a victory for the Bolsheviks in Russia would be the "prologue of the world socialist revolution."[23] Although Russia's backwardness prevented her from carrying the revolution forward alone, the Western proletariat would assure its spread, and the very effort of Europe's governments to resist it would bring the revolution "a hundred times closer."[24] The first official act of the new government, on November 8, 1917, was to issue the Decree on Peace, calling upon the workers of Europe to take up the task of "the liberation of mankind from the horrors of war" if their governments did not comply with Bolshevik terms.[25] The new commissar of foreign affairs, Leon Trotskii, set the tone of the new diplomacy of revolution in one of his first notes to the Allies:

The government of the victorious revolution [he declared] does not
need the recognition of professional capitalist diplomacy. But we
ask the peoples: does reactionary diplomacy reflect their ideas and
aspirations? Do the peoples agree to permit diplomacy to bypass
the great opportunity for peace opened by the Russian revolution?
. . . Soldiers, workers, and peasants of France, England, Italy, the
United States, Belgium, Serbia. . . . We await your representatives.
Act![26]

None of this, of course, relieved the Bolshevik regime of the problems of power, either domestically or internationally, It could not,
even if it wished, abdicate from the world of international politics.
Nor could it ignore the delapidated condition of Russia's political
institutions and armed forces. The peace decree, therefore, was still
an appeal for peace. Neither Trotskii nor Lenin wanted to negotiate
a separate peace with Germany. In fact they did not want to negotiate
a peace in the traditional sense with any of the existing governments.
But both recognized at least the necessity of a truce to allow their
propaganda to work and permit time to prepare for whatever future
action had to be taken.

In the meantime, the Bolshevik slogan of peace was a major asset in
the regime's efforts to remain in power and extend its control over
the country. In so far as the peace slogan, together with the slogans of
land and bread, would attract the support of the war-weary and land-
hungry peasant masses as well as the proletariat, the Bolshevik government could count upon significant strength throughout the country.
However there were, generally speaking, two serious obstacles which
stood in the way of immediate success for the reintegration of Russia
under Bolshevik leadership. In the first place, the Bolshevik party
remained in a distinct minority, with its continuance in power largely
dependent upon its ability to retain its initial identification with popular desires which were in fact closer to Socialist Revolutionary and
Menshevik thinking than to the peculiarly internationalist revolutionary outlook of the Bolshevik leadership. Secondly, the new regime, as
its opponents, would have to contend with the seriously debilitating
consequences of Russia's disintegration along nationality lines which
had been gaining momentum throughout 1917.

*   *   *   *   *   *

Russian had already begun to fall apart at its national seams during
the period of the Provisional government. A polyglot conglomeration
of nationalities, the Russian Empire had been held together by the

power and dominant position of the Russians over the non-Russian elements. With the disappearance of that power, symbolized by the person of the Tsar, the subordinate nationalities had begun to demand their rights, particularly in the form of political and cultural autonomy within a new democratic state. The coming to power of the Bolsheviks only heightened the determination of the geographically peripheral peoples to govern themselves, not simply because the Bolsheviks propagated the slogan of national self-determination (while, of course, having a long-range goal of amalgamating all nations into one), but primarily because of the concern among most of the borderland leaders over the consequences of continued association with a Soviet Russia. While this suspicion was only vaguely defined at first, it would in time become the basis of the continued disintegration of the former Russian state into its many parts. This was particularly true in the case of the southern borderlands. It was thus of major significance that non-Bolshevik, and in some cases strongly anti-Bolshevik, governments were in power in almost all of South Russia when the Soviet regime was established in Petrograd.[27]

In the Ukraine, the Rada (parliament) and its executive body—the Secretariat, headed by a Ukrainian Social Democrat, Volodimir Vynnychenko—had been recognized as an autonomous government by Kerenskii in September. Following the Bolshevik coup, this government refused to recognize the Soviet government's authority over the Ukraine and on November 20 declared instead the establishment of a Ukrainian People's Republic.[28] Only one day later this new Republic began the process of regrouping all Ukrainian troops on Ukrainian territory. General D. G. Shcherbachev, the former commander of Russian forces on the Rumanian front, tentatively agreed to accept command over them.[29]

In the Crimea, to the south, the Tatar National party (founded in July 1917 on a moderately liberal platform of federation with Russia and cultural autonomy) and the Kadet party organization (chiefly representing the Crimean Russian inhabitants) were the most important politically active elements.[30] Although neither took an extreme political position, their rivalry for control of the Crimea and their diametrically opposed attitudes toward the Turks kept them in opposition to each other even though they shared a mutual hostility toward the Bolsheviks.

On November 26, 1917, a Tatar constituent assembly, elected from the Tatar population, assumed authority in Simferopol, introduced a

Crimean constitution, and appointed a five-man directorate headed by the Crimean Mufti and a leader of the Tatar National party, Chelibidzhan Chelibiev. Another National party member, Dzhafer Sejdamet, was named military commander and minister of foreign affairs. These two leaders, however, subsequently split over how to deal with the Bolsheviks, who were entrenched in Sevastopol but not fully supported by the soviets. This struggle within the Tatar government, with Chelibiev favoring some agreement with the Bolsheviks and Sejdamet strongly opposing such a move, gravely weakened its position, and a Bolshevik victory seemed likely. However, the Kadet party organization, led by S. S. Krym and M. M. Vinaver, provided a relatively strong pro-Allied element also contending for power.

To the southeast, the Cossacks had also established their own provisional autonomous governments, mainly by electing representative assemblies (Krug in the Don and Rada in the Kuban) and establishing military executive heads, called "atamans," in their respective territories (voiskos).[31] Relations between the Cossack authorities and the Provisional government had not been very satisfactory to either, especially after Kerenskii became prime minister, although the Cossacks made an effort to prevent a full break. Typical of the Cossack reaction to events of this general period was that of the Don which in April 1917 had voted (1) to recognize the Provisional government, (2) to work for the establishment of representative government with wide autonomy for constituent areas of the republic in close union with Russia, (3) to formulate a land reform which would divide the great estates and turn over repartitional lands to the peasants, and (4) to elect a representative assembly based on universal, equal, direct, and secret suffrage. The Provisional government in turn had recognized the Don government as the local authority. A general Congress of Cossacks held in Petrograd in March had pledged itself to indivisible union with Russia and continuation of the war to victory; the new Don Krug which met for the first time on June 8 confirmed these decisions and on July 2 elected General A. M. Kaledin ataman.[32]

Despite the formal recognition thus established, however, relations between the central government and the Cossacks deteriorated during the summer of 1917. It was the Kornilov affair in particular which precipitated a rupture between the Provisional government and the Don. When the Kornilov-Kerenskii clash occurred, Ataman Kaledin was sharply denounced as a counterrevolutionary by Leftist elements in the Don on the charge that he was a secret ally of Kornilov and implicated in a plot against the government. Giving credence to this allegation, the Provisional government ordered his arrest along with the other generals. From September 18 to 27 the second Krug debated the issues involved and acquitted Kaledin of the charges. Refusing to turn their ataman over for arrest, the Krug demanded instead that Kerenskii send a commission of inquiry to Novocherkassk to clarify the situation. Further identifying its own position, the Krug also, having already elected representatives to the forthcoming Constituent Assembly, declared its refusal to send representatives to the planned Congress of Soviets on the grounds that the Provisional government was still the only valid central government.[33]

Although there was thus officially no secession of the Don from Russia at this point, this sequence of events, coupled with the growing anarchy throughout South Russia, prompted Cossack leaders to act on their own. Thus on October 3 a conference of representatives of the Don, Kuban, Terek, Astrakhan, Kalmyk, Ural, and Dagestan Cossacks was held in Vladikavkaz and agreement was reached on the formation of what was styled the "Southeastern League" (or Union). In the treaty of union then drawn up, the Cossack voiskos guaranteed to each other their "absolute independence . . . in regard to the management of their internal affairs" and set as their goal "the establishment as soon as possible of a Russian democratic federal republic. . . ." Pledging themselves to a mutual struggle "with the enemy" (the Bolsheviks), they declared it their intention to establish a confederation with a government of their representatives at Ekaterinodar in the Kuban voisko, the new government to be headed by V. A. Kharlamov as president.[34]

This initiative on the part of the Cossacks, an effort to unify at least a portion of Russian lands under stable government while declining to go so far as to demand independent status permanently, was a major asset for the anti-Bolshevik movement in general. Although the confederation as such never really materialized beyond the stage of a Cossack alliance with joint consultative bodies formed at a later date, both the Ukrainian Rada and the Moslem Congress in Kokand in November 1917 considered joining the League.[35] In particular the effort meant that those who sought to found a new Russian army could look to the Cossacks for aid and a protected staging area in which to organize an army of liberation for Russia.

An attempt was also made in September to unite the numerous "nationalities" of the Caucasus Mountain region into a "Union of

Mountain Peoples," largely under the leadership of Moslem clerical and secular spokesmen, such as the Imam Nazhmudin Gotsinskii and Prince Nuh-Bek Tarkovskii. During October a merger of the Mountain Union with the Terek Cossacks was agreed upon on the basis of affiliation with the Southeastern League. However, these efforts failed to overcome the obstacles of tribal feuds and Leftist opposition. By early 1918 the Bolsheviks were gaining a strong foothold in Vladikavkaz, where they declared their intention of establishing a Terek Soviet Socialist Republic, and in Petrovsk on the Caspian coast, where a Revolutionary committee was installed. Conservative Moslem authority was subsequently confined largely to central Dagestan.[36]

Farther south, in Transcaucasia, the de facto federation of Georgia, Armenia, and Azerbaidzhan at the same time proved to be highly resistant to Bolshevik advance. The Transcaucasian Commissariat under E. P. Gegechkori, which took over control in November 1917, included representatives of the Armenian Dashnak party and the Azerbaidzhani Mussavat party, but it was based primarily upon the strong Georgain Menshevik organization, which controlled the soviets of the area. Their union was not really a firm one, since the Georgians wanted socialism, the Azerbaidzhanis preferred a more conservative Moslem theocracy, and the Armenians (unlike either) looked to an alliance with the Russians. But in the autumn and winter of 1917–1918, Transcaucasia presented a significant anti-Bolshevik entity on the Turkish Front, where the disintegration of the Russian army posed a serious threat to British operations.[37] The situation across the Caspian in Transcaspia and Turkestan was, however, considerably less stable. A Moslem anti-Bolshevik regime under Mustafa Chokaev in Tashkent was already being driven out of its capital by the Bolsheviks as early as October. Nevertheless, Chokaev was able to stem the tide temporarily and establish a new government in Kokand. Bukhara and other Moslem strongholds also remained unconquered.[38]

This kaleidoscopic array of nationalities and governments in South Russia posed obstacles to Bolshevik conquest, but it also presented almost insurmountable barriers to unification. Each territory had its own peculiar characteristics and traditions, including in many cases a deep-seated hostility toward the Russians engendered by decades of unequal treatment. Where, as in the Central Asian region, the non-Russian native populations were often primitive and illiterate, forming the lower classes of society, national differences were often intensified by class differences. Both the Bolsheviks and the anti-Bolshevik Russians represented a Great Russian ambition to reintegrate the southern borderlands into Russia, although the former significantly showed greater tactical skill by offering "self-determination" under regional Bolshevik regimes.

In most cases the regional governments established before the Bolshevik seizure of power had shown a notable restraint and willingness to look toward some form of federation with a democratic Russia once a Constituent Assembly had been convoked to resolve the problems of reunification. However, in January 1918, when the Bolsheviks summarily dismissed the Constituent Assembly, these governments found themselves compelled either to succumb to Bolshevik control or to become "separatists," declaring their "independence" at least until some acceptable government was established in Great Russia.

* * * * * *

For opponents of Bolshevik rule the disintegration of Russia thus posed both a problem and an opportunity. A united opposition would have been more effective, but, given the situation, it was necessary to take the existence of many separate governments as a fact and try to find in them elements capable of preventing a capitulation to the Bolsheviks and, if possible, capable of continuing the war against the Germans which the Bolsheviks appeared determined to end. However, there was really only one element in the South which was specifically dedicated to this proposition, General Alekseev's Volunteer Army in the Don, an army founded, significantly, not on a nationality or regional basis but on a platform of reintegration of Russia.[39]

When, at the invitation of Ataman Kaledin, General Alekseev arrived in the Don capital, Novocherkassk, on November 15, he set to work immediately to recruit a new army to continue the alliance with the West, but he also encountered serious obstacles. In the first place, the younger Cossacks, despite Kaledin's urging, proved highly susceptible to Bolshevik propaganda and demonstrated the effectiveness of the Bolshevik slogan of peace by "voting with their feet" (in Lenin's words) against more fighting.[40] The only men really available for Alekseev's army were the Russian officers and cadets who could make their way from all over Russia to the Don, no small task despite the financial assistance of officer's organizations and political groups supporting Alekseev. The fact that these men had by the end of 1917 begun pouring in by the hundreds, and later would come by the thousands, was testimony to the existence of a potentially strong force in favor of continuation of the war in alliance with the West. But it would be no easy task to realize that potential under the circumstances existing in the Don.[41]

Ataman Kaledin, himself now nearly exhausted by the burdens of his office, sincerely, almost desperately, hoped to be of assistance to Alekseev, but he was painfully aware of the limitations. Because of the growing opposition to his policies, Kaledin found it necessary even to suggest what he personally knew would be undesirable, that Alekseev might have to move farther south to organize his new army. It was in view of this problem that Alekseev accepted an invitation to address a conference of Don Cossacks and peasants shortly after beginning his work. He explained to them why he had come, assured them that he would guarantee in writing that no troops of the "Alekseev organization" would interfere in politics, and pointed out that his troops would be financed and supplied only by private donations and, he hoped, Allied aid. He, finally, appealed for the support of democratic elements in the area and promised that the army would fight only to save Russia and not for any political party or program.[42]

Alekseev's infectious sincerity plus the fact that he had loyally served the Provisional government even during the Kornilov affair gained him some sympathy in the Don and at least temporarily smoothed relations. It did not, however, bring him any real support for the idea of Cossack participation in continuing a war, either against the Germans or against the Bolsheviks. The latter continued their propaganda campaign to discredit Kaledin, arouse enmity against Alekseev, and organize disturbances. If Alekseev was having problems, however, he was not long alone in facing them, for the generals who had escaped from their confinement in Bykhov soon joined him in the Don.

The "Bykhovtsy" left their jail by various routes and means so that they arrived in the Don at different times, Kornilov being one of the last of the group because of his attempt to lead the detachment of men who had remained loyal to him. However, most of the group had managed to reach Novocherkassk by the third week of December. Denikin, Markov, and Romanovskii arrived on December 5, Lukomskii on December 6, and Kornilov finally on December 19.[43] This notable influx of leadership gave added strength to Alekseev's efforts but also posed problems.

The arrival of Kornilov, in particular, confronted the Volunteer Army with the question of who was to be its supreme commander, General Alekseev, who had begun its organization in the Don, or

General Kornilov, who had simultaneously conceived similar plans in Bykhov and was considered the most capable military leader in Russia. Secondly, the arrival of the "Bykhovtsy" posed anew the issue of hostility in the Don toward the "counterrevolutionaries." If Alekseev could be tolerated because of the mollifyingly neutral role he had played between Kornilov and Kerenskii, the same could hardly be said for Kornilov himself or for most of his associates at Bykhov. And, finally, there was a serious difference of opinion as to what kind of political affiliation to accept, particularly whether to attempt to establish a government as a civil authority in addition to the army command.[44]

At a conference of both military and political leaders in the area, called by Kornilov on December 31, the question of organization was finally thrashed out. Despite Kornilov's insistence that an army must have only one supreme commander, the weight of opinion was in favor of Alekseev's argument that he and Kornilov could best share the burden of leadership by dividing their functions, he assuming chief responsibility for political relations, financial questions, etc., while Kornilov took responsibility for military organization and command. With the aid of pressure from leading Kadets, who provided the chief political backing of the army, a solution was soon found to which Kornilov consented.[45] The formula adopted also simultaneously answered, at least for the moment, the other question, that is, that of the Volunteer Army's relations with the Don.

The agreement, as drawn up by General Denikin, specified that (1) Alekseev was to have primary authority in matters of civil affairs and external relations, (2) Kornilov was to have military command over the armed forces, and (3) the highest authority in all major questions affecting the movement in general was to be vested in a triumvirate consisting of Alekseev, Kornilov, and Ataman Kaledin, the latter thus uniting the Don with the leadership of the Army. Each of the three was to have chief responsibility in his particular sphere, but all questions of "national significance" were to be considered and decided upon jointly.[46] This agreement, signed by all three in January, was the basis of operations henceforth until the death of Alekseev in October 1918, and it was the first formal establishment of authority by the Volunteer Army.

The question of political affiliation was then worked out by Alekseev, who decided against forming a government but organized an advisory Special Council,[47] composed of both military and political leaders, to assist in the formulation of political, social, and financial policies and the coordination of activities. The first persons to be invited to participate in this body, besides Alekseev's own assistants, were those civilians who had been most closely associated with the establishment of the Volunteer Army, such as Peter B. Struve (a former Social Democrat turned conservative), P. N. Miliukov (the former foreign minister), and Prince G. N. Trubetskoi. However, aside from a preference in military circles for political "neutrality," no real agreement existed as to what the exact limits of the Army's involvement with politics should be. From the beginning, its chief support had come from the Kadets, but there was still the question of bringing in persons who leaned farther "Left," moderate socialists who would support the Army's goals.[48]

The question was, in fact, made unavoidable by the presence of the renegade Socialist Revolutionary, Boris Savinkov. One of those ebullient characters who most epitomized the revolutionary in action, Savinkov had once served as a private in the French army, had returned to Russia to become one of Kerenskii's chief deputies, and, upon his arrival in the Don, had with what seemed to the generals as "unbounded pertinacity," immediately plunged into the disputes and intrigues of local politics, particularly those affecting the Volunteer Army. He was among the first to urge Alekseev to establish a political council to advise the army and was quite outspoken in declaring that a purely military leadership would be disastrous because it would certainly thwart popular support. The solution which he suggested, therefore, was the inclusion of men like himself in a civil council to demonstrate to the populace, and to foreigners, that the movement was not only patriotic but also genuinely democratic.[49]

The validity of Savinkov's views had been recognized by Alekseev, but the inclusion of Savinkov himself in the Special Council was another matter. Alekseev was in favor of attracting a broad following, but he had in mind chiefly moderate elements such as the Kadets, and with this middle-of-the-road approach he was indeed somewhat more tolerant and liberal than many of his fellow officers. Kornilov, in particular, identified Savinkov with the worst aspects of Kerenskii's policies toward the military and was quite adamant at first in opposing his inclusion.[50] However, Alekseev and Kaledin finally agreed that a compromise was necessary, and Kornilov bowed to their judgment. Consequently four socialists were admitted to membership in the Special Council: Savinkov, Ageev, Vendziagol'skii, and Mazurenko.[51]

This particular arrangement was short-lived, but it did establish a precedent which was of lasting significance for the political outlook of the Army. While the principle of including a broad representation in the Special Council was not consistently followed, and never reflected the wishes of the majority of the officers, the Volunteer Command made a practice of seeking the advice of both Kadets and socialists on political and social questions from this time on.[52] When, much later, a government was finally formed, it was just such a coalition as Alekseev had established in the early days, including socialists, Kadets, and conservatives. Savinkov himself, however, soon grew restless in the Don and left in mid-January 1918 with a commission from Alekseev to make further contacts in the north.

Alekseev's work with the political problems of the Army also led to the issuance of a statement of its goals. On January 9, 1918, Kornilov and Alekseev thus jointly released a statement declaring:

> The first goal of the Volunteer Army is to stand against an armed invasion of South and Southeastern Russia. Hand in hand with the valiant Cossacks answering the call of their Krug, their government, and the Voisko Ataman, in union with the provinces and nationalities of Russia which are rising against the German-Bolshevik yoke and all the Russian peoples gathered in the South from all corners of Russia, it will defend to the last drop of blood the autonomy of the provinces which give it refuge and which are the last stronghold of Russian independence, the last hope of the restoration of a Free, Great Russia.
>
> But, along with this goal, the Volunteer Army also sets forth others. This army seeks to be that active force which will give Russian citizens the possibility of realizing the construction of a Free Russia. The new army will stand guard over civil liberties until the day when the master of the Russian land, the Russian people, can express its will through the election of a Constituent Assembly. Before the will of the people, all classes, parties, and groups of the population must bow. It alone will be served by the establishment of this army, and all who are participating in the army's creation will incontrovertibly subordinate themselves to the legal authority established by it through a Constituent Assembly.[53]

This declaration, which remained the essence of the Volunteer Army's program throughout its existence, was designed as much to indicate the absence of a partisan political platform as to state the Army's aims. Born of the patriotic impulses of soldiers who regarded themselves as defenders of their country rather than its future rulers,

the Army's chief goal was to save the country from attack from within
or without. Its founders had no desire to restore the tsarist autocracy
which had long since been discredited in their eyes. Their hope was
that, if order could be restored in Russia, another, and firmer, provisional government could be established to carry through the election of a constituent assembly. In so believing, they felt themselves
actually to be expressing the will of the Russian people and presenting
a platform which the Allies would readily support.

This latter consideration was important because the Don was coming under heavy Bolshevik attack by December,[54] and the Volunteer
Army was in desperate need of money. The Don government and
existing anti-Bolshevik organizations, especially the Kadet party,
promised support, but they were hard pressed to keep what funds
they had out of Bolshevik hands. Pledges of several million rubles were
received from wealthy individuals in Rostov and Novocherkassk, but
the Bolshevik invasion precluded the actual collection of all but a
fraction of these amounts.[55] The one real hope, in short, was the
Allied governments. The latter were indeed soon to be heard from, as
will shortly be noted, but in the meantime the situation grew
steadily worse in the Don.

Both the Don government and the Volunteer Army had about
reached the limit of their resources by the beginning of 1918. Although the third Krug had in December voted "supreme powers" to
the voisko government "until the formation of an all-Russian authority" and had re-elected Kaledin as ataman on January 11, there was
little he could do to stem the tide running against him.[56] The Bolsheviks were hard at work organizing both Cossack and peasant elements
against the government and by January were already claiming to represent a "Don Soviet Republic." On January 28 the Bolshevik Revolutionary Committee for the Don presented terms to the government,
demanding (1) that the ataman cede authority to the Committee,
(2) that the government disarm troops in the area, including volunteer
organizations, and (3) that the Krug be dismissed.[57]

Kaledin refused to give in, but the frustration of being unable to
act bore down upon him unmercifully. The final blow for him came
on February 11 when the Volunteer Army Command informed him
that it would be compelled to leave the Don if it were ever to have
a chance to build up its strength. This was a hard choice but undoubtedly a realistic one for the Volunteer Army. For Kaledin, however,
it was the end; in abject despondence, he committed suicide the same
day.[58]

The desperate efforts of the Krug and Ataman Nazarov, elected to succeed Kaledin, all failed to get results. On February 25, Bolshevik forces occupied Novocherkassk and the whole Don shortly fell to their control. Most of the Cossack forces, seeking their self-preservation, adopted a policy of neutrality and submitted. Only 1500 followed the Volunteer Army in its retreat to the south. Ataman Nazarov, Krug President Volochinov, and others in the Don government were arrested and executed.[59]

For the Volunteer Army the retreat in February meant the beginning of a new phase, one in which its operations and further development would for some time be conducted largely in the Kuban territory. The establishment of the Kuban government as an independent entity had taken somewhat the same path as that described for the Don, but with a significant variation. The legislative body of the Kuban, the Rada (meaning the same as Krug in the Don but using the Ukrainized language for greater distinction), had been to a much greater extent under socialist influence from the start and had consequently inclined both toward a more separatist and a more democratic cause. Unlike the Don Krug, the Rada held jealously to its powers and never granted great powers to the ataman. On the contrary, the real power in the Kuban rested with the government, which was largely formed by political rather than military leaders, while the ataman was restricted to the role of military commander. The situation was in fact very much like that which existed in the Provisional government under Kerenskii, and with the same tensions and suspicions between the government and the military. The Kuban ataman, A. P. Filimonov, remained a weak commander dominated by the Rada, and the Rada in turn was most of the time dominated by the so-called Chernomortsy (Black Sea group, so designated because its members largely came from the Black Sea province of the area) headed by the separatist socialist L. L. Bych.[60]

The Kuban Rada had declared its independent existence as early as mid-October 1917, explaining subsequently its conviction that "The formation on the territory of the former Russian state of independent state formations and their assumption of supreme authority was an unavoidable act and, at the same time, an act of self-preservation."[61] The Rada retained the formula of provisional independence until the future convocation of a constituent assembly and the creation of an all-Russian federation of states, but at the same time the prominent role played by the Bych group assured that, until such time, the emphasis in Kuban policy would be upon its independence and its persistent refusal to risk any of its prerogatives in any really close association with the Volunteer Army.

Imbued with the same spirit which animated Kerenskii earlier, Bych repeatedly proclaimed that if left alone the Kuban could build the most democratic state in the world and that alliance with the Volunteer Army would jeopardize that development and probably mean subjection to reactionary dictatorship. "To aid the Volunteer Army," he warned, "means to prepare a new absorption of the Kuban by Russia."[62] Fearful that both his government and democracy would be destroyed if the Volunteer Army Command was given any leeway, especially through control of Kuban armed forces, Bych's group from the beginning asserted its hostility toward the Army and continued to act independently to the extent of its powers both internally and in foreign relations, seeking ties with like-minded governments in Georgia and the Ukraine.

The movement into the Kuban was thus not a very promising one for the Volunteer Army, although it was considered essential when the Don fell. It also cost the Volunteer Army dearly at the time because it was not just a withdrawal into open territory. Bolshevik forces invaded the Kuban also and in mid-March seized Ekaterinodar, forcing the government to flee. The campaign of the Volunteer Army into the Kuban to find itself a new base of operations was therefore a bloody one, ultimately costing it the lives of hundreds of men and even its commander.

Early in March Kornilov called a council of war, including Alekseev, Denikin, Romanovskii, and Erdeli of the Volunteer Army and leaders of the Kuban forces, to plan future operations. At this conference, Kornilov put the issue point-blank to the Kuban representatives: to liberate the Kuban the Volunteer Army would require the full subordination of Kuban forces to his command. Pokrovskii, the chief Kuban representative, objected strenuously that while cooperation was essential, the Kuban must retain its own army if it were to be inspired to fight at all. He therefore proposed instead merely an operational subordination to Kornilov for the duration of the campaign to liberate the Kuban and restore its government. True to form, Kornilov refused to compromise on this point. As he put it simply: "One army and one command. I will not consider any other position."[63]

Even while getting under way the campaign into Kuban territory, Kornilov on March 30 called another meeting to try to resolve this question, this time with both Ataman Filimonov and representatives of the Rada in attendance (including Bych as head of the government). Again one side argued adamantly on the grounds of military necessity and the other countered with firm assertions of "Kuban sovereignty," demanding preservation of the Kuban army with only operational subordination to Kornilov. Kornilov did not retreat from his position on the military question, but he did now give assurances that the Volunteer Army was not trying to "swallow up" the Kuban. He finally persuaded the Kuban representatives to accept a unification of forces on his terms by guaranteeing noninterference in civil affairs and recognition of existing Kuban authority in the Rada and its government. Although Bych at first refused to accept this compromise arrangement, he too agreed to it after the terms were put into writing and signed by Kornilov.[64]

Actually no real or permanent solution to this question was found. Kuban forces were brought under the operational command of the Volunteer Army but retained much of their separate identity despite being incorporated into the Volunteer organization.[65] The issue was, in fact, to come up again and again, but at this critical juncture, and with the Kuban government temporarily without power in its own territory, the military leaders in effect let the question ride for the sake of the liberation. When Kornilov on April 9, after a council meeting on the occupation question, designated General Denikin as provisional "Governor-General for the Kuban," the Kuban government accepted the appointment with sullen silence.[66]

The subsequent campaign, the hardest the young Volunteer Army ever had to fight, was a struggle for its very life. It began with the awful "icy campaign" across the marsh lands and rivers which stood between the Army and liberation of the Kuban. When the Volunteers finally reached Ekaterinodar on April 10, they had only some 500 ablebodied men left and, still carrying with them some 1500 wounded, were exhausted and almost bereft of supplies. It was because of this extreme depletion of the Army's ranks that Kornilov issued his first conscription order and thus ended the purely voluntary phase of its existence. In this struggle, under the most severe conditions, the Volunteer Army was forged into a real fighting force. Whatever its shortcomings, and there were many, this was its noblest hour in terms of sheer endurance and patriotic devotion. But on the very eve of the capture of Ekaterinodar, on April 12, Kornilov was killed by a grenade as he sat alone in a small house being used for his command post. The staff of the Army immediately asked Denikin to take command, and he did so.[67]

Anton Ivanovich Denikin, the inheritor of Kornilov's mantle, had none of the dash or vibrant intensity of the wiry little man whom he succeeded, nor did he have the charismatic hold over subordinates which had made Kornilov such an effective commander. He did, however, have many other traits in common with the dead hero. Both were men of humble origin who had risen to their high military ranks by virtue of ability rather than class. Denikin's father was a serf to the age of thirty when his emancipation came in the form of the military draft. In the army, where he served for twenty-two years, he had risen to become an officer and left his son with the inspiration of his success as well as a deep sense of dedication to his country's service. Following his father's example, Denikin in turn had joined the army as a private, soon qualified for officer training and, after receiving his commission, entered the Staff College. He remembered his climb through the ranks as a struggle against prejudice and privilege in the officer corps, but World War I had brought him rapid advancement to the important post of chief of staff and then command of the western and, finally, southwestern fronts.

As was the case with Kornilov, Denikin had renounced tsarist autocracy and fully supported the democratic revolution in Russia only to become disillusioned with the fumbling of the Provisional government, on which he blamed the subsequent disintegration of the army and the collapse of authority. The dramatic encounter with Kerenskii had left him embittered against the "politicians" and the "socialist babblers" who, in his opinion, were toying with the very survival of Russia. Denikin thus came to the command of the Volunteer Army convinced of the absolute necessity of disciplined, firm, and nonpolitical leadership for the salvation of Russia. Although he looked forward to the day when democracy, civil liberties, peasant farms, and worker prosperity would flourish in a new Russia, he believed that none of this would be possible without first saving the Motherland from destruction by the Bolsheviks and the Germans. He took up that crusade, with the same naive honesty which had characterized Kornilov, and would eventually become its chief leader in South Russia, where he more than any other would dominate events during the next two years. Under the slogan, One Great and Indivisible Russia, he set himself to the single task of military victory, determined that neither he nor any politicians would "predetermine" Russia's future structure, which was to be left to a freely elected national assembly. Until then authority would have to be exercised by a temporary military dictatorship, and even debate on reforms should be postponed so as to reduce antagonism within the anti-Bolshevik camp.[68]

When he succeeded Kornilov, Denikin had only the battered remnant of an army with which to begin the struggle, but under his command the Army, with the assistance of risings by the Kuban population against the Bolsheviks, gradually cleared the Kuban during the spring and summer of 1918.[69] The second Kuban campaign, which returned the Kuban government to power, enabled the Volunteer Army to establish for itself a new base of operations with Ekaterinodar as its headquarters, but if it was to become more than a borderland army, if it was to fulfill its mission of liberating Russia, it would have to expand far beyond the limits permitted in the Kuban. Such expansion would, in turn, require substantial assistance from the outside, at least in the form of supplies and equipment, and would necessitate dealing with the borderland governments which controlled the territory between Ekaterinodar and Moscow. The ability of the Army to cope with these problems would depend to a considerable extent upon the response of the Allied Powers.

* * * * * *

The Allied Powers had, of course, been deeply concerned with the developments in Russia. The ominous Soviet appeal to the "class conscious workers" of Europe over the heads of their governments, and the publication of secret Allied agreements and correspondence, which was begun on November 23, 1917, had further disturbed the already anxious Allied policy makers, but the most crucial issue remained that of whether the war against the Central Powers could be kept alive on the eastern front. When the Bolsheviks persisted in their avowed intention of ending the war even in the absence of European revolution—or rather for that very reason—their action was naturally viewed in the light of its likely contribution to a German victory over the Allies.[70] The United States had entered the war in April, but if Germany was able to transfer the full weight of its forces to the western front before American troops arrived in significant numbers, the Allies' hope of victory could easily be shattered.

The gnawing fear of this possibility, coupled with reports that Lenin had been allowed to return to Russia across German territory and was receiving German funds, had given rise readily to the belief that the Bolshevik revolution had been part of a German plot to get Russia out of the war.[71] The apparent determination of the Bolshevik leaders to do just that had only seemed to confirm this erroneous contention. On November 20 the Soviet government had officially approved fraternization with enemy troops at the front and ordered the incumbent commander of the army, General Dukhonin, to contact the

German Command to arrange an immediate armistice preparatory to peace negotiations.[72] In an effort to encourage Dukhonin to disobey this order, the Allied military missions at Russian headquarters at Mogilev had appealed to him to "repudiate all criminal negotiations with the enemy and keep the Russian Army on the Front facing our common enemy," but the effort was in vain.[73] Dukhonin's attempt to cooperate with this advice accomplished little other than earning him the Bolshevik brand of "enemy of the people."[74] The Allied missions were forced to flee to Kiev just before the arrival of the new Soviet commander, Krylenko, at the beginning of December, and Dukhonin himself had soon met death at the hands of a mob which dragged him from Krylenko's railway coach.[75]

On the heels of this failure, the long-postponed inter-Allied conference on war aims had finally met in Paris on November 29. It seemed to many to offer an opportunity for a fresh approach to the problem of keeping Russia in the war. British Ambassador Buchanan had, for example, reported that leading Russian socialists who opposed the Bolshevik regime, such as N. V. Chaikovskii, believed that if the Allies showed a willingness "to discuss peace terms with a view to bringing the war to a speedy conclusion," then Russia would be inspired with new courage and a will to fight.[76] However, the conference had been unable to reach agreement on what approach to take toward this question and was only further frustrated in its efforts by the news that the German government had agreed to enter negotiations among all the belligerent powers for a general peace.[77] While the Allies did then decide that an unofficial mission should be sent to investigate developments in the borderland regions of South Russia, particularly the Don on which some information had been received,[78] there was still no Allied policy as such, other than the common goal of keeping Russia in the war—an ambiguous aim which bespoke more desperation than plan. When on December 15 the Bolsheviks signed an armistice with the Germans, Allied hopes for keeping the eastern front alive were dealt a further blow. The door seemed open for the shift of German might against the Allies.[79]

Formal peace negotiations had subsequently been opened at Brest-Litovsk on December 22, and Trotskii's appeals to the Allied countries to join in the negotiations had given way to sharp blasts at the West's "blind stubbornness which characterizes decadent and perishing classes" and the warning that the time was rapidly approaching when "the working classes will be confronted by the iron necessity of taking power out of the hands of those who cannot or will not give the people peace."[80] Trotskii's orations were the product of an unyielding faith in the imminence of world revolution, but they also betrayed Bolshevik impotence in the face of German military power. It was still possible that the Soviet government might be compelled to fight rather than accept the terms which a separate peace would force on them, but, meanwhile, Bolshevik actions had also led Allied policy makers to the conclusion that they could not afford to ignore alternative possibilities.

Therefore, as the Bolshevik policy of peace was gradually taking shape, the Allied governments initiated steps to prepare contacts with anti-Bolshevik elements in the South. Even before the two unofficial representatives, dispatched as a result of the November conference, had reached their destination in the Don, both the British and French governments had followed up this decision with new ones. On December 3 the British Cabinet had agreed in principle to offer aid to the Don Cossacks under Ataman Kaledin and subsequently, on December 14, approved extending financial support to this force.[81] On December 7, the French government had moved in this same direction by establishing a special commission under General Janin to study the Russian question and make recommendations concerning the possibility of supporting anti-Bolshevik elements.[82] The French representative, Colonel Hucher, then arrived in the Don capital on December 23 and was soon joined by the British representative, General de Candolle. DeWitt C. Poole, the former United States consul in Moscow,[83] had already arrived in Novocherkassk on December 18.

As Poole's presence suggested, the United States was also interested at this time in establishing contacts and had even indicated a willingness to help support the Russian armies forming in Cossack territory. While direct intervention in the South by the United States was ruled out, both Secretary of State Lansing and President Wilson approved indirect American support for Allied actions. Ambassador Page in London was thus advised on December 13 that the Russian situation had been carefully considered and the conclusion had been reached that "the movement in the south and southeast under the leadership of Kaledine and Korniloff offers at the present time the greatest hope for the reestablishment of a stable government and the continuance of a military force on the German and Austrian fronts." It was deemed unwise for the United States to grant support openly "because of the attitude which it seems advisable to take with the Petrograd authorities," but it was believed necessary that Kaledin "be shown that the Allied Governments are most sympathetic with his efforts." The "practical course" proposed, therefore, was "for the British and French Governments to finance the Kaledine enterprise in so far as it is necessary, and for [the United States] to loan them the money to do so." Page was instructed to take up this matter with British and French authorities confidentially; the initiative for intervention would, however, be left to Paris and London.[84]

These preliminary steps reached a culmination of sorts when on December 22, the day of the reopening of the Brest peace negotiations, an Allied conference met in Paris to consider a special memorandum by the British Foreign Office. This memorandum, formulated largely by Lord Milner, and subsequently approved by Clemenceau and French Foreign Minister Pichon, stressed the necessity of keeping the eastern front active by every means possible and suggested the approaches by which this aim could be achieved. It recommended especially the further development of relations with General Alekseev and the Don Cossacks, but it also suggested the need for a more active Allied policy in the Ukraine and Transcaucasia.[85]

The Ukraine, it was noted, provided the one source of provisions and refuge for the Rumanians, who, having entered the war against the Germans earlier, had been driven back virtually to the borders of Russia.[86] Moreover, if the rich resources of the Ukraine should fall into German hands, the Allied blockade against Germany would be rendered meaningless. Transcaucasia, likewise, was the one real barrier to a German-Turkish penetration which might ultimately reach "from Constantinople to China." It was, therefore, considered essential to "induce the southern Russian armies to resume the fight" in Transcaucasia, the Ukraine, and the Cossack territories, and this, it was agreed, would require both money and instruction. To get both into South Russia, Allied agents and officers would have to be sent in to "advise and support" those governments and armies which would continue the war.

In order to coordinate this activity, an agreement on "zones" was drawn up and signed on December 23.[87] According to this agreement, French operations were to be "developed north of the Black Sea," while the British concentrated on the area "southeast of the Black Sea." Specifically, the French zone would include Bessarabia, the Ukraine, and the Crimea, while the British would assume chief responsibility for the Cossack territories, the territory of the Caucasus, Arme-

nia, Georgia, and Kurdistan. At the same time, both would supply
financial assistance to Alekseev, and other expenses were to be "pooled
and regulated by a centralized inter-Allied organ." All such activities,
however, were to be kept secret so as "to avoid the imputation" that
the Allied governments were "preparing to make war on the Bolshe-
viki." Consequently Allied agents sent into South Russia from Rumania were to be dispatched under the pretext of buying food stuffs for
the Rumanian population.[88]

It was under this cover that the British and French representatives
from the Allied military missions in Rumania made their way to
Novocherkassk in December and January carrying offers to 10 million
pounds and 100 million francs credit respectively.[89] Actually Alekseev
seems to have received only a small fraction of this in a usable form
before the Volunteer Army was forced to retreat into the Kuban in
February, but the Allied agents had brought invaluable moral support
by their mere presence.[90] Likewise, special Allied representatives (the
French General Tabouis and the British Major Fitzwilliams) had
already, in November, been accredited to the Ukrainian government
to bolster its resistance to both the Bolsheviks and the Germans.[91]

On December 18 the Bolshevik government in Petrograd had issued
an ultimatum to the Ukrainian Rada designed to facilitate a coup
against it by the Ukrainian Bolsheviks, but the Rada had replied with
a demand for self-determination and a rejection of the claims of the
Bolsheviks to negotiate on behalf of the Ukraine.[92] Allied offers of aid
to the Rada, however, had also encountered the obstacle of a Ukrainian request for recognition before making any commitments. Neither
Britain nor France was willing to extend formal recognition, but a
diplomatic device to placate Ukrainian sensitivity was adopted. General Tabouis was given the title of "Commissioner of the French
Republic to the Government of the Ukrainian Republic" in creden-
tials issued on December 29 by the French minister in Rumania,
Saint-Aulaire, and the British appointed John Picton Bagge, a former consul-general in Odessa, as "British Representative in the
Ukraine."[93] Both Tabouis and Bagge followed the policy of the Allied
agents in the Don by offering promises of extensive support in return
for loyalty to the Allied war effort.[94]

Such efforts as these, however, were not enough to enable the Allies
to achieve the results needed. Bolshevik forces were well on their way
toward overrunning both the Cossack territories and the Ukraine.
Moreover, British plans now just being worked out, to organize an

expedition into Transcaucasia through Persia, under Major General L. C. Dunsterville, were still only in the organization stage in Baghdad, while the Turkish military drive threatened to conquer the area in a short time.[95] Even with Allied agents in South Russia, no substantial aid was practicable so long as the Straits remained closed, and openings were yet to be made through Persia and Rumania. It was, therefore, imperative for the Allies also to continue efforts to prevent the Bolsheviks from signing a separate peace with Germany. Since the Bolshevik regime was not to be recognized, however, the December 22 memorandum had recommended that contacts with it be kept open "through unofficial agents" on the same basis as contacts with non-Bolshevik governments.[96]

For this purpose Lloyd George delegated a man who had previously served in the Moscow consulate, R. Bruce Lockhart. To smooth his path to Bolshevik contacts, the British Cabinet agreed to grant freedom of action to the Bolshevik "ambassador" in England, Maxim Litvinov, and Litvinov in turn wrote a letter of introduction for Lockhart to Trotskii, declaring him to be an "honest man who understands our position and sympathizes with us."[97] Lockhart then set out for Russia, arriving in Petrograd during January. His only instructions were "to do as much harm to the Germans as possible, to put a spoke in the wheels of the separate peace negotiations, and to stiffen by whatever means [he] could the Bolsheviks' resistance to German demands."[98] The French had a similarly useful agent already on the spot in the person of Captain Jacques Sadoul, who had gone to Russia in October with the military mission under General Niessel. As a socialist and former acquaintance of Trotskii, Sadoul had already established himself as a proponent of contacts with the Bolsheviks and as one whose ideas generally conflicted with those of Ambassador Noulens, with whom Soviet relations were quite strained.[99]

Through Lockhart and Sadoul, it was agreed, the British and French governments would attempt to convince the Bolsheviks that they had "no desire to take part in any way in the internal politics of Russia" and were not in favor of a counterrevolution. The Allies could not condone "the treachery of the Russians in opening peace negotiations" with the enemy, the Milner memorandum had noted, but they were prepared "to accept the principles of self-determination" and to aid in Russia's defense, providing the Bolsheviks did not let themselves be deceived by "empty phrases from the Germans." As Foreign Minister Pichon explained to the Assembly on December 27, the Allies wished to establish contact "with all healthy elements in Russia" which retained the "instinct of legitimate defense" of the country against German aggression, and they had not ruled out the possibility that the Bolsheviks might be persuaded to join this category once they found out what dealing with the Germans would involve.[100]

* * * * * *

The Bolsheviks had, in fact, begun to discover that their lack of a real policy was bound to pose grave difficulties. The Soviet delegation had in reality gone to Brest not to sign a treaty but to drag out the talks in order to agitate for revolution, and initially all of the Bolshevik leadership had agreed with Trotskii's "excellent use" of the negotiations for this purpose.[101] However, during January the Ukrainian Rada had ended its talks with Allied representatives in Rumania, replaced Vynnychenko's government by one willing to negotiate with the Germans, and sent its own delegation to Brest.[102] The Germans then entered separate talks with the Ukrainians and denied Bolshevik competence to negotiate for any territory outside that of Great Russia.[103]

These developments, which threatened to disrupt the talks and lead to a resumption of hostilities had, therefore, provoked a crisis in Soviet policy making. It was rapidly becoming clear that a choice would have to be made: either the Bolsheviks would stake everything on a renewal of the war, or they would have to sign a capitulatory separate peace with the Germans. Lenin, disturbed by the delay of revolution in the West, by the increasingly aggressive tone of the German negotiators, and by a survey of Soviet armed forces which indicated their complete lack of fighting capability, had by January 1918 reached the conclusion that it would be impossible to resume the war, even as a revolutionary war, and that therefore the signing of a separate peace was mandatory, regardless of the terms so long as they permitted the survival of the Soviet regime.[104] Lenin's conclusions could not be applied to policy immediately, however, because the majority of the Bolshevik Central Committee opposed his new position and could be persuaded to adopt only the compromise policy (between making peace at once and conducting a revolutionary war) proposed by Trotskii, which was to prolong the negotiations as much as possible so as to give the German proletariat time to become aroused and prepare a revolt.[105]

On January 9, 1918, Trotskii left for Brest to carry out this policy, but not without arming himself in advance for the possibility that the talks might be broken off by the Germans before the hoped-for revolution arrived. Before facing the Germans again, he talked with the unofficial French representative, Sadoul, and the chief of the American Red Cross mission, Raymond Robins, who was also serving as an unofficial contact. From both he obtained verbal assurances of assistance in case hostilities should be resumed.[106] Nine days later at Brest, Trotskii received an outline of the harsh terms to be demanded by Germany as the price of peace and returned to Petrograd for consultations.[107] Then, on February 9, the Germans signed a separate peace with the Ukraine, giving them a forced invitation to occupy its territory, and presented their "final" terms to Trotskii for his answer.[108] Trotskii, whose position had again received approval from the Party Central Committee, chose to regard the German move as a bluff prompted by fear of imminent revolution and again rejected the terms, despite a mandate from Lenin to capitulate to an ultimatum."[109]

On February 16 this whole question was given a sudden new urgency by the German announcement that the truce would be considered ended and a state of war resumed at noon on February 18.[110] Given this situation, nothing could have proved the powerful hold of old revolutionary ideas on the minds of the Bolsheviks (with the notable exceptions of Lenin and Joseph Stalin) more strikingly than the decision by a majority of the Central Committee on February 18 to try even now to renew and drag out the negotiations, while preparing for a revolutionary war, in the belief that the German attack on Russia would at last provoke the revolution in Germany.[111] It was not, in fact, until the evening of February 18, when disaster was imminent, that the Central Committee finally voted to accept the German terms, and the vote shifted to Lenin's favor even then only because Trotskii changed sides to support him.[112]

Unfortunately for the Soviet government, the immediately dispatched offer to accept the German terms did not stop the German attack. It did not even bring a response from the Germans for several days, and during this interval the Bolsheviks were driven toward that last resort, an appeal to the Allies for help. Relations between the Allies and the Soviet government had, however, deteriorated considerably during January and February, largely because of Allied activities in the Ukraine and the acquiescence of the Allied Powers in the occupation of Bessarabia by Rumanian troops in order to enable them to prevent its falling into German hands. A sharp exchange between the Allied embassies and the Bolsheviks had followed the Soviet arrest of the Rumanian ambassador, Diamandi, and the seizure of Rumanian gold reserves left in Russia for safekeeping, and the Soviet government had both broken off relations with Rumania and charged the Allies with attempting to use Rumania as a base for intervention on behalf of the counterrevolutionaries.[113] Then, on February 10, the Bolsheviks had added to the tension by annulling the Russian state debt, a large part of which was owed to Britain and France, and on February 12 both Allied and neutral representatives had issued a strong protest against this action.[114]

Despite these developments, however, Trotskii had kept up his contacts with the unofficial Allied representatives, now including Lockhart, and had raised the question of Allied aid almost immediately upon his return from Brest. In an interview with Lockhart three days before the German attack, he had hinted that the circumstances in which the Soviet government found itself offered a "big opportunity for the Allied Governments." Lockhart had in turn added to the earlier statements by Sadoul and Robins his own assurances that the Allies, specifically Britain, would aid the Bolsheviks if they took up the fight against the Germans.[115] Thus armed with these assurances, and ignoring their unofficial nature, Trotskii on February 22 proposed to the Central Committee to accept Allied aid in the apparently unavoidable war with the Central Powers. They had no choice, declared Trotskii, but to supply their army with whatever means were available, regardless of their origin. It was extreme desperation which led the Central Committee, with Lenin's grudging consent, to accept this proposal by a vote of 6 to 5, but this curious and revealing turn of events lost most of its significance during the next few days.[116]

On February 23 an answer finally came from the Germans; they were willing to make peace. Despite the fact that their terms were now even harsher than before, the Central Committee voted 7 to 4, with 4 abstentions including Trotskii, to accept them unconditionally. The next day the Soviet Central Executive Committee also voted, 116 to 85, to accept the peace terms, and a new delegation was sent off to Brest to carry out this decision.[117] Trotskii thereupon resigned as commissar for foreign affairs and, taking the post of commissar for war, began the great task of organizing the Red Army. He revealed the logic of his action, and of continuing relations with the Allies even now, in a talk with Lockhart shortly after the Central Committee had voted. The Allied Powers, he charged, were "playing roulette and scattering chips on every number" in their intrigues in Russia, but their help might still be necessary because, in his view, the peace was not likely to last and he, for one, was going to see that they were better prepared to fight when and if it became necessary in the future.[118]

Lockhart himself, while admittedly now having little more than indications of skepticism on the part of the British Foreign Office, believed that the door was still open to obtaining Bolshevik consent for Allied efforts to prevent further German penetration.[119] The growing danger of German occupation of the northwestern area of Russia so as to obtain the Allied supplies there had indeed prompted a hasty flight of the Allied ambassadors and their staffs from Petrograd to Vologda at the end of February, and the Soviet government itself began moving the capital to Moscow in March.[120]

Allied-Soviet contact was maintained in this change, and an ad hoc "miniature Allied council" was established in Moscow consisting of Lockhart, Sadoul, Robins, and a delegation of Allied military representatives, including Major Riggs of the United States, General Lavergne of the French military mission, and General Romei representing the Italian High Command.[121] Lockhart has recorded the rationale behind their activities:

> We knew that the burning anxiety of the Allied High Command was to detach as many German soldiers from the West as possible. But taking every factor into consideration, we could not believe that this object could be attained by support of Alexeieff or Korniloff. These generals . . . were not immediately interested in the war in the West. They may have been sincere in their desire to reconstitute an Eastern front against Germany, but before they could do so, they had to deal with the Bolsheviks. Without strong foreign aid they were not powerful enough for this task. . . . Although we realized that the Bolsheviks would fight only if they were forced into war by German aggression, we were convinced that this situation might easily develop and that by a promise of support we might help to shape events in the form we desired.[122]

The activities of these Allied representatives, however, failed to prevent agreement between the Germans and the Bolsheviks. They not only could not prevent the signing of the treaty on March 3 but also failed, even with the help of the Bolshevik "Left," to head off its ratification by the Fourth Congress of Soviets on March 15.[123] By this treaty (or treaties, since a separate one was signed with each of the Central Powers) the Bolsheviks showed that they would go a long way for the sake of peace. They had, in effect, given over to the Germans an enormous expanse of territory from the Baltic to the Black Sea, with all of its wealth of resources. They had also relieved the armies of the Central Powers of fighting on the eastern front, although many thousands of troops were necessary for the occupation.

These circumstances did, indeed, represent a turning point in Allied relations with Russia, although they did not, as might have been expected, bring an immediate end to the unofficial contacts or the efforts of Lockhart and Sadoul to reach a modus vivendi with the Bolshevik regime. Sadoul, with Trotskii's constant encouragement, even worked out a plan of Allied technical assistance in the organization of the Red Army. The personnel for such assistance was already on hand; General Berthelot had just arrived in Moscow from Rumania and brought with him a rather large French military mission. Since Trotskii sanctioned the formation of a special committee of Allied officers to advise the Commissariat for War, the military members of the Allied "council" in Moscow proposed to use the Berthelot mission to help train the Red Army. In accordance with Sadoul's plan, General Henri Niessel then prepared a program of military development for Trotskii which would employ the French officers as instructors.[124] Things were going so well, from Sadoul's point of view, that by the end of March he could report enthusiastically that "the collaboration of the Allied missions with the Bolsheviks directed toward the building of a new, disciplined army . . . is underway." He expected at any moment to get Soviet agreement to an Allied military intervention in the North to protect that area from the Germans.[125]

Sadoul's joy was short-lived, however, for the French ambassador, Joseph Noulens, who had originally approved the Sadoul-Niessel plan, now intervened from Vologda to stop it. General Lavergne was reprimanded for having allowed Sadoul to become so involved, and the prospective military instructors were ordered to return to France at once. The frustrated Sadoul, whose close association with the Bolsheviks had had its effect, ultimately threw in his lot with Communism, but the remainder of the French mission fell into line with the policy now advocated by Noulens, which was characterized by General Lavergne as "intervention without Bolshevik consent and without asking for it."[126]

The arrival of the new German ambassador, Mirbach, and his formal reception on April 26, consummated Soviet efforts to put relations

with Germany on a normal and more secure basis and served to confirm Noulens' view that it was pointless to pursue further the hope of
getting Bolshevik approval for intervention against the Germans. In
a public statement issued on April 28, in connection with the landing of a small Japanese detachment in Vladivostok and the appearance of Allied ships at Murmansk, Noulens warned that, in view of
German success "extending far beyond the limits which it was possible to foresee after the Brest treaty," the Allied Powers "may be
obliged to intervene in order to meet this threat directed both against
the Russian people and against them."[127] Although Noulens declared
that if the Allies resorted to military operations in Russia, they would
not do so for the purpose of "intervening in the internal affairs of
Russia" or for "any ulterior motives with regard to any kind of conquest," the Soviet government immediately exercised its right to
demand his recall.[128] This incident thus demonstrated, on the one
hand, the Allies' great concern over the rapid expansion of German
influence and occupation, and, on the other hand, the Bolsheviks'
willingness now to accept this situation in preference to cooperating
with the Allies. Meanwhile, the very effort of the Allied Powers to
keep open the possibility of such cooperation with the Bolsheviks had
begun to alienate many in anti-Bolshevik circles who believed that
they detected in the duality of Allied policy an element of indecision and vacillation, if not outright duplicity.

2: THE IMPACT OF GERMAN OCCUPATION

By the spring of 1918 the Bolsheviks had invaded and conquered a large part of the Ukraine and the Cossack territories. The Don government had fallen, and the Volunteer Army had been forced to retreat into the Kuban. During the subsequent campaign in April, Kornilov himself had been killed. When his successor, General Denikin, took command of the Army, it consisted of a handful of men fighting for their very survival against the Bolsheviks, while the Germans ominously approached from the west, and the Allies seemed incapable of action sufficient to stem the tide.

German occupation authorities in the Ukraine were, of course, concerned primarily with exploiting the economic fruits of their victory. When the Rada government proved incapable, in German opinion, of maintaining the degree of control necessary to deliver the goods desired, and seemed in fact to be more interested in socialist agrarian reforms, the Germans were quite prepared to turn to other elements more suited to their requirements. Not surprisingly those found to be more amenable were of a conservative outlook, groups hostile toward the socializing "experiments" of the Rada government and the "agrarian anarchy" in the countryside.[1]

Open conflict over grain harvests between the German Command, under Field Marshal von Eichhorn, and the Rada government thus led the German ambassador, Baron Adolf Mumm von Schwarzenstein, to suggest to his superiors on April 18 that the conservative opposition be used as the basis of a transfer of authority in the Ukraine.[2] Although the exact nature of the shift was not yet clearly formulated, the German authorities were agreed that it was necessary to install a government fully under German control. The candidate then selected by the Germans for the post of chief of state was, appropriately enough, the former Russian general, wealthy Ukrainian landowner, and brother-in-law of the German Commander, Paul Skoropadskii. The descendant of a Ukrainian Cossack "hetman" who had ruled 200 years earlier, General Skoropadskii was ideally suited for the restoration of a "monarchist" dictatorship under German auspices. With the support of Russian officers and the Ukrainian League of Landowners, Skoropadskii was solemnly installed on April 29, while the Rada, having just adopted a constitution for the Ukrainian People's Republic, was dispersed with little resistance.[3]

Just south of the Ukraine, the Crimea, with its strategic location on the Black Sea, was also of immediate concern to the Central Powers. Moscow attempted to hold off the Germans, and keep the Black Sea fleet out of their hands, by having the Bolshevik government in Sevastopol proclaim the independence of the Crimea, but this maneuver was to no avail. As soon as the Germans began to approach the Crimea, the Tatars staged a revolt, reinstated their assembly, and set up a new government under Sejdamet, with the hope of obtaining German support. To their chagrin, however, the welcomed Germans duplicated their behavior in the Ukraine and quickly replaced the Tatar government with a puppet regime under the nominal head of General Sul'kevich, a Lithuanian Moslem who had commanded a special Moslem Corps for the German forces in Rumania. Efforts by the Tatars to obtain Turkish intercession on their behalf failed to move the Germans. The Kadets were also kept out of power by the German occupation, of course, but their organization would be of considerable significance in later months.[4]

After the Ukraine and the Crimea, German influence penetrated most effectively into Transcaucasia, especially into Georgia. In this case the chief reason was, ironically, the menace posed by Germany's ally, Turkey. The Transcaucasian government under Gegechkori was confronted not only by the usual Bolshevik threat but even more importantly by the imminent threat of a Turkish invasion, which had the barely concealed sympathy of Azerbaidzhan. When the Bolshevik regime in Russia had in March entered a separate peace with the Central Powers, it had presumed *inter alia* to cede the territories of Batum, Kars, and Ardahan, populated largely by Georgians and Armenians, to the Turks. When efforts by Transcaucasian leaders to counteract the Brest treaty ran head-on into a Turkish refusal to enter negotiations except with an independent state, the Transcaucasian Federation, under the pressure of attack, on April 22 declared its independence and formed a new government.[5]

This new government, headed by Georgian Menshevik, A. Chkhen-keli, thus preserved temporarily the union of Georgia, Armenia, and Azerbaidzhan for the purpose of negotiating peace with Turkey. The result of its negotiations, however, would undoubtedly have been most unfavorable but for the remarkable fact that the Germans chose to intervene on its behalf.[6] The German representative in the ensuing talks at Baku, General von Lossow, provided a protective shield for the Transcaucasian Federation which enabled it to negotiate a relatively favorable, if somewhat temporary, truce with the Turks.[7] But von Lossow was not interested in preserving the Federation as such; on the contrary, in secret talks with Georgian leaders he recommended its dissolution. Following his suggestion, the Georgians then not only declared their independence as a separate state but put themselves under German protection, a protection which was not extended to the Armenian and Azerbaidzhani governments, which then also declared their independence.

On May 25, a force of some 3,000 German troops was landed at Poti under the command of General Kress von Kressenstein, and an agreement was signed giving the Germans full use of all Georgian rails and ships as well as the port of Poti. A Georgian delegation (consisting of Avalov, Chkhenkeli, Tseretelli, and Nikoladze) then left for Berlin where more detailed agreements could be negotiated and arrangements made to reconcile Georgia's independence with the Brest treaty. The German Foreign Ministry wished to avoid straining relations with the Bolsheviks, however, and therefore urged the Georgians to reach a settlement with Moscow before formal German recognition and economic support were confirmed.[8]

On the other hand, the Germans chose to ignore the Azerbaidzhani government and deal directly with Moscow concerning the fate of the strategic Azerbaidzhani port of Baku. The fact that local Bolsheviks, under the leadership of Stepan Shaumian, had been able to win sufficient support to establish a soviet government in Baku in April gave the Germans reason to believe that they could negotiate special arrangements with Moscow for the exploitation of that city's great oil industry. At the same time, the Turks had taken the dissolution of the Transcaucasian Federation as a signal to renew their attack. Quickly overrunning the isolated Armenians, the Turks signed a treaty of alliance with neighboring Azerbaidzhan in June, and a combined Turkish-Azerbaidzhani army under Nuri Pasha began moving toward the Caspian.[9]

In the summer of 1918 German influence thus seemed firmly entrenched in Transcaucasia; and what the Germans did not have, the Turks did. Moreover, German penetration across the Caspian appeared not unlikely, since the expansion of Bolshevik control throughout most of Turkestan during this time had been accomplished in part by the arming of thousands of German and Austrian prisoners-of-war as soldiers of the Red Army.[10] Even in the Caucasus Mountain region, conditions favored the Germans to the extent that both the Bolshevik and anti-Bolshevik forces there offered possibilities of intervention, the former by their dependence on support from Astrakhan and Baku, and the latter by the appeal of the leaders of the defunct Mountain People's Union to Georgia for German protection of the North Caucasus state proclaimed on May 11.[11] In fact, however, it was not in Turkestan or in the Caucasus Mountains where German influence had the greatest prospects for further advancement in the summer and autumn of 1918 but rather in the Don and among conservative Russian circles in the South.

*   *   *   *   *   *

The advent of a conservative regime in the Ukraine, one which, while maintaining the semblance of Ukrainian statehood, opposed the anti-Russian nationalism of the Rada, proved to be a major inspiration to the Russians not only in the Ukraine itself but throughout South Russia. Actually the inclination of Skoropadskii's regime toward a Russophile and reactionary character resulted as much from default as from intent. The hetman actively sought the support of moderate Ukrainian parties, but both the nationalists and the Leftists persisted in their hostility toward him. As a result, political posts were filled with former Russian bureaucrats, and the regime was used by reactionary elements to regain their lost positions in control of the land and the administration.[12]

To many conservative Russians the Skoropadskii regime thus seemed to provide exactly what was needed: a base of operations, a curb on nationalistic separatism, and immediate and powerful foreign aid. To these same conservatives these features of the German occupation contrasted quite favorably with the procrastination of the Allies and their inclination to prefer liberals and socialists.[13] Moreover, the Germans were interested in finding out what they had to offer, and German inquiries helped to stimulate a debate within anti-Bolshevik circles which led to a splitting of the latter into pro-Allied and pro-German factions.

Among nonsocialist anti-Bolshevik circles the efforts to organize a center of resistance had first resulted in the secret establishment in Moscow of a group of leaders of many shades of opinion who, originally known as the "deviatki," subsequently took on the name of "Moscow Center." It was basically a conservative-liberal coalition initially inspired by the efforts of the former minister of agriculture, A. V. Krivoshein. The declared object of the Center was to unite all nonsocialist elements for the struggle against the Bolsheviks. In addition to attracting to its organization numerous political leaders, it also fostered the formation of a military section for officer members.[14]

The somewhat Rightist inclination of this coalition, however, was unsatisfactory for the more liberal elements. Therefore, early in 1918, a second, or "Left," Center was also founded to attract liberal Kadets, Right Socialist Revolutionaries, and Populist Socialists. This Left Center, which rejected outright any possibility of dealing with the Germans or of compromising with the Right even on grounds of a constitutional monarchy, was chiefly important as the forerunner of the "Union for Regeneration of Russia," which became the leading spokesman for the anti-Bolshevik moderate Left.[15] The Moscow Center, meanwhile, failed to hold even the conservatives together when they clashed over the issue of foreign aid.

The success of the Germans, together with the rather modest prospects for Allied aid, had by the spring of 1918 led some members of the Moscow Center to raise the question of turning to the Germans for assistance, especially since after Brest it seemed to many that Germany would win the war. The debate over this issue was sharp and long. Those in favor of a positive response to privately extended German hints of support believed that the Germans could be persuaded to alter their Brest policy and install a conservative pro-German government in Moscow.[16] The opponents, of course, decried the allegedly devastating effects that a Germanophile course would have on the "national spirit," held that Allied aid would be forthcoming and the eastern front re-established, and, perhaps most importantly, branded the Germanophile policy as monarchist, while the Allies were identified with "republicanism."[17]

As the latter point illustrates, the division which occurred in this debate was not solely based on military considerations. Under the circumstances, it inevitably also assumed some of the features of a Left-Right split within the Moscow Center itself. Soon, however, even the pro-Allied liberal element was beginning to lose faith in the Allies, whose vacillation before Brest had been understandable but whose inaction since then provoked serious doubts. As a Kadet spokesman secretly warned Lockhart, even his party was on the verge of bolting to the enemy.[18] Lockhart himself was now convinced that it was unlikely that the Bolsheviks would ever consent to Allied intervention, and his reports to London recommended seizing the initiative quickly, and massively, so as not to lose the support of the major anti-Bolshevik parties. However, he was in no position to make any promises to his contacts and was indeed poorly informed of Allied plans for intervention.[19]

The Kadet Party itself retained a majority against dealing with the Germans at its conference in May, but the minority, especially those associated with the Kadet organization in Kiev, went ahead with plans to seek German aid.[20] Then in June the majority of the Moscow Center voted for dealing with the Germans, and the minority walked out. Despite the efforts of several influential members of the Center to prevent a schism, it came and brought with it an even further sharpening of differences. The Moscow Center itself broke up into a "Right" Center and a "National" Center. The latter, largely composed of liberal Kadets, sought to establish closer links with the Allies, while the former, relieved of internal opposition, became the spokesman for the monarchist bloc and set about seeking an agreement with the Germans.[21]

The Rightist policy was explained to Russian Ambassador Maklakov in Paris as the product of difficult circumstances, of expediency, rather than of Germanophile inclinations. In truth it was a combination of both, but its spokesman wished to avoid alienating the Allies unduly if at the same time they could use German assistance. Thus, Prince G. N. Trubetskoi even tried to persuade French Consul General Grenard in Moscow that an arrangement with the Germans would actually be in the interest of the Allies in the long run, since the object was to restore order and a legitimate national authority in Russia. Grenard, however, rejected this argument and warned that no government installed by German hands would be recognized by the Allies.[22]

Trubetskoi was not deterred by this rejection. On the contrary, he proceeded to establish contact with the German authorities in the Ukraine and brought word of a division in German opinion which provided hope for success but also required quick action. The German High Command, he reported, favored support for the reunification of Russia under a monarchy, but its position was opposed by the Foreign

Ministry, which advised continuing a policy of dismemberment which involved maintaining relations with the Bolshevik Russian government as well as with existing governments in the South. It was, therefore, most important to impress the Germans with conservative strength as quickly as possible and thus sway the decision in favor of the High Command's point of view. The most obvious way to do this, in the eyes of Trubetskoi and those associated with his efforts, was to bring over to their side the one serious anti-German force in the South, the Volunteer Army.[23]

The result of this situation was that considerable pressure was then brought to bear on Alekseev to agree to accept German aid and discard the Army's "idealistic" dedication to the Allies. The most notable, and effective, advocate of such a shift by the Volunteers, however, was not Trubetskoi's group, but a leader of the National Center, Paul Miliukov, one of the Army's closest political collaborators and, of course, previously one of the staunchest supporters of a pro-Allied policy. Miliukov had temporarily retired from public life in the spring of 1918, but visits from such persons as Trubetskoi, and his own observation of the advantages of cooperation with the Germans in Rostov, led him to take an active part in the effort to draw the Volunteer Army into an alliance with the Germans.[24]

In a remarkable correspondence with Alekseev during May and June, Miliukov revealed how far the disillusionment with Allied aid had gone.[25] Although he himself had reached the conclusion that it was necessary to turn away from the Allies only after a "deep struggle" with his own conscience, he wrote, he was now convinced that in such a reorientation lay Russia's one real hope. Facts, he declared, could not be ignored. The failure of the Allies to come to their aid in a substantial way had forced anti-Bolshevik leaders to turn to the Germans, whose support would make it possible to oust the Bolsheviks from power and restore unity to the country.[26] Besides, he noted, reactionaries were already seeking to turn German aid to their own purposes, and if they succeeded they could destroy all hope of preventing a restoration of the old order and perhaps remove the one chance of establishing a constitutional government, even a constitutional monarchy on the British model.[27] The Volunteer Army could not do any good to anyone by attacking the Germans, he argued, but it could serve not only Russia but the West as well by using the Germans to destroy the Bolshevik menace which threatened them all. In any case, he concluded, the principle of *rebus sic stantibus* applied to the complete change in the situation which had come about since the alliance with Britain and France was signed and thus relieved the Army of any legal obligation in this regard.[28]

Despite the fact that Alekseev rejected the "possibility of entering into negotiations and much less of concluding any sort of treaty or understanding" with the Germans and warned Miliukov that the Germans might even be setting a trap for him and the Army, Miliukov went ahead with his plan to negotiate in Kiev.[29] There on June 21 he had an interview with General Haase of the German Command. Haase expressed doubts about Miliukov's ability to speak for the Volunteer Army and about Germany's own willingness to give up its gains in the Brest treaty, but he was quite prepared to recommend further negotiations if Miliukov could assure strong support for a German alliance.[30] Miliukov, indeed, not only gave such assurances but suggested that a "popular" (narodnyi), or constitutional, monarchy would attract support from both the "republicans" (including the Volunteer commander, General Denikin, and his chief of staff, General Romanovskii) and the monarchists, because it would combine constitutional government with traditional forms. Even the common people would support it if it restored unity and order, he declared, since they were tired of war and civil strife.[31]

In this conversation, Miliukov made it clear that he was advocating Russo-German cooperation on the basis of mutual need and not because of any other consideration. He therefore called not for an alliance but simply for "friendly neutrality" and rejected the idea of direct German participation in Russian military operations, as for example through supplying instructors, which was a suggestion made earlier by Haase. Miliukov also refused to compromise on the question of the restoration of Russian borders before the Brest treaty, indicating that only the separation of Poland had been or could be recognized by Russia. His firm principles, he declared, were "unity of citizenship, unity of territory, and sovereignty of the central organs." With the possible exception of some special status for the Ukraine, he opposed the idea of federation, he told Haase, and indeed had believed all along that strong central government in a unitary state was essential to prevent chaos in Russia. For this reason he had preferred to see Grand Duke Mikhail Aleksandrovich take the throne of a constitutional monarchy rather than have the monarchy destroyed entirely. Now, he added, he believed that the best hope of Russia and the most rewarding policy for the Germans would be to support the establishment of a constitutional monarchy under Mikhail, not as autocrat, but as chief of a popular monarchy. In a final remark intended to impress Haase with his sincerity, Miliukov recalled that he had, indeed, opposed the war with Germany from the start and had suffered some persecution from the tsarist government in 1914 because of his opposition.

Haase appeared to be favorably impressed and asked Miliukov to remain available for future negotiations. However, Miliukov's claim that he represented the element favored by history to rebuild Russia did not subsequently impress Ambassador Mumm, who had just returned from Berlin with new instructions. Mumm maintained a tight-lipped scepticism toward Miliukov's arguments at their meeting on June 27. Evading references to General Haase's discussion with Miliukov earlier, he confined himself to declaring simply that the idea of restoring Russia's old borders would be rather "difficult" to implement and glumly remarking that Miliukov had a reputation for pro-Allied policies which put in question the degree of confidence Germany could place in persons like him.[32] According to Miliukov, the very next day Mumm went to Skoropadskii and demanded that he, Miliukov, be expelled from the Ukraine for opposing Ukrainian independence and spreading anti-German propaganda.[33] When later Miliukov once more spoke with Haase, the latter apparently had been instructed to reject any consideration of a revision of the Brest treaty and on that basis to end the talks. Having thought it over, the Germans had obviously decided to continue their policy of divide and rule.[34]

While Miliukov's effort thus accomplished little other than to do irreparable damage to his own reputation, it did serve to clarify German policy. The Germans would continue to work with the Bolsheviks where Russia proper was concerned, and in fact now sought new agreements with the Soviet government which would result in the desired Russian renunciation of claims to territories occupied by German troops, but they would also continue to work with the pro-German regional leaders of the dismembered South Russian territories. In particular they indicated an interest in the new Don ataman, General Krasnov. Unlike Miliukov, Krasnov had an army at his command. Through a combination of a new Cossack rising, some aid from the Volunteers in the Kuban, the arrival of a small force under Colonel M. G. Drozdovskii from the old Rumanian front, the appearance of the Germans along the eastern boundary of the voisko, and Kras-

nov's dynamic leadership, the Don had been rather quickly liberated
from Bolshevik control in May. Krasnov had then rapidly assumed
the powers of a virtual dictator of the Don state, which declared
itself independent.[35]

Although German troops had occupied Rostov and Taganrog, both
cities claimed by the Don, a delegation sent to see Krasnov soon
after his election as ataman on May 16 found him quite amenable
to cooperation. In fact he had already prepared an appeal to Germany
for aid and was organizing a delegation of his own to be sent to Kiev
to enter into relations with the German Command and with Skoropadskii. Krasnov's quick action and obvious desire to cooperate in
order to obtain aid thus convinced the Germans that the Don could
be used as a counterforce to the Volunteer Army and possibly even
as a barrier to Allied efforts to reopen the eastern front, particularly
if a truce could be maintained between the Don and the Bolsheviks.[36]

A Napoleonic figure, Krasnov made utmost use of both his powers as Don ataman and his flair for the dramatic. Upon assuming
office, he immediately demonstrated his remarkable talent for being
simultaneously pro-Russian and a border state nationalist, a monarchist and a defender of the "conquests of the revolution," an ally of the
Volunteer Army and a collaborator with the Germans. The contradictions which he personified caused no little confusion and resentment,
but no man of his day was more successful at being all things to all
men. An extreme centralist at home, he favored decentralization to
the point of federation for the future Russia which he would help
restore. The staunch protector of "Cossack rights," he was also the
author of land reforms which would limit Cossack holdings and dis-
tribute confiscated lands to the peasants. With it all, this picturesque
and dynamic leader not only evaded foreign occupation of the Don
but gave it the unity and strength it had so lacked before—and that
while others were still weak.[37]

Telling his Cossacks that the Germans had come "to help in the
struggle against the Red Army bands and to restore law and order,"
Krasnov hastily sent off to Kiev a Don delegation led by Generals
M. A. Svechin and A. V. Cheriachukin to enter formal negotiations
with the Germans and with Skoropadskii. For this delegation he set
six major tasks: (1) to establish friendly relations, (2) to obtain arms
and supplies for the Don army, (3) to get German and Ukrainian
cooperation in the movement of Russian and Cossack officers and
men to the Don, (4) to secure Ukrainian acceptance of Don claims

to the Taganrog district, (5) to restore rails and other means of communication between the two states, and (6) to establish trade.[38]

When the delegation shortly thereafter held its first meeting with the Germans, it found, of course, that the latter also had certain aims. In particular they wanted a guarantee from the Don that it would not in any way support Allied activities in Russia, either directly or indirectly. This meant above all not allowing Don territory to be used in Allied schemes for reopening the eastern front, and in this regard, Ambassador Mumm pointed out, it was important for the Don to clarify its position vis-à-vis the Volunteer Army. The German Command, said the chief of staff, General Groener, required definite assurances that any arms given to the Don would not fall into the hands of the Volunteer Army "which does not want to recognize that we have concluded peace with Russia and continues to consider us as its enemy." If a clear understanding were reached on these matters, General von Eichhorn informed Krasnov a few days later, the Germans hoped to interest the Don in participating in its long-range plan to establish a series of large independent states on the territory of the former Russian Empire. The Ukraine and Central Russia would be two such states, and a third might be a "Southeastern League" similar to that attempted earlier in the Cossack areas. Krasnov himself could head such a state if he agreed to prohibit the use of its territory by any outside forces other than the Germans.[39]

In reporting on his negotiations with the Germans, General Svechin strongly advised accepting these German offers and the conditions which accompanied them. He therefore recommended that the Don henceforth "refrain from expressing any hope of seeing Russia united," maintain friendly relations with the Germans, and "have no relationship" with the Allies, who thus far, he noted, "have given us nothing and in many ways have betrayed us." The Don, he believed, should declare its readiness to defend its own territory on the terms suggested by the Germans and offer "a commercial agreement with Germany on the basis of the most favored nation principle." In return, the Don could obtain "all necessary arms, supplies, and military equipment," settle its boundary disagreements with Kiev and Moscow "in accordance with our aspirations," and assume leadership of "a stable organization of the League of the Southeast."[40]

In a second letter to the German emperor three weeks later, Krasnov indicated his willingness to follow this advice. Said the Ataman to the Kaiser: the "glorious Don Cossacks" had fought "for the freedom of their country" with a "courage equalled only by that displayed in recent years in the war against the English by a people of Germanic stock, the Boers. . . ." The Don, he continued, was already in the process of forming, on "federalist" principles, an "independent state consisting of the Great Don Voisko, the Astrakhan Voisko. . . , the Terek Voisko, and the peoples of the Northern Caucasus." These "powers," he declared, had "already given their consent" and had decided "to be neutral in the present international conflict." Therefore, wrote Krasnov, he was requesting the Emperor's recognition of both the Don and the "Dono-Caucasian League" and hoped to receive German support for Don claims to Tsaritsyn, Kamyshin, and Voronezh, in addition to Taganrog, against the claims of others.[41]

Finally, the Ataman asked that Germany "exert pressure on the Soviet authorities in Moscow" to evacuate Don territory and refrain from further attacks. To help secure the Don, he also hoped that Germany would not only grant it "cannon, rifles, ammunition, and supplies" but also, if it saw fit, "set up in Don territory factories for the manufacture" of these things. In return for all this, the Don would "observe strict neutrality in the World War . . . and grant to Germany the exclusive right to export foodstuffs and raw materials" in addition to "special privileges in investing capital in Don industries and in developing new enterprises." Such an arrangement, Krasnov believed, would be "certain to bring mutual benefits," and their friendship, "cemented in bloodshed on common battlefields," would strike a major blow "against our common enemies. . . ."

Krasnov subsequently took steps to implement these claims and promises, for example by inviting representatives to a founding congress in Novocherkassk and presenting a proposed constitution for the league referred to in the letter.[42] Krasnov's efforts were of little effect, however, since the other "members" of the league failed to accept the idea after General Denikin came out against it.[43] Nevertheless, his new German allies accepted his work as convincing and supplied considerable quantities of military aid. Through the German envoy in the Don, Major Cochenhausen, agreements were entered providing for currency exchange, military equipment in return for grain, and tentative plans for joint military action if the need arose. The latter never materialized, but reportedly during the summer of 1918 alone the Germans supplied the Don with 11,651 rifles, 46 cannons, 88 machine guns, 109,104 rounds of artillery shells, and 11,594,721 rounds of rifle ammunition.[44]

For the most part the Germans appear to have tried to stay out of the question of relations between Krasnov and the Bolsheviks, but in so far as they did become involved they attempted to play one against the other and hoped to use both against the Volunteer Army and the Allies. Thus in a meeting between German representatives and a delegation of Rightists in Moscow on July 21, the former declared that German cooperation with Krasnov was aimed at action against the Bolsheviks,[45] but in a note on August 27 to Soviet Ambassador Ioffe, German Foreign Minister von Hintze indicated that both German and Bolshevik forces should do all possible to suppress the Volunteer Army and, in consideration for such cooperation, Germany would support Soviet claims to the Donets basin and would require the Ukraine and Georgia to supply Soviet Russia with specified natural resources (iron ore and manganese in particular). In reply the Bolsheviks indicated that they understood that the Germans would also see to it that Krasnov did not undertake military action against Bolshevik-held territory. Later Soviet Foreign Commissar Chicherin wired the Ukrainian Bolshevik leader, Rakovskii, that the German Embassy had informed him confidentially of "steps by von Hintze with Krasnov in order to isolate the Volunteers, with whom it will then be easier to deal."[46]

In accepting German aid, Krasnov, of course, encountered strong opposition from the Volunteer Command, especially from General Denikin. It was true that the majority of the officers of the Volunteer Army were conservative in outlook, and there was even a fairly strong Germanophile tendency among them, but General Denikin used his position as commander to prevent the identification of the Army with either a monarchist or a pro-German policy. To his mind, the Army could not be allowed to become the "agent of any one political party or public organization" precisely because it was the Army of the Russian state. Besides, as a man of moderate liberal views, he was convinced that a monarchist policy was both undesirable and unpopular among the people generally. He also considered that the Army's duty to save Russia was inseparably bound up with loyalty to the Allied cause, not only because of past commitments but also because of German support for the Bolsheviks on the one hand and for dismemberment of Russia, manifested in the backing of separatist regimes in the Ukraine, Georgia, and the Don, on the other hand. Cooperation with the Germans, in Denikin's view, offered little prospect for either defeating the Bolsheviks or reuniting Russia. Therefore, in his opinion the policies of Krasnov, just as those of Skoropadskii, bordered on treason to the "One Russia" which he was pledged to defend, and which he believed the Allies would also defend. Although he, too, was disappointed with Allied action thus far, he would not accept the alternative represented by Krasnov.[47]

Krasnov repeatedly appealed to Denikin to cooperate with his efforts, and especially to aid in his attempt to take Tsaritsyn from the Bolsheviks, but he refused to subordinate himself to Denikin for the sake of a unified command or to relinquish his "separatist" pro-German policies. Denikin in turn refused to accept anything less as a basis for joint action, and as a result each went his own way. The Volunteers turned their operations to the south, first to clear out the Kuban and then to move toward the Caucasus Mountain region, a campaign which was to last through the summer and into the autumn.[48] It would be incorrect to say, however, that there was no cooperation between the Don and the Volunteer Army, for it was indeed the Don which supplied the Volunteers with much of their arms and equipment during this time.[49] Although such a transfer of supplies was contrary to his agreement with the Germans, Krasnov explained his action with a sarcastic quip aimed as much at Denikin as at the Germans: "I wash them in the clear waters of the Silent Don and present them clean to the Army of the Don and to the Volunteer Army."[50]

* * * * * *

The great success of the Germans in South Russia, and their simultaneous offensive on the western front which reached to within forty miles of Paris, made it all the more imperative for the Allies to do something more substantial to restore the eastern front. Thus at the same time that some disillusioned Russian conservatives, and even liberals, were turning to the Germans for aid, Allied agents were establishing closer relations with the socialists and laying plans for further intervention. Consideration of more extensive Allied action had, notably, been greatly stimulated in May by the rising of a corps of Czech troops in Russia.

During the war certain minority nationalities, chiefly Slavs, resident in Russia had been permitted to form separate, and generally small, military units which were used primarily for reconnaissance and similar duties. One such unit was the Czech Druzina which had been formed after much delay, resulting from internal rivalries and hesitation on the part of the Russian Foreign Ministry, and in mid-1916 this unit had begun recruiting Czech prisoners captured from engagements with the Austrian army on the southwestern front. It was not until after the March Revolution of 1917, however, when obstacles had been cleared away by the support of Miliukov and Kerenskii for the project, that the Druzina, later called the Czech Legion, had become a significant military organization. From May 1917 to March 1918 the leadership and reorganization of the Legion had been taken over directly by Tomas Masaryk on behalf of the Czech National Council in Paris, and recruiting expenses had been assumed by France, where a similar Czech force was already in being under Allied command.[51]

After meritorious service in the short-lived Brusilov offensive launched by Kerenskii in July 1917, the Legion was concentrated in the Ukraine. There, after the Bolshevik coup in November, it had inevitably become involved in the local situation despite Masaryk's desire to avoid such involvement. Chiefly because of the need of Ukrainian cooperation for provisioning the troops, Masaryk had permitted the Legion to be cast in the role of ally of the Ukrainian Rada late in November, an action which coincided with mounting Allied interest in the Ukraine. In December, the Allied Supreme Council had officially designated the Legion as an Allied force, and Masaryk had been encouraged to employ it in the defense of the Ukraine.[52] With the signing of a separate peace between Germany and the Ukraine in February 1918, however, Masaryk's alliance with the Rada had lapsed, and a decision had to be made as to how the Legion was to respond to the Bolshevik invasion of the Ukraine and the approaching German occupation.

At this point, General Berthelot, Allied commander in Rumania, had proposed the transfer of the Legion to that area to aid in its defense against the Germans, while General Alekseev had relayed through General Tabouis an appeal that it be sent to aid the Don, then being overrun by the Bolsheviks. Although sympathizing with the latter because of his past association with Alekseev and Kornilov, Masaryk rejected both of these suggestions on grounds that they would plunge the Legion into highly precarious circumstances with little prospect of success.[53] Instead he had found it expedient to turn to the Bolsheviks, now in virtual control of the Ukraine, for an agreement to permit the evacuation of the Legion to the east. At the same time, Masaryk had obtained Allied approval for the withdrawal of the Legion from Russia via Vladivostok, and late in February the French military mission in Moscow had assumed responsibility for this operation.[54]

However, the Legion's troubles had only begun. While negotiations with Stalin and Trotskii had resulted in agreement in March for the peaceful evacuation of the Czechs with their arms and equipment, local Bolshevik commanders had insisted upon and got from Legion officers a commitment to surrender a considerable part of their arms as condition for passage to the Transsiberian railway from the Ukraine. In Penza, on March 22, 1918, the first incident of open conflict had occurred when the local soviet authorities stopped the trains carrying the Czechs and ordered them to surrender their weapons. During a lengthy delay at this point, the efforts of Bolshevik agitators to turn Legion soldiers against their officers, particularly against the Russian officers still assigned to the staff, further irritated Czech tempers. A second incident, the one usually credited with setting off a full-scale revolt by the Czechs, occurred in Cheliabinsk on May 14, when a fight erupted between the Czechs and some Hungarian prisoners of war being moved to the west, and the Czechs seized control of the city. Moscow now ordered a complete surrender of arms by the Legion, and the latter resolved to defy this order and any other effort to interfere with its movement. Within a few days the younger officers of the Legion had assumed full control of its actions and began a determined campaign to fight their way to Vladivostok against what they now regarded as a joint Bolshevik-German plot to disrupt their plans to leave Russia.[55]

The Czech force of some 60,000 men was soon strung out the length of the Transsiberian railway, taking control of the towns along the way in an open struggle with Bolshevik authority. This development suddenly, "as if by magic" in Churchill's words, changed the whole situation and opened up the question of a new anti-German (and anti-Bolshevik) front in the east.[56] The Allies had in fact had virtually nothing to do with the Czech revolt; both Allied officers and Russian officers attached to the Legion had advised against it.[57] Indeed, the immediate aim of the revolt had been to enable the Legion to get out of Russia as soon as possible. Yet the consequences of the revolt could hardly now be ignored, particularly since a spontaneous alliance had immediately developed on the spot between the Legion and anti-Bolshevik Russian elements, chiefly Socialist Revolutionaries. Although General Lavergne finally conveyed French approval for the Legion's actions on June 27, there were no Allied plans for the Legion other than its evacuation.[58] However, proposals for an Allied intervention in the north were being considered at this time, and this question was naturally affected by the Czech action and by the response of the Socialist Revolutionaries to it.[59]

At the beginning of the Legion's troubles with the Bolsheviks, General Lavergne had suggested rerouting the Czech force to Arkhangelsk, and on May 2 the overburdened Allied leaders had been requested to approve this proposal. Because of objections from both Clemenceau and the Czech National Council, however, a compromise proposal was adopted according to which only a part of the Legion, that still in western Siberia, was to be rerouted through Arkhangelsk. While there was no mention of using the Czech force in support of Allied intervention at this point, the two ideas naturally coalesced after the revolt. On May 17 the British Cabinet, in a decision to reinforce the small naval detachment in Murmansk, dispatched General F. C. Poole to reconnoiter the area in the north for future Allied landings, and on May 18 a British suggestion to employ the Czechs as an intervention army was put to the French government for its consideration.[60]

It was at about this same time that Lockhart and Lavergne conferred with the Allied ambassadors in Vologda and reached agreement on the necessity of a massive and swift Allied military intervention. As Lockhart reported, a "more favorable moment" for such an intervention would not likely recur, and delay, he warned, would only further disillusion those anti-Bolshevik elements who were ready to cooperate, particularly the socialists.[61] The Allied Supreme Council did, indeed, on June 3 give approval to the northern intervention after the United States had indicated its willingness to support this operation, and on June 23 the advance party of Allied troops landed at Murmansk, with plans calling for later landings in Arkhangelsk.[62] It was another month, however, before the Allied Council finally reached agreement on a larger intervention to extend into Siberia for the purpose of establishing a new eastern front. Meanwhile the major development shaping circumstances in Russia was the series of revolts staged by the Socialist Revolutionaries in July.

The Murmansk landing and rumors that a major Allied invasion was scheduled for some time in July had stimulated action by various socialist groups to prepare uprisings against the Bolsheviks.[63] The socialists did not represent a united front any more than the conservatives, but the Socialist Revolutionary party had been shown by elections to the Constituent Assembly to have a mass popular following unmatched by any other party.[64] The decision of the "Left" Socialist Revolutionaries in November to enter the Bolshevik government had split the party into pro-Bolshevik and anti-Bolshevik factions, but by the summer of 1918 both Right and Left Socialist Revolutionaries were plotting against the government, the former from without and the latter from within, and in both cases on a platform of opposition to the German alliance of the Bolsheviks.[65] When the Allied Supreme War Council declared on July 2 that "practically all elements of the Russian population" now appeared willing to support an intervention against both the Bolsheviks and the Germans, its statement therefore had some basis in fact.[66]

The events of July, however, illustrated at once both the strengths and the weaknesses of the socialist opposition to the Bolsheviks. On July 4 and 5, at the opening session of the Fifth Congress of Soviets, the Left Socialist Revolutionaries, led by Maria Spiridonova, bitterly denounced the Germans and the Brest treaty, and the following day their forces, including a part of the Soviet security police, began a revolt against the government by assassinating the German ambassador.[67] During these same days, revolts by Right Socialist Revolutionaries under the leadership of Boris Savinkov were carried out in several cities north and east of Moscow. Moreover, the Socialist Revolutionary members of the disbanded Constituent Assembly had now organized themselves in Samara as a new "all-Russian" government, and the acting commander of Czech troops in the area, General S. K. Cecek, temporarily assumed command of both Russian and Czech forces to form the "vanguard" of an "anti-German front in Russia in conjunction with the whole Russian nation and our Allies."[68]

With the exception of the Samara government, however, all of these socialist efforts were soon suppressed by the Bolsheviks. Although advance knowledge of the plan to land Allied troops in Arkhangelsk played an important role, and Allied agents even reportedly suggested the July timing, these uprisings were not actually coordinated either with each other or with Allied actions. They were certainly not simply the result of Allied machinations, for both the Right and the Left Socialist Revolutionaries acted largely on their own initiative. To the extent that they were really influenced by rumors of Allied plans, they were, as it turned out, actually misled, for those rumors did not accurately represent Allied policy, either officially or unofficially, in so far as they suggested an intention of moving a large Allied force into the interior of Russia from the north.[69]

Final plans for Allied intervention on a significant scale were not fully elaborated and approved by the Allied Supreme War Council until July 2, and even then they were partially conditioned upon future American acceptance, which was not conveyed to the Allies until July 17.[70] Moreover, these plans called for major action not in the north but through Vladivostok into Siberia. At the same time, however, it would not be surprising if the Socialist Revolutionaries had been misled on these matters, for indeed their informers were rather poorly informed themselves. Even Lockhart, according to his later account, expected a large Allied force to land at Arkhangelsk and march to Moscow. In fact, however, the Allied landing which finally took place there on August 2, after a Socialist Revolutionary government had taken power under N. V. Chaikovskii, was not only too late to be coordinated with the Russian uprisings around and in Moscow but also was so small (about 1500 men) as to constitute, in the view of the astonished Lockhart, a "blunder comparable with the worst mistakes of the Crimean war."[71]

It should also be noted, in connection with the landings in the north, that the immediate justification of Allied action had not been the possibility of revolts against the Bolshevik regime but the threat of a German advance into the area, particularly through Finland. The breakdown of the Brest negotiations late in February had followed upon the outbreak of civil war in Finland between Reds and Whites in January. The latter, under the leadership of Marshal Carl Gustaf Mannerheim, had been reinforced in February by German-trained Finnish troops and some German officers. When some of the White forces followed retreating Red units into the area of the Murmansk railway early in March, both Allied and Bolshevik authorities had reacted with alarm. Possibly also informed of the decision of the German High Command at this time to send regular German troops into Finland, Allied military authorities had felt it imperative to act to block an anticipated extension of German operations into northern Russia to seize the Allied military stores there. Even the Bolshevik-led Murmansk soviet had experienced panic at this prospect and had decided to call upon the Allies for help. Most notably, Trotskii himself, following the pattern of his actions at this time, had on March 14 advised the Murmansk soviet to "accept any and all assistance from the Allied missions" in order to stop the expected invasion.[72]

It had thus been on this basis that Allied landings had taken place first in March and then more substantially in June in Murmansk. By the time the latter landing was carried out, however, the Soviet government had become alarmed at Allied actions, had come under pressure from the Germans to resist Allied intervention or risk rupture of relations and repudiation of the Brest treaty, and had concluded that the Allies intended to use the Czechs and anti-Bolshevik Russian elements to stage a major intervention aimed at the overthrow of the Soviet government. As has been implied, the subsequent, and somewhat haphazard, expansion of Allied intervention plans had taken place without careful consideration of their effects in Russia. The aim, in so far as the Allied military planners were concerned, was still to frustrate German plans, and for this purpose to link up with the Czechs and ultimately establish a new eastern front from Arkhangelsk to the Volga and southward. By the time the Arkhangelsk landings had taken place in August, of course, such action could no longer be based upon even a tacit agreement with the Bolsheviks (either locally or at the center) but on the contrary involved overthrowing local Bolshevik authority and ignoring the protests of the Soviet government. Nevertheless, the point remains that the Allies by these actions had not prepared themselves to march on Moscow with overwhelming force but rather to introduce a relatively small number of troops in order to establish a link through the north with the Siberian front.

This intervention by the Allies had, at the same time, inevitably led to a final breakoff of contacts with the Bolsheviks. On August 4 both the British and French consulates in Moscow were raided, and their staffs were arrested. For a time Lockhart and his assistant, Hicks, were excepted from this wholesale action, but following an attempt on Lenin's life by a Socialist Revolutionary on August 30, both were added to the Bolsheviks' collection of hostages. The "Lockhart Plot" then became the theme of Bolshevik propaganda which now branded him, in Trotskii's words, as a "tool used by the British government to keep the Bolsheviks quiet while it was preparing an anti-Bolshevik coup."[73] The Allied Powers themselves still viewed the intervention as a part of the war against Germany and her allies, but the Bolsheviks were now definitely considered one of the latter.

* * * * * *

On August 27 formal supplements to the Brest treaty were signed, giving Germany control over the occupied Baltic territories and providing for the recognition of Georgia by the German government. The understanding included an informal agreement that the Turks would be kept out of Baku and its oil reserved for Soviet and German use alone.[74] A German military mission had already been dispatched in July via Astrakhan to work out the details with Shaumian. During July and August the Georgians also entered additional agreements with German industrial firms for the establishment of joint (50–50) stock companies with monopoly rights in the exploitation of manganese and the use of the rail heads serving the mines, and arrangements were made for loans to Georgia through German banks. As one of the Georgian delegates in Berlin described it, the Germans "rushed passionately to all the stocks, underground riches, all the possibilities which had suddenly appeared" with the breaking of the Allied blockade.[75]

At the same time, the German Command in Kiev took steps to head off the rumored possibility that the Allies would soon have the eastern front reopened as far south as Tsaritsyn. Having found the Volunteer Army unalterably opposed to any dealings more cooperative than "armed neutrality," they decided to permit the formation of new Russian forces in the Ukraine, with the hope of splintering even further the efforts to organize idle Russian officers into a single force and at the same time with a view to developing units which might ultimately be used against the Allied front on the Volga.[76] From mid-June they therefore suppressed the recruitment of troops for the Volunteers in the Ukraine and contributed funds to finance the organization of new "armies" there, not for the Ukraine notably, but independent of Ukrainian authority. Eventually three such rather motley armies were formed under monarchist banners, with German money, German arms, and German purposes behind them, and all three ultimately wound up under Krasnov's control, after he had promised the Germans specifically not to allow the Czechs to enter Don territory if they should move south.[77]

The only real effect of this was to add a few thousand troops to Krasnov's growing forces and extend his domain. He, in effect, added the Voronezh and Saratov districts to the Don in August by issuing orders naming the commanders of two of the new armies, the "Southern Army" and the "Russian National Army," as military governors of these districts under the Don Command. Later he converted all three of the armies into corps of the Don army, jointly forming of them a so-called "South Russian Army" under General N. I. Ivanov.[78] Not all of Krasnov's plans could be realized, but he continued to maintain his German ties and, indeed, broadened his activities to establish relations with the "Belorussian People's Republic," with the Poles, the Bulgarians, and even the Turks.[79]

When the first full Krug ("Great" Voisko Krug) began meeting on August 28, there was considerable cirticism of Krasnov's policies among the delegates, and the pro-Volunteer and pro-Allied element had clearly grown in strength. The future prospect of Allied intervention therefore played a major role in the Krug's deliberation, especially in view of the obvious disadvantages that Krasnov's leadership would pose, but the risk of immediate German retaliation and the danger of internal disunity which Krasnov's defeat would entail led the Krug to approve Krasnov's foreign policy and keep him in power.[80] Despite a threat from the German representative, Major von Cochenhausen, however, the Krug also declared its "feelings of admiration" for the Volunteer Army.[81] On the other hand, relations with it were bound to remain difficult as long as the Germans were present. Krasnov and Denikin continued to clash, and in fact their differences tended to increase rather than diminish.[82]

The Allies hoped to counter these German measures, and more importantly to unify the anti-Bolsheviks, by promoting the establishment of a national government which could rally all Russian forces under a liberal program. The effort of the Socialist Revolutionary committee in Samara to form such an all-Russian government therefore attracted considerable attention and raised hopes that it would supply the basis for a unification of pro-Allied and anti-Bolshevik elements all the way from Arkhangelsk to South Russia. General Alekseev, whose name had figured in Allied plans on several occasions, had already been contacted again in June by General Lavergne, who urged him to go to Samara to assume "leadership of all troops operating against the Bolsheviks." In replying to this, however, Alekseev, while expressing interest in the idea, conditioned his acceptance on there being "no division of authority" in the form of a "directorate" (the form favored by the Socialist Revolutionaries), no restrictions on his authority as military commander, and no subordination to Allied authorities.[83]

Alekseev's conditions went right to the heart of the problems contained in the plan to promote the Samara government as an all-Russian government. Despite Allied support, it could not attract a significant following among military and nonsocialist circles. Its socialist membership held firmly to the belief that the government must be a collective directorate rather than a dictatorship, although it was acknowledged that all the armed forces should be united under one commander. The more conservative elements, on the other hand, were convinced that the socialist approach had already proved to be a fatal weakness and that only a strong single leader could exert the authority necessary to the struggle.[84] Moreover, during July a rival government was established in Omsk which rejected the Samara government's claims and offered instead a more conservative regime with strong military backing.[85] Alekseev's candidacy for the position of national military commander, indeed, received more support from the Omsk conservatives than it did from Samara.[86] Any effort to promote an alliance between Omsk and Alekseev in opposition to the socialists, on the other hand, would be complicated by the fact that the Czechs, who still represented the major military force in the area, were supporting the Socialist Revolutionaries.[87]

Despite the obstacles, a compromise was eventually worked out between the Samara and Omsk governments to establish a new all-Russian government in Ufa. On September 23 a five-man directorate was installed under the Right Socialist Revolutionary, N. P. Avksent'ev, and included the Kadet leader, N. I. Astrov; the head of the Omsk government, P. V. Vologodskii; the head of the Arkhangelsk government, N. V. Chaikovskii; and General V. G. Boldyrev, who was acceptable to the Czechs and was substituted for the ailing Alekseev.[88] In supporting this government the Allies sought to bring representatives of all three major fronts of the war into an association at once liberal in political outlook and backed by significant military force. The Czechs, whose alliance with the socialists had been spontaneous, now became by force of circumstances the chief support of the new coalition government. General Maurice Janin, who had been designated commander-in-chief of Allied forces in Russia in August, entered an accord with General Boldyrev on September 24 recognizing the latter as Russian commander under the former's general authority for the Allies.[89] In view of these achievements, the British government was considering recognition of the Ufa Directorate, but before it had taken any action on the matter information was received of new Bolshevik victories which forced the Directorate to flee to Omsk, and so decision on recognition was delayed.[90] In Omsk, a "Council of Ministers" was formed under Vologodskii, with Admiral Kolchak as minister of war, but instead of being assuaged, the old conflict between the conservative and socialist factions again erupted.[91]

Faced with repeated failure to achieve unity, most of the Allied representatives in Omsk then gave their support to a coup which ousted the socialists on November 17 and the next day established a dictatorship under Admiral Kolchak as "Supreme Ruler."[92] Despite the support now given to Kolchak by the British mission chief, General Knox, however, the British Cabinet, which had finally decided to recognize the government in Omsk on November 17, withdrew its decision upon learning of the overthrow of the coalition.[93] On the other hand, General Janin, who disapproved the coup, nevertheless contributed to its success by ordering the Czechs not to interfere. Kolchak's title, however, remained simply a title with little practical significance at this stage. There were still, as Alekseev put it, just too many "centers" bent upon recognition and Allied aid, and the military situation was deteriorating rapidly, in Siberia because of the decision of the demoralized Czechs to resume their evacuation to Vladivostok, and in the South because of the continued extension of German influence.[94]

* * * * * *

The situation in the South had become most critical in the summer of 1918. Not only were the Germans entrenched in the Ukraine, but they seemed to be on the verge of achieving their most ambitious schemes to penetrate Central Asia.[95] British forces intended to combat this threat were only beginning to appear on the southern borders. As noted, work had been begun as early as January and February 1918 on the organization of special military missions, the major one under Major General L. C. Dunsterville to move in through Persia from Baghdad, with the goal of reaching the Caspian and establishing contacts with pro-Allied elements in Transcaucasia. A second mission under Major General Sir Wilfrid Malleson was to move to Meshed with troops from India and establish contacts in Transcaspia, and a third under Colonel P. T. Etherton and Lieutenant Colonel F. M. Bailey was to proceed via Chinese Turkestan (Kashgar) into Russian Turkestan to Tashkent. Plans had called for these forces to be drawn from Empire troops, especially the Indian Army, to be quite small in numbers, and to perform their task largely through recruitment of native support in the areas to which they were assigned.[96] However, such plans had proved to be rather difficult to put into practice.

Dunsterville had taken command of the spearhead force of some 12 officers, 41 men, and 41 Fords and had left Baghdad as early as January 27, 1918.[97] From there he had proceeded into Persia at the rate of about ten miles a day, the Fords being pushed a good deal of the way through the snow. Another 70 officers and 140 men, picked from the South African, Australian, and Canadian units in France, with a special party of Russian officers to act as liaison men, had also set out from Italy in February by ship to join the "Dunsterforce" in Persia.[98] British and French intelligence agents in Transcaucasia provided reports of strong pro-Allied groups there, but first Dunsterville

had to establish a position in northern Persia from which to make contact and prepare for the intervention.[99] And this had proved to be
no small task.

Actually Dunsterville's small band had initially made a startling
dash to the Caspian port of Enzeli during the first two weeks of February, taking advantage of the element of surprise and the terrifying
appearance which a motorized force made in a primitive land. It was
a daring move through roadless terrain, crowds of Russian refugee-
soldiers going home, and hostile Persian bands, but at the end of the
road in Enzeli, Dunsterville had found a Bolshevik committee in control of the port. His whole party could then easily have fallen prisoner
of the Bolsheviks, but at that early date the latter did not yet consider the British force as their enemy. "Stalky" Dunsterville was
therefore not only able to talk his way out of this situation but had
even persuaded the chairman of the Bolshevik committee, Cheliapin,
to give him some gasoline so that his Fords could return to Hamadan.
The upshot of this affair, however, was that Dunsterville had then
found himself stuck at Hamadan, where he had to await a more favorable opportunity to try again. The obstacles were, indeed, so great
that it had taken him over five months just to get back to Enzeli
again.[100]

The real turning point in Dunsterville's efforts had come only when
he entered an alliance with a small force of Russian Cossacks still in
Persia. General Baratov, the commander of the Russian army on the
Turkish front, had been unable to maintain his army after the revolution, but his subordinate, Colonel Lazar Bicherakov, had managed,
by virtue of the personal loyalty of his men, to hold together a small
band of Cossacks who had taken refuge in central Persia. Realizing
that his own small forces would never suffice to achieve his mission,
Dunsterville had sought and obtained Bicherakov's agreement to join
him in an effort to get both of them to Transcaucasia.[101] Although
Bicherakov reportedly demanded rather exorbitant financial support
for his services, Dunsterville defended this subsidy as necessary for
the accomplishment of his mission, and Bicherakov was authorized to
lead a joint Russian-British force, including a newly arrived armored-
car brigade, against the insurgent Persian nationalist, Kuchik Khan,
whose forces stood astride the road to Enzeli. By mid-June Kuckik's
troops were routed, and Dunsterville and Bicherakov conferred on
how to deal with the Bolsheviks at Enzeli and Baku. The tactic which
they settled upon was subversion.[102]

From the time of the revolution Bicherakov had been receiving

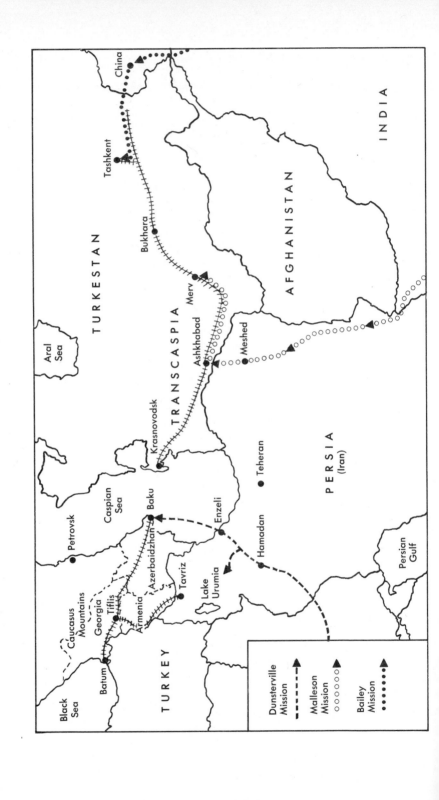

China

Tashkent

TURKESTAN

Bukhara

Aral
Sea

Merv

TRANSCASPIA

Ashkhabad

Meshed

AFGHANISTAN

INDIA

Krasnovodsk

Teheran

PERSIA
(Iran)

Caspian
Sea

Baku

Petrovsk

Enzeli

Hamadan

Persian
Gulf

Caucasus
Mountains

Georgia

Tiflis

Azerbaidzhan

Armenia

Tavriz

Lake
Urumia

Batum

Black
Sea

TURKEY

Dunsterville
Mission

Malleson
Mission

Bailey
Mission

offers from the Bolsheviks, and, with many Russian troops turning Bolshevik in order to get back home, nothing seemed more natural than for Bicherakov to follow the same path. Moreover, with the Turks closing in on Baku and moving into northern Persia, the Bolsheviks were in no position to be particular about their allies. Hence Bicherakov "went over" to the Bolsheviks at Enzeli, accepted appointment as a Red Army commander with the rank of general, and then, through Cheliapin's committee, established contact with the soviet in Baku.[103] With the latter he arranged to move his troops across the Caspian and to take the post of commander of Soviet forces defending that beleaguered city against the Turks. Bicherakov's Cossacks thus left Enzeli on July 1 and moved into a line just south of Baku.[104]

During this same time Dunsterville engineered a rapid infiltration and eventual overthrow of Bolshevik control in Enzeli, negotiated at last a truce with Kuchik Khan, arranged with the defunct Russian Road Company to take over its road, telegraph, and other properties in northern Persia, made a hurried trip to Baghdad for consultation with British headquarters there, and finally established contact with Socialist Revolutionary and Dashnak elements in Baku who were willing to cooperate, and together they worked out a plan for a coup to unseat the Bolsheviks in Baku and issue an appeal for British aid.[105]

The governing power in Baku was held by a coalition of Bolsheviks and Left Socialist Revolutionaries, supported by the Left wings of the Menshevik and Dashnak groups.[106] However, this bloc, led by S. Shaumian, still held only a minority in the soviet itself, a fact which had decisive significance when the soviet began a debate on seeking outside aid in July. Shaumian's coalition had agreed to bringing Bicherakov over, but Bicherakov had found the odds too great in facing the Turks and had ordered his troops to move on to the north. In this situation, the Right Socialist Revolutionaries, Dashnaks, and Mensheviks then demanded an appeal to the British for support. Split once more into its majority and minority factions, the Baku soviet thus on July 25 voted 259 to 236 to seek British help.[107]

Refusing to accept this position, Shaumian's Left coalition was forced out of office, and a new government composed of representatives of the majority factions was installed under the title of "Centro-Caspian Dictatorship." On the basis of preceding secret negotiations with Dunsterville, this government then issued an open appeal for British troops to defend the city.[108] On August 4 a small British advance party under Colonel C. B. Stokes was transported on the hastily prepared ships available in Enzeli and landed in Baku. The German mission which had been sent out earlier to take over Baku in cooperation with Shaumian arrived shortly thereafter. Its members were, to put it mildly, rather surprised to find themselves met by the British and put under arrest immediately. Soviet troops which had been sent to Baku from Astrakhan left on August 12, accompanied by the Bolshevik members of the overthrown government. However, when it was discovered that they had taken away a large part of the arms belonging to the city, the ships were stopped and the arms and the Bolshevik commissars were seized and returned to Baku. On August 17 Dunsterville arrived with the rest of his force and began preparing the defenses of the city.[109]

The second of the British military missions, under General Malleson, had meanwhile, in June, moved along a line from the Indian border northward in eastern Persia to Meshed, filling the gap left there by the withdrawal of Russian troops earlier and taking over what was known as the "East Persian Cordon."[110] By midsummer Malleson had two squadrons of the 28th Indian Cavalry Regiment and two companies of the 19th Punjabi Infantry Battalion in position some 160 miles from Ashkhabad across the Russian border. His mission was to do whatever possible to interfere with an expected German-Turkish move across the Caspian and through Transcaspia, but his instructions made no specific mention of military intervention by his own forces into Russia.[111]

At this time almost all of Turkestan was in Bolshevik hands, but here too the power of the Bolsheviks rested on weak foundations.[112] Their hold on Turkestan was based partly on the recruitment of the German and Austrian prisoners of war in this region and partly on the Russian minority among the population.[113] Rebellious Moslem elements conducted sporadic revolts, and the rising of the Orenburg Cossacks under Ataman A. I. Dutov, in alliance with other anti-Bolshevik forces on the Siberian front, had made contact with Soviet Russia extremely difficult. Moreover, while the Bolshevik government in Tashkent, under F. E. Kolesov, was trying to contend with these problems, its Menshevik and Socialist Revolutionary "allies" in Ashkhabad sought to win over the population, particularly the "proletariat" consisting of the railway workers, to a revolutionary but anti-Bolshevik position. When, in June, the Bolshevik government attempted to force all able-bodied men in the city to register for military service, the opposition seized upon the slogan "soviets without

Bolsheviks" and instigated a rebellion. A punitive force was sent out from Tashkent, but it was repelled, and on July 16 a new anti-Bolshevik government, backed by the railway workers and headed by a Socialist Revolutionary, Fedor Funtikov, was established in Ashkhabad. Soon thereafter supporting revolts in Merv and Krasnovodsk also overthrew Bolshevik control and installed new governments under the general leadership of Ashkhabad.[114]

Contact with General Malleson had already been made through another Socialist Revolutionary and an associate of Funtikov's, Aleksei Dorrer, who had gone to Meshed earlier.[115] It is not unlikely that hopes for support from British troops in northern Persia played some role in the decisions of the rebels, although the revolt itself was clearly a reaction to Bolshevik policy. On July 29 the new Ashkhabad government issued an invitation to the British at Meshed to send aid and authorized its representative, Vladimir Dokhov, to enter negotiations at once for a formal agreement. Malleson in return sent an officer of his staff, Captain R. Teague-Jones, to Ashkhabad to establish liaison and begin talks. In view of a Bolshevik attack which soon overran Merv, Malleson also moved his own troops up to the border and requested permission from Indian army headquarters at Simla to aid the Ashkhabad government. On August 8 this permission was granted, and within less than a week British and Indian troops were sent into action to support the Transcaspian army under Oraz Sirdar in its defense of the railway between Merv and Ashkhabad.[116]

Meanwhile negotiations had proceeded successfully, and on August 19 a protocol of agreement was signed by Malleson and Dokhov. In view of the "common danger from Bolshevism and Turko-German attack in the borders of the Transcaspian region and Turkestan," and to restore order and prepare adequate defenses of the area, said the agreement, the British would (a) defend the city of Baku as the vital gateway to Transcaspia, (b) establish a garrison of British infantry and artillery in Krasnovodsk on the west side of the Caspian, (c) supply artillery, machine guns, rifles, ammunition, explosives, airplanes, instructors, and troops to the limit of their ability, and provide financial assistance to the Ashkhabad government for the continuation of the war and current expenses. For its part, the Ashkhabad government agreed to (a) make every effort to defend its territory, (b) put available ships and the port of Krasnovodsk at the disposal of the British, (c) facilitate the full use of roads, railways, telegraph equipment, and natural resources, (d) halt all export of cotton except as would be agreed upon at a later date, and (e) destroy railway equipment, oil and water reserves, bridges, etc. in case the area should be overrun by enemy troops.[117]

With this agreement as the basis of his support for the Transcaspian government, Malleson sent two companies of the 19th Punjabis to stop a Bolshevik advance at Kaakha, where a major battle took place on August 26. Shortly thereafter reinforcements and artillery were also sent from Enzeli to Krasnovodsk where the Socialist Revolutionary government under Kun was in power, and considerable quantities of arms and ammunition, largely provided by Dunsterville, were supplied to the Transcaspian forces. With a total strength of 950 officers and men, about 500 of whom were at the front, Malleson's small force then made plans for an advance along the railway to the east. Although the Turkman troops proved to be generally unreliable in battle, relations with Oraz Sirdar and with the Russian officers in the Transcaspian army were good, and their cooperation proved effective. By mid-October the offensive had been mounted, and before the end of the month the Bolsheviks had been forced to withdraw beyond Merv.[118]

The third prong of these operations, the mission sent to approach Tashkent from the east via Kashgar just inside China, was both less significant and less successful.[119] Its purpose was largely that of a scouting party intended not for intervention but for gathering information. Colonel P. T. Etherton, Lieutenant Colonel F. M. Bailey, and Major L. V. Blacker had left India for Kashgar with a handful of Indian guards in April 1918. They arrived in Kashgar on June 7 and began a survey of the border area. Etherton then replaced Sir George Macartney as British Consul General there, and Macartney in turn made plans to follow Bailey and Blacker, who left for Tashkent on July 24, to establish a consulate in Turkestan. With the luck which comes from a combination of audacity and a lack of information, Bailey's party reached Tashkent safely on August 14 and immediately proceeded to call upon the soviet "foreign commissar," Domagaitskii.[120] Understandably Domagaitskii found it difficult to believe that a British representative could really be calling upon him with a friendly request to establish a consulate and cordial relations at the very time that British troops were engaged in hostilities around Ashkhabad. However, he agreed temporarily to allow Bailey to go about his business. Whether his leniency at this point resulted from his confusion or from the fact that he was a Left Socialist Revolutionary was not clear.[121]

It soon became quite clear, however, that it was not safe for the British mission to remain in Tashkent. Consequently Macartney decided to return to Kashgar together with Blacker, who was ill. Bailey alone stayed behind. His intention was to conduct intelligence work as long as possible, but, aside from gathering some information on Bolshevik recruitment of German and Austrian prisoners, he could do little.[122] His great hope was that the British forces under Malleson would push on eastward along the railway, a move which he believed would provoke an anti-Bolshevik revolt in Tashkent, where he would be on hand to establish relations with the rebels. This, unfortunately for him, failed completely to materialize, and he soon found himself in the role of a fugitive whose chief "underground" work consisted of avoiding arrest. He managed a fantastic series of escapes for another whole year before finally making his way out to Persia with the help of turn-coat accomplices inside the Tashkent police force, but most of his effort went for naught.[123] Malleson, for his part, did not even know that Bailey was in Tashkent during the first months of his activities and learned of his presence there only after three Soviet "envoys" had been picked up in Meshed, one of whom attempted to defect and reported having met Bailey. No direct word was received from Bailey himself until he was on his way to Persia months later.[124]

Meanwhile Dunsterville had also run into trouble in Baku. He had hoped that the "moral" effect of British presence would arouse active support, especially in the form of troops to defend the city. In this, however, he was sadly disappointed. The Turkish force had a great advantage in size (it numbered around 40,000 men), but it might have been bluffed out of its prize by a determined resistance. Baku, however, was sharply divided between Moslems, who preferred the Turks anyhow and tended to look upon the latter as their potential liberators from their non-Moslem rulers, and Russians and Armenians, who tended to support one another but seemed incapable of organizing themselves properly for the tasks they faced. Moreover, the working class and the crews of the ships in the harbor were revolutionary, even if they were undecided between the Bolsheviks and the Socialist Revolutionaries. This meant that it was virtually impossible to form native forces along traditional lines. Conditions in Baku were, in short, chaotic in the extreme, both politically and economically as well as militarily.[125]

By September 1918, Dunsterville had definitely decided that further efforts to hold Baku would be a waste of time and of British lives. He therefore began secretly making preparations for evacuation, hoping to regroup his forces in Enzeli and then move to Krasnovodsk to link up with Malleson.[126] Bicherakov sent some 500 men back to Baku to help Dunsterville, but there was no hope of withstanding the Turkish attack expected any day. Thus on the night of September 14, with Baku under attack, Dunsterville loaded all but a handful of his men on ships in the harbor under cover of darkness and, in violation of the government's orders, left the city to its fate. The 900 soldiers of the Dunsterville force had held Baku for only six weeks; 180 had been killed, wounded, or left behind, and 30 Fords and armored cars had been abandoned.[127]

In view of the publicity later given to the affair of the "Baku Commissars," it should also be noted at this point that Shaumian and the members of his former government in Baku, who had been jailed during the British occupation, had been released just before the evacuation and had left by ship for Astrakhan. En route, however, the ship's crew and a British officer on board objected to being taken to a Bolshevik-held port and persuaded the captain to put in at Krasnovodsk. There, on September 16, the Bolshevik "commissars," some 26 in all, were arrested and again jailed under the orders of the town commandant, Kun. General Malleson, informed of the situation on September 18, advised that they be put under British guard and transferred to India as hostages to be exchanged for British subjects being held by the Soviet Government. He immediately ordered Captain Teague-Jones, his representative in Ashkhabad, to convey his recommendation to the authorities in both Krasnovodsk and Ashkhabad. Kun, who apparently feared disturbances in Krasnovodsk, had meanwhile resolved to be rid of his prisoners as soon as possible and had wired Ashkhabad requesting their transfer to the latter city immediately. When Teague-Jones inquired of the matter after receiving Malleson's instructions, he found that Funtikov and his associates in Ashkhabad were considering Kun's appeal but were not yet prepared to make a decision. Understanding this to be the case, Teague-Jones failed to press the matter any further at that time.

In fact, however, after meeting with his government and leaving the question unresolved, Funtikov reportedly became intoxicated and suddenly decided to act on his own. That same night he wired orders to Krasnovodsk that the Bolshevik prisoners were to be shot at once. Thus on the night of September 19 the 26 Baku commissars were loaded on a train, ostensibly for transfer to Ashkhabad, were taken well out into the desert, and in the early morning of September 20 were shot "trying to escape." It was not until the following evening, when Teague-Jones casually inquired of the matter again, that he learned what had happened and reported it to Malleson. Malleson protested vehemently, but it was too late to change the fate of the prisoners by then. Several months later a Socialist Revolutionary journalist, V. A. Chaikin, got the story from the now deposed and imprisoned Funtikov and published the latter's evidently vengeful charge that the shooting was the work of the British. When this version reached Moscow, the Soviet Government quite naturally made the case a cause célèbre of Bolshevik propaganda against the British intervention and those whom it aided. It was apparently Funtikov on whom the major responsibility rests, and his inept handling of affairs in general led to his removal from the government, probably at British suggestion, later in the year. But to this day it is not only he but the British who are blamed for the murder of the Baku Bolsheviks in Soviet accounts.[128]

After the evacuation of Baku, Bicherakov provided the only remaining "Allied" foothold in Transcaucasia. Having moved northward, retreating before Nuri Pasha's army, he had established himself in the port city of Petrovsk. From there he hoped to gather enough support to take all of Dagestan with the help of his brother, Georgii Bicherakov, a Socialist Revolutionary member of the soviet in Mozdok. The latter was nominally controlled by the Terek People's Soviet government in Vladikavkaz, but Georgii, just as his brother, had only been playing at being an ally of the Bolsheviks and had secretly established contact with the Volunteer Army. The two Bicherakovs thus hoped to take a major part in clearing the Caucasus area and would probably have opened the way for the Volunteers if their plans had succeeded.[129]

General Bicherakov's position, on the other hand, was seriously complicated by the fact that the most important anti-Bolshevik forces in the area of his operations, those under Nazhmudin Gotsinskii and Uzun Haci, were Moslem forces which had appealed to Nuri Pasha for aid against the Bolsheviks. So long as he was known as a "soviet" military commander fighting Nuri Pasha, Bicherakov thus found himself also fighting the anti-Bolsheviks. This awkward situation was partially resolved when Bicherakov revealed his true character and succeeded in negotiating an agreement with the Moslem Prince Nuh Bek Tarkovskii. Tarkovskii then shifted his alliance from Nuri Pasha to Bicherakov, and an understanding was worked out according to which

Bicherakov would control the coast and Tarkovskii the interior.[130]

However, by October Bicherakov's troops in Petrovsk and Derbent were on the point of being driven into the sea. Although the Turks officially surrendered to the Allies by the Armistice of Mudros on October 30, Nuri Pasha continued the war on his own. Consequently only direct aid from the British could save Bicherakov. The British had in fact been working diligently to prepare new troops and to outfit a "fleet" in Enzeli and Krasnovodsk under the command of Commodore D. T. Norris, but this was a very difficult process since there were few ships available. Despite the obstacles, including Russian objections, a small flotilla had been organized by late October and went to Bicherakov's aid.[131] When the British reached Petrovsk on November 6, however, the city was already under heavy artillery fire, and therefore Bicherakov was advised to evacuate. At Bicherakov's insistence a decision on this was postponed so that a mixed Allied delegation could seek a truce with Nuri Pasha, but this proved to be a hopeless gesture. The Turks claimed to be "instructors" in the army of the Azerbaidzhani Republic and refused to cease hostilities since Azerbaidzhan "had declared war upon Bicherakov." Consequently Bicherakov's troops were obliged to abandon their positions and to return to Enzeli with the British.[132]

British efforts in the northern Caucasus were thus, as in Baku, brought to an unsuccessful conclusion. A renewal of the intervention was only a few days away, but, somewhat ironically, the assembling of a larger force under Major General W. M. Thomson in northern Persia for this purpose had been accomplished only on the very eve of the end of World War I. The introduction of this force into Transcaucasia would still be necessary to expel the Turks and to restore order, and the French had already in October begun similar preparations for operations of the same nature in the Ukraine, but the end of the war was bound to confront this new intervention with a different set of problems. One year after the Bolshevik revolution, the Allies had still not really succeeded in reopening the eastern front, and now the very need for such a front would be subject to question. At least, however, it can be said that Allied efforts up to this point had helped to restrict, if not to stop, the expansion of German and Turkish influence and had to a degree limited the transfer of men and materials from Russia to the west.

PART II

ALLIED INTERVENTION IN SOUTH RUSSIA

3: THE POST-WAR INTERVENTION

In view of the fact that the Allied intervention in Russia had been undertaken largely in order to continue the war against the Central Powers, logic would seem to suggest that it should have ended in November 1918, with the final defeat of Germany. In fact, however, the end of the European war only brought a continuation of Allied efforts in Russia, and, indeed, a commitment to military action in the South far beyond what had been the case earlier. This was in part simply a result of the fact that the Allied Powers had been unable to commit large numbers of troops to the many obligations assumed prior to the end of the war, but it was also a consequence of the conviction that the war against the Central Powers would not be complete until the forces unleashed by them in Russia—Bolshevism and anarchy— were also eliminated or at least effectively restricted.

The continuation of the intervention in November 1918 did not, therefore, involve a sudden shift of purpose from defeating Germany to defeating the Bolsheviks. The change often described as that from a "little" intervention to a "big" intervention was really a very gradual and rather obscure change. To the Allied Powers, the Bolsheviks and the Germans were both enemies who had worked hand in hand against the Entente. In the eyes of Allied leaders, the war against Bolshevism was, of course, a struggle against a subversive ideology and militant revolutionism, but these same leaders maintained that it was not this so much as the identification of Bolshevik policy with German aims which led the Allies to continue to do battle.

It was, thus, not surprising that even after the Armistice the intervention continued to be spoken of in the context of World War I, in terms of loyalty to international commitments versus anarchy. Over a month after the end of the war French Foreign Minister Pichon explained to the Chamber of Deputies:

Russia, our ally, was withdrawn from the war by the action of the Bolshevik Government which conquered her. She has tossed aside all the contracts which had been made with us and annulled the obligations to which she subscribed. Then she signed in her own name a shameful treaty which delivered her into the hands of Germany and Austria-Hungary. . . . How could we, our allies and ourselves, have remained impassive in the presence of such an act which constituted . . . for our enemies an undeniable victory of incalculable consequences? . . .

Why have we sent troops to [Russia]? We and our allies have done so from the beginning to prevent the withdrawal of German troops destined to be sent to the Western front, to combat German infiltration and the assault by Germany on Russia, to save the Czechoslovaks, our allies threatened with destruction by the Germans and the Bolsheviks, to come to the aid of associations and groups in Russia devoted to the Entente and to permit elements faithful to our alliance and respectful of our contracts . . . to organize themselves effectively and fight against ruin and anarchy, the consequences of which can extend to ourselves. Nothing in all this constitutes any interference in the internal affairs of Russia. . . . We have simply defended ourselves, looking out for our vital interests in this country where we have ties of great importance. . . .[1]

Whatever justification there may have been for stressing continuity as a "legitimizing" factor in the intervention, however, such statements evaded the real question. The most important point was that intervention after the end of the war with Germany was a different intervention precisely because its purpose was no longer simply to defeat Germany. Acting directly in the context of the Russian revolution and civil war would require a much broader consideration of policy questions and goals than had been the case before November 1918. So long as the World War had been the focus of all decision-making, the Allied Powers could avoid serious consideration of Russian problems as such, but when the purpose of the intervention had indeed become that of overthrowing the Bolshevik government, it was no longer possible to carry out such a policy successfully without facing up to both the fact of interference in the internal affairs of Russia and the need for clear and firm decisions on the course which that interference should take.

"A peace which was made in the rest of the world and left Russia in a state of civil war, with an odious, abominable government,"

Pichon declared, "would not be a durable peace, would not be a peace of justice." But what were the alternatives to that "abominable" Bolshevik government? This was the question left without a definite answer, although it was fundamental to an adequate Allied policy. Despite the fact that it was no longer enough simply to base Allied policy on the proposition of aiding "allies" against Germany, the "new" intervention was apparently to be only a continuation of the old, and it was precisely this which would ultimately be its undoing.

When, on October 7, 1918, Clemenceau first issued orders initiating French military intervention in South Russia, his instructions to General Henri Berthelot, commanding French forces in Rumania, were simply to make contacts with Russian groups which had remained loyal to the Allies in the war against Germany.[2] When, three weeks later on October 27, Clemenceau sent General Franchet d'Esperey, commander of Allied forces in the east, a more detailed plan of military operations in South Russia, he stated that these operations would be aimed not only at Germany but also at the "isolation of Russian bolshevism with a view to bringing about its destruction," but he still did not provide anything more than this negative shell of a policy to guide French forces.[3]

The British, of course, faced the same problem. The Armistice in November (in Churchill's words) "had altered all Russian values and relations. The Allies had only entered Russia with reluctance and as an operation of war. But the war was over. . . . Therefore every argument which had led to intervention had disappeared."[4] Lloyd George later echoed this point when he noted that with the end of World War I "every practical reason for continuing our costly military efforts in Russia disappeared."[5] Yet the British government did not decide to end the intervention. On the contrary, on November 14 it decided to grant extensive aid to Denikin, and at the end of November it dispatched to its representatives a statement on the general line of policy in Russia containing the following list of immediate purposes:

> To remain in occupation at Murmansk and Archangel for the time being; to continue the Siberian Expedition; to try to persuade the Czechs to remain in Western Siberia; to occupy the Baku-Batum railway; to give General Denikin at Novorossiisk all possible help in the way of military material; to supply the Baltic States with military materials.[6]

These objects, as Churchill has noted, "not only comprised existing commitments, but added to them large new enterprises in the Caucasus and in South Russia" in accordance with the recently reaffirmed zone agreement. What was the logic of such a policy and what did it mean in practice? As in the case of the French, it was explained in terms of commitments assumed as a part of the World War and a temporary show of force to enable loyal Russian allies to gather strength to fight their own battles. The British foreign secretary, Lord Balfour, thus declared in a memorandum to the Cabinet on November 29 that Britain had no intention of seeing "its forces, after more than four years of strenuous fighting, dissipated over the huge expanse of Russia in order to carry out political reforms in a State which is no longer a belligerent Ally." The Russians, he declared, would "choose their own form of government," and Britain would not intervene in domestic affairs.

However, he added, none of this meant that Britain could "disinterest" herself entirely from Russian affairs, for the obligations already acquired would "last beyond the occasions which gave them birth." The Allies were indeed responsible for the "new anti-Bolshevik administrations" which had developed "under the shelter" of Allied aid. Yet, and this was the crux of the matter, he admitted that the British government (just as the French) did not as yet know how aid to such anti-Bolshevik forces would be handled in the future. "How such a policy will ultimately develop, we cannot yet say," he noted. All that was clear was that where troops had been committed there would be an effort made to use them "to the best advantage," and where no troops were to be sent the policy would be "to supply arms and money." A policy of this sort, Balfour owned, would "necessarily seem halting and imperfect," but it was all, in his opinion and that of Lloyd George, that Britain could do "or ought in existing circumstances to attempt."[7]

Such was the status of Allied policy in November 1918. Officially little recognition was given to the basic change which had occurred with the end of the World War. On the contrary, every effort was made to bypass the issue by letting policy and action drift on with no basis other than that which had in fact evaporated. Even the extension of the intervention through the sending of Allied troops to key points in their respective zones was to be treated as merely a follow-up to the Armistice, an action chiefly designed to cover the withdrawal of German and Turkish forces. If as a result there was a further development of anti-Bolshevik armies and the mounting of offensives against the Soviet center, this would be the affair of the Russians. Such efforts would be supported in order to honor previous commitments, but no attempt would be made to "intervene in domestic affairs" in the sense of trying to direct anti-Bolshevik actions or to participate directly in such military operations. In actuality there was thus no clear policy of intervention other than that associated with the fact of Allied presence in Russia. The Allied governments had no plans for accepting the burdens which a thoroughgoing policy of intervention would necessarily impose, for they believed that a token presence would be sufficient.

*   *   *   *   *   *

Clemenceau's decision to extend French military operations into Russia followed upon successful Allied operations in Rumania. The capitulation of Bulgaria in September 1918 and the re-entry of Rumania into the war on the Allied side in November had brought Allied forces into a position to make direct contact with pro-Allied elements in South Russia. In response to Clemenceau's proposal of sending troops into the Ukraine, the Allied theater commander, General Franchet d'Esperey, was himself quite unenthusiastic. Opposing any diversion of troops from the Balkans, he complained to Clemenceau that their numbers were inadequate and their morale too low to undertake an intervention in that "huge frozen country," Russia.[8] However, Franchet d'Esperey's pessimism was more than matched by the optimism of General Berthelot, who could point out that a close relationship already existed between Allied representatives in the temporary Rumanian capital at Jassy and General D. G. Shcherbachev, who in turn was in close touch with the Volunteer Army.[9] Therefore, while Franchet d'Esperey retained general command of operations, the specific task of preparing the intervention was turned over to Berthelot on November 2. On November 3 French naval forces were ordered to prepare to escort troops to Odessa and to establish liaison with the Volunteer Army.[10]

While French action was thus being prepared, some important events were also taking place in the Ukraine with vital implications for the Allies. Skoropadskii's regime proved to be a source of serious complications. By October a full-blown crisis had developed in the government, and Skoropadskii had been forced to undertake efforts to form a new cabinet at the very time that his German support began to crumble. An attempt to organize a coalition government with the participation of the Ukrainian National Union led by Vynnychenko failed, and thenceforward Skoropadskii found himself faced with both a renewed opposition from the nationalist Left and the likelihood of a resumption of hostilities on the part of the Red Army.

The only solution, it appeared, lay in persuading the Germans to remain in control until, it was hoped, Allied forces could replace them. On October 22 Foreign Minister Doroshenko was, therefore, dispatched to Berlin to plead this point with the German government. There, however, he obtained only the sympathetic advice to appeal at once to the Allies. This he then hoped to do, either through the Allied representatives in Jassy or through the Ukrainian mission in Switzerland under E. K. Lukasevich.[11]

Realizing that his government was handicapped by its identification as a "separatist" and pro-German regime, Skoropadskii took steps to create a new image favorable for the Allies. A new government, headed by S. N. Gerbel, was established and immediately appealed to the Allies on the platform of reunification of Russia and repudiation of the nationalist cause.[12] Following reports from a Ukrainian mission sent to Jassy that the Allied ministers would approve aid to the Ukraine only if a complete break were made with the past, the Hetman issued on November 14 a proclamation calling the Allies the true friends of Russia and declaring that the "All-Russian State" must be restored "as a federation."[13] Even while Skoropadskii was thus frantically seeking Allied aid, however, his German support was evaporating, and Vynnychenko's National Union secretly formed a five-man Directorate which declared war on him in the name of revolutionary democracy. Simon Petliura, who took command of the Directorate's armed forces, even managed to conclude an armistice with some of the German troops over the heads of the German Command.[14]

While these events were in progress, General Shcherbachev had seized the opportunity of establishing close relations with the French commander, General Berthelot, who had just returned to Rumania. Shcherbachev's short-lived association with the Ukrainian Rada earlier had ended with the signature of the peace treaty with Germany. Since that time he had remained in Jassy acting as an unofficial representative of Russian interests, along with the Russian ambassador, Poklevskii-Kozel, and others. As former Russian commander on the Rumanian front, Shcherbachev had agreed to Rumanian occupation of Bessarabia and control over Russian supplies on this front on the condition that both would be returned to Russian authorities whenever circumstances permitted. Rumanian incorporation of Bessarabia and subsequent difficulties in regaining possession of the Russian supplies there had put Shcherbachev in an awkward position and made it all the more essential for him to obtain Allied support. Even more important, however, Shcherbachev had used the time prior to Berthelot's arrival to consult with leaders of the Volunteer Army and together with them had agreed on a plan to identify the Allied intervention as closely as possible with the Army and to present its proposals directly to Allied authorities.[15]

When Berthelot arrived in Bucharest on November 15, Shcherbachev was, therefore, prepared to present carefully outlined recommendations representing both his own views and those of the Volunteer Command. Shcherbachev had at first assumed that consultations with Berthelot would merely be preliminary to taking his plan to Franchet d'Esperey and possibly even to Paris. As it turned out, however, this was not to be necessary, or at least it so appeared, for in their secret talks on November 15 and 16 Berthelot not only agreed with Shcherbachev's recommendations but also indicated that he was already fully authorized to carry them out without reference to others. As Shcherbachev reported to Denikin immediately after his conference with the French Commander:

> In Bucharest I succeeded in obtaining results which significantly exceeded expectations. Through direct contact and exchange of opinion with General Berthelot . . . we have now succeeded in bringing talks in Bucharest to such a thoroughly decisive stage that the trip to Paris and to Franchet d'Esperey have for the present become unnecessary.
>
> General Berthelot, who has the personal sympathy and strong support of M. Clemenceau, President of the Allies' Versailles Conference, is empowered with the full authority of "Commander in Chief of Allied Armies in Rumania, Transylvania, and South Russia" and in this capacity is able to formulate and execute all political and military questions which concern South Russia and its salvation from anarchy. I have succeeded in pushing this question forward so far that there now remains hardly anything to be desired. . . .[16]

Shcherbachev's enthusiasm was the result of some remarkable promises made by Berthelot. The French Commander indicated that a large part of South Russia would be occupied in the near future by an Allied force (chiefly French and Greek) of some twelve divisions. This army, he promised, would soon move into Odessa, where its local commander, General d'Anselme, would make his headquarters. From Odessa it would move into Sevastopol, Kiev, Kharkov, the Donets and Krivoi Bog basins, and even the Don, if necessary. Its purpose would be to maintain order, to see to the evacuation of the Germans, and to provide a military shield "to permit the Volunteer Army and the army of the Don to reorganize solidly and have freedom to prepare for wide action." Moreover, Berthelot stated that Russian forces would be granted significant financial assistance and full access to "all military supplies located in the zone of the old Rumanian front in Bessarabia and Little Russia [the Ukraine]."[17]

As Shcherbachev reported to Denikin, Berthelot had thus implicitly rejected any separate French dealing with the Ukrainians and had taken a "clearly negative attitude toward all who have worked with the Germans."[18] At Berthelot's suggestion these promises were to be kept secret at this point, but Shcherbachev was advised to work out further plans with Denikin and to act as his military representative to the Allied Powers.[19] Shortly after this, in fact, Shcherbachev left for Volunteer headquarters in Ekaterinodar where he received appointment as Denikin's special envoy. Denikin in turn then began mapping his own strategy on the basis of this long-awaited support from the Allies.

Meanwhile in Jassy plans were being made to call a special conference of Russian political spokesmen to lend support to the proposed intervention. The idea of a political conference designed to provide the grounds for a united effort had been discussed a number of times among the Russians in Jassy who congregated at the Russian "embassy" there, but it got its chief impetus from the French "consul," Emile Henno, who had previously been attached to General Tabouis' mission in Kiev, where he had established personal contacts with the leading Russian organizations and personalities.[20] The French minister in Jassy, de Beaupoil de Saint-Aulaire, had in October given some support to the idea by encouraging the prominent political figure V. V. Shul'gin, then at Denikin's headquarters, to help "work out a program of political action" to accompany the intervention, but it was Henno's personal initiative which brought these tentative ideas to a head in the proposal for a conference.[21]

The need for coordination of the various fronts of the civil war, and especially for more adequate political preparations, was indeed great. In response to this need, it was the intention of the Allied ministers in Jassy to try to give the anti-Bolshevik movement, and particularly its military leadership, a stronger political foundation by encouraging the affiliation of a broad range of organizations and groups in the South. It was in this general context that they supported the proposal of a conference in Jassy on the eve of the intervention.[22] Through Poklevskii-Kozel and envoys sent to Kiev, invitations were extended to all major political organizations representing the all-Russian and pro-Entente outlook, including the Council for State Unity (an organization of former members of the Duma and provincial and city administrations), the National Center, and the Union for Regeneration, representing conservative, liberal, and socialist views respectively.

While these three organizations sent previously selected delegations, the conference was really a meeeting of individuals, of merchants, bankers, churchmen, and politicians. Some had been active in government before the revolution, such as the former minister of agriculture, A. V. Krivoshein, and the former head of the land section of the Ministry of Internal Affairs, V. I. Gurko; two had been ministers in the Provisional government, Miliukov and M. M. Fedorov; others had been in the soviets and were prominent socialist leaders, such as the former mayor of Moscow V. V. Rudnev and I. I. Bunakov-Fundaminskii. In short, there was a fairly broad representation of South Russian groups which stood for Russian unity and Allied intervention, ranging from moderate socialists to staunch reactionaries.[23]

Altogether there were apparently around thirty persons who attended one or more of the meetings of the conference. Sixteen of these were recognized as full delegates, and an additional five (or possibly eight) were admitted as delegates with an advisory voice. Persons such as Shcherbachev (who represented Volunteer interests in the absence of Shul'gin, the official delegate, who fell ill en route), Ambassador Poklevskii-Kozel, some other military officers, and Allied representatives were not delegates to the conference although they occasionally attended. The conference met daily, usually twice a day, in Jassy from November 16 through November 23, thereafter moving to Odessa, where it continued until December 6. In Jassy some Allied representatives were present at most of the sessions, but only three meetings were held with the Allied ministers (Sir George Barclay, Saint-Aulaire, Charles Vopicka, and Giacinto Auritti).[24]

The major task of the conference was to draft a protocol to the Allies which would set forth the political views and aims of anti-Bolshevik South Russia, make recommendations for future action, and above all appeal for aid. Even before the drafting of the protocol could be got under way, however, news of the Directorate's rebellion against Skoropadskii was received, giving rise to an impromptu two-part appeal to the Allied governments on November 17 and 18 urging that orders be given to the Germans to keep peace and that immediate occupation of Kiev and Kharkov be undertaken to prevent the eruption of anarchy instigated by Bolsheviks and "chauvinistic Ukrainians."[25] At the same time Colonel I. M. Novikov was sent to see Generals Berthelot and Franchet d'Esperey to explain the urgency of the Ukrainian situation.

When discussion was begun on the content of the protocol, the chief issue was to whom aid should go, since all the delegates agreed on the necessity of Allied intervention. Three basic positions came out in the debate, involving both the form of authority and the persons to be included in the authority to be recognized. The most conservative faction, led by A. V. Krivoshein, urged the recognition of Grand Duke Nikolai Nikolaevich as supreme commander and dictator for South Russia. On the opposite end of the scale, the socialists urged the creation of a three-man directorate, including the military commander and two political leaders, which would exercise full authority. In the middle stood the moderate elements, for whom Miliukov was a leading spokesman, urging the necessity of a one-man military dictatorship but rejecting the monarchist candidate. It was the moderates' feeling that only a "democrat" could win the Allies' confidence politically, but at the same time it was felt necessary to concentrate authority in the hands of a military commander.[26]

Debate between these factions ran on for two days (four sessions) before agreement was reached through a compromise, or at least a partial compromise. The moderates strongly supported Denikin for the post of military dictator on the grounds that he was a "democrat"; those favoring a directorate were agreeable to Denikin as the military commander among the three members, and the conservatives who insisted on the Grand Duke were only four in number. When the vote was taken on the question of dictatorship or directorate, the socialists abstained, giving the decision to the former. Then when the candidate was voted upon, they and the center voted for Denikin, thus giving him a clear majority.[27] In fact, however, the conference had not settled the question at all.

The split was indeed so fundamental that the British military attaché, General Ballard, suggested that this question be omitted entirely from the Protocol.[28] Following his advice, this was done, and at least the appearance of unity was preserved. It was agreed simply to urge the Allies to assist in the preservation of Russian unity in its 1914 borders (with the exception of Poland), and to do this by (1) refusing to recognize or support any of the border states as independent states and (2) granting large-scale and rapid assistance of every kind to the Volunteer Army. Since the conference also called for Allied support for the establishment of a single Russian command over Russian forces in the South, however, the logical implication was that Denikin should have that post.[29]

The latter suggestion was in fact already agreed upon by Allied authorities. During the conference Berthelot confided that he had already sent one of his staff officers to see Ataman Krasnov about this question in response to the latter's attempt to deal directly for aid by sending a representative to Jassy. Berthelot indicated that Krasnov would have to subordinate himself to Denikin and that aid would be handled only through the Volunteer Army Command.[30] Pressure was indeed subsequently applied to Krasnov (most effectively, however, by the British as will be noted) which led to his recognition of Denikin's authority. Such a relationship with Skoropadskii, however, was quite another matter. Despite his policies, Krasnov had maintained close ties with the Volunteers throughout the German occupation, but relations between Skoropadskii and the Volunteer Army had been consistently hostile and continued to be so even after the sudden tranformation of Ukrainian policy in November. This became apparent even as the Allied representative, Henno, was taking steps on the contrary assumption.

Because of the increasingly urgent need for a show of Allied determination to prevent anarchy in the Ukraine, some of the delegates to the Jassy conference urged that consul Henno be given extraordinary powers as spokesman for the Allies and that he be sent to Odessa at once. The exuberant Henno was all in favor of this suggestion and, together with M. S. Margulies, drafted the text of a document authorizing him to go to Odessa and issue an appeal to the Ukrainian population to maintain order until Allied forces arrived. To have any validity, of course, this document had to have the Allied ministers' signatures. The latter were indeed obtained but in a manner revealing the haste with which "Allied" policy was being made.

Desiring to leave at once on his mission, Henno, accompanied by Margulies, rushed to the French minister's residence to obtain his signature. There they were told that the French minister would sign only if the British minister, Sir George Barclay, also did. Rushing then to the latter's residence, they found him in bed but managed to arouse him and get his signature. He signed with the comment that he would undoubtedly "catch hell" for it from London, but he planned to resign anyhow.[31] This done, the French minister then agreed to sign. The next day, revealingly, Saint-Aulaire requested a copy of what he had signed only to discover that Henno, now on his way to Odessa, carried the only copy.[32]

The Allied ministers in Jassy, eager for months to push forward with the intervention, had been bombarding Paris with joint telegrams urging the landing of Allied troops before the German occupation disintegrated.[33] The latter, of course, moved rapidly ahead with the end of the World War, but from Jassy the question of intervention seemed little affected by the end of the war itself except insofar as it was regarded as making speed all the more essential. Indeed the obsession with which Allied representatives in Jassy viewed the urgency of the intervention apparently led them to take steps of fateful significance without clear and prior authorization. The conduct of events following the Jassy conference illustrated how easily this happened under the pressures then being felt.

An Allied squadron was already operating in the Black Sea. On November 23 official Allied representatives were put ashore at Novorossiisk enroute to Denikin's headquarters at Ekaterinodar, which they reached on December 3. On November 25, Allied ships arrived in Sevastopol, where they were to receive the surrender of the German fleet (i.e., the Russian fleet previously seized by the Germans) and establish contact with the new Kadet government being set up in the Crimea under Solomon S. Krym, with M. M. Vinaver as foreign minister.[34] But of even greater importance was the arrival of Henno in Odessa. The city was already cut off from Kiev by Petliura's troops. Although the Hetman's authority was still technically recognized in Odessa, the only troops there were a small brigade of Polish soldiers organized by Denikin to be sent back to Poland and a small, recently recruited detachment of Volunteers, neither of which was capable of holding the city against a full-scale attack. In this awkward situation, Henno turned to his own ingenuity for salvation and proceeded to act in the name of the Allies on his personal initiative.[35]

The first thing necessary, he believed, was a declaration of Allied policy. Therefore, to the previously authorized appeal to the people to maintain order until Allied troops arrived, he now added a specific declaration of support to the Hetman:

The powers of the Entente state through their special delegate, the French Consul at Kiev, that they will not permit that the work of the reestablishment of order and the reorganization of Russia begun by patriotic Russians and powerfully supported by the Allies shall be disturbed in any manner whatever. The regeneration of Russia as a power . . . shall be carried out in conformity with the desire of all patriots and of all elements which stand for the maintenance of order in Russia. . . . The powers of the Entente declare their firm purpose to maintain order there. This decision will be carried out within the shortest possible period by an armed force as large as circumstances may require. Furthermore, they declare that from the present they will render personally responsible all political leaders for every attempt to create trouble and anarchy. The French Consul at Kiev declares the Entente powers intend to support, with all their force, the existing authority at Kiev represented by the hetman and his government, in the hope that he will be able to maintain order in the cities and provinces until the arrival of the Allied troops in the country. . . . Every attack upon the existing authorities, every revolt which will render [harder] the task of the Allies, will be severely punished. . . .[36]

When the Allied ministers in Jassy forwarded the text of this declaration to Paris, they hastened to construe it as only "a denunciatory declaration to the Bolsheviks" authorized after the urging of the "Russian delegation."[37] It is true the words "threatened by Bolsheviks" did appear as a descriptive phrase for the Ukraine (or rather South Russia, since even the use of the name Ukraine was considered nationalistic and separatist), but the object of the warning was clearly the Directorate and Petliura's troops, and the impact of its wording certainly derived from the outright declaration of Allied support for the Hetman. Moreover, if by "Russian delegation" was meant the Jassy conference, the statement as it was issued by Henno was hardly what they had called for. On the contrary, the conference was entirely anti-Ukrainian in the sense of opposing any recognition of a Ukrainian government or support for it. What the conference urged was the retention of German control until the Allies arrived. Even if it were acknowledged that temporary retention of the Hetman's regime was implied in this as a practical necessity, they would very probably have preferred to leave it as an implied matter and not have it so bluntly declared in the name of the Allies.[38]

The Jassy ministers explained that the second part of the declaration was added by Henno on his own initiative, "exercising the latitude which we had given him," because he felt that "the present system of government should be supported as it represented the only organization which could at present be utilized against Bolshevism."[39] This of course both suggested that the Directorate was not anti-Bolshevik and that the Hetman's regime could in fact be used effectively against the Bolsheviks, although neither of these assumptions was quite true. The action of the Allied ministers in Jassy was, however, the result not merely of confusion but also of a lack of clear policy directives from home.[40] As they stated in their explanation of Henno's position, they were doing what seemed necessary to prepare for the expected intervention, "although the decisions of the Entente in this regard have not yet been notified to us."[41] On the other hand, it was obviously anticipated in Jassy that a major intervention in force was imminent, and for this Berthelot was probably to blame. As previously noted, he had from the start assumed an extraordinarily sanguine outlook and apparently believed that he would be supported in Paris since Franchet d'Esperey's initial objections had seemingly been overruled.

Berthelot had assumed too much, however, in taking Clemenceau's vagueness for approval. When the plans which he had presented to Shcherbachev were subsequently submitted to Clemenceau, supposedly as a formality, they were in fact rejected. Berthelot, therefore, could not, as he had intended, triumphantly present his plans to the Jassy conference because he had been cautioned from Paris that they could not be fulfilled—for the very reasons given by Franchet d'Esperey earlier. But, instead of telling Shcherbachev that the plans would have to be changed, he simply informed him that their implementation would be delayed. In view of the troops' exhaustion and their lack of will to enter new operations after the World War had ended, he said, Clemenceau proposed "to form new French divisions" which, along with Greek units, could be used for the intervention. Both Shcherbachev and the Volunteer Army, therefore, continued to assume that Allied occupation of the Ukraine would provide the cover and base from which to launch future operations.[42]

Meanwhile Henno's action in Odessa had put the Allies on record in support of both Denikin and Skoropadskii, a somewhat contradictory position in itself. It had presumably been his assumption that Skoropadskii and Denikin would make natural allies after the Hetman's change of policy; at least he had hoped to keep Skoropadskii in power, with the help of both Denikin and the Germans, long enough to maintain order until the Allied occupation force arrived.[43] This, however, was a most unrealistic approach. Neither Skoropadskii nor Denikin had any real military forces in the Ukraine, and, in any case, Denikin had not ceased to regard Skoropadskii as a traitor to Russia.[44] The only real force in the Ukraine capable of military action at this time was the Directorate and its troops under Petliura, and Henno had chosen to denounce it.

Henno's appeals to the German Command to maintain order had little effect in stemming the tide of the Directorate's victory. On the contrary, Petliura's forces quickly swept southward toward Odessa, while Skoropadskii's regime collapsed and the Hetman fled to Berlin in German disguise. On December 17 the Directorate proclaimed from Kiev the restoration of Ukrainian independence and pledged to fight unceasingly against the idea of a federation with Russia.[45] Henno thus found himself directly threatened not by the Bolsheviks but by a new Ukrainian government which opposed almost everything which he, personally, stood for. For the French this situation was to add another confusing dimension to the problems of intervention; more immediately, it forced Henno to shift his tack. After consultation with political and military leaders in Odessa, who had organized an unofficial council of defense, he decided that it would be necessary to seek a truce with Petliura before Ukrainian troops completely overran the city.[46]

Intending only to stall for time by this maneuver, Henno in fact got himself in deeper than ever. Petliura immediately outmaneuvered him by interpreting his proposal as an offer of recognition and used this in turn to induce the Germans to surrender Kiev and the surrounding area without resistance.[47] In a futile attempt to extricate himself, Henno appealed to Denikin to send troops against Petliura, but Denikin was hard pressed by the Bolsheviks and could not help. Berthelot wired that French troops would be there soon, and meanwhile Henno could inform Petliura and Vynnychenko that the French Command would "hold them personally responsible for all hostile movements and acts tending to disturb the peace," but it was obvious the Ukrainian troops could take Odessa as soon as Petliura gave the order.[48] The only troops Henno had at his disposal were the handful of Polish and Volunteer soldiers also stranded in Odessa and a few French sailors.

What saved Henno was Petliura's decision not to drive him out. While his troops occupied a part of the city, he issued orders to avoid any clash with Henno and his little band and reserved a "French zone" for them. At Henno's suggestion, General Grishin-Almazov, formerly one of Admiral Kolchak's assistants and now a stranded delegate to the Jassy conference, took charge of the Polish and Volunteer troops and stationed them on a ship in the harbor for their protection. This done they all, Henno, Grishin-Almazov, and Petliura, settled down to await the arrival of Allied troops.[49] It was clear that Petliura had in mind something other than a war with the Allies. The joint campaign of the Red Army and the Ukrainian Bolsheviks had just been resumed, and the Directorate needed assistance. Petliura, who had far less desire than Vynnychenko to seek accommodation with the Bolsheviks, believed that aid should be sought from the Allies, and that was why he stopped short of victory in Odessa and waited.[50]

On December 17 the French 156th Division, consisting of Moroccan and French troops brought from Salonica, finally arrived in Odessa harbor under the command of General Borius. Before they disembarked, however, General Grishin-Almazov offered to clear the city for them by the use of the Volunteer detachment, so that the French troops would not have to fight their way into the city. Thus on December 18 the Volunteers opened an attack on the Ukrainian forces, which while superior to their attackers were persuaded by the accompanying bombardment from French naval guns to withdraw from the city, and Odessa was then occupied by General Borius' troops.[51] General Borius, whose orders reportedly instructed him simply "to make common cause with patriotic Russians," not only followed Henno's advice in this matter but also on his suggestion then designated General Grishin-Almazov as military governor of the city and approved the establishment of a Volunteer civil administration under him.[52] Since Grishin-Almazov then declared his subordination to General Denikin, pledging that "nowhere and under no circumstances would he follow any policy other than that ordered by his directives," it appeared that a direct relationship between the Volunteers and the French Command was to be established on an exclusive basis.[53] Under Henno's guidance, and with only the vaguest instructions from higher authority, the intervention had been got under way on the basis of an alliance with Denikin and hostilities with the Ukrainian Directorate.

At the same time, however, the direction of French policy was being shaped by different factors in Paris. After a reaffirmation of the Allied zone agreement in November,[54] Clemenceau had begun to clarify somewhat his understanding of the intervention. He had, indeed, earlier spoken of bringing about the destruction of Bolshevism, but he had also indicated to Franchet d'Esperey that the course of the intervention would be determined by "the possibilities which are opened to us. . . ."[55] Whatever others may have been led to believe, Clemenceau apparently did not now regard the "possibilities" as including either military operations against the Bolsheviks or a full-scale occupation of the Ukraine. On December 24 a statement released to the press indicated that no major military occupation was anticipated,[56] and on December 29 in a message to the Assembly Clemenceau described the purpose of the intervention simply as that of establishing a "defensive front." Any military operations necessary to defeat the Bolsheviks, he declared, would "have to be carried out subsequently by Russian forces. . . ."[57]

In the Chamber debates which followed this statement of policy, Foreign Minister Pichon was still hard pressed to defend the intervention in the face of strong criticism from the Left. He too denied that it had any offensive objectives and declared that it was merely a matter of the "encirclement" of Bolshevism. "Sincere revolutionaries" had requested the intervention, he said, and France had an obligation to help those who, unlike the Bolsheviks, had remained loyal to the Allies in the struggle against German control over Russia, but at the same time he wished to make it clear that France had no intention of fighting a new war. A few troops would be sent as a show of force to give the anti-Bolsheviks time to organize and begin their march to victory, but French policy was not to participate in the civil war but rather to construct a "cordon sanitaire" to fence off the Bolshevik menace while the "healthy elements" in Russia, with the assistance of material aid, carried out their tasks themselves.[58]

The divergence between Berthelot's promises and Henno's actions on the one hand and the government's description of its policy to a skeptical parliament on the other hand was obvious, but the fact that France would not continue to follow the Berthelot-Henno lead did not become fully apparent until the commander of French forces based on Odessa, General d'Anselme, and his chief of staff, Colonel Freidenberg, arrived to take up their duties in January 1919. They, unlike Henno, came to Odessa with some, albeit still rather general, instructions from Paris stating that all anti-Bolshevik forces capable and genuinely desirous of cooperating in the task of restoring a non-Communist Russia should be supported. The Volunteer Army was to be given full cooperation as an Allied army and the major force in the

South, but it was not to be regarded as an all-Russian authority or supported to the exclusion of others. Operations were to be based upon de facto situations so as to make use of every ally but at the same time to avoid the political issues which would inevitably accompany the concentration of support upon one element alone.[59]

As General Franchet d'Esperey put it, French policy was "neither to dismember Russia nor to impose on her this or that form of government . . . [but] simply to support local governments in order to enable them to reestablish order and proceed freely with election of a Constituent Assembly," which in turn would establish a national government.[60] This, in effect, was what was meant by not "intervening" in internal affairs, but it did not receive clear application in Odessa before the arrival of d'Anselme's staff because of the rush of events in which individuals like Henno had attempted to "make" policy on their own under the pressure of circumstances and because of the lack of clear instructions from Paris earlier.

Even now the French commander, d'Anselme, did not himself take up the duties of applying this policy to local political affairs. Preferring to avoid politics, he put Colonel Freidenberg in complete charge of relations with local and regional groups and left it largely to him to work out the problems involved. Freidenberg, who was endowed with a great fascination for political manipulation but little diplomatic talent, assumed his duties with a burst of energy which led him to seek out new directions and to ignore both Henno's past actions and Henno's presence. From the beginning of his work in Odessa, Freidenberg subtly made himself clear as to the major change to be made. France, he declared, remained faithful to the principle of a United Russia, "but it is now not a matter of decision of this or that political question, but exclusively a matter of making use of all anti-Bolshevik forces, including the Ukrainians, in the struggle against the Bolsheviks."[61]

What this meant, it was soon to become clear, was that Freidenberg planned to enter relations with the Ukrainian Directorate. This was, to put it mildly, something of a shock to both Henno and Denikin. Henno, indeed, then took up a position of open but futile opposition which soon ended in his resignation.[62] His demise marked the beginning of a new phase in Volunteer-French relations in which mutual antagonism rather than cooperation became the dominant theme.

* * * * * *

The British had, meanwhile, returned to Transcaucasia in November 1918. In fact the initial landing in the new intervention took place on the same day that the Jassy conference opened. On November 16 a new Allied "armada" of some twenty ships set sail from Enzeli and was met en route to Baku by the Russian flotilla carrying Bicherakov's troops. The international character of the expedition was stressed by the flying of all four "Allied" flags—i.e., those of Britain, France, the United States, and Russia—and by the hasty addition of French and American advisers to the staff of the British commanding officer, General Thomson.[63] The immediate goal and only clearly specified task of the expedition was to enforce the Armistice of Mudros and to expel any remaining Germans in the area.

Russian sanction for the landing of Allied troops in Transcaucasia was personified by General Bicherakov, participating in the self-made role of Russian commander in the Caucasus and leader of the "Pre-Caspian" government which he had established at Petrovsk in alliance with Krasnovodsk and Ashkhabad and which claimed Russian state authority over the Caspian coastal area.[64] Since he had links with other Russian authorities, including Denikin, it thus appeared that the new British intervention was to be put squarely on the side of those elements which stood for the reunification of Russia, following the pattern established by Henno for the French intervention at its inception. Such a clear and simple procedure, however, was no more applicable in Baku than it was in Odessa. Once again the complexity of the situation would not fully be appreciated until it was actually encountered.

The British Command could not avoid the question of what attitude to adopt toward the "states" whose territory it was occupying. Should these states be labeled creations of a German-Turk scheme to dismember Russia and thus denied support? Or, on the contrary, should their claims to self-determination and independence be regarded as the legitimate right of nationalities formerly contained in an oppressive empire and thus given support? These were, indeed, the only "simple" alternatives. But the former would very probably involve the British in hostilities with existing Transcaucasian authorities, an undesirable prospect, while the latter would be inconsistent with aid to Denikin and contrary to the avowed policy of support for Russian unity supposedly being pursued by all the victorious powers. Whereas one would open the intervention to the charge of reactionary oppression incompatible with Allied principles, the other would invite charges of dismemberment, imperialistic duplicity, and betrayal of

Russia in a manner similar to that perpetrated by the Germans. The British would find, as the French did in Odessa, that the only way to avoid a choice between these alternatives was to steer a course right down the middle, to become a buffer and mediator seeking at once to keep hostile factions apart and engender their cooperation in a common effort. General Thomson's handling of this problem in the case of Azerbaidzhan established the pattern of British involvement in Transcaucasia.

The Azerbaidzhani government of Fathi Ali Khan had undeniably been a pawn of the Turks just as the Ukrainian government of Skoropadskii had been a tool of German policy.[65] However, this had not been entirely to the liking of Azerbaidzhani leaders themselves, most of whom were identified with the nationalistic and socialistically inclined Mussavat party. It had rather been a result of the fact that after Turkish occupation the real control of the area was in the hands of Nuri Pasha. The latter had indeed intervened to force the reorganization of the government and the postponement of any socialistic projects.[66] With the collapse of the Turks, and British refusal to deal with Nuri Pasha on any terms except surrender, however, the Azerbaidzhani government was to some extent relieved of its dependence on the Turks and thus free to press its own claims. This it set out to do by sending a delegation to see General Thomson in Enzeli even before the new intervention began.

Thomson received this delegation but took a reserved attitude toward it. Rejecting the request that the intervention be delayed, he informed the Azerbaidzhani representatives that Baku would have to be completely cleared of all troops—both Turkish and Azerbaidzhani—by the morning of November 17 when his troops would occupy the city. Moreover, he flatly declared that British authority would be established in the city under himself as governor-general and that this would involve the installation of British authority over the city militia, military and naval facilities, and whatever accommodations were necessary for housing the staff and maintaining supply lines.

On the other hand, Thomson indicated that these conditions applied only to the city of Baku. All Turkish forces would have to withdraw completely, of course, but no objections were raised to the continued existence of Azerbaidzhani forces outside Baku. Moreover, while no official recognition would be extended, Thomson indicated that he did not intend to intervene in internal affairs and would deal on a de facto basis with the Azerbaidzhani government, providing it had rid itself of Turkish influence and could maintain peace and order in its territory. The question of self-determination, he noted, would have to be decided by the Peace Conference, and Azerbaidzhan would be free to present its case there.[67]

This formulation of the British position did not meet all the desires of the Azerbaidzhani government, but it was a good deal more generous than might have been expected in view of the alliance between the British and Bicherakov. When the British arrived in Baku on November 17, Thomson was warmly greeted on the pier by the Azerbaidzhani government. In a note, the acting foreign minister welcomed the Allies to the "capital of Azerbaidzhan," spoke glowingly of the ideals and victories of the Allied Powers, and urged "in the name of the exalted and sacred ideal of humanity" that Azerbaidzhan be admitted into the family of European states.[68] Thomson replied, in a friendly tone, that the Allies' purpose was merely to enforce the armistice and assured the government that the British Command had "no intention of intervening in [Azerbaidzhan's] internal affairs either at the present or in the future."[69] The semi-official newspaper *Azerbaidzhan* that evening even went so far as to suggest that Thomson's statements were tantamount to Allied recognition of the Republic of Azerbaidzhan.[70]

The same day, however, Bicherakov appealed to the local population, in the name of Russia, "to forget all party and political differences and to unite to bring all forces to the aid and support of our dear suffering Russia, and thereby, lightening the task of our allies, make it possible for them to return to their homeland soon." Bicherakov's appeal was addressed to "citizens of Russia," and it clearly indicated that he regarded Azerbaidzhan as a part of Russia.[71] Since Azerbaidzhani troops were obliged to leave Baku, and Bicherakov's were allowed to occupy the city along with the British, the contradictions in Thomson's position were hardly removed. Indeed the situation was, if anything, made even more confusing when on November 18, at Thomson's request, the newspaper *Azerbaidzhan* ran a retraction of the statement concerning recognition, and on November 19 (in accord with instructions from London) Thomson himself issued a new statement of British purposes. It declared in part:

> Baku is being occupied by British troops on behalf of the Allies. I am accompanied by representatives of France and the United States, and we are here with the full knowledge and agreement of the New Russian Government. . . .[72]

In the hour of victory we have not forgotten the great services rendered by the Russian people to the Allied cause in the earlier part of the war. The Allies cannot return home without restoring order in Russia and placing her again in a position to take her proper place among the nations of the world.

Unrest still exists in the Caucasus. It is my duty to remove this from the Baku area. It is caused entirely by our enemies.

Democratic government is unknown in Turkey and Germany. When they talk of setting up republics outside their own territory they do so for their own ends, and not in the interest of the people.

There is no question of the Allies retaining possession of a single inch of Russian territory. They have given their word to the Russian people on this.

The internal government of any portion of Russia is a question for the Russian people and one in which the Allies will in no way interfere.

We come simply to restore order by removing the Turkish and German centers of unrest which remain and prevent the establishment of peace and prosperity. All races and religions will receive the same treatment at our hands. Local and municipal administrations will be appointed provisionally by me and will have our support, and we shall confine our attention to the restoration of law and order. In carrying out this I appeal confidently to the large mass of the public; I enjoin them to return to their lawful work and to do their duty as citizens in observing public order. For my part the orders that will be issued will be as little irksome as possible; trade will be encouraged and every possible assistance will be given.

I look forward, with the assistance of all moderate and thinking men in Baku, to the easy and early accomplishment of the duty which lies before me and the troops under my command, so that we may return at an early date to our country, having helped Russia to take her share in the victory which has been achieved over our common enemies. . . .[73]

Thomson added to this the statement that martial law would be enforced in Baku "until the civil authority is in a position to relieve the troops of responsibility for the maintenance of public order" and indicated that all arms were to be surrendered by persons in the city. British officers were put in charge of the local police, and British authorities were soon in control of virtually the entire economic apparatus of the city. Special mixed commissions were created under British supervision to reorganize, repair, reopen, and operate the shipping industry, the railroads, local industries (especially oil), and the Baku branch of the Russian state bank.[74] By the end of December this

Herculean effort had succeeded in reopening the Baku-Batum railway, and oil production was once more available for shipment to the Black Sea either by rail or pipe line.

Thomson's November 19 statement, plus the fact of the full take-over in Baku, seemed to put the British once more on the Russian side of the question of authority. The statement was unmistakably pro-Russian in character and, in so far as it implied that "republics" supported by Germany and Turkey were only instruments of the Central Powers' foreign policy, pointed to an anti-Azerbaidzhan conclusion. But again this was deceptive. Thomson had plans designed to end the confusion in a manner which he hoped would be acceptable to all concerned.[75] What he had in mind was first indicated in his talks with representatives of the Russian National Council (R.N.C.), the only organization acting as spokesman for Russian opinion in the city. (It, together with the Azerbaidzhani and Armenian National Councils, reflected the views of the major elements in Baku.) The R.N.C. had been quite pleased with the November 19 statement because it seemed to accord with the Council's view that Azerbaidzhan was an integral part of Russia and should, therefore, with a reasonable degree of autonomy, be put under Russian authority.

At a meeting with three representatives of the R.N.C.—B. Baikov, M. F. Poshibiakin, and I. N. Smirnov—Thomson revealed that he hoped to see negotiations begun between the major groups and the Azerbaidzhani authorities for the removal of the existing government and its replacement by a coalition which would represent all of the national groups in Azerbaidzhan. Such a government, he felt, would end the stigma of Turkish influence, prevent outbreaks and disputes by national elements not now represented in the government, and provide the transitional authority necessary to maintain peace and order until the Paris Peace Conference could determine the ultimate fate of the Transcaucasian territories.[76]

Both the R.N.C. and the Armenians supported the idea of a coalition. The Russian Council would have liked to see authority entirely in Russian hands, of course, but prospects for this were full of uncertainties. Not only did the British prefer a coalition, but the Russian element itself was crucially divided into four (if not more) factions, each one of which had only itself in mind when favoring a "Russian" authority. Bicherakov had already asserted his claim on behalf of the "Pre-Caspian" government, that is, calling for the elimination of the Azerbaidzhani Republic and the recognition of himself as the bearer

of Russian authority in this area. The R.N.C. held several meetings
with Bicherakov and his "government," but drew from them not a
new sense of unity but rather the conclusion that Bicherakov's success
would mean their exclusion from a position of power. The R.N.C.,
therefore, tended to regard Bicherakov's forces and his leadership more
as a source of trouble than a source of strength.[77] The majority in the
R.N.C. consequently felt it necessary to seek agreement with moderates among the Moslems and Armenians as the only basis for a peaceful return to Russia.[78]

A third potentially important spokesman for Russian opinion existed in the person of General N. N. Golovin, acting as representative
of the "Ufa government." However, there appeared to be a good deal
of confusion concerning Golovin's authority and his views. As a representative of Ufa he was expected to be quite liberal or even socialist,
but then it was reported that he was involved in the plot to overthrow
the socialist directorate and seat Kolchak as dictator. The R.N.C.,
for its part, got the impression that there were ties between Bicherakov and Golovin and that the two of them were seeking to establish
a Russian authority not subordinate to Denikin, so it refrained from
supporting Golovin.[79]

On the other hand, General Thomson purposely delayed final execution of his plans for a coalition government until conferences could
be held with Golovin so as to coordinate these plans with the desires
of "an all-Russian government." But when Thomson and Golovin
met, it developed that the latter refused to deal with Bicherakov or
anyone else. He apparently insisted that he alone should be recognized as the representative of Russian authority. Thomson turned this
question over to his American advisor, Dr. Post, but all the latter
could elicit was the information that the Ufa Directorate had been
succeeded by a new government in Omsk which was "now the all-
Russian government," through which all British aid should be distributed. Golovin wished to take over affairs in the Caucasus in the name
of that government.[80]

The prospects for achieving a workable solution to the problem of
authority thus seemed rather slim. For a while it looked as though the
R.N.C. might be able to negotiate an agreement with the Azerbaidzhanis to establish a provisional coalition authority based on the understanding that the question of the reunification of Azerbaidzhan
with Russia would be determined by an all-Russian constituent assembly in the future.[81] However, negotiations to this end were suddenly

repudiated by the Azerbaidzhani government, and its delegation was recalled. Further talks were eventually held, but to no avail.

After Thomson, in an effort to remove one of the points of dispute, declared in a statement on November 24 that the future of the Transcaucasian territories would be decided at the Paris Peace Conference, the Azerbaidzhani government used this as the basis for rejecting any commitment to the decision of this question by an all-Russian constituent assembly or to reunion with Russia as conditions for organizing a coalition. For the Azerbaidzhani government henceforth the only question subject to negotiation was that of participation by the Russians and Armenians in the Azerbaidzhani government and parliament. The Armenians, fearing any further exacerbation of tensions, reluctantly agreed to this, but the R.N.C. voted to refuse to participate in the government on this basis, believing that it would be tantamount to supporting the separation of Azerbaidzhan from Russia.[82]

This stand by the R.N.C. apparently angered Thomson. He was virtually accused by the Council of aiding the Azerbaidzhani government to reject the only acceptable compromise, and he in turn accused the Council of refusing to accept reality and adopting an unjustifiably narrow view. The R.N.C., he told its representatives, did not represent all Russians, and if it refused to cooperate he believed that others could be found who would.[83] From this point on the R.N.C. took a critical and hostile attitude toward both the British and the Azerbaidzhani government, and Thomson became more convinced than ever that the Russians (Bicherakov, Golovin, and the R.N.C.) were incapable of the adjustments necessary to maintain a stable authority in the area.

Just as Thomson had predicted, the Azerbaidzhani government subsequently found some Russians who, while not representative of the majority, were willing to cooperate on its terms, and, with British approval, a new parliament was then convoked on December 7. Its composition was predominantly Moslem, but small delegations were allowed for the Armenians, Jews, and Russians. The leading party, holding over one-third of the seats, was the Azerbaidzhani Mussavat, which, together with other Azerbaidzhani parties, held a dominant position.[84] The new parliament was, however, an expression of compromise to a degree and at least partially representative of the population.[85] Not only were five members of the Slavic Russian Society, a minority which had split off from the R.N.C., seated in the parliament, but two of its members (Vinogradov and Lizgar) were included in the new government organized under Fathali Khan-Khoiskii, a leader of the Neutral Democratic Group.[86]

In view of the fact that other efforts had failed to achieve what the British wanted, Thomson decided to accept the new Khan-Khoiskii government as the legitimate government of Azerbaidzhan. Without taking a position on Azerbaidzhani statehood as such, Thomson issued a statement on December 29 that this coalition government would receive the "full support" of the Allied Command as the "only legal local authority in the borders of Azerbaidzhan."[87] Less than two weeks later the Azerbaidzhani government announced that it had sent a delegation to Paris "for the defense of our political interests and for the recognition of our independence by the Great Powers."[88] Meanwhile, General Sul'kevich, former head of the Crimean government under German auspices, was put at the head of the Azerbaidzhani general staff with the duty of organizing a new army.

The British theatre commander, General George Milne, came from Constantinople in January and gave his approval to these developments. In a note to the minister of foreign affairs on January 22, Milne assured the Azerbaidzhani government that the Allied victory in the war meant the guarantee of the "right of peoples to dispose freely of themselves," and in a meeting with Khan-Khoiskii the next day he affirmed Thomson's statement that the new government would be dealt with de facto as the only legal authority. The Azerbaidzhani delegation to the Peace Conference would be allowed to present its views in Paris, Milne added, and while the British would not interfere in Azerbaidzhan's internal affairs, they would do all possible "to develop the industry and the commerce of your country." This cooperation, he believed, would assure both peace and justice in prosperity for Azerbaidzhan.[89]

With some changes in personnel later in the year, this arrangement of authority in Azerbaidzhan lasted until the end of the civil war. So long as the British remained in Baku they controlled that city and used it as their chief base of operations on the Caspian, but the rest of Azerbaidzhan was put into the hands of the Azerbaidzhani government. This solution was, however, only a partial one. It did not remove the basic issues involved. There was still the anomalous status of Bicherakov, who commanded both his Cossacks and the Russian Caspian fleet. There was also the even more important question of relations with Denikin and the Volunteers, whose views were similar to those of the R.N.C. and hardly in accord with British action in

Azerbaidzhan. More immediately, however, there was the question of British occupation of Georgia.

The landing of British troops in Baku had been only part of the British plan to occupy strategic points in Transcaucasia. The utmost importance of Baku as a military base and source of oil was matched on the Black Sea side by the importance of Batum as the key port for entrance from the west and the chief outlet to the west for that oil, and the rail and pipe line connections between these two cities ran through Georgia. Its capital at Tiflis (Tbilisi) was the logical place for British headquarters in Transcaucasia. Furthermore, Georgia was both involved in the disputed claims to Batum (which had been previously taken by the Turks) and, as Azerbaidzhan, implicated in the earlier German penetration which had first prompted British intervention.[90]

In view of the uncertainty of British attitudes on these questions, the Georgians had not waited for the actual arrival of Allied troops to begin a campaign for recognition. As soon as the British arrived in Baku, a Georgian envoy (Kartsevadze) was sent to see Thomson to present the official explanation of Georgia's earlier behavior. The appeal to Germany, he declared, had been made purely out of desperation; the Bolsheviks threatened in the north and the Turks in the south, and the Allies, with whom Georgia had all along wished to establish close relations, were unable to send adequate aid. On November 26 Georgian Foreign Minister Gegechkori supplemented this explanation by a letter to Thomson assuring the British Command that "during the whole of its existence [Georgia] had not allowed a single step to be taken which could affect the interest of the Allies and hopes that it will have the sympathy of the Allies as regards the prosperity of an independent Georgia in the future."[91]

Gegechkori thus sought from the moment of British appearance in Baku to convince the British Command that there had in fact been no establishment of German influence in Georgia and, moreover, that the Georgian government had already established "complete tranquility" in its borders, guaranteeing all that was necessary for its continued existence as a "strong and normal state." More specifically, when the question of the entrance of British troops into Georgia was broached, the Georgian government on December 22 informed the British mission that had just arrived that it did "not consider as necessary the introduction into Georgian territory of foreign troops for the maintenance of order, since the Government itself has adequate forces at its disposal for this purpose." And, this note added, if the purpose of British troops should be anything beyond the maintenance of order, "the Georgian Government decisively declares that this introduction cannot take place without the agreement of the Georgian Government."[92]

Repeating the standard phrases, the British Command informed the Georgian government that British forces would in no way interfere in internal affairs, that their purpose was merely to assist in the restoration of "order and normal conditions" in the area, and that all territorial and similar major questions would be "decided in the peace conference in Paris."[93] Realizing the inexpediency of generating any hostility between themselves and the Allies, the Georgian government then hastened to reply to the British representative on December 24 that "having in view your statement that the entry of troops into Tiflis . . . will be carried out in accordance with the general plan of the Entente Powers, the Georgian Government, animated by a desire to work in agreement with the Allies for the realization of the principles of law and justice proclaimed by them, gives its agreement to the entrance of troops. . . ."[94]

During December the British fully occupied Batum and stationed a small garrison in Tiflis where their headquarters were subsequently established.[95] While relations with the Georgian government were not entirely smooth, there was no repetition of the problem of organizing a new government experienced in Azerbaidzhan. Georgia retained its existing government and continued to pursue a notably independent policy. The Georgian representative, Avalov (Avalishvili), who arrived in London in December, found the British committed in general to the restoration of Russia under democratic principles, but he also found them willing to listen to his view that the Transcaucasian states should not be included in that restoration but rather retained as buffer states.[96] This appeal to old imperialist rivalries found support in high places, especially in the British Foreign Office.[97] From the latter Avalov received on December 31 assurances that "His Majesty's Government view with sympathy the proclamation of independence of the Georgian Republic and are ready to urge its recognition at the Peace Conference."[98] This actually meant at this time only what was being applied to Azerbaidzhan—holding the status quo and letting each send its own delegation to Paris where final decisions would be made—but it demonstrated the quality of a British policy that left much freedom for Georgia to act in its own interest.

Batum, however, was quite another matter. It was claimed by both Russian and Georgian authorities, of course, but it was taken over by the British as successors to neither of these but to the Turks. Batum therefore, in itself, posed not only the same problems as those encountered in Baku but still more serious ones. Some sort of local authority had to be established under British auspices and, even more difficult, this had to be done without prejudicing the decision as to Batum's future status. This latter question, of course, as the oft-repeated magic words declared, would be decided by the Peace Conference. Meanwhile the British general in command of troops occupying the city held the authority of governor-general and bore the responsibility for organizing a local administration.

General Forrestier-Walker, commander of the British forces which moved into Batum and then Georgia, set in motion plans for a solution to this problem along lines similar to those sought by Thomson in Baku. The population of Batum was extremely mixed, so any authority established, it was felt, should be as representative of all resident nationalities as possible. As in Baku, there existed in Batum a Russian National Council which spoke for the majority of the Russian element and stood for the interests of the Russian state. Also as in Baku, the R.N.C. strongly supported Denikin and, in this case, took its position in accordance with Volunteer directives.[99] The Batum R.N.C., however, was somewhat more moderate in its views, being largely under the influence of Kadet leadership.

P. M. Maslov, chairman of the Batum R.N.C., consulted with Walker when the British arrived and was asked by the General to help organize a "council on government" representing Batum's chief elements. This council, it was made clear, would not be an independent government but rather an advisory body under the British governor-general, which post Lt. General W. J. N. Cooke-Collis would assume. Such a council was in fact organized—including two Russians, two Georgians, one Greek, one Moslem, one Jew, one Pole, and one Armenian—under Maslov's chairmanship and largely under Russian influence.[100] The British Command then issued a statement concerning authority in the city and British policy. Noting the creation of the local administrative council, this declaration went on to assert that "all decisions of the Council must before execution receive the approval of the Military Governor." Moreover, while the population was assured that so long as it behaved properly the British would "not interfere in your affairs nor infringe upon your freedom," it was made clear that any offences which interfered with British policy or control would be tried by court martial and punished by penalties up to and including death.[101]

There was, however, a flaw in this arrangement. The object of the British plan was to stabilize conditions locally on a neutral platform which would prevent an internecine struggle for control of the city until its fate could be decided in Paris, and which would in the meantime provide the orderly conduct of affairs necessary to the full exploitation of Batum as a British base. The R.N.C., on the other hand, felt itself bound by duty and loyalty to Russia to promote the eventual return of the port to Russia, and meanwhile it sought to do all in its power to facilitate its use by and subordination to the Volunteer Army. The Georgians, of course, pursued precisely the opposite policy of trying to exclude Russian interest and bring Batum under Georgian control. There were, in short, no neutrals except the British, and they were, by virtue of their stand, bound to clash with both sides.

The administrative council headed by Maslov was subordinate to the British governor-general, but Maslov also considered it an agency of the Volunteer Army Command. Anticipating the conflict of interest which would inevitably arise, Maslov thus inquired of Denikin exactly what should be done in case the British should order a course interpreted to be injurious to Russian interests. Denikin's reply, while advising his supporters not to quarrel over "trivialities," insisted that in any question touching basic Russian national interests they must "directly, openly, and strongly defend the Russian view, not letting anything stand in the way."[102] This advice soon clashed with British efforts to enforce a rule prohibiting any agitation in the city for its reunification with Russia or otherwise concerning its future disposition. No refugees were permitted to return to the Kars or Batum regions who were identified with a position on this question. Volunteer officers conducting recruiting activities were temporarily ordered to cease such work. Political meetings involving agitation on this question were prohibited.[103]

The council was naturally involved in these matters and, in dealing with them, did not function in the manner hoped for by the British. The result was that by April tensions had reached the point where the British Command intervened decisively, dismissing the council and putting both civil and military administration directly under British authority.[104] Henceforward Batum was administered solely by

British officers or agents, and neither Georgian nor Volunteer authority was permitted. When later a native of the area, General Natiev, was commissioned by Denikin to resume recruiting activities, protests were immediately raised by both Georgia and the British. Not long thereafter the general was attacked in the streets and killed, demonstrating how fierce the hostilities had become and indicating what the British were seeking to avoid.[105]

Thus even in Batum, where direct British controls were established, internal squabbles continued to be a serious problem. Holding the status quo was no simple matter, for, however it was interpreted, it appeared to one party or another to favor its adversaries. In Transcaucasia alone, bitter fights ensued between the Armenians and Georgians over strips of territory claimed by both, and similar quarrels, though always less serious, beset Azerbaidzhani-Georgian relations, while the Azerbaidzhanis and the Armenians continued their old hostilities. In these areas the British would be obliged to intervene, in some cases with force, to stop the conflict.[106] Local Transcaucasian problems, serious as they were, however, would still not be as difficult to deal with as the larger question of the conflict between the Transcaucasian states and the Volunteer Army which had already erupted along the borders to the north.

*   *   *   *   *   *

It was almost inevitable that an intervention undertaken in the confused crosscurrents of civil-war politics in South Russia would soon find the Allies engulfed in a perplexing tangle of disputes and claims among the various anti-Bolshevik elements. The subsequent history of their stay in South Russia would, indeed, have to be written more in terms of these disputes than in terms of the war to liberate Russia from Bolshevism. The Allied commands would find one of their major functions to be that of mediating between the Volunteer Army and the border states. This thankless task would in turn lead to some curiously contradictory relationships between the Allies and those whom they had come to aid. The politics of intervention in the civil war were to be full of troubles for the well-meaning Allies.

Meanwhile, however, the Allied problem was not merely the result of confusion in South Russia but just as importantly the result of a lack of a coordinated policy among the Allied Powers themselves. The busy Allied leaders, wearied by a long war and now confronted with the even more taxing questions of peace-making, were not blessed with either a ready-made policy adequate for the post-war intervention in Russia or the time needed to formulate one. The "Russian question" was not taken up again by the Allied Powers jointly until the meeting of the Peace Conference in Paris in January 1919.[107] Actually the Peace Conference as such never really dealt with the Russian problem, but there were in the course of the conference a few discussions in the Council of Ten, and it was in these meetings that what policy there was of a joint nature was shaped in some rather dramatic ways.

The Council of Ten began its discussion of the Russian question on January 12, and one of the first questions to arise was that of Russian representation at the Peace Conference. Foreign Minister Pichon noted that none of the quite numerous delegations from Russia in Paris could be recognized officially, since no Russian government had been recognized. He suggested, however, that there was no reason why selected persons—such as the former prime minister, Prince L'vov, or the former foreign minister, S. D. Sazonov—should not be given an unofficial hearing. Lloyd George agreed that the Russian question should be discussed, since the Allies still "had no definite policy in Russia," but he also suggested that the persons named by Pichon to testify on Russia's behalf "represented every opinion except the prevalent opinion in Russia." The latter, he said, was Bolshevism, and that fact "must be accepted." Perhaps the Bolsheviks had no right to represent Russia, he added, but then neither did L'vov nor others in Paris. The Council voted in the spirit of Lloyd George's remarks against recognizing any representatives of Russia at the Peace Conference, but it did tentatively accept Pichon's proposal to allow some personal interviews.[108]

As Pichon pointed out, the acceptance or rejection of Russian delegations in Paris was intimately linked with the question of recognizing some over-all Russian authority or else all the various individual governments. Russian Ambassador Maklakov in Paris had foreseen this problem and had been working vigorously since the autumn of 1918 to effect a united representation for at least the major Russian anti-Bolshevik forces so as to make recognition more likely. On his initiative a conference of Russian ambassadors and representatives was held in Paris during January 1919, and it was decided to organize a special representative body there to be called the Russian Political Conference.[109] Former Prime Minister L'vov was designated as its chairman, and he was to be assisted by the Russian ambassadors or other representatives in Paris (Maklakov), Rome (Giers), London (Nabokov),

Washington (Bakhmetev), Madrid (Stakhovich), Berne (Efremov), and Stockholm (Gulkevich.)

Others invited to participate were former Foreign Minister Izvolskii, former Provisional government members Konavalov and Tretiakov, P. Struve, B. Savinkov, and other acknowledged Russian leaders. Both the South Russian (Denikin) and Siberian (Kolchak) governments were to be represented by former Foreign Minister Sazonov, and the Northern government by its leader, N. V. Chaikovskii. Such a composition, it was believed, would not only unite the three governments most powerfully representing all-Russian interests but also present a liberally oriented representative coalition, containing both former leaders of the Provisional government and outstanding socialist spokesmen such as Savinkov. The efforts of the ambassadors abroad could be coordinated, the specifically military representatives such as General Shcherbachev could be backed in their appeals for aid, and Russia could at last speak with a strong voice in Paris.[110] In practice this voice was to be expressed by an inner body of the Conference subsequently referred to as the Russian Political Council, consisting of L'vov, Maklakov, Sazonov, and Chaikovskii.

This development marked a notable achievement due largely to Maklakov's credit, but it never succeeded either in fully uniting Russian spokesmen in Paris or in obtaining Allied recognition. The Council was always in competition with the innumerable delegations of the non-Russian nationalities, and even of the Cossack states, which inundated Paris and the Allied chancelleries with appeals and demands. Despite various efforts to achieve some unity with these delegations, the Council never overcame their determination to go their own way in distrust of Great Russian designs.[111] Especially those representing the South Russian border states tended to take the view, expressed by a Georgian representative in London, that their chief duty was "to explain and to accustom people's minds to the idea that the re-establishment of Russia in no way necessitated the inclusion of [their particular state]."[112]

Moreover, the Russian Political Council encountered differences with both Kolchak and Denikin, but particularly with the latter because of what Denikin regarded as its overzealous efforts to act not simply as a joint ambassador but also as a government in its own right. This resulted both from the efforts at leadership on the part of the Council and from Denikin's feeling that his own representatives were muffled and restricted by its attempt to appeal to liberal opinion in

Europe. It was, in this sense, unfortunate that a former tsarist minister, Sazonov, had been chosen to represent the two major military forces in Russia. Denikin had named Sazonov as his director of foreign affairs in November 1918 and had sent him to Paris over Cossack objections.[113] In January 1919 Kolchak in turn had also designated Sazonov as the representative of the Omsk government. Both had instructed him to seek the territorial status quo ante bellum for Russia, with the exception of Poland, and to oppose any compromise of Russia's territorial integrity or political unity for the sake of popularity in the Allied countries.[114]

The other members of the Russian Political Council—L'vov, Maklakov, and Chaikovskii—did not disagree with Kolchak and Denikin in principle, but they did believe that it was necessary to be more flexible, and they were particularly determined to avoid identification with the tsarist past. The importance of having representatives acceptable to the Allied governments had, indeed, already been illustrated by the fate of the delegation sent by the Jassy conference to Paris. This delegation, including both conservatives and socialists, had been expanded at the last minute to include Miliukov. This had proved to be a fateful decision, for when the delegation reached Constantinople it was immediately confronted with French hostility toward Miliukov because of his "collaboration with the enemy" earlier. Only after British intercession had been obtained did the delegation receive permission to continue on to Paris, and once it had arrived there it was given a very cool reception. In fact Clemenceau had ordered some of its members, particularly Miliukov, expelled from France. Miliukov then received a warmer reception in London, and some of the delegation's members were later welcomed back to Paris, but this incident indicated how ineffective an unpopular representative could be.[115]

So it was with Sazonov. L'vov and Maklakov regarded his membership in the Council as unfortunate not only because they wished to take as liberal a stand as possible but also because he too was distasteful to Clemenceau. Refusing to have any personal dealings with Sazonov, Clemenceau even warned the Council of Ten against hearing him "lest it be alleged that the Conference was conspiring with tsarism."[116] Clemenceau himself thus thwarted Pichon's attempt to get the Council of Ten to hear Sazonov's testimony. The ultimate result of this situation was that Sazonov, and to a lesser extent even General Shcherbachev, were obliged to rely upon Savinkov, who had the most extensive contacts in Allied circles, to act as their intermediary.[117]

Indeed, for various reasons, the influence not only of Sazonov but of the entire Russian Political Council was generally confined to friendly circles in the French Foreign Ministry and in the British War Office, which Winston Churchill, a staunch defender of the Russian anti-Bolshevik cause, took over on January 15.

The lack of Russian participation in the Peace Conference did not, of course, automatically preclude decisions favorable to anti-Bolshevik hopes. On the contrary, Russian representatives in Paris had been given reason prior to the first session of the Council of Ten to believe that plans for a full-scale intervention would soon materialize. A proposal for the formation of an international army including Allied, East European, and Russian forces to liberate Russia from Bolshevism had, indeed, been drafted by Marshal Foch and was known to the Russian representatives before its presentation to the Allied conference in January.[118] However, when this proposal was finally debated in the Council of Ten on January 22, immediate objection was raised by Wilson and Lloyd George, both of whom doubted the feasability and wisdom of opposing Bolshevism by force of arms from outside.[119] Instead, what the Council of Ten proposed as an answer to the Russian problem was not an expansion of the war but peace.

The lack of Russian anti-Bolshevik influence in the Peace Conference was thus never better illustrated than by Lloyd George's suggestion to the Council of Ten on January 16 that the Allies should propose a truce in the Russian civil war and invite all of the various factions to meet in Paris for a conference to settle the Russian problem. As one of the most outspoken opponents of the intervention among the Allied chiefs, Lloyd George argued that this was the only logical course, because (a) no one really knew what was going on in Russia, (b) conditions in Russia were obviously bad and would only get worse with a continuation of the intervention and civil war, and (c) those centers of resistance to the Bolsheviks which had been supposed to be so strong, such as the Ukraine, had been toppled "with a few thousand men." In other words, he said, the Allies had only three possibilities. They could declare Bolshevism to be a menace to all civilization and go all out to destroy it, a policy which he believed no one could seriously advocate; they could attempt to isolate Bolshevism in Russia with a so-called *cordon sanitaire* or blockade, a policy which he believed would condemn thousands of innocent people already starving to a sure death and thus could not be supported "on grounds of humanity"; or they could demand a truce and call a con-

ference of the belligerents to reach some settlement, which was the
only policy which he personally could support.[120]

Despite the fact that, at Pichon's suggestion, former Ambassador
Noulens testified on January 20 that the Bolsheviks held power only
"by terror alone . . . a terror unexampled in history," that the Bolsheviks were out "to conquer the world," and that the Bolshevik regime
would never really make peace with anyone, Lloyd George continued
to press his point of view with notable success.[121] At the January 21
meeting his position was, moreover, greatly strengthened by Wilson's
reading of a report on peace overtures being made by the special Bolshevik representative, Maxim Litvinov, in Stockholm. The Bolsheviks, Litvinov reportedly declared, were "prepared to compromise
on all points," including amnesty for their opponents, renunciation of
"imperialistic designs" on Finland, Poland, and the Ukraine, and
acceptance of a reasonable solution to the questions of the Russian
state debt and foreign economic interests in Russia.[122]

At first Clemenceau took issue with both Lloyd George's ideas and
with the Bolshevik overtures. Bolshevism, he said, presented a "very
great danger" to the world, and the Bolsheviks were unworthy of
being accepted in such a conference as that proposed. And as for Litvinov's offers, they were only a clever trap designed to embarrass the
Allies, as it were, by inducing them to take a bribe. If time were available, he would simply advocate taking a wait-and-see attitude in the
confidence that "eventually sound men representing common sense
would come to the top" in Russia, but, he added, he recognized that
a speedier solution was necessary. Therefore, while he would not have
the Bolsheviks, or for that matter certain other Russians, invited to
confer on French soil, he would nevertheless go along with the idea
of a conference since President Wilson supported it and had suggested
that it could he held elsewhere. In any public announcement of
such a proposal, Clemenceau added characteristically, it should be
made clear that the Allies had no intention whatsoever of contributing
to a restoration of tsarism.[123]

Thus came about the famous "Prinkipo Proposal," the first public
proposal on the Russian question to emerge from the Paris Peace
Conference, the international authority to which the Russians had
repeatedly been told by Allied representatives to look for solutions.
Initiated by Lloyd George, drafted by Wilson, and grudgingly consented to by Clemenceau, it was approved on January 22 and ordered
relayed by radio and the press to all governments contending for power

in Russia. It invited them to confer jointly on Prinkipo (Prince's) Island near Constantinople. The only condition to attendance was cessation of hostilities.[124] The Allied leaders thus put themselves on record against the intervention and, even more important, implied a willingness to accept a negotiated settlement which very probably would leave the Bolsheviks in Moscow and possibly would leave Russia dismembered.[125]

The Prinkipo conference was scheduled for February 15, but in fact it never met. The Soviet government implied a willingness to accept the invitation in a note of January 28, and some of the anti-Bolshevik groups in the South sent favorable inquiries at first, but both Denikin and Kolchak categorically rejected the idea.[126] It was subsequently charged by some proponents of the conference that Pichon deliberately torpedoed the conference by putting pressure on all anti-Bolshevik elements receiving Allied aid to refuse to attend. For example, George D. Herron, then representing the United States in Geneva, wired the American delegation in Paris on February 13:

> Since the announcement [of the Prinkipo conference] . . . delegation after delegation of Russians, and of nationalities formerly constituting part of the Russian Empire, has been here to talk with me. It has become entirely clear to me that none of the Russian parties or nationalities understands the nature of the Prinkipo Conference. . . . But in the next place, and what is far more important is this: that the representatives of each one of these parties explains that officials of the French Government persuaded or commanded them not to go. It has become clear to me that the refusal of all the parties except the Bolsheviks to participate is due to French intervention . . . especially by M. Pichon.[127]

The truth of this statement lies not solely in the charge that Pichon opposed the conference but also in the fact that the initially favorable response of some of the anti-Bolshevik groups was based upon a misunderstanding of the purpose of the conference. They had apparently believed that it was to be a conference to bring anti-Bolshevik elements together to present an overwhelming front against the Bolsheviks if the latter refused (as expected) to accept the terms which would be presented, i.e., that the whole purpose was to discredit the Bolsheviks and rally opposition against them.[128] This interpretation was, indeed, encouraged by some of Clemenceau's comments on the conference and probably represented his view.[129] On the other hand, the Foreign Ministry apparently regarded such a maneuver as too risky.

In view of Lloyd George's quite different intentions, and of the Bolshevik "acceptance" of participation, Pichon undertook an immediate campaign against the conference. South Russian groups were quickly disabused of the idea that the conference could be used as an anti-Bolshevik rally, and French representatives both discounted the likelihood that the conference would ever meet and warned that Bolshevik overtures of peace were merely a deception.[130] Moreover, Pichon personally aroused the ire of supporters of the Prinkipo proposal by publicly criticizing it and declaring that France would not have any dealings with the Bolsheviks.[131]

The French Foreign ministry, of course, had a considerable advantage in the fact that it had direct contact with almost all anti-Bolshevik groups, an advantage which it naturally did not refrain from using in this affair. The Bolsheviks were thus put at a disadvantage by the fact that the Council of Ten had decided to send the invitations only by press and radio so as to avoid any implications that might accompany direct address.[132] The Bolsheviks, as it turned out, heard the proposal by radio and thought that a direct invitation would follow; when none did, and their delay in sending a full reply was being taken as a refusal despite their request that it not be, they responded on February 4 with a slightly insulting statement of agreement in principle to negotiate. However, they indicated a preference for dealing with the Allies themselves, leaving their position on the actual question of a conference among Russian parties rather unclear.[133] By contrast with this indirect and delayed communication with Moscow, the French Foreign Ministry made its views known directly to Maklakov and Sazonov in Paris and wired instructions to its representatives in Russia. The tenor of Pichon's advice was clearly indicated by Sazonov's report to both Kolchak and Denikin on February 5: "The conference on Prinkipo Island is being regarded as doomed to failure. France intends to continue support with supplies and does not intend to withdraw its military units in Russia."[134] The reply from Omsk read: "We . . . have received a communication from Pichon in the spirit of the first part of your telegram, i.e., on the apparent failure of the meeting on the Prince's Island. . . ."[135]

The fact remains, however, that, regardless of whether Pichon opposed the Prinkipo proposal or not, the suggested conference could not have met on the basis proposed by Lloyd George. Neither the Whites nor the Reds were prepared to make a truce or to accept a real compromise with their opponents.[136] Denikin, among others, had made it abundantly clear long before that he would not sacrifice his goals for anything, even if it meant a "fight to the death" against the Bolsheviks.[137] The charge against Pichon was therefore exaggerated in so far as it gave him credit for the failure of the conference. Prinkipo was bound to be a failure. About all that was accomplished in proposing it was to point up the differences in the views of Lloyd George, Clemenceau, and Pichon. On the other hand, the very call for such a conference could have produced a sharp reaction of hostility and disillusionment among the anti-Bolsheviks if it had not been for the quick reassurances received first from Pichon and then from Churchill.[138]

In sharp contrast to Lloyd George's effort to end the intervention, Churchill (as Foch) had boldly assumed the initiative to continue it. Arriving in Paris on February 14, he quickly took advantage of Lloyd George's failure and proposed the immediate establishment of an Allied Council for Russian Affairs to take responsibility for further Allied action, particularly to determine "what resources were available and how they could be co-ordinated" in Russia.[139] Lloyd George, who left for London after the Prinkipo failure, now merely urged Churchill not to commit Britain "to any costly operations which would involve any large contribution either of men or money." There was a moral commitment not to pull out abruptly on the Russians, he conceded, but he wanted Churchill to keep in mind that the intervention could be justified only to the extent that Russia "wanted" it and would use the opportunity afforded to "save herself" by her own efforts.[140] As it turned out, Churchill's proposal of a special Allied body to direct the intervention was rejected because of opposition from the foreign secretary, Lord Balfour, but he was not deterred. In the face of what he called "the lack of any policy on the part of the Allies," Churchill undertook to lead what was left of the intervention, but he would obviously be rather limited in what he could do.[141]

Meanwhile the Bolshevik acceptance and the anti-Bolshevik rejection of the invitation to meet at Prinkipo had put the Allies in the awkward position of having to find an excuse for dropping it.[142] This was done, at Churchill's suggestion, by means of a deadline for a cessation of hostilities, with which no one complied.[143] Clemenceau's was now again the strongest voice against keeping the question of the conference open. The anti-Bolsheviks, he conceded, had foolishly refused "the unique opportunity offered by the Conference of indicting Bolshevism and its abuses before the whole world," and they had put the

Allies on the spot by doing so. However, he too had really been "completely opposed" to the conference all along and believed that it had only contributed to the disintegration of anti-Bolshevik forces since they did not know whether to fight or to wait for an armistice. There was certainly no need now to drag out the embarrassment, he declared, and the Council of Ten agreed.[144]

While, on the one hand, the idea of a negotiated settlement of the civil war was not entirely dead—it was revived, for example, in connection with the trip of W. C. Bullitt to Moscow in March 1919 to sound out the Bolsheviks on behalf of Wilson, and in the discussion of the Hoover-Nansen relief project in April[145]—the Allies were, on the other hand, still only haphazardly committed to the intervention. A report by General Alby to the Council of Ten on February 15 indicated that there were two French divisions, two Greek divisions, one Italian division, one English division, and some 100,000 Rumanian soldiers which could be used to effect a reinforcement of the intervention, particularly in South Russia, but this information was received sceptically.[146] Even Foch now expressed doubts on further intervention in Russia, and in March modified his plan so as to suggest not an Allied army for invading Russia but the creation of an armed cordon around Bolshevik territory through the mobilization of armies in Poland, Rumania, and other East European states.[147] It was revealing of the division in allied opinion that Lloyd George suspected even this armed cordon idea as a cover for an East European assault on Russia and denounced it as "a great mischief."[148] Any further expansion of the intervention, either by way of Allied or other non-Russian forces, was thus rejected without any clear indication as to what the limited intervention already undertaken was expected to accomplish. Allied representatives in the field would have to contend with circumstances as they found them, with or without policy directives from their governments.

4: THE FRENCH AND THE VOLUNTEERS IN ODESSA

A curiously distorted relationship had been established in Odessa between the Volunteers and the French, partly as a result of Berthelot's promises but more directly because of Henno's frantic and futile efforts to build an alliance between the Volunteers and the Allies against the Ukrainian Directorate. The subsequent arrival of the commander of French forces in Odessa, General d'Anselme, and the efforts of his staff under Colonel Freidenberg to rectify this situation, from the point of view of their instructions to avoid singling out or favoring any one anti-Bolshevik element to the exclusion of others, had immediately resulted in misunderstanding and tension between the Volunteers and the French Command.

The French Command was faced with an urgent need to remedy the frustrating situation there resulting from the latent but paralyzing state of war between the Russians and the Ukrainians. Odessa was cut off from the interior on which it depended for its supply of food, water, and other necessities. Since the French found it impossible to keep the city supplied from the outside, either by land or sea, conditions steadily grew worse and, in fact, threatened to provoke open rebellion among the poorly fed, unemployed, and Bolshevik-agitated workers.[1] The Volunteer Army Command was also aware of these difficulties and repeatedly urged the French to expand into the interior by force to establish an economically secure base, or at least to allow the Volunteer units in the city to undertake this mission. This would, however, involve a Volunteer offensive, or French military action, against the Ukrainian forces under Petliura which surrounded the city, and the French Command refused either to use its own troops to force Petliura back or to allow the Volunteers to move out beyond the city limits.[2]

Preferring to negotiate rather than to fight with the Ukrainians, the French Command therefore brushed aside Volunteer objections and in January 1919 opened talks with Directorate representatives in Odessa.[3] In these negotiations, which were arranged through General Michael Grekov (who had deserted Skoropadskii and negotiated the German withdrawal from Kiev in December on behalf of the Directorate), an agreement was soon reached to lift the blockade of Odessa and permit French and Greek troops to move into the interior beyond Odessa along a line from Tiraspol on the Dnestr River, through Berezovka and Nikolaev, to Kherson on the Dnepr River.[4] With this matter settled, Freidenberg then agreed to enter further negotiations with the Directorate on other aspects of relations between them, and the Directorate's delegation in Odessa was expanded to include Dr. Osip Nazaruk, director of press relations for the Directorate, and Serhi Ostapenko, then minister of trade and industry.[5]

Freidenberg's plans called for a division of South Russia into two zones of civil authority, one Ukrainian and one Russian, with the French Command providing the necessary links between them.[6] Each of these zones, he envisaged, would be governed by its own directorate, but at the same time the military forces of both would be integrated into a single force under French supervision. To implement this plan, Freidenberg proposed nothing less than a reorganization of the entire political and military structure in the South, and since he had begun talks with the Ukrainians, he put his demands to them first, presumably in the belief that whatever agreement he could make with the Directorate could then be coordinated with a similar agreement with Denikin. His exact intentions toward the latter were not clear, but, as for the Directorate, it soon became evident that he wished to bring it entirely under French influence.[7]

His first demand to the Directorate, and the condition for continuing negotiations with it, was the staggering proposal that Vynnychenko, the founder and leader of the Directorate, be ousted. The name of Andrievskii, another leader of the Left wing of the Directorate, was soon added to this demand. The fact that the Directorate agreed, that these two leaders and even a third, Chekhovskii, resigned, and that a new government was formed under the moderate Ostapenko, testified to the desperation of the Directorate and its strong desire to obtain French aid.[8] It was a victory for Petliura's point of view, but it was not complete surrender, for Petliura then demanded recognition of the Directorate (as the government of an independent

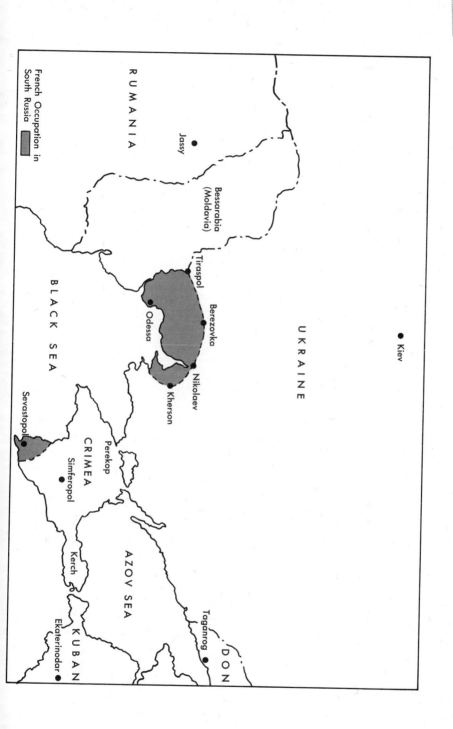

French Occupation in
South Russia

RUMANIA

Jassy

Bessarabia
(Moldavia)

Tiraspol

Odessa

Berezovka

Nikolaev

Kherson

BLACK SEA

Sevastopol

CRIMEA

Perekop

Simferopol

Kerch

AZOV SEA

UKRAINE

Kiev

Taganrog

DON

KUBAN

Ekaterinodar

Ukraine) as his condition for further negotiations, declared that no interference in the internal affairs of the Ukraine would be tolerated, and stipulated that any cooperative military operations against the Bolsheviks would be limited to the "ethnographical border" of the Ukraine.[9] To this Freidenberg countered with a sharp rebuke to Petliura and the suggestion that he too might have to be removed from the Directorate.[10]

*   *   *   *   *   *

This exchange temporarily resulted in a stalemate and a cessation of the talks, but during this interval the activities of the various political organizations in Odessa, which were already taking sides on this question, assumed a new significance. The organizations which had participated in the Jassy conference had not only continued to take an active part in local politics in Odessa but they had even for a time continued to meet jointly as the "Jassy conference." Singly and as a body, these organizations maintained close contact with the French Command and were in turn kept well informed on problems which arose. Each also took a stand on the basic questions posed and raised new issues on its own.

Because these organizations (chiefly the Council for State Unity, the National Center, the Union for Regeneration, and the Zemstvo-City Union) were the major spokesmen for the Russian intelligentsia in Odessa, they commanded attention.[11] Moreover, Freidenberg hoped to use them to support his moves in Odessa. However, there remained an obstacle to smooth cooperation between the French Command and the Odessa organization: the latter were divided by serious differences in outlook. The Council for State Unity, headed by Baron Meller-Zakomelskii and listing Krivoshein as vice-chairman, stood generally on the conservative Right, while the Union for Regeneration (successor to the Left Center and predominantly composed of moderate Socialist Revolutionaries) had retained a basically socialist character, although it also included liberal Kadets in its membership.[12] The National Center, somewhere between these two, was limited in its activities by the fact that it was more closely tied to the Volunteer Army, by its past history of internal division and separate operations by the Kiev branch under Shul'gin, and by the overlapping connections of some of its members with the other organizations. The Zemstvo-City organization, a union of civic leaders from the zemstvo and city duma organizations which still existed, tended to line up with the Union for Regeneration because many of its members were socialists, but it too was divided internally. In other words, the differences which had appeared in the Jassy conference were just as much and perhaps more in evidence in Odessa.

These differences and their implications became apparent as three major issues were faced: (1) the question of some agreement with the Ukrainian Directorate, (2) the problem of authority in Odessa itself, and (3) the possibility of the establishment of a new regional authority for southwest Russia, corresponding to the Ukraine. All three of these questions were closely intertwined and each bore directly on the four-cornered relationship which existed in Odessa involving the French Command, the Odessa political organizations, the Ukrainian Directorate, and the Volunteer Army. Literally months of debate and negotiation over these issues took place before the climactic moment was reached. A detailed account of these is impossible here, but certain features must be noted in order to indicate how serious misunderstandings subsequently arose.

To begin with, many in Odessa, and especially the conservatives, had grown dissatisfied with the Volunteer authority there, and in this they had Freidenberg's complete sympathy. There were several reasons for this dissatisfaction, all of which had a bearing on the general debate. The military government under Grishin-Almazov had been established on an ad hoc basis at a time when nothing else seemed expedient, but this authority had proved to be weak from the start. It put Odessa under Denikin's command, but at the same time it provided no solution to the problem of completely inadequate communication between Ekaterinodar and Odessa. The result was that the Volunteer government in Odessa had little power to act on its own and even less initiative, since Denikin's insistence on centralization of authority precluded autonomous government in Odessa, while Denikin himself was too far removed from the scene to provide the necessary leadership. Consequently administrative authority in Odessa grew steadily weaker at the same time that circumstances increasingly demanded that it be strengthened. The economic situation became chaotic, speculation ran wild, but the military government did nothing to stop it. Complaints therefore grew in volume daily, and demands for a change took on greater insistence.[13]

The question, of course, was what kind of a change should be undertaken. Denikin would certainly not countenance a simple removal of the Volunteer government, even though he knew of some of its shortcomings, and it was quite clear that he would be totally opposed to bringing in the Ukrainians involved in negotiations with the French because he considered them no better than traitors to Russia and fore-runners of Bolshevism.[14] The Council for State Unity, the chief critic of the Volunteer government in Odessa, regarded Denikin as an acceptable military commander but believed him incapable of the necessary political leadership and, for its part, challenged Denikin's right to claim control over regions not occupied by the Volunteer Army, particularly the Ukraine. Furthermore, it was the general feel-ing in conservative circles that Denikin was dominated by the middle-of-the-road Kadets and National Center, who jealously guarded their position against all other political organizations.[15] The Union for Regeneration, on the other hand, preferred Denikin's moderate polit-ical position to that of the Right, but at the same time it opposed the Volunteer policy of military dictatorship and would rather have seen some form of directorate established in Odessa.[16]

None of these groups supported the Ukrainian Directorate, but their positions on the question of negotiations with it were strongly influ-enced by their views toward what should be done about changing the situation in Odessa.[17] Thus the Right and Left in Odessa tended either to oppose or to support French plans for agreement with the Ukrainians, and in turn either to stand by Denikin or to oppose him, not on the basis of any simple political position, but rather on the basis of a very complex analgam of considerations. It was the Right which most opposed Denikin and favored a French-dominated reor-ganization of the Ukraine by way of an agreement with the Directo-rate, or more accurately, by way of the negotiation of a subordination of the Directorate to the French Command and its absorption into a new government under Russian influence. The Left, by contrast, opposed such French plans and supported the Volunteers because it disliked the prospect of domination either by the French or by the conservatives.[18] To make this peculiar situation even more confused, it need only be added that the French, while agreeing with the Right element in Odessa, nevertheless put constant pressure on it to bring the socialists into any negotiations and to plan for their inclusion in any new authority or government which might ultimately be estab-lished. French intelligence sources indicated that only a moderate socialist platform could gain the support necessary to establish an effective government, and it was evident that only a clearly democratic Russian authority could persuade the French parliament to support an intervention adequate to the tasks.[19]

At the end of January Freidenberg began a series of conferences with representatives of all of these groups in the hope of working out answers to the problems at hand.[20] In these negotiations M. S. Margulies took the initiative, on behalf of the Council for State Unity, to propose the creation of a southwest Russian regional government in Odessa with authority over the entire territory of the Ukraine. This government, a council of ministers which might include some Ukrainians, would be composed primarily of representatives of the four Odessa organizations. Only ministers of war and foreign affairs, it was suggested, should be named by General Denikin as commander-in-chief of all armed forces in South Russia.[21] However, this plan immediately encountered strong Volunteer opposition, both from General Lukomskii, the chairman of Denikin's Special Council then on a tour of inspection in Odessa, and then from Denikin himself, who sent orders to General Grishin-Almazov to insist on continued subordination of the government in Odessa to his command.[22]

A counterproposal then submitted by Prince E. N. Trubetskoi, which was designed to prevent a clash with Denikin, called for the establishment of a civil advisory council composed of local political leaders, but it would retain the governor-general appointed by Denikin and would simply specify that the authority of such an administration could be expanded to include whatever territory Denikin designated for it.[23] Trubetskoi's alternative proposal, however, also failed to obtain Denikin's support because he believed that it would compromise Volunteer authority in Odessa and open the door to French dominance. He categorically rejected any changes which implied the formation of an autonomous regime in Odessa.[24] The efforts of the Council for State Unity to reach a compromise agreement with Denikin thus came to naught.

Another attempt at agreement was initiated, apparently at the urging of General Berthelot, when the French Command announced in mid-February that a French delegation would be sent to Ekaterinodar to seek Denikin's approval of the appointment of a new governor for Odessa as a minimal step toward improving conditions in the city. It was believed that A. I. Pil'ts would be the most acceptable candidate since he already headed the civil section under Grishin-Almazov and had only a few days before been invited by Denikin to take a position in the Department of Internal Affairs in Ekaterinodar.[25] However, when this delegation met with Denikin, it coupled the recommendation of Pil'ts with a proposal to establish an autonomous military and civil authority in Odessa and indicated that the French Command wished to use such an authority as the basis for the organization of mixed Franco-Russian detachments which would form the nucleus of a new army to operate in the Ukraine. The details for such a plan, it was suggested, could be worked out directly in a meeting between Berthelot and Denikin in the near future. For Denikin, however, it was not a question of details but of the basic idea itself, and he still refused to accept it. In fact, he agreed to nothing proposed by the French delegation except the suggestion that he and Berthelot should meet.[26]

The failure of these negotiations, coupled with the extremely poor communications between Ekaterinodar and Odessa, did much to foster misunderstanding on the part of both Denikin and the French Command. Such was all the more the case when certain persons in Odessa who were close to the Volunteer Command, particularly V. V. Shul'gin, harbored deep personal resentment against the French Command as represented by Freidenberg and did all they could to discredit French efforts to find solutions to the problems which beset the anti-Bolshevik cause.[27] Denikin himself was not unaware of the correctness of many of the French complaints, but his one real answer was to appoint Lt. General A. S. Sannikov to replace General Grishin-Almazov. Sannikov had in fact arrived in Odessa on January 26 but, on seeing for himself just how complex the situation was, had requested Denikin to withhold official announcement of his appointment until he could orient himself to local conditions and problems. Sannikov's position in Odessa was thus an anomalous one from this point on. He represented Denikin's desire to put a new man in charge but, especially in view of objections voiced by General d'Anselme, delayed indefinitely the assumption of Grishin-Almazov's position. Instead he sought to reach some understanding with the French Command and prevent a full break between it and Denikin.[28]

In February, while Sannikov was working at this task, General Berthelot made his last visit to Odessa. In talks with both Sannikov and Shul'gin at this time, Berthelot assured them that his personal preference would be to reject any plan of cooperation with the Ukrainians and to give full support solely to Denikin and "One Russia." However, he added that it was not a question of his personal ideas but of what was best under the circumstances. There were some in the French Command, he noted, who felt that agreement with the Directorate and a political and military reorganization were essential, and he was not in a position to contradict them. He hoped that it would still be possible to bring in Allied reinforcements which would make such changes unnecessary, but until then he had no choice but to allow the reorganization to proceed as planned. When Sannikov indicated that he would convey Berthelot's desire to Denikin, Berthelot replied: "It is not my desire, but my order."[29]

The Allies' chief duty, the French Commander explained to Sannikov, was to "unify all political groupings fighting against the Bolsheviks" and to assist "all forces useful for this struggle."[30] To General Gerua, who had been assigned to Odessa earlier as liaison officer for General Shcherbachev, Berthelot further indicated that he was disturbed by the misunderstanding with Denikin and had approved Freidenberg's plans solely because he viewed them as a good way to resolve the Ukrainian problem and to bring all military forces under a unified command. At the same time, he could not understand Denikin's refusal to cooperate with these efforts and still could see no other way out of the dilemmas which confronted the French Command in Odessa.[31] As Sannikov observed, this meant that the French would go ahead with Freidenberg's plans, for they believed it more important at this point to do what they could to save the situation in the Ukraine than to aid the Volunteer Army which was in a better position to help itself.[32]

When Berthelot then left Odessa, full responsibility for operations there was temporarily turned over to General d'Anselme. Accompanying the order giving d'Anselme this authority was also a directive stating that General Sannikov would have to subordinate himself to the French Command "in all matters of a political and administrative character." Upon hearing about this directive, Denikin wired Sannikov: "In all respects, military, political, and civil, you are subordinate to me and only from me can you receive orders." However, Denikin still hoped to see Berthelot before he left for Paris in order to work out their differences, so he added: "I suggest that you coordinate your actions in all matters with the French Command. . . . Our detailed relations will be determined in my meeting with General Berthelot."[33]

Unfortunately Berthelot was never able to meet with Denikin, and on February 23 Sannikov reported that General d'Anselme had ordered an immediate reorganization under French direction of all military forces in Odessa. Denikin replied bluntly:

I categorically forbid you to carry out experiments with the Russian Army by foreign orders. . . . I will not permit any interference in the question of the formation of the Russian Army. Announce that anyone under my command who carries out such an illegal order will be court-martialed.[34]

At the same time Denikin appealed to Berthelot again, condemning both the idea of a military reorganization under French direction and the negotiations with the Directorate as steps likely to undermine the unity of command under the Volunteer Army. "Decision of important questions of Russian life by representatives of foreign powers without consultation with me and without the participation of representatives appointed by me," he wrote, "will bring to ruin the idea of a united command and unity of authority."[35]

General d'Anselme did not conceal his irritation at Denikin's stand on these questions and on occasion expressed his dissatisfaction most pointedly. The French Command, he told Baron Meller-Zakomelskii (head of the Council for State Unity), was fed up with this situation and was now determined to go ahead and organize the southwest on its own terms.[36] Freidenberg also expressed his opinion, adding the interesting observation that he believed Denikin's obstinacy was directly related to the fact that he was under strong British influence. For his part, Freidenberg now saw only two possibilities for the Russians in Odessa: either they would organize a new regional government in Odessa themselves and cooperate in a regrouping of the armed forces under the French Command, or he would take upon himself the organization of a new Ukrainian Directorate, which would be given authority over all of southwest Russia, and joint military units would be organized by agreement with it.[37] He hoped the Russians would find some way of obtaining the cooperation of the Volunteers, and he assured them that he intended to include Russians in either plan and to see that southwest Russia was prepared for entry in a future Russian federation, but there could be no further delay now.[38]

* * * * * *

Freidenberg was, indeed, prepared to introduce the second alternative, for he had come a long way in his negotiations with the Directorate by the beginning of March.[39] He had not pressed further for the removal of Petliura after the latter had resigned from the Social Democratic party, and the Directorate for its part had sent new negotiators to Odessa who were authorized to accept French demands.[40] Outstanding among these new representatives was the eminent Urkainian jurist, deputy foreign minister, and Jewish Socialist-Federalist, Dr. Arnold Margolin, who was ideally suited for negotiations with Freidenberg.[41] Not only was Margolin a skilled diplomat but his own political views were moderate and included a belief in the feasibility of "federation from below"—that is, preparing a future federation through the temporary formation of independent state units which would ally themselves together for the military struggle now and later unite politically in a new Russian state.[42]

One of Margolin's first tactical steps in Odessa had been to contact the representatives of other South Russian states and negotiate with them a cooperative effort. Through these contacts Margolin had achieved the significant breakthrough of producing a joint Belorussian-Kuban-Don-Ukrainian note to the French Command setting forth their position.[43] While this note, published on February 5, consisted chiefly of a reasoned argument in favor of "federation from below" and against "federation from above," it also presented the idea of separate regional armies coordinated by a common general staff, which would be supreme in military matters but prohibited from interfering in political affairs. It also offered a demonstration of voluntary cooperation among the representatives of the South Russian states in seeking French aid and thus gave the Ukrainian appeal considerably more force.[44]

It had been this effort on Margolin's part more than anything else which had opened the way for new talks with Freidenberg and gave him reason to believe that his plans could be achieved. Freidenberg was not authorized to enter any formal commitments with either the Ukrainian or other South Russian governments, but it was his prerogative to negotiate terms for agreements which might subsequently be approved in Paris, and that is what he did. Circumstances were entirely in his favor, for, in the face of severe defeats from the invading Bolsheviks, the Directorate proved to be willing to make extensive concessions.[45]

Freidenberg's first aim was to reorganize the military forces in such a way as to use all anti-Bolshevik troops in the war. This was especially necessary if "not one drop of French blood" could be spilled to save Russia.[46] Hence the first proposed agreement to come out of the negotiations was one designed to do this in a way calculated to be acceptable to both sides and at the same time to give the French Command supervisory powers. The most significant part of this agreement was the stipulation that all existing armed forces of the Ukraine and all new formations (together expected to reach 300,000 men) were to be put under the command of a joint general staff consisting of representatives of: (1) the French Command (General d'Anselme), (2) the Polish Legion (Colonel Dzewatinski), (3) the Volunteer Army (General Grishin-Almazov,) and (4) the Ukrainian army (General Manissov).[47]

Under this agreement all (non-Bolshevik) military hostages held by either the Ukrainians or the Russians were to be released, and mobilization of the army was to begin forthwith under the direction of the new general staff. Freidenberg further indicated that the French plan was to form this army into "mixed brigades" each of which was to be organized by French instructors and to contain Russian officers. This force, under general French supervision, would then fight alongside of General Denikin's Armed Forces of South Russia, and their operations would be coordinated through the joint command of which the Volunteer Staff in Odessa would become a part.[48] Having obtained approval of this project from the Ukrainian delegation, Freidenberg then began negotiations for a political agreement to back it up.

Political negotiations were now conducted with Ostapenko as the head of a newly formed government which replaced the old Directorate in mid-February. The terms which Freidenberg presented to this new Directorate included the understanding that it would eventually enter a reconstituted Russian state on a federated basis. Equally important, the Ukraine was asked to accept certain economic arrangements designed to protect French interests and at the same time provide the basis for future development, namely, (1) French control over all Ukrainian railroads as long as the economic situation required (some sources indicated a fifty-year concession), (2) assumption by the Ukraine of its share of the Russian state debt, the interest on which was to be guaranteed by income from the operation of the railroads, and (3) supervision by French experts over all industrial, financial, commercial, and military policies for a period of five years.[49]

In this manner France hoped to secure the reunification of Russia and at the same time protect her own substantial economic interests in the South. In return for agreement on these terms, France for her part was to (1) grant temporary de facto recognition to the Ukrainian government in its reorganized form until such time as the Peace Conference or the Allied governments made a decision on the status of the Ukraine, (2) extend the fullest possible assistance to the Ukraine through technical advisors and through the new General Staff, (3) permit temporary economic, social, and agrarian reforms in the Ukraine by the new government so long as they did not create disorder and retained the principle of compensation for confiscated land or other property, and (4) use her good offices and influence to bring an end to hostilities between the Ukraine and Poland over Galicia, to obtain a favorable settlement of other questions of disputed territories, and to do all possible to improve Ukrainian relations with Rumania.[50]

France thus offered to concede that the Ukrainian government was the legitimate authority in the Ukraine and should have its views taken into account in the settlement of the Russian question, providing that it guaranteed French interests, cooperated fully in a joint military struggle against the Bolsheviks, and accepted the goal of a reunification of Russia through federation of its parts. The real significance of this plan lay not in its details (on which the sources disagree to some extent) but in what it revealed of French policy. The French Command wanted unity within the anti-Bolshevik camp and sought to achieve it by forcing a reasonable compromise on its diverse elements. If there was hostility between the Volunteers and the Ukrainians because of extremists on both sides, then both sides would be moderated to make cooperation easier. If there was military disunity and even conflict, then a reorganization was in order so as to direct all the fighting against the Bolsheviks. And the only force able to do these things, able to act as a buffer and at the same time to bring sufficient pressure to bear for unification, was the French Command in its capacity as spokesman for the Allied Powers and dispenser of Allied aid.

Unfortunately, however, what looked good in principle completely failed in practice. Freidenberg had apparently hoped that he could, in defiance of Denikin's objection, enter an agreement with a movement branded as a band of traitors by the Volunteers, and still create unity between them by virtue of the terms which he would force upon the desperate Ukrainian Directorate. It was not Freidenberg's fault, of course, that Denikin's policies were what they were, but in the light of those policies his approach could hardly have produced harmony. Indeed it alienated Denikin long before the negotiations with the Directorate were completed. No matter how much Denikin might have stood to gain from the terms of the agreements after they were negotiated, his relations with the French Command had deteriorated to such an extent by that time that nothing Freidenberg offered could restore Volunteer confidence.

It appeared from the Volunteer point of view that the French
Command had suddenly reversed Henno's policy without any clear
explanation, had proceeded to work through personal contacts in
Odessa rather than through the Volunteer government, and had deliberately ignored repeated warnings from Denikin about such interference. Denikin objected to negotiations with the Ukrainians chiefly
because he feared the separation of the Ukraine from Russia, but he
also feared that the French were secretly attempting to exclude the
Volunteers from that area and deprive them of its vast sources of supply. The purpose of the intervention, in his view, was to provide a
shield for the formation and supply of the Volunteer Army, and he
had been led initially to believe that was its purpose by Berthelot
himself. But if the French recognized a separate government in the
Ukraine and even went so far as to form a separate army to fight
there, they would, he believed, betray that purpose and even turn the
intervention against him.[51]

Denikin's fears were largely unfounded, for in fact the negotiations
with the Directorate were intended as a step toward eliminating the
source of them. Indeed, on March 3 in a dispatch to the French
ambassador in London, Pichon expressed concern over separatism in
the non-Russian borderlands and declared that, even if it should be
necessary to make certain arrangements with the ethnic minorities,
"nevertheless the dismemberment of our ally cannot be the end
sought by our policy." Allied policy in South Russia, he declared,
"must be based on the one force which exists there, the Volunteer
Army, mediocre though it may be."[52] It was thus all the more ironic
that after the misunderstanding which they had helped to provoke,
the agreements negotiated with the Directorate were never really
adopted or made official.[53] The negotiations had finally reached their
culmination at a time when the forces of the Directorate were being
driven from the Ukraine and it no longer had any real power at all.
Since the basis of French efforts to deal with the Directorate was
the assumption that it represented a significant force which must be
employed in the common struggle, the evaporation of this basis rendered the effort itself futile and costly.[54] Meanwhile, Bolshevik successes in the Ukraine, in the Crimea, and in the Don threatened to
end hope of a victory in any form and forced the French Command
into even more drastic actions.

*   *   *   *   *   *

By mid-March French troops were being forced to pull back from the perimeter around Odessa by the advance of Grigorev's pro-Bolshevik partisans. Red forces occupied Kherson on March 10 and Nikolaev on March 12, and the defenses of Odessa itself were in a poor state.[55] At the same time the Crimea found itself under attack and equally ill-prepared to meet it. Denikin proposed to institute martial law in the Crimea and ordered the Volunteer units in Odessa to prepare for transfer there. Once again, however, his orders conflicted with those of the French Command. In this case the French Command in Odessa refused to allow the Volunteers to leave the city for fear of undermining its defenses, and the French Command in Sevastopol opposed the introduction of martial law in the Crimea as an unwarranted interference on Denikin's part.[56]

On March 13 it became known in Odessa that the French Command there was preparing to declare a state of siege the next day as a preliminary step before the appointment of a new military commander and the establishment of a new government.[57] The latter was to be headed by D. F. Andro de Langeron, a "Ukrainian" of French ancestry who had formerly served in the Skoropadskii regime and had for some time in Odessa sought unsuccessfully to persuade the French Command to support the restoration to power of the elements which had once backed the Hetman.[58] On the same day, d'Anselme and Freidenberg held a conference with Grishin-Almazov and Sannikov to discuss this plan and to learn the Volunteer attitude toward it. The Volunteer generals raised no objections to a declaration of martial law in Odessa but strongly opposed the creation of any new authority, especially in view of Denikin's order that Volunteer officers were to be subordinated only to the Volunteer Command. Nevertheless, Freidenberg indicated that these objections would not be allowed to stand in the way of the planned action.[59]

The next day, March 14, a group of Volunteer representatives, including Sannikov, Grishin-Almazov, Shul'gin, General Timanovskii, M. V. Bernatskii (head of Denikin's Finance Department), and V. A. Lebedev (head of the Department of Trade and Industry), held a secret conclave among themselves to decide what to do. They all agreed that the French action was highly objectionable but also that a public rift with the French Command should be avoided as long as possible since this would only encourage both the local opposition and the Bolsheviks. It was, therefore, decided that they would seek privately to clarify the situation, "without a scandal" as Shul'gin put it, and meanwhile follow a policy of wait-and-see. Only when confronted publicly with French rejection would they make an open break and take a public stand of opposition.[60]

Meanwhile the Council for State Unity, which had been invited to provide several members in the proposed new government, approved the French plan, and Margulies was slated to take the position of minister of finance. The question of who should compose the government, however, was less important than the vital issue of the selection of a new military commander (who would also be minister of war in the new cabinet). The candidate proposed by Freidenberg, General A. V. Shvarts, was (just as Andro) out of favor with the Volunteers, but in addition to that he was already committed to other plans of his own and therefore not very interested in the post. Rejected for Volunteer service some months before because of his earlier acceptance of the Red Army command in Petrograd, Shvarts had joined a group in Odessa (led by the former minister of war in the Provisional government, A. I. Guchkov) which was secretly laying plans for the organization of a new army among Russian prisoners in Germany to open a campaign against Petrograd. Because of his involvement with this scheme Shvarts initially rejected the French offer.[61]

Subsequently, however, not only d'Anselme but Franchet d'Esperey, who arrived on March 20 to investigate the difficulties in Odessa, visited Shvarts and offered terms designed to induce him to accept the appointment. What they offered was the promise that (1) a southwest Russian government would be established on an equal basis with the Siberian, Transcaucasian, Crimean, and Volunteer (Ekaterinodar) governments, (2) a mass mobilization would be carried out immediately in the Odessa area to organize a large new army, into which Ukrainian forces would also be incorporated, (3) Allied reinforcements would be sent to provide for a strong defense of Odessa and give Shvarts adequate time to organize his new army, (4) Allied aid would be forthcoming in substantial quantity to assure supply, and (5) a real effort would be made to obtain Denikin's cooperation and support for the reorganization by a formal recognition of his position as commander-in-chief of all South Russian forces and by inviting his Finance Department chief, Bernatskii, to assume the same post in the new government at Odessa.[62]

Shvarts was impressed, but he still hesitated, since none of these promises could be fulfilled without considerable delay. Franchet d'Esperey even admitted that the plan to establish a new government would not be implemented at once but rather in two stages, the first stage being simply to name Shvarts as governor-general to replace Grishin-Almazov and to install a special political council (the nucleus of Andro's cabinet) under the French Command. Moreover, it would take some time for the nine battalions of African troops and a Greek Corps, which were promised as reinforcements, to be assembled and transported to Odessa, although in the meantime, Shvarts was told, French troops in Rumania would be readied to protect the flank on the west. Shvart's doubts were finally overcome, however, and he agreed to accept the French offer on condition that Denikin be consulted first.[63]

About all that was done to fulfill this condition by the French Command was the sending of a telegram by d'Anselme to the new French mission chief in Ekaterinodar, Colonel Corbeil, reading: "Avoid a break in relations with the Volunteer Army. Insist on . . . Shvarts whom I know personally. I have had enough of Sannikov and Grishin; the former is a disorganizer and the latter is an adventurer."[64] In any case, without Denikin's approval, the French Command proceeded to name Shvarts as commander of Russian forces in the Southwest and to establish the new political council under Andro. D'Anselme took pains to explain that the creation of the new council, or "Council for Civil Affairs," was only a "temporary measure provoked by the serious situation," which also made martial law and an assumption of full authority by the French Command necessary. "If the appointment of M. Andro as my assistant for civil affairs was made by me without waiting for the approval of General Denikin," d'Anselme noted, "this is explained solely by existing circumstances which prevent rapid communication with Ekaterinodar."[65]

Whether rightly or not, however, this assumption of authority by the French in Odessa was taken by the Volunteers both there and in Ekaterinodar as a virtual coup d'état.[66] Despite d'Anselme's "explanation" and an effort by Shvarts himself to inform Ekaterinodar of the reasons for these steps, Denikin ordered General Sannikov "not to enter any relations with Andro and not to carry out any of his orders." While instructing Sannikov to keep negotiations open as long as possible, Denikin added: "In case of a complete break of connections, I recommend that you take extraordinary measures in my name for the maintenance of the dignity of Russia and the interests of the Volunteer Army."[67]

Andro's authority in Odessa was challenged, moreover, not only by Denikin but also by local groups which took a stand against it. In a rare demonstration of unity among the liberal and socialist groups in the city, a statement was issued in defense of Denikin's position. This statement, bearing the signatures of individual Kadets, Socialist Revolutionaries, and even Mensheviks, was presented to d'Anselme by a five-man delegation from the Odessa organizations and the city duma.[68] It declared:

> If, in the place of the Volunteer government of Odessa, the French Command establishes a governmental organization under its own aegis, it will stir up sharp discontent among the population of Odessa. In the present quarrel between the Staff of the French Command and the Volunteer Command, the Odessa duma and highly influential democratic and socialist organizations join with the Volunteer Army in opposing all attempts on the part of the French staff to establish any sort of "South Russian Authority" which has the character of a colonial regime and which violates the sovereignty of Russia.[69]

The French Command had certainly miscalculated Andro's following.[70] Instead of obtaining cooperation, it had stirred up an opposition within the city which was clearly not simply a reflection of Denikin's intransigence. Two leading spokesmen of the Union for Regeneration and of socialist opinion generally, Braikevich and Titov, for example, protested that with all its faults the Volunteer Army was still the best hope against the Bolsheviks, and they were joined in this opinion even by members of the Council for State Unity who were having second thoughts on the advisability of making major changes now. In opposition to French plans some socialist leaders even threatened to call for a workers' demonstration to back the Volunteers![71] Such was the curious outcome of the long French efforts to obtain a united front for the formation of a new government.

Spokesmen for the French Command now denied vigorously any intention of displacing the Volunteer government, and Franchet d'Esperey in particular insisted that the French "had no intention of establishing a colonial regime here."[72] The new council, declared d'Anselme, would "by no means be called upon to replace the present authority established by General Denikin" but would act exclusively as "an auxiliary technical apparatus for the duration of the state of siege" for the purpose of improving defense and supply operations.[73] Despite these protestations, however, the expression of opposition to its plans seems to have spurred the French Command toward further implementation of them rather than the reverse.

After the formal announcement of Shvarts' appointment as commander of all Russian troops in the French zone (on March 20), Andro's council was slightly reorganized as a "Committee of Defense and Supply" and a supplemental "Extraordinary Advisory Organ" was created, consisting of the socialist city duma leader, Braikevich, and the socialist Zemstvo head, Butenko, in addition to Shvarts.[74] This was obviously a move designed to placate socialist opposition. With regard to the Volunteers under Shvarts' general command, General Timanovskii of the local Volunteer Staff was designated as the officer specifically in charge of Volunteer troops in the area, but at the same time the dismissal of Grishin-Almazov and Sannikov was curtly announced by a simple statement reading: "Tomorrow, March 22, General Sannikov will leave for Ekaterinodar, and General Grishin-Almazov will accompany him."[75]

General Franchet d'Esperey, as previously noted, had been dissatisfied with the course of the intervention from the start, but, much against his will, he had been obliged to take over personal direction of affairs in Odessa by the illness of Berthelot and the latter's request to be relieved to return to Paris.[76] Prior to receiving instructions on March 15 to proceed to Odessa, Franchet d'Esperey had been in Paris for conferences with Allied military and political leaders on the problems of the occupation, and he had come away from these meetings more opposed to the intervention than ever.[77] In view of his low opinion of the Volunteers—he thought the Bolsheviks had shown more ability to form a "serious army"—and of his belief that the intervention itself was an "absurdity," it was not surprising that Franchet d'Esperey authorized steps which could result in a complete break with Denikin, and it is quite probable that he subsequently recommended pulling Allied troops out of Odessa entirely.[78]

During the last days of March, however, no plan of evacuation was mentioned in Odessa. On the contrary, the French Command undertook a feverish and intensive fortification of the approaches to the city. General Berthelot, then departing Rumania for Paris, on March 23 offered optimistic reassurance to Ambassador Poklevskii-Kozel. The French Command, he said, had made a "resolute decision" to hold Odessa, and Allied reinforcements would soon be on their way.[79] In Odessa itself the papers printed an "official" communique stating that Paris had ordered a concentration of forces to defend the city and repeated the assertion that new troops would be sent.[80] General Shvarts meanwhile ordered a general mobilization in the area and took some 15,000 Ukrainian troops under his command, and Andro announced to the disturbed population that the city would not be surrendered.[81]

Franchet d'Esperey himself, it is true, warned that if their plans did not work out, "the French Government would be obliged to recall its troops and end the occupation of the South Russian region,"[82] but on March 26 two ships carrying French and Greek troops did appear, and four days later another arrived with a detachment of Algerian troops.[83] With these, and a sizable naval force in the port, it seemed likely that evacuation would not be necessary. On the other hand, the real question from the French point of view was not whether the city could be held but whether it would actually be worth the effort under existing circumstances. Military preparedness was only one side of the picture; on the other was the fact that conditions in Odessa had grown steadily worse until by the end of March it was on the verge of anarchy.

Thousands who had fled the Bolsheviks had congregated in the city and had formed mobs of homeless, foodless people.[84] Less than one-third of the economic enterprises in Odessa were functioning in March, and unemployment seemed likely to spread to a large majority of the population. The city was vitually without heat or electricity because of the fuel shortage, and other shortages had brought about a ten-fold inflation of prices generally. Such conditions led one newspaper to declare: "Never before has Odessa passed through such a tragic, nightmarish period as now. The population is succumbing . . . to starvation and cold. . . ."[85] The Bolsheviks were, of course, taking advantage of the situation for propaganda and agitation. Organized into special "colleges," French-speaking agitators, both men and women, stirred up the workers, inspired mutiny among the soldiers and sailors, and from a hidden press circulated "incredibly large quantities of literature in Russian and French."[86] By this time the Bolsheviks were also finally making headway in undercutting the popular appeal and influence of the socialists who had in the past dominated the worker and peasant movements in Odessa.[87]

Bad conditions and skillful propaganda combined to make the French troops even less reliable than they had been five months earlier when Franchet d'Esperey had expressed concern over their low morale. Greek and colonial troops succeeded in maintaining a higher esprit de corps, but neither the Greek nor the French soldiers had expected to have to fight and had been disillusioned by what they found in

Russia. When they came under attack, and especially when in Kherson and Nikolaev the local populations had joined the Bolsheviks in firing on them, many of the French troops had refused to fight, and the Greeks had in turn blamed their own losses on the French.[88] These incidents, plus the subsequent mutiny of a sizable number of the sailors of the French squadron, were among the many factors which had to be taken into consideration in deciding whether to remain in Odessa or not.[89] Although the French Command probably overrated the Bolsheviks' strength, it did appreciate the inferior condition of its troops and their unwillingness to fight a Russian war.[90]

Despite the many obstacles to successful military operations, however, it was not so much the difficulty of defending Odessa as it was the difficulty in keeping it supplied which finally led to the decision to evacuate it. Franchet d'Esperey's reports to Paris stressed most of all the food and fuel problem and the lack of adequate Russian leadership to cope with it. In discussion of this problem in the Allied Council of Four in Paris on March 17, 25, and 27, Marshal Foch, who saw more to be gained in building the cordon in Eastern Europe, advised that it would be better under the circumstances to send what supplies were available to Rumania instead, and on March 27 it was agreed that evacuation of Odessa was advisable.[91] Thus when the decision to evacuate was announced in Odessa, it was stated:

> The Entente Powers have given notice that it will be impossible for them . . . to assure the supply of Odessa. This is why, in order to diminish the number of mouths to feed, it has been decided to evacuate the city.[92]

This decision was conveyed to Franchet d'Esperey's headquarters in Constantinople on April 1 and reached d'Anselme in Odessa on April 2. It ordered the evacuation to be carried out within three days, but d'Anselme decided that it could be done in 48 hours and on April 3 issued the order to begin.[93]

The French evacuation of Odessa followed Foreign Minister Pichon's public statement to the Chamber on March 29 that the government's policy was one which opposed any further use of French troops against the Bolsheviks,[94] but it was a severe shock in Odessa, where the preceding defense preparations had given assurances against it. Faced not only with a withdrawal of Allied forces but a 48-hour deadline to get out, the population panicked and mobbed the docks.[95]

On April 3 the Council of Trade Unions demanded the release of

all Russian ships held by the French, but their demand was rejected.[96]
A workers' delegation then presented an ultimatum to d'Anselme
insisting that no Russian property or persons be taken from the city
and threatening a general strike to block the evacuation if he refused.
D'Anselme, however, informed them that he would order his naval
guns to level the workers' homes if they carried out their threat or
attacked a single French soldier. At this the Bolshevik-led workers
backed down and agreed not to obstruct the evacuation, but they
knew now that the city was theirs. Bolshevik newspapers were being
sold on the streets only two hours after the last ship pulled away, and
after April 6 communications from Odessa were conducted in the
name of the Ukrainian Soviet Socialist Republic.[97]

Under the circumstances it was remarkable that the French were
able to evacuate 30,000 civilians and 10,000 Volunteer and other
troops in addition to their own.[98] The achievement, however, is far less
impressive when it is noted that thousands were left behind, partly
because of the insistence on carrying out the evacuation as rapidly as
possible. In the panic, many committed suicide or were killed, equipment was destroyed needlessly, and part of the Volunteer troops were
left behind virtually empty-handed. The Volunteer brigade under
General Timanovskii was even refused money by the French on the
excuse that the necessary treasury operations would take two or three
days. With practically no supplies, the brigade was ordered by the
French to leave Odessa and move inland to Bessarabia. After making
their way to Bessarabia, these Volunteers were arrested and disarmed
and only after some difficulties returned to Denikin.[99]

The suddenness of the evacuation also meant that Denikin was
taken by surprise. Informed of the decision only after the evacuation
was in progress, Denikin immediately demanded that Russian troops
be provided with assistance and "immediate shipment by sea with
full supply and artillery . . . to Novorosiisk." He wrote to Franchet
d'Esperey:

> Only yesterday did I learn that the French Army was leaving
> Odessa. . . . The French Command did not even find it necessary
> to forewarn me of this. It is difficult at this point to foresee the
> historic consequences of this step, but in any case I believe the
> Volunteer brigades have a moral right to assistance. . . .[100]

The fact that some Volunteer troops were left behind and that the
evacuation left Denikin's left flank and the Crimea open to Bolshevik

attack added to the bitterness already felt toward the French. This feeling came out particularly in a subsequent report which charged the French with having secretly prepared the whole thing in advance. Citing the prearrangement of certain organizational features of the evacuation, the Volunteer account in effect accused the French of betrayal.[101]

* * * * * *

The evacuation of Sevastopol, which followed three weeks later, was carried out slowly. Yet it presented almost a repetition of events in Odessa. As in Odessa, the French had a sizable fleet in the harbor, had established a fortified defense line around the city, and had spoken of holding the city. They had even once again announced that reinforcements were on the way. On March 26, Franchet d'Esperey had indicated that new Allied troops should arrive in about two weeks, and in fact between April 12 and 14 some Algerian and Senegalese troops, which had come too late to help in Odessa, were moved to the Crimea and put under the French commander, Colonel Trousson.[102] However, the situation in the Crimea was still not good.

The Crimean government was in no position to defend its territory, and its relations with the Volunteer Army had been complicated by incidents connected with Volunteer efforts to mobilize troops there and by Denikin's announcement that he might move his headquarters to the Crimea and thus take over control of it.[103] Raids by guerrilla bands, Bolshevik propaganda, and the French refusal to permit the transfer of Volunteer troops into the Crimea earlier had left the entire peninsula in a precarious state even before the fall of Odessa.[104] And the French withdrawal from the Ukraine had in turn relieved Bolshevik forces for a concerted attack. While the French Command had taken some steps to strengthen the Crimean government, the effort was half-hearted and was largely wiped out by the emergency. On April 8 the government was moved out of Simferopol for its own safety and thereafter, in virtual exile in Sevastopol, lost all control over events. It called upon the zemstvos throughout the Crimea to assume the responsibility of administration, but by the end of March the French were applying martial law wherever their authority extended.[105]

The fortress of Sevastopol was technically under the control of the Volunteer commander, General Subbotin, but, following the pattern of events in Odessa, Colonel Trousson also, on April 3, set up a defense committee and named himself military governor, making Sub-

botin his assistant.[106] In practice this simply meant that Trousson
took over command, since the defense committee was never able to
take any action or even to agree on a plan for the defense of the city.
About all the creation of the committee accomplished was to bring
to a head a dispute between Trousson and Subbotin as to what measures were necessary. Trousson insisted that no extensive effort need
be put into constructing a ground defense on the north side of the
city, since naval guns could cover that approach. Subbotin disagreed,
but his objections were overruled.[107]

Beneath this disagreement over strategy, however, there lay a much
more serious dispute over the very presence of Volunteer troops in
Sevastopol. Colonel Trousson accused the Volunteers of being plun-
derers and considered them more of a hindrance than a help to his
task of defending the city. Even the Sevastopol city treasury, he
claimed, had been robbed and the money put on Volunteer ships.
Accordingly he ordered that no ships be allowed to leave the harbor
without his permission, that all members of the Crimean government
be detained until the money was returned, and that no Volunteer
soldier be permitted to leave with anything other than his personal
baggage.[108]

The issue here was really who had authority to take responsibility
for the acts of the Crimean government. After the declaration of a
state of siege in Sevastopol on April 10, Trousson claimed such powers. However, Subbotin asserted that the authority had devolved on
him after the break-up of the government and its move to Sevastopol,
and he refused to subordinate himself to Trousson except in purely
military matters. On the basis of this claim to authority, Subbotin
had already made arrangements with the finance minister of the Crimean government to assume control over the state funds which had
been deposited in Sevastopol. Volunteer troops were, indeed, being
paid out of these funds, and for safekeeping the money had been
transferred from the state bank to a Volunteer ship in the harbor.
Nevertheless, Colonel Trousson refused to countenance this arrangement and decided to end it by confiscating the funds involved.[109]

The Crimean government was then caught in the middle of this
dispute, despite the fact that it had abdicated its powers and its
remaining members had already boarded a ship to leave the Crimea.
Trousson refused to allow their ship to depart and ordered them to
come ashore to see him on this matter. They immediately informed
the French commander that all the funds had been appropriated

according to Crimean law or had been allotted to General Subbotin for the expenses of defense and evacuation. Only 500,000 rubles had been retained by the government itself to cover the cost of its own departure.[110] Colonel Trousson, however, retorted that Crimean law was no longer valid and declared that he had not only ordered the arrest of General Subbotin and the Volunteer naval commander, Admiral Sablin, but would do the same to the government if it did not turn over the money by eleven o'clock the following morning.

The startled Crimean ministers thus found themselves under a kind of house arrest and faced with a demand that some 11 million rubles, for which they were being held responsible, be turned over to the French Command at once. An attempt to protest this situation to the ranking French naval officer, Admiral Amet, was rejected, and the government then began hastily gathering all the treasury and bank records it could find to show where the funds had gone. These records were presented to Trousson the next morning, but he still refused to release the government until the money itself was found. In view of this the government decided that the only way out was to sign over all funds, wherever and whatever they might be, to the French Command. Consequently a document was drawn up on April 12 giving Colonel Trousson control over all assets of the government, the only condition being that any surplus left after the evacuation be returned to Russian authorities.[111]

With this document as authorization, Colonel Trousson then ordered French troops to board the Volunteer ship on which the money was being held, and the funds were forcibly seized. The Crimean minister of finance, for his part, collected all the money he could find elsewhere (mostly short term notes) and turned it over to the French Command also. Finally, on April 28, the government was allowed to leave. The protests of the Volunteer Command over this action were ignored. On April 12, the day the Crimean government had capitulated to his demands, Trousson had ordered all Volunteers to leave Sevastopol and move to the Kerch peninsula, which they were told to hold at all cost.[112] This action, together with a curt rejection of an offer from Denikin to send more troops, had put a decisive end to Volunteer authority in Sevastopol even before the Crimean government had been sent on its way.[113]

While these events had been taking place, Trousson had ordered French ships to take stations for the defense which he had planned. However, his strategy of using the naval guns fell through when the

battleship *Mirabeau* promptly ran aground and made it impossible
to get the ships into position.[114] In this situation Trousson concluded
that it would be foolish to fight, and so he decided to negotiate a
truce with the Bolsheviks, specifically with the soviet already established in the city, so as to permit a more orderly evacuation as soon
as the *Mirabeau* could be refloated. Under this truce, which lasted
until the end of April, Red troops bided their time outside Sevastopol
while the soviet prepared to assume control inside the city. The military revolutionary committee of the soviet actually held power after
April 19 when the city duma conceded defeat, but the full evacuation of the city was not completed until April 30.[115]

So ended the French occupation of Sevastopol and of the Crimea.
Once again a break with the Volunteer Command had been brought
about over the defense of a city which was then surrendered without
a fight. The evacuation of Sevastopol had avoided a last-minute panic,
but at the same time the French force had not only failed to offer
resistance but had negotiated with the Bolsheviks instead. As a result,
relations between the French and the Volunteers were, as Denikin
put it, "extremely strained."[116]

*   *   *   *   *   *

In the aftermath of these evacuations, the charges hurled at the
French from sources associated with the Volunteer Army were so hos-
tile and bitter that Franchet d'Esperey was prompted to write to
Denikin:

> It is extremely regrettable that Russian public opinion can
> believe that the evacuation of Odessa by the French Command
> was carried out by design and that although it had sufficient mili-
> tary means at its disposal, it intentionally failed to make use of
> them. You know as well as I do that the real causes of the evacua-
> tion of Odessa are the same that have now compelled us to leave
> Sevastopol. The evacuation of both of these cities resulted exclu-
> sively from the impossibility of supplying provisions for them, in
> consequence of which disorder threatened to break out. From a
> military point of view we did not suffer any sort of defeat, and if
> there had been no fear of dooming the populations of these two
> cities to starvation, we would have remained in position.[117]

Denikin did not debate this point, but he noted that if the French
had brought sufficient forces to occupy the area, as he had urged,
instead of negotiating with the Directorate, defense and supply would
have been possible. The French, he declared, were therefore properly

accused of backing down on their promises and of taking a hostile attitude toward the Volunteers which seriously hampered his efforts to establish unity of command and to implement effective political and economic as well as military policies.[118] While Denikin's argument in his own defense betrayed a certain blindness to Volunteer faults in relations with the French and to the limitations imposed on the French Command, there is no doubt that the troubles experienced in Odessa contributed substantially to the failure of the intervention and, in turn, of the anti-Bolshevik effort.

The strained relations between the Volunteers and the French were, indeed, to persist long after the French evacuation of South Russia. And, as Freidenberg had hinted, this situation had in turn put a serious burden on inter-Allied relations. French troubles in Odessa and considerable criticism from British circles of the policies adopted to deal with those troubles had suggested the need for new inter-Allied consultations. Indeed, even now Allied policy still lacked the full benefit of joint planning and coordination.[119]

On April 4 an Anglo-French conference had, therefore, been called in Paris to discuss, among other things, the operation of the zone agreement in South Russia and the problem of French relations with Denikin. This conference then produced a protocol which, as a supplement to the December 1917 agreement, was expected to help in avoiding further conflict. It had a curious air of unreality about it, since it ignored the evacuation of Odessa then taking place and was couched in terms of a compromise of Freidenberg's earlier plans, but its main purpose was to state the French desire to work cooperatively with Denikin and to suggest the terms under which that could be achieved. Thus the French agreed with the British that:

1. The French High Command will not interfere with General Denikin and his representatives in the formation of Russian contingents on the condition that no disorder follows in the zone placed under the authority of the French Command;

2. Command of Russian units formed in the field will be assumed by Russian officers belonging preferably to the Army of Denikin or to other organizations in the case where units motivated by a desire to fight the Bolsheviks do not agree to serve in Denikin's Army;

It is agreed that these formations will be composed of Russians only, and will not include Allied and French troops, but they will be provided with Allied instructors and technical advisors;

3. Russian troops in the French zone which have recognized the authority of Denikin can, by joint agreement between General Denikin and the French High Command, be used by the former in his theater of operations or can be put at the disposal of the latter;

4. General Denikin and the French High Command are to come to an agreement on the question of Russian material located in the zone of French operations, to be used for the formation of Russian forces in the territory of the zone in question or to be put at the disposal of General Denikin. The latter will not interfere with the transfer of surplus material in his zone to the French zone;

5. General Denikin and the French Command will work together in the course of their operations and in their mutual needs through the intermediary of special missions charged with liaison service. . . .[120]

The protocol further provided for a settlement of the dispute over the possession of Russian transport ships seized by the French during the occupation of Odessa. The French agreed that these ships would be returned and also stated that Russian military ships under Denikin's command would be authorized "to navigate under the Russian flag" and that there would be no further interference with chartered shipping on the Black Sea. Acutally, however, the further needs of the evacuation had led to a seizure of even more ships by the French and to new protests from the Volunteers before anything was done about implementing this agreement. Compliance with Denikin's request to have the ships returned came only after lengthy and rather troublesome negotiations between French and Volunteer representatives during the summer and autumn of 1919.[121]

In the April protocol the French unquestionably indicated a willingness to compromise with Denikin. They had acknowledged that Denikin's authority was the only one left in their zone with which to deal on major questions, and they had agreed not to interfere. But they had done these things, Denikin noted, "on condition" and in a tone of granting permission and "authorizing." Furthermore they specifically retained the right to exercise influence over troops in their zone "who refuse to submit to General Denikin's authority," and promised to turn over Russian materials only after an agreement of unspecified terms had been made with Denikin. "Mutual" needs were stressed, and the clause referring to transfer of "surplus" material to the French hinted openly that they intended to seek compensation for whatever they might give to Denikin. It was in fact in the subsequent negotiations concerning return of Russian ships that the French first formally raised the question of economic concessions.[122]

France had from the beginning held Russia responsible for the state debt and made acceptance of this obligation a condition for aid to any group.[123] Beyond this, moreover, the French Foreign Ministry had also shown as much, if not more, interest in new economic concessions. In a note written during April 1919, for example, one French official stated:

> The French government must take into consideration the fact that the payment of interest on the Russian state debt has not been made. It is therefore obliged to consider all the natural wealth of Russia at the same time as the source of revenue that can be created as a guarantee of repayment for the creditors of the Russian state, such as railroads, mines, forests, etc.[124]

The terms presented to the Ukrainian Directorate had, perhaps, reflected what the application of this reasoning might mean in practice.

Denikin's position on this question was related to his conception of himself as the appointed guardian of the Russian land and its unity but not one authorized to bind a future government. Any economic concessions, he believed, would have to come from a national assembly after the war. Furthermore, he resented any attempt by a foreign power to bypass his authority and deal with individual governments in South Russia on economic questions, as the French had done in the Ukraine and to a lesser extent in the Don. Such attempts, of course, thwarted his efforts to force all regional authorities, of which the Cossack governments were the most important and also at times the most stubborn, to accept centralized control over economic policy and external relations. To Denikin's mind the Allies should not have to be "bribed" to live up to their moral obligations, and besides that he insisted that the Volunteer Army would not "even temporarily bow the knee to the foreigner or hamper in any way the free course of the Russian ship of state."[125]

On the other hand, this did not in any way mean that Denikin did not recognize Russia's past commitments or that he was unwilling to negotiate trade agreements. He did not deny the fairness of an exchange or of payment for the aid which he received. However, he felt that this matter should be dealt with on an ad hoc basis, taking into account the state of war which existed in Russia and the absence of a central authority competent to make long-term arrangements. In

August Denikin thus consented to a French request to begin talks on a trade agreement as the basis of possible future French aid.[126] As a note from the Russian chargé d'affaires in Paris explained the French position: "The French government has agreed in principle to send provisions, but only in exchange for our wheat."[127] However, the talks did not result in any acceptable arrangement at this stage, and Maklakov soon wired from Paris that the French government would not send any more military supplies because Denikin had failed to promise delivery of suitable quantities of wheat in exchange.[128]

Volunteer relations with the French thus showed no real improvement despite the April protocol. Indeed there were even indications that they were perhaps getting worse during the summer of 1919. An American observer in the Kuban reported increasing hostility on both sides and thought he detected a French "diplomatic offensive" against Denikin "to have him replaced by someone more Francophile."[129] Making matters worse, the Bolsheviks captured and published in May a letter from Denikin to Kolchak in which he called the French evacuations "shameful" and contrasted the "extensive aid" which he was receiving from the British with the "extensive opposition" which he was getting from the French. Denikin was subsequently informed in June that this letter had "roused the extreme wrath of M. Clemenceau."[130]

It was actually almost two months before the text of the new protocol was delivered to Denikin, and at the same time he was for the first time officially informed of the Anglo-French zone agreement. His response to the latter was that it could possibly apply only to arrangements for Allied aid and could in no way be permitted to suggest an actual division of Russia or be allowed to interfere with the movements of the Volunteer Army. And as for the protocol, it is interesting to note that Denikin's reply, rejecting in effect its basic ideas, was sent after the British representatives at Volunteer headquarters had indicated to him that they would support him fully, both militarily and politically.[131] Since Volunteer operations were bound, if they succeeded according to Denikin's plans, to take place largely through the French zone, the protocol had also clearly failed to eliminate the problems involved here in relations between the two Allies.[132]

Notably, in the question of Denikin's status as supreme commander of Russian forces in the South, it had not been the lower-ranking French mission in Ekaterinodar headed by a Captain Fouquet but the strikingly superior British delegation under General F. C. Poole (who had earlier commanded the Arkhangelsk expedition) which had successfully applied pressure on Krasnov and brought about his recognition of Denikin as commander-in-chief in January. Fouquet, it is true, had joined this effort, but his methods had served only to intensify Denikin's feeling that the French Command was seeking primarily to establish its own influence. In response to Denikin's request for backing, Fouquet had sent Krasnov a note demanding his subordination not only to the Volunteer Command but also to the Allied Command under Franchet d'Esperey. Moreover, the French captain had chosen to use this same occasion to demand that the Don assume responsibility for its share of all losses by French citizens caused by the revolution.[133] In contrast to this, shortly after arriving in Ekaterinodar, Poole had asked Denikin bluntly whether it would be necessary "to overthrow Krasnov" in order to eliminate his opposition to a single command. Denikin had replied that he only wanted Poole to use his influence to change Krasnov's attitude, and Poole had then arranged the conference between Krasnov and Volunteer leaders which had finally led to the accord formalized on January 8, 1919, giving Denikin the command over all forces in South Russia. The achievement of a unity of command was thus attributed by Denikin largely to British rather than French support, although this conclusion reflected the unequal influence of the two missions more than it reflected the facts.[134]

In February British influence had grown even more as a result of the arrival of the new British mission under General Briggs, which brought with it several shiploads of equipment and supplies for the Volunteers. Although, following the recall of Fouquet, the French sent a mission of higher rank under Lt. Colonel Corbeil, General Briggs' status was further elevated over that of his French counterpart by arrangements permitting him to deal directly with the British War Office rather than being subordinated to the command center in Constantinople. Moreover, Briggs subsequently showed a special concern for the setback suffered by the Volunteers in Odessa and the Crimea. It was in part because of the strained relations between the Volunteers and the French, and particularly because of the criticism at that time of the Volunteers as reactionary and Germanophile, that Briggs urged Denikin in April to issue a statement to clarify his policies and counteract the unfavorable image being presented abroad. It was indicative of the influence of the British mission that Denikin, who was inclined to evade political questions and ignore advice to

give more attention to public relations, accepted the British suggestion and issued one of his infrequent policy statements in the form of
a note to the Allied missions on April 23. In it he set forth a list of
Volunteer objectives along the lines proposed by Briggs, including
election of a national assembly, guarantee of civil liberties, land reform, protection of labor, and decentralization of power through the
extension of regional autonomy and broad local self-government.[135]

This statement could be regarded as an honest reaffirmation of
Denikin's personal goals, but the significance of its release at this time
was reflected in the fact that it satisfied virtually no one but the British mission. Neither liberal nor conservative elements in the Volunteer
leadership approved of it, and Denikin himself would have preferred
to stick with his "nonpredetermination" stand at this point so as to
restrain the expression of political differences within Volunteer ranks
and maintain the nonpartisan authority of the military dictatorship.
Moreover, after the experience in Odessa the French could hardly
have regarded the statement as much more than a propaganda move
aimed principally at them. The episode of the April policy statement
thus once again illustrated the delicacy of the three-way relationship
between the Volunteers and the Allies and the increasing tendency
of the Volunteer Command to rely on the British for both aid and
advice. The tension existing after the French evacuation, and the attitude of the British Foreign Office toward Volunteer-French relations,
were bluntly expressed in a letter from Lord Curzon (then acting
foreign secretary) to Lord Balfour on June 11:

> French actions at Odessa and in the Ukraine have so embittered
> French relations with the Russians that it is inconceivable we shall
> ever be able to co-operate with them again in those regions.
> We have always maintained that we could not regard the Ukraine
> independently of Russia, and that General Denikin's Government
> was the only one in South Russia worthy of support. . . .
> The Ukraine, when it is reconquered, should properly fall within
> General Denikin's sphere of influence, and consequently under our
> control, and we should make a strenuous endeavour to obtain a
> modification of the existing agreement with the French to secure
> the elimination of their activities in those regions forthwith.[136]

Apparently, however, Curzon found that the French would not
give up their zone, regardless of the British "right" to control Denikin
and territory under his command. In any case, he soon decided that
a formal modification of the existing agreement would not be neces-

sary. The French certainly had no desire to impede the struggle against the Bolsheviks and would hardly interfere to stop Denikin. Therefore, he reasoned, the British could proceed without too much concern for the anachronistic and really defunct zonal demarcation. As he then wrote Balfour in July:

> To propose that the Ukraine should now be appointed to Great Britain would certainly increase . . . the ill feeling shown by the French towards the Volunteer Army and General Denikin personally. . . . it does not seem likely that the French will dispute our right to exert a controlling influence over Denikin in regard to the regions occupied by his troops. [137]

When Denikin did, during the summer of 1919, begin his march into the Ukraine, he requested the British to help him organize a new army in the Crimea, and they agreed. Curzon had the tact to consult the French, however, and requested British representatives in Paris to inform the Quai d'Orsay of Denikin's desire and state that "while we maintain the old agreement of December 23, 1917, in principle . . . we are acceding to the request in view of the desirability of giving all the assistance we can to Denikin."[138] The French consented but, still clinging to their zone, replied to Curzon that they reserved the right to act in the zone either to reinforce their military or other representation there or to establish new organizations, especially in the Crimea and the Donets area "where very considerable French interests require appropriate protection."[139] France, indeed, retained her contacts in the Ukraine and would yet play a significant role in determining the directions of Allied policy when the Volunteer Army's offensive in the summer and autumn of 1919 brought it into new contacts with both Ukrainian and Polish operations.

5: BRITAIN AS A BUFFER

Both of the Allied Powers had begun their interventions in South
Russia to aid the struggle against the Bolsheviks only to find themselves engulfed in a confusing tangle of disputes and claims to authority. In dealing with these problems the British were not much more
successful than the French. A clash between the Volunteers and the
Georgians on the Black Sea coast had erupted just prior to the arrival
of British troops in Transcaucasia, and contrary to the expectations
of the British Command the presence of Allied troops did not serve
to end that conflict.

The northern Caucasus region might have provided a natural buffer
between the Volunteers and Transcaucasia, but, having been blocked
to the north earlier by the Germans, Denikin had decided to make
his first task that of clearing the mountain region and the coasts between the Kuban and the Transcaucasian states. He hoped to expand
his base of operations, to protect his Black Sea outlets, and, if possible,
to establish control over the northern part of the Caspian Sea so as
to cut off the highly strategic Volga route uniting Moscow with
Transcaucasia and Turkestan. From Denikin's point of view these
were vital military objectives, all necessary to the establishment of a
secure base for a later drive to the north.[1] The failure of Bicherakov
to hold on to his northern Caucasus outpost and the invasion of the
area first by the Turks and then by the Bolsheviks had made this
Volunteer task all the more imperative.

At the same time, however, Denikin's operations had almost immediately brought the Volunteers into direct contact with Menshevik
Georgia. It was, indeed, just a month before the new British landings
that the two had clashed and a pattern of hostile relations had been
established between them. Georgian troops had begun operations
against the Bolsheviks in the area as far north as Tuapse on the Black

146

Sea coast in the summer of 1918. The Volunteers, then pushing the Bolsheviks out of the southern portion of Kuban territory, had initially regarded this action favorably. Alekseev had in fact established contact with the Georgian commander, General G. I. Mazniev, and had expressed the hope that a cooperative relationship might be established between them as "allies fighting for the same thing."[2] In the hope that mutually advantageous arrangements could be worked out, Alekseev and the Georgian Command had then agreed to call a conference in Ekaterinodar to discuss their differences.

Before such a conference could meet, however, a marked change had come over the attitudes of both sides. Georgian troops had been pushed back by Bolshevik forces in the direction of Sochi, and as the battle line moved southward, the Volunteers had advanced behind the Bolsheviks and occupied Tuapse. Viewing this movement with concern, the Georgian government had recalled General Mazniev and had sent a larger force of national guard units under General Koniev to hold the line.[3] Also at this time anti-Georgian elements among the population of the Sochi and Sukhum areas had begun sending requests to Volunteer headquarters for assistance and "liberation."[4]

It was in the context of these events that the conference of Volunteer and Georgian representatives had opened in Ekaterinodar on September 25. Participating were E. P. Gegechkori and General Mazniev for Georgia, Generals Alekseev, Denikin, Romanovskii, Dragomirov, and Lukomskii for the Volunteer Army, a delegation headed by L. L. Bych for the Kuban, and V. V. Shul'gin and V. A. Stepanov as political observers.[5] The conference had been opened on a fairly friendly note by Alekseev's assurances to the Georgian delegation that the Volunteer Army made "no claims whatsoever" against Georgia's independence and recognized it "in full measure." This cordiality had quickly disappeared, however, when the Volunteers had then voiced their complaints about Georgian treatment of Russian residents and about its dealings with the Germans.[6] Accusations leveled against Georgia in these matters had immediately provoked Gegechkori's ire and resulted in a heated exchange between the delegations.

It had soon become evident in this debate, however, that the issue on which their relations ultimately depended was that of the border between Georgian and Russian territory. Gegechkori was willing to concede Volunteer occupation of Tuapse, but he categorically refused to accept the Volunteer contention that the highly mixed territory southward from there to Sochi, and even to Gagri, was "purely Russian" and that, therefore, the 1905 border was the only acceptable one. The Volunteer Army, he argued, was not a "state" but a military force whose task was to fight the Bolsheviks and not to set borders.[7] The Volunteers, however, had stubbornly refused to accept this argument and would not negotiate further so long as Georgia insisted on retaining the Sochi district.[8]

Efforts by Bych to mediate between the Volunteer and Georgian delegations had come to naught save a further deterioration of Kuban-Volunteer relations.[9] The conference had been a complete failure, and in its aftermath increasingly hostile attitudes had developed on both sides.[10] Relations between Georgia and the Volunteer Army were thus already off to a bad start when the British arrived in Transcaucasia.

The situation in the North Caucasus region remained quite fluid in the winter of 1918–1919 when British occupation had begun. The so-called Mountain Republic had never succeeded in uniting the numerous elements in the area. Real control had passed in turn to the Bolsheviks, to Bicherakov and his allies, and to the Turks, all in a short period preceding the new arrival of the British. Even after the British order requiring all Turkish troops and officers to leave the area, the Mountain government had attempted to retain the services of some of the remaining Turkish troops by means of a technical change of their national status.[11] However, the British Command prohibited such an arrangement and in December sent a military mission to Shura to see that the evacuation order was carried out. This was not to be the end of Turkish actions in this area, but for the time being the Mountain region was left without any forces capable of ruling it. With the exception of a British detachment stationed in Petrovsk, the North Caucasus presented a military and political vacuum.[12]

Chermoev, the head of the Mountain government at this time, had sought to fill this vacuum by obtaining Allied support for his government. Leaving a secondary figure, Pshemakho Kotsev, in charge, Chermoev and his foreign minister, Gaider Bammatov, and his minister of internal affairs, Ibraq bek Gaidarov, had set out on this mission which was eventually to carry them to Paris. Chermoev obtained an audience with General Thomson in Baku in December and used the opportunity to explain the previous reliance on the Turks and the present necessity of British aid to prevent a reconquest of the entire area by the Bolsheviks.[13] Thomson's reply was the issuance on December 18 of a proclamation appealing to the peoples of the North Caucasus to put aside their differences for the moment and unite against the Bolsheviks. All disputes, he declared, would "be decided in the forthcoming World Conference," and meanwhile the Allies had come as the "enemies of Bolshevism," to occupy the Caucasus so as to maintain order and "to secure justice and peace for all."[14]

This appeal was cast in the usual spirit of de facto cooperation with existing authorities, but it offered no immediate assistance to the alarmed Mountain government. The fate of the government was, indeed, hanging by a thread, for its authority was already being challenged by two outside forces seeking to establish control over the North Caucasus: the Bolsheviks and the Volunteers. Moving first into the Terek region, Denikin's troops had fairly rapidly overwhelmed the Bolshevik force there and clearly intended to continue this line of march until the whole Mountain area was secured.[15] The Terek Cossacks were united with the Volunteers with little difficulty, the only problem being the issue which had also affected Denikin's relations with the other Cossack territories, namely, the degree of authority to be vested in the ataman and Krug. And the solution was the same: autonomy for the local government accompanied by recognition of the authority of the Volunteer Command in military matters and questions of Russian national interest.[16]

Denikin's policy emphasized the restoration of law and order and autonomy for local authorities, but it also included the goal of reuniting with Russia not just the Terek but the North Caucasus area in general, a policy concretely expressed in the appointment of General Liakhov as governor-general of the Mountain region, including Dagestan. The full implication of this policy was brought home to the Mountain government when it sent a delegation to negotiate with the approaching Volunteers.

This delegation was instructed to inform the Volunteers that the Mountain Republic would join the struggle against the Bolsheviks but must insist upon its independence, and the exclusion of Volunteer forces from its territory, "until the final decision of this question along with analogous questions concerning other new state formations in the world conference in Paris, to which a special Mountain Government delegation has been sent."[17] When, after a rebuff in Ekaterinodar,[18] representatives of the Mountain government finally succeeded in contacting General Liakhov, the latter explained that his authority covered the entire area but indicated that each of the various Mountain peoples could form an autonomous government for local administration. Under the Governor-General a special local governor of native birth would be appointed for each region, and administration organs could be developed as each saw fit within this framework. In short, the Mountain Republic as such did not exist for the Volunteers, and the compromise offered by Liakhov was the only concession which would be made.[19]

The Mountain Republic parliament (Medjlis) debated this situation at some length after the interview with Liakhov and finally resolved to stand firm on its demand for independence until a decision by the Peace Conference. It therefore issued a statement, declaring, "before all the Great Powers and all state formations on the territory of the former Russian Empire and before the democracy of the world, a determined protest against such profound coercion by the Volunteer Army. . . ."[20] The parliament backed this stand with authorization to mobilize armed forces to defend the territory if the Volunteers should persist in invading. Since the Volunteers were at this point encountering resistance from the Chechens, the first step taken was the dispatch of a detachment to aid the latter.

The Mountain government, however, was in no position to enforce such bold words. The detachment sent to the Chechens was not willing to fight, and the government itself was widely split over the course to take. The division of opinion within the government became especially apparent when, with a view to avoiding any further conflict, Denikin personally journeyed to Grozny in April to meet with Mountain representatives. After hearing Volunteer policy explained once again at this conference, the two leading Mountain government representatives parted company. One, Kaplanov, who was president of the parliament, tried to rally Chechen warriors against the Volunteers, and the other, Gotsinskii, sought support for an agreement with the Volunteers.[21]

With the government divided and helpless, and a Bolshevik invasion threatening, Mountain Republic military leaders (chiefly Dagestanis led by Khalilov) acted on their own to restore order and prevent a Bolshevik takeover. In a belated acknowledgment of the situation the parliament then accepted Kotsev's resignation and authorized General Khalilov to form a new government. With British assistance from Petrovsk, Khalilov then suppressed a Bolshevik effort to seize power and was assured by the British commander in Petrovsk that an agreement with Denikin had been arranged which would exclude Volunteer occupation of Dagestan if it separated from the Mountain Republic and proved itself capable of keeping order and ousting the Bolsheviks.[22]

Following this advice, the Dagestan section of the Mountain Republic parliament, on May 23, 1919, decided to separate from the Mountain Republic "for an indefinite time" to establish a provisional Dagestan government under General Khalilov and to authorize the latter to enter an agreement with Denikin along the lines suggested by the British.[23] This development, however, was not as uncomplicated as it would seem. In the first place the remains of the Mountain government, refusing to acquiesce in its demise, took refuge in Azerbaidzhan and Georgia to continue the struggle.[24] And, in the second place, the alleged agreement with Denikin was not yet a reality. There was in fact a misunderstanding in this case, one of a long series of misunderstandings which had already developed in Denikin's relations with the British Command in Transcaucasia.

As early as December 1918, Denikin had grown concerned about reports that General Thomson in Baku was actively backing the Mountain elements and that the British Command was allowing the confiscation of Russian military supplies from the old Caucasian front by Azerbaidzhan and Georgia.[25] This concern was undoubtedly increased during January by Volunteer intelligence reports that the British were constructing a heavily fortified base at Petrovsk, from which they allegedly intended to expand their operations into Dagestan. It was even reported that the British mission sent to Shura was conducting a mobilization of troops to be placed under the British Command in Transcaucasia.[26] At the same time Volunteer representatives in Baku reported to Ekaterinodar that the British mission was recommending the drawing of a demarcation line from Petrovsk over the *northern* border of Dagestan to separate the area of Volunteer activities from the "zone of English influence," and that General Thomson regarded General Liakhov's appointment as "intervention" in British affairs.[27] Finally, Russian suspicion of British policy in Transcaucasia was probably reinforced in February and March 1919 by the knowledge that the French, initially Colonel Chardigny in Tiflis and then Foreign Minister Pichon, were complaining that the British were intervening, particularly in the case of the Mountain area, in a manner which tended to encourage separatist tendencies and promote the dismemberment of Russia in contradiction to agreed Allied policy.[28]

While this issue was thus building steam, the similar dispute on the Black Sea side also reached a new crisis. The "neither war nor peace" stalemate in which Volunteer and Georgian troops faced each other just below Tuapse had also taken a turn for the worse in December.

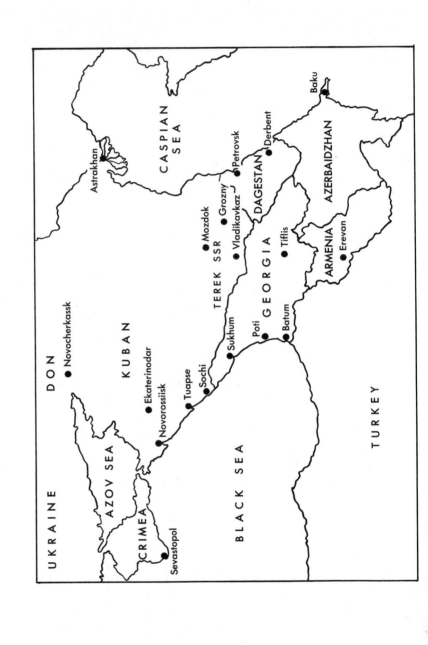

Probably because of the outbreak of hostilities between Georgia and Armenia to the south, Georgian troops had begun withdrawing from the Tuapse-Sochi area. When this happened, Denikin immediately ordered Volunteer troops to occupy the opened territories, the line thus being moved southward to the Loo River. The Georgian commander, General Koniev, indicated that he had been informed from Tiflis that "in agreement with the English, Sochi district is recognized as neutral territory. In accordance with this agreement no armed forces of any kind, neither those of an army nor those of a state, will be permitted into the territory of this district."[29]

Both of these situations thus pointed to potentially serious disputes between the Volunteers and both the Transcaucasian states and the British. Denikin had early in January 1919 sent a high-ranking personal representative to Transcaucasia to make contact directly with the British Command and clear up any misunderstanding. This representative, General I. G. Erdeli, had at first encountered unexpected difficulties in seeing the British generals. The Allied theatre commander, General Milne, then in Tiflis, refused to see Erdeli on grounds that he was not an accredited representative and that his (Milne's) instructions included the establishment of relations only with the Transcaucasian governments but not with Volunteer representatives.[30] As Milne explained three months later, after a bitter protest by Denikin over the snub of his special envoy, the letter of accreditation given to Erdeli by the British mission in Ekaterinodar had somehow been overlooked, and because of the numerous imposters afoot, Milne preferred to avoid any contact not fully cleared in advance. Moreover, he pointed out, relations between Denikin and the British were supposed to be handled through General Poole and not through representatives in Transcaucasia.[31]

However, Erdeli had been able to see both the British commander in Transcaucasia, General Walker, in Tiflis, and General Thomson in Baku. The tenor of the relations thus established was clearly indicated by what these two told Erdeli for relay to Denikin. Walker had made it clear that the British Command considered it necessary to maintain the status quo until the Peace Conference had decided outstanding questions and that this meant supporting the existing governments and borders. As for the future, he said, the Transcaucasian states might be reunited to Russia, or they might remain independent, or they might form a United States of Transcaucasia, but in any case this would not be determined until the Peace Conference acted, and meanwhile no agitation or forceful action designed to influence the future could be allowed.[32]

Thomson had been even more blunt in his statements. He indicated that he not only disapproved of the recruitment or movement of Volunteer troops in the entire area south of Petrovsk but proposed to remove those already there, including such detachments in both Baku (Bicherakov's) and Petrovsk (detachment under General Przheval'skii, who had moved there from Baku). As for military supplies in the area, said Thomson, the Volunteer authorities must either negotiate with the local governments or await a decision by the Peace Conference.[33]

In an effort to lessen the British concern thus expressed with regard to Volunteer intentions, General Erdeli had made a point of assuring both British generals that the Volunteer Army had no aggressive intentions.[34] This assurance was apparently the basis of subsequent British assurances to Georgia and to the Mountain Republic government that Volunteer troops would cease operations on these fronts and move no farther south. These assurances were apparently in turn interpreted by Georgia and Azerbaidzhan to mean that Denikin would be precluded from occupying either Dagestan or Sochi (or any territory farther to the south on the Black Sea). This, unfortunately, was not at all Denikin's intention or what he expected the British to assume.

On January 22 General Poole conveyed to Denikin a note from General Walker, authorized from Constantinople, stating that so long as Georgian behavior was "satisfactory," the British Command would support the Georgian government and, further, that in view of the difficulties which would be provoked, Volunteer troops must not be moved farther south (into Sochi district) without prior consultation with the British Command.[35] Denikin was thus confronted with an interdict from General Walker to prohibit what until this point had been in no wise opposed by the British representative in Ekaterinodar, General Poole. In fact, Poole had apparently taken Denikin's side in both this question and the Dagestan issue. Poole may have been unaware of such a contradiction before this time, since the note of January 22 was apparently the first telegram which had come through defining British policy to the contrary, but it appears that he still did not unequivocably support General Walker's position.[36]

On January 27, Denikin replied directly to Milne that the Sochi district was a part of Russia, had never been part of Georgia, and must be placed under Russian authority at once. The latter, he added, was especially necessary in view of the oppressive policies of the Georgians after their unjustified seizure of the area and the numerous appeals from the peoples of Sochi district for Volunteer support. Georgian annexation of this district, said Denikin, was an outrage to the dignity and interests of Russia, and it had been the result of policies engendered earlier by the Germans with a view to the dismemberment of Russia. As commander of the Volunteer Army and guardian of Russian interests, Denikin concluded, he could neither understand nor accept British support for such policies and therefore would ask that this "unjust attitude toward Russian interests" be reconsidered and modified.[37]

A few days later Denikin informed General Thomson that once the North Caucasus area was cleared of Bolshevik forces, each of its regions would be placed under local governments under the authority of General Liakhov, and he therefore requested that corresponding instructions be given to British authorities in this area, including Dagestan.[38] On the same day, February 6, in response to a revolt of the Armenian population in Sochi against Georgian rule, Denikin ordered the Volunteers to move into the district and occupy it. Forcing the Georgians out of the entire district, the Volunteers then came to a halt at a still more southerly point, on the Bzyb River, taking Georgian General Koniev prisoner in the process.[39]

Volunteer occupation of the Sochi district almost immediately provoked a rebellion of anti-Georgian elements in the neighboring Sukhum district (Abkhasia) to the south, and Denikin fired off still more telegrams to the British Command calling attention to the disorder and the necessity of pacifying the area. Rather noticeably ignoring previous British suggestions that Volunteer troops not continue moving south—Tuapse had been the original demarcation line proposed—Denikin now suggested that Sukhum district should be neutralized under British supervision to avoid further bloodshed, thus taking an earlier Georgian suggestion for Sochi and applying it farther south.[40]

This, of course, was immediately protested by the Georgian government, which called the occupation of Sochi "crude coercion and treachery" violating written assurance from the British Command that the Volunteer Army would refrain from hostile action against Georgia. In response to this protest, the Georgian government was quickly informed that the British government had "ordered General Denikin to withdraw his troops from Sochi" and that a British occupation of the area would be undertaken to establish a neutral zone.[41] Denikin, however, refused to comply with the request to withdraw, and in February 1919, perhaps because of his failure to support the British Transcaucasian Command's position, General Poole was replaced as British representative to the Volunteer Command by General Briggs.[42] Unlike Poole, Briggs was reputedly a close friend of General Milne, but, also unlike Poole, Briggs was not subordinated to Milne but rather directly to the War Office and Churchill.[43]

Meanwhile, on February 15, General Walker arranged an urgent conference with Georgian Prime Minister N. N. Zhordaniia, Georgian Foreign Minister E. P. Gegechkori, and the chief of the French military mission, Colonel Chardigny, to attempt to resolve the conflict before it turned into war.[44] In his opening remarks at this conference Walker honestly admitted the embarrassment resulting from the movement of Volunteer troops after his assurances to the contrary to the Georgian government in January. He had sent a mission to investigate, he added, and while he could not assign any blame until more information was available, he deeply regretted the state of affairs and would do all possible to see that no repetition of the recent events occurred.

Walker's effort to appease Georgian wrath was not successful, however. The Georgians, Zhordaniia in particular, adopted a very bitter attitude not only toward the Volunteer Army but toward the British as well. Threatening to drive the Volunteers back at least to Gagri, with or without British support, Zhordaniia insinuated that Walker had been naive to think that Denikin would be deterred by the proposal of a neutral zone under British guard or that the Volunteers would stop now in their drive to the south. "The General apparently does not know the Russians," Zhordaniia declared, for at the least opportunity Denikin would deceive the British again in his drive to destroy Georgia. Georgia, he added, had been the real victim because it had taken the word of the British.

Walker, noticeably irritated by this attack, informed the Prime Minister that he had not been at the scene of the Volunteer action to judge it, and he could not in any case force one side or the other to take orders from the British Command. His purpose was to mediate and help keep the peace, not to support either side, but, he added, if Georgia chose to refuse this mediation, as it could, then responsibility for the consequences would be on Georgia and not on someone else. Zhordaniia's retort was that before the British arrived Georgia was peacefully building a new life of independence, but ever since their arrival Georgia had found itself "fighting all the time," with the Volunteers, the Armenians, and the "Turko-Tatar hordes."

When his examples of alleged British mishandling of situations were protested by Walker as unheard of, Zhordaniia called the general "badly informed." Gegechkori, fortunately, took a rather less polemical approach and calmed the atmosphere with the frank admission that the Georgian government's protests over many incidents were influenced by the necessity of taking a stand which would "prove to the people that the work of the government of Georgia was directed toward the defense of the interests and dignity of both the whole population of the republic and of its individual citizens." Finally, after nearly three hours of this kind of debate the question of resolving the Sochi-Sukhum question was put squarely to the Georgians by Walker with this comment:

> Georgia stands at the cross-roads and its whole future depends on the policy of its leaders. . . . Georgia is going along the road of independence with such powerful support as that of Great Britain, and I do not think Georgia will reject it. I am not a diplomat, I am simply a soldier, but I request a frank answer to me on this question: will Georgia be a sincere ally of England?

Professing in reply to be the most devoted supporter and admirer of the Entente Powers, Zhordaniia attributed the difficulties with the British Command to "the unreliable information of its irresponsible agents." He called for the closest cooperation in their future economic relations and declared that Georgia sought only to preserve its own rightful borders and did not seek anything north of Gagri.[45]

Little more was achieved to moderate the Georgian-Volunteer feud at this point except the stationing of a small British detachment between them at the Bzyb River.[46] A Georgian representative, accredited to the Kuban government with Denikin's permission at the end of February, was assured that no movement beyond the Bzyb would take place, but nothing more was done about a resolution of the territorial questions.[47] During March the ailing Walker was obliged to turn over his post to General Thomson, but before leaving he had conveyed another warning to Denikin that action against Georgia would "not in any way facilitate your operations against the Bolsheviks, which is the purpose for which the British Government is supplying you with arms and military equipment."[48]

Meanwhile the demarcation issue was likewise being played out on the Caspian side. When General Briggs had arrived in Ekaterinodar, he had assured Denikin that a solution acceptable to the Volunteers could be worked out in Dagestan if restraint and patience were applied. As Poole before him, Briggs thus assumed the Volunteer side of this question, although perhaps more skillfully.[49] Denikin still intended to take over Dagestan, but he now had decided to replace Liakhov and agreed to postpone any further movement until the situation could be clarified.[50] To this end he also accepted Briggs' suggestion that all Volunteer messages and relations with British authorities be directed through him alone.[51] This, however, did not prevent further misunderstanding. When Denikin's confidential promise to Briggs to postpone action in Dagestan was conveyed to the British mission in Petrovsk, the latter used it to issue a public statement that, at British request, General Denikin had agreed not to move Volunteer troops into Dagestan and would replace Liakhov.[52] And, adding to Denikin's chagrin, a series of notes was received by him from London (through Briggs) in February and March lecturing him on his recent behavior.

Carrying out instructions from the War Office, Briggs warned Denikin that if he crossed the demarcation line to occupy new territory in the North Caucasus, the British government might be obliged to withhold further aid to the Volunteers.[53] Further, Briggs conveyed a telegram, identified as coming from the Allied Supreme Council, noting the concern of the Allied and Associated Powers over the use of force in many places to seize territory rather than resolving such questions by peaceful means. All those involved in such conflicts, said the telegram, were warned that the Peace Conference in its decisions would hold it against anyone who used force and therefore advised that all such questions be left to the Peace Conference "with full confidence in its impartiality."[54] In March the British War Office added to this series a more specific statement of what was expected of Denikin. Briggs was instructed to inform him that:

> In response to the full sympathy which has been extended to him in his efforts to free Russia from the Bolsheviks, and which is manifested not only in words but in the sending of arms, supplies and equipment in great quantity to Novorossiisk, it is expected from him that he will loyally adhere to the general policies of the Allies with regard to the small states. Great Britain does not intend to leave its troops in the Caucasus. They were sent there to enforce

the conditions of the armistice and to maintain peace. . . . General Denikin must understand that the presence of Allied troops in Transcaucasia now secures him against attack from the rear and puts the Caspian Sea in the hands of the Allies. These facts should influence him to concentrate all possible effort against the Bolsheviks in Russia. The question of the final organization of the Caucasus in any case cannot be decided until order has been restored in Russia, and it would behoove Denikin to avoid any action which would prejudice this question.

Therefore his troops should not move into Dagestan except for the purpose of active military operations against the Bolsheviks, and it is necessary to request him to reconsider seriously the question of the appointment of General Liakhov as governor of this region. His Majesty's Government looks upon this appointment with great displeasure. . . . It is important that General Denikin avoid any activities, military or otherwise, likely to increase the existing friction between his followers and the Georgians and other Caucasians. On the other hand every effort will be made to have these nations maintain a neutral position. . . .

. . . General Denikin now has the opportunity, if he is supplied with the necessary military material, to inflict jointly with Admiral Kolchak a decisive blow against Bolshevism, and it would be most regrettable if, by allowing his impatience to take a direction in any matter not acceptable to Great Britain, he compelled His Majesty's Government to deny him its support and to stop the shipment of supplies now enroute.[55]

Denikin quickly pointed out to Briggs that the so-called demarcation line had been differently defined by different sources. Briggs described it as running through Zakataly, putting most, if not all, of Dagestan on Denikin's side, although, as noted, he had asked for a delay in occupation. The British Transcaucasian Command, however, continued to define it as running north of Petrovsk, leaving most, if not all, of Dagestan outside Denikin's jurisdiction. Moreover, Denikin noted, the strategic importance of Dagestan, as the key to contacts with Allied elements across the Caspian and the center of defense against attack from Astrakhan, made it impossible for him to accept the British position, since it would not really guarantee the rear or assure order. Denikin's staff held long talks on this question with Briggs and then, in April, with Milne, and out of these talks the Volunteers got the impression that both, once they understood the situation, sympathized with the Volunteer point of view.[56]

Whether this were entirely true or not, Briggs then publicly withdrew the statement issued by the British mission in Petrovsk, and Denikin gave orders that Dagestan was to be occupied up to the line Kizil-Burun, Zakataly, Caucasus range. This in fact led to the full occupation of Dagestan during May, since a modus vivendi was quickly reached between General Khalilov and the Volunteer forces commander, General Dratsenko.[57] Without any resistance the Volunteers moved into Petrovsk and Derbent, the chief coastal cities, on May 21 and 23 respectively. On June 13, General Erdeli, now appointed to replace Liakhov, arrived in Dagestan and officially designated Khalilov as the Volunteer choice for governor.[58]

With Dagestan thus under Volunteer authority, Denikin ordered his representative in Baku, General Lazarev, to inform the Azerbaidzhani government at once that no hostilities against its territory would be undertaken. Lazarev was instructed to tell the new Azerbaidzhani prime minister, Ussubekov, that "we consider Azerbaidzhan a part of Russia but until the restoration of a supreme authority in Russia we shall respect the independent existence of Azerbaidzhan." Although Lazarev, on his own initiative, omitted the first half of this sentence in his statement to the Azerbaidzhani government and instead suggested the possibility of a federation negotiated among the border states as a means of future reunification, the Azerbaidzhani government rejected this offer of a truce and instead stepped up preparation for its defense.[59]

The Azerbaidzhani protests to the British Command may have been what inspired a wire to Denikin from Churchill on June 11 advising against the occupation of Derbent. In any case, five days later the British mission in Petrovsk renewed the proposal of a demarcation line and now suggested that it should begin at a point five miles south of Petrovsk and follow a route five miles south of the Petrovsk-Vladikavkaz railroad to the Georgian border and thence along that border to the Bzyb River, following the river to its mouth on the Black Sea.[60]

The suggestion that the Volunteers pull out of some of the territory just occupied was irritating enough to Denikin, but even more so was a later report that this line had actually been set after meetings between the Georgian government and the British Command without his having been informed. Moreover, when the information to this effect was received by Denikin, it came in the form of a note from the Azerbaidzhani government, dated June 22, which demanded fulfillment of the British instructions. Denikin's immediate response was to order Erdeli to ignore the proposal and to make it clear that he (Denikin) was the "highest authority" in this region and the only one who could issue orders to his troops.[61]

Actually a whole series of meetings between the British generals, Beech and Cory, and Georgian representatives, including Zhordaniia, had taken place during May while the Volunteers were occupying Dagestan.[62] But, contrary to Denikin's impression, the British generals involved in them had made a great effort to resolve the issue on Denikin's terms and in the process had to put up with a rather stubborn attitude on Zhordaniia's part. Earlier, during April, with the line established at the Bzyb and Denikin's forces voluntarily pulled back beyond Gagri to provide a neutral zone under British supervision, the Georgians had boldly gathered forces and attacked across that zone, moving up to the Makhadyr River. In an effort to avoid bloodshed, General Milne, when informed of what the Georgians were about to do, had wired Denikin on April 16, warning that "the Georgians propose to attack despite the fact that they were aware that this will be an act hostile to [Great Britain]." He urged Denikin to pull his men back until he could stop the Georgian attack.[63] The Georgians, who justified the attack by references to Bolshevik propaganda and uprisings in the Sochi district,[64] had then called for a shift of the neutral zone northward to accord with their advance.

Enraged by this attack—which this time had been specifically protested in advance by the British Command—Denikin had heavily reinforced his troops in the Sochi district and had declared an absolute blockade against Georgia, which closed the border and prohibited any trade or shipping between them. Briggs informed Denikin that General Milne regarded the Georgian action as a "direct violation of orders given by British authorities" and assured him that British forces were being sent to prevent any further movement of Georgian forces. Meanwhile, Briggs urged, Denikin should avoid any counterattack and give him time to arrange negotiations.[65]

Briggs was subsequently supported by General Beech, temporarily acting as British commander (after Thomson's departure and before his replacement, General Cory, had arrived) in efforts to arrange a special conference to resolve the demarcation line issue. At a meeting with Zhordaniia on May 24, Beech had obtained Georgian agreement to participate in such talks, although Zhordaniia, upon hearing that Briggs would be participating, had branded him as an out-and-out "partisan of General Denikin in questions concerning Georgia" and scoffed at assurances made by Briggs that the Volunteers would not attack Georgia if the Bzyb line were restored.[66] Despite Beech's warning that Georgia was in the wrong and inviting undesirable consequences, Zhordaniia had put himself flatly on record as refusing any agreement except one which would keep the Volunteers at the Mekhadyr and post British troops between them and the Georgians. If Denikin refused and attacked, he added, he would consider it a British attack, and he would activate an already prepared propaganda appeal to British and European public opinion against their government's policies, which were already unpopular.[67]

Briggs did then hold two meetings with representatives of the Georgian government, but no compromise or agreement was reached. He conveyed Denikin's insistence on the Bzyb line and his proposal for neutralization of Sukhum district, but the Georgians insisted on the Mekhadyr line and brushed aside the warnings of the British that Allied troops would eventually be withdrawn, while the Russians would remain. Gegechkori reminded the British general that the Peace Conference was supposed to decide broader questions and that the British government had assured Georgia of its support at the Peace Conference.[68] After these futile efforts to mediate the dispute, Briggs was in turn replaced by General Holman as head of the British mission in Ekaterinodar.[69]

This was the background to the statement issued by the British Command to the Georgian and Azerbaidzhani governments on June 11, stating that instructions from London had been received which declared:

> The demarcation line between General Denikin and the Caucasian states must be the following: from the mouth of the Bzyb river northward along this river to the border of Sukhum district, thence eastward along the border of Kutai and Tiflis provinces and Dagestan region to a point five miles south of the Petrovsk-Vladikavkaz railroad, and from there toward the south-east paralleling the railroad to a point on the coast of the Caspian Sea five miles south of Petrovsk.[70]

> General Denikin has received instructions that his troops should not cross to the south of the indicated line; those of the Transcaucasian states must not cross to the north of it. In accordance with the foregoing, Georgian troops must withdraw to the south of the Bzyb. The Transcaucasian states must refrain from any aggressive action against the Volunteer Army, cooperate with General Denikin in

the delivery of oil and other supplies to him, and prohibit access to these supplies by the Bolsheviks. Nonfulfillment of these conditions by them will entail the complete cessation of British support in the future and will make it impossible for His Majesty's Government to prevent General Denikin from crossing to the south of this line.[71]

This statement thus supported Denikin on the Black Sea side but excluded part of Dagestan from Volunteer occupation. However, in July the British position was significantly modified to take into account the Volunteer occupation of Dagestan. A joint note from the War and Foreign offices, dated July 17, was sent to the British mission in Ekaterinodar instructing that Denikin was to be advised that:

> his troops must not penetrate south of the following line: from (the) mouth of (the) Bzyb river northward along that river to the frontier of Sukhum province, thence eastwards along (the) northern frontiers of (the) provinces of Sukhum, Kutais, Tiflis, thence south-eastwards along the southern boundary of (the) province of Dagestan. . . .[72]

The British commander in Baku then informed the Azerbaidzhani government that the demarcation line had been modified to include Dagestan in Denikin's territory. Subsequently a statement was also issued to the anti-Volunteer elements in the North Caucasus branding their opposition as a Bolshevik-provoked movement rather than a real national movement, and equating hostilities against Denikin to hostility toward the Allied Powers.[73]

The summer of 1919 thus marked at least a relative improvement in Volunteer-British relations. Once the demarcation line issue was settled to the satisfaction of the Volunteer Army, tension was greatly reduced, although never fully eliminated; and the British, soon to evacuate most of their forces, ceased intervening to defend Transcaucasian interests against Russian interests. They were for the moment satisfied that little more could be done and satisfied that Denikin would respect the Georgian-Azerbaidzhani borders and concentrate his attack against the Bolsheviks to the north.

Relations between the Volunteers and Georgia and Azerbaidzhan, however, continued hostile, although partially stabilized by the completion of Volunteer operations in the North Caucasus. During June Azerbaidzhan and Georgia concluded a military alliance for defense against "any attack which threatens the independence or territorial integrity" of either.[74] They clearly had not only the Bolsheviks but also the Volunteer Army in mind and intended to continue support for anti-Volunteer elements in the North Caucasus. Georgia and Azerbaidzhan, going over the heads of the British Command in Tiflis through their delegations in Paris, issued to the Allied Powers on June 28, 1919, a protest which was joined by the representatives of Estonia, Latvia, Lithuania, and the Republic of the North Caucasus. It declared:

> The Allied and Associated Powers have proclaimed several times that they were pursuing in Russia a policy tending toward the right of nations to self-determination. . . .
> Now, the occupation of the (North Caucasus) Republic by the troops of General Denikin and the threatening attitude of these troops towards the Republics of Georgia and Azerbaidzhan seem on the contrary to be inspired by the avowed plan of the Russian reactionaries, who wish to bring back under their yoke the independent national states newly formed within the limits of the former Russian Empire; these reactionaries are trying to present to the Peace Conference a *fait accompli* by the military occupation of these states. . . .
> The undersigned delegates emphasize the fact that General Denikin is accomplishing this fatal work with the military and financial assistance of the Allied Powers. . . .
> They proclaim that in view of a sincere application of the right of self-determination it is necessary to maintain the territorial integrity of these states at present existing in the Caucasus, while waiting for the establishment of a definitive regime which will be instituted not by a Russian Constituent (Assembly) but by the Peace Congress, acting according to the will of the populations. . . .
> Consequently, the undersigned delegates bring their protests to the knowledge of the Allied and Associated Powers. They request them to put an end at once to the aggressive moves of General Denikin against the Republics of Georgia and Azerbaidzhan, and to make him evacuate the occupied territory of the Georgian Republic. . . .[75]

In all of this Armenia's position had been an especially awkward one. She refused to associate herself with the Azerbaidzhani-Georgian alliance or with the protests against the Volunteer Army to the Allies and found herself in frequent conflict with her two neighbors. Moreover, the British Command had not been entirely sympathetic with

Armenian claims, even less so with Armenian determination to take by force if necessary the territory in dispute.[76] The British effort to maintain the status quo had in effect favored the Georgians and Tatars, who were in a more advantageous position at the time when British troops were introduced to prevent further clashes.[77] This situation had in turn affected Armenian relations with the Volunteers. While the British took what the Armenians regarded as an unfair attitude toward them, Armenia developed a more and more friendly attitude toward the Volunteers. At the same time, however, she was afraid to establish close relations for fear of further damaging relations with the Allies.

In the spring of 1919, when British relations with Georgia and Azerbaidzhan grew cooler and evacuation was being contemplated, a more favorable view was adopted toward Armenia. During April the British supported Armenian occupation of previously denied territories and turned over to Armenia the entire province of Kars.[78] In May, on the first anniversary of the declaration of independence, the Armenian parliament, with British approval, declared the Transcaucasian and Turkish territories of Armenia united in a single Republic.[79] But this was as far as the British would go in any positive support, with the result that the Armenians then again began looking elsewhere for backing. Concern over the real aims of the Azerbaidzhani-Georgian alliance and the prospect of a British withdrawal thus led to the establishment of closer ties with the Volunteers.[80]

During July the Volunteer Army took the unusual step of supporting the issuance of Armenian bank notes in the name of the Russian state bank. The same month the approval of this source of funds for raising Armenian troops was supplemented by success in getting aid through to Armenia from the Volunteer Army. Denikin states that "several million cartridges" were shipped via Batum into Ardahan, despite Georgian efforts to prevent it.[81] Moreover, during August the Armenian chief of staff, Colonel Zinkevich, visited Volunteer headquarters in Ekaterinodar and returned home as "military representative of the AFSR" (Armed Forces of South Russia), thus acquiring a rather unique combination of titles. However, according to a subsequent report from Zinkevich, the Allied high commissioner prohibited further direct communication with Denikin and thus prevented any development of this tie for the moment.[82] It was not until November that the first official and formal exchange of representatives took place, the Volunteer Army sending a Colonel Lesli to Erevan and the Armenians sending a Colonel Vlas'ev to Ekaterinodar.[83] Even, then, however, the Armenians were divided as to the course to pursue and refrained from carrying the relationship any further. No alliance ever developed, and in fact Colonel Lesli's status was subsequently reduced to that of an informal "scout" as had been the case in the past.

Denikin never tried to press the Armenians on this matter, and he was willing to let matters rest as they were with respect to Georgia and Azerbaidzhan. On July 15, 1919, he issued secret instructions to his chief representative in Transcaucasia, General Baratov. They included the following statement of general policy toward Transcaucasia:

> Having in view the fact that all of Transcaucasia, in the borders existing before the beginning of the war in 1914, must be considered an inalienable part of the Russian State, you are instructed to prepare the ground for the painless reunification of these regions into one whole with Russia under the supreme government of an all-Russian state authority.
>
> As regards future state structure, which must not be predetermined before an expression of the will of all the peoples of the Russian state, it is necessary to keep in mind that the representatives of all regions and peoples of Russia will have a share in the decision of these questions, and that broad internal autonomy in local affairs of regional and national life will compose one of the bases of the future state life of Russia.
>
> Meanwhile, until the final decision of an all-Russian state authority, independent government will be permitted in those areas where it has been established and now exists.[84]

In addition to the job of seeking military material and officers in Transcaucasia, Volunteer representatives were given instructions that if Georgia should recognize its ties to Russia and withdraw its troops beyond the Bzyb River, then they should work "to establish completely friendly relations and a restoration of free trade," but if Georgia refused these conditions, then the trade restrictions would remain and only a military truce should be sought. The same in general was said of Azerbaidzhan: the existing government was accepted as independent until a future all-Russian authority could decide such questions, and no military action would be taken against it except in self-defense. Closer economic ties were recommended if political differences could be shelved. Although this provided the basis of the subsequent truce between the Volunteers and Transcaucasia, no real reconciliation was possible so long as a basic distrust and fear existed between them.[85] As Denikin put it: "After all else is said, the major, indeed the only, cause of the struggle in the Caucasus was the conflict between the idea of one Russia and the idea of fully independent Caucasian state formations."[86]

The relative settling down of affairs, in the summer of 1919, was not achieved, however, without first removing one of the obstacles previously mentioned, namely, the Russian presence in Baku. This concerned chiefly the question of Bicherakov's troops but also involved control over the Russian Caspian flotilla and Volunteer activities. Only the British could negotiate the removal of these Russian forces without violence, and even they were bound to encounter difficulties. To avoid trouble as much as possible, the British had approached these questions carefully and with considerable skill, using the tack of apparent support rather than opposition. Specifically this took the form of recognizing Denikin's authority over Russian military units in Baku and honoring Bicherakov with a citation to be presented by the king himself—in London.

As early as January 1919, British naval authorities under the Black Sea Fleet commander, Admiral Seymour, had notified Denikin of the recognition of his authority over Russian forces in Baku and had at the same time expressed grave concern about the conduct and reliability of these forces. Particularly, it had been noted, the crews of the Russian ships operated virtually independently of any outside authority and therefore constituted a menace, especially in view of their tendency to become "infected with Bolshevism."[87] Denikin had therefore been urged to order the removal of such crews, and this request had been passed on to General Erdeli, then acting as the chief Volunteer representative in Baku.

When Erdeli had conferred with General Thomson on this question, he found that the British Command was preparing not only to deal with the flotilla but also to arrange the removal of all Russian troops from the area. The first step, cutting off further financial support, was already under way, and Bicherakov was being plied with requests to give up his command and to go to London to receive recognition for his contribution to the British war effort.[88] Bicherakov had in fact turned over his affairs to his followers in February and had been escorted by a British honor guard to Batum to await passage to England. Bicherakov's forces were then, at Thomson's suggestion, placed under the command of General Przheval'skii. Contrary to the hopes of Erdeli, who confirmed the appointment in Denikin's name, Thomson refused to countenance any continuation of the formation of Russian troops and ordered Przheval'skii to direct his efforts entirely to preparations to move the troops to Petrovsk as soon as possible.[89]

The removal of the flotilla had not been quite so simply accomplished. Once Bicherakov had gone, the ships' crews, which made their own decisions through committees, had declined to honor Przheval'skii's authority. Erdeli had conducted negotiations with them but succeeded only in obtaining their agreement to cooperate in "tactical relations" with the Volunteer Army. They refused to adhere to Erdeli's proposal that they submit entirely. To complicate this matter, the crews found considerable support among the working class in Baku, which had strong revolutionary tendencies. In view of this, Erdeli and other Russian military authorities in Baku hesitated to make any attempt to use force against the crews, despite Thomson's insistence that "the Russian crews must be disbanded, peacefully if possible, but forcibly if necessary."[90]

Fortunately for the Volunteers their hesitation then provoked Thomson into seizing the ships himself, an act which eliminated the "infected" crews without bloodshed and at the same time put all the odium upon the British.[91] Even the spokesmen of the workers protested, in the name of Russian patriotism, demanding Russian rather than British control.[92] Thomson was at first in no mood to turn the ships over to the Volunteers, but with the intercession of General Briggs on Denikin's behalf in June the flotilla was remanned under Volunteer officers and sent to Petrovsk.[93]

The issue of the ships was not merely a matter of unreliable crews. It was also a question of who would command the Caspian Sea. The Bolsheviks were known to be preparing a naval force at Astrakhan by arming merchant ships and bringing several torpedo boats down the Volga from the Baltic. Who would command the naval force to keep this menace bottled up at the northern end of the Sea? The British clearly intended that it should be themselves, for they had been organizing such an operation since the Dunsterville mission.[94] This implied British command of Russian ships, since only a small number of British boats could be brought in from the Black Sea by land, and consequently it implied a certain rivalry with the Volunteer Command, which claimed authority on the Caspian and over the Caspian fleet. The British practice of retaining Russian captains as figureheads and of flying the Russian flag was a gesture of appeasement, but it did not resolve the issue, and after March these practices were abandoned.[95]

Following the dispute with Thomson in Baku over possession of the Russian ships there, the British flagship *Kruger* visited Petrovsk, and there Commodore Norris was asked for an interview by the Volunteer naval commander. The Volunteers requested British cooperation in the fitting out and manning of a larger Russian flotilla to be based at Petrovsk. Norris, however, rejected this idea on grounds that the British flotilla was quite adequate for the tasks at hand and there was no need for another naval force. According to the account given by a Russian officer then in British service, the Volunteer commander bluntly reminded the British commodore that he was in Russia and that Russian authorities had no need to ask British permission to sail the Caspian.[96] Later in the year the Volunteers were also to submit a stern warning to Azerbaidzhan that under the Treaty of Turkmanchai (1828) only Russia and Persia were permitted to operate commercial ships, and only Russia could have a military fleet on the Caspian.[97]

Despite this difference of opinion, the British did indeed dominate the Caspian as long as the intervention continued, both with regard to naval operations and with regard to civilian shipping, which was prohibited north of the latitude of Petrovsk.[98] Although the small British flotilla was described by one of its officers as "a squadron of 'tubs' armed by obsolete guns" facing superior Bolshevik equipment, the British managed until the autumn of 1919 to keep most of the Caspian free of Bolshevik incursions by patrolling the northern waters regularly.[99] The one major battle with the Bolsheviks occurred late in May when the Bolsheviks attempted to establish a new base at Fort Aleksandrovsk but were driven off by the massed British flotilla.[100]

* * * * * *

The Caspian operations were, of course, closely tied to operations in Transcaspia and Turkestan. Indeed, by virtue of their hold on the sea the British were even able to send some aid to the Ural Cossacks by way of Gurev.[101] Of utmost importance was the base at Krasnovodsk, which served not only as a naval base but also as the chief link between the British forces in Transcaucasia and the small missions across the sea to the east. For the anti-Bolshevik governments of Transcaspia "the moral effect of British support was the mainspring of the resistance to the Bolshevik advance."[102]

As previously noted, British intervention was never pushed farther into Turkestan. Colonel Bailey's virtually one-man operations had consisted largely of escaping capture and picking up information on the run. At the start of the British occupation of Transcaucasia, the Bolshevik government in Tashkent had begun efforts, on orders from Moscow, to locate and arrest all Allied personnel in the area.[103] Without British aid the anti-Bolshevik underground, with which Bailey was in contact, had been unable to effect any real resistance against the Bolsheviks, much less overthrow the government.[104] The trouble for the Bolsheviks came instead from a persistent feud with the Left Socialist Revolutionaries, who were a part of the ruling coalition, and from personal rifts within the Bolshevik group itself, During January 1919 a socialist rebellion against the government had been started by its own 23-year-old "commissar of war," Osipov. This had in turn set off "war" in the villages between the Bolsheviks and the Socialist Revolutionaries which could have provided an opening for counter-revolution, but the opportunity was not readily grasped.

The military weakness of the Bolshevik regime had been the result not only of Osipov's revolt but also of the British presence in Merv. Reliable Red forces had been sent to form a line against a possible British invasion from that quarter, thus depleting forces in Tashkent. The failure of the British to move in at this decisive moment thus contributed to the Bolsheviks' ability to suppress both the counter-revolutionary group and Osipov.[105] The hostility which existed between the Left and the Right anti-Bolshevik groups, however, was more immediately the cause of their failure. Osipov's movement was really a call for socialism without Bolshevik oppression, and the leaders of the counterrevolutionary movement apparently refused to have any dealings with it.[106]

Turkestan thus remained Bolshevik, and it was really only a matter of time until neighboring territories, such as Bukhara, would come under attack. Bailey, who eventually succeeded in getting himself hired as a "Bolshevik agent" by a defecting Bolshevik agent, went with his accomplice on a mission in October 1919 to investigate reports of British aid to Bukhara.[107] Enroute he had a rare interview with the famous Indian revolutionary, Mahendra Pratap, then hiding in Kagan under Bolshevik protection, but in Bukhara he found no British forces.[108] British aid consisted simply of a camel caravan which, with the escort of two Indian army guards, had carried some guns and ammunition across the desert in February after a meeting between a Bukharan representative and General Malleson, who had indeed advised the former not to take military action against the Bolshevik regime in Tashkent. Bailey then left Turkestan in December, accompanied by a few fleeing Russians, and made his way to Meshed.[109]

The small British force under Malleson, which had played so important a role in keeping an anti-Bolshevik government in power in Transcaspia, had long since ceased its advance. Having achieved a significant victory in pushing Bolshevik forces back beyond Merv late in October 1918, the British-Indian force had been ordered to halt its march at that point. The order came from Indian army headquarters, which had from the beginning demonstrated an "extraordinary lack of interest in the work of the Mission" and was now far more concerned about threatening developments in India and Afghanistan. When the Turkish armistice followed on October 30, Indian headquarters saw no purpose in continuing operations in Russia.[110] However, Malleson had not yet received indication of any intention to withdraw his troops and continued his efforts to strengthen the Ashkhabad government's position economically and militarily while holding the line at Merv.

The problem of building adequate military forces was complicated by political considerations. The Ashkhabad government, while having Turkman advisers and a Turkman field commander, never succeeded in establishing good relations with the predominantly Turkman population. Malleson urged the government to include more Turkman representatives in order to assure support, but instead it deliberately kept Oraz Sirdar's forces small because of its fears of the anti-Russian sentiment and the somewhat anarchic tendencies among Moslem troops. The chief alternatives considered by the government were appeals to Bicherakov and to Denikin to send detachments into Transcaspia. Bicherakov did in fact quickly respond to a request by the Transcaspian foreign minister, Zimin, and in December had sent over a detachment of Dagestani cavalry. The latter, however, by its untamed behavior, had tended more to alienate the population than to aid the government's defense efforts. Denikin also sent an advance party over from Petrovsk in February 1919, but it was not until later in the spring that more substantial relations could be established with the Volunteers.[111]

Meanwhile, Oraz Sirdar repeatedly urged the government and Malleson to seek an alliance with the Emir of Bukhara, but neither the government nor Malleson favored such a step, the former for the same reasons that it opposed any extensive enlargement of Moslem forces and the latter because he believed that it would only result in Bolshevik attacks on Bukhara.[112] Since the Russian working class in Ashkhabad strongly resisted recruitment into military service and prevented a general mobilization, and since, therefore, Ashkhabad's total force numbered only some 2,500 men, the one real hope for survival lay in further victories by the Volunteers, Kolchak, and Ataman Dutov at Orenburg. However, for the time being British forces were stationed in Ashkhabad to prevent an untimely overthrow of the government and at the same time to prod it into taking steps to solve its many problems.[113]

British presence was indeed probably all that prevented the government's collapse at the end of December 1918, when the railway workers had threatened to rise against it. With Captain Teague-Jones' participation, a new government, now called a Committee of Public Safety, was formed on January 3, 1919, at the peak of the crisis.[114] With the exception of Funtikov and his closest associates, who had already been removed, the new committee was composed largely of the same men, but an additional Turkman commander, Obez Baev, was named to the field command of the armed forces. New British promissory notes issued at this time temporarily staved off a new financial crisis.[115]

While these events were in progress, the Malleson mission was transferred from the Indian army command to the British War Office and put under General Milne's authority. In mid-January 1919 the Bolsheviks had again launched an attack but failed to move the British defenses. It was generally agreed that a strong push against the Bolsheviks at this point would have brought significant victories, and the Osipov revolt in Tashkent made success all the more likely, but this was the time of the Prinkipo proposal and the policy emanating from London was disengagement, especially in peripheral areas like Transcaspia.[116] A few days after a visit by Milne on January 21, Malleson received notice that his troops were to be withdrawn from Russian territory as soon as possible.[117] By this time the Red Army had broken through the barrier posed by Dutov's forces at Orenburg and was on its way to aid Tashkent. In view of the danger which this would eventually create for Ashkhabad, Malleson requested a delay in the evacuation of his troops and was granted time, until the end of March, to prepare more adequately for the withdrawal.[118]

Malleson did not inform the Ashkhabad committee of his orders

until February 4, after having worked out further plans with General
Kruten for obtaining aid from Denikin. He intended to turn over
most of his own arms and supplies to the Transcaspian army before
leaving, but he knew that it had not been arms alone but British
presence which had protected the Transcaspian government.[119] Both
Malleson and Denikin, along with General Kruten, hoped that the
Volunteers would be able to fill the gap left by the British withdrawal, and preparations had to some extent already been undertaken
after the visit to Volunteer headquarters by General Savitskii, who
had returned to Transcaspia with Denikin's authorization to act as
his representative in this matter. During March 1919 the Ashkhabad
committee went beyond these tentative arrangements and, through
General Erdeli, proposed that all Transcaspian military operations be
put under the Volunteer Command.[120]

Although several small Volunteer detachments had arrived in Transcaspia by the end of March and general responsibility for the defense
of this area was put under General Lazarev in April, Denikin refrained
from making any formal announcement of incorporation of the area
into Volunteer territory because of the possibility of undesirable reactions both in Transcaspia and in Azerbaidzhan.[121] Very close relations
were established, however, and further military support was provided
by the assignment of additional units of Bicherakov's old force to
Transcaspia. Moreover, financial assistance of some six million rubles
was extended by the Volunteer Command to the Transcaspian government.[122] However, these steps were not enough to stem the tide of
the Bolshevik advance.

After the overthrow of Emir Habibullah of Afghanistan in March
and his replacement by Amanullah and a militant faction which
favored an anti-British policy, the withdrawal of Malleson's forces
was stepped up. The British and Indian elements were separated, the
former being sent to Krasnovodsk and the latter being pulled back
into Persia, where they subsequently conducted "political warfare"
against a possible Soviet-Afghan alliance and saw action against a
Bolshevik supported revolt in northern Persia.[123] By April 1 all of
"Malmiss" had been evacuated from Russian territory, with the
exception of the few officers who remained in Krasnovodsk.

Oraz Sirdar kept up the fight to save Ashkhabad for some time,
but he could not match the massive Red offensive which began in
May. On July 15 Ashkhabad was itself finally evacuated, and the government moved to Krasnovodsk, which was still a British outpost.[124]

On August 5, with nothing left but the Krasnovodsk area, the Trans-caspian government dissolved itself and turned over all authority to the military command, now under General Lazarev. It was not until autumn that the picket around Krasnovodsk could be penetrated by the Bolsheviks, after additional Red troops had been sent down from the north, but in December the remaining Transcaspian troops, under General Kazanovich, began a gradual evacuation to Petrovsk by sea, thus ending the Transcaspian campaign.[125]

The North Caucasus territories, which had been incorporated into the Volunteer administrative system, had meanwhile become, in Denikin's words, a "boiling cauldron," which would in any case have prevented greater aid to Transcaspia by the Volunteers.[126] In June an insurrection of the Ingush had revived their old feud with the Cossacks. In July Ali Khadzhi had raised a short-lived rebellion in the mountains of Dagestan. Late in August new eruptions broke out in Chechen territory led by Sheikh Uzun-Khadzhi with a force of around 1500 men, which soon grew to 4000. This movement in fact spread rapidly until by mid-September 1919 it covered most of Dagestan as well.

As Denikin has pointed out, there were many reasons for this "senseless and ruinous" struggle—poverty, ignorance, age-old feuds, ineptness and injustice on the part of local officials, instigation by previously displaced governments, and outside aid from Transcaucasia and Turkey.[127] It unquestionably affected the Volunteer military effort by pinning down thousands of troops needed elsewhere, and it also affected prospects for better relations with Transcaucasia. From the summer of 1919, however, the Volunteer Army concentrated its efforts on an offensive to the north, and in this it was to have greater success. Indeed, the spring and summer of 1919 marked a turning point in both the civil war and the intervention in the South. While the Allies were beginning a withdrawal from their military entanglements in South Russia, the Volunteer Army was just emerging to make its bid for victory in the direction of Moscow.

* * * * * *

On April 16, 1919, Lloyd George told the House of Commons that military intervention in Russia was "the greatest act of stupidity that any Government could possibly commit." By that he meant chiefly intervention in the form of sending troops to conquer Russia, for at the same time he acknowledged that those parts of Russia where "there is no doubt that the populations are anti-Bolshevist" still had to be given the material support already promised "to arrest the flow of the lava."[128] Churchill in turn agreed that British troops were not the answer and should be withdrawn as soon as it became feasible to do so, but he was also determined to see that the British discharged their pledges "faithfully and fully by arming and equipping the anti-Bolshevik forces" from the "immense surplus of munitions" still available and by helping them "to train efficient armies of their own."[129] He therefore played a major role in preparing for the shift of British policy from occupation toward a concentration on aid to Denikin.

While not ignoring the difficulties in the question of relations between Denikin and the border states, the British adopted an attitude of considerable optimism, believing that, with Denikin's attention turned north and his success likely with massive aid, Allied influence could be brought to bear sufficiently to keep the peace between the Volunteers and the non-Russian nationalities.[130] On July 1, 1919, Curzon expressed this view in a note to Balfour on British policy in Russia. He noted the problems, especially in terms of public opinion, stemming from the reactionary reputation of the anti-Bolshevik Russian forces, but he was confident that their real views and those of the border states could be reconciled. What was needed now, besides military aid, was the effective use of Allied "good offices" to bring about the political rapprochement necessary to a common front against the Bolsheviks.[131]

Foreign Office memoranda circulated at this time also noted that this course would require the services of competent political representatives assigned to Denikin's headquarters and to Transcaucasia, since experience had shown the inadequacy of military representatives to handle such affairs.[132] As Balfour put it, British policy was to aid all cooperating in the anti-Bolshevik movement but at the same time to do this in such a way as to promote unity and avoid any encouragement to separatist tendencies.[133] And to this Curzon added that every effort should be made to restore normal economic relations and stability in South Russia and promote trade with the outside.[134] A major step in preparing this line of policy, the shift from military intervention to political guidance and economic relations, was the appointment in July of Mr. Oliver Wardrop as British commissioner to Transcaucasia, a civilian role and one superseding the military command. Wardrop's instructions drawn up by Curzon specifically noted that recognition had not been granted to the Transcaucasian states and impressed on him that he was to use his office "to do your utmost to prevent friction between the Volunteer Army and the Transcaucasian Republics. . . ."[135] Enforcement of the established demarcation line upon the Transcaucasian states was to be central to this duty.

The appointment of a political representative to Denikin was delayed until considerably later, but London was reassured on the "guiding principles by which General Denikin and his Military and Political Advisers are inspired" in a memorandum submitted by Denikin's acting Director of the Foreign Affairs Department, A. A. Neratov, and transmitted through the Russian representative in London, Nabokov, on August 8, 1919. The heart of the memorandum centered directly on the question of the border states, declaring that the Volunteers had no desire or intention of suppressing self-government even in territories occupied by them. "In fact," the statement declared:

> General Denikin and the Volunteer Army are already putting into practice the idea of a federation of peoples under the supreme authority of the Russian State. General Denikin has negotiated with and acted towards Georgia, Azerbaijan and other national groups in the Caucasus in the same spirit. They were repeatedly given definite assurances that the Volunteer Army had no intention whatsoever of infringing upon their rights. . . . In the opinion of the political leaders who surround General Denikin the same principle applies to all the nationalities inhabiting the borders of Russia, viz. that under the new Russian régime they will receive the fullest measure of self-government, but as integral parts of the Russian State. General Denikin believes that in so doing he is in full accord with the spirit of the League of Nations. . . .[136]

This statement was a clear exaggeration, but it, along with other developments, undoubtedly contributed to the optimistic outlook which accompanied the withdrawal of British troops. Ironically Neratov's memorandum and similar efforts by the Transcaucasian states to impress the British by their moderation at this time were intended to persuade the British to stay rather than to encourage them to withdraw. The first official notification in South Russia that a gradual withdrawal was being undertaken by the British had been made in May, but the implications were not fully appreciated until later in the summer, at which time the campaign to persuade them to stay gained momentum.[137] One reason for this delayed reaction was that the announcement, in addition to specifying a fairly gradual withdrawal of British forces, indicated at first that other Allied troops would be brought in to replace them. Many were probably drawn to the conclusion that, regardless of whose troops were sent, the British would still be running the show.[138]

Actually the British were active in efforts to persuade other powers to take over this responsibility, although undoubtedly they expected to retain a considerable, if not predominant, political and economic influence in Transcaucasia. It was in this context that the question of a mandate over Transcaucasia or parts of it was discussed in Allied councils, and it was also at this time that the United States was being drawn into participating in these questions. Indeed it was the Foreign Office's strong hope that British evacuation would be based upon some such substitution and would not be carried out without arrangements necessary to retain Western leadership in this area until the Russian problem was resolved. Simply to evacuate and leave a vacuum here would endanger all that had been accomplished and what was hoped for in the future. It was a matter of sharing the burden, not of dumping it. At least this was the plan which the Foreign Office put to Lloyd George, who was apparently in rather a hurry to bring the intervention to an end.[139]

Among Britain's allies there were really only two prospects for a military replacement in Transcaucasia: Italy and the United States. Neither had troops in the area, of course, but both had observers, and both had shown some interest in parts of Transcaucasia. In January 1919, for example, at the suggestion of Brigadier General Marlborough Churchill, and upon the proposal of Secretary of State Lansing to the President, it had been decided to send a special United States mission to South Russia "to study and report on political, economic and military conditions in such parts of southern Russia and the Caucasus as its members may be able to visit." Lieutenant Colonel E. F. Riggs, former military attaché in Petrograd, had been named chief of the mission.[140]

Upon reaching Constantinople on March 1, Riggs' mission had been divided into three sections assigned to Odessa, Ekaterinodar, and Tiflis, under the direction of Major James Steinberg, Captain William R. Berry, and Mr. Benjamin B. Moore, respectively. Each had established an active American post at these key points and had begun supplying the United States with regular dispatches of information on affairs in South Russia, supplementing the reports of American consular personnel also located at these cities.[141] Yet before the end of May the American Commission to Negotiate Peace, under whose authority these missions were acting, had expressed doubts as to continuing them.[142]

Although lack of funds was mentioned as a reason for recalling them, it is not at all unlikely that the members of the missions turned out to be rather more enthusiastic than was desirable: two of the Odessa party intervened as mediators in Polish-Ukrainian negotiations over Galicia; Captain Berry in Ekaterinodar was unusually emphatic in urging the immediate recognition of General Denikin as commander-in-chief of all anti-Bolshevik forces in South Russia; Moore and other members of his party in Tiflis were attacked and robbed in the streets and presented a demand for reparations to the Georgian government, with which their relations were none too good.[143] Moreover, differences of opinion concerning American involvement apparently developed between Colonel Riggs and the American operations commander in this theatre, Admiral Mark L. Bristol.[144]

In view of such factors, United States authorities in Paris decided definitely on July 12 to dispense with the military missions and ordered their recall.[145] Only the Moore mission in Tiflis was authorized to remain temporarily on duty pending the arrival of Major General J. G. Harbord, whose mission was to be confined to the Armenian question.[146] As this move suggested, American interest would henceforth be limited in its geographical scope, but it was not necessarily any less significant for this. Indeed, as one British historian puts it, the United States had thereby "nibbled at the bait" being dangled by the British.[147] On July 5 United States Colonel W. N. Haskell was appointed *Allied* high commissioner to Armenia, a post he was to hold for over a year. And in August Admiral Bristol was named American high commissioner in Constantinople, putting the United States on an equal footing with the Allies.[148]

For the British the position taken by the Italians and the desire to commit the United States to the Armenian question were closely related. When the British had publicly announced their decision to withdraw their troops in May, they had simultaneously declared that the Italian government had agreed to send troops to replace them. This solution might also have helped to appease Italy's irritation over her clash with Yugoslav aspirations, which threatened to deprive her of her anticipated compensations in Dalmatia. In any case the prospect of a mandate in Transcaucasia, or at least temporary occupation and all it offered, apparently held some attraction for Italy. The Italian delegation in Paris had hinted to the British as early as March of Italy's willingness to occupy Transcaucasia, and on April 2 Lloyd George had told Clemenceau that an agreement to this effect had been reached with Orlando.[149] This pleased the British since it would not only relieve them of a burden but at the same time help appease an ally.

On the other hand, Wilson's opposition to the secret wartime agreements, and especially his opposition to Italian claims against Yugoslavia, also helped to explain the delicacy of the American position in Transcaucasia. Since Wilson had been particularly known as a defender of the Armenians, this situation might, however, have been resolved by a division of responsibility in Transcaucasia between the two, with Italy replacing the British in Georgia and Azerbaidzhan and the United States doing so in Armenia. At least this appears to have been what the British had in mind. The difficulties in working out such an agreement, however, were very great. Even if the United States and Italy both agreed, the general hostility between Armenia and the other two republics, and especially the recent history of armed clashes among them, and the Turks, over the disputed territories in Kars and Ardahan provinces, would raise serious obstacles. And, not to be neglected, the Russians (of whatever political persuasion) would likely regard any arrangement which prolonged the separation of Transcaucasia from Russia as improper interference and dismemberment.

In May the advance party of an Italian mission had arrived in Transcaucasia with the purpose of surveying the situation and presumably to make the necessary preparations for the later arrival of Italian troops.[150] Both the Georgian and Azerbaidzhani governments took a dim view of this mission and privately urged the British not to leave, but to no avail, at least with regard to British evacuation in general.[151] British troops would remain only in Batum, Wardrop told the Georgian government, and there, after the establishment of a new city government, only the port would be retained for military purposes, while the city itself would probably be turned over to Georgia (a promise which as yet did not have official sanction).[152] The internal crisis faced by the Italian government in June 1919, however, had soon changed this situation. In the midst of negotiations in Paris, on June 19, the Orlando government was toppled and replaced by Nitti's cabinet.

This turn of events upset whatever plans had been made, for Nitti now reversed the Italian position on Transcaucasia and cancelled preparations for sending troops.[153] As late as August 7, the Italian ambassador in Paris, Count Sadino, stated that he still expected Italy to be given the mandate by the League of Nations and that Italy would promote the formation of a Transcaucasian confederation to be joined to a Russian federation in the future, but nothing ever came of further Italian involvement other than tentative promises of aid.[154] During August British troops left Azerbaidzhan for Persia, and those in Georgia were moved to Batum for evacuation. On August 18 Balfour wrote to Lloyd George urging that every effort be made to bring the United States into Armenia in view of the Italian reversal and the prospect of renewed clashes between the Transcaucasian republics in the absence of Allied controls.[155]

Colonel Haskell's appointment in July had gone far to achieve what Balfour sought, but Haskell's mission had been conceived not as a political but as a relief mission. It had been Herbert Hoover's suggestion which prompted the appointment, and it was under the general supervision of the Relief Administration that Haskell's mission operated. The American contribution in this regard was a significant and generous one, for it brought over $21 million in aid, but it did not solve the political dilemma.[156] The latter aspect of the problem was approached seriously only with the appointment of a special mission under General J. G. Harbord to investigate the circumstances which would affect "possible American interests and responsibilities in that region."[157]

General Harbord and his mission traveled Transcaucasia "from north to south and east to west" for thirty days in the late summer of 1919, interviewing representatives of every established government and individuals of every major nationality, enduring train wrecks, gun fire, miserable conditions, and inevitable involvement in the numerous squabbles besetting the area. When the survey was completed, Harbord had reached some conclusions on the "Armenian" question. The General could only find that this question was completely inseparable from the broader question of the fate of the entire region. Consequently he recommended that not only (1) was a mandate necessary but (2) it should also include all three Transcaucasian republics and contiguous territory in Anatolia, and that (3) "from the standpoint of peace, order, efficiency, and economy" the same power should assume the mandate for all of this area and should be given special status in Constantinople.

General Harbord believed that only the United States could do this job (requiring a steadfast devotion to the task "for at least a generation" and an initial assignment of 59,000 troops with an expenditure of $88 million a year for the first two or three years), so he recommended the acceptance of a mandate as he had described. But although the War Department estimated that only 27,000 men would be necessary for occupation, the burden was clearly more than the United States wished to assume.[158] The most that came of the American mandate idea was Wilson's agreement to act as mediator for the determination of Armenia's boundaries.[159] This, for all practical purposes, could be said to have ended the Allied military intervention in Transcaucasia. Later the United States State Department did appoint Admiral Newton H. McCully as "special agent in South Russia," but his assignment was not to Transcaucasia but to General Denikin and later to General Wrangel, who succeeded Denikin as commander of the Volunteers.[160]

The Transcaucasian republics did not let up in their efforts to retain Great Power protection, especially through the League of Nations, but no more troops were ever sent. On August 5, 1919, the British War Office announced its intention thenceforth to concentrate British military and financial support on the Volunteer Army.[161] A few days later, in a memorandum to Balfour, Curzon opined that this course was now clearly the best hope for bringing the civil war to a successful conclusion. Toward both Denikin and the border states, he noted, the Allies had followed an inconsistent and often unclear course, and consequently the results produced by the intervention had thus far been "incommensurate either with the objects for which they were undertaken or with the enormous expenditure involved." However, he was still optimistic about the possibility of correcting this situation and coordinating Allied policy more effectively in the future.[162]

In particular Curzon continued to oppose the recognition of the Transcaucasian or other border states so long as he believed that the Volunteer Army had a chance of success, despite repeated recommendation of such recognition by numerous persons, including Wardrop.[163] Even against the specific argument, made by Wardrop, that recognition would serve the cause of protecting British interests in Persia and India, Curzon insisted as late as October 1919 that it was "most important that at this moment when Denikin's progress against the Bolsheviks promises great success he should not be hampered by fear of attack in the rear." The defeat of Bolshevism, he continued in his reply to Wardrop, was the interest of Great Britain, and therefore it should do all in its power to aid Denikin and to prevent any unfriendly action against him.[164] This, wrote Curzon, had to take precedence over any consideration of the claims of the Transcaucasian states or particular interests there.[165]

In keeping with these views, Curzon then acted on his earlier stated

intention of attempting to reconcile the claims of these states with
the aims of the Volunteer Army. In November he appointed Sir Halford Mackinder as special British high commissioner to Denikin, with
the specific assignment of negotiating for unity between the various
anti-Bolshevik elements.[166] A private French envoy, Dr. J. Loris-
Melicof, was also authorized by Clemenceau at this time to seek
greater cooperation between the Volunteers and the Transcaucasian
states.[167] However, Mackinder did not arrive in South Russia until
January 1920, and Loris-Melicof soon found that his efforts were
resented as interference by both British and French official representatives in the area. The problem of relations with the Transcaucasian states, in any case, did not assume major importance again
for some time.

British withdrawal from both Transcaucasia and Transcaspia had,
of course, not been unrelated to the general crisis of affairs in the
East, especially in India where a nationalist rebellion had broken out.
The vastly important British position in India, moreover, had been
threatened by the sudden intervention by Emir Amanullah of Afghanistan. Taking advantage of the weakness of both Russia and Britain,
and hoping to silence internal opposition, the new Emir had proclaimed holy war on the British in May 1919 and ordered an invasion of India. This, the "Third Afghan War," was shortly ended by
a successful British counterattack and a peace settlement which left
Afghanistan independent, but it had greatly complicated the situation for Britain and limited its ability to give more attention to the
Russian question.[168]

It should also be noted that it was likewise in the summer of 1919
that General Mustafa Kemal had begun his nationalistic rally of Turkish troops, which was ultimately to overthrow the Ottoman regime,
which had capitulated to the Allies, and thus to undermine the plans
of the Allies in Turkey. At the same time, however, British policy
had been much more successful in Persia. The treaty concluded by
Britain with the Teheran government in August put that country in
a thoroughly dependent position.[169] However, while these events undoubtedly affected British policy, they had little direct bearing on
events in Russia. There the main concern and the most important
development in the summer and early autumn of 1919 was the
beginning of the Volunteer's major offensive toward Moscow.

PART III

THE RISE AND FALL OF THE VOLUNTEER ARMY

6: DENIKIN'S MILITARY AND POLITICAL STRATEGIES

The rise of the Volunteer Army to the position of being the major challenger to Bolshevik power and its subsequent fall in almost total defeat took place in the short span of the second half of 1919. To some extent it was in fact the very effort to do or die in 1919 which led to the disaster, but the failure was also in part a result of the fact that the Army tried to attain victory without a coordination of action with others and without adequate political and diplomatic foundation. The Army was, indeed, the victim of circumstances in many ways and was not to blame for all that happened, but at the same time Volunteer military and political strategy did not always provide the best basis for success.

Following the conquest of the North Caucasus, Denikin intended first, in the spring of 1919, to press toward Astrakhan and Tsaritsyn to seal off the lower Volga before launching a major offensive against the Russian heartland. However, he soon decided that this operation would be difficult because of the weakness of the Don forces facing a large Bolshevik concentration at Tsaritsyn and the necessity of maintaining adequate strength on the left flank protecting the vital Donets basin. Believing it impossible to move in both directions at this time, he found it necessary to choose between them. His decision to shift his strength to the western flank was thus motivated, on the one hand, by the crucial strategic value of the Donets and, on the other hand, by the strength of Bolshevik forces around Tsaritsyn.[1]

Volunteer successes early in the spring on the left flank were thus accompanied by a pull back on the right. Denikin hoped to stabilize and hold the right flank by uniting the troops in that area under one commander, and he asked General Baron P. N. Wrangel, who had achieved much success in the North Caucasus, to take this post.

185

Wrangel, however, at first refused to accept it unless priority were given to the right flank, a move which Denikin had already rejected. Denikin himself therefore took temporary command of the troops involved and managed to reverse the tide on the right during April, only to be confronted with a turn for the worse on the left, where General Mai-Maevskii's Volunteer Corps was operating. It was thus not until May that these initial difficulties were overcome by a re-grouping which created two large forces on the left and right under Mai-Maevskii and Wrangel respectively, the latter now having agreed to take the post, while continuing his demands for a change of strategy. This reorganization, plus the bringing of British tanks into play and anti-Bolshevik uprisings in the North Don and the Ukraine, made May a turning point for Denikin. He now sought to expand and secure his base by spreading his forces in a great arc from the Volga on the right to the Black Sea west of the Crimea on the left.

Operations in May began with a fairly balanced fan-like movement pushing outward on radii leading east, north, and west simultane-ously. Troops from the North Caucasus moved toward Astrakhan; Wrangel's force headed toward Tsaritsyn; the Don army directed its attack toward Voronezh; and Volunteer units on the left drove toward Kharkov, Kiev, and Odessa. By mid-June the span of Volun-teer victories reached from the Dnepr in the west to the outskirts of Tsaritsyn in the east. Only the Astrakhan front saw no notable suc-cess, partly because of strong Bolshevik defenses there and partly because Volunteer operations were plagued by poor supply and native rebellions in Dagestan and the Mountain area. Denikin did not receive the Caspian flotilla from the British until July, but it subse-quently kept the Bolsheviks bottled up in Astrakhan, while land forces held a line 35 miles from the port.

On July 1 Wrangel succeeded in capturing Tsaritsyn, and a great celebration was held in the city to honor this achievement and hail the dawn of a new day of liberation. In this spirit of great optimism and rejoicing, Denikin on July 3 announced his plan for culminating his offensive in Moscow. His order issued on this day, subsequently dubbed the "Moscow Directive," was to be the guide for the trium-phant march on the Bolshevik capital so long awaited. The plan was a simple one. Operations thus far had been along diverging lines in order to secure the flanks and form a broad base for future move-ments. Now operations were to proceed along converging lines from points along the front to Moscow, thus inverting the fan so that it focused all operations on the heart of Soviet Russia. This pattern would, of course, draw the two flanks toward the center by its very nature, and Denikin proposed to concentrate his attention and the largest body of men and supplies possible along the shortest path to Moscow, that is, through Kharkov, Kursk, Orel, and Tula.

The Moscow Directive thus put the focus of effort and attention upon Mai-Maevskii's Volunteers, leaving the impatient Wrangel on the periphery in a supporting role. Denikin put the main burden of responsibility upon Mai-Maevskii, a rather uninspiring commander, simply because he commanded the hard core of the original Volunteer Army, a force which Denikin believed to be the most reliable and the most deserving, in addition to its being already in the central position. Wrangel's troops were composed largely of Cossacks, with whom he worked extremely well, but who were not expected to be reliable outside their own territory. Kuban Cossacks were already noticeably poor in their contribution, and the valiant Don Cossacks were expected to be much less enthusiastic when moved northward beyond Don borders. As good as Denikin's reasons appeared, however, they could be tested only as the plan was executed.

During July and August the Red Army was put on the run all along the front except on the right flank. So precipitous was their retreat that full victory seemed almost inevitable for the Volunteers. The superiority in number of men possessed by the Bolshevik forces diminished rapidly as the Volunteers advanced northward. Each of the corps operating at the front recruited new men in large numbers as it moved, and a sizeable number came over from the Bolshevik forces, which were beset with frequent desertions. At the beginning of the May operations Denikin had only 64,000 men in the line, but by midsummer he was commanding some 150,000 men, not including rear personnel.[2] At the same time, however, the length of the front was now hundreds of miles long, so there were no forces to spare. In these circumstances, Denikin's basic tactic was to keep the Bolsheviks on the run so as to prevent them from regrouping or building up their strength and also to obtain the arms and supplies which the retreating Red Army left behind. The psychological significance of this approach in a civil war was also very important, Denikin observed:

> Strategy [traditionally] does not permit dispersal of strength and demands a front size proportional to it. But we spread over hundreds of versts, sometimes intentionally sometimes of necessity. . . .

In enthusiasm called forth by victories, in maneuver, and in the inertia of progressive movement lay our strength. . . . When we widened the front to hundreds of versts, we therefore became not weaker but stronger as a result. . . . Only under such conditions did we have the possibility of continuing the struggle. Otherwise we would have been smothered by the vast superiority of strength of our opponent, who possessed inexhaustible resources of manpower. . . . Theory speaks of securing borders but the practice of civil war, with its vast distances and front, and with its exceptional predominance of psychology, not only in the army but also in the population of areas affected by the war, testifies to the insurmountable difficulty and frequently the complete worthlessness of the methods of positional warfare.[3]

Although this thesis was subject to question, Denikin achieved remarkable success so long as his forward wave remained in motion. Through the summer the Red Army continued to make its major effort in the Volga-North Don area on Denikin's right. A two-pronged offensive by the 10th Army along with Budenny's cavalry (with a total of some 90,000 men) struck a hard blow against Wrangel's position north of Tsaritsyn and the right section of the Don line. This succeeded in pushing Wrangel back to Tsaritsyn itself and forced the Don army to pull back south of the Don River, but there the advance was stopped. On this flank Denikin's forces then held their ground with minor fluctuations in September and October. During August there was also a temporary break in the line between the Volunteer corps and the Don army around Voronezh, but Denikin ordered the Don army to assume a defensive position on the right and concentrate its efforts subsequently upon support of the center thrust by the Volunteers. This pulled the Don forces to the left, leading them outside Don territory, but it served the purpose of plugging the hole and allowing the Volunteers to continue pressing forward in the center. During September and October Denikin's strategy staked everything that could be mustered on this central thrust, and it paid off in the advance of the Volunteers to within striking distance of Moscow itself, with the spearhead around Tula.

As Denikin knew, the divided counsels of the Red Army had been one of his chief assets in this offensive. A dispute between Trotskii and Stalin over strategy in the South had plagued Bolshevik operations since the fall of 1918. With Stalin and Voroshilov, commanding the 10th Army on the Tsaritsyn-North Don front, insisting on priority for their flank and apparently failing to execute orders contrary to that point of view, Trotskii had been frustrated in his efforts to coordinate operations in the South and shift forces to meet Denikin's main attack. As he had put it in a telegram to Lenin, "Operations in strength are impossible without coordination of operations with Tsaritsyn. There is no time for diplomatic negotiations. Tsaritsyn must either obey orders or get out of the way. We have a colossal superiority in forces but total anarchy at the top." To avert "ruin for the entire cause," Trotskii had demanded the removal of Stalin and Voroshilov and the reorganization of the southern front, but he had failed to dislodge them and the conflict had resulted in a serious delay in mounting an effective counteroffensive.[4]

The concentration of Bolshevik efforts on the Don side of the line had brought them up against Cossacks fighting for their own homeland, put their chief operations east of the strategic Donets area, and kept them occupied in a sector where Denikin was content to hold the defensive. The Volunteers were thus able to advance into the Ukraine and on toward Moscow with far less resistance than might have been provided. This situation did not last long enough, however, for Trotskii did eventually succeed in stepping up the transfer of men from the Siberian front and shifted his main effort away from Tsaritsyn toward the center. Trotskii had his way, but only after the failure of Kolchak's offensive in Siberia and the retreat of the anti-Bolshevik forces on that front during the summer, a retreat which removed the threat of a link-up between Denikin and Kolchak at the Volga, a threat which had been the justification of Stalin's position. The Bolshevik victory on the Siberian front, a clear victory by early autumn, thus both justified and made more feasible a concentration against Denikin's forward advance.

Red Army forces, notably Budenny's cavalry, were thus moved westward to Voronezh during November; and Denikin, instead of consolidating his line there to stop this threat, continued to concentrate on keeping the center moving forward. Because of the increasingly difficult supply situation, the lack of reserves, and the general instability in the rear of Mai-Maevskii's army, Denikin even felt compelled to pull troops away from the left flank of the Don army where it joined the Volunteer corps, thus weakening the line at precisely the point where Budenny was preparing to strike. The decisive Bolshevik break-through, assisted by the resulting gap between Volunteer and Don forces, thus occurred in the form of a penetration moving in a

southwesterly direction from Voronezh toward Kharkov. This successful movement in effect cut Denikin's forces in two and put his most
advanced units in the extremely dangerous position of being cut off in
the rear. During November and December the Volunteer bubble collapsed and a general withdrawal was made unavoidable. This retreat,
which Denikin hoped to make merely a regrouping operation after
which the offensive could be renewed, in fact turned into a rout. The
gamble of the Moscow Directive had come close to success, but in
failing to achieve its goal it had also deprived Denikin of a second
chance.

One of the most obvious causes of the failure of the anti-Bolshevik forces to win their war against the Soviet regime was the failure
of Denikin and Kolchak to coordinate their operations. Denikin has
written that there was "perfect solidarity" between himself and
Kolchak, but this was true only in principle. On the understanding
that an amalgamation of their respective territories was to take place
after the two fronts had been brought together, for example, they had
"temporarily divided the territories within the spheres of influence of
Omsk and Ekaterinodar, the territory west of the Volga and also the
Transcaspian region falling to [Denikin]." They were also in general
agreement on political questions. When the Allied Powers offered to
recognize Kolchak's government in May 1919, at the peak of the
Admiral's military success, both Kolchak and Denikin agreed to the
conditions stipulated, including the calling of a constituent assembly,
holding free elections, protecting civil and religious liberties, recognition of Poland and Finland, and League of Nations mediation of
relations with the Baltic and Transcaucasian nationalities.[5]

In the matter of military strategy there was indeed also a general
agreement from the beginning of 1919 that their forces should con-
verge at the Volga and then march jointly to Moscow. It was with
this in mind that Denikin initially planned his campaign so as to seal
off the lower Volga at Astrakhan and then execute a drive through
Tsaritsyn which would meet Kolchak's forces coming from the East.
Such a plan had the support of the Allies, and the agreement on
zones between Kolchak and Denikin had been intended to implement their cooperation and serve the common goal of restoring Russian unity through the establishment of a moderate and constitutional
government in Moscow. Moreover in June, at Allied suggestion and
despite personal disappointment and considerable opposition in his
own camp, Denikin formally confirmed his recognition of Kolchak as

supreme commander so as to avoid even the appearance of rivalry between them and to facilitate coordination of their operations.[6] Yet when it came to the actual fact of military operations, there was not only no coordination but even almost a complete lack of communication between them. At the farthest point of Kolchak's advance in May Denikin was not concentrating his forces in the direction of Tsaritsyn at all but rather had them moving in all directions at once. His main drive was, indeed, not toward the Volga but northwest into the Ukraine. In July, when the troops under General P. N. Wrangel, one of the sharpest critics of Denikin's strategy, finally took Tsaritsyn on the Volga, Kolchak was already in retreat and the distance was too great to bridge.[7] Kolchak's subsequent withdrawal, of course, also enabled the Red Army to shift its main weight from Siberia to Denikin's front and thus to destroy in turn his separate march toward Moscow through Rostov, Kharkov, Orel, and Tula.

Denikin's offensive came much closer to Moscow than Kolchak's, but this was in part because of the slowness of the Bolsheviks in shifting their own troops to meet the main drive of Volunteer forces. When in July Denikin issued his controversial Moscow Directive, he caught the Bolsheviks off guard because they assumed that he would concentrate on joining Kolchak through Tsaritsyn, but in the long run even two skillfully executed offensives (in fact there were three, since General N. N. Iudenich led a campaign against Petrograd from the Baltic in September) could not achieve separately the success which their coordination might have assured. It was with this in mind that General Wrangel charged that Denikin's Moscow Directive and the whole strategy of a separate drive on the Bolshevik capital amounted to "nothing more or less than a death sentence for the Armies of South Russia."[8] Denikin's failure to follow up on the plan to move through Tsaritsyn to link up with Kolchak, moreover, he blamed upon a selfish rivalry between the two commanders and claimed that Denikin's strategy was deliberately designed to beat Kolchak to Moscow so as to keep power for himself.[9] Similar charges were, indeed, made by some of Kolchak's subordinates as well, accusing him of failing to make a real effort to make contact with the Volunteer forces in the South and blaming this upon a desire to avoid having to share power with Denikin once the victory had been won.[10] From the actual movements of their respective forces and the lack of coordination between them, it did in fact appear that such charges were well founded. It was certainly true that feelings of rivalry existed in both

Kolchak's and Denikin's staffs which could easily have influenced the two chiefs.

However, this explanation considerably oversimplified the problems involved. In the first place neither Kolchak nor Denikin ever indicated any desire to remain in power once the military victory had been achieved. Both were pledged to turn over authority to a provisional government and a constituent assembly. Moreover, it is unlikely that Denikin would have subordinated himself to Kolchak, even under Allied pressure, if a strong rivalry had really existed between them. The real explanation of their failure to coordinate their operations seemed to lie rather in the fact that while to some extent both mishandled their military offensives, neither had full control over the directions they took. When in May Denikin was just beginning his fan-like expansion into the Ukraine, Kolchak was already at the peak of his offensive, and it looked as though he would soon reach Moscow by way of a route far to the north long before their two forces could be united.

There was in fact a running dispute over whether Kolchak should concentrate on linking up with Denikin and therefore give his main attention to his left flank, the strategy apparently favored by the French representative and Allied commander, General Maurice Janin, or should give special consideration to a drive toward Arkhangelsk in order to join forces with the Allied units there and give the Czechs a chance, at last, to move out in that direction, which was what the British seemed to prefer and General Knox recommended.[11] The British, generally, argued that the northern route would be more likely to bring results and proposed to assure its success by coordinating a simultaneous movement of Siberian army forces under General Gajda and Allied forces in Arkhangelsk toward the city of Kotlas, taking advantage of the fact that Bolshevik forces were weak in this area.

On June 23 Churchill suggested that the Czechs should be routed either to the north or to the south rather than continuing their evacuation toward Vladivostok, and both he and Clemenceau seem to have been convinced that if the Czech evacuation was reversed, the Legion could then be counted upon to continue fighting.[12] However, despite orders to General Janin to this effect, the now demoralized and mutinous Czech forces refused to change their plans, rejected any further participation in the war, and continued their evacuation toward Vladivostok.[13] At the same time, the Czech General Gajda, now in Russian service as commander of the Siberian army, became involved in a violent clash with Kolchak over the advance of his forces to the northwest in accordance with the British plan. Gajda, it seems, operated without coordinating his actions with Kolchak's headquarters, and, according to Denikin, the unauthorized extension of the right flank by Gajda forced Kolchak to drop whatever plans he may have had for directing his forces toward Tsaritsyn.[14]

It was thus not Kolchak, but a combination of circumstances which really brought about the failure of his army to reach out to the southwest to meet Denikin. While Denikin himself had decided in May that advancing into the Ukraine was essential to his further success, it is also true that even if he had decided, *at that time*, to make his first goal a closing of the gap between his own forces and those of Kolchak, it would have been too late to achieve this result. Kolchak's forces began falling back very early in the summer and were in full retreat on the left flank by the time Denikin's troops reached Tsaritsyn. Denikin's Moscow Directive was then aimed at rushing in to take Moscow while Kolchak could still oblige the Bolsheviks to keep their major force on the Siberian front.

The lack of effective communication between Kolchak and Denikin played an important role in these miscalculations, but there was little either could do to speed the flow of messages, which were frequently a month or more in transit.[15] It is also true, however, that if Kolchak's offensive was started too soon, Denikin's was by the same token started too late. And the reason for the latter was undoubtedly Denikin's insistence on bringing the entire North Caucasus area under his control before moving northward.[16] Denikin had valid reasons for being concerned about the Mountain area in his rear, and he could point to the failure of the Allies to secure it to his satisfaction, but his devotion of so much time and energy to the Caucasus region not only cost him heavily in troops and delayed action but was also directly responsible for his most serious conflicts with Georgia, Azerbaidzhan, and the British Command in Transcaucasia.

Denikin's actions in this regard, moreover, presaged some of his most difficult problems in the Ukraine once his offensive did get under way. Even if no fault could be found with the military strategy of moving into the Ukraine, which did, after all, offer the shortest rail line to Moscow in a war where rails were often decisive, this decision immediately raised once more the question of relations with the Ukraine and indeed made it as important as relations with Kolchak. Here in particular Denikin could blame the Allies for having failed to prevent the influx of Bolshevik forces after the German withdrawal, but in resolving to reconquer the Ukraine he too was not prepared to deal with the extremely complex situation which existed there. His conviction that he could win the war under the banner of "One Russia" did not prove to be one of his greatest assets in separatist territory.

*   *   *   *   *   *

The Ukraine had provided a decidedly unsuccessful arena for Russians in general and conservative Russians in particular since the fall of the Hetman regime. With the exception of Georgia, no territory in the South had given greater support to the non-Bolshevik Left, and nowhere else was the anarchist movement so strong. Moreover, by the time the Volunteer offensive reached its peak, the Ukraine had become a complex battleground involving several different local forces and foreign powers.

None of the small forces in the Ukraine constituted a military power comparable to the Volunteers or the Red Army, but all of them posed a menace to both of the latter. Neither Denikin nor Trotskii ever had any of them securely on his side, although the inclinations of most of them, it must be noted, were to the Left rather than to the Right. When Denikin's troops first entered the Ukraine, the forces of disintegration in this area were actually de facto allies of the Volunteers insofar as they disrupted the Bolshevik rear and made it more difficult to stop the Volunteer offensive. By the same token, however, once the Volunteers had seized a large part of the Ukraine, such elements assumed the same troublesome significance for them. The subsequent defeat of the Volunteer Army can, indeed, be attributed in a significant measure to the problems raised by Volunteer relations with forces in the Ukraine which were not Bolshevik, such as the army of Nestor Makhno.

Makhno was an uneducated peasant—and one of the greatest revolutionary leaders produced by the Russian civil war. No one came even close to his achievement in rallying the peasants to a political and military cause. He reflected a deep stream of peasant aspirations in his own person, but he was also a remarkably brave and shrewd military leader who knew and practiced the most clever, and brutal, guerilla tactics. More often than not he served the Bolshevik cause, because it was a revolutionary cause, but he was fundamentally opposed to dictatorship, whether it be Bolshevik or anti-Bolshevik in character. This colorful vagabond, who did so much with so little, was an anarchist. He advocated the destruction of all government and all authority except direct communal democracy, but he also learned from personal experience the necessity of power to achieve his goals. He thus offered to his fellow peasants the combination which no one else could: freedom from both landlords and governments and an organized military force with which to realize these ends.[17]

The inconsistencies in Makhno's position thus did not prevent his organizing a real fighting force. His appearance as a revolutionary leader in South Russia, in the area north of the Sea of Azov, dates from his release from prison during the Provisional government's rule. He had been forced into inactivity and exile by the German occupation, but during the French occupation he had returned to his native territory and had begun to build up a peasant army to renew the struggle. The Bolsheviks planned to destroy him the instant his usefulness ended, but this did not prevent their collaboration against the Volunteer Army, which was regarded as a common enemy.[18]

Thus, when Denikin's Volunteers pushed the Red Army out of the Ukraine, there still remained in the rear the elusive Makhno and his roaming army. In fact, at the peak of Denikin's success Makhno was able to rally possibly up to 40,000 men, plus a sizeable cavalry, to wreak havoc behind the Volunteer lines. During October he reconquered a great swath of territory north of the Sea of Azov and forced Denikin to pull his best troops out of the forward line to face the anarchists in the rear, a decisive event at this crucial point.[19]

Denikin was urged by Wrangel to try to induce Makhno to come over to the Volunteers, but the Volunteer Commander refused to offer any concessions for this purpose. He specifically rejected the suggestion that Makhno's troops be allowed to maintain their own units and organizations if they agreed to cooperate, the arrangement by which the Bolsheviks had effected an alliance with the peasant leader.[20] Denikin was probably correct in believing that Makhno could not have been won over by anything the Volunteers could offer, but his failure to come to terms with the peasants was undoubtedly one of the chief causes of his defeat. Another was his failure to come to terms with Petliura and the Poles.

The situation was, indeed, quite different when Denikin's forces once more encountered the question of relations with Petliura, for in the summer and fall of 1919 it was not simply the Directorate which was involved in the old Ukrainian question but also the Poles and the independent Galician authority. It was in fact the Galician question more than any other which brought the Allies directly into this question again and which most complicated relations with both Petliura and the Poles, since the former had taken refuge in Galicia, and the latter were bent on incorporating the area into Poland.

The Ukrainian Directorate had never been its former self after the spring of 1919. After the French evacuation it had split up, and Petliura was the only real spokesman for its policies left in the Ukraine itself, although a strong delegation still existed in Paris, where A. Shul'gin and A. Margolin, among others, continued to represent the Ukrainian cause. The overriding problem for both Petliura and the Ukrainian representatives in Paris in mid-1919, however, was the reconquest of a large part of the Ukraine by the Red Army. It was this, of course, which had forced Petliura to retreat with what was left of his troops into the western borderlands of Galicia.[21]

The autonomous West Ukrainian (or East Galician) government, headed by E. Petrushevich, had cooperated with the Directorate earlier in the hope of uniting former Austrian territories to the Ukraine, but now its one concern was survival. The Galicians had strong leaders and an army of their own, and their policies were neither as revolutionary nor as anti-Russian as those of the Directorate, but they now hoped that an alliance with Petliura would strengthen their position. From the Galician point of view the most dangerous enemy was not Russia, although the Bolsheviks were of course a recognized menace, but Poland.[22]

Under the leadership of Jozef Pilsudski, Poland had embarked upon a rather imperialistic policy of uniting neighboring areas (parts of Lithuania, Belorussia, and the Ukraine) to the Polish state or at least bringing them under dominant Polish influence.[23] This policy, designed to make Poland a strong counterweight to Russian power, had led to a direct conflict between Poland and the Galician government, which was converted to a dictatorship by Petrushevich in an effort to mobilize against Polish incursions. By June, however, the Poles had invaded with such power as to force the Galician army, still joined by Petliura's troops, to retreat across the Zbruch River into East Ukraine. The combined Ukrainian-Galician forces used this situation, however, to make a successful drive to Kiev in July and August with the object of restoring Petliura to power there.

By now the Galician question had become a major international issue in Paris, involving the Allies directly in the problem of Polish-Ukrainian-Russian relations. As early as February the Peace Conference had taken up the Galician problem and had sent a mission to investigate. A proposed truce line, one of several in this period, had failed to end the Polish advance, however, and the issue had become a source of tension between the British and French points of view. In March 1919 in the course of discussion of the Galician issue, Marshal Foch had quickly taken up the defense of Poland's position, going even so far as to propose bringing Rumania into the military operations. However, Lloyd George had denounced this idea as a plot to form a new international army to invade Russia and squelched its acceptance by the Allied Council.[24] A special Inter-Allied Commission had been established to study the problem further and seek a solution. Its efforts to maintain a cease-fire until decisions could be made, however, had been in vain. Having received French aid which enabled them to put new troops into the field in April, the Poles were not inclined to listen to appeals to refrain from further action.

After new hearings on the Commission's work in May, the Polish prime minister, Paderewski, had been called upon in June to explain Poland's behavior.[25] He had done so quite bluntly, claiming that all of East Galicia rightfully belonged to Poland and would be taken.[26] In the Council of Foreign Ministers the British and French had then continued for a time in June to debate the validity of Poland's claim, while Polish troops overran Galician territory,[27] but the only result of this was that on June 25 the Allied Supreme Council had publicly acknowledged the fait accompli of the Polish conquest.[28] This acknowledgement was said to contain no prejudice to future decisions on the status of Galicia, but as the Supreme Council itself had once noted a fait accompli had a way of predetermining political decisions whether one liked it or not.

This question was, of course, also closely related to the larger question of the future of the Ukraine, and the Ukrainian delegation in Paris had used the opportunity to seek new support. During May the Ukrainian delegation had appealed to the French Foreign Ministry to help restore French-Ukrainian contacts by sending a mission to Petliura. In view of later misunderstandings as to the French position on this, it is worth noting here at some length the reply of the Foreign Ministry. According to Margolin the following statement was received by the Ukrainian delegation on May 19:

The French Government is happy to express full accord of its own views with the position of the Ukrainians with respect to the

Bolsheviks, who are above all enemies of mankind. The French Government cannot remain indifferent toward appeals submitted to it on this question. It is disposed therefore to send a military mission to Galicia at the present time, the scope of which will depend upon the settlement of several disputed questions in accord with the views of the Peace Conference.

In any case, in view of present political conditions, the support of France must be based on the following considerations:

At the present time the French Government is denied the possibility of any sort of intervention between the Ukrainians and the Poles with regard to the possession of Lemberg, since this question is subject to the consideration of the Peace Conference. It is necessary, however, for the Ukrainians and Poles to be united in their struggle against the common enemy, bolshevism, and that they forget their mutual individual claims and cease hostile activities against one another without further delay. In connection with this it must be made clear that French officers will in no case be sent to serve on the front of Galician operations, nor will they participate in the organization of the struggle on this front.

Finally, the aid of France must not be used by anyone for the organization of troops aimed at a struggle against the stable elements of Russia or those groups which the French Government recognizes as such, namely against the armies of Kolchak and Denikin, in case their attack against the Bolsheviks should lead into Ukrainian territory. This reservation applies particularly to the participation of any French officers, who will be given the most precise instructions on this matter upon their departure. They will be given orders to withdraw immediately from Rutheno-Ukrainian territory if they should be confronted with the risk of entering into conflict with the above named Russian military elements.[29]

A. Shul'gin subsequently assured the Foreign Ministry that these conditions were acceptable and thanked the French government for the "material aid" which was now anticipated. Actually, however, little seems to have come of this. Later, when Denikin got word through Russian representatives in Bucharest that the French hoped to mediate between himself and the Ukrainians, he asked the British to inquire in Paris about French intentions and to find out whether a military mission was actually to be accredited to Petliura.[30] The answer then returned was that the French had no intention other than to send in "counterintelligence" officers for the purpose of "gathering information."[31] Moreover, the rumor that the purpose of these officers was primarily to seek accord with the Volunteers led the Ukrainians in Paris to conclude that Pichon was still under the influence of the Russians.[32]

In any case, it is clear that both British and French representatives in Rumania undertook efforts during the summer of 1919 to promote a reconciliation between the Ukrainians and the Volunteers to head off a clash as the latter also moved into Ukrainian territory. In mid-July the Ukrainian representative in Bucharest, Colonel Strizhevskii, contacted the Volunteer representative, General Gerua, reportedly at the behest of the Allied missions, and proposed a compromise arrangement which would enable the Ukrainians and the Volunteers to cooperate in the military struggle against the Bolsheviks. According to General Gerua the proposal called for a suspension of all political questions, especially the question of Ukrainian independence, for the duration of the war so as to make possible an alliance within which each would retain autonomy for internal purposes, while Denikin would be recognized as commander-in-chief. Such an arrangement, as Gerua reported to Denikin, would not require either side to relinquish its political objectives but would recognize that neither could succeed without first defeating the Red Army. "After the victory over the Bolsheviks," Gerua wrote, "the struggle between the two 'allies' can be resumed."[33]

While this overture was being considered, however, Denikin received further reports from Bucharest which indicated, on the one hand, that Strizhevskii did not speak for Petliura and, on the other hand, that he himself was taking a highly anti-Russian position in his talks with Rumanian officials, warning the latter that if Denikin won the war against the Bolsheviks, the Volunteers would then try to take Bessarabia back by force.[34] At the same time, on August 23, Churchill sent a personal message to Denikin urging him "to meet Ukrainian separatist tendencies half way" for the sake of accord "at the present critical juncture,"[35] and Ukrainian representatives in London were advised to seek an alliance with the Volunteers to make possible a successful struggle against the Bolsheviks.[36]

This was, indeed, the time for decisions on this question, for at the end of August Ukrainian and Volunteer troops came face to face at Kiev, and the Volunteer commander in charge, General Bredov, declared that he intended to occupy the city and that, therefore, the Ukrainians and Galicians would have to withdraw. In this situation the outcome hinged, not so much on the position of the Allies, but on the relationship between Petliura and the Galician commander, General Tarnovskii.

Despite the contacts in Bucharest and in the Allied capitals, Petliura's attitude had remained unclear up to this point. However, it soon developed that he had already entered secret negotiations with the Poles behind the back of his Galician allies.[37] Tarnovskii, who probably suspected Petliura's intentions anyhow, was at the same time inclined to accept the Volunteers not only as the only hope against the Bolsheviks but also as potential allies against the Poles. This divergence came out into the open, and the two parted company when Tarnovskii informed the Volunteers that he was willing to cooperate whether Petliura went along or not. Thus on August 31 Bredov and Tarnovskii agreed on Volunteer occupation of Kiev and decided that Galician troops should be moved to the south to await the negotiation of a more detailed accord with Denikin.[38] The next day Petliura concluded a separate truce with the Poles and began a fateful relationship with Pilsudski which was to be of great importance in future months.

This, it should be noted, did not immediately rule out some agreement between the Volunteer and Ukrainian forces, for Petliura himself had still not specifically rejected the possibility, and besides he had little control over individual units of his "army" which were scattered throughout the western portion of the Ukraine. Thus on September 11 a detachment of Ukrainian troops operating north of Odessa made it known that it would favor a truce arrangement with the Volunteers based upon a demarcation line separating their zones of activity. Likewise, on September 13 the Volunteers were approached by a Ukrainian field commander, General Omelianovich-Pavlenko, who stated that, at the suggestion of Allied representatives who had contacted him, he was proposing the establishment of a demarcation line between their forces so as to make it possible for both to concentrate on the war against the Bolsheviks.[39] General Edgar Jadwin, an American military observer then in the Ukraine, gave his support to such proposals and urged Denikin to seek at least a truce with Petliura.[40]

There was thus apparently the possibility of an arrangement of some sort between the Ukrainians and the Volunteers, and Allied pressure was definitely being applied to this end. However, even in assuming that political differences could have been put aside for the time being, it would probably have been necessary for Denikin to agree to leave at least the western half of the Ukraine under Petliura—that is, under a separate Ukrainian government—since the demarcation line most frequently suggested was the Dnepr River. It was never entirely clear whether Petliura himself would have agreed to the terms proposed in his name, but in the end it mattered little, since Denikin refused to countenance the possibility of such an agreement.[41]

Denikin's reasons stemmed both from practical considerations and from his determination to stand by the policy of "One Russia." None of the mentioned proposals convinced him that the Ukrainians were in the least willing to renounce their separatist aims, and he believed that to compromise on this issue would both undermine the morale of the Volunteer Army and encourage other separatists to demand similar concessions. Moreover, he was certain that Petliura's forces were on the verge of disintegration and thus believed that the suggested demarcation-line arrangement would simply give them a protected area in which to regroup and prepare to attack from the rear.[42] In these circumstances the only agreement which Denikin would accept would be one requiring the Ukrainian forces either to lay down their arms and disperse or else to allow themselves to be incorporated into the Volunteer Army. Otherwise they would be considered as "opponents just as the Bolsheviks."[43] The latter proved to be the case.

Petliura's forces in the South were mostly beaten in subsequent battles, while he and a small contingent of those remaining took refuge in Poland. Allied naval units participated in the defense of Odessa by the Volunteers against a Ukrainian attack during September, but at the same time a new rash of rumors was started to the effect that the French were going to intervene on Petliura's behalf. To some extent such rumors were a product of the fact that Russian Ambassador Maklakov continued to seek French mediation in the Ukrainian question not only to prevent further clashes with the Volunteers but also to avoid having this question stand in the way of possible cooperation between Denikin and the Poles.[44]

A Polish delegation had arrived at Denikin's headquarters in September, and Maklakov sought to persuade the Allied governments of the necessity of full support for the negotiations to follow. One immediate result was that the British envoy, Mackinder, appointed as high commissioner to Denikin in November, was instructed to go first to Poland and try to persuade Pilsudski to take a conciliatory attitude toward the Volunteer Army.[45] It was at this point, in November, that Denikin announced the accord which had finally been worked out with the Galicians. There was no direct connection between this accord and either Petliura's actions or the arrival of the Polish delegation, but the timing inevitably lent itself to such an interpretation.

The Galician forces recognized Denikin as commander-in-chief and entered a military alliance with the Volunteers. It was agreed that they would be allowed to retain their own autonomous organization and would not be required to fight against the Ukrainians under Petliura. It was also agreed between Denikin and the Galician authorities that political decisions regarding Galicia's future status should be postponed to a more convenient time. Until then Petrushevich's government was recognized as the only legitimate government of East Galicia.[46] In other words, Denikin had accepted the Galician government as an ally on approximately the same terms as those governing his relations with the Cossacks and, for a time, with the Crimean government. In return for accepting his supreme military command, they were recognized as an autonomous government with authority over the internal affairs of their own territory.

This kind of accord might have provided a solution to the problem of Volunteer relations with other military and political forces in South Russia, as Denikin apparently thought it should, but only if the other party was prepared to accept a clearly unequal relationship. The weakness of the Galicians, their opposition to the Poles, their distrust of Petliura, and their inclination to look to the Russians for help (in a position not unlike that of the Armenians) were undoubtedly the ingredients which made such an agreement possible in their case. Moreover, they had succeeded in convincing Denikin that they were not really "separatists," something which Petliura did not do. However, this agreement with the Galicians had little if any military value, and although Denikin himself did not see any grounds for considering it as such, it was bound to be a bad omen for Volunteer-Polish relations, which were of much greater importance in the decisive days of November and December 1919.

* * * * * *

Contact between the Volunteers and Polish troops was not new, for, as previously noted, Polish units in South Russia, cut off from their homeland by the German occupation of the Ukraine, had established close relations with the Volunteers even at that early date. During the summer of 1918 representatives of these Polish troops had worked out with Denikin an arrangement whereby he assisted their reorganization into a Polish brigade and agreed to give them the status of an autonomous unit under his operational command in return for their support of Volunteer military operations. After participating in a few engagements, this brigade was sent by Denikin to Odessa, where it joined the Volunteer-French occupation and was subsequently enabled to return as a body to Poland. Relations between the Volunteers and these Poles had been excellent and their cause a common one.[47] Desiring to achieve a similar relationship with the Polish government, Denikin had in fact during this time already begun efforts to establish contacts with Warsaw.

Establishing communications on a regular basis actually never proved possible, but General Cheriachukin, who had been Krasnov's representative to the Ukraine earlier, had taken up an assignment as a Don-Volunteer representative in Warsaw during June 1919, and had begun sending regular reports to the Don and to Denikin concerning events and attitudes in Poland. However, when he finally decided to leave in October to return to South Russia, he noted in one of his last dispatches that he had received no instructions for seven months.[48] It also appears unlikely that all of his reports got through to the South, for Denikin indicates that no word was received for months from his own military representative, Colonel Dolinskii, who had also been sent to Warsaw.[49]

The work of these military representatives in Poland, while it thus provided no real contact between the Volunteers and the Poles, was nevertheless of some significance. For one thing they worked during most of their stay on the project of reorganizing and transferring to the South those Russian troops which had been stranded or had taken refuge on Polish soil. This required Polish cooperation, Allied intercession and financial assistance, and permission from Rumania to cross its territory. Securing such cooperation and support was no small feat under prevailing circumstances.

The actual transfer of such troops was not achieved until much later, but in the process of negotiating on this matter Cheriachukin reported some interesting facts. He detected a division in Polish opinion toward Russia from the start, for example, and noted that Pilsudski did not represent the pro-Russian faction. However, he was also convinced that Pilsudski would attack the Bolsheviks and could thus be of great assistance if some cooperative arrangements were made.[50] A few weeks later, still during the summer, Cheriachukin began warning in his dispatches that such arrangements were indeed being made, not for the Volunteers, but for Petliura. The deal, he predicted, would give part of the Ukraine to Poland.[51]

With French help Cheriachukin did obtain permission for some of the Russian troops to pass through Rumania to Galats by train, but the Poles continued to force delays. Even though, at French request, they had agreed to the transfer in principle, they continued to propose that these troops be sent north instead of south, and their attitude stiffened with time. Just before he left, Cheriachukin reported that information had been received in Warsaw that Denikin was dealing with the Galicians, but had refused to negotiate with Petliura, a position which the Poles interpreted as anti-Polish. The implication drawn was that Denikin clearly would refuse the borders demanded by Poland.[52]

Cheriachukin's reports had thus revealed the delicacy of relations with the Poles. There was a definite possibility of anti-Bolshevik military operations by the Poles, but there was no assurance at all that such operations would be pro-Volunteer. The Poles were quite hesitant about supporting any Russian elements and would not do so except on their own terms. These conclusions also appeared in a report from Russian representatives in Poland during November. Both military and nonmilitary envoys in Poland, said this report, found the Polish government quite anti-Russian and uncooperative. Moreover, it concluded, "an alliance with Poland is possible only if Russia gets out of Belorussia [and West Ukraine] as far as the Dnepr. . . ." Even then, the report added, such an alliance "will not be sincere" and "will not be long lasting" because Poland opposed the restoration of Russia and proposed instead to aid in the establishment of "all the little independent states" which had grown up in neighboring territories.[53]

At first the pessimism of such reports was not accepted by Denikin. He saw no reason why the two brother Slavic nations could not cooperate in their common cause, especially since, despite difficulties regarding other nationalities of the old Empire, he and Kolchak and the Russian Council in Paris all agreed fully with the Provisional government's recognition of Poland's right to independence in March 1917, and accepted the principle of placing the border according to ethnographic lines. Moreover, as he informed Sazonov in September, he intended to follow a very conciliatory policy in his own relations with Poland.[54] What then could stand in the way of cooperation, he asked, for it was clearly a fact that both were menaced by Bolshevik power and both had sizeable military forces whose lines were destined to be in close proximity in the fall of 1919 with the great prospect of crushing the Red Army between them?[55]

It was thus with a certain enthusiasm that Denikin greeted the Polish military and trade mission sent to Volunteer headquarters in September to open direct negotiations on their mutual relations. The character of the mission seemed in itself to suggest strong evidence of cooperation, since it was headed by a former Russian general, Karnicki, and included the former Polish minister of trade, Iwanicki. At a banquet welcoming the mission, Denikin declared:

> After long years of mutual misunderstanding and internecine conflict, after the grievous blows of the World War and general disorder, our two fraternal Slavic nations are emerging into the world arena in new mutual relations based upon an identity of state interests and upon a common defense against opposing forces. From my heart, I hope that our paths will never diverge. I raise my glass to the rebirth of Poland and to our future vital alliance.[56]

General Karnicki assured Denikin with great feeling that he viewed the success of his mission in achieving an alliance as a matter "of life and death," and he wanted nothing to stand in the way. His chief of staff, Major Przezdziecki, on the other hand, caused a stir even before the banquet was over by protesting the reference to Poland as an ally. Pressing his point on succeeding days, Przezdziecki bluntly asserted that Poland had a "vast army" capable of handling the Bolsheviks "entirely independently" and would help the Volunteers only if what it was to get in return was clearly spelled out in advance. Specifically, he said, Poland must have a border agreement before any talk of an alliance would be accepted. When Volunteer spokesmen objected that a specific border agreement could be entered only by a future Russian authority, the Major's answer was: ". . . then there is no point in our being here."[57]

This turn of events apparently disturbed both Denikin and Karnicki. Denikin's position was that he had no authority to commit the Russian state to a border agreement, but that this question was no reason for hostility, since Poland's independence in its ethnographic borders had been fully accepted by all. If the implication of Przezdziecki's remarks was that Poland demanded more than this, then, he felt, there was neither justification nor sincerity in its proposals. This view, moreover, was supported by the Allied missions, notably by the head of the French mission, who had information that the Polish government had instructed the delegation to demand borders creating a "Great Poland" and who took the initiative in warning Karnicki

against presenting excessive demands to the Volunteers.[58] The upshot
of this phase of the negotiations was that Karnicki apologized and
sent Major Przezdziecki home.

This effort by the head of the Polish delegation failed to change the
situation in any real sense, however, for succeeding events were to
show that not he, but Przezdziecki, more accurately expressed Pilsudski's views. The crux of the problem which confronted Volunteer-
Polish relations was the distrust on the part of the Poles of all Russians
who wished to restore Russia as a great state, and their consequent
determination to obtain security by establishing control over territories beyond the purely ethnographic line.[59] Their claims to such
territory were based upon borders existing before the first partition of
1772 and upon the cultural predominance of the Polish intellectual
and upper classes in these areas even though they were a minority.
Past Russian oppression, cultural and religious differences, the highly
charged atmosphere of the period, and many other reasons can be
given to explain the Polish position. It was understandable, but it
decidedly put great barriers before a genuine alliance with the Volunteers—and by the same token with the Bolsheviks, although the
latter were prepared to make significant territorial concessions in order
to gain time.

The logic of Pilsudski's position, based on opposition to any restored Russia, produced a policy of strength and unswerving independence for the new Poland standing between Russia and Germany.
It also naturally favored support for the borderland separatists, particularly the Ukrainians, rather than support for Denikin. Pilsudski's
view was thus indicated by his rejection of the provisional border
suggested in November by the studies initiated under the auspices of
the Peace Conference. This border, later designated as the Curzon
line, was based partly upon ethnographic factors and partly upon
consideration of the compensation of Poland by the addition of lands
taken from Germany in the west. In view of the difficulties of the
case, it was judged by the Allied Supreme Council to be the best basis
for a final demarcation which could be worked out later through
negotiations between Poland and Russia. However, in Pilsudski's
view it not only denied to Poland territories which he wished to
incorporate directly into the Polish state, but also implied the restoration of a Russian state which would include the Belorussian and
Ukrainian borderlands, whose independence he wished to maintain
under Polish influence and protection.[60]

Sazonov telegraphed Denikin from Paris that the provisional border proposed by the Allies corresponded to the declarations of the Provisional government in 1917, and he therefore, on behalf of the Russian Council, recommended its acceptance. Denikin was in fact quite satisfied with the Allies' proposal and made it the basis of his own proposals to the Poles, adding only that the final settlement would of necessity not be his but that agreed to jointly by Poland and the government established by a Russian constituent assembly after the war. In talks with Karnicki, Denikin expressed this view and added that if military cooperation could be achieved, he would agree to the subordination of Russian civil authorities in areas of Polish military action to the Polish Command for the duration of military operations. Such proposals were, finally, written down in a memorandum which the former British mission chief, General Briggs, carried personally to Pilsudski to seek his agreement.[61]

The position of the Volunteers around Kiev daily grew more critical as this exchange was taking place, but no reply came from Warsaw and no action came from the Polish troops strategically poised to the west and northwest. Denikin's urging that the Poles help by moving toward the upper Dnepr was ignored. Pilsudski told those who inquired about this inaction that he had offered to help Denikin but that Denikin had refused to recognize Poland's independence, making an agreement between them impossible.[62] Iwanicki explained the army's inaction by Poland's concern over complications with Germany in the Silesian question and the threat posed by German troops under Von der Goltz operating in East Prussia and the Baltic states. Karnicki opined that the Polish government probably felt it had no "right" to move troops any farther into Russian territory. Later he added that Poland was waiting for approval from Kolchak before entering any agreement with Denikin.[63]

The truth, however, was that Pilsudski neither expected nor wanted Denikin to win the war.[64] He was not impressed by the urgings of General Briggs, particularly since, as General Karnicki later revealed, the Polish delegation at Denikin's headquarters had reported pessimistically on the prospects for either military cooperation or political agreement.[65] Pilsudski had in fact become convinced that, on the one hand, Denikin's troops "were not worth much" and would soon fall back, and, on the other hand, no satisfactory agreement on a territorial settlement could be negotiated with Denikin because of the latter's policy of "Russia One and Indivisible" and the predominance of reactionary elements at Volunteer headquarters. Despite this negative view of the Volunteers, Pilsudski did make it clear to Allied representatives, particularly the British, that Poland would consider independent action against the Bolsheviks provided that such operations were requested and financed by the Allied Powers. However, this suggestion, put to the Allied Supreme Council in September at the same time that the Karnicki mission had been sent to sound out Denikin, was rejected; and Pilsudski subsequently took the position that Poland would have nothing to gain by intervening in the Russian civil war under existing circumstances.[66] This did not preclude Polish action in the future, under changed conditions, but it did rule out the kind of assistance sought by Denikin at the time it was requested.

In view of the assumed military weakness and political obstinacy of the Volunteers, and in view of the Allies' negative response to possible independent Polish action, the only feasible policy in Pilsudski's judgment was that of biding time in order to await further developments and meanwhile to strengthen Polish forces. To facilitate this policy, Pilsudski indeed proceeded to establish a neutral stance by means of a truce with the Bolsheviks. After talks between Polish and Soviet Red Cross missions at the front, a de facto truce was established unofficially on October 30. On November 2 this was supplemented by an agreement on hostages and a demarcation line, and finally on November 9 a formal agreement on an exchange of prisoners was signed between the two governments.[67] It is clear that Pilsudski decided to make this approach to the Bolsheviks even while the negotiations with Denikin were in progress. His decision to do so did not mean that he trusted the Bolsheviks any more than he trusted Denikin; it simply meant that he chose not to aid Denikin.[68]

It would be an exaggeration to suggest that Pilsudski's behavior was responsible for the defeat of the Volunteer Army which followed shortly or even to assert that Pilsudski "shamefully betrayed Denikin and the Entente" as Bolshevik leader Karl Radek has written.[69] Pilsudski was, after all, acting on the basis of Polish interest as he saw it. However, the fact remains that his failure to come to the rescue of the Volunteers in November and December when they were in retreat certainly facilitated the advance of the Red Army and contributed to the failure of Denikin's forces to prevent the retreat from turning into a rout. Soviet forces facing the Poles, although they were perhaps not as numerous as Denikin thought, were pulled out and sent against the Volunteers during those fateful last weeks of 1919. As Denikin wrote with some bitterness to Pilsudski in December: "The Bolsheviks are so sure of the passivity of the Polish front that . . . they are calmly advancing with their backs to it."[70] By the beginning of 1920 the Volunteers had been driven back to their Kuban base and the Crimea. Pilsudski had at least helped to fulfill his own prediction; it remained to be seen whether this would turn out to be in the interest of Poland.

At a meeting of the Allied prime ministers and foreign ministers on December 12, Clemenceau stated that in his opinion the policy of aiding the Russian anti-Bolshevik armies had failed. The only sensible thing to do now, he felt, was to adopt seriously the policy of erecting a "barbed wire entanglement around Russia in order to prevent her from creating trouble outside, and in order to stop Germany from entering into relations with Russia. . . ." In short, he said, the Allied Powers should give up the intervention in Russia as a lost cause and concentrate on aiding Poland and other countries on Russia's western border "in order to dam up the Russian flood and to provide a check to Germany." A statement released to the press by Allied spokesmen on December 13 echoed these sentiments when it indicated that while no specific commitments were anticipated, "a strong Poland was in the interests of the Entente Powers."[71]

The position thus taken by the Allies under French influence undoubtedly helped Petliura to reach the decision at this time to put himself entirely at the disposal of Pilsudski's Poland. In return for Polish military support to restore him to power in Kiev, Petliura agreed to accept the Zbruch River as the border with Poland, thus giving East Galicia to Pilsudski.[72] The significance of the fact that Pilsudski had not made peace, so long requested by the Bolsheviks, but only a truce, was thus to be revealed in the spring of 1920 when the Polish army put aside its secret agreement with the Bolsheviks and resumed its march into the Ukraine to carry out the promise to Petliura.

It was indeed Pilsudski's plan to do this which enabled the British envoy, Mackinder, to carry from Warsaw to Denikin in January 1920 the news that Pilsudski had finally agreed to enter the war against the Bolsheviks in the spring. The Polish leader, said Mackinder, had indicated that he would accept the borders proposed by the Peace Conference as a point of departure for negotiations and would not oppose the settlement of disputed claims to areas around the border through plebiscites.[73] The promise of Polish action which Mackinder thus brought might have been a great boost to hopes for a Volunteer recovery from the rout recently suffered, but it came now, as Denikin put it, with the ring of malicious irony.[74]

* * * * * *

Of all the potential alliances which might have been possible for the Volunteer Army, that with Poland was undoubtedly the most significant. The failure to obtain it was a major factor in Denikin's defeat. As Churchill put it: "The lines of Denikin embraced the whole of South Russia and were moving steadily northward. An arrangement between him and the Ukraine, combined with a steady pressure by Poland, might well have been decisive. But everything fell to pieces."[75] There were, however, three Balkan states—Rumania, Bulgaria, and Serbia—which also might have helped, especially with stronger encouragement from the Allies.

By virtue of the early contacts established in Jassy and the promise of turning over materials from the earlier Russian front there, Rumania had been very close to the Russian civil war from the beginning. She had sympathized with the Polish position, but she was also a great enemy of Bolshevism, having lost her gold reserve in the earlier breakoff of diplomatic relations with Moscow. Bulgaria, likewise an opponent of the Reds, was a Slavic state with less reason to dislike the anti-Bolshevik Russians and more cultural identification with them. Both Rumania and Bulgaria had accredited representatives to the Volunteer Command. Serbia, unlike the others, was not a neighboring state but had long regarded Russia as its patron, and its leaders had expressed a desire to help the Volunteers.

None of these prospects was ever translated into real aid, however, for various reasons. In the case of Rumania the reason was primarily the problem of Bessarabia. When during August 1919 an inquiry was put to Prime Minister Bratianu by the British military mission concerning cooperation with Allied efforts to aid Denikin, the Rumanian position on this issue was stated flatly: "We are prepared to extend every cooperation to General Denikin's army," Bratianu said, "but only under the condition that he sign an act of renunciation of Bessarabia."[76] When, shortly after this, Volunteer forces occupied Odessa and began moving into territory bordering on Bessarabia, the Rumanian government ordered the borders closed and sent troops into Tiraspol. Meanwhile the Rumanian press cited the activities of a so-called "Committee for Liberation of Bessarabia" formed in Odessa as evidence of Volunteer plans to seize this area.[77]

Denikin ordered his troops to exercise extreme caution so as to avoid any clash with the Rumanians, and he hastened to assure the Rumanian government that the Volunteers would not cross the Dnestr. The Bessarabian question, he said, must be settled by negotiations and not by war, but he, as a military leader, had no authority to decide such questions, which must be left to a constituent assembly.[78] At the same time he thanked the Rumanian army for "their desire to give us assistance" but asked that they too observe the Dnestr dividing line.[79] The Rumanian government agreed to this, but it still made the recognition of Rumania's claim to Bessarabia a sine qua non of further cooperation. This position, moreover, affected the previously guaranteed access to Russian war material left in Bessarabia and Rumania.

The military supplies left by General Shcherbachev under Rumanian protection and Allied supervision originally amounted to enough to equip some 43 divisions with arms and ammunition.[80] Its status as Russian property had been clearly set forth in a note from the Allied representatives to the Rumanian government in March 1918, and the Rumanian government had agreed.[81] Yet nothing proved more difficult than getting this material out of Rumania, even with Allied support, largely because Rumania imposed obstacles of various sorts to its release. Fears of Russian restoration, the loss of their gold reserve in Moscow, the arming of at least six divisions of their own out of the Russian stocks, and the shipment of Rumanian arms to Petliura[82]—all were reasons for the Rumanian attitude, but the consequence was still that the largest part of the enormous quantities of military equipment so close by never got to Denikin.

Despite the earlier Rumanian agreement to release certain quantities of the stocks, in April 1919 all shipment was stopped. New appeals were made and negotiations reopened in May, with promises again made to release the material, but again only token shipments followed. During August Maklakov succeeded in getting the French Foreign Ministry and the Allied ministers in Bucharest to make a strong appeal to the Rumanian government on the urgent need of equipment by Denikin,[83] and again the Rumanians seemed willing to cooperate and even to deliver large quantities during the fall. But once more delays appeared, and by January the change in Volunteer fortunes had provided new reasons for halting any transfers. As late as August 1920 the French legation could thus report to Paris that, even with all the token deliveries made to both Denikin and the Ukrainians, only a fraction of the material left by the Russians had been released.[84]

Neither Shcherbachev's appeals[85] nor Allied notes effected a real change in this situation until after the defeat of the Volunteers and their evacuation to the Crimea, and even then the change was minimal. Meanwhile, the Peace Conference subcommittee assigned to study the Bessarabian question reported in favor of Rumania's claims, thereby strengthening its resistance to Denikin's requests. The Allied Supreme Council suggested a plebiscite in Bessarabia to legitimize the Rumanian incorporation of it, but Bratianu rejected that, and finally, in March 1920, the Supreme Council approved the Rumanian acquisition.[86]

In discussion of these questions in the Peace Conference attention had also been turned to Bulgaria, which reportedly possessed some 181,300 rifles, 600 machine guns, 900 cannons, and over 200 million cartridges in excess of the limits allowed by treaty.[87] These too might have been made available to Denikin, not only because the Bulgarian government raised no objections but also because they were near at hand and could be shipped in by sea. The Bulgarian government in fact even offered to send a contingent of Bulgarian volunteers along with these arms to Denikin.[88] But this again was not to be, for Clemenceau envisaged that with Denikin's forces in retreat the chances were that any supplies sent to Russia would simply fall into the hands of the Bolsheviks. Besides, he said, any aid available should go to Poland, and he objected to the involvement of Bulgaria. In any case the Bulgarian offer to Denikin was viewed as a scheme to get around the treaty obligations limiting the Bulgarian armed forces. In a compromise motion the decision was made to leave the use of these supplies to the discretion of General Franchet d'Esperey.[89] His views have already been noted, and it is sufficient to state that he agreed with Clemenceau in this case. Denikin never got the material involved.

None of the objections raised in these cases was present in the case of the aid offered by Serbia, however, for there were no territorial disputes involved, and Serbia was in a very real sense one of the Allied countries. Moreover, the Serbian aid offer came when the Volunteers were on the rise rather than in retreat. When General Shcherbachev left South Russia to go to Paris as Denikin's special military representative, he had passed through Belgrade, where he was warmly greeted by Prince Alexander of Serbia. During February the Prince himself had gone to Paris, where he participated in discussions of the Russian question and made a special effort to enable Shcherbachev to obtain the aid he sought. Once the Prinkipo proposal had been removed from the scene, Prince Alexander even worked out a plan along with Shcherbachev to form an international expeditionary force to be sent to South Russia to aid the Volunteers.[90]

This plan, which was discussed with Poincaré and Wilson among others, proposed the formation of a corps of 30,000 Serbian volunteers and looked to a similar contribution by the Czechs. Aside from the geographical problem, however, there was an important condition. As Sazonov stated in his March 27 report to Kolchak on the Serbian proposal, Prince Alexander made the offer "on condition that the Allies send clothing, supplies, arms, and technical means without payment of money now but through the opening of credits for such maintenance for ten months."[91] Sazonov was apparently enthusiastic about the possibilities of thus obtaining up to 80,000 Serbian and Czech troops for Denikin, but Kolchak's council took a skeptical view in its reply. It was especially doubtful of Czech cooperation after its own experience, but it also noted the unlikelihood of being able to finance and supply such troops in any case.[92]

The judgment "impractical" was also made by the Allied governments on whom the implementation of the plan depended. As late as the following January, when Denikin was in talks with Mackinder, he was still urging British support for the Serbian and Bulgarian offers, but nothing ever came of them.[93] Since the Allied governments had rejected Foch's earlier proposal for a general East European mobilization against Bolshevism, they were not interested in having parts of the same plan adopted piecemeal. Nor was any way ever found to get Russian prisoners of war in Germany to the South, a project also diligently sought by Shcherbachev.[94] It foundered on the same problems as those raised in the Serbian case.

7:   RETREAT AND THE END OF
ALLIED AID

So went the prospects for new allies for South Russia. Those capable of offering aid refused it because Denikin would not accept the price. Those who demanded no such price were unable to send any aid. Denikin, for his part, remained devoted to "One Russia" and in so doing sacrificed some potential support from sources outside the Great Powers. At the same time he undoubtedly also adversely affected the chances of continued aid from the latter. The fault was not all Denikin's, however, for the Allies might have exerted a far more decisive influence in these matters. In the fall of 1919 Churchill provided one of his typically direct and concise, if somewhat exaggerated, summaries of the situation. Taking the broader context of the whole civil war, he noted the failures of both Allied policy and coordination of effort in Russia:

> Large sums of money and considerable forces have been employed by the Allies against the Bolsheviks during the year [1919]. . . . Admiral Koltchak's armies, equipped mainly with British munitions, reached in May a total of nearly 300,000 men. General Denikin's armies aggregate at the present time about a quarter of a million combatants. Besides these there were the Finns, who could place 100,000 men in the field. There were also the Estonians, the Letts and the Lithuanians. . . . Lastly there are the powerful Polish forces, and help could also have been obtained from Roumania and, to a lesser extent, from Serbia and Czechoslovakia.
>
> It is obvious from the above that the elements existed which, used in combination, would easily have been successful. They have, however, been dissipated by a total lack of combination, and this has been due to a complete absence of any definite or decided policy among the victorious Allies. Some were in favour of peace

and some were in favour of war. In the result they made neither peace nor war.

. . . Meanwhile the Bolsheviks succeeded in gradually developing their armies. These armies were far weaker than the forces potentially opposed to them; but, as they lay in the centre of the circle, and could, subject to the limits of their transportation, throw their weight from one part of its circumference to the other, they have been able to attack in detail and in many cases to overwhelm the forces opposed to them. Thus, while Denikin was getting on his feet Koltchak was broken and defeated. . . . During the last three months the very large numbers of men which the Bolsheviks were able to transfer from in front of Koltchak, from in front of the Poles, and from in front of the Baltic States, . . . have given them a large superiority of numbers over Denikin. His army . . . spread out in practically a single line on a front of more than 1,200 miles, has now been thrown back everywhere by these superior forces. . . . The inactivity of the Poles has enabled the Bolsheviks to concentrate against Denikin; the destruction of Denikin will enable them, if they choose, to concentrate against the Poles. . . .

Whereas by taking the proper concerted measures we could, without any large additional employment of men or money, have established an anti-Bolshevik and modernized Russia friendly to the Entente, we are now within measurable distance of a Bolshevik Russia thoroughly militarized, with nothing but its militarism to live on, bitterly hostile to the Entente, ready to work with Germany, and already largely organized by Germany. The idea that Poland will serve as a barrier to such dangers is illusory. The idea that by standing on the defensive on the east until every other anti-Bolshevik force has been destroyed, she will be able to maintain a strong attitude toward Germany in the west, is equally ill-founded. What is the wisdom of a policy which seeks to strengthen Poland by allied money and munitions and yet calmly acquiesces in the destruction of Denikin and the consequent liberation of the main Bolshevik armies to treble and quadruple the enemies with whom Poland has to contend? What is the justice or logic of recognizing every State, and even to a large extent guaranteeing the independence and security of every State which has torn itself away from the Russian Empire, while refusing to recognize and aid in preserving the great territories and populations in the south of Russia from which General Denikin's armies are drawn and which are unquestionably anti-Bolshevik?

It is a delusion to suppose that all this year we have been fight-

he battles of the anti-Bolshevik Russians. On the contrary,
...cy have been fighting ours. . . .[1]

When Churchill wrote these lines, however, he had already largely
lost the battle to direct British policy. Allied policy had taken a
decided turn away from further intervention. As the fall of 1919
marked the decisive turning point in Denikin's military offensive, so
it also brought equally important and corresponding developments in
Allied aid policies. Between February 1919, when aid had begun to
arrive in substantial quantities, chiefly from British stores, and the
winter of 1919, supplies had been given generously and freely. They
had come largely from materials left from the war with the Central
Powers and were thus mostly surplus to those giving them, but they
nevertheless represented an invaluable assist for the Volunteers. Britain alone in this period supplied Denikin with over 500 cannons,
250,000 rifles, 30 tanks, a million and a half shells, and 160 million
rounds of rifle ammunition, plus substantial and costly support in
naval power and aerial reconnaissance.[2] Similar supplies in smaller
quantities had been obtained in France, and the United States had
given generously of its stores of medical supplies.[3]

But the policy of making such grants merely as additions to the
Russian national debt had been questioned from the beginning. Moreover, Allied aid had always had vocal opponents in both Britain and
France, and even for its advocates it had its limitations both as to
time and as to quantity. Doubts concerning continuation of aid on
credit became decisions against it late in the fall, for that aid had
inevitably been linked to the performance of those aided and thus
involved a continuing judgment of the character and effectiveness of
Russian policies and actions. In short, it was tied to success. A lost
cause, no matter how attractive it had once been, could not continue
to draw support from those who had to live on after its failure and
who would only be handicapped by continued identification with it.

As already stated, the French had been the first to show signs of a
shift in Allied policy. Hints that the French minister of finance
opposed any further credit operations in supplying Russian forces had
been heard earlier, and in August the minister of war had circulated
a warning that further shipments of supplies would depend upon
some better arrangement for compensation.[4] Thus, when in September it became known that the Salonika army was being demobilized,
making a significant stock of military supplies available for the Vol-

unteers, it was made clear that economic difficulties made it impossible for the French government to send any more supplies on credit.[5] War surplus would henceforth have to be released only for cash or goods in exchange.[6] This, Maklakov wrote, was deemed essential not only for economic reasons but also because of the political opposition. Direct aid by the government was believed so unpopular in socialist worker circles that shipments were being kept secret from them.[7]

All was not necessarily lost for the anti-Bolsheviks, however, and Maklakov quickly called attention to the alternative which would make it possible to continue to receive goods and supplies from Europe. If the Allied governments were going to end the intervention as such and reopen trade relations through private organizations, the anti-Bolsheviks would have to do all they could to steer the exchange in their own direction.[8] Trade would have to replace aid. Private organizations would have to take over where strictly governmental operations left off.[9] During October and November this idea received active attention on all sides. Official notes from both the British and French governments indicated a definite interest in reaching agreement on the exchange of supplies for Russian raw materials and wheat, and Denikin authorized his Supply Department to enter negotiations on this question.[10]

This, however, was no simple matter or an easy step to take. As previously noted, Denikin had always been opposed to bargaining Russian resources for aid and especially to the granting of specific concessions to foreign powers. As far as he was concerned, the "Varangians" should have reason enough to help without being paid for it. Moreover, South Russia was not exactly bulging with an excess of wheat or anything else which could be traded for the needed supplies. It was in fact already exporting all that it could to finance government operations quite apart from military supply.[11] Nor was the notion of setting up trade companies as intermediaries likely to appeal to Denikin's strong convictions on the selfish and disorganized behavior of private operators in the past, to say nothing of the dubious political position of the cooperative societies so often mentioned in Allied circles. Finally, as Maklakov warned, trade relations would raise the delicate question of whether to deal equally with both the Allied Powers.[12]

It was therefore not with great enthusiasm that Denikin agreed to negotiations on trade with the Allies. That he did so at all was indicative of his plight rather than of his desire. In November Denikin's

Special Council wired Maklakov that the offer of supplies in exhange for Russian grain would be acceptable in principle, but certain problems would have to be met before specific agreements could be worked out. Particularly, Maklakov was informed, two points had to be kept in mind: first, the wheat itself could be obtained from the peasants only if goods were avialable which could be given to them in exchange and also as an inducement for growing and harvesting future crops; secondly, military supplies were essential at once and must not be delayed until the wheat was actually shipped.

These obstacles, the Special Council felt, could be removed only if the British and French governments could assure the continued delivery of goods and supplies by establishing sizeable credits immediately (100 million francs was suggested) and agreeing to accept in payment two separate deliveries of wheat, the first to be available not later than May 1920 and the second to follow in the second half of 1920. Payment, in other words, would have to be correlated with the harvest, but the supplies thus bought were needed at once.[13] When the wheat did become available, that part of it to be exported would be divided into equal shares for Britain and France if the terms proposed were acceptable to both.[14]

These terms were, however, not acceptable. Early in the talks Major Pindar, the British economic affairs representative at Volunteer headquarters, expressed some disappointment that Britain was being regarded on equal terms with France. Britain, he suggested, could handle the problem more effectively if it were the only party in an arrangement with South Russia, especially in view of the uncertainties of the harvest. Moreover, he pointed out, the British were prepared to pay for the grain with either currency or goods, thus making the exchange more flexible for the Volunteers. To ask for new credits or an additional loan under existing conditions, however, was to impose "grievous" conditions which might frustrate any agreement, he added.[15]

The French also disliked the proposed conditions. They wanted a guaranteed priority on a definite portion (later specified as 50 per cent) of all wheat (and other goods) exported, would not agree to establish a credit as the condition to any agreement, and insisted that some percentage (preferably 10 per cent) of the value of the exchange be set aside as amortization of the debt that would result from supplies sent after October. They also asked that tariff and license fees be either set aside or considered a part of the amortization fund. What

France proposed to do to meet these conditions was to set up, or enter contracts with, trading companies that would be authorized to ship up to 100 million francs' worth of supplies to South Russia, but these supplies would have to be exchanged in South Russia for agreed quantities of raw materials, the total amount of which the French government would retain the right to buy in turn from the trading companies.[16]

Several versions of a possible trade agreement with France were drawn up during the fall, and negotiations were conducted simultaneously in Paris and Ekaterinodar, in the former case between a special delegation organized by Sazonov and the French Inter-Ministerial Commission on Russian Financial Affairs, and in the latter case between Denikin's representatives, Neratov and Maslov, and the French mission, with a newly arrived fact-finding mission under General Mangin playing a major role. However, there was little progress to be reported. In December Maklakov forwarded to South Russia a final proposal in the form of a contract which contained the indicated provisions and gave France a priority claim on 50 per cent of all exports of wheat, coal, wool, leather, and cotton seed oil from South Russia.[17] Denikin, however, did not accept the agreement on these terms for many reasons, but particularly because of the French demand for such a large share of the exports, a demand which would not only preclude favorable arrangements with other countries but was also considered inconsistent with Russian sovereignty in view of the implied foreign control over trade.[18]

The French, for their part, continued to refuse any further commitment to ship military supplies until an agreement was signed. Earlier, in October, Clemenceau had agreed, in response to a special appeal, to make an exception and permit the sending of 30 million francs' worth of equipment, including 80 cannons, 240,000 shells, 75 machine guns, and other items such as swords and clothing, to South Russia without waiting for an exchange agreement, but now that too was cancelled.[19] The small delivery made in January 1920 brought only the swords and clothing, since, it was explained, Generals Franchet d'Esperey and Mangin had advised against sending the other supplies because of the changed military situation.[20] No further aid from the French was forthcoming until later when a somewhat different relationship was established with General Wrangel in the Crimea, as will be related below.

Meanwhile, in November British policy had been subjected to similar reconsiderations when the House of Commons took up debate on the Russian question. The weight of opinion was leaning heavily toward Lloyd George's position by this time and was further influenced to do so by the conciliatory overtures coming from the Bolsheviks, via Litvinov in Stockholm,[21] and by the outspoken opposition to aid to Denikin on the part of the former prime minister, Alexander Kerenskii. Kerenskii did a most efficient job of keeping the newspapers supplied with denunciations of Kolchak and Denikin as reactionaries, indicating that aid to them would be ruinous for Russia.[22]

Churchill had not ceased his eloquent appeals for continuation of aid to Denikin and in September had succeeded in getting Parliament to grant a credit of 15 million pounds for the Volunteers. This had extended British aid into the spring of 1920, but only to Denikin, for at the same time Churchill had to inform Kolchak that there would be no more aid for him.[23] In November it was clear that no further aid would be forthcoming for Denikin either. Lloyd George helped to insure this by taking a strong stand against any action which would contribute to a continuation of the Russian civil war and by raising anew the spectre of the old imperialist rivalry with Russia, recalling warnings once voiced by Disraeli about the Great Russia which had absorbed the borderland areas and threatened British interests.[24] He implied that Denikin's Russia would be such a Russia. Privately he even stated that he would now oppose the restoration of Russia and instead favored its dismemberment and the recognition of all of the border states.[25] The only alternative which he would even consider was the French concept of fostering an alliance of the states ringing Russia from the Baltic to Transcaucasia.

Churchill hastened to reassure Denikin that aid would continue, but Maklakov, who conveyed Churchill's message, warned that little more could be expected.[26] During November and December Lloyd George gave evident substance to this warning in his speeches touching on the Russian question. He in effect said to Denikin that the Allies had done all they could but that their resources had now been exhausted and any continuation of policies which prolonged the war would be both inexpedient and wrong. This, he stated, was the view of both the British and the French governments.[27] Moreover, the talk of ending the blockade against Bolshevik Russia and opening trade relations through the cooperative societies, which by now were fully Bolshevik dominated, was indicative of the prevalent attitude in both civilian and governmental circles. British aid, of course, would continue for a while because of the September credit, but no further arrangement could be worked out with them either. In both France and Britain the policy makers had simply decided against any further commitment in aid, and there were just no adequate conditions for trade.

For a time there was some hope of obtaining significant quantities of equipment from the United States to fill the gap which would be left by the termination of Allied aid.[28] Kolchak had in fact been granted credits in the United States which had previously been intended for the Provisional government but which were never used or withdrawn, yet Denikin had gotten little benefit from this before Kolchak's defeat, only two ships having made the run from New York to South Russia before the autumn of 1919.[29] However Denikin now hoped to obtain at least a part of the millions of dollars' worth of supplies contracted for by Kolchak's economic representatives, S. A. Ughet and P. A. Morozov, but still not shipped to Russia. Under terms required by the United States Shipping Board, ships carrying supplies to Russia were to return with at least a two-thirds capacity load of raw cargo in exchange.[30]

On the basis of this plan, which was accepted by Ughet and Morozov on Denikin's behalf, four additional freighters delivered cargoes valued at over $10 million to South Russia from the United States between October and December.[31] One of these, carrying over half of this total value, however, was not able to unload in the Crimea until April 1920.[32] Moreover, Denikin was not able to live up to the agreement to pay for the supplies by return cargoes, and Ughet and Morosov were soon compelled to scrap much of the ordered military material in order to pay their storage and freight debts.[33] Hundreds of thousands of rounds of ammunition and artillery shells, rifles, and all sorts of other supplies thus went to junk instead of to South Russia, and the War Department subsequently interdicted further aid shipments despite Secretary of State Lansing's approval of them.[34]

An equally frustrating outcome resulted from General Shcherbachev's diligent efforts throughout 1919 to obtain Russian material held in Germany.[35] Articles 116 and 169 of the Versailles Treaty finally conceded the obligation of Germany to return all such Russian material, but no formal arrangement was ever made to expedite this obligation. In any case, prior to the signing of the Versailles Treaty in June 1919 Clemenceau had objected on principle to allowing Germany to dispose of any war material and, after the signing of the

treaty, continued to block efforts to have material released to the
Russians.[36] In a compromise resolution eventually adopted by the
Allied Supreme Council in December at Foch's suggestion, Denikin
was granted permission to buy munitions available in Germany. However, this slightly insulting gesture was at best a bit too late and did
not resolve the problem, since the money was not available for such
purchase.[37]

                              *   *   *   *   *   *

In January 1920 Maklakov summed up the situation in frank letters
to acting Volunteer Foreign Minister A. A. Neratov. The Allies, he
said, had concluded that the policy of attempting to overthrow the
Bolsheviks by force had failed, not just temporarily but irreparably.
They would now turn their attention to the East European states and
the former Russian border states. But it was also a fact, he added,
that the Allied governments regarded the failure as chiefly the fault
of the Russians themselves, and they put the blame directly upon
inadequate and even wrong political and social policies followed by
Russian authorities. Such things as the agrarian problem and the
demand for democratic government had not been faced properly.
Equally important, the attitude toward non-Russian nationalities
seeking guarantees of their autonomy and self-government had been
foolish and self-defeating. Finally, said Maklakov, they pointed to the
failure to appeal to and attract a broad popular support, especially
among liberal and socialist elements. There was even a growing feeling, Maklakov concluded, that the support given to those who had
made these mistakes had only helped to drive the people into the
arms of the Bolsheviks.[38]

As Maklakov pointed out, the purely military side of the struggle
was not the only area of shortcomings. The judgment made by the
Allies had equally often centered upon social and political policies.
The results and ultimate fate of Denikin's leadership were thus bound
up with the burdens of administration and domestic problems as
much as they were with his military strategy and alliances. During his
visit to Volunteer headquarters early in 1920, Sir Halford Mackinder
urged Denikin to form a "real" government as soon as possible, thus
pointing to the fact that even at this late date the Volunteer Army
still had not developed a real political organization.[39]

In part this lack of political development had resulted from Denikin's desire to avoid politics and leave social issues in abeyance until
the war had been concluded, a policy which he called "nonpredeter-

mination."[40] Denikin did not fully realize the folly of this position until the spring of 1919 when the Army's offensive and Allied pressure together forced him at last to take a stand. To his credit, he did then outline a positive liberal program, listing the following as the goals of the Volunteer Army:

1. defeat of Bolshevik anarchy and restoration of law and order;
2. re-establishment of a strong united and undivided Russia;
3. convocation of a National Assembly on the basis of universal suffrage;
4. decentralization of power through the establishment of regional autonomy and broad local self-government;
5. guarantee of full civil liberties and freedom of religion;
6. immediate preparation of land reforms to meet the land needs of the laboring population;
7. immediate development of labor legislation safeguarding the working class against exploitation by capital or by the state.[41]

In other statements Denikin had also committed himself to the principle of popular sovereignty, in the sense that the future form of government must be decided by a constituent or national assembly elected by the people, and he stood always for loyalty to Russia's international commitments.[42] It would indeed be quite accurate to state that in most things he stood for the same policies and goals that the Provisional government had stood for. Standing for something and putting it into practice, however, were two different things. He, for example, appointed a commission to study the land problem and draw up reforms "to facilitate the transfer of land to small holders," and while it was working, he issued interim orders to protect peasant holdings against reseizure by former owners.[43] However, the conservative opposition successfully blocked even the formulation of a reform law until November 1919, after which time it was bound to be "completely ineffective" by Denikin's own admission.[44]

Meanwhile the army in the field, because of severe shortages of supplies, was compelled to live off the land by forced requisitions, a practice which alienated the peasants. Moreover, the former owners followed the army wherever it went and used its presence to coerce the peasants, regardless of Denikin's orders.[45] Such practices could have been controlled only by an effective and efficient administrative apparatus in the rear of the army, and under Denikin's system of military government such an apparatus was completely lacking. On the contrary, the only people whom Denikin could attract into the bureaucracy were old bureaucrats who were in many cases both reactionary and corrupt. Such persons, as Denikin himself described them, were "so alien to the upheaval that had taken place that they could neither understand it nor deal with it."[46] All they could do was to try to resurrect the past.

Denikin made a valiant, and typical, attempt to correct all this in the winter of 1919–1920 by reorganizing the entire governmental structure at the top. Plans for "real" government had, indeed, been under preparation for months by the legal adviser of the Special Council, K. N. Sokolov, but strong Cossack objections and the entrenched autonomy of the Cossack governments had prevented their implementation.[47] At this crucial stage, however, Denikin forced a showdown with the Cossacks and put through in February 1920 a reorganization which called for a legislative assembly, a council of ministers responsible to it, and a president with limited veto powers and the responsibility for naming the chairman of the council and the ministers of war and communications.[48]

It was particularly notable that Denikin, who would assume the post of president, introduced this democratic alternative to the dictatorship at the very time that Kolchak, just before his own death, designated him as successor to "supreme all-Russian authority."[49] In reality, of course, neither the reforms nor the new titles meant very much. When Denikin named N. M. Mel'nikov, a Don Cossack leader, to form the new government and recommended the inclusion of Socialist Revolutionaries in the cabinet, his plan was denounced by the conservatives as a capitulation to the "Leftists," by the liberals as a surrender to Cossack predominance, and by the Cossacks as a violation of their rights.[50] Moreover, Denikin's efforts to reform the government came at the very moment when the Army was disintegrating under the blows of the Red Army.

* * * * * *

By the spring of 1920 the Volunteers' last foothold in the Kuban at Novorossiisk had become a hellhole of disease, insurrection, chaos, and confusion.[51] All the hostility of miserable refugees, disillusioned officers, rebellious troops, and fanatics had welled up into a common chorus of denunciation of those held responsible, especially Denikin and his chief of staff, Romonovskii; and a new threat from the south, the "Green" movement, was making even an orderly evacuation of Novorossiisk extremely difficult.

This movement, concentrated in the coastal zone between Georgia

and Novorossiisk, was symbolic of the collapse of resistance to the
Red Army. Technically neutral in the war between Reds and Whites,
the Greens represented in practice a peasant socialist revolt against
the latter with illusory hopes of reaching a truce with the former. It
had taken an organized form in November 1919 with the election of
a "Committee of Liberation" headed by the Socialist Revolutionary V. N. Filippovskii-Samarin and a military staff headed by N.
Voronovich.[52]

Having organized a small striking force initially under the wing of
Georgian neutrality, Voronovich had attacked the Volunteers early in
the year and had then pressed on northward to Tuspse and beyond,
incorporating into his forces deserting Kuban troops sent to stop him.
In their position on the coast the Greens posed not only a military
threat, with the possibility that they would be able to cut off Volunteer communications with the Mountain region and obstruct a retreat
to the south, but also a political threat. In effect the Green movement
represented both a peasant revolt against Volunteer authority and an
outgrowth of the "neutrality" movements in the Kuban and Transcaucasia. The Green attack had in fact first been reported as a Georgian attack supported by Kuban traitors, and Denikin had been led
to break off relations abruptly with Georgia again at the end of January, just as Volunteer forces were being isolated in the mountains and
being driven toward the Georgian border on one side and toward
Petrovsk on the other.[53]

Denikin refused to be swayed by the advice of some members of
the Don Command, who believed negotiations with the Greens to
be the only way out, or by the fact that various Kuban leaders were
known to be closely associated with the movement. A Don-Kuban
delegation, seeking a truce and some agreement to prevent further
clashes, did contact Green leaders late in March, but nothing came of
the effort, since the Greens claimed that they could obtain recognition of their independence from the Bolsheviks but could be assured
of nothing from Denikin.[54] The pressure for negotiations, however,
also surprisingly came from another direction—the British.

The British diplomatic representative, General Keyes, apparently
felt that this was one of the cases in which British mediation would
be most helpful, for on February 6 he had sent a member of his staff
to Sochi to meet with Voronovich and Filippovskii-Samarin. Through
this contact the British envoy satisfied himself that the Georgian
army had no part in the attack and that the arms acquired had largely

been captured from the Volunteers. He had then inquired whether the liberation committee would accept the status quo as the basis of a truce if it was recognized and supported by the British, and he was told that the British guarantee would have no meaning if Denikin intended to try to retake Sochi. However, the committee did not at this point completely reject the offer of mediation.[55]

General Keyes himself had then gone to Sochi and there talked with V. Chaikin, a representative of the committee and a Socialist Revolutionary journalist whose account of the murder of the Baku commissars had provided the basis of the charges of British complicity in their deaths. Upon being told by Chaikin that the Green rising had been provoked by Volunteer atrocities, Keyes replied that the committee should have reported this to him at the time. He knew that the Volunteers had acted badly, said Keyes, but he hoped that the committee would now accept his mediation of differences with the Volunteers. Taking personal credit for some of Denikin's recent political concessions, Keyes indicated that Britain would aid all legitimate governments opposing the Bolsheviks, including the committee if it was willing to cooperate.[56]

Going then to Gagri, Keyes met with Voronovich and offered the use of his boat to carry the Green Commander to Novorossiisk to meet with Kuban and Volunteer leaders. Unable to contact the committee for authorization, Voronovich nevertheless agreed to go in a personal capacity. In Novorossiisk, however, Volunteer authorities (specifically General Lukomskii, who was then governor-general of the Black Sea province) refused to admit Keyes' guest, and so he was returned to Sochi, where the committee had meanwhile repudiated any negotiations with the Volunteers.[57] Despite the apparent opposition to negotiations on the part of both the committee and the Volunteers, however, Keyes continued his efforts.

When a peasants', workers', and soldiers' congress was convoked in Sochi later in February, another British representative, General Cotton, attended and addressed the meeting to urge a truce through British mediation. He assured Green leaders that once previous commitments had been fulfilled, British aid to Denikin would cease, and he offered to guarantee that any prisoners held by the Greens would not be allowed to take any further part in the war if they were released. His promises were also to no avail, however, since the Greens refused to agree to negotiate or even to refrain from an attack on Novorossiisk. The latter, they said, was a part of the Black Sea province, and if, as Cotton warned, the British tried to defend it, the resulting clash would be unavoidable. Even after this rebuff, Keyes accompanied Cossack Supreme Krug Vice-President Ageev to Sochi on March 7 to seek some arrangement with the Greens, but he was told that only a complete break with Denikin would make negotiations possible with anyone.[58]

These efforts to reach a compromise with the Greens were futile, and they aroused Denikin's resentment,[59] but they possibly also helped to produce a rift within the Green movement. By the end of February a factional split had developed between the peasant-oriented liberation committee and the associated military revolutionary committee, which was backed by the Bolsheviks and based upon worker support. As Red Army units moved into the Kuban from the east, the Bolshevik faction in the movement proposed to invade the Kuban in order to join forces with them. Voronovich and the liberation committee opposed this suggestion, but, having lost control over a part of the Green forces to the military revolutionary committee, they were unable to stop the attack.[60]

Kuban forces, now retreating southward under the command of General Shkuro, clashed with the "Red" Greens shortly thereafter, successfully routed them, and then proceeded on toward Sochi. The chairman of the Kuban government at this time, V. Ivanis, made a hasty trip to Gagri and got the liberation committee's belated agreement to a truce at least to cover Kuban troops, but this had little effect, since the committee no longer had any influence with the Green units in the field.[61] The latter, under Bolshevik leadership, continued to attack, and Shkuro renewed his drive against them. The Kuban commander then succeeded in forcing the Green army to retreat into the hills, but all that he himself could do after that was to continue with his own troops toward the south, followed by swarms of refugees carrying a plague of typhus and cholera.[62] This movement, of course, once again raised the question of relations with Transcaucasia.

* * * * * *

Despite the renewed hostility initially provoked by the Green attack, Denikin had begun efforts almost immediately afterward to restore relations with Georgia and establish a basis for cooperation.[63] The military situation, the burden of over 40,000 civilian refugees, and particularly the clear necessity of sending some troops southward since there were not enough boats to carry all of them directly to the

Crimea, made better relations with Georgia essential. The common threat posed by the Red Army also seemed to offer to Georgia an imperative justification for ending past differences. Moreover, Georgia was badly in need of supplies herself and now had far less to fear from Denikin than in the past. In short, the opportunity for cooperation seemed open, and Denikin, for his part, took steps toward that end. The fate of both Transcaucasia and the Volunteers, however, depended also on the response of the Allies to their mutual needs at this time.

At the conference of Allied prime ministers and foreign ministers in December both the Volunteer retreat and the question of what to do about the Transcaucasian states had already received special attention.[64] On December 13 the Allied leaders had adopted a resolution setting forth the decision "not to enter into any further commitment beyond what has already been promised." The resolution continued:

> The Conference agreed that no useful purpose would be served by attempting to summon any general conference of the representatives of the anti-Bolshevik States at the present.
>
> As regards the border communities with non-Russian populations which have been struggling for freedom and self-government, the Allies will give them such assistance in defending their liberties as may be found desirable in the circumstances of each case as it arises.[65]

It was not until January 10 that Curzon, on Lloyd George's instructions, had finally raised specifically the question of granting formal de facto recognition to Georgia and Azerbaidzhan. As he pointed out to the foreign ministers present, these states were in grave danger, and the British government now believed that recognition would be a major aid to their preservation against Bolshevik attack.[66] It had then been decided that the Allied Powers would jointly extend de facto recognition to the governments of Georgia and Azerbaidzhan.

On January 16 the prime ministers had further considered the question of the defense of the two republics and their requests for aid, but Lloyd George had cast doubt on the feasibility of a serious aid program and had turned the discussion instead to the question of reopening trade with all of Russia as the "best way . . . to ruin Bolshevism."[67] The extent to which Allied policy had turned toward Lloyd George's point of view was indicated by the fact that on the same day the Allied Supreme Council had approved ending the blockade of Bolshevik Russia and opening trade relations through the cooperative societies, an indirect approach designed to get the benefits of trade without granting recognition of the Soviet government.[68]

Finally, on January 19 the question of Allied policy toward South Russia and Transcaucasia had been brought to a head when Foch and Sir Henry Wilson were called upon to analyze the military situation, and representatives of Georgia and Azerbaidzhan were invited to testify on the plight of their countries. Foch surveyed the state of affairs in the civil war and concluded that Denikin's forces were at the point of complete collapse. He therefore recommended that the Allies concern themselves chiefly with building a strong alliance among Poland, Rumania, the Baltic States, and Finland. Sir Henry Wilson agreed with Foch that the Allies could not seriously consider a reintervention in South Russia and Transcaucasia unless they were prepared to devote at least three full divisions of troops to this purpose. And as for further aid in supplies, he believed that unless they were willing to make the necessary effort to hold the Caspian, any material sent in would probably soon fall into Bolshevik hands.[69]

On the other side of the debate, the Transcaucasian representatives (Tseretelli, Avalov, Chkheidze, Topchibashev, and Mageramov) declared that Georgia and Azerbaidzhan were prepared to defend themselves but could do so successfully only if they received full Allied recognition and supplies so as to assure their position against both the Bolsheviks and Denikin. The inclusion of the Volunteers in the category of enemies of Georgia and Azerbaidzhan was particularly stressed by Tseretelli, who even suggested that it would be easier for them to deal with the Bolsheviks than with Denikin. Indeed, of all those present at this discussion (Lloyd George, Clemenceau, Curzon, and Churchill in addition to the names already mentioned) only Churchill put in a word on Denikin's behalf and suggested that he deserved more than just being written off as either a defeated man or a threat to Transcaucasia.[70]

At the end of this discussion the Allied leaders reached three decisions: (1) they agreed to extend de facto recognition also to Armenia, on condition that this not prejudice a future decision on Armenia's border, but not to grant de jure recognition to any of the three Transcaucasian states as yet; (2) they agreed that no more troops would be sent to Transcaucasia; and (3) they agreed to supply arms and material aid to the Transcaucasian states if they should be threatened with attack. Italy, whose representatives now admitted to having secretly supplied some arms to Dagestan already, joined in these decisions and offered to contribute arms if the British and French would take responsibility for delivering them.[71] The United States and Japan were also to be invited to adhere to these policies.[72]

While these decisions were being made, Mackinder had taken up his post at Volunteer headquarters and had begun work on the task of encouraging better relations between the Volunteers and Transcaucasia.[73] His task had, of course, taken on new significance after the January 10 decision by the Allied governments to grant formal recognition to the Transcaucasian states. Mackinder apparently was favorably impressed to find that Denikin was not opposed to acknowledging the de facto existence of his neighbors to the south, although the Volunteer Commander still maintained that he had no authority to accept formally any territorial change in the Russian state.

Denikin had thus assured Mackinder that he recognized the Georgian and Azerbaidzhani goverments and wanted to negotiate with them if they were willing to cooperate in the fight against the Bolsheviks and to refrain from making claims which could be judged only by a future all-Russian authority.[74] There was nothing new in this, of course, but Denikin had at this time agreed to go beyond his previous position and to commit himself in writing to the proposition that reunification might be achieved through negotiation with the borderland governments rather than solely through the medium of an all-inclusive constituent assembly.

Therefore on January 14 Denikin had issued a statement, declaring in part:

> 1. I recognize the de facto independence of the border governments which are carrying on the struggle against the Bolsheviks;
> 2. the settlement of the future relations of the border states with Russia should be accomplished by means of an agreement between the all-Russian government and the border governments;
> 3. the mediation of the Allies can be accepted in this matter....[75]

Moreover, when Denikin had created his new government, he had appointed General Baratov, who had formerly been in charge of the Volunteer mission in Tiflis, to the post of foreign minister. Convinced that better relations could be established with Georgia and Azerbaidzhan, Baratov had immediately begun efforts in that direction with Denikin's approval. By February both sides had agreed to begin new negotiations, and special representatives were exhanged for this purpose. The Volunteer representative still in Georgia, Colonel Den, was commissioned on March 7 as plenipotentiary envoy and instructed to seek agreement with Georgia as soon as possible.[76]

The instructions given to Den contained the following points: (1) the South Russian government, having extended recognition to the government of Georgia, agreed that future relations between Georgia and Russia could be established by treaty between the Georgian gov- ernment and a future all-Russian government, with the mediation of the Allied governments if desired, and it was now prepared to supply Georgia with grain to the greatest extent possible and join with Geor- gia in a joint defense of its territory against attack; (2) Georgia, for its part, was asked to allow military supplies to be sent through its terri- tory to Volunteer troops in the North Caucasus region in case they were cut off from other sources, to permit Russian troops to retreat into Georgian territory if necessary and to be transferred with their arms to Batum as a port of exit, to undertake cooperative military operations against the Bolsheviks if they should attack Georgia, and to permit the use of Georgian ports and supplies of coal for shipping between South Russia and Georgia.[77]

Baratov's instructions to Colonel Den in effect proposed an alliance with Georgia, and Den himself was quite optimistic about the pros- pects. Less than a week after receipt of the above proposal he reported that the Georgian government had reacted quite favorably to the sug- gestion of a trade of coal for grain and was giving serious consideration to the other points.[78] The only obstacle to full agreement, Den indi- cated, was the element of uncertainty in Georgia's present situation, especially with regard to the position of the Allied Powers.[79] "My impression from talks with Gegechkori," he reported, "is that the Georgian Government is anti-Bolshevik in principle, and if only it could get a full guarantee from the Allies that they would give active aid in case of a Bolshevik attack, it would readily enter an anti-Bolshe- vik agreement and accept the conditions proposed by us."[80]

In his conversation with Gegechkori, Den even confidently re- quested the Georgian government to permit recruitment of new troops on Georgian soil, but, as he reported it, all would now depend upon the cooperation of the Allied governments, whose decisions would be the crucial factors in future relations with Transcaucasia. Without firm Allied support, he warned, Georgia would probably feel it impossible to "drop its neutrality and run the risk of Bolshevik retaliation. . . ." Volunteer representatives pursuing the same task as

Den's with regard to Azerbaidzhan reported essentially the same situation: Azerbaidzhan favored friendly relations and trade but hesitated to go beyond this or violate its neutrality unless assured of Allied protection.

The situation grew more desperate for Volunteer troops in the North Caucasus and north of the Georgian border daily, since new uprisings in Dagestan and the Greens' attack on the Black Sea coast coincided with Red Army advances which threatened any day to force a retreat into Transcaucasia. For Georgia and Azerbaidzhan, however, the situation was critical in a different way. Being wooed now by both the Bolsheviks and the Volunteers, they were at the same time threatened with the entry of the troops of both and, unable to stand alone, could hope to meet the situation only with renewed Allied military assistance. Soviet Foreign Commissar Chicherin had already, in January, called it to the attention of Georgia and Azerbaidzhan that the Red Army was "dealing a shattering blow to the White Guard bands of the Tsarist General Denikin," and he called upon them "to enter immediately into negotiations with the Soviet Government for the conclusion of a military agreement . . . for the purpose of accelerating the defeat of the White Guard armies in South Russia."[81]

The initial reaction of both Georgia and Azerbaidzhan had been to renew their efforts to obtain Allied support, but their hopes in this regard were in vain. Britain and France would do what they could to erect a legal barrier against Bolshevik attack, promote cooperation with the Volunteers, and continue the shipment of supplies to the extent possible, but a new intervention was not in the works. At the London conference which began on February 12 the Allied leaders took steps toward defining Armenia's borders and the status of Batum in preparation of the peace treaty with Turkey, but only in these cases was there further discussion of the defense of Transcaucasia.[82] Despite new expressions of scepticism by French representatives, the conference followed Lloyd George's lead in calling for peace. The appeal of Colonel Stokes in Baku for Allied support of the defense of the Mountain area was specifically overruled, and Wardrop was obliged to countermand Azerbaidzhani plans to extend its military defense line into Dagestan.[83]

A temporary exception was made in the case of Batum. The immediate threat of disorder, together with the approach of the Bolsheviks, led Curzon to appeal for French and Italian battalions to be sent so as to permit continuation of the occupation until the question of the fate of that city had been resolved. It was then agreed that each of the three Powers would supply one battalion for this purpose and that Batum should be a free port in Georgia, with the latter guaranteeing access to Azerbaidzhan and Armenia under League supervision.[84] With regard to questions other than the border with Turkey and Batum, however, the Allies would be unable to accept any further direct responsibility. In a statement conveyed to the Transcaucasian delegations on February 24, 1920, the Allied Supreme Council informed them that while the Allied governments were not entering political relations with the Soviet government, it had been decided that "to establish commercial relations was the proper way to beat Bolshevism" and that the border states were advised to follow this example and enter peaceful relations with Moscow. Only if they should be attacked "within their legitimate frontiers" could aid be expected.[85]

Meanwhile Chicherin continued to inquire where Georgia and Azerbaidzhan stood, reiterating that Denikin was their common enemy, while the Soviet government stood for the right of self-determination.[86] In a reply in February, Azerbaidzhani Prime Minister Khan-Khoiskii stated the position to which both Georgia and Azerbaidzhan adhered. Noting Azerbaidzhan's past record of noncooperation with the Volunteers and its determination to remain "neutral in the struggle which is taking place in Russia," Khan-Khoiskii declared:

> The Government of Azerbaidzhan, welcoming in every way the firm decision of the Soviet Government to be undeviatingly guided by the principle of recognition of the right of peoples to national self-determination, must, however, state with the feeling of profound regret, that in neither of the two radiotelegrams of the People's Commissar, Chicherin, was there clearly and categorically expressed the unconditional recognition of the independence of the Azerbaidzhani Republic. . . .
>
> Therefore the Government of Azerbaidzhan, which considers the establishment of good neighborly relations between the Russian and the Azerbaidzhani peoples both necessary and desirable, finds that any negotiations on this matter can take place only upon the basis of unconditional recognition by the Soviet Government of the independence and sovereignty of the Azerbaidzhani Republic.[87]

This in effect said that Azerbaidzhan would continue to hold to the policy of neutrality. Georgia had already done likewise.[88] When

in March and April Volunteer troops were obliged to take refuge in
Georgia and Azerbaidzhan, they were interned as prisoners and disarmed. Colonel Den had been informed that this would be necessary
because of the neutrality, but he was also assured that the Transcaucasian countries would defend themselves against a Red attack
and would cooperate in the evacuation of the prisoners.[89] However,
Den was also warned that the Georgian and Azerbaidzhani governments could not risk doing anything which would destroy the possibility of reaching an agreement with the Bolsheviks later if the
situation came to that.[90] Volunteer troops under General Dratsenko
in Petrovsk, which left there by sea on March 29, had made arrangements to proceed to Enzeli in Persia, but en route a ship had been
disabled and the flotilla had proceeded to Baku. There the men were
disarmed and interned, but an agreement was reached with the Azerbaidzhani government by which the troops, upon surrendering all
claim to their supplies and arms, were permitted to go to Poti to join
those held by Georgia.[91]

Georgia, which thus found itself host to most of the Volunteers
retreating to the south, agreed to permit those who wished to do so
to enter the Georgian army, but balked at Den's efforts to obtain the
release of the troops, and their arms, to be sent to the Crimea. As
it turned out, Georgia even refused to be saddled with the burden of
maintaining the refugees, because their numbers, greatly increased by
civilians, soon grew into thousands. Since Volunteer money was no
longer any good, Den also found it impossible to solve this problem.[92]
Ultimately the misery of those caught in this situation was relieved
largely by the Allies and through a good deal of deception to accom-
modate Georgian and Azerbaidzhani neutrality. After most of the
Volunteer troops had been concentrated at Poti, they were eventually permitted, without their arms, to board Allied ships purportedly
bound for Constantinople, that is, removing them from further participation in the civil war. In fact, however, they were then transported
to the Crimea.[93]

These precautions were necessary, for on April 27 the Bolsheviks
led a rebellion in Baku and appealed to approaching Red Army troops
for aid. The next day Bolshevik forces occupied Azerbaidzhan and
established a new Soviet republic.[94] This victory had undoubtedly
been facilitated to some extent by the inability of the Transcaucasian
delegations to agree among themselves and the resulting failure of
Curzon's efforts at the San Remo conference in April to bring about

an alliance among the three border states.[95] One week after the Bolshevik conquest of Azerbaidzhan the Georgians entered negotiations which on May 7 resulted in the signing of a treaty with Soviet Russia. The latter, holding the line at this point to consolidate its forces,[96] now unconditionally recognized the independence of Georgia and promised "to desist from all interference in the internal affairs of Georgia." In return Georgia agreed to legalize the Communist party, to prohibit the presence of any foreign troops on Georgian soil directed against Soviet Russia, and to disarm and intern all anti-Bolshevik military forces which entered the country.[97]

After a vain effort in May to revive the unfulfilled plan to have French and Italian troops join the British in Batum, this project was finally dropped, and on June 11 the British informed Georgia that they were removing their troops. The last British troops left Transcaucasia on July 10. In August the Allied governments tried to write some security for Georgia and Armenia into the Sevres Treaty with Turkey by providing for their recognition, but the revolt of the Turks under Kemal soon undid this effort. Subsequently, Georgia also applied for admission to the League of Nations but was turned down, a setback viewed by many to mean that no one would accept the obligation to aid Georgia if it were attacked. Both Britain and France voted against the acceptance of Georgia, although they did later, in January 1921, extend de jure recognition. The conquest of Armenia and Georgia by the Red Army, which was delayed but not prevented by such moves, took place in December 1920 and March 1921 respectively.[98]

* * * * * *

At the end of March 1920 the remainder of the troops under Denikin's command had been evacuated to the Crimea with extensive Allied assistance. Even while this was happening, it had been made known to Denikin unofficially that the Allied governments viewed the situation as hopeless.[99] British aid had been scheduled to end at the beginning of April 1920,[100] and in the Crimea Denikin now had only some 35,000 men capable of active service, 100 field guns, and 500 machine guns. Most of the other equipment and supplies, including horses, which the Army had in its possession in Novorossiisk had been left behind for lack of space and time.

Denikin refused to consider the struggle over, but he was compelled to take immediate steps to deal with the critical conditions which existed if there was to be any hope of a future for the Army.

He therefore set in motion at once a reorganization of the forces left and initiated action to rectify the political chaos in the Crimea.[101] General Romanovskii, on whom so much of the criticism from the Right had fallen, was relieved from duty as chief of staff at his own request, and the only recently organized South Russian government was dissolved.[102] The government under Mel'nikov had officially been in office less than a month, but there was no place for it in the Crimea now in Denikin's opinion, since under the circumstances it could no longer serve the purposes for which it had been established and would simply complicate matters. Most of the members of the government opposed this step, but they bowed to Denikin's judgment and left for Constantinople. Only a small executive staff under Bernatskii was retained.[103]

These matters taken care of, Denikin then took the final step to eliminate internal conflict and give the Army a chance to continue its struggle: he announced his intention to resign and issued orders calling all senior officers to a conference to be held in Sevastopol on April 3 for the purpose of selecting his successor as commander-in-chief.[104] Considerable objection was raised to this method—that is, the "election" of a commander-in-chief—but Denikin insisted upon it. In view of the strong opposition which had formed against him in Rightist circles supporting General Wrangel, Denikin refused to remain in the post himself, but he was determined to have a successor who would be acceptable to the officer corps. The official appointment of the new commander would be made by him, but the senior officers were asked to recommend the best man for the job.

General Dragomirov, who was designated as presiding officer of the conference by Denikin (who refused to attend personally), called the meeting to order on the evening of April 3.[105] When the full gathering was unable to agree on procedure, however, Dragomirov invited the highest ranking officers (corps commanders and up) into a private session. This smaller group was also divided on the question, but at least the emotional element was eliminated. Volunteer officers who had spoken out earlier against approving anyone other than Denikin were not invited; some had in fact already left in protest.[106] The senior men in the smaller meeting all agreed that a choice had to be made, since to refuse would destroy the authority of the man eventually named to be commander. They also agreed that the only real task for the new commander would be that of putting things in order and preparing for the final evacuation of the Army abroad. His would therefore be a brief tenure in any case.

With these points in view, the small meeting then agreed upon General Wrangel as the man to recommend to Denikin.[107] This selection of Wrangel was based upon his leadership ability, but there was a certain irony in the choice, for during the preceding weeks the increasingly hostile relations between Denikin and Wrangel had resulted in an open break. It had, indeed, been this rupture, as much as the military defeat, which convinced Denikin of his inability to continue to lead the Army. Baron General Wrangel, a popular commander of noble birth who regarded Denikin as both too weak and too liberal, had for some time been an outspoken critic of the latter's policies, both military and political. He had on a number of occasions condemned what he termed Denikin's "colossal mistakes" that he believed were leading the Army to ruin.[108] Moreover, leading conservative politicians and officers (including Krivoshein; Struve; Admiral Neniukov, the fleet commander; and his chief of staff, Admiral Bubnov) had formed an opposition bloc in the Crimea during Wrangel's assignment there and had actively promoted a movement to oust Denikin and put Wrangel in his place. Their activities and Wrangel's own public criticism had finally provoked Denikin into requesting Wrangel to leave the country.[109]

Wrangel had complied with this request but not without first issuing (in the form of a letter to Denikin) a strong statement of his unrelenting opposition. In it he portrayed himself as much as Denikin:

I fought for eighteen months in the ranks of the Armed Forces of South Russia [wrote Wrangel], invariably leading my troops to victory, and more than once saved the general situation in a moment of grave danger. . . .

[But] the Army, brought up on arbitrary rule, plunder, and drunkenness, under the leadership of men who depraved their troops by their own bad example, such an army could not save Russia. . . . The enemy's success grew and the ineffectiveness of your strategy and your policies became more manifest with every day. The eyes of the public were gradually opened. Louder and louder grew the voices of those who demanded the replacement of some whose blamable conduct was apparent to all by others whose names remained unblemished amidst the general moral decline. But the poison of ambition had entered your soul, and, drunk with power, surrounded by dishonest flatterers, you thought more of safeguarding your own power and authority than of saving your country. . . .

Military chiefs, statesmen, and social leaders repeatedly pointed out to you the necessity of availing yourself of my services, of using the powers and abilities I possessed. . . . But instead I was spied upon . . . and rumors about my alleged intentions of making a coup d'état were spread abroad by your Staff. . . . Both the Army and the people, worn out by anarchy, having lost all faith in the principles proclaimed by their leaders, deeply revolted by the criminal actions of their representatives . . . saw in me the man who could give them what they were longing for. . . . But it was in vain, for you, jealous of your power, clinging to the authority slipping from your grasp, and compromising with the separatists, you decided to declare war against your closest assistants. . . .

Since I have resigned I consider myself free from any obligation toward you and consider your orders in no way binding upon me. You have no way whatsoever of forcing me to obey. Nevertheless I have decided to leave Russia, smothering the flame in my heart.[110]

Denikin's reply to this tirade, of which the above was only a small sample, was quite brief. He accused Wrangel of fabricating lies in a deliberate effort to undermine his position and seize power. His letter, said Denikin, dispelled all doubt about his "role in the struggle for power." Now all that could be added, Denikin's note concluded, was a prayer that God would forgive Wrangel for the harm which he had done to the "Russian cause."[111]

Just before this exchange, General Holman, as British military representative, had sought to intervene in the feud in the hope of reconciling the two Volunteer leaders.[112] Through British Admiral Seymour he had asked Wrangel to accept his offer to arrange a meeting with Denikin. If Wrangel were "prepared to abide by Denikin's final decision regarding his future movements . . . and to state publicly his adherence to Denikin's new domestic policy and sternly discountenance reactionaries now using his name," Holman wrote, then he felt sure that the misunderstanding between them could be cleared up.[113] Denikin had not rejected this offer of mediation, but Wrangel, while agreeing to send his trusted assistant, General Shatilov, refused to go personally to see Denikin.[114] Holman then conferred with Denikin and, on learning the seriousness of the dispute, himself suggested that Wrangel should leave the country and wrote to Wrangel to this effect a few days later.[115]

When Wrangel subsequently returned to the Crimea in April to attend the conference which selected him as Denikin's successor, he brought with him official notification of an end to British aid. The message conveying the British view of the situation had been addressed to Denikin, under the date of April 2, but in view of Denikin's decision to resign it was delivered to Wrangel instead.[116] It put its main point bluntly, calling the prolongation of the civil war "the most disturbing element in the present European situation." The British government, it continued:

> desires to submit for General Denikin's consideration the suggestion that in the present situation, an arrangement with the Soviet Government with a view to requesting amnesty for the population of the Crimea in general and for the personnel of the Volunteer Army in particular would be in the best interest of all concerned. Filled with the conviction that abandonment of this unequal struggle would be the most advantageous step for Russia, the British Government would undertake this demarche itself, once General Denikin's consent is obtained, and would put at the latter's disposal and that of his principal followers the full hospitality of Great Britain.
>
> The British Government, which has furnished in the past a large measure of the assistance which alone made possible the continuation of the struggle to the present time, believes itself justified in its hope that this proposal will be accepted. If, however, General Denikin should feel it his duty to refuse in order to prolong a manifestly hopeless struggle, the British Government will find itself obliged to renounce all responsibility for his action and to cease immediately to furnish him any assistance or subvention of any kind.[117]

When Wrangel revealed this message to the officers who had agreed to recommend him as commander-in-chief, he gave it as one reason for his insistence upon having a statement signed by all those present setting forth the conditions under which he would take command. This statement declared that the meeting had been informed of the British advice to end the war as an "unequal and hopeless struggle" and of the offer by the British government to appeal to Moscow for amnesty. "Under these conditions," the statement continued:

> the Council expressed the desire to request the Commander-in-Chief to appoint General Wrangel as his successor, in order that he, having taken upon himself the high command, could seek the inviolability of all persons who have fought against the Bolsheviks and could establish the most favorable conditions for the personnel of the Armed Forces of South Russia, namely, for those who will

not find it possible for themselves to accept a guarantee of security from the soviet government.[118]

After this agreement was made with Wrangel by the top officers in secret session, Denikin was informed of their decision. In a letter to Dragomirov, Denikin had already confided his feelings at this time:

> For three years of the Russian turmoil, I have led the struggle, giving it all my strength and bearing the heavy cross of authority handed down by fate. . . .
> Faith in the Army's vitality and its historic mission is still alive, but the intimate ties binding the Chief to his men are broken, and I no longer have the strength to command them.

Now he wired Dragomirov the order appointing Wrangel as his successor:

> Lieutenant General Baron Wrangel is appointed Commander-in-Chief of the Armed Forces of South Russia. . . .
> May God give victory to the Army and save Russia.[119]

The great crusade seemed to be over, since Wrangel had pointedly taken responsibility for concluding it, and Denikin, who could not end it himself, now left for exile abroad. For Denikin the depth of the tragedy could not have been greater, for, having lost the struggle, he now lost his closest friend. During their stopover in Constantinople en route to England, General Romanovskii was assassinated by a man wearing a Russian officer's coat.[120] Denikin himself continued his lonely voyage under British guard.

8: THE CRIMEAN EPILOGUE

At the time of Denikin's resignation Wrangel claimed to be really confident of only one thing: he had "no doubt" that he would be chosen as the new commander-in-chief. Otherwise he gave the impression (later proved to be false) of being completely pessimistic. "I see no possibility of continuing the struggle," he told General Dragomirov. The conditions in which Denikin had left the Army and the British "ultimatum," he said, made absolutely clear the necessity of immediate preparations for evacuation.[1] Consequently he ordered his chief of staff, General Makhrov, to set to work at once on the task of readying all available facilities to take the Army abroad. The reply sent to the British on April 4, while posing certain conditions, suggested the same conclusion:

> The categorical demand of the British Government that we cease fighting [wrote Wrangel] makes it impossible for my army to continue. Putting upon the British Government all the moral responsibility for the consequences of the decision it has made and absolutely denying the possibility of direct negotiations with the enemy, I leave the fate of the army, the navy, the population of the territories occupied by us, and all those who have taken part in the present struggle on our side to the good offices of the British Government.[2]

Holding the British responsible for securing the inviolability of all the members of the armed forces and civilian refugees either abroad or in Russia, Wrangel called for a settlement of the "armistice questions" as soon as possible and added that he would need at least two months from the conclusion of peace terms in order to handle properly the "liquidation of administrative, military, and civil organs" in the Crimea. During this interval, Wrangel stated, he would expect the Allies to continue to supply the Crimea with everything necessary

241

for its maintenance and the preparation of its evacuation.

The Crimea was indeed, according to Wrangel, desolate. It was "completely lacking in natural resources," while the Army had virtually no supplies on hand and direct responsibility for feeding over 150,000 people. Administrative machinery was in a "state of complete decay," and even evacuation was impossible until coal and oil could be obtained from outside to power the ships helplessly standing in the harbors. The situation was "almost hopeless."[3]

Both the British and the French governments apparently took this situation and Wrangel's position at face value at this time. On April 19 Admiral Seymour informed Wrangel that Curzon had proposed to the Soviet government the cessation of hostilities and establishment of peace on terms comparable to those stated in Wrangel's note.[4] Meanwhile the British navy would stand by to assist in maintaining the status quo. Four days later General Mangin forwarded a message from Paris stating that the French government would "coordinate its actions with those of the British Government in order to support General Wrangel . . . until he has obtained from the Soviets armistice conditions which will assure his army of proper treatment."[5]

These statements, both Wrangel's and those of the Allied representatives, however, gave a somewhat misleading impression. Curzon was unquestionably sincere in the position he took, but he equally surely overestimated the prospects for a rapid achievement of his proposals. British authorities in Constantinople confidentially expressed doubts as to chances for successful negotiations with the Bolsheviks along the lines proposed by Curzon,[6] and Churchill for his part strongly criticized Curzon's policy and refused to associate himself with it.[7] Late in April Curzon himself was obliged to wire Admiral de Robeck that the Soviet response had not been encouraging.[8]

Moreover, Wrangel himself was contemplating something more than just preparations for evacuation. He had, in fact, made up his mind from the start not to go along with the British proposals. His reply suggesting that he would do so had been a deliberate maneuver to keep the British involved long enough to enable him to reorganize his forces. On the same day that he took command Wrangel told his closest associates that he intended to continue the war, but for the moment the important thing was "to avoid giving England an opportunity to leave us in the lurch."[9] The demand for two months' time would meanwhile provide the opportunity for sounding out other possible sources of aid, both abroad and among forces in and around

Russia. This, in essence, was the explanation of policy which Wrangel sent to Maklakov in Paris, setting forth the aim of restoring the Army, introducing impressive social and political reforms, and in general preparing the Crimean base for future operations.[10] In his own account of these first days of his command, Wrangel's statement that the situation was "almost hopeless" was thus followed almost immediately by the remark that he was in fact "preparing to continue the struggle."[11]

Nothing demonstrated Wrangel's intention better than the impressive list of actions taken even before the end of his first month as commander. He immediately initiated efforts to register and restore all available military material to re-equip the Army, set in motion a complete reorganization of the Army into three corps, and began the elaboration of plans for a campaign to secure the passes leading into the Ukraine. Further, in the matter of military organization he issued new regulations concerning discipline and the operations of courts martial, removed all restrictions upon service of deserters from Red forces and issued an appeal to attract more of them, took action to remove from command those who disagreed with his policies (especially the policy of new military action), undertook the further evacuation of Kuban troops to the Crimea, and (in May) ordered a new mobilization of recruits to enlarge the Army.

In the area of civil authority and policy, finally, he began the organization of a new government, issued a new statute on administration of occupied territory, appointed a commission to formulate new agrarian reforms, took steps to increase revenue from customs and taxes, and, along with a reorganization of the propaganda effort in the West, declared in an interview with the press that he sought a new path for the "resurrection" of Russia which must begin with the immediate establishment of a "strong and unified power" in the Crimea.[12] There was no call for a new march to Moscow, but there was a clear call to hold the Crimea.

On May 2, while still professing to be seeking an end to the war and the facilitation of British negotiations with the Soviet government, Wrangel informed the British military representative of his intention of assisting the Kuban Cossacks and expressed the view that peace efforts were futile so long as "the people themselves are not willing to tolerate Bolshevik rule." Reports of uprisings in the Don and elsewhere during April, he declared, proved this point. The "sole method" of saving Russia from anarchy, Wrangel concluded, was "to preserve a healthy nucleus around which all the movements which have broken away from the tyranny of Bolshevism by sheer force can group themselves."[13] Peace, ran Wrangel's logic, depended upon the elimination of the cause of anarchy and war; that cause was not his army but Bolshevik conquest.

Before discussing the circumstances under which Wrangel did subsequently mount the offensive, however, it is worth noting here some of the changes in policy adopted under his command. Wrangel had been highly critical of Denikin's policies and was now equally vocal in declaring his intention to correct past mistakes. Included among the latter in Wrangel's view had been, on the one hand, the compromises made by Denikin in the area of authority and, on the other, his failure to make necessary compromises in the area of relations with the Allied governments and the various non-Russian authorities in the South. Thus, Wrangel condemned Denikin's relaxation of the power of the commander-in-chief both in terms of permitting liberal influences on policy and in terms of changes in the administrative structure that allowed for greater participation on the part of the Cossacks and permitted a closer approximation to a parliamentary government.

As Wrangel himself phrased it, Denikin had allowed the administration to fall into "complete decay" by countenancing its evolution "from a personal dictatorship to a democratic government. . . ."[14] On the other hand, Wrangel also condemned what he called Denikin's "narrow and uncompromising policy" of persecuting those who disagreed with him or in any way could be identified with elements taking a different stand, such as the Ukrainians, the Georgians, subordinates who advised different tactics, etc.[15] Included in this latter category as mistakes were likewise Denikin's failure to use liberal policies, especially in the field of agrarian reform, for their propaganda value and also his "obstinate refusal to use the enormous natural wealth of South Russia to attract foreign capital," that is, by granting concessions.[16]

These criticisms revealed a great deal about the differences between the two men. Wrangel's position appeared to be full of contradictions, but in fact there was a notable consistency in his approach. He was in essence calling for what had sometimes been labeled a "Left" policy in "Right" hands. Where Denikin had sought to maintain an administration staffed by moderates and to follow moderate policies, Wrangel would reserve administrative control in the hands of staunch conservatives under a tight dictatorship and at the same time advance policies of reforms, compromise with the border states, appeasement of the Allies, and appeal to the peasants. The ideal combination of control and appeal—something the Bolsheviks seemed to accomplish so skillfully—was what Wrangel sought, as contrasted to the instability and fluctuating laxity of Denikin's approach. At least this was the way Wrangel saw it.

What Wrangel's ideas meant in practice was seen first in his organization of authority. In the first place he quickly promulgated, on April 11, a new statute on government which assigned unlimited powers to himself. He would personally exercise "the fullest civil and military powers, without any limitations whatsoever," and to symbolize this authority he took the title of "regent" as well as commander-in-chief.[17] There would be no government or parliament in the usual sense, only the regent and his assistants. By the same token, and in view of his scorn for Denikin's selection of persons "from Liberal circles,"[18] he chose as his chief assistant for civil affairs a man from "the old school of statesmen" who would not be "one of those who were ready to throw in their lot with the Revolution," A. V. Krivoshein.[19] As a conservative and former tsarist minister, Krivoshein would know how to choose "good colleagues," Wrangel believed, but equally importantly he was an advocate of the kind of agrarian reform suitable to the situation. As one of the authors of the Stolypin land reform after the Revolution of 1905 and also the minister of agriculture from 1908 to 1915, Krivoshein knew the problem well.

Wrangel approached the problem of appointing representatives abroad in the same spirit. It was quite clear that the Russian Political Council in Paris would have to be eliminated because of its independence and its criticism, and Sazonov had proved to be incapable of the kind of initiative and influence now needed.[20] There was, however, a man most admirably suited to the job. He had a widespread reputation as one of the founders of the socialist movement in Russia. But he had also long since been converted to conservatism. He better than any other would command the attention of Western circles and create the image of liberality but at the same time enthusiastically devote this service to Wrangel's cause. He was P. B. Struve. Struve entered at once into the duties of Wrangel's chief assistant for foreign affairs and began the arduous task of obtaining support abroad.[21]

The character of this new regime was reflected in the basic features of its internal policy and its external image. Aside from future military campaigns, the two chief concerns of internal administration were relations with the Cossacks and the agrarian reform. With regard to the former Wrangel was determined to undo Denikin's compromises with Cossack "separatism." Technically he returned to the administrative policy of combining a single military command with internal autonomy for the Cossack territories, but since both the Cossack authorities and Wrangel's command were limited now to the Crimea, this had little meaning.[22] It had even less meaning in view of Wrangel's determination to see that the Cossack forces were "purged of traitors and cowards."[23]

When the commander of the Don corps, General Sidorin, and his chief of staff, General Kel'chevskii, allowed the corps newspaper to criticize Wrangel's policies and take a pessimistic tone toward continuing the war, Wrangel ordered them removed from their posts and tried for treason, along with the paper's editor, Count du Chaila. Although the defense argued that the accused had said no more than Wrangel himself concerning ending the war, Sidorin and Kel'chevskii were found guilty and sentenced to four years at hard labor. Wrangel himself reduced the sentence to dismissal from the service and prohibition from wearing the uniform of the Russian army. The paper's editor, whose trial was delayed because of his hospitalization after a suicide attempt, was acquitted. This affair, Wrangel noted, "put an end to the machinations of the Don Command, and the intriguing and lying of the dissatisfied generals ceased. . . ."[24]

The agrarian reform question presented, with a certain amount of contrast, the other side of internal policy. Wrangel was determined "to tear the enemy's principal weapon of propaganda from him, kindle the imagination of the Army and the populace, and make a favorable impression on foreign opinion," and land reform was considered the key to this.[25] The first drafts of the land and local-government laws were ready late in May, and the reform was inaugurated in June. In each district an agrarian assembly consisting of those holding land was to elect at least four persons to membership in a district agrarian soviet (a name chosen by Krivoshein for its propaganda value).[26] The remaining members of the soviet were to be specialists appointed by the central government, including a district "agrarian mediator" who would serve as chairman, the president of the district zemstvo, a justice of the peace, and a representative of the ministry of finance. This soviet was, according to Wrangel, to be given the "widest powers" to apply the reform, that is, to determine the size of plots to be allotted in accordance with local circumstances and to select the owners. The latter in turn were to be required to pay for their allotment (if they were new owners) by delivery of at least one-fifth of the crops to the government for 25 years. The decisions of the district soviet would, however, be subject to annulment by the provincial governors.[27]

While this system was declared "more advanced than any other in Western Europe" by Krivoshein, it did not do fully what was claimed. In particular, it did not simply legalize peasant seizures, and it did not put control over redistricting or local government in peasant hands. As Wrangel himself noted, those elected to the soviets included a rather large number of intellectuals, civil officers, and even "great landed proprietors." They in turn, when setting the size of holdings, allowed allotments to be as large as 1600 acres.[28] Moreover, when local government based upon the reorganized district administrations was subsequently introduced, the population showed "great moderation and common sense" by electing largely the "wealthier peasants" and big landowners.[29] Wrangel's land reform thus fell somewhat short of being revolutionary, but there is no doubt that it served a major propaganda purpose. Wrangel at least put a reform into effect and not just on paper, and that helped create a good impression in Western Europe. Krivoshein even called it the major factor in attracting support for Wrangel.[30] This failed to give proper credit to other elements influencing events, but one of the chief services of the land reform was duly noted.

*   *   *   *   *   *

Struve meanwhile used all such aids to the fullest in his efforts abroad. Two facets of policy were particularly notable: the repudiation of the "One-Russia" concept with respect to the border areas and the attempt to renew European support by way of economic concessions. "The future organization of Russia," he declared, "must be based on an agreement between the existing new separate entities. . . . They must unite into one great federation based on an arrangement to which they have all freely consented."[31] While Denikin had at the end accepted this view in principle and had applied it in the recognition of the Transcaucasian states, this statement indicated that Wrangel would apply it to all the new borderland governments, and he would not shun but openly espouse the idea of federation from below.

Again a better reputation abroad could be expected as a result of this change in policy, but little difference was noticeable in relations with particular governments in South Russia. Some trade with Georgia and the evacuation of prisoners (this time under the ruse of the use of force) continued, but no closer alliance developed than had been the case with Denikin. Wrangel did, however, undertake negotiations with the Ukrainians unprecedented during Denikin's term, but here as before the relationship was intimately tied up with relations with Poland and will be noted in that context below.

The question of aid was more important and more difficult. As previously noted, Wrangel believed that Russian natural resources should be used to attract foreign investment; Struve's telegram to Maklakov in April reiterated this point of "attaching vast significance to the correlation between Russian interests and the economic interests of the Allied Powers, especially France, in the economic resources of Russia. . . ."[32] This policy was a reversal of Denikin's position, but it was also an acknowledgment that this was the only method likely to obtain aid. At conferences between Struve and other Russian representatives in London and Paris, it was made clear that Allied funds were exhausted and simple credits were quite unlikely to be obtained.[33] The problem was to use long-range interests in such a way as to attract immediate assistance. Struve's task would obviously be a difficult one, but he prepared the ground very effectively.

To begin with, he inaugurated an expensive but invaluable propaganda campaign in the British and French press, using his socialist past and the image of liberal reforms and democratic local government to the limit of their credibility.[34] Russian funds were poured into Western newspapers, and frequent interviews and statements of the desired character were soon forthcoming.[35] Even more importantly, efforts were made to attract the highly useful services of certain strategically placed persons of known Russophile inclinations. In this capacity the assistance of the former French ambassador to Russia and currently secretary general of the Foreign Ministry, Maurice Paléologue, was to be outstanding. At the same time every prospect for a renewal of negotiations with the Allied and United States governments and the encouragement of their continued involvement was to be sounded out.[36] After all has been said, however, the events of the spring and summer months depended at least as much upon developments entirely beyond Wrangel's control as they did upon his own efforts. The situation was one in which circumstances changed with staggering rapidity.

Officially both Britain and France (where Clemenceau had been replaced by Millerand) anticipated an end to the war shortly, even if a certain amount of pessimism was apparent as to the prospects for obtaining desirable terms. Yet it was not long before this picture changed. As previously noted, the French government had indicated its dissatisfaction with the idea of negotiations with the Soviet government in the London conference of February and March 1920, and Millerand had not only urged renunciation of such negotiations, even those relating to trade, but also called for an Allied policy of aiding the border states, particularly Poland. There were thus "very serious differences of opinion" among the Allies, as Lloyd George observed, since Britain favored talks aimed at restoring trade with Russia and urged Allied pressure on the border states to make peace with Soviet Russia at once, while Italy even proposed entering full diplomatic and economic relations with Moscow. Lloyd George had been particularly disturbed to hear from Millerand that France had advised Poland against making peace with the Bolsheviks, and, for his part, he had categorically rejected the idea that Britain should encourage Poland to "continue war against Russia," part of whose territory it already occupied. At Lloyd George's suggestion a resolution had been adopted stating Allied opposition to continued hostilities with Soviet Russia and directly warning against "a policy of aggression towards Russia." Yet, as Lloyd George later observed, France had continued to encourage precisely such a policy by its opposition to efforts to bring peace.[37]

Whether or not the French attitude was to blame, Lloyd George's prediction of new conflict was soon fulfilled. A joint Polish-Ukrainian offensive into the Ukraine was launched at the time of the signing of a military alliance between Pilsudski and Petliura on April 24. Three days before they had formalized their earlier understanding in a treaty which recognized the right of the Ukraine to independence under Petliura's government and established the border at the Zbruch River, giving East Galicia and Volynia to Poland.[38] Simultaneously with these events, Maklakov received assurances in Paris that the French government was taking a negative view toward the British proposals, would oppose any pressure on Wrangel to surrender, and would in fact not participate in mediation efforts even if the British persisted.[39] On May 7, as he was preparing to leave Paris to take up his duties in the Crimea, Krivoshein wrote to Paléologue that he would like very much to carry with him the "assurances of the sympathy of the French Government for the continuation of the struggle against the Bolsheviks. . . ."[40] Paléologue responded the next day, on the official stationery of the Foreign Ministry, that he had taken up this request with Millerand and could state that the French government recognized the importance of Wrangel's position and would certainly support the defense of the Crimea against Bolshevik attack.[41]

It should be noted that this encouraging response, which Paléologue significantly urged be kept strictly confidential,[42] was still couched in defensive terms. It was not suggested yet that Wrangel should take the offensive against the Bolsheviks, but developments were clearly leading in that direction. Not only had efforts to develop the Polish-Soviet truce into a peace failed but also Pilsudski was now liberating a most important part of the South, a part which happened to be close by Wrangel's position. The day that Krivoshein requested a statement of support was the same day that Kiev was recaptured by Petliura, while the Poles occupied territory west of the Dnepr. In his request Krivoshein had notably added to his statement on the continuation of Wrangel's struggle the phrase "in coordination with that of Poland and all others able to take part in the battle."[43] French interest in this idea was made apparent by the fact that General Mangin, then with the French mission in Sevastopol, began making repeated inquiries about Wrangel's feeling on cooperation with the Poles and Ukrainians. Nor did Mangin restrict his questions simply to a general coordination of military operations. Indeed, he apparently wished to prepare for the most extensive collaboration, since he sought to raise all aspects of the question of mutual relations which might be encountered in the case of a unified command of all three forces involved.[44]

Trubetskoi, as acting foreign minister, informed General Mangin on May 30 that Wrangel did not wish to raise political questions which might be involved because he feared that, as in the past, they might interfere with what was primarily a practical and military problem at this stage. Wrangel was, however, very much interested in collaborating with the Polish offensive and was thus "quite disposed to cooperate with the Polish and Ukrainian forces." As proof of his desire, it was added, he would propose immediately that zones of operations be laid out, principally directing Polish efforts southward to the west of the Dnepr and assigning to his own forces the territory to the east of the Dnepr and as far north as Ekaterinoslav.[45] Mangin, Trubetskoi noted in a letter to Struve, was not satisfied with this cautious reply and continued to press for an even more extensive plan. Wrangel, for his part, hoped to leave the negotiations up to the French at this stage because of the difficulties of a direct approach to Pilsudski in view of the latter's anti-Russian statements and his position on Ukrainian independence.[46]

Wrangel was, indeed, preparing to move his forces northward into North Taurida in the direction of Melitopol, and he had intimated as much to the Allied governments, but he too wished to move cautiously. French inquiries as to his plans had been kept strictly secret, but the implication of a movement of troops could not be so concealed from the British. Trubetskoi thus informed Struve on May 27 that the anticipated operations could easily involve a clash with official Allied policy and therefore must be carefully prepared diplomatically. It was necessary for Struve to insist in the Western capitals that "the operation was undertaken for one goal, to secure a base for provisioning without which the A.F.S.R. and Crimean population would be doomed to starvation and ruin."[47] It was, of course, quite true that the territory north of the Crimea was necessary to the provisioning of a permanent base in the Crimea, barring massive outside aid, but the implications were clear.

The question was how would the British react to any such step? The answer was not so clearly a foregone conclusion as might be expected, at least not at first. British military authorities in Constantinople, as previously noted, had confidentially taken a dim view of the peace proposals from the start. They had in fact privately suggested that Wrangel would do well to undertake vigorous action as soon as possible—to put himself in a more favorable position to negotiate.[48] Although the latter context kept this suggestion technically within the official bounds of British policy, the attitude was hardly the same. There was thus an interesting divergence between British military representatives near the area of concern and British political leadership in London. General Percy, chief of the British mission in Sevastopol, made it quite clear that he favored continued support for Wrangel and a continuation of the struggle. While admitting that it was not his place to make policy, he simultaneously indicated that he was doing all he could to persuade his government that its policy was wrong.[49]

Even more notable was the attitude taken by General Milne when he arrived in Sevastopol for a visit on May 15. Milne professed to be most interested in Wrangel's work and complimented him highly on the reorganization of the army. In response to Milne's questions as to future operations, Wrangel confided his plans to move north to secure a more adequate base. The Russian Commander declined to disclose anything more at this point, but the British Commander not only appeared to understand this reticence but even expressed his full support. Noting that Wrangel would undoubtedly need supplies for future operations, Milne offered to do all he could to obtain what was needed. He issued orders immediately to facilitate the shipping of fuel from Batum.[50] Meanwhile the British high commissioner in Constantinople, Admiral John de Robeck, took a similarly encouraging stand. Wrangel's chief representative there, General Lukomskii, was told that British naval forces would facilitate and protect oil shipments, and Krivoshein reported after a personal talk with de Robeck that, despite the government's position, the Admiral "shares our views" and would do what he could to help. This, Struve was then advised, made it all the more necessary "to play for time" with the British government, using the sympathies of British military authorities and "the mood of the French" to the best advantage.[51]

Actually, however, Admiral de Robeck had been rather pessimistic about the possibility of a change in British policy, and his pessimism was a more accurate reflection of the real situation. On May 29 General Percy forwarded to Wrangel a new statement of official British policy. It instructed the British mission to have no further conversation with the Volunteer Command on the subject and stated categorically that Wrangel must not expect any change whatsoever in the British position. That position, the statement continued, was still based upon the determination to bring hostilities in South Russia to an end. The Soviet government, it concluded, had accepted in principle the proposals of peace negotiations and a general amnesty, and on this basis Lord Curzon urged that talks be initiated as soon as possible some place in South Russia. For this purpose he was sending a diplomatic representative who would arrive shortly.[52] On June 3 a second message was relayed to Wrangel stating that the British government was very much "disquieted by rumors of your intention to take the offensive against Bolshevik forces." It was therefore felt necessary to warn Wrangel that such an attack would undoubtedly destroy plans for peace negotiations, and in that case "His Majesty's Government will be unable to concern themselves any further with the fate of your army."[53]

It was under these circumstances that on June 5 Admiral de Robeck sent word that it would be impossible for British naval forces to take part in the planned offensive, but it was also characteristic of de Robeck that he added that he still had authorization to assist in the defense of the Crimea against a Bolshevik attack![54] It was likewise in keeping with General Percy's views that he informed his government that he would not participate in any talks with the Bolsheviks. He also argued that Wrangel's plan to enlarge his base was impossible to change, but the reply of the British government was to order his recall.[55] All but a small skeleton staff of the British mission was, in fact, withdrawn in June, and orders were dispatched to Admiral de Robeck to suspend all military shipments destined for the Crimea, whether under British flag or in Russian ships.[56]

In response to such actions by the British, Wrangel on June 5 sent off a long note to London. In it he stated categorically that he would continue to refuse to negotiate directly with the Bolsheviks. The British had taken that task upon themselves, and it would be for them to carry it out. However, he added, his plan to move into Taurida did not necessarily contradict British efforts as they seemed to claim. Such a move was not only necessary to hold the Crimean base until negotiations could be completed, he argued, but would also favor those negotiations by prodding the Soviet government into a positive response. A successful outcome to the campaign would in fact "greatly facilitate the task of the British government in its talks with the Soviets." Moreover, he declared, the Bolshevik record made it essential to obtain real guarantees that any negotiated agreement would actually be carried out in practice. Until such guarantees were explicitly assured, he hoped that the British government would not refuse that assistance which it had promised and which was "so precious" to him.[57] In any case, Wrangel noted, the order to advance had been issued the day before the receipt of the message of June 3, and it was too late to stop it now.

Actually Wrangel's offensive did not begin until June 7, but he was clearly hedging to avoid an open break with the British.[58] On June 8 Struve wired that he had met at length with Millerand, and the French Premier, while reaffirming French support, urged that Wrangel not alienate the British if at all possible. The tack recommended was that Wrangel patiently receive British proposals as friendly advice and at all times adhere publicly to the view that negotiations with the Bolsheviks to end the war were desirable. If this were done, said Millerand, the question would be kept open, and

Wrangel could legitimately make counterproposals. He could certainly refuse outright capitulation, even on the basis of amnesty, for example, and could even put as a condition to future negotiations the clearing of the Cossack and Transcaucasian territories and guarantees of the inviolability of the Crimea. If Wrangel remained tactfully firm and indicated full readiness to cooperate with the Poles, Millerand told Struve, France would do its part.[59]

Struve was assured of Wrangel's cooperation along this line and urged to do all possible to encourage French initiative with the British.[60] Meanwhile, Wrangel wrote again to the British to indicate that he sought their views so as to plan his actions accordingly in the future, and also to remark that now the Bolsheviks had opened an offensive against him, thus revealing their duplicity. His own offensive had barely managed to anticipate the Bolsheviks' move to seize the initiative by only two days![61] Moreover, in keeping with his previous justifications, Wrangel halted his military advance on June 17 after having secured northern Taurida and the base he claimed necessary. What was not yet announced was his intention of preparing now a new advance into the Kuban with the hope of liberating the Cossack territories from which only shortly before the British had helped him evacuate remaining anti-Bolshevik troops. Meanwhile, however, the questions of inter-Allied relations and of relations with Poland were to become rather suddenly more critical.

*   *   *   *   *   *

During June 1920 the military situation took a decided turn for the worse. Despite Wrangel's operations, the Bolsheviks were able to hold the front against him and at the same time begin a new offensive against the Polish-Ukrainian front. By June 11 Kiev had been lost, and Petliura's government was once more displaced. But, worse still for the anti-Bolshevik camp, the Red Army managed to rally patriotic support against the foreign invaders to such an extent that Poland itself was soon threatened.[62] By mid-July it did indeed look as though the previous hopes for new opportunities to defeat the Bolsheviks would be reversed by a possible Bolshevik conquest of both Russia and its biggest neighbor to the west. It was this ominous situation which instigated a flurry of activity on all sides during July and August.

Both France and Britain were, of course, deeply concerned with what was happening, the British because of their initiative in efforts to conclude peace and the French because of their great concern for

Poland. The differences between the two powers, however, more than ever threatened to erupt into the open. As Struve reported, Lloyd George had categorically denounced Wrangel's Taurida campaign and had assured Moscow that Britain in no way supported it.[63] Moreover, Lloyd George was more insistent than ever on peace, including Poland, and was continuing trade talks, putting the French in an awkward position. After a brief conference between the two premiers in Boulogne, a communique had been issued favoring economic talks and peace but not recognition, and on June 24 Millerand had explicitly declared that he did not intend to recognize any Russian government which did not recognize its international obligations.[64]

On July 5 a twelve-day conference between the two Allied governments was opened in Spa to discuss the problems involved and particularly to coordinate policy in the Polish question. Here the Polish prime minister, Grabski, confessed that Poland had been misled "by strong men who had great visions" which, unfortunately, neither corresponded to commonsense nor the desires of the people. "M. Pilsudski," he stated, "now acknowledged his mistake," but Poland was in desperate need of help to survive. Lloyd George "thought that it might be possible to do something if the independence of Poland were assailed, but nothing could be done unless Poland abandoned in deed, as well as in words, its imperialist and annexationist policy." The Polish prime minister was told bluntly that Poland would have to accept the Curzon line and seek a renewal of peace talks with Moscow; only under these conditions, said Lloyd George, could any support be given, but if Poland did comply and Soviet troops crossed the Curzon line the Allies, including Britain, would defend Poland's independence.[65]

Under this pressure Grabski signed an agreement "to initiate and sign an immediate armistice on the basis that the Polish army retires to and stands on the line fixed by the Peace Conference on the 8th December, 1919, as the provisional boundary of Polish administration, and that the Soviet armies halt 50 kilom[eters]. to the east of this line," to send representatives to a peace conference to be held in London, and to accept the decision of the Allied Supreme Council on "the future of Eastern Galicia" and other territorial questions. Despite Millerand's objections and refusal to join in the British demarche, the Spa conference then concluded its consideration of this question with a call to the Soviet government on July 11 to cease military operations and accept an invitation to the proposed peace conference.[66] If this were done, Lloyd George indicated, obstacles to the establishment of normal relations between Britain and the Soviet government could be removed. Shortly after the conclusion of the conference, Curzon reiterated the point that the demand for an armistice applied to both sides.[67]

This conference had brought the Allies no closer to agreement. Millerand stood by his refusal to enter official relations with the Bolshevik government unless it accepted all previous obligations of Russian governments, and Lloyd George went ahead with his plans for a peace conference. As Struve noted in his report from Spa on July 17, Lloyd George's proposals to the Bolsheviks also included a truce on the southern front on the basis of Wrangel's withdrawal to the Crimea proper and the establishment of a neutral zone on the Perekop peninsula. This would be followed by an invitation to Wrangel to attend or send an observer to the peace conference but apparently not to participate in it as a full partner. When Millerand was consulted on this point, he advised that Wrangel should refuse to accept these terms and demand full representation and the preservation of territory now held.[68] Struve was then instructed to present this position in Wrangel's name to the Allied governments, stating that withdrawal behind the Perekop isthmus would be tantamount to condemning the Army and the population to death by starvation and noting that justice demanded not only fair treatment for Wrangel's government but also at least the opportunity for the peoples of the territory it was called upon to evacuate to decide their own fate by plebescite.[69]

Meanwhile, the Bolsheviks themselves provided one of the greatest aids to blocking British efforts. Chicherin's reply to Lloyd George's most recent effort did not reject peace but did question Britain's right to pose as an objective mediator. Branding Wrangel as a British puppet, the Soviet note of July 17 offered only amnesty in return for capitulation in his case and declared that Moscow could handle its own relations with Poland.[70] On July 20 Curzon warned the Bolsheviks that if Red troops crossed the Curzon line, Britain would be compelled to aid Poland, and on July 22 Poland proposed an immediate cessation of hostilities, but Soviet troops continued their drive toward Warsaw.[71]

An Allied commission including both British and French representatives soon thereafter arrived in Warsaw to investigate the situation. They found the newly formed Polish cabinet headed by Witos now prepared to end the war, but the Bolsheviks were less likely than at any other time to accept any terms which would be offered. The Bolsheviks were in fact so elated by their victories that they were eagerly awaiting the establishment of a Communist government in Warsaw and therefore would not be deterred by peace offers.[72] Millerand responded to this situation by authorizing General Weygand, a member of the Allied commission, to put his services at the disposal of the Polish government to help organize its resistance.[73] Moreover, on July 20 Millerand had spoken to Parliament in highly favorable terms with regard to Wrangel's government, calling it a "real de facto Government" with the sympathy of the people and a program of agrarian reform and plans for a "popular representative Assembly" to establish a democratic government in the Crimea.[74]

This same day Millerand had sent for Struve and informed him confidentially that he had decided to recognize Wrangel's government. Before this could be announced, however, it was necessary for Wrangel to issue a statement confirming certain points. These were (1) recognition of that portion of all debt obligations of previous Russian governments corresponding to the territory held, (2) approval of the division of the land among the peasants with ownership rights, and (3) announcement of plans to convoke a popularly elected assembly as the basis of a democratic government. In addition to these, of course, the statement should, Millerand indicated, include an appeal for de facto recognition. Struve immediately recommended not only full acceptance of these terms but the recognition of the entire Russian debt since "we consider ourselves the bearers of the national idea and representatives of the Russian State."[75] A few days later Wrangel replied as recommended. Pointing out the agrarian reforms and the governmental reorganization in his answer, appropriately exaggerating their content, he added that it was his aim "to make it possible for the people to voice their opinion freely on essential problems of the form of government to be established as soon as circumstances permit."[76]

Millerand withheld official recognition for the time being, but at the Anglo-French conference in Boulogne on July 27 to 28 he frankly expressed his disapproval of British policy and indicated that he did not wish to see a peace conference with the Soviet government at this time.[77] Although once again the British initiative for peace was renewed, French policy took a decided turn in favor of aid to Wrangel. French ships in the Black Sea had already been alerted to stand by to defend the Crimea, and, in response to Wrangel's proposal to mine coastal waters to prevent supplies reaching the Bolsheviks through the Black Sea, French Admiral de Bon now indicated that this would not be necessary since he had orders to prohibit any maritime commerce whatsoever with Soviet ports.[78] Somewhat more indirectly, the French undertook to enable Wrangel's mission in Constantinople to bypass secretly a ruling against it by the Allied commissions on the matter of a radio station.

Negotiations had been under way for several months to obtain Allied permission to establish a radio communications center at the site of the Russian Embassy at Buiuk Dere, but they had been stalled by British opposition. However, Wrangel's representative, Captain Shcherbachev, was enabled to bypass the British veto by a confidential arrangement with Admiral de Bon. The latter agreed that if after one more appeal the British still said No, the station could be built and operated under the guise of a French station. Thus, although on August 7 a final British rejection of the project was issued through Admiral de Robeck, Wrangel's representative was able to inform him a few days later that the station would soon be in operation.[79]

Even more importantly, the French intervened during July and August in the hitherto frustrated efforts to obtain more of the Russian military supplies in Rumania. Wrangel had tried unsuccessfully to get the Rumanian government to cooperate, but it declined such relations on grounds of its neutrality.[80] He had then urged the French to intercede on his behalf in Bucharest, and this too had failed to bring much of a response in the past. Then on July 12 the Foreign Ministry gave its official sanction to the Ministry of War to undertake steps to obtain the supplies sought by Wrangel.[81] From that moment French representatives in Bucharest took the initiative and quickly obtained a change. It was noted that the Rumanian government was especially concerned not to arouse Moscow and that consequently precautions would have to be taken.[82] Therefore, during August, Marshal Joffre paid a call on Rumanian Prime Minister Averescu, and together with the French Minister in Bucharest, they worked out a plan by which Rumania would turn over the materials in question to France, supposedly in payment for past French aid. The French in turn would make the necessary arrangements to have them delivered to Wrangel without compromising the neutrality of the Rumanian government.[83] The actual execution of these plans took a good deal of time, and the Rumanian government never cooperated fully, but the small shipments finally obtained were significant developments in Wrangel's desperate drive for outside aid.[84]

None of these steps, however, quite got to the heart of the matter, and more direct French action was delayed until the Allied conference at Hythe on August 8 to 9. This conference came at the most crucial time of the Polish war, and this was the question uppermost on the agenda. Just prior to the conference, in talks with the Soviet trade delegation in London headed by Kamenev and Krasin on August 4 and 6, Lloyd George had revealed his irritation with the continuing Soviet advance into Poland and threatened to issue orders to the British fleet to sail to the Baltic in three days to resume the blockade unless Moscow halted its forces and presented reasonable terms for peace which could be accepted by Poland. Armed with what he believed to be Kamenev's agreement to comply, Lloyd George then entered the Hythe conference with the aim of persuading Millerand to join in bringing the war to a close.[85]

Declaring that Pilsudski had betrayed his own people and was an enemy of the Allies and that, because of their aggressive policies, the Poles were now hated by everyone except the French, Lloyd George argued that there was no acceptable policy other than pressure on Poland to accept the reasonable terms which he expected to receive momentarily from the Soviet government. In direct opposition to this view, Millerand again denounced negotiations with the Soviet government as both unacceptable and "quite futile," since the Bolsheviks could not be trusted to keep any promises which they might make. In his opinion, "all that remained for them to consider was the way in which that Government could be fought." While he might be willing "to sacrifice Pilsudski" to appease Lloyd George, he believed that the main task now was to rally resistance against the Bolsheviks by promising aid to the border states and encouraging all of them to ally against Soviet Russia.[86]

No final resolution of this debate was possible until a definite reply on Soviet terms was received, and the conference ended with only a tentative agreement on policy. Lloyd George conceded that if a truce had not been obtained by August 15 because of Soviet obstinacy, he would expel the trade delegation and give support to Poland, to the other border states (including the Ukraine and Transcaucasia if they should rebel), and even to Wrangel; but the first aim was still peace and he would not take any such action until he had exhausted every possibility of attaining it. Consequently it was decided to repeat the peace offers and obtain a clarification of Soviet terms. If the latter were acceptable, Poland would be advised to accept; but if they infringed on Poland's independence, it was agreed that the Allies would continue to aid Poland.[87]

The position to be accorded to Wrangel was still left rather obscure, although it was decided at Hythe to re-establish an Allied naval mission at his headquarters and to prepare plans to use his forces if Bolshevik action against Poland could not be stopped. Paléologue had assured Wrangel's representatives that Millerand would do everything possible to persuade Lloyd George not to display "excessive submissiveness" toward the Bolsheviks. In any case, he said, France would insist upon the participation of Wrangel's representatives in any peace conference and would retain freedom of action for itself. Lloyd George had agreed to restate the proposal to Moscow in terms which would require not only a preliminary truce but also participation in a peace conference by all interested parties before the establishment of normal relations with Moscow would be considered, but, it was noted, the British still seemed prepared to accept the stated Soviet terms for Wrangel's army, that is, amnesty for surrender.[88]

The slight variation in British policy which occurred at this time really modified Lloyd George's stand only with regard to Poland, and that only temporarily. He backed efforts to send aid to Poland through Danzig and ordered British ships and troops in the area to assist,[89] but at the same time he believed, on the basis of tentative Soviet responses made through the trade delegation, that Moscow now really wanted peace and would accept reasonable terms.[90] Millerand, by contrast, denied that Soviet peace offers were adequate or that the Soviet regime could be dealt with as the legitimate government. This different interpretation of the situation made the agreement of August meaningless, but it also put the French government back in the situation it had hoped to avoid, that is, confronting an open divergence of policy with the British. As Struve had reported earlier, this situation would very likely have a grave influence on open French support, although concealed or indirect aid might be expected in any case.[91] And, as Trubetskoi had pointed out, Wrangel's offer to undertake diversionary action to draw the Red forces away from Poland would depend upon receipt of aid.[92]

Fortunately for those who faced this dilemma, an unexpected boost was received at the decisive moment. On August 10 United States Secretary of State Colby released a note to the Italian ambassador setting forth the American position on the Russian-Polish question. In this note Colby reasserted American support for a strong and free Poland and for the preservation of Russian unity, with the exception of Armenia, Finland, and Poland. More importantly, the Secretary of State took issue with the view held "in some quarters" that the Russian and Polish questions could be properly resolved by a general peace conference or by dealing with the Soviet government. Such proposals, he declared, inevitably leaned toward dismemberment of Russia and the recognition of the Bolshevik regime, "from both of which this country strongly recoils." The United States thus opposed efforts to obtain peace at the expense of "true" Russian interests, which could not be properly protected "while it [Russia] is helpless in the grip of a nonrepresentative government, whose only sanction is brutal force. . . ." The Bolshevik government, said Colby, "is based upon the negation of every principle of honor and good faith, and every usage and convention underlying the whole structure of international law, the negation, in short, of every principle upon which it is possible to base harmonious and trustful relations. . . ." No faith could be placed in Bolshevik pledges or agreements, he concluded, and therefore the United States would not support pressures to bring about their acceptance.[93]

The French government saw the opportunity immediately and expressed its deep gratitude to the Secretary of State for stating the French position so well.[94] As the Russian envoy, Girs, wired to Struve, the American declaration led France "out of a difficult position of isolation" and provided "moral support for its anti-Bolshevik policy, thus blocking the obstinate inclinations of Lloyd George to reach agreement with the Soviets."[95] The same day that Colby's note appeared, Millerand (to the perplexity of the British) informed Wrangel that he was announcing de facto recognition publicly and informed the United States that this step was being taken in the "spirit" of their common policy toward the Russian question.[96] Millerand had just the day before, on August 9, confidentially informed Marshal Foch that he could begin at once taking steps to supply Wrangel with everything "necessary for him to take the offensive." Although British policy called for an end to the flow of material to South Russia, he added, Wrangel's case acquired "particular urgency" at this time.[97] Foch in turn informed Wrangel's military representative in Paris, General Miller, that he should henceforth keep him informed "day by day" of the exact needs of Wrangel's army.[98]

An equally important boost to French policy came, coincidentally also on August 10, in the form of the Soviet government's statement of terms to be presented to Poland. These terms—including a limit of 50,000 men on Polish armed forces, the establishment of a strictly proletarian militia, the dismantling of the arms industry, and an end to all outside aid—were deemed totally unacceptable by Lloyd George, who as promised subsequently expelled Kamenev (whom he accused of duplicity in this matter) and suspended the trade talks. Soviet-British relations were, indeed, brought to a new low by the discovery that an antigovernment newspaper in London was receiving a Soviet subsidy.[99] None of this, however, meant that Britain had "now accepted the views of the French Government," as the French commissioner in Bulgaria reportedly declared,[100] nor did it mean that massive French aid was on its way to Wrangel. What did happen was that Soviet forces opened a new attack, and military action was renewed both in Poland and in South Russia. This time, however, the tide of battle quickly turned against the Bolsheviks, who badly mishandled their operations. The Poles were soon recovering the lost territories west of the Curzon line and even threatening Bolshevik control eastward from there.

Wrangel, for his part, had already laid plans for a move into the Kuban and, despite the fact that this would probably have been the best time to move north into the Ukraine instead of east, he launched his Kuban campaign on August 11. His action undoubtedly aided in the general struggle, but the campaign in itself was a rather pathetic failure. Before August was over he had been forced to withdraw the expedition to the Crimea, although more troops returned than had gone over. Wrangel covered his failure, however, by declaring that he hoped to achieve more direct coordination with the Poles and therefore decided to shift his forces to the west for strategic reasons. Moreover, there were reports that Poland could be expected to sign a truce with the Bolsheviks soon. Any effort to head off that possibility would be worth trying, since it would spell the doom of the Crimea.[101]

French assistance would be essential in these questions, both in the matter of supplies to keep Wrangel's army going and in the matter of Polish policy with regard to entering a truce or continuing the war. Wrangel knew this, and he was willing to take radical action to achieve that support. On September 1 he sent the following urgent statement to the French mission and to Paris:

General Wrangel wishes to submit to the French Government and High Command the following observation on the general military situation:

Poland's great success in her fight against the Red Army makes it possible, for the first time since the beginning of this war, to strike a decisive blow at Soviet power and to assure general tranquility and social peace by means of concerted action by the Polish and Russian Armies under the supreme direction of the French High Command. Conclusion of a separate peace between the Poles and the Bolsheviks would leave the question unresolved and the Bolshevik danger unchecked.

For these reasons the Commander-in-Chief places before the French Government and High Command the question of the creation of a common and connected front in cooperation with the Poles against the Bolsheviks and under the leadership of the French High Command. . . .

If the Poles begin active operations on their right flank in the Ukraine, while our efforts are concentrated on our left flank, a common united front can be developed with the aim of finally destroying Soviet power and restoring tranquility to Europe on the basis of a general peace.

The Commander-in-Chief urgently requests a speedy reply.[102]

Struve followed up this appeal by a reminder of the necessity of supplies and an offer of Wrangel to go to Paris personally if this should be considered necessary for the coordination of action.[103] The latter, Foch replied, would be unnecessary, but he was doing all he could to facilitate Wrangel's requests. There were, he noted, several difficulties which slowed down action, especially the strong pressures in Poland to end the war now and the obstacles to an effective supply program. He therefore advocated not rushing into an offensive before it could be adequately organized.[104] Foch's comments were revealing, for in fact the general picture, which should have been brightest now, was clouded by many uncertainties. The long appeals and negotiations for aid, for example, had resulted only in the proposal by the French of an exchange treaty, the terms of which illustrated the weaknesses rather than the strengths of Wrangel's position. French aid was to be had only for payment; the offer, in short, was the same type made to Denikin earlier. The difference was that Wrangel was willing to negotiate seriously on the concessions necessary.

According to the text of a proposed treaty, which was published in the British press on August 30,[105] in return for assurances of the

French government in facilitating exchange of goods, Wrangel would have to agree (1) to recognize all financial obligations of Russia to France and establish a priority of payment for the latter, (2) to accept a conversion of the Russian debt into a single loan payable at 6½ per cent interest over a period of 35 years, and (3) to guarantee the payment of the loan and interest by conceding to France (a) the right to exploit all railroads in European Russia, (b) control over customs and duties in ports on the Black and Azov seas, (c) disposal of all exportable grain obtained in the Ukraine and the Kuban, and (d) rights to three-fourths of oil and benzine production, and to one-fourth of the coal output, of the Donetz basin. In addition, it was stipulated in this text that French agents would be incorporated into the ministries of Finance, Trade, and Industry, with their functions and powers to be established in a separate agreement. The span of years to be set for each of the concessions noted was also to be determined by special agreements. However, it was stated that the alliance upon which the agreement was based would be a 20-year pact.

The evidence as to negotiations on such a text is quite obscure, however, and there is no clear indication that this text was signed in August as alleged by those who made it public. There is evidence, however, that its terms were at least approximately those asked by France, in return for which an extension of 100 million francs on the debt would be granted.[106] A similar agreement was mentioned in October by Maklakov as being the proposal of the French government. In this text the demand was for one-half of all wheat, coal, wool, tobacco, hides, and cotton seed oil exported from Russia as guarantee on the debt. Here it was specified, moreover, that the new credit would have to be repaid by the end of 1921. As Maklakov viewed this proposal, it asked an exorbitant price for "less than one-tenth of the materials requested by us." The rest would have to be paid for in cash. Maklakov recommended at least holding out for a two-year term on the loan and a reduction of the export concession to one-third instead of one-half.[107]

If, indeed, this was the status of aid negotiations as late as mid-October, the situation was virtually hopeless, regardless of whether or not such an agreement were eventually signed. Some aid had been sent apparently, since Maklakov indicated that 40 million of the proposed new loan would be absorbed by supplies already shipped, but such a figure represented a mere drop in the proverbial bucket.[108] Wrangel had attempted to prepare the ground for a trade agreement by establishing a governmental monopoly on grain, and Krivoshein convoked a financial and economic conference on this problem in October. Together they worked out private contracts with individual firms to export some 10 million poods of grain, but even this was proceeding rather slowly.[109] As late as the end of October Struve wired from Paris that he still had hopes of getting a loan,[110] but when these negotiations were completed, the situation in South Russia had completely changed.

All of this in effect meant that Wrangel's one real hope lay in an alliance with the Poles (and Ukrainians), and for this he would have at least the moral support of the French. The prospects for such an alliance, however, dimmed rapidly with the passage of time. Wrangel had designated his chief of staff, General Makhrov, as special envoy to Poland as early as June, but his departure was delayed and the trip to Warsaw had taken a devious and time-consuming route through Belgrade and Vienna. Makhrov thus did not arrive in Warsaw until mid-September. Even then he had authorization to negotiate only with the Poles and solely on military cooperation.[111] Moreover, he found the situation there quite complicated, not only because of the Polish situation itself but also because of the division of Russian leadership inside Poland, where there were several thousand Russian troops, numerous organizations, and a number of political and military factions contending with each other.[112] One unit of Russian troops, the 10,000-man Bredov corps, had been returned to the Crimea through Rumania after long and difficult negotiations by Cheriachukin, but others still remained on Polish soil.[113]

The leading political figure among Russians in Poland was none other than Boris Savinkov. Having served with both Alekseev and Kolchak in the early days of the war, and, of course, having raised rebellions of his own, Savinkov had subsequently gone abroad, as previously noted, to work with the Russian Political Council in Paris. There he had struck up many eminent acquaintances, but he had soon grown restless in this diplomatic role. Now he was in Poland to head a Russian committee which sought to give political leadership to the diverse military groups there. It was apparent to Makhrov from the start of his mission in Warsaw that he would have to work with Savinkov, since he alone—and to a remarkable degree—had the full confidence of Pilsudski and had obtained extensive financial backing from Polish sources.[114] In fact he had a secret agreement with the Polish High Command that all Russian forces in Poland were to be subordinated to his political leadership and would receive funds on the basis of additions to the Russian state debt.[115]

This posed complications, but at the same time Savinkov indicated a willingness to cooperate, and both Pilsudski and Foreign Minister Sapieha assured Makhrov that they were doing everything possible to prolong the recently resumed negotiations with the Bolsheviks, despite British pressures.[116] More specifically, the Polish chief of staff, General Razwidowski, informed Wrangel's envoy fully on the military situation and declared that even if Poland were forced to conclude a truce, there was still time to organize Russian troops in Poland as an independent force which would not be bound by the truce.[117]

These initial assurances of Polish support were encouraging, but they did not yet solve the problem. There were many details to resolve, both with regard to organizing Russian troops and with regard to certain questions concerning relations with Poland. Pilsudski frankly told Makhrov that he detested both tsarist Russia and the Russia of Kolchak and Denikin, but he would, he said, happily work with "a third Russia, a democratic Russia." If Wrangel represented this Russia, they could fight side by side, "in full confidence in one another." Savinkov, he added, did represent the Russia of which he spoke.[118] Makhrov must have had some doubts about the compatibility of Pilsudski and Wrangel, or even of Savinkov and Wrangel, but he did not express them. In subsequent interviews with Savinkov and commanders of the various Russian units, however, he found their outward willingness to accept Wrangel's leadership qualified by certain reservations.[119] One of the most important of these was a noticeable disinclination to accept transfer to the Crimea. There was a definite desire among the Russian officers involved to remain in Poland or at least to operate from it into Belorussia rather than going south.[120] Moreover, it would clearly be difficult to find military leadership in Poland acceptable to all the groups in question.[121]

The issue of transferring the troops in Poland was also complicated by the fact that they were almost entirely equipped and supplied with Polish money, and there were no funds at all to supply their needs once they left Poland. Added to this, of course, were the other problems of organizing them and obtaining their cooperation in a doubtful venture which would remove them from the sanctuary hitherto enjoyed.[122] Makhrov recommended that Wrangel help resolve these problems, and still obtain the available assistance, by appointing a special commander for troops in Poland acceptable to the Polish

Command, approving the committee of Savinkov as their political representative, and dropping his insistence upon the transfer of troops to Crimea, leaving them the opportunity to operate in whatever area was most favorable.[123]

Wrangel agreed to these recommendations generally and, with the blessing of the Polish representative in Sevastapol, on October 16 authorized the formation of a "Third Russian Army" in Poland. The condition stated was that it would be placed on the right flank of the Polish-Ukrainian front so that when the two fronts were joined, this army could be transferred to his command. Meanwhile it was to be placed under the command of someone appointed by himself, providing an acceptable candidate was found.[124] Finding such a man, however, proved difficult. General Kirei, recommended by Makhrov, was rejected by Wrangel, presumably because of his Ukrainian origin and past hostility toward both Wrangel and his assistant, General Shatilov. General Miller, the military representative in Paris, was rejected by the Polish Command; and General Boboshko, the leading commander of forces in Poland, was rejected by Savinkov. Finally, a fourth mention, General Palen, was considered unsuited by Makhrov. After much trouble and a waste of valuable time Makhrov finally settled upon a young officer, General Permykin, and designated him as commander, pending Wrangel's confirmation.[125]

Subsequent to this action Makhrov was virtually left on his own as a result of the extreme difficulties of communicating with the Crimea. Messages had frequently to go by way of Paris and often took several weeks to reach their destination, if indeed they arrived at all.[126] This situation resulted in a good deal of confusion and a great lack of coordination in days when every hour was precious. The Polish-Soviet negotiations, resumed in September in Riga, were less than a month from conclusion even when Makhrov began his work. The days available to him were therefore of necessity filled with desperate efforts to fulfill his mission. And one of the most difficult questions had still not been answered, that is, that of relations with the Ukrainians.

Makhrov believed that circumstances would make possible a union between the 20,000 Russian troops in Poland and the approximately 15,000 men whom Petliura commanded. Savinkov apparently favored this, and Pilsudski's willingness to negotiate with Wrangel indicated that he would not likely oppose it, especially in view of his earlier disappointment with Ukrainian strength. To avoid isolation, Petliura might himself accept a compromise arrangement.[127] Makhrov therefore recommended establishing contacts, which he could easily do, and negotiating an alliance. According to his account, Wrangel did in fact authorize such contacts, a circumstance confirming Makhrov's impression that this was the policy favored.[128] However, Wrangel had meanwhile entertained several other Ukrainian delegations in the Crimea.

During August a group of independent Ukrainian military leaders conferred with Wrangel's government in Sevastopol and was granted arms and money for operations in the Ukraine.[129] Later a delegation under Markotun of the Ukrainian National Committee, which was established in Paris in January 1920 after splitting with Petliura over the latter's submission to Polish leadership, visited Sevastopol and was accorded a grand reception by Wrangel. He "made a point of showing the greatest attention to the delegation" and expressed his "complete agreement with its principles."[130]

These delegations in effect brought virtually every Ukrainian group into contact with Wrangel, who had earlier even tried unsuccessfully to attract Makhno.[131] Even Petliura's close associate and commander of the main Ukrainian force, General Pavlenko, visited the Crimea at the same time as the Markotun delegation, which in keeping with its earlier disagreement with Petliura denounced "separatism" and proposed to cooperate with Wrangel on the basis of unity with Russia.[132]

Wrangel's earlier declarations of his willingness to unite with the border states in a free federation were thus tested by his position now toward the Ukraine. What he offered, and what the Ukrainians were willing to accept according to him, was support for "autonomous national units on the same lines as those adopted in my agreement with the Cossacks."[133] It was thus on this basis that negotiations were continued into October with the combined Pavlenko and Markotun groups. Apparently only a lack of time precluded the elaborate development proposed at the time, such as the establishment of a Ukrainian political center in the Crimea.[134] However, it appears that these negotiations were not coordinated with Makhrov's efforts in Warsaw.

Even while Makhrov was struggling with such problems virtually on the eve of the truce, he received word from General Miller in Paris that an urgent conference was being called there of representatives of Poland, Wrangel, and France to establish a council under Foch's staff to coordinate operations against the Bolsheviks.[135] Since he had already made contacts with Petliura's chief of staff and had obtained agreement for cooperation, and since the French mission chief in Warsaw, General Niessel, urged formal conclusion of an agreement as rapidly as possible, Makhrov thought he might resolve this and the question of a political agreement with Poland by attending the meeting in Paris.[136] Just before he left, however, another crucial factor was raised. Pilsudski called him in on October 13 and confided that the truce with Soviet Russia had been signed the day before, giving him less than a week, according to Pilsudski, to do whatever he could before it would come into effect on October 18. If Russian troops were not out of the country by then, the terms of the truce would require that they be disarmed and interned.[137] Everything had to be done in six days!

That same day Makhrov met with Savinkov, who advised him that no time was left to await Wrangel's orders. Makhrov agreed that the troops had to be started toward the Ukrainian border at once, and Savinkov indicated that he would continue work toward some kind of agreement with Petliura. General Bulak-Balakhovich refused to accept this plan but was given to understand that the Poles would allow his partisan forces to remain on the border of Belorussia as a safeguard against a possible resumption of the war.[138] The Polish chief of staff, Razwidowski, offered to protect the movement of the Russian and Ukrainian troops until October 18, and even suggested that Makhrov still seek a political agreement before the truce went into effect.[139]

Having done all he could to meet this deadline, and still having no further word from Wrangel, Makhrov then left for Paris on October 22. There he found, to his chagrin, that the plan mentioned by Miller had fallen apart and that no one had an alternative. Wrangel's representatives in Paris, including Struve, appeared now to regard broader political and economic questions as more important than the immediate military question and therefore declined to act with the haste urged by Makhrov.[140] At Makhrov's insistence, however, he received Struve's authorization to proceed with negotiations with representatives of Petliura in Poland. Meanwhile separate negotiations with the Ukrainian delegation in the Crimea were apparently continued.

Upon his hurried return to Warsaw, Makhrov immediately contacted Ukrainian representatives there and began working out an agreement. The "Third Russian Army" had already moved into the border area with some 6000 men, putting themselves in a "reserve"

position behind Ukrainian troops numbering about 10,000 men who
were facing the Red Army. In this position the Ukrainians under
General Pavlenko took the offensive in mid-November but were
almost immediately routed, while the Russian forces were simultaneously drawn into the struggle out of necessity.[141] The two armies had
in fact already concluded their own temporary working agreement in
the field, and Makhrov himself apparently found it impossible to
achieve any more than this.

Later in the month Makhrov received word from Struve that an
agreement had been reached with the Ukrainians which would grant
recognition to them in return for the establishment of a single high
command under Wrangel and future cooperation toward unity, an
arrangement which Petliura was expected to accept, but this development made little difference now.[142] Even while these somewhat
unreal negotiations were taking place, Wrangel was making his last
effort to renew the struggle. Just before the Poles had signed the truce
with the Bolsheviks, he had launched a new offensive across the
Dnepr to the west. For several days it looked as though this effort
might succeed, but Soviet forces, then relieved of the danger of a
Polish attack by the truce, were massed for a counterattack, and by
mid-October Wrangel's army was in full retreat.

* * * * * *

The logical conclusion to be drawn from this situation was not
accepted immediately, although ultimately it would have to be. Even
after news of the Polish truce had arrived in Sevastopol, the Polish
diplomatic representative in the Crimea was still stating flatly that
Poland did not want a truce and indeed was still seeking an alliance
with General Wrangel.[143] Moreover, Wrangel was informed that a
special French mission was even now en route to the Crimea for
further negotiations, leading him to believe that France might still
induce the Poles to delay peace and themselves provide aid to enable
the army to continue.[144] On October 9 Admiral de Bon conveyed his
assurances that he was continuing to do all possible to assist in the
struggle and still believed new advances could be made.[145] On October 22 Struve reported from Paris that he had been received by Millerand and had presented new proposals on aid; he felt that there was
much hope for success, especially on the matter of a loan.[146]

The French mission headed by Count de Martel had arrived in the
Crimea on October 19 and had been greeted with pomp and ceremony. The following day conferences were held between Wrangel and

his assistants and the French representatives, including Martel, Admiral de Bon, and General Brousseau. Martel announced that he was accredited to Wrangel's government as French "High Commissioner" and had come to solidify their "alliance." He congratulated Wrangel on the establishment of a "democratic Government" and promised "full moral support and as much material help as possible."[147] However, while these remarks were being made, Red forces were pushing their way toward the passes into the Crimea, and Wrangel shortly began disguised negotiations to have everything ready for evacuation in case the defenses failed. His own realization of what could be expected was concealed even from his government, which was told as late as November 4 that a new campaign could be started after rest and the distribution of additional equipment.[148]

On November 8 General Kutepov reported that Red troops had broken through, and Wrangel immediately initiated preliminary evacuation procedures, including appeals to France, Britain, and the United States to assist with ships and in finding refuge when evacuation came. On November 10 Wrangel frankly informed French Admiral Dumesnil that the situation was hopeless and asked for all the assistance available to evacuate both the troops and as much of the civilian population as possible. Such assistance would involve a financial burden, he noted, but he was willing to put up the fleet as security.[149] The next day the final evacuation order was issued, and an exchange of notes was prepared on the subject of entrusting Russian properties to France.

Wrangel put his army, the navy, "and all those who have followed" under the protection of France and declared his decision to offer the military and merchant fleets as "securities for the payment of the expenses which France has already incurred or will in future incur in giving the help which our present circumstances make necessary."[150] Count Martel replied on the same day, November 13, that this arrangement was acceptable, and for the next three days a massive embarcation took place.[151] It involved 126 ships and the saving of 150,000 persons who did not wish to remain behind, and most remarkably this great operation was carried out smoothly and in complete order.[152] It was the last evacuation and signaled final defeat, but it was a triumph in itself.[153]

The war was over. At least almost everyone but Wrangel thought so. The British government, which had had a draft trade agreement with the Soviet government ready since September, decided on

November 18 to reopen the suspended talks with the Soviet trade delegation under L. B. Krasin.[154] A few days later French Premier Leygues authorized similar negotiations on behalf of the French government, noting that Wrangel's government had ceased to exist and with it all formal obligations as far as France was concerned.[155] This did not mean that France would not continue to be of service to those who evacuated the Crimea, but such service would henceforth be in the nature of "humanitarian" assistance to individuals in a refugee status. It would primarily take the form of efforts to place such persons in new homes wherever they could be found.[156] Wrangel, however, had a rather different view of the situation.

Even while putting his troops under French protection, Wrangel had stated that he reserved the right to maintain his command and even to use his troops again in the future if and when the opportunity arose.[157] He therefore hoped to keep the Army intact and in close proximity to Russian territory, and to this end he proposed to his French protectors that his troops be used as occupation forces in and around Constantinople.[158] This request was, of course, categorically rejected. It was considered impossible to maintain the Volunteer Army any longer, not only for financial reasons but also because it would be a political embarrassment so long as it existed. The French government therefore instructed its representatives to see to the dispersal of the troops to whatever points were expedient, including the return of those who would go to Soviet Russia.[159]

During the first months of 1921 these instructions were carried out over Wrangel's repeated protests, the refugees being sent to Russia, Serbia, and Brazil primarily.[160] Wrangel remonstrated in vain against the French practice of ignoring his orders as commander, declaring that he would prefer to return to Russia with his troops and fight to the death rather than submit to the humiliations of being treated as a refugee, but his strongest protests concerned the refusal of the French government to continue to provide maintenance for his troops even in exile as refugees.[161] The French had taken over the Russian fleet as French property on grounds of the debt already owed, but Wrangel vigorously denied their right to do so if they refused to extend further assistance.[162] The Russian property turned over to them was only security for the debt, not payment of it, Wrangel contended, and therefore the "liquidation commission" established by the French government to dispose of such property was acting in violation of their agreement.[163]

This tragic state of affairs soon reached such proportions that Wrangel expected any day to be arrested by his French allies. He even secretly prepared orders for a transfer of command to General Kutepov in case he should be jailed "for refusing to influence the Army to return to Soviet Russia."[164] Fortunately for both Wrangel and his men his fears were exaggerated, and the issue never came to that. The French relaxed their demands and agreed to provide maintenance for the troops still on the Straits Islands until a residence could be secured for them elsewhere.[165] While negotiations for the latter were in progress, the fate of the Russian troops which had been in Poland was also being decided.

The evacuation of the Crimea had, of course, left the troops which were leaving Poland for the South without a place to go. The "Third Army" and what was left of the Ukrainian forces had therefore been forced to reverse their course and retreat once more into Poland. Savinkov and Bulak-Balakhovich continued for a time to operate in Belorussia, with Pilsudski's blessing, but they too were soon, in December, obliged to pull back into Poland. All of these troops were then disarmed and eventually released as civilians.[166] Polish negotiations with both the Russian and Ukrainian Soviet governments had been continued during this time and were finally brought to a successful conclusion in 1921. The Treaty of Riga, formally signed in March, gave Poland extensive territories beyond the Curzon line, including Eastern Galicia and Western Volynia, and recognized the "independence" of the Soviet Ukraine and Soviet Belorussia. It categorically prohibited the signatory governments from supporting or encouraging any organization which sought to attack or subvert forcibly the territory, government, or institutions of another party to the treaty.[167]

During the spring the problem of the Russian refugees in uniform, the remainder of Wrangel's troops, was also taken care of by the agreement of Bulgaria, Czechoslovakia, and Yugoslavia to admit those for whom homes had still not been found. Wrangel continued to lead his scattered men for several years yet, but now in the capacity of a commander of welfare funds and refugee settlement administration.[168] The era of the emigration had taken over, with all of its attendant factional clashes, but until his death in 1928 Wrangel continued to live in the spirit of the Army's long struggle. History, he said in 1927, would ultimately vindicate and praise what had been done:

History, which knows no favouritism [he declared], will tell the importance of our struggle. . . . It will know that the fight we carried on for love of our country, for the resurrection of Russia as a nation, was indeed at the same time to safeguard the culture of Europe, the struggle for an age-long civilization, for the defense of Europe against the Red terror. On that day the nations of Europe will salute the Russian Army, paying homage to its valour, its sufferings, and its death agonies.[169]

9: POST MORTEM

When it was all over, the Bolsheviks had won. It was a beaten, starving, disintegrated, and devastated country which they took over, but the victory was decisive. Many years later Churchill would remark to the leaders of the Soviet regime that they should have awarded him the Order of Lenin for his services to the Red Army. To his startled hosts' question of why, he would reply: "I taught the Red Army how to fight. . . ."[1] Churchill's remark was facetious, but it brings out the thread of irony which ran through the entire effort of the Allied intervention.

There is perhaps no better authority than Lenin to attest, as he has, to the fact that the Bolsheviks won the civil war not so much because of their strength as because of the weakness of their opponents.[2] The anti-Bolshevik forces, he observed, never succeeded in rallying popular support or even in coordinating their own efforts. And the Allies, who could have defeated Soviet forces "in a few months if not a few weeks" by even a modest effort if they had applied their strength, failed to take full advantage of the opportunity. Instead "at every step they squabbled among themselves." The unquestionably superior force of the Allies and Whites failed, Lenin concluded, because "they could not unite," because "their own interests divided them. . . ."[3]

This conclusion applies to the civil war and intervention in general, and it is perhaps particularly valid when applied to that part which occurred in South Russia. The events which took place in the South have, indeed, a history of their own, but they must also be viewed in the general context of the years 1917 to 1920, as the preceding account has sought to do. The "Russian problem" was many problems, although at the same time they constituted a whole. And the intervention was disjointed and multiple in character, although its parts merge into a single pattern in perspective. It is therefore impor-

275

tant to understand both the broad outline of events of the period and
the particulars of the war in South Russia.[4]

The upheaval of Russia in 1917 proved to be one of the great turning points of history, not only for Russia, but for the world. To some
extent the significance of the revolution was appreciated at the time,
but nothing would be more misleading than to judge the reactions
of its contemporaries solely in the light of historical hindsight. In
the first place there were no inevitable laws at work which predeter-
mined the outcome of the following years. In the second place the
most that can be expected of rational human beings is that they act
in accordance with the best information available at the time, and
in 1917 circumstances looked much different from what they would
some 50 years later. Later generations have condemned World War I
severely, but the conditions which it produced and the commitments
which it engendered at the time of the fall of the tsarist autocracy
in Russia and after were vital ingredients of the problem presented
to an unprepared and somewhat startled Europe.

The origins of the Allied intervention and the beginning of the
civil war in Russia thus must be viewed in the context of (1) a stale-
mated war which had exhausted both its Western and its Eastern
participants, (2) the disillusionment which set in when the Provisional government proved unable either to take Russia out of the war
or to revive her waning military energy so as to continue the war,
(3) the tragic disunity in the ranks of democratic Russians and the
general ignorance of what "Bolshevism" could mean in power, (4) the
inability of Western statesmanship to rise above the pressures and
confusion of the closing year of the war and the following year of
peacemaking, and (5) the bitter heritage of overwhelming internal
problems to be faced in a vacuum of political experience, leadership, and institutions which confronted those in Russia on whom any
alternative to Bolshevism depended.[5]

The Provisional government, which provided a real hope of democracy in Russia, found the collapse of the country simply too great to
cope with. The Allies in turn found it impossible not to become
involved in this situation because in their judgment winning the war
against Germany demanded a continuing Russian effort. The fall of
Kerenskii did not lessen this imperative, but rather heightened it,
especially since the leaders of the new Soviet government were suspected of secret dealing with the Germans. "In such circumstances,"
Churchill has written, "it would have been criminal negligence to

make no effort to reconstruct an anti-German front in the East. . . ."[6]

In the subsequent initial effort to build this new front in Russia, the Allied governments proceeded to acquire the commitments which were to keep them involved into 1920. But the manner in which they went about it proves the stupendous falsity of later Soviet efforts to portray the intervention as a massive and coordinated conspiracy on the part of Western "imperialism." The intervention was in the first place directed against the Germans, and the remarkable, albeit furtive, effort to prod the Bolsheviks themselves into reviving the war against Germany is evidence not only of this fact but also of the desperation of the Allies.

On the other hand, it has been said that it was not this phase of the intervention but the postwar intervention which was a fatal mistake and engendered the everlasting hatred and suspicion of the West on the part of the Bolshevik regime and the Russian people.[7] But how true is this evaluation? One suspects that this conclusion is almost as much a product of highly effective Soviet propaganda as the image of an imperialist plot. The view that there must be a clear distinction made between the intervention before November 1918 and Allied actions after that date is a valid one, but not for the reason given here.

The Allies intervened in Russia during World War I because, in the judgment of those responsible for their countries' leadership, it was in their national interest, in fact, imperative in order to protect that national interest. Initially the intervention took the form of aid to an allied government and was thus "legitimate." It is equally true that the Allies intervened during the next two years because those responsible for such decisions believed their interests to be at stake. However, in this case, it is noted, the intervention evolved into support of those opposing the government in power and could, therefore, be labeled "illegal" and even "immoral." This conclusion, however, ignores both the moral commitment and the legal situation which actually obtained.

In November 1918 Russia was in a state of civil war. There were several governments claiming authority in Russia, and none was really "in power." In these circumstances the Allies were merely continuing to honor the moral commitment made to those who had cooperated when the survival of the Western nations had seemed at stake. It may, on the other hand and more to the point, be asserted that the Allies misjudged their real interests and that they handled their commitment so poorly that their conduct was blameworthy even in terms of morality.

As for the legality of intervention in a civil war as such, international law traditionally required only that the intervening party could not claim the rights of a neutral. As E. V. Gulick has noted in his study of the theory and practice of the European state system in the nineteenth century, it was indeed characteristic of legal thought in the traditional pattern that even those commentators who stressed most emphatically the principles of sovereign independence and non-intervention usually admitted the possibility of justifiable interference when internal change constituted a threat to other states and to the established system of states.[8] A modern authority on international law points out that intervention must be regarded as an exceptional act in the normal course of relations between states, but at the same time a strictly legal definition of the cases in which it may be justified has in the past been precluded by the very nature of the international system. Moreover, he notes, even an intervention technically stigmatized as "illegal" may deserve moral approval if the provocation has been great. The question of the rule of law on intervention thus remains uncertain, since

> Neither the practice of states in their relations with one another, nor the opinions of writers on international law, afford any clear answer to the question when an intervention . . . is legitimate. Practice on the matter has been determined more often by political motives than by legal principles. Moreover, the extremest form of intervention is war, and until recently modern international law . . . has not attempted to distinguish between legal and illegal occasions of making war.[9]

The claim that the postwar intervention assured the subsequent hostility of the Bolshevik regime is also questionable. Bolshevism was by its own admission at war with everything which the Western governments stood for, a position which had been declared long before World War I and had become a sacred doctrine of Leninism from its beginnings. As a leading historian of Soviet-Western relations has phrased it:

> . . . hostility from the Communist side was preconceived, ideological, deductive. In the minds of the Soviet leaders, it long predated the Communist seizure of power in Russia. Anti-Sovietism in the West, on the other hand, was largely a confused, astonished, and

indignant reaction to the first acts of the Soviet regime. Many people in the Western governments came to hate the Soviet leaders for what they *did*. The Communists, on the other hand, hated the Western governments for what they *were*, regardless of what they did. . . .

Moscow's attitude toward the Western powers does not really flow, as Soviet apologists have so often alleged. . . , from the fact that Soviet feelings were injured by the Allied intervention in 1918. The intervention increased Soviet contempt for the Western adversary; it did not increase the hatred and rejection that stamped him as an adversary from the very day of the Revolution.[10]

While it is true that Bolshevik leadership was notably flexible and opportunistic in its tactical adjustments to circumstances, these shifts were made in the context of Communist doctrine and interpretation. To attribute Bolshevik ideology to the postwar actions of the Allies is thus both to misunderstand the character of that ideology and to do scant justice to its founders, especially Lenin. On the other hand, it was indeed largely because Bolshevik ideology was misunderstood that the Soviet regime gained all of the advantages of being called "socialist" in the West.

As for the attitudes of the Russian people at large, a subject beyond the scope of this study, perhaps the only clear evidence of the political preference of the population was the election of the Constituent Assembly in November 1917, and it indicated that the Bolsheviks did not attract a majority following. The largest vote went to the Socialist Revolutionaries, all but the minority of whom were in friendly contact with the Allies throughout the period. Indeed, some of the first firm contacts linking resistance against the Bolsheviks with the intervention were with socialists. This beginning, however, did not solve the problem involved here.

When Lloyd George declared in a February 16, 1919, note that the only justification for intervening in Russia was that Russia wanted it, he did in fact seem to be suggesting that Allied policy should be guided by the majority opinion in Russia.[11] But how was one to know what that opinion was under changing circumstances? As the preceding account has attempted to indicate, one of the built-in problems of the Russian turmoil was a fatal division between those parties which had generally attracted the largest following and the military forces and leadership which were capable of a real war against the Bolshevik regime.

It was this situation which led to the fact that in its later stages the intervention aided, not the Socialist Revolutionaries directly, but the military forces led by Kolchak, Denikin, and Iudenich, with whom the majority of the socialists ultimately split. In this situation the question was, therefore, not simply a moral one; it was the practical one of combining popular support with the formation of military forces. The implementation of Allied policy did, moreover, include an effort to put some pressure on the military leaders to adopt "democratic" policies and include socialists among their political advisers. The shortcoming here was not so much in the "legitimacy" of the policy, which did imply a respect for the interests and desires of the people, but in the halfhearted character of the effort made to carry it out.

In fact the "people" were largely peasants, and while they were traditionally hostile toward all outside influences, their hostility, in so far as it was a factor, was directed at least as much toward Russian authority as it was toward the Allies, and it probably depended mostly upon immediate contacts. Dozens of memoirs of the civil war indicate that the peasants welcomed both Reds and Whites as their "liberators" on suitable occasions but also note that the same peasants also turned on their liberators when a clash of interests occurred. Advancing military forces on either side of the struggle found it necessary to act to establish their authority and to requisition supplies wherever they went. Sufficient outside aid to make the latter unnecessary for the anti-Bolsheviks might have made a significant difference in their favor, but aid on such a scale was not available. Equally important, a new authority was not likely to secure even the neutrality of the peasants without a land program acceptable to them. If neither Whites nor Reds had such a program, the latter at least had the slogans.

Churchill has provided a description of this situation given to him by Savinkov as they talked one day over lunch:

The peasant millions . . . had the land. They had murdered or chased away its former owners. . . . No more landlords: no more rent. The earth and its fullness—no more—no less. They did not yet understand that under Communism they would have a new landlord, the Soviet State—a landlord who would demand higher rent to feed his hungry cities. . . .

Meanwhile they were self-supporting. Their rude existence could be maintained apart altogether from the outer world or modern apparatus. . . . There was bread; there was meat; there were roots. They ate and drank and squatted on the land. Not for them the causes of men. Communism, Czarism; the World Revolution, Holy Russia; Empire or Proletariat, civilization or barbarism, tyranny or freedom—these were all the same to them in theory; but also whoever won—much the same in fact. . . . One morning arrives a Cossack patrol. "Christ is risen; the Allies are advancing; Russia is saved; you are free." "The Soviet is no more." And the peasants grunted, and duly elected their Council of Elders, and the Cossack patrol rode off, taking with it what it might require up to the limit of what it could carry. On an afternoon a few weeks later, or it may be a few days later, arrived a Bolshevik in a battered motor-car with half a dozen gunmen, also saying, "You are free; your chains are broken; Christ is a fraud; religion is the opiate of democracy; Brothers, Comrades, rejoice for the great days that have dawned." And the peasants grunted . . . [and] swept away the Council of Elders and re-elected with rude ceremony the village Soviet. But they chose exactly the same people who had hitherto formed the Council of Elders and the land also remained in their possession. And presently the Bolshevik and his gunmen got their motor-car to start and throbbed off into the distance, or perhaps into the Cossack patrol.[12]

What one can, perhaps, safely say is that the belief of the peasants as to who were their friends and who their enemies was an important factor in the struggle, and in this respect propaganda images were an important weapon. To the extent that the Bolsheviks were more adept than their opponents at purveying such propaganda, the people could be swayed to their favor and against their enemies. However, it is also true that no amount of propaganda was likely to be sufficient to overcome immediate experience, and the experience which produced the most hostility among the peasants was that of being deprived of land and material goods. This was particularly true when it was the old landowners who did the taking, and the former owners followed the White forces, not the Red. One may surely venture a guess that this fact did considerably more than the Allied intervention as such to shape popular attitudes, but, of course, the intervention was thereby identified with the hated landowners and suffered accordingly.

Yet perhaps the most important consideration in judging the intervention in the civil war is the fact that an outstanding characteristic of both the Allied and the anti-Bolshevik efforts was disunity. Instead of a coordinated plot on either side, there was rather a desperate and

muddled attempt to bring some order out of sheer chaos. If either is
to be condemned, therefore, it should indeed be for the failure to
produce a sensibly organized and adequate action rather than for acting at all. There was in fact a real possibility that the Allies could
have supplied the decisive action and backing necessary to establish
a regime in Russia which would have been in accord with Western
ideas of representative government and, at the same time, would have
respected Allied interests. The opportunity was genuine, and it was
compelling, for successfully pursued, it could have meant the reintegration of Russia into the community of states with undoubtedly
beneficial results both for Russia herself and for her neighbors. Simultaneously it would probably have spelled the failure and perhaps even
the disappearance of the undemocratic Leninist offshoot of Marxism
which was dedicated to remaking the world in its own image through
violence and dictatorship.

What condemned the intervention, and made it condemnable, was
its inadequacy. The crime was that of failing to measure up to the
opportunity. The Allies muddled through when the times called for
vigor, cohesion, and quick action. One may, indeed, say that a major
conclusion to be drawn is that it would have been better not to have
intervened at all than to have done so in such an irresolute manner.
Admittedly this condemnation is still based upon hindsight to a large
extent, upon the known fact that the intervention failed to achieve
its purpose. It was true that the prospect for success seemed good at
the time when the decisions were being made to grant major assistance
to Kolchak and Denikin, but when in the spring and summer of 1919
weaknesses began to appear, the Allies acted too slowly both in the
matter of coordinating their efforts and in supplying moral and material aid. Hoping to win their victory with the least sacrifice, they abdicated the responsibility which the intervention inevitably imposed.

Given the lack of coordination and the hesitations of the Allied
governments, the rosy views held by many during the latter half of
1919 were false views in more ways than one. The military situation in Russia was too disjointed to be as good as the most sanguine
supporters of the intervention supposed. At the same time, aid in
supplies and equipment was limited by both financial and strategic
considerations, and large-scale aid in the form of troops was severely
hampered by popular opposition in the Allied countries and by the
poor military morale which prevailed among Allied troops.

The disunity of the Allied governments—not only disagreements

between Britain and France but also between factions of both governments—coupled with the popular demand for an end to all war once
the Great War was over, made it unlikely that a major Allied effort
could be mounted without serious dedication to the task. Instead of
such a dedication there was a rush to demobilize. Instead of concentration on the problem of Russia, the Great Powers took on the overwhelming burden of peacemaking on a global scale. One of the most
often repeated and most revealing phrases of the day was thus "wait
until the Peace Conference decides."

The Peace Conference could not even resolve the items first on the
agenda, much less the secondary one of Russia. Never was so much
demanded of a handful of men in a "summit" conference, and never
were the circumstances so bound to produce disillusionment. The
result was procrastination and indecision—or, whenever decisions were
made, contradiction and confusion. What possibilities of real aid to
the Russian forces there were were "frittered away by doubtful or
contradictory convictions and disjointed inconsequent actions."[13]

Churchill was one of the very few leading Allied statesmen who
displayed the single-minded will and energy to make the postwar intervention decisive, and his efforts were continually stymied by a lack
of support from higher authority. The most serious fault was not that
either the policy of war (Churchill) or the policy of peace (Lloyd
George) was "wrong," but that both were haphazardly pursued at
the same time. To repeat Churchill's observation to Lloyd George in
February 1919, the Allied governments could not decide "whether
they wish to make war upon the Bolsheviks or to make peace with
them. . . , pausing midway between these two courses with an equal
dislike of either. . . ."[14] Both possible policies were thereby inevitably deprived of whatever effectiveness they may have had. The
"either-or" imperative was blindly ignored.

Continuation of the intervention after the end of the World War
required precisely a choice either to intervene wholeheartedly and to
accept political as well as military responsibility or to withdraw on
grounds that the reasons for the wartime intervention had disappeared.
Instead the Allied governments, perhaps falling victim to their own
propaganda claims that the postwar intervention was simply a continuation of the anti-German war, deluded themselves into thinking
that they had only to station a few troops on Russian soil to overcome
the forces of anarchy and chaos. The enemy, as if he were simply an
opposing army, was to be overwhelmed by a mere show of force which

could easily be managed by the same officers and men who had just won the great World War. Such thinking not only failed to grasp the meaning of revolutionary upheaval but it even fell short of being an adequate military policy. As it was (according to Churchill) "enough foreign troops entered Russia to incur all the objections which were patent against intervention, but not enough to break the then gimcrack structure of the Soviet power."[15]

This military inadequacy itself was, more importantly, a result of the inadequacy of political leadership. Nothing so revealed the lack of understanding in the Allied governments of the nature and demands of a revolutionary situation, and all the more so of involvement by outside powers in such a situation, as the persistent failure to give the intervention political leadership and competent political representation at the scene of action. When the World War ended and the Allied governments provided nothing by way of such leadership other than a baseless continuation of old and consequently obsolete commitments, the intervention was doomed to failure. In this sense it is possible to say, as Churchill has, that the Armistice of November 1918 "proved to be the death-warrant of the Russian national cause" to the extent that it marked the end rather than the beginning of effective Allied policy in Russia.[16]

And in the absence of effective leadership from the statesmen in Paris and London, the responsibility for conducting so momentous an action as intervention in a foreign civil war fell willy-nilly to subordinates who had neither the experience nor the political perspective necessary to the task. General Franchet d'Esperey saw the hazards of inadequate military action, and General Thomson recognized the pitfalls of divided authority, but neither Franchet d'Esperey nor Thomson, nor most of the other Allied representatives in South Russia, had the necessary comprehension of, or the desire to deal with, the complex problems they faced in a war of ideologies, nationalities, and classes, as well as armies.

The failure was, of course, not merely that of the Allies. In truth it was always more the failure of the moderate forces, both military and political, in Russia. Though it was inadequate, the Allied effort might have been both significant and praised in history had those aided lived up more effectively to the fulfillment of their part. Unfortunately for one seeking to understand the failure on the Russian side, an even more complex situation must be taken into account. Ironically, issues which the Allies failed to comprehend were often clear to Russian leadership, but the latter in turn failed to see the significance of many factors which the Allies appreciated.

In January 1918 the Volunteer Army issued its proclamation of aims, stating that "the Volunteer movement is an all-national movement" which "seeks to be that active force which will give Russian citizens the possibility of realizing the construction of a Free Russia . . . [and to enable] the master of the Russian land—the Russian people—to express their sovereign will through the election of a Constituent Assembly."[17] Commenting on that proclamation in his memoirs, General Denikin admits that the Volunteer movement "did not become an all-national movement. . . . From its inception . . . the army acquired a distinct class character."[18] This was undoubtedly one of the major reasons why the Volunteer movement failed to meet the Bolshevik challenge.

Denikin, who must bear the chief responsibility for this failure in South Russia (since Wrangel's period consisted largely of a side show staged under French sponsorship for the benefit of Poland), was not entirely prepared for his task. As Wrangel has written of him:

> Destiny had laid on his shoulders the burden of a gigantic task in a sphere quite foreign to him, and had plunged him into a whirlpool of passions and political intrigue. He felt lost, he said, at this unsuitable work, was afraid of making mistakes, trusted nobody, and yet failed to find sufficient strength in himself to enable him to navigate the ship of state with a firm hand. . . .[19]

One of the reasons why this was true was that others, both military and political leaders, were not above creating such a "whirlpool of passions and intrigue" in the Volunteer camp. While on the one hand they condemned Denikin for failure to navigate with a "firm hand," on the other they denounced him, as previously noted, for clinging to authority blindly, "poisoned by the venom of ambition, drunk with power." Destiny had indeed given Denikin a gigantic task: to deal with arrogant commanders around whom the reactionary opposition collected, with drunken commanders who failed him at the critical moment of attack, with Cossack atamans who were proud and independent, and at the same time to deal with a myriad of political groups ranging from socialist to ultraconservative, with a bureaucracy wed to the tsarist past by corruption, and with a civil war in microcosm between landowners and peasants—all while fighting a war for the highest stakes.

It is little wonder that Denikin "began to imagine sedition and rebellion" around him and to try to draw all the reins of power into his own hands. He was not imagining; he was acting in self-defense. Yet the fact that such a situation existed had grave implications for the whole Volunteer movement. It meant that the initiative to take the leadership of a really bold program corresponding to the challenge was stifled. Perhaps a bolder leader than Denikin could have appealed directly to the people and could have gained a mass following. An appeal made directly, specifically, and strongly in the name of democracy and social justice may, indeed, have been the way to win both popular support in Russia and enthusiastic assistance by the Allies, who would certainly have welcomed the prospect of some other alternative to the bleak choice between "Red" and "White."

To have made such an appeal, however, would not have been without grave difficulties, even if Denikin personally had been convinced of its necessity. Indeed, had Denikin done so, it is doubtful that it could have been convincing to the people without at the same time destroying the Army. Denikin argued, perhaps correctly, that the moods of both the Russian population and the populations of the Allied countries were transient and unstable things which could not win a war for either side, that the military task was the real one. But even if he was correct in this belief, it was surely a serious mistake on his part not to supplement the military effort with an adequate political program. The latter was clearly essential for consolidation behind the front line during the war and for assuring the possibility of taking advantage of a military victory in the future to achieve the political, social, and economic reforms which could not be carried out during the war itself. Unfortunately Denikin equated the necessity of postponing execution of reforms with the necessity of avoiding declaration and even discussion of reforms as the basis of a politico-social platform which would attract support—at least he did so until it was really too late.

Denikin inherited the Volunteer Army by the accident of the deaths of Kornilov and Alekseev early in its development. His purpose was to lead that Army in such a way as to give it strength and to appeal to the Allies. For this task he was probably the best suited and most capable of all the leaders available in South Russia. To understand his predicament and accept his relative ability, however, is not to dismiss his failings. The fact remains that, in addition to his questionable military strategy, the failure to change the predominantly class character of the movement, to balance military necessity with popular appeal, and to adopt a flexible policy toward the non-Russian nationalities, were major shortcomings. Given the nature and situation of the Allied governments, these failures were of decisive significance in the matter of getting aid. They were also crucial to the problem of internal disunity.

Denikin was, as he repeatedly stated, first of all a soldier; he was not a politician. As a soldier he was really neither liberal nor reactionary. When political decisions were forced on him, he tried to hedge and take a middle course. He distrusted the extremes on both sides, and he refused to commit the Army to any political program. When his middle course failed, he took a somewhat more liberal stand, but he could not carry it into practice. At best his revised stand was an expression of his personal views as they developed under continuous testing, but neither he nor the Army believed that he had any right to allow his personal conclusions to prejudice the future course of Russia. Russia would be different after the war, he said; the people would be free; the peasants would have small farms; the workers would have safeguards against exploitation; the nationalities would have their civil liberties and autonomy. But the war had to be won first; things should stay as they were until a constituent assembly, the counterpart of the Peace Conference as a *deus ex machina* in Allied thinking, could act.

This was, perhaps, proper for a soldier. But winning the civil war required more than soldiers. Denikin himself may, indeed, have sincerely desired a more liberal course than those whom he represented, but the stark fact is that the landowners used the army to seize land back from the peasants. His military administration, which was quite unsuited to correcting such faults, never really became a government, despite the shift in the last months, and in fact it could not so long as it was dominated by the Army. His very act of proclaiming the intention of instituting land reforms alienated Army sentiments, and if in turn the liberal elements complained, they were told to wait for the constituent assembly as always. Policy and personnel, proclamation and act, simply did not correspond. Denikin belatedly proved himself capable of evolving a policy, but his reactionary subordinates carried it out in reverse.[20]

The consequence of this situation was that Denikin himself was

The Volunteer Army

taken for a reactionary dictator. Except for a few who knew his moderate personal aims, those on the outside naturally saw the movement as it was rather than the inner soul of the man. Even when they did look upon the man, he seemed to be defending his own authority against all others, demanding but refusing to compromise or to give any concessions to achieve cooperation or get aid. During the intervention he did not seem even to have the full support of the Cossack armies on whom he depended heavily. This was not just appearance, and the Allied governments, together with many of the Russian and non-Russian peoples, could easily be led to ask: Does such a weak and reactionary class army stand a chance against the Bolsheviks or really deserve support? The answer was frequently in the negative.

Miliukov took the Allies to task for drawing such a negative conclusion after observing conditions in the Volunteer camp, for as he put it, Europeans were "unhappily too much inclined to brand every attempt to use military force for restoring order in Russia as being 'counter-revolutionary'. . . ."[21] The restoration of order by a strong military hand in Russia, he said, did not exclude liberal policy as soon as order was restored but was in fact the first condition for such a policy. This reasoning had some merit, but even assuming that the Allies should have judged the Volunteers on this basis, would their conclusion have been different? Indeed, could it not more accurately be said that the Allies were in fact not too hesitant but too prone to accept the arguments of military necessity as a substitute for political maturity, both in Denikin's case and in the case of their own representatives?

The Volunteer Army was in reality rent with internal cleavages. It helped to undermine faith in itself both at home and abroad by its actions. The case of war booty was a clear example. Denikin's Supreme Council tried to channel all booty through the central command in order to prevent plunder and speculation, but it failed. Commanders in the field claimed the right to hold all captured materials, and the practice of "self-equipment," in Denikin's own words, soon "transgressed all legal limits and became bald plunder and violence."[22]

There remains, finally, the failure of the anti-Bolshevik Russian forces to attract the support of the non-Russian nationalities. The Allied governments, for their part, did make an effort, although an ineffective one, to produce the winning combination of a united military offensive and a democratic political backing which would provide an answer to the so-called "nationalities" problem. Even if one discounts other shortcomings of Russian leadership, their failure to cooperate with Allied efforts in this matter might still have been decisive for the outcome of the struggle. Denikin could not execute a land reform in chaos, and he could not force the Allies to secure his supply lines, but he might have filled the gap to some extent by adopting a policy of joint cooperation with all the borderland governments on the basis of federation. He refused. The slogan of "One Russia" was interpreted to mean not only a united Russia but a unitary state, and it remained absolute until the time when its modification ceased to have any practical meaning.

The Army had actually worked with the Cossacks on a federal basis all along, and in February 1920 Denikin established the South Russian Authority, which was essentially a federation with a legislative council and a council of ministers responsible to it. But this pattern, achieved with the Volunteers' closest allies only at the end, was never tried with the non-Russian nationalities, where it would have had much greater significance. Volunteer policy persisted in its tendency to view the demands of the latter as treasonous separatism. During the decisive phases of the war Denikin insisted that any change in the Russian constitution had to come from above, from a constituent assembly after the war was won. When, after his own defeat, he accepted the idea of reunification through negotiations with the borderland states, it was too late to affect the outcome.

The unity of Russia and federalism, of course, need not have come into such conflict; they were not necessarily contradictory concepts. "You cannot deprive a great empire of the vital sources of its economic welfare without the greatest upheavals, without endless wars. . . ," Denikin insisted quite rightly, and indeed the complete dismemberment of the country could not have been accepted by any of the major Russian parties or forces.[23] But that was only the negative side of the issue. The upheaval was already a fact. The split between the empire and its economically vital borderlands had already taken place. By refusing to recognize, until too late, that there was no longer a Russia in the old inclusive sense, Denikin simply encouraged the disintegration which he was fighting to prevent.

The question, which was not faced up to, was how Russia could be reunified. Instead of providing a rallying point for the new governments, Denikin fought them. He insisted on a unitary Russia when the demand was for federation, and he appeared willing to make some concessions in the direction of autonomy only after the demand had passed to independence. The Bolsheviks admittedly achieved the reunification of Russia by force, but there can be little doubt that their espousal of the doctrine of self-determination (albeit deceptively) and subsequent advocacy of federation greatly facilitated their victory.

A policy of federated reunification would have aided the Volunteers at least as much as it aided the Bolsheviks and probably more, since it would have gone far to dispel the fear of Great Russian chauvinism in the borderlands and would have made Denikin's claim that he wanted to establish a basically democratic union more convincing not only in Russia but also in the West. To have been really effective, of course, it should have been adopted from the beginning, from the early days of the war, rather than after defeat was predictable.

Denikin hesitated to accept such a policy not only because he felt that he was not competent to change the political status quo but also because he distrusted politicians and especially those with Leftist inclinations who predominated in the most important border areas. Besides preferring the traditional noninvolvement of the army with political parties, he believed that winning the war was the prerequisite to any political decisions, and he believed that he could win the war alone. A quick victory was the easy answer to his opponents, he felt, especially since the questions at stake were too complex to be resolved fully during the war. Once the victory had been achieved, all would see, or could be made to see, the necessity of cooperation in determining the future structure of the country through a constituent assembly. In holding these views, Denikin had a good case as far as it went, but unfortunately he was both too optimistic in his hopes for military success and unreasonably obstinate in his demand that everyone trust his motives.

It was at least in part because of Denikin's obstinacy that the borderland governments refused to put faith in his leadership. Instead they in turn adopted an equally futile obstinacy on less important matters as well, while turning a deaf ear to the argument of military necessity. The failure of both Denikin and the border states to seek reunification on the basis of a mutually acceptable compromise was thus in large measure the cause of their disunity and of their ultimate defeat.

Outside pressure from the Allies to bring about such a compromise was also never properly coordinated or consistent; it was short-lived when it did appear and too weak to provide the necessary mediation.

Indeed, the actions and statements of British military representatives in Transcaucasia and of French military representatives in Odessa frequently provoked misunderstanding and antagonism rather than served the cause of reconciliation. By conducting themselves along an erratic course which appeared to lean first one way and then the other, Allied representatives in South Russia at one time gave the impression that dismemberment was their policy and at another time appeared to favor reintegration.[24] The lack of qualified diplomatic representation at the key points in South Russia undoubtedly contributed to this situation.

In justice to the Allied governments it must at the same time be kept in mind that such pressures did constitute a degree of interference in internal affairs which was unacceptable even to many advocates of military intervention, and it was extremely difficult to arrive at a concensus on such issues. Even what little pressure the Allies did apply, moreover, was resented and resisted by the recipients of Allied aid. In defending his position on this matter, for example, Denikin has written:

> From Paris they wrote to us often that aid from the Allies was slight because the struggle of the South . . . was not popular among the European democracies and that to win their sympathy we had only to say two words: Republic and Federation.
> These words we did not say. But, if another authority had tolerated such intervention from outside in Russian affairs and had gone beyond the limits of not predetermining basic questions of state structure of Russia before a free expression of the will of the people in one manner or another, what would have been changed in the history of the past? Would the new state armies, poisoned by the sweet venom of dreams of full independence, have closed their ranks with us sincerely and unselfishly? Would the regiments of General Walker have gone to Tsaritsyn, and would the riflemen of General d'Anselme have gone to Kiev? Finally, would the morale of the Russian Army have been buoyed up going into battle for a "Federal Republic?"
> Of course not.
> The wheel of history was not turned by declarations and formulas.[25]

Perhaps Denikin was right. Both sides were clearly at fault. On the other hand, it was he and not the Allies who stood to lose the most. When it became clear that the Allied governments would not provide the kind of intervention which he sought—that is, more military assistance and still less political lecturing—would it not have been wise to compromise his ideals on grounds of expediency? Would not the little aid that was given have been far more effective if the major forces in the South had accepted the opportunity to unite which the Allies tentatively offered instead of fighting among themselves?

At least it can be said for Denikin that he did not stoop to a policy of deception on this matter. He would not declare support for the separation of parts of Russia just as a *ruse de guerre*, with the intention of turning on the allies thus won over once he had been victorious.[26] Denikin was, indeed, a man who (in Churchill's words) "possessed both the qualities and limitations of a tough, sensible, steady and honourable military man."[27] History and not he prepared the antagonism which created this great problem, and the absence of a "national consciousness" embracing all of the peoples of Russia deprived even liberal Russians of the appeals for unity which would have been effective in another land.[28] It was this lack of the very foundations of democracy and unity in Russia which had for so long frustrated her liberal idealists.[29]

Denikin was in a very real sense a bearer of the traditions of the Russian idealists. His idealism would allow him to answer the most important questions only in the "correct" way; expediency, compromise, maneuver—the hallmarks of Leninist tactics—were alien to his nature. And in the long run his convictions, which led him to devote so much effort to opposing the very compromises which would have served his cause most, prevented him from doing what was necessary to win. As Miliukov has commented, the moderates of Russia remained too conscientious all through the revolutionary period to cope with the reality confronting them, and events quickly passed them by.[30] Herein lay the gap between heroism and statesmanship.

Ultimately one must conclude that despite the courageous efforts of some—and both Denikin and Churchill may be included here—the lack of policy, the kind of policy and program required for a struggle in the context of revolution and civil war, was fatal for both the Allies and the Volunteers in Russia. The whole bloody and costly affair of the Allied involvement and the anti-Bolshevik war, although it might have resulted in a momentous victory with far-reaching international consequences, was in the end reduced by divided counsels, procrastination, and incompetence to the point where "it did the utmost harm and gained the least advantage."[31] History has written the epitaph to this failure in what followed.

NOTES

CHAPTER I: THE DISINTEGRATION OF RUSSIA

[1] On the circumstances of the arrest of the generals, see R. P. Browder and A. F. Kerensky, eds., *The Russian Provisional Government, 1917: Documents,* 3 vols. (Stanford: Stanford University Press, 1961), Vol. III, p. 1523 ff., and A. S. Lukomskii, *Vospominaniia* (Berlin: Otto Kirchner, 1922), Vol. I, p. 245 ff.

[2] For the Western response to the March Revolution, see, for example, the London *Times,* March 19, 1917; *Petite republique* (Paris), March 18, 1917. British Labour leaders and French socialist ministers both sent congratulatory notes to Kerenskii as the representative of the Left in the new government. See London *Times,* March 17, 1917, and David Lloyd George, *The War Memoirs of David Lloyd George* (London: Ivor Nicholson and Watson, 1936), Vol. III, pp. 505–508. For more detailed accounts of the events related in this chapter, see David Footman, *Civil War in Russia* (London: Faber and Faber, 1961); Richard Pipes, *The Formation of the Soviet Union, Communism and Nationalism, 1917–1923* (Cambridge: Harvard University Press, 1954); R. D. Warth, *The Allies and the Russian Revolution* (Durham: Duke University Press, 1954); G. F. Kennan, *Soviet-American Relations, 1917–1920,* Vol. I, *Russia Leaves the War* (Princeton: Princeton University Press, 1956); and R. H. Ullman, *Anglo-Soviet Relations, 1917–1921,* Vol. I, *Intervention and the War* (Princeton: Princeton University Press, 1961).

[3] See C. K. Cumming and W. W. Pettit, eds., *Russian-American Relations, March 1917–March 1920: Documents and Papers* (New York: Harcourt, Brace and Howe, 1920), pp. 4–6. Cf. Maurice Paléologue, *An Ambassador's Memoirs* (London: Hutchinson, 1923), Vol. III, pp. 248, 254; Sir George Buchanan, *My Mission to Russia and Other Diplomatic Memories* (London: Cassell and Co., Ltd., 1923), Vol. II, pp. 90–91; and Major General Sir Alfred Knox, *With the Russian Army, 1914–1917* (London: Hutchinson, 1921), Vol. II, p. 584.

[4] F. A. Golder, ed., *Documents of Russian History, 1914–1917* (New York: Century, 1927), pp. 325–329. See also *Izvestiia* (Petrograd), March 31, 1917.

[5] See Browder and Kerensky, *op. cit.,* II, 989 ff.

[6] See, for example, the statement issued on April 9, appealing for support to the war effort, quoted in Golder, *op. cit.,* pp. 329–331.

[7] Humiliated by this situation, Kornilov resigned his post on May 13 to return to the front. The minister of war, Guchkov, also resigned. See Golder, *op. cit.,*

pp. 335–336; and W. H. Chamberlin, The Russian Revolution, 1917–1921 (New York: Macmillan, 1935), Vol. I, p. 143.

[8] See Miliukov's statements in an interview in the Manchester Guardian, April 26, 1917. His resignation was one condition stipulated by the soviet before it agreed to approve the participation of other socialists in the government. At the same time the government withdrew the appointment of former Foreign Minister Sazonov as ambassador in London. That post remained vacant with Constantin Nabokov (Nabokoff) serving as chargé d'affaires. See Ullman, op. cit., I, 7; and C. Nabokoff, The Ordeal of a Diplomat (London: Duckworth and Co., 1921), pp. 82–84. Despite the change, the new foreign minister, M. I. Tereshchenko, quickly reaffirmed Russia's alliance with the Western Powers. See United States Department of State, Papers Relating to the Foreign Relations of the United States, 1918, Russia, 3 vols. (Washington: Government Printing Office, 1931–1932), Vol. I, pp. 75–77 (hereafter cited as Foreign Relations, 1918, Russia).

[9] Victor Chernov, The Great Russian Revolution, trans. P. E. Mosely (New Haven: Yale University Press, 1936), p. 303. Cf. A. I. Denikin, The Russian Turmoil (London: Hutchinson, 1922), p. 294.

[10] Knox, op. cit., II, 648.

[11] On Kerenskii's position, see Browder and Kerensky, op. cit., II, 1003 ff. For a review of the Menshevik and Socialist Revolutionary views during this period, see I. G. Tseretelli, Vospominaniia o fevral'skoi revoliutsii, 2 vols. (Paris: Mouton and Co., 1963), particularly Vol. II, Chap. 6 and appendix, pp. 401–417.

[12] Kornilov had already in July spurned monarchist overtures to join in a plot to restore the old regime and had assured fellow commanders that he would positively "take no part in any Romanov adventures." Denikin, op. cit., p. 307.

[13] That this dispute resulted from a misunderstanding was later testified to by Savinkov, a Socialist Revolutionary and Kerenskii's "political commissar" in the War Ministry, who tried unsuccessfully to mediate the dispute. See Ispoved' Savinkova: protsess Borisa Savinkova (Berlin: "Russkoe Ekho," 1924), p. 5, and B. V. Savinkov, Bor'ba s bol'shevikami (Warsaw: Izdanie Russkago Politicheskago Komiteta, 1920), pp. 3–6. For a statement of Kornilov's position and documents on the activities of his supporters, see Browder and Kerensky, op. cit., II, 998; III 1527 ff. Kornilov had been named commander-in-chief in July. See also accounts in Lukomski, op. cit., I, 245 ff.; Chamberlin, op. cit., Vol. I, Chap. 9; and materials in Golder, op. cit., pp. 521–522.

[14] That the Allied military representatives would have favored a coup to establish a stronger government is apparent from the positions of General Knox and General Henri Niessel. See Knox, op. cit., II, 677–678; and Henri Niessel, Le triomphe des bolcheviks et la paix de Brest-Litovsk; souvenirs, 1917–1918 (Paris: Librairie Plon, 1940), passim.

[15] See Buchanan, op. cit., II, 75–76. For a statement of the Allied governments' concern, see the joint note composed in September and finally sent to Kerenskii on October 9, in Foreign Relations, 1918, Russia, I, 196–197, 207–208. Cf. A. I. Denikin, Ocherki russkoi smuty, 5 vols. (Berlin: Russkoe Natsional'noe Knigoizdatel'stvo 1921–1926), Vol. II, p. 63.

[16] A. F. Kerensky, The Crucifixion of Liberty (New York: John Day, 1934), p. 351; Lloyd George, op. cit., V, 103; Buchanan, op. cit., II, 183–184; J. Nou-

lens, *Mon ambassade en Russie Sovietique, 1917–1919* (Paris: Plon, 1933), Vol. I, p. 71. See also Ullman, *op. cit.*, I, 12.

[17] Lukomskii, *op. cit.*, I, 250 ff.

[18] Denikin, *The Russian Turmoil*, p. 322 ff. On Denikin's views, see also Browder and Kerensky, *op. cit.*, II, 991 ff.

[19] See Savinkov, *Bor'ba s bol'shevikami*, p. 6 ff.; R. H. Bruce Lockhart, *Memoirs of a British Agent* (London: Putnam, 1932), p. 166; Ullman, *op. cit.*, I, 3–4; *Foreign Relations, 1918, Russia*, I, 224 ff.

[20] For a treatment of Lenin's thought and his influence on Bolshevik ideology, see Alfred G. Meyer, *Leninism* (Cambridge: Harvard University Press, 1957). In Lenin's own works see especially V. I. Lenin, *Polnoe sobranie sochinenii*, 5th edition, 55 vols. (Moscow: Gospolitizdat, 1960–1965), Vol. VI, pp. 1–183; Vol. XI, pp. 1–131; and Vol. XXVI, pp. 45–93, 209–265. All future references to Lenin's works are from the 5th edition (unless otherwise specified), which is cited simply as *Sochineniia*.

[21] Lenin, *Sochineniia*, XI, 45; XXVI, 162, 311 ff.; XXX, 39–40; XXXI, 91–92.

[22] *Ibid.*, XXVII, 50–51. See also XXVII, 325, 327–328, 341, and XXXI, 90–91, where he repeats this statement almost word for word in March 1917.

[23] *Ibid.*, XXXI, 90–92; see also XXVII, 51.

[24] *Ibid.*, XXXIV, 148–149, 233–234, 411; see also XXVI, 354–355, XXXI, 406.

[25] USSR, Ministry of Foreign Affairs, *Dokumenty vneshnei politiki SSSR*, Vol. I (Moscow: Gospolitizdat, 1957), p. 11.

[26] *Ibid.*, I, 41, 43–44.

[27] For an account of the formation of the many governments in South Russia, see Pipes, *op. cit.*, especially Chaps. 2–5.

[28] See V. Vynnychenko, *Vidrodzhennia natsii* (Kiev and Vienna, 1920), Vol. II, p. 74 ff.; P. Khrystiuk, ed., *Zamitky i materialy do istorii ukrains'koi revoliutsii* (Vienna: Ukrains'kii Sotsiol'ohichnii Instytut, Drukernia J. N. Vernay, 1921), Vol. II, p. 51 ff.; and A. Shul'gin, *L'Ukraine contre Moscou* (Paris: F. Alcan, 1935), p. 125 ff. A history of the Ukraine during the civil war period may be found in J. S. Reshetar, Jr., *The Ukrainian Revolution, 1917–1920* (Princeton: Princeton University Press, 1952).

[29] See D. Doroshenko, *Moi spomyny pro nedavne-mynule, 1914–1918*, 4 vols. (Lvov: Chervona Kalyna, 1923–1924), Vol. II, p. 26 ff. General Shcherbachev declined the Ukrainian request that he move his headquarters to Zhitomir, preferring to retain his contacts in Rumania. His association with the Ukrainian government lasted only until January 1918. On his activities, see E. G. von Val' (Wahl), *K istorii belago dvizheniia; deiatel'nost' General-ad" iutanta Shcherbacheva* (Tallin: Izdanie avtora, 1935), pp. 5–23.

[30] A highly mixed area, the Crimea had a population roughly one-half Russian or Ukrainian, one-fourth Tatar, and the remainder Jews, Germans, Greeks, Poles, and Armenians. For a general account of events in the Crimea, see Pipes, *op. cit.*, pp. 79–81, 184–190; for a detailed documentary history, see A. I. Gukovskii, ed., "Krymskoe kraevoe pravitel'stvo v 1918–1919 g.," *Krasnyi Arkhiv*, Vol. XXII (Moscow: Gosizdat, 1927), pp. 92–152; and "Krym v 1918–1919 gg.," *Krasnyi Arkhiv*, Vol. XXVIII (Moscow: Gosizdat, 1928), pp. 142–181; and Vol. XXIX

(Moscow: Gosizdat, 1928), pp. 55–85. For memoir accounts from the Tatar and Kadet points of view respectively, see D. Sejdamet, *La Crimée: passé, present* (Lausanne: G. Vaney-Burnier, 1921); and M. M. Vinaver, *Nashe pravitel'stvo; Krymskiia vospominaniia, 1918–1919 gg.* (Paris: Izdanie posmertnoe, 1928). Cf. E. Kirimal, *Der nationale Kampf der Krimtuerken, mit besonderer Beruecksichtigung der Jahre 1917–1918* (Emstetten: Verlag Lechte, 1952).

[31] For a first-hand account of events in the Don, see V. Dobrynin, *La lutte contre le bolchevisme dans la Russie meriodionale; participation des Cosaques du Don à lutte, Mars 1917–Mars 1920* (Prague: Imprimerie "Melantrich," 1920) (also in Russian, *Bor'ba s bol'shevizmom na iuge Rossii*), and S. V. Denisov, *Zapiski: grazhdanskaia voina na iuge Rossii, 1918–1920 gg.* (Constantinople: Izdanie avtora, Tipografiia "Pressa," 1921), Bk. I. For developments in the Kuban, see A. P. Filimonov, "Kubantsy, 1917–1918," in A. A. von Lampe, ed., *Beloe delo: letopis' beloi bor'by* (Berlin: Russkoe natsional'noe Knigoizdatel'stvo "Mednyi Vsadnik," 1926–1928), Vol. II; Ignat Bilyi, ed., *Tragediia kazachestva; ocherk na temu: Kazachestvo i Rossiia,* 4 vols. (Prague and Paris: Vol'noe kazachestvo, 1933–1938), Vol. I. See also N. N. Golovin, *Rossiiskaia kontr-revoliutsiia v 1917–1918 gg.* (Paris: Biblioteka "Illiustrirovannoi Rossii," 1937), Vol. V, Bk. 2, Chaps. 23–24.

[32] See Dobrynin, *op. cit.,* pp. 29–32.

[33] *Ibid.,* pp. 34–35. Although the charges against Kaledin were exaggerated, he had earlier been closely associated with the arrested generals as commander of the Eighth Army on the southwestern front and had not concealed his sympathy with Kornilov's position.

[34] The texts of this treaty and declaration may be found in the V. A. Maklakov Archives (Arkhiv Russkogo posol'stva v Parizhe, 1918–1923), (Hoover Library) Series B, Packet I, Dossier 7. See also Deniken, *Ocherki russkoi smuty,* II, 182. A Don Cossack leader and a Kadet, Kharlamov had earlier served as commissioner for Transcaucasia.

[35] See Pipes, *op. cit.,* p. 93.

[36] On these events in the Caucasus Mountain area in 1917–1918, especially in Dagestan, see Haider Bammate, *The Caucasus Problem: Questions Concerning Circassia and Daghestan* (Berne: Staempfle et Cie., 1919), p. 22 ff.; and A. A. Takho-Godi, *Revoliutsiia i kontr-revoliutsiia Dagestane* (Makhach-Kala: Dagestan-skii Nauch.-Issl. Institut, 1927), pp. 61–65, 70 ff. Cf. N. Samurskii, (Efendiev), *Dagestan* (Moscow: Gosizdat, 1925), p. 131 ff.; N. L. Ianchevskii, *Grazhdanskaia bor'ba na severnom Kavkaze* (Rostov-on-Don: Gosizdat, 1927), pp. 134–136, 189 ff.; I. Borisenko, *Sovetskie respubliki na Severnom Kavkaze v 1918 godu* (Rostov-on-Don: Gosizdat, 1930), Vol. II, pp. 231–236. Cf. W. E. D. Allen and Paul Muratoff, *Caucasian Battlefields: A History of the Wars on the Turco-Caucasian Border, 1828–1921* (Cambridge: Cambridge University Press, 1953), "The Dagestan Revolt," p. 501 ff.

[37] For an account of this period in Transcaucasia, see F. Kazemzadeh, *The Struggle for Transcaucasia, 1917–1921* (New York: Philosophical Library, 1951). Cf. Pipes, *op. cit.,* pp. 98–107, 193–195, 204–214. A documentary record may be found in *Dokumenty i materialy po vneshnei politike Zakavkaz'ia i Gruzii* (Tiflis: Tip. Pravitel'stva Gruzinskoi Respubliki, 1919). Good, although some-

times partisan, accounts may be found in Z. D. Avalov (Avalishvili), *The Independence of Georgia in International Politics* (London: Headley Bros., 1940); and J. Loris-Melikof, *La révolution russe et les nouvelles républiques transcaucasiennes* (Paris: F. Alcan, 1920). See also J. Buchan, ed., *The Baltic and Caucasian States* (Boston: Houghton, Mifflin Co., 1923), section by W. E. D. Allen, p. 212 ff.; and Ia. M. Shafir, *Secrets of Menshevik Georgia; the Plot Against Soviet Russia Unmasked: Documents* (London: Communist Party of Great Britain, 1922).

[38] A more complete review of these and subsequent developments in Turkestan may be found in Pipes, *op. cit.*, p. 88 ff., and A. G. Park, *Bolshevism in Turkestan, 1917–1927* (New York: Columbia University Press, 1957). On the Soviet side, see S. M. Dimanshtein, ed., *Revoliutsiia i natsional'nyi vopros*, Vol. III (Moscow: Gosizdat, 1930). See also P. Alekseenkov, "Natsional'naia politika Vremennogo Pravitel'stva v Turkestane v 1917 g.," *Proletarskaia Revoliutsiia*, No. 8/79, (Moscow, 1928), pp. 128–132.

[39] The name "Volunteer" was used throughout the civil-war period to designate the army units organized by Alekseev and subsequently expanded by Generals Kornilov and Denikin, although the army soon ceased to be entirely voluntary and, after Don and Kuban Cossack troops were added to it, its official name became the Armed Forces of South Russia (AFSR). Because of the continuity of Volunteer leadership for all of the forces involved here after their unification, the name, Volunteers, will be used to refer to the AFSR as well as to the original organization.

[40] See Dobrynin, *op. cit.*, pp. 33, 37, 40. For a speech by Kaledin describing the situation and setting forth his plans, see "Kazach'ia kontr-revoliutsiia," in Piontkovskii, ed., *Grazhdanskaia voina v Rossii, 1918–1921 gg.: khrestomatiia* (Moscow: Izdat. Kom. Universiteta im. Ia. M. Sverdlova, 1925), pp. 395–398. The Bolsheviks played upon the old hostility between the Cossacks and the peasants, which was based largely upon the latter's resentment of the traditional privileges, especially in land ownership, held by the former, and also attempted to organize what small "proletariat" there was in the area. See Dobrynin, *op. cit.*, pp. 41–42.

[41] For a first-hand description of the life and psychology of Russian officers in this period, see I. A. Poliakov, "General Kornilov" (MS, Columbia University Russian Archive). The Army's dependence almost entirely on officers in its first months, and to a lesser extent throughout the war, tended to give it a conservative leaning which it could never quite shake off. As General Denikin has noted: "Under the existing conditions of recruitment, the army from the very beginning bore a deep organic deficiency and acquired a class character." Denikin, *Ocherki russkoi smuty*, II, 199. On the formation of the Army and events in the Don, see also David Footman, *Civil War in Russia*, p. 33 ff.

[42] Dobrynin, *op. cit.*, pp. 38–39.

[43] See Denikin, *Ocherki russkoi smuty*, II, 160; Lukomskii, *op. cit.*, I, 273.

[44] Denikin, *Ocherki russkoi smuty*, II, 187· Lukomskii, *op. cit.*, I, 276. General Romanovskii was notably excepted from the charge that the generals were counter-revolutionary. His reputation for liberal views was later, however, to cause him the opposite embarrassment of being denounced by fellow officers as a "socialist." The majority of the officers were conservative, but, contrary to widespread belief, both

Kornilov and Denikin were men of humble origin who had taken a stand not only against a restoration of tsarism but also against class or special privileges. On Kornilov's beliefs and plans formulated by him at Bykhov, as well as Romanovskii's position, see Denikin, *Ocherki russkoi smuty*, II, 98; III, 137; *The Russian Turmoil*, pp. 294, 307.

[45] In this and subsequent meetings the chief political leaders participating were P. N. Miliukov, N. N. L'vov, P. B. Struve, M. M. Fedorov, and G. N. Trubetskoi. See Denikin, *Ocherki russkoi smuty*, II, 188 ff.; Lukomski, *op. cit.*, I, 279 ff. Both Alekseev and Kornilov offered to leave the area if no agreement could be reached, expressing a perference for moving further east, Alekseev to the central Volga region in Siberia and Kornilov either to his birthplace, Ust-Kamenogorsk, or to the place of his early military service, Turkestan. Kornilov did not give up his interest in the eastern territories, although he stayed on in the South; he sent several representatives to establish contacts with forces in other areas. See, for example, the anonymous account of the mission of General Flug to Siberia which was organized in January 1918, "Otchet o komandirovke iz Dobrovol'cheskoi Armii v Sibir v 1918 godu," *Arkhiv Russkoi Revoliutsii*, Vol. IX (Berlin: Izdatel'stvo "Slovo," 1923), pp. 243–304.

[46] Denikin, *Ocherki russkoi smuty*, II, 189.

[47] The Russian word for council here was originally soviet. This term, which came to be associated primarily with the Bolsheviks, was still found in frequent use by anti-Bolshevik groups at this time. To avoid confusion, it will be translated as council when it is used by the Volunteer Army and similar organizations and left as soviet when it is used by organizations on the Left, chiefly by the Bolsheviks and Mensheviks.

[48] Denikin, *Ocherki russkoi smuty*, II, 190.

[49] Lukomskii, *op. cit.*, I, 283.

[50] For Savinkov's own account of his role in the earlier Kornilov-Kerenskii dispute, see *Ispoved' Savinkova*, p. 5.

[51] Vendziagol'skii was formerly commissar of the 8th Army, and Ageev was a representative of the Don Peasant Conference. Denikin, *Ocherki russkoi smuty*, II, 191.

[52] According to Denikin, by mid-1919 the Special Council contained 13 "Rightists" out of a total membership of 24. Denikin and Romanovskii continued to consult with liberal Kadets and socialists who were not on the Council, however. See *ibid.*, IV, 206–207.

[53] *Ibid.*, II, 198–199.

[54] Trotskii declared the Don area to be in a state of war with Soviet Russia on December 7 and ordered Krylenko "to wipe off the face of the earth the counter-revolutionary rebellion of the Cossack Generals and Kadet bourgeoisie." J. Bunyan and H. Fisher, eds., *The Bolshevik Revolution, 1917–1918* (Stanford: Stanford University Press, 1934), p. 407.

[55] Denikin, *Ocherki russkoi smuty*, II, 192. In addition to the subsidy provided by the Don government, the chief source of income at this stage seems to have been an allotment of several million rubles obtained, with the help of the Don government, from the Rostov branch of the Russian state bank.

[56] In its effort to increase its public support, the Don government had begun

to bring non-Cossack representatives into the government and, appealing to their Leftist tendencies, had declared that the Volunteer Army must "be under the strict control of the Unified Government and, in case of the discovery of the presence in the Army of counterrevolutionary elements, such elements will be removed immediately beyond the borders of the Don oblast." The government also consented to the organization of a delegation to be sent to the Bolsheviks to seek "a cessation of the civil war" within Don territory. See Piontkovskii, op. cit., pp. 398–400.

[57] Dobrynin, op. cit., p. 47.

[58] Ibid., p. 48. Although Kaledin himself had foreseen the possibility of a Volunteer withdrawal, and had been specifically warned of the likelihood by Alekseev on January 29, he apparently could not face the reality of this situation. See Ia. M. Lisovoi, ed., Belyi arkhiv: sborniki materialov, 3 vols. (Paris: 1926–1928), Vol. I, pp. 99–100.

[59] Dobrynin, op. cit., p. 52.

[60] For accounts of the entry of the Volunteers into the Kuban, see A. P. Filimonov, "Kubantsy, 1917–1918," loc. cit., and K. N. Nikolaev, "Pervyi Kubanskii pokhod," M. A. Golubov, "Sil'nye dukhom," and A. Filimovov, "Kazach'i nastroeniia," in the Nikolaev Papers (Columbia University Russian Archive). Bych had earlier been a member of the Baku municipal government and was affiliated with the Socialist Revolutionary party. For a statement by the Kuban Rada and speeches by persons associated with Bych setting forth their position, see Piontkovskii, op. cit., pp. 461–467.

[61] G. K. Pokrovskii, Denikinshchina: god politiki i ekonomiki na Kubani, 1918–1919 gg. (Berlin: Izdatel'stvo Z. I. Grzhebina, 1923), pp. 62–63. See also Piontkovskii, op. cit., p. 461 ff.

[62] Denikin, Ocherki russkoi smuty, II, 254.

[63] Ibid., p. 277.

[64] For a slightly different version of these events, see A. P. Filimonov, "Nash dolg," in "Pervopokhodnik," pp. 9–10, Nikolaev Papers. For the text of the agreement, see Denikin, Ocherki russkoi smuty, II, 279. It was signed by Generals Kornilov, Alekseev, Denikin, Erdeli, Romanovskii, Ataman Filimonov, Bych, Riabovol, and Sultan Shakhim-Girei.

[65] Kuban infantry was placed in General Markov's brigade, and Kuban cavalry in General Erdeli's.

[66] Denikin, Ocherki russkoi smuty, II, 283.

[67] See accounts in V. N. Birkin, "Povesti minuvshikh let," Vol. VII, "Kornilovskii pokhod," MS, and "Pervopokhodnik," Nikolaev Papers.

[68] For a review of Denikin's career, see his The Russian Turmoil, passim. An exposition of his views and policies may be found in his Ocherki russkoi smuty, IV, 201 ff.

[69] See Denikin, Ocherki russkoi smuty, II, 303 ff.

[70] See Warth, op. cit., p. 168 ff.

[71] Ambassador Francis, for example, telegraphed a report to Washington in which he deemed it "not improbable" that Lenin was "working for Germany[,] whose plan is to encourage civil strife in Russia so that German troops will be called to restore order and then [a] separate peace [can be] negotiated on terms

favorable to Germany and disastrous to Russia." *Foreign Relations, 1918, Russia,*
I, 245. It is clear that Germany supplied "large amounts of money" (in General
Ludendorff's words) to the Bolsheviks both before and after the November coup,
but it is unlikely that the Bolsheviks felt any obligation toward Germany on this
account. Indeed, Lenin and his party came to power with a program which called
for the immediate spread of revolution to Germany, but it is true that the ability
of the party to seize power and keep it was improved by German financial support.
Germany had made it possible for Lenin and others to return to Russia because it
was deemed in the interest of the Central Powers that "the influence of the radical
wing of the Russian revolutionaries should prevail." However, the motives of the
Bolsheviks were not trusted by the Germans, and the latter would soon begin
considering the overthrow of the Soviet regime at the same time as continuing to
support it with money for some months. For documentary evidence on this question, see Z. A. B. Zeman, ed., *Germany and the Revolution in Russia, 1915–1918:
Documents from the Archives of the German Foreign Ministry* (London: Oxford
University Press, 1958), especially documents Nos. 15, 51, 57, 71, 92, 124, 131,
133, and 135.

[72] Bunyan and Fisher, *op. cit.,* pp. 233, 243.

[73] *Ibid.,* pp. 245, 403. The Allied ambassadors ordered a statement of protest
against the armistice proposal on November 22 after receiving instructions from
their governments. See *Foreign Relations, 1918, Russia,* I, 248; Ullman, *op. cit.,*
I, 22; Kennan, *op. cit.,* I, 90–91, 93. The quotation cited here is from the French
appeal to Dukhonin, sent to Mogilev through General Berthelot's headquarters in
Jassy, Rumania, which also sent a similar note to General D. G. Shcherbachev,
Russian commander on the Rumanian front. See also E. Moulis and E. Bergonier,
eds., *En marge du conflict mondial; la guerre entre les alliés et la Russie, 1918–
1920* (Paris: Librairie generale de doit et de jurisprudence. Imprimerie H. Jehan,
1937), pp. 21–22; *Foreign Relations, 1918, Russia,* I, 272; and Louis Fischer,
The Soviet in World Affairs (Princeton: Princeton University Press, 1951), Vol.
I, p. 20.

[74] *Foreign Relations, 1918, Russia,* I, 251.

[75] Bunyan and Fisher, *op. cit.,* pp. 267–268. When the Bolshevik detachment
under Krylenko was approaching Mogilev on December 1, Dukhonin informed
Kornilov and the other generals at Bykhov of the danger and offered to aid in their
escape, although he made no attempt to escape himself. Most of the generals at
Bykhov left individually in disguise, but Kornilov left at the head of the small
band of troops, his "guards" at the prison, who had remained loyal to him. All
of the Bykhovtsy headed south for the Don.

[76] Buchanan, *op. cit.,* II, 225–226. Buchanan himself expressed doubts as to
the validity of this view and stated that "every day that we keep Russia in the war
against her will does but embitter her people against us." *Ibid.,* p. 221. See also
Foreign Relations, 1918, Russia, I, 238.

[77] See Ullman, *op. cit.,* I, 25–28.

[78] See *Foreign Relations, 1918, Russia,* I, 244 ff.; and J. F. N. Bradley, "The
Allies and Russia in the Light of French Archives," *Soviet Studies,* Vol. XVI, No.
2 (October 1964), p. 177.

[79] The text of the armistice is in *Dokumenty vneshnei politiki,* I, 47–51. It

was to extend only until January 14, and under its terms there was to be no further transfer of German troops to the west. However, the prohibition against the transfer of troops applied only to those not already ordered to move, and apparently the Germans had already issued orders for the major transfers. See J. W. Wheeler-Bennet, *The Forgotten Peace: Brest-Litovsk, March 1918* (London: Macmillan, 1938), p. 89; Ullman, *op. cit.*, I, 32.

[80] *Dokumenty vneshnei politiki*, I, 70. On Trotskii's attitudes and actions during this time, and in the peace talks, see I. Deutscher, *The Prophet Armed* (New York: Oxford University Press, 1954), p. 346 ff.

[81] See Ullman, *op. cit.*, I, 42–43, 46, 52.

[82] Bradley, "The Allies and Russia," *loc. cit.*, p. 177.

[83] *Ibid.* See also *Foreign Relations, 1918, Russia*, II, 609, and Denikin, *Ocherki russkoi smuty*, II, 192.

[84] United States Department of State, *Papers Relating to the Foreign Relations of the United States: The Lansing Papers, 1914–1920*, Vol. II (Washington: Government Printing Office, 1940), pp. 345–346. See also Kennan, *op. cit.*, I, 168, 177.

[85] *Foreign Relations, 1918, Russia*, I, 330–331. See also Ullman, *op. cit.*, I, 46, 51, 53–54.

[86] Among the several plans proposed during this period for rescuing the Rumanian government and army was one envisaging the evacuation of the former, via South Russia, to Transcaucasia, and the joining of the latter to Kaledin's army in the Don. No such evacuation proved necessary, but the king of Rumania did confidentially offer to join a military alliance with the Cossacks if the Allies would support it. See Kennan, *op. cit.*, I, 197; Ullman, *op. cit.*, I, 42; Paul Cambon, *Correspondance, 1870–1924* (Paris: Editions Bernard Grasset, 1946), Vol. III, p. 203. The British Cabinet had on November 22 approved encouraging Rumania to cooperate with the Cossacks, but it had decided against suggesting any particular Cossack government so as to avoid the appearance of recognition. Nothing further came of the idea of a Rumanian-Cossack alliance, but once the British had decided on December 3 to give Kaledin full financial support, it was assumed that Rumania would be a major base of future operations by Allied agents. See Ullman, *op. cit.*, I, 42–43, 46.

[87] See Great Britain, Foreign Office, *Documents on British Foreign Policy, 1919–1939*, First Series (hereafter: *Documents on British Policy*), Vol. III (London: His Majesty's Stationery Office, 1949), pp. 369–370. See also A. I. Gukovskii, *Antanta i Oktiabr'skaia revoliutsiia* (Moscow: Gosudarstvennoe Sotsial'no-ekonomicheskoe Izdatel'stvo, 1931), p. 100 ff., and Fischer, *op. cit.*, II, 836. As many have noted, the Anglo-French accord corresponded to some extent with the pattern of British and French investments in Russia prior to the war. The Transcaucasian area, bordering on the Middle Eastern countries, and its oil had been of concern to the British, while French interest had centered especially on the Ukraine and the Donets basin. See A. I. Gukovskii, *Frantsuzskaia interventsiia na iuge Rossii, 1918–1919* (Moscow: Gosizdat, 1928), p. 31. According to one source, French investment amounted to around 70 per cent of all investment in the South, with up to 97 per cent in some areas. See A. G. Shlikhter, ed., *Chernaia kniga: sbornik statei i materialov ob interventsii antanty na Ukraine v 1918–*

1919 gg. (Ekaterinoslav-Kharkov: Gosizdat Ukrainy, 1925), p. 20. On these economic influences, see also R. Labry, "Notre politique en Russie, les methodes, les hommes," *Mercure de France,* Vol. CXXXVIII (1920), pp. 7–10. However, both Soviet sources and certain works published in the West have tended to exaggerate the significance of this factor by reading into the confusion of 1917 motives and policies which appeared only later and were secondary even then. See, for example, L. I. Strakhovsky, "The Franco-British Plot to Dismember Russia," *Current History,* Vol. XXXIII, (March 1931), p. 839, and Louis Fischer, *Oil Imperialism, the International Struggle for Petroleum* (New York: International Publishers, 1926). In view of the preoccupation of the Allied governments with the war effort at this time, a primarily economic interpretation seems unwarranted. Cf. D. Lloyd George, *The Truth About the Peace Treaties* (London: V. Gollancz, Ltd., 1938), Vol. I, pp. 316–317.

[88] That the Bolsheviks suspected Allied use of Rumania as a base of operations was indicated by the so-called Kalpashnikov affair in which a Russian officer serving in the Red Cross was arrested for allegedly attempting to aid Kaledin. A shipment of ambulances in Kalpashnikov's care was to be sent from Petrograd to Jassy, Rumania, but, fearing German capture of them in Rumania, the American Red Cross mission in Rumania had on December 5 ordered their destination changed to Rostov-on-Don where it was presumed they would be safe. When the danger of German capture diminished, this order was changed, but in the meantime the Bolsheviks suspected a trick and not only arrested Kalpashnikov but believed others, including Raymond Robins of the American Red Cross, to be implicated in a plot to aid the counterrevolutionaries. See Kennan, *op. cit.,* I, 191 ff. It might also be noted that in January Bolshevik commissars on the old southwestern front were advised to take "the most resolute action against the counterrevolutionary Roumanian command, and against Kaledin's forces and the accomplices of the Kiev Rada." See Jan M. Meijer, ed., *The Trotsky Papers, 1917–1922,* Vol. I (The Hague: Mouton and Co., 1964), p. 9.

[89] See *Foreign Relations, 1918, Russia,* II, 591, 595, 609; Denikin, *Ocherki russkoi smuty,* II, 192; Ullman, *op. cit.,* I, 52, 56. The British offer was the result of the Cabinet decision of December 14 to allot 10 million pounds for Kaledin and Alekseev and another 10 million pounds to be distributed in South Russia as deemed advisable by British representatives in Rumania. The French support had also been approved prior to the zone agreement and was specifically cited in the text at the figure given.

[90] Practical realization of funds on the basis of the Allied credits seems to have been unexpectedly difficult. The American consul, DeWitt Poole, Jr., then in the Don, reported at the end of January that Colonel Hucher, the French military agent who contacted Alekseev in December, thus far had only some 5 million rubles "in sight," which he had raised through selling French drafts to bankers in Rostov and other South Russian cities. He estimated that Alekseev's expenses were already running to 20 million rubles per month and were expected to total over 200 million during the next four months. See *Foreign Relations, 1918, Russia,* II, 613. Alekseev's own financial records show a receipt of only 300,000 rubles from the "French Mission" during January. See M. V. Alekseev, Account Book (MS, Hoover Library); and "Denezhnye dokumenty Generala Alekseeva," *Arkhiv Russkoi*

Revoliutsii, Vol. V (Berlin: Izdatel'stvo "Slovo," 1922), p. 352.

⁹¹ For an account of these early contacts, see A. Shul'gin, *L'Ukraine, la Russie et les puissances de l'Entente* (Berne: Imprimerie Reunies S. A. Lausanne, 1918), p. 32 ff.; and Reshetar, *op. cit.*, p. 98. A Ukrainian note to the Allied ambassadors, dated November 23/December 6 and signed by Shul'gin, assured the Allies that "a separate peace without the consent of [our] allies produces in us feelings of indignation and disgust. . . ." *Foreign Relations, 1918, Russia*, II, 649. Cf. Vynnychenko, *op. cit.*, II, 242.

⁹² See Lenin, *Sochineniia*, XXXV, 143–145; Reshetar, *op. cit.*, pp. 95–96; Chamberlin, *op. cit.*, I, 486 ff.

⁹³ For documents on Tabouis' appointment, see Khrystiuk, *op. cit.*, II, 198; E. Evain, *Le problème de l'indépendance de l'Ukraine et la France* (Paris: Librairie Felix Alcan, 1931), pp. 100–108; A. Margolin, *Ukraina i politika Antanty* (Berlin: Izdatel'stvo S. Efron, 1921), Appendix No. 2, pp. 365–368. On Bagge's activities, see Great Britain, *Parliamentary Papers*, 1919, Vol. LIII, Cmd. No. 8, "A Collection of Reports on Bolshevism in Russia," p. 50. When the French ambassador informed the United States on January 9 that de facto relations were being established with the Ukrainian government, Lansing wired Ambassador Francis that the United States was not prepared "to recognize any independent governments until the will of [the] Russian people has been more definitely expressed on this general subject." *Foreign Relations, 1918, Russia*, II, 655, 657. Although Tabouis reportedly declared that "official recognition" had been given to the Ukraine (Evain, *op. cit.*, p. 100 ff.), it was generally understood at the time that the appointment of Tabouis and Bagge did not constitute diplomatic recognition. See *Foreign Relations, 1918, Russia*, II, 659. When the question of whether recognition had been given came up again several month later, French Foreign Minister Pichon declared flatly that "the allegation . . . that France and England have recognized the Ukraine is incorrect. Even if the idea had been envisaged last December, the attitude of the Ukraine vis-à-vis the Germans would have dissuaded us." See the telegram from Pichon to Berne, November 7, 1918, in the Maklakov Archives, Series B, Packet I, Dossier 6 (the Ukraine). French Ambassador Noulens took a strong stand not only against recognition of the Ukraine but also against the appointment of Tabouis. See Noulens, *op. cit.*, I, 241. Speeches in the French Assembly long after this time advocated recognition of the Ukraine and implied that it had not been given because of the hostility of the Foreign Ministry toward national movements in Russia. See, for example, the speech by M. de Monzie, in France, Assemblée Nationale, *Débats Parlementaires, Journal Officiel*, (March 27) 1920, Vol. I (Paris: Imprimerie des Journaux Officiels, 1920), pp. 392–394.

⁹⁴ Tabouis promised significant "financial and technical aid . . . to the Ukraine to assist it in its gigantic task," and Bagge stated that the British government would "support to the utmost of its ability the Ukrainian Government in the task which it has undertaken of introducing good government, maintaining order, and combating the Central Powers who are enemies of democracy and humanity." See Evain, *op. cit.*, p. 100 ff.; and Vynnychenko, *op. cit.*, II, 242. Cf. Reshetar, *op. cit.*, p. 99.

⁹⁵ See British Foreign Office intelligence report of February 9, 1918, in United

States National Archives, Foreign Affairs Section, Doc. No. 861.00/1277. The British Cabinet had also authorized financial support for Russian troops in Persia on December 3, and in January a Russian committee was established to deal with relations with non-Bolshevik elements and areas. See Ullman, op. cit., I, 51, 83.

96 The British Foreign Office had already on November 20 authorized in principle the establishment of informal contacts with the Bolshevik government. See Ullman, op. cit., I, 30.

97 Lockhart, op. cit., pp. 201–202. Lockhart had acted as consul general in Moscow until November 1917, when he was recalled to London, where he served temporarily as a Russian expert under Sir Arthur Steel-Maitland in the Department of Overseas Trade. After several meetings with members of the Cabinet, he found Lloyd George "greatly impressed" by those who criticized "the folly of the Allies in not opening up negotiations with the Bolsheviks," but he also found Lord Robert Cecil, the under secretary for foreign affairs, "supremely sceptical of the usefulness of establishing any kind of relations with the Bolsheviks," since he believed that "Lenin and Trotsky were paid agents of Germany. . . ." Ibid., p. 197 ff. Ambassador Buchanan now felt that some relations with the Bolsheviks were necessary, since "a complete rupture would leave the Germans a clear field in Russia. . . ." See Buchanan, op. cit., II, 246.

98 Lockhart, op. cit., p. 205. For an explanation of Lockhart's mission to Secretary of State Lansing, see Foreign Relations, 1918, Russia, I, 337. Cf. Ullman, op. cit., I, 58 ff.

99 For Sadoul's own account of his activities in Russia, see Jacques Sadoul, Notes sûr la révolution Bolchevique, Octobre 1917–Janvier 1919 (Paris: Editions de la Sirene, 1919).

100 France, Assemblée Nationale, Annales de la chambre des députés, Débats parlementaires, 1917, Tome III, pp. 3794–3795, session of December 27. The Allied military representatives in the Supreme War Council had already in December declared their opinion that the Bolsheviks were "assisted and controlled by the Germans." See Ullman, op. cit., I, 56.

101 See Lenin's statement to the 7th Party Congress on March 8, 1918, in Sed'moi ekstrennyi s"ezd RKP(b), Mart 1918 goda, Stenograficheskii otchet (Moscow: Gospolitizdat, 1962), p. 111.

102 For reports by the Allied ministers in Rumania on negotiations with the Ukrainians, see Foreign Relations, 1918, Russia, II, 660–665. The Ukrainian delegation sent to Jassy for these negotiations was headed by Vice Minister of Foreign Affairs Halip and Minister of Finance Halisinskii. The Allied ministers involved were Charles Vopicka (United States), Sir George Barclay (Britain), Saint-Aulaire (France), and Auritte (Italy). For statements on Ukrainian policy at this point, see Khrystiuk, op. cit., II, 95 ff., and Vynnychenko, op. cit., II, 244 ff.

103 See Mirnye peregovory v Brest-Litovske; polnyi tekst stenogramm, Vol. I (Moscow: Izdatel'stvo NKID, 1920), especially pp. 94–96, 126, 156.

104 See Lenin, Sochineniia, XXXV, 179–180, 246–247, 472.

105 See Sed'moi ekstrennyi s"ezd RKP(b), prilozheniia, pp. 299, 321; and Protokoly tsentral'nogo komiteta RSDRP(b), Avgust 1917–Fevral' 1918 (Moscow: Gospolitizdat, 1958), pp. 169–171, 198.

106 Ambassadors Francis and Noulens both informally authorized this assurance

but without any commitment of their respective governments. See Noulens, *op. cit.*, I, 153–154; *Foreign Relations, 1918, Russia*, I, 418. Cf. Kennan, *op. cit.*, I, 234–239, and appendix pp. 521–522.

[107] *Mirnye peregovory v Brest-Litovske*, I, 126.

[108] For an English translation of the peace treaty between the Ukraine and the Central Powers, see *Foreign Relations, 1918, Russia*, II, 665–671. The Ukrainians at first asked Germany only for assistance in joining Galician troops to other Ukrainian forces for defense against the Bolsheviks and for the release of Ukrainian prisoners of war being held by the Central Powers. When it became obvious that direct German military aid would be necessary, the Ukraine then sought German agreement to a limited military intervention along the border with Russia without occupation of the interior. The Germans rejected all such halfway measures, however, and ultimately the Rada was obliged to accept unrestricted German "aid." However, it publicly announced that Ukrainian sovereignty and independence would be respected by the "liberators." See Khrystiuk, *op. cit.*, II, 139–143. For the statement of the German position to Trotskii on February 9, see *Mirnye peregovory v Brest-Litovske*, I, 185.

[109] *Protokoly tsentral'nogo komiteta RSDRP(b)*, pp. 173, 190–191; *Sed'moi ekstrennyi s"ezd RKP(b)*, pp. 111, 283. Even Lenin's faith in German revolution had been revived at this point by reports of the formation of "soviets" in Berlin and Vienna, and he optimistically predicted that the German Communist leader, Karl Liebknecht, would "soon stand at the head of the German Government." A few days later, however, his pessimism had returned. See Lenin, *Sochineniia*, XXXV, 251–252, 321.

[110] *Dokumenty vneshnei politiki*, I, 105. For a discussion of the German decision to attack and to justify this action by Trotskii's refusal to sign the peace, see E. Ludendorff, *Ludendorff's Own Story* (New York: Harper and Brothers, 1919), Vol. II. p. 181 ff.; M. Hoffmann, *War Diaries and Other Papers* (London: Martin Secker, 1929), Vol. II, p. 218 ff. Cf. Warth, *op. cit.*, p. 225 ff.

[111] *Protokoly tsentral'nogo komiteta RSDRP(b)*, pp. 194–195, 198–199.

[112] *Ibid.*, pp. 200–204. See also Deutscher, *op. cit.*, pp. 383, 391.

[113] *Dokumenty vneshnei politiki*, I, 79, 82–84, 89–90. See also Noulens, *op. cit.*, I, 171–174; Niessel, *op. cit.*, pp. 157, 161–163. Cf. Kennan, *op. cit.*, I, p. 330 ff. In connection with the rupture of relations with Rumania, the Soviet government declared General Shcherbachev an "enemy of the people."

[114] *Dockumenty vneshnei politiki*, I, 97–98; *Foreign Relations, 1918, Russia*, III, 32–33. The Inter-Allied Council on War Purchases and Finance also adopted a resolution in protest on February 13. See *ibid.*, p. 34. By the end of October 1917 British war loans to Russia totalled 597,300,000 pounds, France had loaned 4 billion francs (making the combined British and French war loan some $3,528,-000,000), Japan 296 million yen, Italy 221 million lire, and the United States had established a credit of $450 million, of which the Provisional government had used about $188 million. An additional $125 million in credit was offered by the United States in September, but this also remained unused. Combining the prewar debt with that of the war loans, the total of Russian state debts in 1917 was approximately six billion dollars. See H. E. Fisk, *The Inter-Ally Debts* (New York: Bankers Trust Co., 1924), p. 111; A. M. Michelson, P. N. Apoltol, and

The Volunteer Army

M. W. Bernatzky, *Russian Public Finance During the War* (New Haven: Yale University Press, 1928), pp. 302–320; and R. P. Browder and A. F. Kerensky, *op. cit.*, II, 502–508. Figures on the wartime loans may also be found in the Papers of M. V. Bernatskii (Provisional government minister of finance), "Kreditnyia operatsii vo vremia voiny," (MS, Hoover Library).

[115] Lockhart, *op. cit.*, pp. 225, 227–228. On the day of the German attack Noulens also repeated the offer to this effect made earlier by Sadoul, this time addressing it to Chicherin. See *Foreign Relations, 1918, Russia,* I, 383.

[116] *Protokoly tsentral'nogo komiteta RSDRP(b)*, p. 208. See also Deutscher, *op. cit.*, pp. 385–386.

[117] *Protokoly tsentral'nogo komiteta RSDRP(b)*, p. 215, and notes Nos. 223 and 224, p. 287; *Sed'moi ekstrennyi s"ezd RKP(b)*, p. 268. Earlier Soviet sources (e.g. the 3rd edition of Lenin's *Sochineniia*, XXII, 608) gave the vote in the C.E.C. as 116 to 84, with 26 abstentions. For the German terms, dated February 21, see *Dokumenty vneshnei politiki*, I, 112–113. See also Lenin's comments to the Seventh Congress of the party, which approved the Brest peace on behalf of the party, in *Sed'moi ekstrennyi s"ezd RKP(b)*, pp. 19–24, 112–114.

[118] Lockhart, *op. cit.*, pp. 228–229. See also L. Trotsky, *My Life; An Attempt at an Autobiography* (New York: Scribner's, 1930), p. 389.

[119] Lockhart complains in his account of this period that the Foreign Office failed to reply to most of his telegrams. Instead of giving him the answers he needed, it "insisted on keeping my own position as vague as possible." Lockhart *op. cit.*, pp. 235, 238, 260. For a statement by Balfour on the rationale behind the British policy which Lockhart found so frustrating, see Ullman, *op. cit.*, I, 166.

[120] The British ambassador, Buchanan, had already left the country, and the British chargé d'affaires, Sir Francis Lindley, now accompanied Francis and Noulens to Vologda. Lindley was the only one who managed to arrange immediately for the further transfer of staff personnel out of the country through Helsinki. Others, caught in the Finnish civil war, were obliged to return to Vologda, where they stayed until the summer of 1918, when it was possible for them to leave through Arkhangelsk. See Ullman, *op. cit.*, I, 77.

[121] See Lockhart, *op. cit.*, pp. 240–243, 253.

[122] *Ibid.*, p. 245. Lockhart also records that Foreign Secretary Balfour commented in one of his notes: "If you can, indeed, persuade Trotsky to resist German penetration, you will have earned the gratitude of your own country and of all humanity." *Ibid.*, pp. 271–272.

[123] See *Dokumenty vneshnei politiki*, I, 117–119, 119-204, 212–213.

[124] Lockhart, *op. cit.*, p. 247. Later, according to Lockhart, Trotskii also suggested the possibility of having a British naval mission to reorganize the Russian fleet and of the use of British railway experts to help put the transportation system into working order. Lockhart's account indicates that the transmission of these suggestions to London brought no response. *Ibid.*, pp. 271–272. However, at about this time a British economic mission was being formed in London by the Department of Overseas Trade to investigate prospects for economic relations. This mission traveled to Russia with the returning Lindley in June and arrived in Moscow on July 22, after receiving assurances of protection from Radek. Nothing but confusion was accomplished by this strange development, however, since

by then almost all relations with the Soviet government had been disrupted by events earlier in July. The mission did well just to get out again with the Allied diplomats then hastily departing from Vologda. See Ullman, *op. cit.*, I, 232–234.

[125] Sadoul had been led by Trotskii to believe that the Soviet government might agree to the intervention if (1) the Japanese were not included, (2) it would be purely military, directed against the Germans, and not involve any interference in domestic affairs, and (3) the Allies provided the Soviet government with a clear and precise statement agreeing to these conditions. See Sadoul, *op. cit.*, pp. 277, 284–285, 295.

[126] Lockhart, *op. cit.*, p. 268. See also Noulens, *op. cit.*, I, 151–152; Sadoul, *op. cit.*, p. 289; and Bradley, "The Allies and Russia," *loc. cit.*, p. 184.

[127] With regard to German relations with the Bolsheviks, it is notable that the German Foreign Office informed Mirbach on May 18 that he should use whatever funds were necessary to keep the Bolsheviks in power. On June 3 he in turn indicated that three million marks per month would be required "due to strong Entente competition." See Zeman, *op. cit.*, pp. 128–129, 130. It may also be noted that both the United States and the anti-Bolshevik representatives in Paris, particularly Russian Ambassador Maklakov, at this time objected to Japanese intervention as a part of joint Allied action to restore the eastern front. See *Foreign Relations, 1918, Russia*, II, 37, 41–42. For an account of the negotiations leading to the Japanese intervention, see Ullman, *op. cit.*, I, 85–109. Noulens' statement on Allied intervention first appeared in *Izvestiia*, April 28, 1918, and is quoted in *Foreign Relations, 1918, Russia*, I, 509.

[128] The French government did not accept the Soviet demand for Noulens' removal, but according to Chicherin (who was now acting commissar for foreign affairs and received formal appointment to that post on May 30), the Soviet government as of this time "began to regard him as a private person, absolutely ignoring his political status." G. V. Chicherin, *Two Years of Foreign Policy* (New York: Russian Soviet Government Bureau, 1920), p. 12.

CHAPTER II: THE IMPACT OF GERMAN OCCUPATION

[1] See the telegram from Colonel von Stolzenberg in Kiev to the German commander of the eastern front, March 9, 1918, in I. I. Mints and E. N. Gorodetskii, eds., *Dokumenty o razgrome germanskikh okkupantov na Ukraine v 1918 godu* (Moscow: Gosizdat, 1942), p. 16. Cf. I. I. Mints and R. Eideman, eds., *Krakh germanskoi okkupatsii na Ukraine (po dokumentam okkupantov)* (Moscow: Gosizdat, 1936), p. 30. For a more detailed account of events in the Ukraine, see J. S. Reshetar, *The Ukrainian Revolution, 1917–1920* (Princeton: Princeton University Press, 1952), p. 145 ff. On German policy, see the study of D. S. Fedyshyn, "German Plans and Policies in the Ukraine and the Crimea," Ph.D. dissertation, Columbia University, 1962.

[2] Mints and Gorodetskii, *op. cit.*, p. 71. Mumm favored caution but stated that he believed further cooperation with the Rada would be impossible "because of their socialist theories" which kept them from comprehending "the real state of affairs." *Ibid.*, p. 44.

[3] D. Doroshenko, *Istoriia Ukrany, 1917–1923 gg.* (Uzhgorod: Nakladom dok-

tora Osipa Tsiupki, 1930–1932), Vol. II, pp. 37–39. Cf. Reshetar, *op. cit.*, pp. 130–132; M. A. Svechin, "Dopolnenie k vospominaniiam" (MS, Columbia University Russian Archive), Part II, "V Kieve," p. 12.

⁴ A. I. Gukovskii, "Krym v 1918–1919 gg.," *Krasnyi Arkhiv*, Vol. XXVIII (Moscow: Gosizdat, 1928), pp. 142–144. See also Richard Pipes, *The Formation of the Soviet Union: Communism and Nationalism, 1917–1923* (Cambridge: Harvard University Press, 1954), pp. 186–187. M. M. Vinaver, a leader of the Crimean Kadet party, was subsequently sent to Kiev to investigate the activities of Kadet party members who advocated cooperation with Skoropadskii and the Germans. See the policy statement which he drafted for the Party of National Freedom (Narodnoi Svobody), a Kadet organization, in May 1918, in the Miliukov Personal Archives; and P. N. Miliukov, "Dnevnik" (MS, Columbia University Russian Archive), diary entries for June 22 and 23, 1918, pp. 28–31. A later report by Vinaver may also be found in the Wrangel Military Archives (WMA), File 129.

⁵ Gegechkori's government resigned to protest continuation of negotiations with the Turks on the latter's terms. Chkhenkeli's government which then took power was the only government which the short-lived Transcaucasian Federation had as an independent republic. The next government formed, under Zhordaniia, was for independent Georgia alone. See Z. D. Avalov, *The Independence of Georgia in International Politics, 1918–1921* (London: Headley Bros., 1940), pp. 29, 97.

⁶ Transcaucasian officials did confer with Allied representatives still in Tiflis but were told by them that Allied aid could not yet be obtained and that therefore it would be advisable to seek as favorable a peace with Turkey as possible. See J. Loris-Melikof, *La révolution russe et les nouvelles républiques transcaucasiennes* (Paris: F. Alcan, 1920), pp. 112, 124.

⁷ Records of the negotiations with the Turks may be found in Georgia, Ministerstvo Vneshnikh Del, *Dokumenty i materialy po vneshnei politike Zakavkaz'ia i Gruzii* (Tiflis: Tip. Pravitel'stva Gruzinskoi Respubliki, 1919). Von Lossow was German High Command representative in Turkey at this time. He was accompanied at the negotiations by the German consul-general in Tiflis, Count Schulenburg. Also present at these talks was the leader of the North Caucasus Mountain Republic, Chermoev, who later accompanied a Georgian delegation to London. See Avalov, *op. cit.*, p. 34. German-Turk rivalry was obviously an important factor in German support for the Transcaucasian government at this time and in subsequent German efforts to beat the Turks to Baku. General Ludendorff thus urged strong support for Georgia to give it "security against the greedy Turks" and suggested that an attempt by the Turks to occupy Baku or to take over the rail line from Tiflis to Baku should be regarded "as an act of hostility" toward Germany. See Z. A. B. Zeman, ed., *Germany and the Revolution in Russia, 1915–1918: Documents from the Archives of the German Foreign Ministry* (London: Oxford University Press, 1958), pp. 134–135. Cf. Firuz Kazemzadeh, *The Struggle for Transcaucasia, 1917–1921* (New York: Philosophical Library, 1951), p. 147; L. Fischer, *Oil Imperialism* (New York: International Publishers, 1926), p. 25; and G. Lenczowski, *The Middle East in World Affairs*, 2nd ed. (Ithaca: Cornell University Press, 1956), p. 65.

⁸ Avalov, *op. cit.*, pp. 54–68. See also John Buchan, ed., *The Baltic and Caucasian States* (Boston: Houghton, Mifflin Co., 1923), pp. 215–216.

⁹ Since the Turks' main objective at this time was Baku, they agreed to peace treaties with Georgia and a rump Armenia also in June and concentrated on a joint military effort with their Azerbaidzhani allies. See Avalov, *op. cit.*, pp. 38–43, 81–84; and Kazemzadeh, *op. cit.*, pp. 124–127. On the establishment of an independent Azerbaidzhan, see its government's collection of documents in *Le 28 Mai, 1919; Le jour du premier anniversaire de l'indépendance de la République d'Azerbeidjan* (Baku, 1919), Azerbaidzhan delegation propaganda (Hoover Library), pp. 8–9.

¹⁰ According to the best estimates there were probably some 1,600,000 German and Austrian prisoners-of-war in Russia, of whom the Bolsheviks recruited and armed about 15,000. At least 5,000 of the latter were in Turkestan, out of a total of about 35,000 there. See G. F. Kennan, *Soviet-American Relations, 1917–1920*, Vol. II, *The Decision to Intervene* (Princeton: Princeton University Press, 1958), pp. 71–73. See also R. H. Ullman, *Anglo-Soviet Relations, 1917–1921*, Vol. I, *Intervention and the War* (Princeton: Princeton University Press, 1961), pp. 156, 311. Cf. J. Bunyan, ed., *Intervention, Civil War and Communism in Russia, April–December 1918: Documents and Materials* (Baltimore: Johns Hopkins Press, 1936), p. 92; and P. T. Etherton, *In the Heart of Asia* (London: Constables and Co., 1925), pp. 1–2.

¹¹ See Haider Bammate, *The Caucasus Problem: Questions Concerning Circassia and Daghestan* (Berne: Staempfli et Cie., 1919), pp. 30–32. A map showing the borders claimed is included.

¹² See Paul Khrystiuk, *Zamitky i materialy do istorii Ukrains'koi revoliutsii, 1917–1920 gg.* (Vienna: Ukrains'kii Sotsiol'ohichnii Instytut, Drukernia J. N. Vernay, 1921), Vol. III, pp. 15 ff., 39; Doroshenko, *Istoriia Ukrainy*, II, 86, 260, 265; and V. Vynnychenko, *Vidrodzhennia natsii* (Vienna: Dzvin, 1920), Vol. III, p. 67. However, two Socialist Federalists joined the Hetman's administration. D. Doroshenko, who resigned from his party for the purpose, became foreign Minister, and A. Shul'gin accepted the post of ambassador to Bulgaria. See Reshetar, *op. cit.*, pp. 151, 184. Vynnychenko resumed active leadership of the opposition, as president of the Ukrainian National Union, in September.

¹³ See A. I. Denikin, *Ocherki russkoi smuty*, Vol. III (Berlin: "Slovo," 1924), p. 87.

¹⁴ For an account of the development of the Center and other anti-Bolshevik organizations, see Denikin, *Ocherki russkoi smuty*, III, 73 ff.

¹⁵ In its bimonthly organ later published in Paris, the Union defined itself as a coalition of "democratic elements, socialist and non-socialist, which are united on the following platform: (1) organization of the armed struggle against the Germans and the Bolsheviks in alliance with the Allies, (2) convocation of a constituent assembly on the basis of universal, equal, direct, and secret suffrage, and (3) institution by the Constituent of a political regime which will be based on popular sovereignty, which will assure land to the peasants and free development to all nationalities and all classes." For the duration of the civil war the Union favored a three-man directorate to lead the struggle. For the Union's position see *La Russie Démocratique* (Paris organ of the Union), Année I, No. 3, June 12, 1919. See also Denikin, *Ocherki russkoi smuty*, III, 74–75.

¹⁶ The Germans were at this time, as a Foreign Ministry spokesman put it, "reckoning with the possibility of the overthrow of the Bolsheviks," a possibility

which made it necessary to prepare German influence with anti-Bolshevik elements. The German counsellor of legation in Moscow advised his superiors to indicate a willingness to revise some parts of the Brest treaty. See Zeman, op. cit., pp. 131, 133.

[17] See Miliukov, "Dnevnik, 1918 section, p. 46 ff. Cf. Denikin, Ocherki russkoi smuty, III, 75. It is interesting to note that both the pro-German and the pro-Allied factions opposed a Japanese intervention, although the former were the most outspoken critics of Japanese aid.

[18] See dispatch from Lockhart to the Foreign Office, May 17, 1918, in the U. S. National Archives, Foreign Affairs Section, Doc. No. 861.00/1897½. Cf. Miliukov, "Dnevnik," 1918 section, pp. 4–5, 44–45, 49–50.

[19] See Lockhart's reports to the Foreign Office of May 27 and May 30, 1918, in U. S. National Archives, Foreign Affairs Section, Doc. No. 861.00/2080½ and Doc. No. 861.00/2072.

[20] The Kadet (or National Freedom) party was thrown into considerable confusion by the tendency of branch units in the South to formulate their own policies, often in contradiction to the central organs. In a thesis by N. I. Astrov adopted at the May conference in Moscow, the party forbade any member to enter any agreement with the Germans concerning the establishment of state authority, but it admitted the possibility of members participating in local governments under German aegis if the purpose was solely to serve the people's interest in accordance with local conditions. See protocols, resolutions, etc. of the Central Committee of the Party of National Freedom in the P. N. Miliukov Personal Archives. Correspondence to and from party members in Kiev expressing opposing positions on the question of seeking German aid may also be found here. See also Miliukov, "Dnevnik," 1918 section, p. 28.

[21] The split-up of the Moscow Center made possible a greater degree of cooperation between the National Center and the Union for Regeneration, a coalition which French Ambassador Noulens had been working to produce since May. The National Center and the Union tentatively reached a working compromise on the basis of their mutual hostility toward German aid. The Center thus indicated that it would not object in all cases to the principle of a directorate as proposed by the Union, and the latter agreed that if a directorate were established it should include the commander of the military forces (particular reference was to the commander of the Volunteer Army) along with one socialist and one nonsocialist (probably a Kadet). Both also agreed in principle that the future of Russia should be determined by a new constituent assembly. Cooperation between these two groups facilitated the task of obtaining Allied aid, but it had little other practical effect. See P. N. Miliukov, Russia Today and Tomorrow (New York: Macmillan, 1922), pp. 130–132. See also Denikin, Ocherki russkoi smuty, III, 78.

[22] See Denikin, Ocherki russkoi smuty, III, 77, and Piontkovskii, op. cit., p. 157 ff.

[23] See Trubetskoi's letters from Kiev relating his experiences (particularly those dated August 11 and August 12, 1918) in the Miliukov Personal Archives.

[24] During this time Miliukov was living incognito (as "Professor Ivanov") on the estate of the Korostovetz family in Chernigov guverniia as the guest of his former personal secretary in the Foreign Ministry, V. Korostovetz. See V. Korostovetz, Seed and Harvest (London: Faber and Faber, Ltd., 1931). Korostovetz's

uncle, a former Russian minister to Persia and China and an advocate of cooperation with the Skoropadskii regime, accepted appointment from the latter as a Ukrainian envoy. An account of his mission may be found in his "Moia komandirovka iz Kieva v Jassy v 1918 godu," in the Miliukov Personal Archives.

[25] Seven letters of this correspondence, dated from May 16 to July 1, 1918, are in the Miliukov Personal Archives. Copies of four of them (dated May 16, 19, and 21, and June 20) are in the Wrangel Personal Archives, Kotliarevskii Section, File I, section b. Some were also later published in issues of *Novoe Vremia* (Belgrade) for April 26, May 7, May 28, June 7, and June 23, 1921.

[26] See Miliukov's letters to Alekseev from Rostov-on-Don, May 16 and May 19, 1918, Miliukov Personal Archives.

[27] Miliukov's letter to Alekseev from Novocherkassk, May 21, 1918, Miliukov Personal Archives. Miliukov's warning about the possibility of others seeking German aid was borne out by negotiations which subsequently took place between representatives of the extreme Right and the Germans. On July 21, for example, two representatives of the Right Center met with an official of the German Embassy in Moscow to discuss the possibility of cooperation. The German representative declined active participation in an effort to overthrow the Bolsheviks, however, and he expressed great scepticism concerning the reliability of the so-called Germanophiles in Russia. It was also clear from the conversation that the Brest treaty posed a most serious obstacle to cooperation. However, it is notable that these Rightist representatives sought in particular to act independently of the Volunteer Army and to seize power in the center, with German help, before the Volunteers had a chance to move in. A stenographic record of this conference may be found in the Miliukov Personal Archives. For another first-hand account of negotiations with the Germans, see V. I. Gurko, "Iz Petrograda cherez Moskvu, Parizh, i London v Odessu," *Arkhiv Russkoi Revoliutsii*, Vol. XV (Berlin: Izdatel'stvo "Slovo," 1924), pp. 8–20.

[28] Miliukov letter to Alekseev, May 19, 1918, Miliukov Personal Archives.

[29] Letter from Alekseev to Miliukov from Mechetinsk, May 5/18, 1918, Miliukov Personal Archives. See also Miliukov's letter of May 21 and Alekseev's reply of May 12/25 in Miliukov Personal Archives and *Novoe Vremia*, June 2, 1921. In a later account of his activities at this time, given to a French journalist, Miliukov stated that "It was the Germans who, on their own initiative, came to see him in Kiev. . . ." Strictly speaking this was true, but it is clear from his letters and from entries in his diary that he went to Kiev specifically for such talks and himself arranged the "invitation." See the interview in *Le Temps* (Paris), December 26, 1918, and compare with Miliukov's letter to Alekseev from Kiev, June 20, 1918, Miliukov Personal Archives, and with entries for this period in his "Dnevnik," 1918 section, pp. 10–14.

[30] It is notable that the counsellor of the German Embassy in Moscow had just prior to this recommended drawing Kadet leaders into any negotiations with anti-Bolshevik elements, first because they represented a major party and secondly because it would be useful to "compromise them" with the Allies in case no agreement could be reached. However, the German Foreign Ministry had already on May 18 informed Ambassador Mirbach that it regarded the Kadets in general as "anti-German" and even doubted the advisibility of dealing with the monarchists, since these elements would undoubtedly seek a revision of the Brest treaty

and reunification of Russia. The Foreign Ministry, this note stated, favored a policy designed "to prevent Russian consolidation as far as possible" and therefore believed support should go to "the parties furthest to the left." The initiative for talks with Miliukov apparently came from the military command. For the German notes on these matters, see Zeman, op. cit., pp. 128–129, 131. Cf. Ludendorff's appraisal of the situation and his advocacy of dealing with anti-Bolshevik elements, especially the monarchists, in ibid., pp. 134–136.

³¹ See Miliukov's account in his "Dnevnik," 1918 section, pp. 16–24. The Le Temps interview indicates that Miliukov talked with an officer of the political intelligence department of the German Command on June 24 and July 10, and the diary indicates that his talk with General Haase was on June 21 and a second conference was held with the German ambassador, Mumm, on June 27.

³² Miliukov, "Dnevnik," 1918 section, pp. 37–40. Miliukov implies that his contacts with the moderate Left were the cause of Mumm's distrust.

³³ Le Temps, December 26, 1918.

³⁴ See the interview with Miliukov in the Pall Mall Gazette, January 15, 1919. Copies of this interview as well as that in Le Temps may be found in the Miliukov Personal Archives.

³⁵ Although Krasnov's status was to be provisional until the scheduled meeting of the Grand Krug in August, he immediately assumed dictatorial powers. Under the basic law introduced by him, he appointed the government, had a veto on all legislation, and was commander-in-chief of the armed forces. See Donskaia Letopis', Vol. III (Belgrade: Izdanie Donskoi Istoricheskoi Komissii, 1924), pp. 320–326. See also N. N. Golovin, Rossiiskaia kontrrevoliutsiia v 1917–1918 gg. (Paris: "Illiustrirovannoi Rossii," 1937), Vol. V, Bk. 10, Chap. 22 and Appendices Nos. 69 and 70, pp. 49–59; Bunyan, op. cit., pp. 32–35; and V. Dobrynin, La lutte contre le bolchevisme dans la Russie meriodionale (Prague: Imp. "Melantrich," 1920), pp. 58–60. Cf. David Footman, Civil War in Russia (London: Faber and Faber, 1961), p. 74 ff.

³⁶ Golovin, op. cit., Vol. V, Bk. 10, p. 20; K. P. Kakliugin, "Donskoi Ataman P. N. Krasnov i ego vremia," Donskaia Letopis', III, 81. Krasnov also attempted to initiate negotiations with the Bolsheviks immediately after becoming Ataman. His envoy, A. Padalkin, left for Moscow on May 17 and arrived there a week later. He was at first given cordial treatment, but when he attempted to leave Moscow he was arrested. Although he was soon again released, there was no more talk of negotiations. See A. Padalkin, "Poezdka v Moskvu k Leninu s pis'mom donskogo atamana P. N. Krasnova," Donskaia Letopis', III, 261–267. The attitude thenceforth adopted by the Soviet government was expressed in a declaration to the Cossacks on May 30 which stated: "The Soviet of People's Commissars hereby declares that the Don region is an integral part of the Russian Socialist Federated Soviet Republic . . . Krasnov and his helpers and allies [are declared] to be enemies of the people . . . outside the law. Death to the traitors!" See Bunyan, op. cit., pp. 36–37.

³⁷ On Krasnov's policies, see Golovin, op. cit., Vol. V, Bk. 10, pp. 14–19; Kakliugin, op. cit., p. 68 ff. Cf. Krasnov's own defense of his policies against charges of separatism in P. N. Krasnov, Kazach'ia "samostiinost" (Berlin: "Dvuglavyi Orel," 1921), and P. N. Krasnov, "Vsevelikoe voisko Donskoe," Arkhiv Russkoi

Revoliutsii, Vol. V (Berlin: Izdatel'stvo "Slovo," 1922), pp. 190–321.

[38] Svechin, *op. cit.*, Part I, pp. 38–39; Bunyan, *op. cit.*, pp. 35–36; I. I. Mints and E. Gorodetskii, eds., *Dokumenty po istorii grazhdanskoi voiny v SSSR*, Vol. I (Moscow: Gospolitizdat, 1940), p. 230. Cheriachukin's instructions are noted in A. V. Cheriachukin, "Donskaia delegatsiia na Ukraine i v Berline v 1918–1919," *Donskaia Letopis'*, III, 165–173; and in the Cheriachukin Papers, File II, NN. 1–3

[39] Svechin, *op. cit.*, Part II, pp. 52–55. See also Golovin, *op. cit.*, Vol. V, Bk. 10, pp. 21–22; and Kakliugin, *op. cit.*, p. 81. Cf. Miliukov, "Dnevnik," 1918 section, pp. 6, 15, 25.

[40] See General Svechin's report of June 21, 1918, in "Germanskaia interventsiia i Donskoe pravitel'stvo v 1918 g.," *Krasnyi Arkhiv*, Vol. LXVII (Moscow: Gosizdat, 1934), pp. 120–122. Cf. Bunyan, *op. cit.*, pp. 40–42.

[41] The text of this letter, dated July 11, 1918, may be found in Krasnov, "Vsevelikoe voisko Donskoe," *loc. cit.*, p. 210; Cheriachukin, "Donskaia delegatsiia . . . ," *loc. cit.*, pp. 196–198; Kakliugin, *op. cit.*, pp. 92–94; "Germanskaia interventsiia i Donskoe pravitel'stvo," *loc. cit.*, pp. 97, 120; Mints and Gorodskii, *Dokumenty po istorii grazhdanskoi voiny v SSSR*, I, 232–233; and Bunyan, *op. cit.*, p. 43. The letter was apparently not delivered directly to the Kaiser but initially sent to German authorities in Kiev. Cheriachukin, who later carried it to Berlin, was not received by the Kaiser. In view of considerable opposition to his policy within his own government, Krasnov took personal responsibility for the letter and the steps which accompanied. See Golovin, *op. cit.*, Vol. V. Bk. 10, pp. 23–24; Kakliugin, *op. cit.*, p. 75; and the Cheriachukin Papers, File III.

[42] For the text of the proposed constitution, see Denikin, *Ocherki russkoi smuty*, III, 246–247; and Bunyan, *op. cit.*, pp. 44-46. Krasnov's proposals included statements on neutrality in the World War, opposition to "invasion of its territories by any foreign troops," and "peaceful relations with all states." In later years Krasnov, however, denied having really taken the idea of the League seriously. See Krasnov, *Kazach'ia "samostiinost'*," p. 23.

[43] Denikin, *Ocherki russkoi smuty*, III, 248. Only the Astrakhan ataman, Tundutov, who was also seeking German aid, actually signed the proposed treaty. See Kakliugin, *op. cit.*, p. 97. On the Kuban response to German advice to unite with the Ukraine or join the League, see Miliukov, "Dnevnik," 1918 section, p. 12.

[44] See Krasnov, "Vsevelikoe voisko Donskoe," *loc. cit.*, pp. 207–210; and Kakliugin, *op. cit.*, p. 81. Cf. Footman, *op. cit.*, p. 76 ff.

[45] See note 27 above.

[46] See von Hintze's note and the Soviet reply in the Denikin Archives. Chicherin's note is in WMA, File 141, GHQ, Azbuka reports.

[47] See Denikin, *Ocherki russkoi smuty*, III, 75–78, 87, 246–249, 262. On opinions within the Volunteer Army, see B. M. Brofel'dt, "Vospominaniia" (MS, Columbia University Russian Archive), Part II, p. 96; Part III, p. 3 ff. and Ia. M. Lisovoi, ed., *Belyi arkhiv* (Paris, 1926), Vol. I, pp. 138–149. Cf. the Volunteer Army pamphlet, *Kratkaia zapiska istorii vzaimootnoshenii Dobrovol'cheskoi armii s Ukrainoi* (Rostov-on-Don: Tip. "Donskogo akts. o-va. pech. i izd. dela," 1919), pp. 3–4; Golovin, *op. cit.*, Vol. V, Bk. 10, pp. 27–30; and Krasnov, "Vsevelikoe voisko Donskoe," *Arkhiv Russkoi Revoliutsii*, Vol. V (Berlin: Izda-

tel'stvo "Slovo," 1922), pp. 200–202. Alekseev indicated in a letter to Denikin in
July 1918 that Denikin himself and his chief of staff, Romanovskii, were "considered definitely republicans if not socialists" by many of their subordinates. See
Denikin, Ocherki, russkoi smuty, III, 130–133, 137. On Denikin's relations with
Krasnov see also A. A. Smagin, "Vospominaniia" (MS, Columbia University Russian Archive), p. 22 ff. Generally, the most reactionary of the officers were those of
the old elite, the Guards, who continued to exist as the nobility within the officer
corps, although the officer corps had been opened to those not of the nobility
since the reforms of the 1870's. Denikin, who was not included in their number,
never recognized any special status for the Guards, and even made a point of stressing the equality of all in a given rank regardless of their social origin. They in turn
were the most distrustful of his motives and ultimately became the leaders of the
Army faction opposed to his command. For a biased but interesting description
of this internal division, see "Zapiska o reaktsionnom dvizhenii v voennoi sred
i o merakh bor'by s nim," in the Miliukov Archives. See also G. Shavel'skii,
"Vospominaniia," p. 337 and passim (MS, Columbia University Russian Archive).

[48] Although Krasnov could not match the strength of the Bolsheviks in Tsaritsyn, Don efforts did prevent some Bolshevik forces from being sent farther south
to oppose Volunteer operations toward the Caucasus. Denikin felt it necessary, if
possible, to establish a base on the Black Sea through which Allied aid could
eventually come, and he feared that the Germans would try to occupy the Kuban
if the Volunteers did not do so first. See Golovin, op. cit., Vol. V. Bk. 10, pp.
30–37; and Bk. 11, p. 7 ff.

[49] It should also be noted, however, that after considerable urging from Alekseev
the Allied representatives in Moscow, chiefly Lockhart and Lavergne, apparently
did agree to supply financial support to the Volunteers and sent 10 million
rubles in July. The extent of German influence in the South clearly disturbed
Lockhart and probably led him to abandon his previous hesitations in this regard.
See Ullman, op. cit., I, 232.

[50] Krasnov, "Vsevelikoe voisko Donskoe," loc. cit., p. 207. Cf. Footman, op.
cit., p. 83.

[51] The best study of the formation of the Legion and its subsequent role in
Russia is that by J. F. N. Bradley, La Legion Tschecoslovaque en Russie, 1914–
1920 (Paris: Centre National de la Recherche Scientifique, 1965) (On the background see Chap. 2). See also Kennan, op. cit., II, 136 ff.; and Ullman, op. cit.,
I, 151 ff.

[52] Bradley, op. cit., pp. 61–66.

[53] Ibid., pp. 63–65.

[54] Ibid., pp. 67–69. See also Page to secretary of state, summary of British
Foreign Office intelligence report of April 11, 1918, U. S. National Archives,
Foreign Affairs Section, Doc. No. 763.72/9693. It was suggested at this time
that Russian troops in France could be offered to the Soviet government in trade
for the Czechs if it should be necessary in order to obtain Bolshevik permission
for the transfer of the Legion out of Russia. However, this idea was set aside, and
the question of the disposition of Russian troops in France was not revived until
a later date. See also W. S. Churchill, The World Crisis: The Aftermath (London: Thornton Butterworth, Ltd., 1929), p. 92. Cf. materials in Bunyan, op. cit.,
p. 75 ff.

⁵⁵ Bradley, op. cit., pp. 73–80.

⁵⁶ Churchill, op. cit., p. 94.

⁵⁷ Bradley, op. cit., p. 80 ff. The revolt was immediately branded by the Soviet government as a deliberate act instigated by Allied agents against Moscow. The Allied governments denied this allegation and protested Soviet actions against the Czechs, warning that further such interference with their movements would be regarded as "an act inspired by Germany and hostile to the Allies." R. H. Bruce Lockhart, Memoirs of a British Agent (London: Putnam, 1932), pp. 282–284. See also Ullman, op. cit., I, 195, 211–212; and Churchill, op. cit., pp. 94–95. For the Soviet protests, see R.S.F.S.R. Commissariat for Foreign Affairs, Correspondance diplomatique se rapportant aux rélations entre la République russe et les puissances de l'Entente, 1918 (Moscow: Commissariat du peuple pour les affaires étrangerès, 1919), pp. 13–15; U.S.S.R. Ministry of Foreign Affairs, Dokumenty vneshnei politiki SSSR, Vol. I (Moscow: Gospolitizdat, 1957), pp. 326–327, 329, 347–348, 356–358, 367, 376–378, 389; and G. V. Chicherin, Two Years of Foreign Policy (New York: Russian Soviet Government Bureau, 1920), p. 12.

⁵⁸ Bradley, op. cit., p. 86.

⁵⁹ For accounts of the debate over Allied policy and the involvement of the Czech issue in intervention plans, see Ullman, op. cit., I, 153 ff.; and Kennan, op. cit., II, 140 ff. See also G. F. Kennan, Russia and the West Under Lenin and Stalin (Boston: Little, Brown and Co., 1961), pp. 70–71, 97 ff. Memoranda and notes of January and February 1918, indicating various proposals for intervention in Russia, apart from the question of the use of the Czech forces, may be found in Foreign Relations, 1918, Russia, II, 20–21, 35–36, 38–41. See also Reinsch to Lansing, February 15, 1918, U. S. National Archives, Foreign Affairs Section, Doc. No. 861.00/1093.

⁶⁰ The first specific proposals for the use of the Czech Legion as an intervention force were made by the British War Office to Czech leaders themselves on April 1, then to the Allied military representatives in the Supreme War Council on April 8, although the idea had been broached even earlier. See E. Benes, My War Memoirs (Boston: Houghton, 1928), p. 357; and records of the military representatives' meeting of April 8 in the Supreme War Council Records, U. S. National Archives, Modern Army Section. See also British Foreign Office intelligence reports in File No. 763.72; U. S. National Archives, Foreign Affairs Section; and memoranda from and to the French Foreign Ministry in the Maklakov Archives, Series B, Packet I, Dossier 11, Paris Embassy (Hoover Library). Cf. Lloyd George, War Memoirs, VI, 3175–3177. Shortly after the appointment of General Poole it was decided by the British to send an expeditionary force to Murmansk, and later to Arkhangelsk, one of whose functions would be "to equip and train such Czecho-Slovaks as should find their way to that port, and also to take in hand the organization, equipment, and training of a local Russian contingent . . ." as later reported by its commander, Major General C. C. M. Maynard. This expeditionary force was then, on May 23, ordered to proceed to Murmansk. It should be kept in mind, however, that this action was to be directed solely against the Germans (and the Finnish "Whites") and, if at all possible, was to be undertaken in cooperation with the Soviet government and the local soviet in Murmansk. See C. Maynard, The Murmansk Venture, 1918–1919 (London: Hodder and Stoughton Ltd., 1928), pp. 12–14; Ullman, op. cit., I, 154–155, 169–173;

and Kennan, *Soviet-American Relations*, II, 263–264. Cf. Footman, *op. cit.*, p. 167 ff.

⁶¹ Lockhart, *op. cit.*, pp. 280–281; Lockhart to Foreign Office, May 17, 27, and 30, 1918, U. S. National Archives, Foreign Affairs Section, File 861.00, NN. 1897½, 2080½, and 2072. Lockhart remained noncommital toward the anti-Bolshevik elements longer than most of his colleagues and did not take a stand in favor of intervention to help them until late in May.

⁶² See *Foreign Relations, 1918, Russia*, II, 213–214, 471, 474, 476 and *Doku-menty vneshnei politiki*, I, 379, 390–392. For an account of relations with the Murmansk soviet and complications with Moscow, see Ullman, *op. cit.*, I, 178 ff.

⁶³ See Miliukov, *Russia Today and Tomorrow*, pp. 134–135; Lockhart, *op. cit.*, pp. 288–289.

⁶⁴ In the voting for the Constituent Assembly on November 25, 1917, of the 707 members elected 410 were Socialist Revolutionaries (370 Right Socialist Revolutionaries and 40 Left Socialist Revolutionaries), 175 were Bolsheviks, 17 Kadets, 16 Mensheviks, and most of the remainder were members of various "national groups." See I. S. Malchevskii, ed., *Vserossiiskoe uchreditel'noe sobranie* (Moscow: Gosizdat, 1930), p. 115; O. H. Radkey, *The Election to the Russian Constituent Assembly of 1917* (Cambridge: Harvard University Press, 1950), p. 80. For a history of the Socialist Revolutionaries in this period, up to the Constituent Assembly, see O. H. Radkey, *The Sickle Under the Hammer* (New York: Columbia University Press, 1963).

⁶⁵ The Left Socialist Revolutionaries had withdrawn from the government in March in protest against the ratification of the Brest treaty, but they still formed a major faction in the soviets and held important posts in the administrative apparatus and the police. For their part, the Right Socialist Revolutionaries, at a conference in May, had called for the overthrow of the Bolshevik government and the establishment of a "government based on universal suffrage and willing to accept Allied assistance in the war against Germany." See S. A. Piontkovskii, ed., *Grazh-danskaia voina v Rossii* (Moscow: Izd. Kom. univ., 1925), pp. 154–156; E. H. Carr, *The Bolshevik Revolution, 1917–1923*, Vol. I (New York: Macmillan, 1951), pp. 161–162.

⁶⁶ *Foreign Relations, 1918, Russia*, II, 243.

⁶⁷ The Cheka vice-chairman, Aleksandrovich, provided the passes which admitted the assassins of Mirbach to the German Embassy. Ironically, just prior to this Mirbach himself had been speculating on the possible overthrow of the Bolshevik regime by German troops in alliance with some anti-Bolshevik elements, although he excluded the possibility of working with the Socialist Revolutionaries because he believed them to be "financed by the Entente and equipped with Czechoslovak arms, quite openly leading a new Russia back into the ranks of our enemies." See Zeman, *op. cit.*, pp. 137–139, note from Mirbach to Berlin, June 25, 1918. On July 14 the Germans, expressing sharp irritation at the assassination of the ambassador, demanded the right to send a battalion of troops to Moscow to protect the Embassy. However, this demand was not pressed after the Soviet government assured the Germans that a stronger Soviet guard would be provided and that the auxiliary staff of their Embassy could be increased to 300. To the Bolsheviks this relatively easy reconciliation with the Germans, plus the subsequent

appointment of Helfferich, an expert on economic relations, to succeed Mirbach, indicated a decisive shift in the German Foreign Ministry toward a more "conciliatory policy." See *Dokumenty vneshnei politiki*, I, 397–400; Chicherin, *op. cit.*, pp. 15–16.

[68] Footman, *op. cit.*, pp. 98–99. On the efforts of the Socialist Revolutionary members of the Constituent Assembly (the group was sometimes called Komuch for short) to form a new government and prepare for an alliance with the Allied governments, see Golovin, *op. cit.*, Vol. III, Bk. 7, pp. 81–85.

[69] See *Ispoved' Savinkova: protsess* . . ., pp. 49–51; Savinkov, *Bor'ba s bol'shevikami*, pp. 24–28; and Miliukov, *Russia Today and Tomorrow*, pp. 130–133. Miliukov notes that advance information on the Allied landings helped to encourage the uprisings—Ambassador Noulens, for example, had informed both the National Center and the Union for Regeneration that the Allies would send troops—but he also notes that what resulted was largely debate rather than coordinated action. Ullman notes that Lockhart had instructions not to become involved in Savinkov's plans, but Lockhart himself indicates that French representatives were already strongly supporting Savinkov and that both French and British agents were in contact with the Left Socialist Revolutionaries who were plotting in Moscow. See Ullman, *op. cit.*, I, 190, 231; Lockhart, *op. cit.*, pp. 274, 288–289, 292–301. Cf. Joseph Noulens, *Mon ambassade en Russie Sovietique* (Paris: Plon, 1933), Vol. II, pp. 109–110. It seems quite likely, as Footman has noted, that "local Allied liaison officers may well have gone further in their advice and encouragement than was warranted by their instructions." The result was first unfounded expectations and then, after failure, resentment over Allied actions. See Footman, *op. cit.*, pp. 100–101; Bradley, *op. cit.*, pp. 87–92; Miliukov, *Russia Today and Tomorrow*, p. 135–136.

[70] At their meeting on July 2 the Allied leaders agreed that intervention on a substantial scale was not only "urgently necessary in order to save Russia" from German control but also "essential in order to win the war," and it was stated that the "primary object of Allied action" should be "to cooperate with the Russian nation in re-creating the eastern front as a first step towards freeing Russia." The Aide-Memoire of the United States of July 17 constituted only a limited acceptance of the War Council's recommendations and insisted that "the only legitimate object for which American or Allied troops can be employed" was to aid the Czechs and "to guard military stores which may subsequently be needed by Russian forces and to render such aid as may be acceptable to the Russians in the organization of their own self-defense." It should further be noted that the actual execution of a large-scale intervention was considered dependent upon agreement with the Japanese on their participation. The latter was tentatively concluded on July 24 but not publicly declared until August 2. For these statements in the order mentioned, see *Foreign Relations, 1918, Russia*, II, 241–246, 287–290, 301–302, 324–325. For accounts of these negotiations see Ullman, *op. cit.*, I, 211–229; and Kennan, *Soviet-American Relations*, II, 381 ff.

[71] Lockhart, *op. cit.*, p. 308. The addition of American, French and Serbian troops, however, brought the total force in Arkhangelsk to about 8,500 men in September. Also in September the force under General Maynard in Murmansk was reinforced and brought up to about 15,000 men. See Ullman, *op. cit.*, I, 230 ff.; Footman, *op. cit.*, pp. 172–176.

[72] See M. A. Kedrov, *Bez bol'shevistskogo rukovodstva (iz istorii interventsii na Murmane)* (Leningrad: Izdat. "Krasnaia gazeta," 1930), p. 28. For a full account of developments in the north, see Kennan, *Soviet-American Relations*, II, 15–57, 245–276, 363–380; L. I. Strakhovsky, *The Origins of American Intervention in North Russia* (Princeton: Princeton Univ. Press, 1937); and Ullman, *op. cit.*, I, 178 ff.

[73] Lockhart, *op. cit.*, p. 283. Most of the Allied diplomatic personnel, who had gone to Vologda earlier, had already left the country. Those remaining (aside from the very small staffs in Moscow) had taken refuge in Arkhangelsk along with Ambassadors Noulens and Francis. See Ullman, *op. cit.*, I, 234–238; Noulens, *op. cit.*, II, 180–181; Lockhart, *op. cit.*, pp. 312–331, 334. Sadoul and one of his associates, Marchand, remained in Soviet Russia for a time and then returned to France as Communists. Sidney Reilly, a British intelligence agent who had worked with Lockhart, went to South Russia and worked for a while with the Volunteer Army, after which he reportedly joined Savinkov's movement. See M. S. Margulies, *God interventsii* (Berlin: Izdatel'stvo Z. I. Grzhebina—Z. J. Grschebin Verlag—1923), I, 236–237. See also René Marchand, *Why I Support Bolshevism* (London: British Socialist Party, n. d.).

[74] For the texts of the formal agreements, see *Dokumenty vneshnei politiki*, I, 437–453, 692–703, especially 443–444. On the understanding with regard to Baku and its oil see Lenin's telegram to Stalin in *ibid.*, p. 381. Germany was also to seek Soviet recognition of Georgia, but no official statement of such recognition was actually obtained before the German withdrawal. See Pipes, *op. cit.*, p. 211.

[75] Avalov, *op. cit.*, pp. 93–95, 98–99. While the Georgian delegation was in Berlin, Avalov made a side trip to Oslo where he contacted the British and French ambassadors and informed them of the negotiations with the Germans.

[76] For an account of several German attempts to establish contacts with the Volunteer Army and its categorical rejection of relations, see Denikin, *Ocherki russkoi smuty*, III, 114.

[77] See Golovin, *op. cit.*, Vol. V, Bk. 10, p. 37 ff. and Chap. 14; Denikin, *Ocherki russkoi smuty*, III, 118. Cf. Footman, *op. cit.*, pp. 76–77.

[78] Krasnov had tried to persuade General Dragomirov, Denikin's second in command under Romanovskii, to head this army, but Dragomirov bluntly declined and labelled the offer an insult and the army a pawn of the Germans. Denikin, *Ocherki russkoi smuty*, III, 124. Golovin, *op. cit.*, Vol. V, Bk. 10, p. 38.

[79] See the report of the Department of Foreign Affairs of the Don government to the Great Voisko Krug covering Krasnov's foreign policy from May through August, WMA, File 133, pp. 112–120.

[80] Golovin, *op. cit.*, Vol. V, Bk. 10, pp. 43–46. The policy of cooperation with the Germans was approved in so far as it was "based on the principle of mutual and equal satisfaction of both sides in practical questions raised by circumstances, without the Don being drawn into a struggle either for or against Germany." See also Piontkovskii, *op. cit.*, p. 413 ff.

[81] A letter from von Cochenhausen was read to the Krug on September 24 by the Don army commander, General Denisov. In this letter the German repre-

sentative warned that the German High Command would withdraw support from the Don "so long as an Ataman has not been elected in whom the German High Command can place its confidence, who will conduct the policy of the Don state in a direction friendly to Germany, and who will be entrusted by the Krug with the full authority necessary for the present critical period." Denisov was requested to convey this message to Krasnov, "in whom the German High Command has the fullest confidence," as well as to the government. See telegram from Major von Cochenhausen to Lt. General Denisov, WMA, File 133, p. 108. See also Denikin, *Ocherki russkoi smuty*, III, 126, 250; and Golovin, *op. cit.*, Vol. V, Bk. 10, Appendix No. 72, pp. 61–63.

[82] Krasnov himself listed as his "four enemies" 1) the intellectuals, 2) General Denikin, 3) foreigners, and 4) the Bolsheviks. Denikin he called his "most dreadful enemy" and the Bolsheviks he listed last and declared that he feared them "least of all because I conduct an open struggle with them and they do not pretend that they are my friends." Krasnov, "Vsevelikoe voisko Donskoe," *loc. cit.*, p. 198. See also Golovin, *op. cit.*, Vol. V, Bk. 10, p. 41. For Denikin's position see Denikin, *Ocherki russkoi smuty*, III, 251.

[83] Denikin, *Ocherki russkoi smuty*, III, 88. See also Smagin, *op. cit.*, p. 24. Cf. Bradley, *op. cit.*, p. 90.

[84] See Miliukov, *Russia Today and Tomorrow*, p. 131; Footman, *op. cit.*, p. 104 ff.

[85] For an account of these developments and the conflict between Omsk and Samara, see Golovin, *op. cit.*, Vol. IV, Bk. 8, p. 60 ff. See also Bunyan, *op. cit.*, pp. 283–285, 339–356; and Footman, *op. cit.*, pp. 109–110.

[86] Denikin, *Ocherki russkoi smuty*, III, 88. See also the introduction by S. Piontkovskii in V. V. Shul'gin, *Dni* (Belgrade: Knigoizdatel'stvo M. A. Suvorin i ko., "Novoe Vremia," 1925).

[87] Bradley, *op. cit.*, pp. 99–100.

[88] Golovin, *op. cit.*, Vol. IV, Bk. 8 pp. 101–102; *Foreign Relations, 1918, Russia*, II, 406–409. On the Ufa conference which established this government, see also the proceedings in *Russkii istoricheskii arkhiv* (Prague: Izdanie russkogo zagranichnogo istoricheskogo arkhiva v Prage; sbornik pervy, 1929); and V. L. Utgov, "Ufimskoe gosudarstvennoe soveshchanie 1918 goda," in *Byloe*, No. 16, 1921, p. 15, cited in Leonard Schapiro, *The Origin of the Communist Autocracy* (London; G. Bell and Sons, Ltd., 1955), p. 160.

[89] Bradley, *op. cit.*, pp. 105–108.

[90] See Ullman, *op. cit.*, I, 279; Churchill, *op. cit.*, p. 164. Cf. C. Nabokoff, *The Ordeal of a Diplomat* (London: Duckworth, 1921), pp. 251, 276.

[91] See Peter Fleming, *The Fate of Admiral Kolchak* (London: Rupert Hart-Davis, 1963), p. 99 ff.

[92] On the coup and subsequent formation of the Siberian front, see Fleming, *op. cit.*, p. 109 ff.; Golovin, *op. cit.*, Vol. IV, Bk. 9, pp. 30–40, 74–83; Miliukov, *Russia Today and Tomorrow*, pp. 152–155; Footman, *op. cit.*, pp. 118–133, 211 ff. Many Socialist Revolutionaries now became more alarmed by the growth of anti-Bolshevik military dictatorship than by Bolshevik terror; at a conference in Petrograd in February 1919 one faction of the party denounced any further attempts to overthrow the Soviet government by force. See Carr, *op. cit.*, I, 172.

Cf. Miliukov, Russia Today and Tomorrow, pp. 131–136. A valuable account of the rise of Kolchak may also be found in V. G. Boldyrev, Direktoriia, Kolchak, interventy (Novonikolaevsk: Gosizdat, 1925).

[93] Ullman, op. cit., I, 279; Bradley, op. cit., 109. Churchill gives November 14 as the date of the Cabinet's decision. Churchill, op. cit., p. 164.

[94] Denikin, Ocherki russkoi smuty, III, 87; Bradley, op. cit., pp. 114–115.

[95] See Etherton, op. cit., pp. 1–2; Lenczowski, op. cit., p. 44; and Ullman, op. cit., I, 305. Ludendorff, for one, favored a thrust into Persia and India. See O. S. Fedyshyn, op. cit., p. 288. Cf. Churchill, op. cit., p. 89.

[96] See British Foreign Office intelligence report, February 20, 1918, No. 8343, in U. S. National Archives, Foreign Affairs Section, Doc. No. 861.00/1277. See also Ullman, op. cit., I, 305 ff.; and History of the Great War Based on Official Documents: The Campaign in Mesopotamia, 1914–1918, Vol. IV (London: His Majesty's Stationery Office, 1927), pp. 104–105.

[97] The best first-hand accounts of the operations of the "Dunsterforce" are those by its commander and one of his assistants. See L. C. Dunsterville, The Adventures of Dunsterforce (London: Edward Arnold, 1920); and M. H. Donohoe, With the Persian Expedition (London: Edward Arnold, 1919). Additional material may be found in Ullman, op. cit., I, 305 ff.

[98] Donohoe, op. cit., p. 3. According to Major Donohoe's account the Dunsterville mission was at first given independent command status, putting it directly under the War Office rather than under General Sir Stanley Maude's Mesopotamian Command. However, this apparently aroused opposition from the latter and obstructed coordination, and so the Dunsterforce was eventually put under Maude's command. Ibid., pp. 62, 132–133. It should be noted, however, that the Malleson and Bailey missions were under the Indian army command.

[99] A number of British intelligence reports, dating from January 1918 on, may be found in the U. S. National Archives, Foreign Affairs Section, File 763.72, Doc. No. 8757 ff. In connection with reports of pro-Allied elements in Transcaucasia see particularly the report of April 18, 1918, No. 8809, which is Doc. No. 763.72/9780. The British and French military attachés in Tiflis, Colonels Pike and Chardigny, worked together in the Georgian capital until early in 1918, when they left for the North Caucasus and Baku respectively in order to establish better contacts in those areas.

[100] Dunsterville, op. cit., pp. 13–58; Donohoe, op. cit., pp. 62–64. It should also be noted that Persia was officially neutral in the World War, and the British ambassador in Teheran, Sir Charles Marling, objected to the Dunsterforce operation on grounds that British military operations against the Central Powers, using Persia as a base, would probably provoke Turkish and German military intervention. Russian and British troops were already in Persia under the 1907 agreement, which in effect established a Russian protectorate in the north and a British protectorate in the south. However, the movement of British troops out of the zone of the British sphere of influence into the north would violate both the 1907 agreement and Persian neutrality. It seems unlikely, on the other hand, that the operations of the Dunsterforce affected the German and Turkish attitudes toward the latter.

[101] Dunsterville, op. cit., pp. 77–78.

¹⁰² *Ibid.*, p. 159 ff. Financial support for Russian troops in Persia that would continue the struggle had been authorized by the British Cabinet in December 1917, when the Dunsterville mission was first being discussed, but no specific amounts had been stipulated. See Ullman, *op. cit.*, I, 51–52. Dunsterville agreed to an initial payment of 5 million Persian krons, and similar payments were to be made later. No final accounting is available, but it appears likely that Bicherakov's requests were met. See British Foreign Office intelligence reports of April 8 and May 6, 1918, U. S. National Archives, Foreign Affairs Section, Doc. Nos. 763.72/ 9645 and 763.72/10125. The British armored car brigade which joined in this action was that previously known as the Locker-Lampson Armoured Car Unit, which had been attached to the troops approaching Petrograd at the time of the Kerenskii-Kornilov dispute. Late in 1917 it had been reorganized in England and the next spring was sent to Dunsterville, arriving during May. Composed of 21 officers and 450 men, with 8 armored cars, 24 trucks, 30 cars, 44 Ford vans, and 32 motorcycles, it was an imposing force in the Persian situation and contributed substantially to Bicherakov's success. A part of the brigade was later outfitted with Russian uniforms and attached to Bicherakov's force, accompanying it as far north as Petrovsk. See Donohoe, *op. cit.*, pp. 252–270. Kuchik Khan's anti-British stance was undoubtedly nationalistic, but he also had German military advisers. See Dunsterville, *op. cit.*, p. 29.

¹⁰³ Dunsterville, *op. cit.*, pp. 166–167. See also *History of the Great War Based on Official Documents*, IV, 187. Russian diplomatic representatives in Persia were apparently informed of Bicherakov's intention, since even before he left Enzeli they had telegraphed reports of the "fantastic plan" to Russian Ambassador Maklakov in Paris, and Maklakov had replied with full approval. See telegrams from Minorskii to Maklakov, Etter to Maklakov, and Maklakov to Teheran, June 1918, in Maklakov Archives (Hoover Library), Series B, Packet I, Dossier 7.

¹⁰⁴ The Bolshevik faction in the Baku soviet hoped that the arrangement with Bicherakov would help to head off the pro-British inclinations in the soviet. Although the Bolsheviks knew that Bicherakov had worked with the British in Persia, they believed that the Cossack commander was sincere in his offer of aid. Orders from Stalin, which were supported by Lenin, precluded the possibility of any Bolshevik acceptance of British aid. See *Dokumenty vneshnei politiki*, I, 371, 401–402; and S. G. Shaumian, *Stat'i i rechi, 1908–1918* (Baku: Izdatel'stvo "Bakinskii Rabochii," 1924), p. 205. Cf. V. A. Gurko-Kriazhin, "Angliiskaia interventsiia v 1918 i 1919 gg. v Zakaspii i Zakavkaz'i," *Istorik Marksist*, No. 2 (Moscow, 1926), p. 123; and Ullman, *op. cit.*, I, 307.

¹⁰⁵ Dunsterville, *op. cit.*, p. 169 ff. See also British Foreign Office intelligence report, May 28, 1918, in U. S. National Archives, Foreign Affairs Section, No. 763.72/10322.

¹⁰⁶ For Soviet documentary material see *Bol'sheviki v bor'be za pobedu sotsialisticheskoi revoliutsii v Azerbaidzhane, 1917–1918* (Baku: Gosizdat A.S.S.R., 1957). See also Pipes, *op. cit.*, pp. 199–204.

¹⁰⁷ Dunsterville, *op. cit.*, p. 208; Ullman, *op. cit.*, I, 309; and Kazemzadeh, *op. cit.*, pp. 136–137.

¹⁰⁸ See Ia. A. Ratgauzer, *Revoliutsiia i grazhdanskaia voina v Baku*, Vol. I (Baku: Gostip. "Krasnyi Vostok," 1927), pp. 213–215; Gurko-Kriazhin, *op. cit.*, p. 124 ff.

[109] Donohoe, op. cit., pp. 211–212; C. H. Ellis, The British "Intervention" in Transcaspia, 1918–1919 (Berkeley: Univ. of California Press, 1963), pp. 36–37; Kazemzadeh, op. cit., pp. 137–138; Ullman, op. cit., I, 309. See also History of the Great War Based on Official Documents, IV, 213.

[110] The best account of the Malleson mission is that by one of its officers, C. H. Ellis, The British "Intervention" in Transcaspia, 1918–1919. Colonel Ellis indicates that Major General Malleson had served on the intelligence staff of Indian army headquarters and on Lord Kitchener's staff between 1904 and 1914 and was chosen to command "Malmiss" because of his knowledge of the area and his intelligence background. Ibid., p. 25. On Malmiss see also the memoir account of Lieutenant Colonel D. E. Knollys, "Military Operations in Transcaspia, 1918–1919," Journal of the Central Asian Society, Vol. XIII, Part II (London, 1926), pp. 89–110; and Malleson's own brief account in Major General Sir Wilfrid Malleson, "The British Military Mission to Turkestan, 1918–1920," Journal of the Central Asian Society, Vol. IX, Part II (London, 1922), pp. 96–110.

[111] Malleson, op. cit., p. 96; Ellis, op. cit., p. 29.

[112] For collections of Soviet documents on events in Transcaspia and Turkestan which contain some useful material, see Pobeda Velikoi Oktiabr'skoi sotsialisticheskoi revoliutsii v Turkestane (Tashkent: Gosizdat Uz. S.S.R., 1947), and Sh. Tashleva, ed., Turkmenistan v period inostrannoi voennoi interventsii i grazhdanskoi voiny, 1918–1920 gg.: sbornik dokumentov (Ashkhabad: Gosizdat T.S.S.R., 1957). See also Iz istorii grazhdanskoi voiny v SSSR, Vol. I (Moscow: Izdatel'stvo "Sovetskaia Rossiia," Institut Marksizma-Leninizma pri TsK KPSS, 1960), pp. 425–438. Sharp criticism of the inadequacy of Bolshevik leadership in Turkestan, especially with regard to the treatment of the non-Russian nationalities, may be found in some earlier Soviet accounts. See, for example, Z. I. Mirkin, "Interventsiia v Zakaspii," in K desiatiletiu interventsii: sbornik statei (Moscow: Gosizdat, Obshchestvo sodeistviia zhertvam interventsii, 1929), p. 165 ff.

[113] A British agent, sent to Tashkent earlier to investigate Bolshevik arming of German and Austrian prisoners-of-war, reported in May that, out of some 35,-000 in the area, about 3,000 had been recruited into the Bolshevik forces in Tashkent itself and about half that number into a force on the Afghan frontier at Kushk. This agent learned that the Bolshevik government was concentrating many of its troops in the direction of Afghanistan because of a fear that the British would encourage the Afghans to invade. Consideration of such a move was indeed taken up in the British General Staff in June, but the War Cabinet rejected the idea. It was, of course, the Bolsheviks who subsequently took up the policy of urging Afghanistan to attack the British. See Ullman, op. cit., I, 311–315.

[114] Mirkin, op. cit., pp. 166–168; Ellis, op. cit., pp. 26–27. Other members of the Ashkhabad government, or executive committee, were L. A. Zimin, an intellectual specialist on the languages and culture of Turkestan and a Right Socialist Revolutionary, minister of foreign affairs; D. Kurylev, a railwayman, minister of labor and transportation; Dmitrievskii, a banker, minister of finance; and S. L. Drushkin, a Jewish lawyer, director of public security. General Kruten, a former Russian officer in Transcaucasia and Persia who held liberal views, became the

government's chief military adviser. Hadji Murat and Obez Baev, Turkman leaders, acted as its chief advisers on relations with the native Turkman population. Colonel Oraz Sirdar, the son of a Turkman hero who had in earlier times fought to keep the Russians out of Turkestan but who had himself been trained in the Corps de Pages in St. Petersburg and had then served in General Kornilov's "Savage Division" as a cavalryman, commanded the only existing military force in the area. Sirdar put his small force, consisting of Turkman horsemen and Armenian infantry, behind the Ashkhabad government and became its major field commander. Vladimir Dokhov and Alexei Dorrer, the former a railwayman and the latter a former aristocrat and member of the Tashkent administration during the Provisional government period, were to serve as the government's chief envoys in contacts with the British. See Ellis, op. cit., pp. 27, 49, 95, 97, 99, 137. The government of Kun (Kuhn) established in Krasnovodsk shortly after the coup in Ashkhabad was considered subordinate to the executive committee in Ashkhabad. Kun was also installed by a "strike committee" of anti-Bolshevik socialists. See Ellis, op. cit., pp. 27, 59; Ullman, op. cit., I, 321.

[115] Mirkin, op. cit., p. 170; Gurko-Kriazhin, op. cit., pp. 125–126.

[116] Ellis, op. cit., pp. 41–42; Ullman, op. cit., I, 315–316; History of the Great War Based on Official Documents, IV, 209–210; Mirkin, op. cit., 169. Cf. A. Mel'kumov, Materialy revoliutsionnogo dvizheniia v Turkmenii (Tashkent: Ispart TsKKPT, 1924), p. 139.

[117] Ellis, op. cit., pp. 43–44. For the text of the agreement see Mints and Gorodetskii, Dokumenty po istorii grazhdanskoi voiny v SSSR, I, 301–302; Tashleva, op. cit., pp. 93–96; F. Kostiaev, "Interventsiia, na iuge Rossii, Kavkaz'e i v Turkestane, 1918–1920 gg.," in A. G. Shliapnikov, ed., Kto dolzhnik? Sbornik dokumentirovannykh statei po voprosy ob otnoshenniakh mezhdu Rossiei, Frantsiei i drugimi derzhavami Antanty (Moscow: Avioizdat, 1926), p. 333 ff. and Appendix No. 20, pp. 396–399. Ellis gives an English translation of the agreement in his article, "The Revolt in Transcaspia, 1918–1919," in the Central Asian Review, Vol. VII, No. 2 (London, 1959), pp. 122–125. See also his comments on the agreement in "Operations in Transcaspia, 1918–1919, and the 26 Commissars Case," in D. Footman, ed., Soviet Affairs, No. 2 (St. Anthony's Papers, No. 6) (New York: Praeger, 1959), pp. 139–140. Cf. A. H. Babakhodzhaev, Proval angliiskoi agressivnoi politiki v Srednei Asii, 1917–1920 (Tashkent: Gosizdat Uz.S.S.R., 1955). See also Ullman, op. cit., I, 317–319.

[118] Ellis, British "Intervention," pp. 51–58, 68–80.

[119] The best account of this mission is by one of its leaders, F. M. Bailey, Mission to Tashkent (London: J. Cape, 1946). See also Ellis, British "Intervention," pp. 71–75.

[120] Bailey, op. cit., p. 26; Ellis, op. cit., p. 72. In later years (a note of October 15, 1923, for example), Chicherin charged that Etherton used his consular post in Kashgar to foment the Basmachi revolts that plagued the Soviet government for several years. See Dokumenty vneshnei politiki SSSR, Vol. VI (Moscow: Gospolitizdat, 1962), p. 477. For Etherton's own account of his work, see P. T. Etherton, In the Heart of Asia (London: Constable and Co., Ltd., 1925).

[121] Bailey, op. cit., pp. 38–39.

[122] Ibid., p. 43 ff. It is worth noting in connection with the question of the

prisoners that efforts were also being made on an international level to see to the proper handling of the men involved. Arrangements had already been made for neutral Danish and Swedish diplomatic personnel to represent Germany and Austria respectively in the negotiation of a prisoner exchange, and missions had been sent into Turkestan for this purpose. These missions encountered great difficulty and experienced constant frustration in their efforts, however, and were unable to prevent Bolshevik mobilization of some of the prisoners. One Swedish Red Cross official was shot, and others were frequently arrested in this work. For a detailed account of the experiences of the Danish mission, see A. H. Brun, *Troublous Times: Experiences in Bolshevik Russia and Turkestan* (London: Constable and Co., Ltd., 1931).

[123] Bailey, *op. cit.*, p. 51 ff.

[124] Ellis, British "*Intervention*," p. 73.

[125] Rather bitter complaints on the part of the British officers assigned to organize the natives were frequent. See Donohoe, *op. cit.*, pp. 212–214; and Dunsterville, *op. cit.*, pp. 213, 224, 267–269. Even on his flagship, ironically named the *President Kruger*, Dunsterville was obliged to fly the Russian flag upside down as a compromise with the crew, which objected to its allegedly reactionary significance when flown properly. Since the Russian flag inverted was like the Serbian flag, Dunsterville could describe himself as "a British General on the Caspian . . . on board a ship named after a South African Dutch president and whilom enemy, sailing from a Persian port, under a Serbian flag, to relieve from the Turks a body of Armenians in a revolutionary Russian town." Dunsterville, *op. cit.*, p. 219. The only British officer who became directly involved in the Baku government itself was Colonel Stokes, who was given the post of chief of staff by mutual agreement.

[126] Dunsterville, *op. cit.*, pp. 260, 283–286. Krasnovodsk was a better port for naval operations, and location there would also, Dunsterville hoped, enable him to re-establish contact with Bicherakov, with whom Major Rowlandson of the Dunsterforce was working north of Baku and moving toward the Caucasus area, where Colonel Pike was still operating.

[127] Dunsterville, *op. cit.*, pp. 312–313.

[128] Probably the best account in English of the case of the Baku commissars is that in Ellis, British "*Intervention*," pp. 57–65; a similar treatment is given in his "Operations in Transcaspia, 1918–1919, and the 26 Commissars Case," *loc. cit.* Chaikin's version was later extended into book length: V. A. Chaikin, *K istorii rossiiskoi revoliutsii: kazn 26 Bakinskikh komissarov* (Moscow: Z. Grzhebin, 1922). See also Gurko-Kriazhin, *op. cit.*, p. 134 ff.: "Angliiskaia politika v Turkestane v epokhu grazhdanskoi voiny v Rossii," *Voennaia Mysl'*, No. 3, 1921; and L. S. Shaumian, *Rasstrel 26 Bakinskikh komissarov angliiskimi interventami* (Moscow: "Znanie," 1949). Cf. Ullman, *op. cit.*, I, 320–324; Donohoe, *op. cit.*, p. 218; Mirkin, *op. cit.*, p. 180: Kazemzadeh, *op. cit.*, pp. 144–145. Chicherin's protest to the British government, dated April 21. 1919, is in *Dokumenty vneshnei politiki*, Vol. II (Moscow: Gospolitizdat, 1959), pp. 141–142. Chicherin put the blame directly on Teague-Jones. The latter's version (cited by Ullman, *op. cit.*, I, 321, note 59), a rather unsatisfactory explanation of his role, was given in a letter of November 12, 1922, to the Under-Secretary of State for Foreign

Affairs, printed in Cmd. 1846 (Russia No. 1, 1923), *Correspondence between H. M. Govt. and the Soviet Govt. respecting the murder of Mr. C. F. Davison in Jan. 1920*, pp. 6–11. The Soviet propaganda use of the incident has been kept alive through the years, as witness the following comment by L. Shaumian in *Pravda* on September 20, 1963, on the forty-fifth anniversary of the event: "On September 20, 1918, 26 commissars of the Baku commune, true sons of the Communist party, passionate fighters for the happiness of the people, were shot by the English interventionists and their S. R. servants. . . . Malleson acted in full contact with the counterrevolutionary authorities of Ashkhabad and Krasnovodsk."

129 Denikin, *Ocherki russkoi smuty*, IV, 102–104; Kazemzadeh, *op. cit.*, p. 134. By the fall of 1918 contacts were established both between Bicherakov and the Transcaspian governments and between these two and the Volunteer Army. For a time N. N. Golovin even provided a contact between these elements and the Ufa Directorate, going on behalf of the latter first to Krasnovodsk and then to Baku, where he contacted the British. See B. R. Marine telegram dated October 5, 1918, in Maklakov Archives, Series B, Packet I, Dossier 8. A representative of the anti-Bolshevik "Turkestan Military Organization," E. P. Dzhunkovskii, first contacted the British in Meshed in July 1918 in hopes of getting support for plans to coordinate anti-Bolshevik activities in Turkestan, Transcaspia, Transcaucasia, and South Russia, but he had received no encouragement from the Malleson mission. At the latter's suggestion, however, he offered his services to the Ashkhabad government and was subsequently sent by the latter to establish contact with Denikin at Volunteer headquarters. Dzhunkovskii's mission was thus the beginning of a serious effort to unite the various forces fighting the Bolsheviks on a regional basis, including both Transcaspia and Bicherakov. Such efforts, as will be noted later, were only moderately successful, however. See letter from E. P. Dzhunkovskii to Denikin, October 17, 1918, Miliukov Personal Archives; and Report of the Representative of the Provisional Government of Transcaspia, E. P. Dzhunkovskii, Wrangel Military Archives, File 153, pp. 128–130. On contact with the Bicherakovs, see also Margulies, *op. cit.*, I, 49.

130 A. A. Takho-Godi, *Revoliutsiia i kontr-revoliutsiia v Dagestane* (Makhach-Kala: Dagestanskoe Gosizdat, 1927), p. 70 ff.; Allen and Muratoff, *op. cit.*, p. 507.

131 The assignment of building up a "naval" force on the Caspian had been given to the naval command of the East Indies, with the commodore of the Persian Gulf in charge. The job of fitting out and repairing any ships available was taken on by the Inland Water Transport section of the Mesopotamia Expeditionary Force, with a detachment of Naval engineers under the command of a Commander O'Dogherty. Commodore Norris began the work of converting old steamers into gunboats with four-inch guns in Enzeli while the Dunsterforce was in Baku. When Baku was evacuated, the three ships brought from there were added to the force, bringing the total to four, and naval operations headquarters were moved to Krasnovodsk. There the work of preparing more ships and maintaining those on hand was taken over by a Captain Washington. See the account of a participant in these operations, F. J. F. French (Lt. Col.), *From Whitehall to the Caspian* (London: Odhams Press, Ltd., 1920), p. 107 ff. See also Sir Percy Sykes, *A History of Persia*, 3rd ed. (London: Macmillan and Co., Ltd.,

1951), Vol. II, p. 497. A British squadron was also later stationed in the Baltic in order to pose a threat which would keep some Bolshevik gunboats from being sent to the Caspian via the Volga. For an account by a Russian naval officer serving with the British flotilla see N. N. Lishin, Na Kaspiiskom more (Prague: Izd. Mor. zhur., 1938).

[132] See French, op. cit., pp. 119, 123–125; Lishin, op. cit., p. 39 ff.

CHAPTER III: THE POST-WAR INTERVENTION

[1] France, Assemblée Nationale, Annales de la chambre des députés, Débats parlementaires, Tome III (1918), pp. 3334–3335, session of December 29. See also E. Moulis and E. Bergonier, eds., En Marge du conflit mondial (Paris: Jehan, 1937), pp. 165–167. Cf. the Aide Memoire on the intervention in the Maklakov Archives (MA), Series B, Packet IV, Dossier 11 (Hoover Library).

[2] These instructions are quoted in France, Ministere de la Guerre, Etat-Major de l'Armee, Les Armées françaises dans la Grande Guerre (Paris: Imp. Nationale, 1934), Tome VIII, Vol. III, Annexes, vol. 3, pp. 120–125.

[3] Le Matin (Paris), June 17, 1920; A. G. Shliapnikov, ed., Les alliés contre la Russie (Paris: Delpeuch, 1926), p. 285. See also C. H. Sloves, La France et l'Union sovietique (Paris: Rieder, 1935), p. 81. Cf. note on the question of intervention in South Russia by General Canter in MA, Series B, Packet IV, Dossier 11.

[4] W. S. Churchill, The World Crisis: The Aftermath (London: Thorton Butterworth, 1929), p. 166.

[5] D. Lloyd George, The Truth About the Peace Treaties, Vol. I (London: Gollancz, 1938), p. 317.

[6] Churchill, op. cit., pp. 165–166.

[7] Ibid., p. 165.

[8] Franchet d'Esperey's letter is quoted in Jean Xydias, L'Intervention française en Russie, 1918–1919; souvenirs d'un témoin (Paris: Editions de France, 1927), p. 115. See also Paul J. L. Azan, Franchet d'Esperey (Paris: Flammarion, 1949), pp. 240–241; F. J. Deygas, L'Armée d'Orient dans la guerre mondiale, 1915–1919 (Paris: Payot, 1932), p. 297; and A. I. Gukovskii, Frantsuzskaia interventsiia na iuge Rossii, 1918–1919 (Moscow: Gosizdat, 1928), p. 83. Franchet d'Esperey's full name is Louis Felix Marie Francois Franchet d'Esperey.

[9] Foreign Relations, 1918, Russia, II, 663–664, 707. Russian Ambassador Poklevskii-Kozel in Jassy was also accredited as a diplomatic representative of the Volunteer Army. It should also be noted that the Allied ministers in Jassy had reportedly already indicated that plans were being made to aid the Volunteers in conversations held on November 2, and General Erdeli, representing Denikin, met with Franchet d'Esperey on November 15 at Sophia and obtained a promise of immediate arms shipments to Novorossiisk. See MA, Series B, Packet I, Dossier 8.

[10] Clemenceau's order is printed in Les Armées françaises dans la Grande Guerre, Tome VIII, Vol. III, Annexes, vol. 3, p. 459. Orders from Franchet d'Esperey to French forces at Corfu and Monastir are in ibid., pp. 478–479, 514.

[11] Gukovskii, Frantsuzskaia interventsiia, p. 154. In a note addressed to the

Allied Powers, dated October 20 and forwarded from Sophia to Paris on November 6, former Foreign Minister Aleksandr Shul'gin explained that the German occupation had been accepted only out of necessity. The Hetman, who maintained friendly relations with the Germans only to preserve order, now, said Shul'gin, wished to restore the ties with Britain and France that had earlier been exemplified by the appointment of Tabouis in December 1917. See Shul'gin's note in MA, Series B, Packet I, Dossier 6.

[12] See the statement by the Gerbel government (signed by ten of its members) to the Allies, declaring that the Ukraine was an integral part of Russia and calling for a united effort in the fight against the Bolsheviks, in MA, Series B, Packet I, Dossier 6.

[13] See D. Doroshenko, *Istoriia Ukrainy* (Uzhgorod: Tsiupka, 1932), Vol. II, p. 409 ff.; and P. Khrystiuk, ed., *Zamitky i materialy do istorii ukrains'koi revoliutsii* (Vienna: Vernay, 1921), Vol. III, p. 120 ff. When informed by Maklakov in Paris of the efforts to reorganize the Ukrainian government, Foreign Minister Pichon wired the French representative in Berne on November 7, citing these efforts favorably and noting them as one reason for refusing to deal with Lukasevich, who was seeking Allied intervention but on behalf of an independent Ukraine. See the Pichon note and statement by Lukasevich (under the heading Bureau de Presse Francaise, Berne, November 18, 1918), MA, Series B, Packet I, Dossier 6.

[14] The text of the Directorate's statement is in Khrystiuk, *op. cit.*, III, 131. On events in the Ukraine during this period, see also the pamphlet by a member of the Ukrainian Directorate delegation in Paris, M. Kushnir (Kouchnire), *L'Ukraine, l'Europe orientale et la conférence de la paix* (Paris: Bureau de presse Ukrainien, 1919), Hoover Library collection of delegation propaganda.

[15] See E. G. von Val', *K istorii belago dvizheniia* (Tallin: Izd. avtora, 1935), pp. 24–28. Virtually all of Shcherbachev's troops were forced to leave Bessarabia or to hide when, after the Rumanian peace with the Germans, the latter had demanded the disbanding of all Russian forces in Rumanian territory, including Bessarabia. It is notable that from these forces, as they disintegrated, came not only Ukrainian units but also the Polish Corps under Haller, the Moslem Corps which moved to the Crimea under Sul'kevich, and the Drozdovskii detachment which went to the Don. All of these units had been formed earlier in a reorganization along nationality lines. When Shcherbachev dissolved his command officially on April 18, the Allied ministers in Jassy jointly expressed their highest respect for him and his efforts. Bessarabia had declared its "independence" in February and then in April entered a union with Rumania. See *Foreign Relations, 1918, Russia*, II, 715, 719.

[16] Val', *K istorii belago dvizheniia*, pp. 34–37.

[17] *Ibid.* See also Armed Forces of South Russia, *Ocherk' vzaimootnoshenii vooruzhennykh sil' iuga Rossii i predstavitelei frantsuzskago komandovaniia* (Ekaterinodar: Izdano unpravleniem Generala Kvartir-meistera Shtaba Glavnokomanduiushchago Vooruzhennymi Silami na Iuge Rossii, May 1919), in Denikin Archives, and printed in *Arkhiv Russkoi Revoliutsii*, Vol. XVI (Berlin: Izdatel'stvo "Slovo," 1925), pp. 233–262. Cf. Moulis and Bergonier, *op. cit.*, pp. 152–157. On French plans see also the General Staff recommendation of December

9 in *Iz istorii grazhdanskoi voiny*, I, 72–73. This recommendation calls for putting three French and three Greek divisions under Berthelot for the intervention,
only half the size of the force mentioned by Shcherbachev. However, it states
that the six Allied divisions should be combined with an unspecified number of
Rumanian troops at Berthelot's disposal.

[18] Val', *K istorii belago dvizheniia*, p. 38.

[19] Russian Ambassador Poklevskii-Kozel was informed of the talks as were
Shcherbachev's immediate assistants and Denikin, but apparently no one else was
to be told of them. See *ibid*.

[20] The best single source on the Jassy conference is the journal of its meetings
and assorted reports in the Wrangel Military Archives (WMA), File 143. The
best analysis is in Robert H. McNeal, "The Conference of Jassy: An Early Fiasco
of the Anti-Bolshevik Movement," in J. S. Curtiss, ed., *Essays in Russian and
Soviet History* (New York: Columbia University Press, 1963), pp. 221–236.
Denikin's evaluation of the conference is in his *Ocherki russkoi smuty*, Vol. V
(Berlin: "Slovo," 1926), p. 5 ff. Henno had been director of the intelligence
section with the Tabouis mission in Kiev late in 1917, but after the signature of
the peace treaty with Germany he had moved to Kishinev, where his activities
were under the supervision of the French minister in Rumania, Saint-Aulaire. In
Jassy in the latter part of 1918 he is referred to as the French consul at Kiev,
although there appears to be no evidence of his actual appointment and he never
returned to Kiev. As McNeal has pointed out, Henno did later, in March 1919,
produce a letter from Saint-Aulaire indicating that he had been named vice-consul
in Kiev, and this letter was read in the Chamber of Deputies in his defense, but
Foreign Minister Pichon twice disavowed Henno's appointment. Whatever authority Henno in fact had in November and December 1918 came from his support
by the Allied ministers in Jassy. See McNeal, *op. cit.*, p. 222; *Annales de la
chambre des députés, Débats parlementaires*, Tome I (1919), pp. 1250, 1305–
1306, sessions of March 24 and 26; and N. N. Golovin, *Rossiiskaia kontr-revoliutsiia* (Paris: "Illiustrirovannoi Rossii," 1937), Vol. V, Bk. 12, pp. 23–24.

[21] Denikin, *Ocherki russkoi smuty*, V, 6.

[22] See telegrams from the Allied ministers in *Foreign Relations, 1918, Russia*,
II, 699–703.

[23] Report on the Jassy Conference, WMA, File 143, pp. 279–285. This, of
course, did not mean that the conference was fully representative of all South
Russia. As one of its participants has pointed out, what it did represent was the
group of Russian organizations looking to Allied intervention to aid Russian forces
to restore Russian unity. See V. I. Gurko, "Iz Petrograda cherez Moskvu, Parizh,
i London v Odessu," *Arkhiv Russkoi Revoliutsii*, Vol. XV (Berlin: "Slovo,"
1924), p. 50. On the composition of the conference, see also M. S. Margulies,
God interventsii (Berlin: Grschebin, 1923), Vol. I, pp. 27–28. Most of the delegates were listed as "nonparty," but there were those listed as belonging to the
following: National Freedom party (Partiia narodnoi svobody), Socialist Revolutionary party, Monarchist-Constitutionalist party, Octobrist party, and Popular
(Narodno) Socialist party. See WMA, File 143, pp. 287–290. A sizable number of the delegates came from Kiev, and although no Ukrainian governmental
delegation was invited, Skoropadskii cooperated in issuing passports for those
attending. V. I. Gurko, who arrived late but was accepted as a voting delegate,

consulted with Skoropadskii just before the conference. N. N. Shebeko and he indirectly represented the Hetman's interests. See Gurko, op. cit., pp. 36, 46–47.

[24] The sources are not in complete agreement as to who was present or had a vote. The list accompanying the journal of meetings in the WMA, File 143, includes the following: M. V. Braikevich, I. I. Bunakov-Fundaminskii, A. V. Krivoshein, K. R. Krovopuskov, M. S. Margulies, V. V. Meller-Zakomel'skii, P. N. Miliukov, Colonel I. M. Novikov, A. I. Pil'ts, A. A. Titov, S. N. Tret'iakov, M. M. Fedorov, N. A. Khomiakov, A. Ia. Chembers, N. V. Savich, and V. I. Gurko as voting delegates, plus B. E. Maliutin, N. N. Shebeko, V. P. Riabushinskii, V. Ia. Demchenko, and N. F. von Ditmar with advisory voice. V. V. Rudnev was not an official delegate but participated as a representative of the Union for Regeneration. Counting him the number would thus be 17. V. V. Shul'gin was an accredited delegate but was prevented from attending by illness. Present at some of the meetings were also the British and French military attachés, Ballard and Beloir, the Russian Red Cross Colonel Il'in, General Shcherbachev, and Henno.

[25] Documents of the Jassy conference, WMA, File 143, pp. 368, 376. This appeal and an accompanying note from the Allied ministers was apparently not dispatched until December 6. See U. S. National Archives, Foreign Affairs Section, Doc. No. 861.00/3435; and McNeal, op. cit., pp. 227–228.

[26] The three man directorate idea had first been adopted jointly by the National Center and the Union for Regeneration when an all-Russian government was expected to be established at Ufa to get Allied recognition. It was then supposed to include one general, one Kadet, and one socialist. As previously noted, on September 23 the projected directorate had been established at Ufa after negotiations between the Samara and Omsk governments, with five men forming the joint authority. It is important to recall at this point, however, that on November 17–18, just after the opening of the Jassy conference, the Ufa Directorate was overthrown and Admiral Kolchak was installed as dictator, thus breaking the liberal-Left coalition and reopening both the question of the form of authority to be supported and the gap between socialist and non-socialist factions in the anti-Bolshevik camp. See Miliukov's account of this background to the Jassy discussion in the journal of meetings, 2nd session, November 20, WMA, File 143, p. 327. See also a statement by the Union for Regeneration relating to this question in the Miliukov Personal Archives, and Margulies, op. cit., I, 30–31, 35. Journal of meetings, November 7/20 and 8/21, WMA, File 143, pp. 323–340.

[27] There were 14 voting delegates present at these votes. The vote for military dictatorship was 10 to 0; the vote for Denikin was 9 to 4 (the four being for Nikolai Nikolaevich). Both votes thus constituted a majority of the total of 16 or 17 possible if all voted. See journal of meetings, WMA, File 143, pp. 336–340.

[28] Margulies, op. cit., I, 35.

[29] Text in documents of the Jassy conference, WMA, File 143, pp. 377–381.

[30] Ibid., pp. 371–373. Berthelot indicated that in the case of the Ukrainian forces of Petliura he would demand full surrender.

[31] According to Margulies, Barclay was later reprimanded by London for associating himself with Henno's declaration since decisions on such matters had not been made yet by the Foreign Office or the Cabinet. See Margulies, op. cit., I,

136–137. Vopicka was also apparently overstepping his authority when he backed these moves, since Acting Secretary of State Polk wired the United States consul at Irkutsk that the Powers "other than the United States" were proposing to keep order in the Ukraine by supporting the established authorities. See Polk to Harris, December 12, 1918, *Foreign Relations, 1918, Russia*, II, 703.

³² This incident is related in Margulies, *op. cit.*, I, 38–39.

³³ See notes of the Allied ministers in *Foreign Relations, 1918, Russia*, II, 644, 678, 699–703, 709.

³⁴ Denikin, *Ocherki russkoi smuty*, IV, 36–40. On the formation of the new Crimean government, see *ibid.*, V, 54 ff. and Foreign Minister Vinaver's description of the government and its policies in a letter to Maklakov, MA, Series B, Packet II, Dossier 10. See also the new government's memorandum to the Allies in Documents of the Crimean Government and M. Vinaver, File No. 6, Hoover Library. Cf. Gukovskii, "Krym v 1918–1919 gg.," *loc. cit.*, p. 144; and Vinaver, *Nashe pravitel'stvo, passim.*

³⁵ Apparently all Henno had by way of instructions from Paris was simply a statement from the Foreign Ministry declaring that the Allied Powers did not intend to change the form of government in the Ukraine. See documents on "The Ukraine and the Allied Powers," MA, Series B, Packet II, Dossier 3.

³⁶ See the text forwarded by the Ministers in Jassy to Paris, December 7, 1918, in *Foreign Relations, 1918, Russia*, II, 701. See also MA, Series B, Packet II, Dossier 3.

³⁷ *Foreign Relations, 1918 Russia*, II, 702.

³⁸ See Margulies, *op. cit.*, I, 42. It is interesting to note, on the other hand, that Henno's statements apparently made a big impression in Kiev at first. According to one witness, a welcoming committee and speeches were even prepared to greet the expected arrival of the Allies. See Margolin, *op. cit.*, p. 96 ff.

³⁹ *Foreign Relations, 1918, Russia*, II, 702.

⁴⁰ The American minister, Vopicka, provided a good example of the confusion in his reports. On December 19, for example, he telegraphed Washington that Petliura was "now head of the Bolsheviks of Ukraine," and on December 21 he wired that "Petlyura does not head the Bolshevik army . . . but the republican army, which is fighting for independence of Ukrainia. . . ." See *Foreign Relations, 1918, Russia*, II, 704–705. On the character of the Ukrainian Directorate, see A. D. Margolin, *Ukraina i politika antanty* (Berlin: Efron, 1921), pp. 99–100; and J. S. Reshetar, *The Ukrainian Revolution* (Princeton: Princeton University Press, 1952), p. 217 ff.

⁴¹ *Foreign Relations, 1918, Russia*, II, 702.

⁴² Val', K istorii belago dvizheniia, pp. 42–43. On the plans of the Volunteer Army based on Berthelot's promises, see "Ocherk' vzaimootnoshenii vooruzhennykh sil' iuga Rossii i predstavitelei frantsuzskago komandovaniia," *Arkhiv Russkoi Revoliutsii*, Vol. XVI (Berlin: "Slovo," 1925), pp. 235–236. Cf. A. S. Lukomskii, *Memoirs of the Russian Revolution* (London: T. F. Unwin, 1922), p. 218.

⁴³ The Germans were obliged by section B of article 12 of the armistice to remain in place in the territories occupied by them in Russia until they could be replaced by Allied troops, but only in Nikolaev and Kherson did they actually stay in place until Allied troops arrived. For an example of Henno's appeals to the Germans, see *Iz istorii grazhdanskoi voiny*, I, 78.

[44] Some efforts had been made to form troops and coordinate their actions, but these very efforts had only led to new friction. Agents of the Volunteer Army had begun recruiting in Kiev some time earlier, but Denikin made it clear that he had not intended for Volunteer officers to be subordinate to the Ukrainian command or to support Skoropadskii directly. Kiev was soon (December 14) to fall to the Directorate, and the Volunteers there took refuge with the Germans, an ironic end to their campaign against the "pro-German" policies of the Hetman. Many of these Volunteer officers were later picked up in Germany by the British, taken to England, and there sent to a special camp to be given new training and sent back to Russia. On these events, see the Volunteer Army's *Kratkaia zapiska istorii vzaimootnoshenii Dobrovol'cheskoi armii s Ukrainoi* (Rostov-on-Don: Tip. "Donskogo akts. o-va. pech. i izd. dela," 1919), p. 5 ff. An account of the confused Volunteer "participation" in Kiev's defense may also be found in the memoirs of a member of one of the Volunteer units there, B. M. Brofel'dt, *Vospominaniia*, Part III, p. 10 ff. Brofel'dt describes the later re-training in England in Part IV. French sources had, notably, prematurely reported an accord between the Volunteers and the Ukrainian government (Gerbel) in November. See the bulletin of the Bureau de Presse Française for November 22, 1918, in MA, Series B, Packet II, Dossier 6.

[45] See Khrystiuk, *op. cit.*, IV, 6 (note 1), 15 ff.; and Lukomskii, *Memoirs*, p. 212.

[46] For more detailed accounts of events preceding the French intervention in Odessa, see Xydias, *op. cit.*, pp. 123–170; and Denikin, *Ocherki russkoi smuty*, V, 7 ff.

[47] See Gukovskii, *Frantsuzskaia interventsiia*, p. 139; and G. Frants, "Evakuatsiia germanskimi voiskami Ukrainy," in I. P. Petrushevskii, ed., *Istorik i sovremennik: istoriko-literaturnyi sbornik* (Berlin: Olga Diakow Verlag, 1922–1924), Vol. II, p. 268.

[48] Denikin, *Ocherki russkoi smuty*, V, 10; A. G. Shlikhter, ed., *Chernaia kniga: sbornik statei i materialov ob interventsii antanty na Ukraine v 1918–1919 gg.* (Kharkov: Gosizdat Ukrainy, 1925), p. 93.

[49] Xydias, *op. cit.*, pp. 149–160. Both Colonel Novikov, who had been sent to Constantinople by the Jassy conference to urge the sending of Allied troops as soon as possible, and General Erdeli, who had been sent by Denikin for the same purpose, reported that Franchet d'Esperey received them coldly and lectured them on Russia's betrayal of France and on the poor quality of Russian officers. However, the British representative, General Bridges, had welcomed them warmly and promised to help in every way he could. See Margulies, *op. cit.*, I, 82–83.

[50] See J. Bunyan and H. H. Fisher, eds., *The Bolshevik Revolution, 1917–1918* (Stanford: Stanford University Press, 1934), pp. 439–448; Margulies, *op. cit.*, I, 75 ff.; and Gukovskii, *Frantsuzskaia interventsiia*, p. 137 ff. Cf. Reshetar, *op. cit.*, p. 217 ff.

[51] Denikin, *Ocherki russkoi smuty*, V, 11–12. Significantly, Petliura had offered a truce to Borius on condition that Grishin-Almazov be removed. Borius in turn demanded that the Ukrainians disarm, and when they refused, he simply repeated Berthelot's earlier warning. See F. Anulov, "Soiuznyi desant na Ukraine," in A. G. Shlikhter, ed., *Chernaia kniga: sbornik statei i materialov* (Kharkov: Gosizdat Ukrainy, 1925), p. 111 ff.; and Xydias, *op. cit.*, pp. 160, 170–172.

[52] Borius' instructions are quoted in Xydias, *op. cit.*, p. 163 and V. Margulies, *Ognennye gody: materialy i dokumenty po istorii grazhdanskoi voiny na iuge Rossii* (Berlin: "Manfred," 1923), pp. 6–7.

[53] Denikin, *Ocherki russkoi smuty*, V, 11.

[54] *Foreign Relations, 1918, Russia*, III, 143. See also Churchill, *op. cit.*, p. 166.

[55] Clemenceau's letter of October 27 to d'Esperey, printed in *Le Matin* (Paris), June 17, 1920; also in Shliapnikov, *op. cit.*, p. 285. Cf. Moulis and Bergonier, *op. cit.*, pp. 160–161.

[56] See *New York Times*, December 25, 1918.

[57] *Annales de la chambre des députés, Débats parlementaires*, Tome III (1918), pp. 3334–3335, session of December 29.

[58] *Ibid.* See also *Le Petit Parisien* (Paris), December 30, 1918, quoting Pichon's remarks and retorts from the Chamber.

[59] See M. S. Margulies, *op. cit.*, I, 285, 289, where he relates the belated revelation of these instructions to leading individuals in Odessa.

[60] Quoted in Xydias, *op. cit.*, p. 202.

[61] Quoted in Denikin, *Ocherki russkoi smuty*, V, 34.

[62] On Henno's feud with Freidenberg and the outcome, see M. S. Margulies, *op. cit.*, I, 125 ff.; and D. Kin, ed., "K istorii frantsuzskoi interventsii na iuge Rossii," *Krasnyi Arkhiv*, Vol. XIX (Moscow: Gosizdat, Tsentral'nyi Arkhiv RSFSR, 1927), pp. 5–8.

[63] The peripatetic French military representative in the Caucasus, Colonel Chardigny, acted as French liaison officer, and an American physician attached to the American Persian Relief Commission, Dr. Wilbur E. Post, was asked to serve as the representative of the United States. This informal and ad hoc arrangement was made largely so that the British commander could land his force in the name of the Allies. See W. E. Post et al., "A Resumé of Events in the Caucasus Since the Russian Revolution," a manuscript containing personal accounts by Post, Chardigny, and Mr. Harry Pratt Judson, in the Hoover Library; the title used is that of Chapter 1 by Colonel Chardigny. Cf. F. J. F. French, *From Whitehall to the Caspian* (London: Odhams, 1920), p. 127; and N. N. Lishin, *Na Kaspiiskom more* (Prague: Izd. Morskogo zhurnala, 1938), p. 54 ff.

[64] The Pre-Caspian government was described in one account as composed almost entirely of socialists, chiefly Socialist Revolutionaries. The same source also states that Bicherakov received his appointment as "Commander in Chief of troops in the Caucasus and on the Caspian" from Kolchak. See B. Baikov, "Vospominaniia o revoliutsii v Zakavkaz'i, 1917–1920 gg.," *Arkhiv Russkoi Revoliutsii*, Vol. IX (Berlin: Izdatel'stvo "Slovo," 1923), pp. 160–161. Denikin characterized Bicherakov's government as a group of socialists from Petrovsk (including some Armenians) who were "spiritually" associated with Komuch and the Ufa Directorate. See Denikin, *Ocherki russkoi smuty*, IV, 165. The "government" was apparently simply Bicherakov and some of his followers and was intended as a means to lend weight to Bicherakov's claims to authority. Cf. Ellis, *British "Intervention,"* pp. 113–114.

[65] This view was strongly presented by Colonel Chardigny in his report, dated November 21, 1919, which constitutes Chapter 1 in Post, *op. cit.* For Soviet materials on events and conditions in Azerbaidzhan during this period, see *Bol'-sheviki v bor'be za pobedu sotsialisticheskoi revoliutsii v Azerbaidzhane, 1917–*

1918 (Baku: Gosizdat A.S.S.R., 1957).

⁶⁶ See A. A. Takho-Godi, *Revoliutsiia i kontr-revoliutsiia v Dagestane* (Makhach-Kala: Dagestanskoe Gosizdat, 1927), pp. 77–82, 104–105; J. Loris-Melikof, *La révolution russe et les nouvelles républiques transcaucasiennes* (Paris: Alcan, 1920), pp. 144, 160, 170–171; J. Buchan, ed., *The Baltic and Caucasian States* (Boston: Houghton, Mifflin, 1923), p. 237; and Ia. A. Ratgauzer, *Bor'ba za sovetskii Azerbaidzhan* (Baku: Tip. "3-i Internatsional," 1928), pp. 14–15. Cf. Richard Pipes, *The Formation of the Soviet Union* (Cambridge: Harvard University Press, 1954), p. 204 ff.

⁶⁷ Thomson's position is recorded in the report of the Azerbaidzhan delegation to the government on November 16, quoted in A. Raevskii, *Angliiskaia interventsiia i Musavatskoe pravitel'stvo; iz istorii interventsii i kontr-revoliutsii v Zakavkaz'i* (Baku: Gostip. "Krasnyi Vostok," 1927), pp. 32–33.

⁶⁸ This note is included in documents presented in the Azerbaidzhan Paris delegation's brochure, *Le 28 Mai, 1919; le jour du premier anniversaire de l'indépendance de la République d'Azerbeidjan*, p. 13.

⁶⁹ *Ibid.*, pp. 13–14. See also Raevskii, *op. cit.*, p. 40.

⁷⁰ Raevskii, *op. cit.*, p. 36. Cf. A. Popov, "Iz epokhi angliiskoi interventsii v Zakavkaz'i; po materialam arkhiva b. Min. In. Del. Azerbaidzhanskoi Respubliki," *Proletarskaia Revoliutsiia* (Moscow), No. 6–7 (18–19), 1923, p. 226.

⁷¹ Raevskii, *op. cit.*, p. 34.

⁷² Thomson's reference to the "New Russian Government" here recalls a similar reference made by Franchet d'Esperey in Odessa, although the latter spoke of such a government "in Paris." There is evidence that Thomson, however, was referring to the Ufa government, which the Allied Powers had considered recognizing. It is quite possible that Thomson had been informed of the British Cabinet's decision of November 14 to extend recognition but had not yet learned of the coup which put Kolchak in power on November 18. Such an interpretation seems all the more valid in view of the presence in Baku of a "representative" of the Ufa government, N. N. Golovin. See note 94, Chap. 2, above; and D. E. Enukidze, *Krakh imperialisticheskoi interventsii v Zakavkaz'i* (Tbilisi: Gosizdat Gruz. S.S.R., 1954), p. 147.

⁷³ The text of this statement as here presented is taken largely from Post, *op. cit.*, Chap. 2, pp. 1–2, but it has been modified in minor details on the basis of a partial Russian text contained in Raevskii, *op. cit.*, p. 34, since the Post version does not appear to be the original English text.

⁷⁴ The reorganization of the bank and the oil industry is described in the report of its director, Wertheim, to General Thomson in Post, *op. cit.* Cf. the account by Post in *ibid.*, Chap. 2, p. 3 ff., and Raevskii, *op. cit.*, p. 49 ff.

⁷⁵ Post, *op. cit.*, Chap. 2, pp. 3–4.

⁷⁶ Baikov, *op. cit.*, p. 148.

⁷⁷ Thomson was also apparently drawing toward this conclusion. See Post, *op. cit.*, Chap. 2, p. 6. It was even being rumored at this time that Bicherakov was preparing a coup to seize power. See Raevskii, *op. cit.*, p. 44.

⁷⁸ The Russian National Council's position and activities are described in detail in Baikov, *op. cit.*, p. 147 ff. Baikov indicates that both the socialist composition of Bicherakov's "government" and the report that he had received appointment

as commander in the Caucasus area from Kolchak were regarded as evidence of opposition to Denikin and to the Council. *Ibid.*, pp. 160–161.

[79] *Ibid.*, pp. 147, 148.

[80] Post, *op. cit.*, Chap. 2, pp. 6–8.

[81] *Ibid.*, annex to Chap. 2, which is an article from the R.N.C. paper, *Edinaia Rossiia*, entitled "The Allied Policy and the Second Proclamation of General Thomson." See also Baikov, *op. cit.*, pp. 149–150.

[82] Raevskii, *op. cit.*, p. 44; Baikov, *op. cit.*, pp. 150–151. The Armenians, who had previously been involved in an exchange of massacres with the Moslems and were in a minority which lacked power, obviously looked to some moderate coalition as the only hope for peace.

[83] Baikov, *op. cit.*, p. 151.

[84] Post, *op. cit.*, Chap. 2, p. 9.

[85] The figures used by the British for "Baku district" gave the following population count: 390,000 Tartars, 55,000 Armenians, and 40,000 Russians, with considerably smaller Polish, German, and Georgian elements. See Post, *op. cit.*, annex on population.

[86] Baikov, *op. cit.*, pp. 152–157.

[87] Raevskii, *op. cit.*, p. 47; *Le 28 Mai, 1919* . . ., p. 15.

[88] *Le 28 Mai, 1919* . . ., p. 16.

[89] Milne's statements are quoted in *Le 28 Mai, 1919* . . ., pp. 17–18. The delegation actually did not reach Paris until May because of a delay in Constantinople, where the French had been blocking further travel by such delegations (by refusing visas) since the trouble over the Jassy conference delegation. See Raevskii, *op. cit.*, p. 51.

[90] For Soviet documentation on events in Georgia see *Bor'ba za pobedu sovetskoi vlasti v Gruzii, 1917–1921 gg.* (Tbilisi: Gosizdat Gruz, S.S.R., 1958).

[91] Post, *op. cit.*, Chap. 8, quoting a letter from Gegechkori.

[92] Note from Gegechkori quoted in *Dokumenty i materialy po vnesnei politike Zakavkaz'ia i Gruzii*, pp. 425–426.

[93] *Ibid.*, p. 426.

[94] *Ibid.*, p. 427.

[95] According to Volunteer intelligence reports the 27th Infantry Division under General Walker, which occupied Baku, consisted in January of 12 batallions, of which 4 were stationed in Baku, 2 disbursed along the Baku-Tiflis-Batum railway, and 3 located in Tiflis. Others were being deployed at various trouble spots along the borders of Georgia and Armenia. See WMA, File 181, intelligence report No. 15 and *passim*. Churchill has stated that the total British force in Transcaucasia reached approximately 20,000 men. See Churchill, *op. cit.*, p. 166.

[96] Z. D. Avalov, *The Independence of Georgia* (London: Headley, 1940), pp. 152–153.

[97] Lord Bertie, until May 1918 British ambassador in Paris, recorded in his diary his view at this time that Russia "would not be fit to protect or administer Mohammedan khanates in Central Asia or Caucasian principalities" and advocated lining up all the border states as buffers, letting what was left of Russia "stew in their own juice." See F. L. Bertie, *The Diary of Lord Bertie of Thame, 1914–1918*, edited by Lady Algernon Gordon Lennox (London: Hodder and Stoughton, 1924), Vol. II, pp. 310–311.

NOTES   335

⁹⁸ Avalov, op. cit., p. 146.
⁹⁹ Denikin, Ocherki russkoi smuty, IV, 143. The important role played by the Russian National Councils in Transcaucasia was eventually given formal recognition in June 1919, when Prince L'vov, as chairman of the Russian Political Council in Paris, extended to the combined Transcaucasian Russian Councils the official designation of representative of Russian state interests until the reunification of the area with Russia. See MA, Series B, Packet II, Dossier 11 (Maklakov to Denikin, June 14, 1919).
¹⁰⁰ "Proclamation to the inhabitants of the city of Batum," MA Series B, Packet II, Dossier 11.
¹⁰¹ Ibid. See also E. E. Iakushkin and S. Polunin, Angliiskaia interventsiia v 1918–1920 gg. (Moscow: Gosizdat, 1928), p. 40.
¹⁰² Denikin, Ocherki russkoi smuty, IV, 143–144.
¹⁰³ Lukomskii, Vospominaniia, II, 301–302, citing reports from the R.N.C. to Volunteer headquarters.
¹⁰⁴ As one observer put it: "To settle the matter, a number of British officers . . . were marched one fine morning to the various offices of the administration, and relieved the members of the Council of their easy but profitable duties." C. E. Bechhofer-Roberts, In Denikin's Russia and the Caucasus, 1919–1920 (London: W. Collins Sons and Co., Ltd., 1921), p. 17.
¹⁰⁵ Denikin, Ocherki russkoi smuty, IV, 145. The R.N.C. continued to send Denikin accounts of events highly critical of British policy and calling for the dispatch of Russian troops to seize Batum.
¹⁰⁶ See Avalov, op. cit., pp. 148–150. Colonel Chardigny joined in such mediation efforts as the representative of France, supporting the Allied policy of preventing forceful changes in borders and keeping order until decisions could be made by the Powers.
¹⁰⁷ Only a brief review of this question can be presented here. For a detailed analysis of the problems of Allied policy-making at the Paris Conference, see John M. Thompson, "The Russian Problem at the Paris Peace Conference, 1919," Ph.D. dissertation, Columbia University, 1960.
¹⁰⁸ United States, Department of State, Papers Relating to the Foreign Relations of the United States: The Paris Peace Conference, 1919, 13 vols. (Washington: Government Printing Office, 1942–1947), Vol. III, pp. 472 ff., 490–491. Hereafter cited as Paris Peace Conference.
¹⁰⁹ See telegrams from Maklakov on this question in MA, Series B, Packet I, Dossier 5. On the formation of the Conference, see Maklakov's letter to Mr. Fisher, March 31, 1934, concerning the Archives placed in the Hoover Library, attached to the Archives. See also documents in MA, Series B, Packet III, Dossier 11.
¹¹⁰ Generals Shcherbachev and Golovin were accepted by Kolchak as military representatives of his government as well as of Denikin. See Sazonov to Maklakov, February 16, 1919, MA, Series B, Packet III, Dossier 11. Shcherbachev's further activities are detailed in Val', K istorii belago dvizheniia, p. 61 ff.
¹¹¹ See Denikin, Ocherki russkoi smuty, IV, 237–238, and the collection of delegation propaganda in the Hoover Library. See also M. S. Margulies, op. cit., I, 330 ff., for a description of his efforts to promote a "federalist bloc" to unite the non-Russian nationalities' delegations. Federation was also the program supported

by the moderate socialist group which gathered around Kerenskii in Paris. See "Une declaration des Democrates Russes," signed by Kerenskii and others, in the Miliukov Personal Archives. For the invitation of the Russian Political Council to all governments in Russia that opposed the Bolsheviks to join in a single diplomatic representative body, see MA, Series B, Packet III, Dossier 11 (Sazonov to Neratov, April 23, 1919). See also Margolin's account of his experiences in Paris with the Ukrainian delegation in Margolin, op. cit., p. 139 ff. Margolin notes that Kerenskii and other Russian socialists tended to take essentially the same stand on representation as the "Whites," that is the view that there must be one Russia for all. Ibid., pp. 140–143.

[112] Avalov, op. cit., p. 155.

[113] See Denikin, Ocherki russkoi smuty, IV, 237–238, 241–242; V, 86 ff.

[114] See the instructions to Sazonov in the Denikin Archives, and see Denikin, Ocherki russkoi smuty, IV, 236–237. The Don and Kuban Cossacks rejected the suggestion that they also be represented by Sazonov and sent their own delegations. See Neratov to Sazonov, January 16, 1919, MA, Series B, Packet III, Dossier 11.

[115] For further information concerning the activities of the Jassy conference delegation, see M. S. Margulies, op. cit., I, 85, 304 ff.; and Gurko, op. cit., p. 53 ff. For Miliukov's public defense of his record while in England see the interviews and other items in his clipping book in the Miliukov Archives.

[116] Paris Peace Conference, IV, 53–54.

[117] Val', K istorii belago dvizheniia, p. 64. Shcherbachev was also handicapped by the opposition of the former tsarist military representative in Paris, Count Ignat'ev, but his personal acquaintance with Foch was of great assistance.

[118] See P. N. Miliukov, La politique exterieure des Soviets (Paris: Giard, 1934), p. 48. On the Foch plan, see Paris Peace Conference, III, 471 ff. A brief account may also be found in T. Komarnicki, Rebirth of the Polish Republic (London: W. Heinemann, Ltd., 1957), pp. 235, 399–400.

[119] Paris Peace Conference, III, 584.

[120] Ibid., pp. 581–583.

[121] Ibid., pp. 626–628.

[122] Ibid., pp. 643–646.

[123] Ibid., p. 649. Cf. Lloyd George, The Truth About the Peace Treaties, I, 346.

[124] Paris Peace Conference, III, 691–692. For the text of the radio message as received and recorded by Soviet radio on January 23 see Dokumenty vneshnei politiki, II, 45–46.

[125] The implications noted here were those immediately recognized by many in South Russia. See, for example, Gurko, op. cit., p. 70. In the Council of Ten meetings leading up to the Prinkipo proposal, only Italian Foreign Minister Sonnino stood consistently opposed to the idea and in favor of further intervention aiding the anti-Bolshevik elements. Pichon indicated his sympathy for the intervention and especially for the anti-Bolshevik leaders in Paris, but he never spoke out firmly as Somnino did, presumably because of Clemenceau's strong feelings.

[126] Chicherin's first reply noted the radio message but failed to regard it as an "invitation" as such. However, the Soviet Foreign Commissar stated that, while awaiting a direct invitation to which to give a formal reply, the Soviet government

did not want its delay to be interpreted as a rejection. See *Dokumenty vneshnei politiki*, II, 52. Chicherin's note is here dated January 28, but from its content appears to have been written on the same day that the radio message was received, i.e., January 23. For the replies to the proposal from Denikin and Kolchak as well as from the Soviet government, see Cumming and Pettit, *op. cit.*, pp. 298–302, 305–306.

[127] See the Herron Papers, Vol. X, Russia: Prinkipo, Doc. III (Hoover Library). See also W. C. Bullitt, *The Bullitt Mission to Russia* (New York: B. W. Huebsch, 1919), p. 32. In a similar vein the Socialist deputy, Cachin, in a speech in the Chamber of Deputies, accused Pichon of having blocked the conference and called the Foreign Minister the head of "a reactionary internationale." See *Annales de la chambre des députés, Débats parlementaires*, Tome I (1919), p. 1244, session of March 24.

[128] See M. S. Margulies, *op. cit.*, I, 194, 217.

[129] This view was apparently also presented to Russian Chargé d'Affaires Nabokov in London. Believing that the Bolsheviks would refuse, some British spokesmen favorable to the intervention urged Nabokov to seek anti-Bolshevik acceptance of the conference. Nabokov, however, rejected this approach on grounds that he would simply be repudiated by the Russian representatives in Paris. C. Nabokoff, *The Ordeal of a Diplomat* (London: Duckworth, 1921), p. 289.

[130] See M. S. Margulies, *op. cit.*, I, 183. See also Vinaver to Maklakov, February 3, 1919, Documents of the Crimean Government, File 11; and an interview with Berthelot by representatives of the Zemstvo Council and the Union for Regeneration, February 21, 1919, Documents of the Crimean Government, File 3.

[131] See Cachin's attack on Pichon, citing a number of statements by the Foreign Minister in January, in *Annales de la chambre des députés, Débats parlementaires*, Tome I (1919), p. 1244, session of March 24. Cf. W. H. Chamberlin, *The Russian Revolution* (New York: Macmillan, 1935), Vol. II, p. 157.

[132] It has been charged that the invitation was sabotaged by its not being sent directly to Moscow, the latter hearing of it only by radio. See Fischer, *The Soviets in World Affairs*, I, 167. That, however, was the way the invitation was supposed to be sent and was not the result of any "sabotage." Both Wilson and Lloyd George explained this fact in the Council of Ten on February 1 upon receipt of a note from Chicherin concerning this question. See *Paris Peace Conference*, III, 835–836.

[133] For the two Soviet replies, see *Dokumenty vneshnei politiki*, II, 52, 57–60.

[134] Quoted in I. Subbotovskii, ed., *Soiuzniki, Russkie reaktsioneri i interventsiia; iskliuchitel'no po ofitsial'nym arkhivnym dokumentam Kolchakovskogo pravitel'stva* (Leningrad: Vestnik Leningradskogo Soveta, 1926), p. 230.

[135] Quoted in I. Mints, ed., "Vneshniaia politika kontr-revoliutsionnykh 'pravitel'stv' v nachale 1919 g. iz dokumentov Parizhskogo Posol'stva," *Krasnyi Arkhiv*, Vol. XXXVII (Moscow: Gosizdat, 1929), pp. 71-72. See also the series of telegrams on the Prinkipo question in MA, Series B, Packet III, Dossier 1.

[136] The same could be said of the independent border states. The Georgian reply to the Prinkipo proposal, for example, simply declared in essence that "whereas the aim of the proposed conference of Russian parties and groups on Prinkipo was to restore the lost national unity of the Russian people, Georgia, being no part of the latter and endeavoring to obtain international recognition of her inde-

pendence, had no reason to take part in the projected conference." Avalov, op. cit., p. 162.

[137] See Denikin, Ocherki russkoi smuty, II, 342.

[138] The former British ambassador to Russia, Sir George Buchanan, even went so far as to assert that the Prinkipo proposal "was directly responsible for the defection of a large body of Don Cossacks and for the serious set-back in the south that resulted from it . . ." Sir George Buchanan, My Mission to Russia (London: Cassell, 1923), p. 258. Cf. Denikin, Ocherki russkoi smuty, IV, 243. Churchill advised the Council of Ten that anti-Bolshevik troops "were deteriorating rapidly because of the uncertainty of the support they might expect from the victorious Allies." See Paris Peace Conference, III, 1041–1042. Cf. Denikin, Ocherki russkoi smuty, IV, 243.

[139] Churchill, op. cit., p. 172; Paris Peace Conference, IV, 14–15. Cf. D. H. Miller, My Diary at the Conference of Paris, 21 vols. (New York: priv. pub., 1924–1926), Vol. XIV, p. 448.

[140] Churchill, op. cit., pp. 174–175. In his account Lloyd George notes that he warned Churchill not to commit Britain to any "mad enterprise" which would drive organized labor into the arms of the extremists and put Britain in the position of having "to pull the chestnuts out of the fire" for the French. See Lloyd George, The Truth About the Peace Treaties, pp. 371–372.

[141] Churchill, op. cit., p. 177.

[142] On February 16 some Russian representatives in Paris suggested to the Allies that they should call a conference of only the anti-Bolshevik governments in Russia, but this proposal was rejected. See Mints, "Vneshniaia politika kontr-revoliutsionnykh 'pravitel'stv' . . .," loc. cit., pp. 74–76.

[143] Paris Peace Conference, IV, 13–14.

[144] Ibid., pp. 16–18. See also Bullitt, op. cit., pp. 32–34.

[145] See Bullitt, op. cit., passim; and Fridtjof Nansen, Russia and Peace (London: G. Allen, 1923), pp. 22–33.

[146] Paris Peace Conference, IV, 11–12.

[147] Ibid., pp. 122, 379–383.

[148] Ibid., p. 380.

CHAPTER IV: THE FRENCH AND THE VOLUNTEERS

[1] On conditions in Odessa, see Jean Xydias, L'intervention française en Russie, 1918–1919 (Paris: Editions de France, 1927), pp. 138–265 passim; and M. S. Margulies, God interventsii (Berlin: Grschebin, 1923), Vol. I, p. 163 ff. See also E. N. Trubetskoi, "Iz putevykh zametok bezhentsa," Arkhiv Russkoi Revo-liutsii, Vol. XVIII (Berlin: "Slovo," 1926), pp. 194–195.

[2] "Ocherk' vzaimootnoshenii vooruzhennykh sil' Iuga Rossii i predstavitelei frantsuzskago komandovaniia," Arkhiv Russkoi Revoliutsii, Vol. XVI (Berlin: "Slovo," 1925), pp. 237–238. Cf. A. S. Sannikov, "Vospominaniia, 1918–1919" (MS, Columbia University Russian Archive), pp. 15–16.

[3] See A. D. Margolin, Ukraina i politika antanty (Berlin: Efron, 1921), p. 109; and A. I. Gukovskii, Frantsuzskaia interventsiia (Moscow: Gos. sots.-ekon. izdat., 1928), pp. 139–140. In this case the Directorate was represented by a military

delegation under General Matveev, acting under the general instructions of General Grekov, who was then serving as coordinator of these activities for Petliura. In connection with the French decision to authorize negotiations with Petliura, it might be noted that during the testimony of the former Danish minister in Russia, M. de Scavenius, to the Peace Conference (Council of Ten) on January 21, 1919, Clemenceau questioned Scavenius on Petliura and Skoropadskii, and was told that the former had driven the latter out and had captured most of the Ukraine. Scavenius added, speaking of Petliura, that, "while the result of his rule had been identical with that of Bolshevik rule in Great Russia," it seemed likely that he would moderate Ukrainian separatism and accept federation with Russia. See United States Department of State, *Papers Relating to the Foreign Relations of the United States: The Paris Peace Conference* (Washington: Government Printing Office, 1942–1947), Vol. III, p. 640 (hereafter cited as *Paris Peace Conference*).

[4] The "French" troops involved here included one and one-half divisions of French and colonial troops, two divisions of Greek troops, and one brigade of Polish troops. One observer estimated that total French-Greek-Polish strength in Odessa in February was about 12,000 men, about half of these being French. See M. S. Margulies, *op. cit.*, I, 225. Cf. Sannikov, *op. cit.*, p. 45. The new line was only sparsely fortified, and local authorities—Directorate, Soviet, and even German in Nikolaev—continued to exist and compete for power in the zone. See A. I. Denikin, *The White Army* (London: J. Cape, 1930), p. 244.

[5] See J. S. Reshetar, *The Ukrainian Revolution* (Princeton: Princeton University Press, 1952), p. 240.

[6] See A. I. Denikin, *Ocherki russkoi smuty*, Vol. V (Berlin: "Slovo," 1926), p. 35.

[7] Cf. S. Ostapenko, "Direktoriia i frantsuzskaia interventsiia" in A. G. Shlikhter, ed., *Chernaia kniga: sbornik statei i materialov* (Kharkov: Gosizdat Ukrainy, 1925), pp. 267–268.

[8] See Margolin, *op. cit.*, pp. 123–124; and Denikin, *Ocherki russkoi smuty*, V, 35. Cf. V. Vynnychenko, *Vidrodzhennia natsii* (Vienna: Dzvin, 1920), Vol. III, p. 255 ff. Vynnychenko states that he and Chekovskii were already planning to resign and were forced out only because they refused to resign after Freidenberg's ultimatum. In a review of the situation in the Ukraine in January 1919, Trotskii noted some sentiment in the Directorate "to seek support and backing from Soviet Russia" against the "Anglo-French White Guard assault," but he still ruled out agreement with the Directorate on grounds that it would frustrate independent Bolshevik effort in the Ukraine and "would yield us no benefit" militarily because Petliura's army was already "powerless and insignificant." Trotskii concluded that "In the event of any serious Anglo-French thrust Petliura is capable of betraying everyone and everything and rushing into their arms." See J. M. Meijer, ed., *The Trotsky Papers, 1917–1922*, Vol. 1 (The Hague: Mouton, 1964), p. 243.

[9] Gukovskii, *Frantsuzskaia interventsiia*, p. 147.

[10] See Azbuka report, March 8, 1919, Maklakov Archives (MA), Series B, Packet II, Dossier 3 (Hoover Library).

[11] It should be noted that these organizations were not tightly structured but rather loose associations which overlapped one another in membership. The National Center group referred to here, moreover, was only one branch of the or-

ganization by this name and in this case was composed chiefly of the group
headed by V. V. Shul'gin that had moved from Kiev to Odessa. See Gukovskii,
Frantsuzskaia interventsiia, p. 53 ff. The Russian names of the four organizations
mentioned are: Sovet Gosudarstvennogo Ob'edineniia, Natsional'nyi Tsentr, Soiuz
Vozrozhdeniia Rossii, and Zemsko-Gorodskii Soiuz, in that order.

¹² The Bureau of the Union for Regeneration of Russia consisted of three Socialist Revolutionaries, two Social Democrats (Mensheviks), two Populist Socialists, and two Kadets. Ibid., p. 55.

¹³ See M. S. Margulies, op. cit., I, 57 ff. Cf. Gukovskii, Frantsuzskaia interventsiia, p. 118 ff. See also reports on the situation in Odessa from the American
mission to South Russia (Riggs mission) in U. S. National Archives, Foreign
Affairs Section, File No. 184.01602, especially Doc. No. 3.

¹⁴ Denikin, The White Army, p. 234; and Ocherki russkoi smuty, V. 34.

¹⁵ The position of the National Center, which was anti-Ukrainian, pro-Allied,
and a strong defender of Denikin's authority both as political and as military
leader, is set forth in a statement issued February 11, 1919. See MA, Series B,
Packet II, Dossier 3.

¹⁶ M. S. Margulies, op. cit., I, 112. The Zemstvo-City Union, whose membership closely paralleled that of the Union for Regeneration, took a similar position,
standing for popular sovereignty, democracy, a mildly socialist program of reform,
and, most importantly, the superiority of civil authority over the military. Policy
statements and resolutions setting forth the Zemstvo-City Union's position may
be found in the collection of "Zemskii-Gorod" materials in the Miliukov Personal
Archives. An account of events during this period from the socialist point of view,
written as a critique of M. S. Margulies' account, may be found in M. V. Braikevich, "Iz revoliutsii nam chto-nibud'," in P. E. Shchegolev, ed., Frantsuzy v
Odesse; iz belykh memaurov Gen. A. I. Denikina, M. S. Margulies, M. V. Braikevicha (Leningrad: "Krasnaia gazeta," 1928), pp. 225–259.

¹⁷ See, for example, the Council for State Unity's statement on negotiations
with the Directorate as stated in a resolution adopted in February, MA, Series B,
Packet II, Dossier 3.

¹⁸ Examples of the unexpected socialist (Right Socialist Revolutionary, Menshevik, and Populist Socialist) support for the Volunteer Army are given in the
selection from Braikevich in Shchegolev, op. cit., p. 244 ff. A conference composed of thirty Socialist Revolutionaries, thirty Mensheviks, nine Kadets, and five
Populist Socialists which met under Zemstvo Union auspices in Simferopol early
in December, for example, presented a thoroughly democratic program including
a proposal for a directorate as the South Russian authority. But it also issued a
highly favorable resolution praising the Volunteers, which contrasted sharply with
the position taken by the Socialist Revolutionary organization in Moscow. In
Odessa the socialists always insisted that the Volunteer commander be the supreme military authority in the three-man directorate advocated during the
French intervention period. It should also be noted that the Odessa city duma,
which continued to function during this time in accordance with Denikin's order
that such bodies were to continue until the expiration of their terms, was largely
dominated by socialists. The Socialist Revolutionaries held the majority, but its
membership also included Jewish socialists, Mensheviks, Populist Socialists, and
even three Bolsheviks, according to Braikevich, who was a member. During this

period the duma held weekly meetings with General Grishin-Almazov to discuss local matters. See Braikevich in Shchegolev, op. cit., pp. 232, 240; and Gukovskii, Frantsuzskaia interventsiia, p. 97 ff.

[19] An intelligence report which draws such conclusions is cited in Gukovskii, Frantsuzskaia interventsiia, pp. 93–94. It was this same reasoning which lay behind the sympathy of the Allied governments for the Ufa Directorate, which was supposed to unite the Samara and Omsk governments, as previously noted. See Foreign Relations, 1918, Russia, II, 412–413, 426. Cf. M. S. Margulies, op. cit., I, 133, 140–141.

[20] M. S. Margulies, op. cit., I, 133. The following account is also based upon Azbuka reports in February and March in MA, Series B, Packet II, Dossier 3.

[21] M. S. Margulies, op. cit., I, 154.

[22] See Denikin, Ocherki russkoi smuty, V, 88–89; M. S. Margulies, op. cit., I, 156.

[23] E. N. Trubetskoi, "Iz putevykh zametok bezhentsa," loc. cit., p. 198 ff.

[24] Denikin, Ocherki russkoi smuty, V, 140; and M. S. Margulies, op. cit., 202 ff.

[25] M. S. Margulies, op. cit., I, 226, 235, 238.

[26] Ibid., pp. 247–248.

[27] V. V. Shul'gin had been in Odessa since his interrupted trip to the Jassy conference. The paper Rossiia (sometimes called Velikaia Rossiia) which he published in Ekaterinodar was now also published in Odessa, except when the French temporarily closed it down because of its criticism of the Command's policies. The paper apparently on occasion tried to connect Freidenberg with Jewish speculators, Ukrainian Jews, and other allegedly anti-Russian elements. See Xydias, op. cit., p. 251; and V. Maiborodov, "S frantsuzami," Arkhiv Russkoi Revoliutsii, Vol. XVI (Berlin: Izdatel'stvo "Slovo," 1925), p. 125. Shul'gin was a member of the Volunteer Special Council and as such had considerable influence. His influence, moreover, was made greater by the fact that the secret propaganda and intelligence organization established by him, "Azbuka," served unofficially as an intelligence arm of the Volunteer Army. Its reports were thorough, but they also tended to be slanted toward Shul'gin's own views, which were rather conservative and not very favorable toward the Allies. Azbuka reports on events in Odessa during this time are contained in the Wrangel Military Archives (WMA), Files 131 and 132; and in the MA, Series B, Packet II, Dossier 3.

[28] Sannikov's experiences are set forth in his memoirs: Lt. General A. S. Sannikov, "Vospominaniia, 1918–1919" (MS, Columbia University Russian Archive).

[29] Quoted in Denikin, Ocherki russkoi smuty, V, 39. Cf. letter from Shul'gin to Denikin, February 14, MA, Series B, Packet II, Dossier 3. On the question of the French attitude toward the Ukraine, a representative of the Directorate who also talked with Berthelot at this time got the impression that Berthelot "was a proponent of a federative structure" for Russia, in which the Ukraine would have autonomy, a rather different impression from that gained by Sannikov. See Margolin, op. cit., p. 121.

[30] Sannikov, op. cit., pp. 18–19.

[31] Val', K istorii belago dvizheniia, pp. 45–46, 56.

[32] Sannikov, op. cit., p. 19.

[33] Denikin, Ocherki russkoi smuty, V, 39–40. Cf. Sannikov, op. cit., p. 28;

and Neratov to Sazonov, February 21, 1919, telegram in MA, Series B, Packet II, Dossier 9.

[34] Denikin, *Ocherki russkoi smuty*, V, 40; "Ocherk' vzaimootnoshenii vooru-zhennykh sil' Iuga Rossii i predstavitelei frantsuzskago komandovaniia," *loc. cit.*, p. 242.

[35] *Ibid.*

[36] M. S. Margulies, *op. cit.*, I, 263–264. Cf. Azbuka report of February 28, 1919, MA, Series B, Packet II, Dossier 3. French counterintelligence director Portal complained to Margulies at this time that the French Command in Odessa was being "ignored by Berthelot, abandoned by Franchet d'Esperey, and deserted by Paris." However, he added that the Command was now determined to act decisively to hold Odessa. See M. S. Margulies, *op. cit.*, I, 299–300, 305.

[37] M. S. Margulies, *op. cit.*, I, 251, 279.

[38] For a further statement of Freidenberg's position, see the report of a conversation between him and Shul'gin in Azbuka report No. 2, March 1, 1919, MA, Series B, Packet II, Dossier 3.

[39] A chronology of the French-Ukrainian negotiations from December through February may be found in the Ukrainian weekly published in France, *France et Ukraine*, February 20, 1920.

[40] See Vynnychenko, *op. cit.*, III, 264–267; and Ostapenko, "Direktoriia i frant-suzskaia interventsiia," in Shlikhter, *op. cit.*, pp. 260–271.

[41] The fact that both Margolin and Freidenberg were Jewish, of course, had nothing to do with the events being related, but this fact was the basis of frequent charges from anti-Semitic quarters. See V. I. Gurko, "Iz Petrograda cherez Moskvu, Parizh, i London v Odessu," *Arkhiv Russkoi Revoliutsii*, Vol. XV (Berlin: "Slovo," 1924), p. 52; M. S. Margulies, *op. cit.*, I, 71; and V. Maiborodov, "S frantsuzami," *loc. cit.*, p. 125.

[42] Margolin's political beliefs and reasons for supporting the Ukrainian Directorate are given in his memoirs. See Margolin, *op. cit.*, pp. 35–38, 103–105.

[43] *Ibid.*, p. 112 ff. Those joining with Margolin in this demarche were L. L. Bych of the Kuban, Bakhanovich of Belorussia, and General Cheriachukin of the Don. Although accredited to the Hetman's government Cheriachukin had immediately entered friendly relations with the Directorate as soon as its forces captured Kiev in December. The remarkably flexible Cheriachukin subsequently went to Odessa, where on behalf of Grekov and Margolin he "applied every effort to prove to [the French] that support must be given to the Ukraine." See his report to the Don Krug, February 22, 1919, Cheriachukin Papers, File IV, No. 1.

[44] See Margolin, *op. cit.*, pp. 114–118.

[45] See M. S. Margulies, *op. cit.*, I, 219, 221. See also the statement by the Directorate quoted in S. A. Piontkovskii, ed., *Grazhdanskaia voina v Rossii* (Moscow: Izd. Kom. univ., 1925), p. 382.

[46] Freidenberg was also quoted as saying that the intervention must not require "a single French soldier . . . to sacrifice his life on the fields of Russia." Gukovskii, *Frantsuzskaia interventsiia*, p. 122.

[47] The "texts" of both this military agreement and a subsequent political agreement are printed in Gukovskii, *Frantsuzskaia interventsiia*, pp. 142–143, 146; Shliapnikov, *Les alliés contre la Russie*, pp. 286–288; Shlikhter, *op. cit.*, pp. 134–135. It should be noted that these "texts" are based primarily on the reports of

Bolshevik agents in Odessa at the time, but since the agreements are confirmed in somewhat different terms also in P. Khrystiuk, *Zamitky i materialy do istorii Ukrains'koi revoliutsii* (Vienna: Vernay, 1921), Vol. IV, p. 104, and by general statements by Dr. Margolin in Margolin, *op. cit.*, 109–124 *passim*, they may be considered basically reliable. Vynnychenko, who rejected any idea of entering such agreements with the French, states that Grekov and Matveev, whom he describes as a Russophile and a Denikinist respectively, would have done so. In any case he agrees that the texts represent French policy and reflect the demands put to the Directorate by Freidenberg. See Vynnychenko, *op. cit.*, III, 251 ff.

[48] See "Ocherk' vzaimootnoshenii vooruzhennykh sil' Iuga Rossii i predstavitelei frantsuzskago komandovaniia," *loc. cit.*, p. 246; Xydias, *op. cit.*, p. 198; and Denikin, *Ocherki russkoi smuty*, V, 34–40.

[49] See note 47 above. In addition to the sources cited above, the economic agreement appears in Piontkovskii, *op. cit.*, pp. 382–383; and in Iakushkin, *Frantsuzskaia interventsiia*, pp. 31–32. Cf. also the note from the Ukrainian Bolshevik leader, Rakovskii, to Pichon, February 28, 1919, in Piontkovskii, *op. cit.*, pp. 383–385. Virtually these same terms were said to have been presented to Sidorenko, representing the Directorate in Paris, by Foreign Minister Pichon when an inquiry was made into the possibility of obtaining French aid. See Gukovskii, *Frantsuzskaia interventsiia*, p. 146. In an interview with this writer, the late Dr. Margolin, who cites no time limit in his account (Margolin, *op. cit.*, p. 123), stated that the French requested control of the railroads, finances, etc. for "as long as possible." Cf. M. S. Margulies, *op. cit.*, I, 229, 250.

[50] Margolin, *op. cit.*, p. 123; Khrystiuk, *op. cit.*, IV, 104. See also Vynnychenko, *op. cit.*, III, 158.

[51] See "Ocherk' vzaimootnoshenii vooruzhennykh sil' Iuga Rossii i predstavitelei frantsuzskago komandovaniia," *loc. cit.*, pp. 241–242, 245.

[52] Pichon to Paul Cambon, March 3, 1919, MA, Series B, Packet II, Dossier 11. A copy of this dispatch was sent to Maklakov by the French Foreign Ministry.

[53] The negotiators apparently initialled the agreements at the time of their acceptance by the Ukrainian delegation, but negotiations were continued beyond that point (February 21). This probably meant that these terms were accepted as the basis for further negotiations to determine their final form. However, no formal treaty was ever entered by France and the Directorate, apparently because the French gave up the idea under the impact of new developments. Margolin states that the project never became a treaty because the French suddenly broke off the negotiations upon receipt of instructions from Paris. See Margolin, *op. cit.*, pp. 123–124. Ostapenko, on the other hand, simply indicates that the negotiations never reached the final signing. See Shlikhter, *op. cit.*, p. 267. Cf. Vynnychenko, *op. cit.*, III, 254 ff.; and Gukovskii, *Frantsuzskaia interventsiia*, p. 143 ff. The belief that Freidenberg's plan to enter a formal agreement with the Ukraine was cancelled from Paris is supported by the report of a telegram from Pichon made by Azbuka. See MA, Series B, Packet II, Dossier 3, Azbuka report of March 15, 1919.

[54] The criterion for relations with any anti-Bolshevik force was expressed in Pichon's reply to an appeal from the Samara government earlier; said he: "As soon as you prove to us that you have real power in your hands, that you are listened to in Russia, and that real forces will group themselves around—this will

produce a great impression. Thus the key to your significance abroad lies more in your real strength than in your legal claims." Quoted in Gukovskii, *Frantsuzskaia interventsiia*, p. 152; and in I. M. Maiskii, *Demokraticheskaia kontr-revoliutsiia* (Moscow: Gosizdat, 1923), p. 78.

[55] See "Ocherk' vzaimootnoshenii vooruzhennykh sil' Iuga Rossii i predstavitelei frantsuzskago komandovaniia," *loc. cit.*, pp. 241, 246–247; and Sannikov, *op. cit.*, pp. 22–26. See also Iakushkin, *Frantsuzskaia interventsiia*, p. 56; and telegram from Demidov to Maklakov, March 16, 1919, MA, Series B, Packet II, Dossier 9.

[56] "Ocherk' vzaimootnoshenii vooruzhennykh sil' Iuga Rossii i predstavitelei frantsuzskago komandovaniia," *loc. cit.*, p. 243. Denikin's proposal to send more Volunteers to the Crimea was accompanied by a statement that he also wished to move his headquarters there. The Crimean government cooperated closely with the Volunteers, but it was feared by some in the government that if Denikin moved into the Crimea, it would mean the end of any real autonomy for the government, even if its existence were technically maintained. See Nabokov to Sazonov, February 27, 1919, MA, Series B, Packet II, Dossier 10.

[57] M. S. Margulies, *op. cit.*, I, 310. A collection of the orders from the French Command beginning March 13 with the declaration of martial law and the appointment of a new civil authority may be found in MA, Series B, Packet II, Dossier 1.

[58] Andro de Langeron was supposed to be an excellent selection for this post because of his unusual background and experience. See Kin, "K istorii frantsuzskoi interventsii na iuge Rossii," *Krasnyi Arkhiv*, Vol. XIX (Moscow: Gosizdat, 1927), p. 6. However, to many the inclusion of Andro and others who had served under the Hetman meant an effort to restore a puppet regime in the Ukraine. See Sannikov, *op. cit.*, pp. 31–32.

[59] Sannikov, *op. cit.*, pp. 35–38.

[60] *Ibid.*, p. 39. See also the transcript of the conference of Volunteer representatives in Odessa, March 14, 1919, in the Bernatskii Papers.

[61] For background on General Shvarts and the activities with which he was involved, see Ia. I. Kefeli, "S Generalom A. V. Shvartsem v Odesse, osen' 1918-vesna 1919 gg.: vospominaniia" (MS, Columbia University Russian Archive). Earlier in the spring of 1918 it had been rumored that Shvarts was likely to be included in an incoming Socialist Revolutionary government if the Socialist Revolutionaries succeeded in overthrowing the Bolsheviks with Allied aid. See the report of a German officer in Petrograd in Zeman, *op. cit.*, p. 122. Although the plans of the Guchkov group had been kept secret, Denikin knew of them and had given Guchkov his approval, despite the fact that one of Guchov's reasons for urging his plan was that he believed that the Volunteers could at best hold the South while others moved in from the east and north and especially from the west to administer the knock-out blow to the Bolsheviks. See Guchov's memorandum to Denikin entitled "Bor'ba v Rossii s bol'shevizmom i eia perspektivy," in the Miliukov Personal Archives; and Kefeli, *op. cit.*, p. 8.

[62] Kefeli, *op. cit.*, p. 21. In connection with point No. 1, it should be noted that the Volunteer government at Ekaterinodar was proposed as the government of the "Southeast." In connection with point No. 2, the French had up to this time opposed any mobilization in the Odessa area by the Volunteers, partly because of the fact that the most promising source of recruits was the German ele-

ment resident in the area. See Sannikov, *op. cit.*, pp. 13–14.

[63] Kefeli, *op. cit.*, p. 21. Odessa duma leader M. V. Braikevich, who was a Kadet but was regarded as a spokesman for socialist opinion, had urged Shvarts not to accept the French offer or oppose Denikin, since it would "compromise his good name" and merely involve him in a "colonial government which was contrived by Col. Freidenberg together with Margulies and the C.S.U.R. [Council for State Unity of Russia]." See Braikevich in Shchegolev, *op. cit.*, p. 255. Up to this point Shvarts, on Sannikov's advice, had indeed planned to accept the appointment only after joining the Volunteer Army and obtaining Denikin's authorization to take the post. See Sannikov, *op. cit.*, p. 36.

[64] See d'Anselme to Col. Corbeil, received March 21, 1919, Correspondence with the French Mission, Denikin Archives.

[65] This statement and others relating to the reorganization may be found in MA, Series B, Packet II, Dossier 1. See also Denikin, *Ocherki russkoi smuty*, V, 45–46; and a detailed and fairly objective account of events leading up to the change in authority and the break with Denikin in the anonymous article, "Bor'-ba s bol'shevikami v Novorossiiskom krae," MA, Series B, Packet II, Dossier 1.

[66] The official Army report on these events declared that "this coup d'état . . . emanated from the apparent aspiration of the French to obtain unity of command for themselves and . . . subordination of the civil power to that military command." "Ocherk' vzaimootnoshenii vooruzhennykh sil' Iuga Rossii i predstavitelei frantsuzskago komandovaniia," *loc. cit.*, p. 247. For Denikin's personal condemnation of Shvarts for his role, see Denikin to Iudenich, May 8, 1919, MA, Series B, Packet II, Dossier 8.

[67] Denikin, *Ocherki russkoi smuty*, V, 46. Denikin's policy was also under fire at this time from within his own Special Council. While some urged him to accept a French government in Odessa to avoid a break, others were entirely opposed to compromise. Denikin as usual tried to steer a middle course. *Ibid.*, p. 41; and Kin, *op. cit.*, pp. 8–9.

[68] The Council for State Unity, which was backing the French and supporting Shvarts, boycotted this appeal. See Gurko, *op. cit.*, pp. 77, 81–82.

[69] Quoted in Denikin, *Ocherki russkoi smuty*, V, 47. See also Braikevich in Shchegolev, *op. cit.*, p. 257. The general description of the new authority was "South-Western" rather than "South Russian" as used here. However, in view of the previous history of military organization in the Ukraine, it is interesting that the new army to be under Shvarts was to be called the "South Russian Army," and Shvarts' immediate assistant in command was to be General Prokhopovich, who had served as deputy minister of war in the Hetman's cabinet. See "Bor'ba s bol'shevikami v Novorossiiskom krae," MA, Series B, Packet II, Dossier 1.

[70] Xydias, however, presents the view that the break with Denikin was not a miscalculation, but a deliberate move by d'Anselme to make a last ditch effort to form a new Russian army. See Xydias, *op. cit.*, p. 285. Cf. Azbuka report, March 15, 1919, MA, Series B, Packet II, Dossier 3.

[71] M. S. Margulies, *op. cit.*, I, 314–315. What the socialists still preferred was a three-man directorate, but now they wished it to be composed of two socialists and General Sannikov as the Russian government in Odessa under Denikin's general authority.

[72] Quoted in Denikin, *Ocherki russkoi smuty*, V, 49. Franchet d'Esperey's

remark regarding a colonial regime may be compared with the socialist charge, made by Braikevich, that French behavior was in fact clearly representative of a "colonial policy." See Braikevich in Shchegolev, *op. cit.*, p. 254.

[73] Quoted in "Bor'ba s bol'shevikami v Novorossiiskom krae," MA, Series B, Packet II, Dossier 1. According to an unconfirmed Azbuka report, dated March 15, Pichon had wired instructions just prior to this repudiating Freidenberg's policies and calling for support of the Volunteers. See Azbuka report, March 15, 1919, MA, Series B, Packet II, Dossier 3.

[74] Denikin, *Ocherki russkoi smuty*, V, 51. See also "Ocherk' vzaimootnoshenii vooruzhennykh sil' Iuga Rossii i predstavitelei frantsuzskago komandovaniia," *loc. cit.*, p. 248; and "Bor'ba s bol'shevikami v Novorossiiskom krae," MA, Series B, Packet II, Dossier 1. Interestingly, Braikevich has left one of the few written defenses of Grishin-Almazov's work as governor-general. See Braikevich in Shchegolev, *op. cit.*, pp. 241–243. After June 1919 the Socialist Revolutionary organization in the South officially rejected further cooperation with the intervention and associated itself with the Moscow Socialist Revolutionary position. Individual members, however, still went their separate ways, some continuing to support the intervention and the Volunteers. See Gukovskii, *Frantsuzskaia interventsiia*, p. 106.

[75] Denikin, *Ocherki russkoi smuty*, V, 50. Grishin-Almazov's highly critical views of French policy are expressed in a note to the National Council, March 23/April 5, 1919, WMA, File 134, p. 76. Sannikov still hoped, in vain, to save the situation by bringing Denikin and Franchet d'Esperey together for a conference. See Sannikov, *op. cit.*, pp. 43–44.

[76] See Azan, *Franchet d'Esperey*, pp. 247–248.

[77] *Ibid.*, pp. 241–242. Clemenceau, for whom Franchet d'Esperey apparently had little respect, seems to have felt the same way about the general. He wrote later that Franchet d'Esperey had tried to dictate policy "from the East" and had "mistreated me greatly." See Georges Clemenceau, *Grandeurs et misères d'une victoire* (Paris: Plon, 1930), p. 105. A similar impression of Franchet d'Esperey is given in J. J. H. Mordacq, *Le ministère Clemenceau, journal d'un témoin* (Paris: Librairie Plon, 1931), Vol. III, pp. 80–81.

[78] Azan, *op. cit.*, p. 246. See also Gukovskii, *Frantsuzskaia interventsiia*, p. 227.

[79] In reporting this to Denikin, however, the ambassador added rather prophetically of Berthelot: "I did not observe in him any confidence that Odessa would be held. . . ." Denikin, *Ocherki russkoi smuty*, V, 67.

[80] Quoted in "Bor'ba s bol'shevikami v Novorossiiskom krae," MA, Series B, Packet II, Dossier 1. See also Xydias, *op. cit.*, p. 287.

[81] Xydias, *op. cit.*, pp. 281–282. Lt. Col. E. Francis Riggs, of the American mission sent to South Russia, also reported from Odessa on March 23 that while the morale of French troops was very poor, the quality of the French staff was even poorer, and the supply problem was most pressing. French headquarters had assured him, however, that it had been decided to reinforce Odessa and hold it. See Ammission (Odessa) to American Commission to Negotiate Peace (Paris), March 23, 1919, in U. S. National Archives, Foreign Affairs Section, Doc. No. 184.01602/7. The Ukrainian troops mobilized by Shvarts never actually participated in the defense of the city, since they obtained permission from Rumania

through French intercession to pass through Bessarabia and go to Galicia. See Xydias, op. cit., p. 284.

[82] Xydias, op. cit., p. 289. Franchet d'Esperey's recommendations that Odessa be evacuated unless the situation was greatly improved date from early January. See U. S. Embassy, Paris, E.S.H. Bulletins, 1919–1920, No. 73, Hoover Library.

[83] Gukovskii, Frantsuzskaia interventsiia, p. 219. See also intelligence report No. 76, WMA, File 181; and Denikin, Ocherki russkoi smuty, V, 69.

[84] Xydias, op. cit., pp. 294–299.

[85] Odessa Novosti, March 2, 1919, quoted along with statistics on the economic situation in Gukovskii, Frantsuzskaia interventsiia, pp. 75–77.

[86] Gukovskii, "Krym v 1918–1919 gg.," loc. cit., p. 172.

[87] A detailed account of Bolshevik underground activities during the intervention may be found in Gukovskii, Frantsuzskaia interventsiia, p. 158 ff. Copies of some of the handbills distributed by the Bolsheviks in Odessa are in WMA, File 132, pp. 115-117. Among the rumors apparently circulated at this time was one very effective story that the Clemenceau government had fallen because of opposition in the Chamber to the intervention and had been replaced by a Socialist government that had ordered evacuation of Odessa. See Xydias, op. cit., pp. 299–302; and M. S. Margulies, op. cit., II, 70.

[88] According to Xydias, the Greek and African troops were less affected by Bolshevik propaganda, partly because of their better morale and partly because of the language barrier. Xydias, op. cit., pp. 271–273. An account of the military operations and the problems of the French Command may also be found in F. J. Deygas, L'Armée d'Orient dans la guerre mondiale, 1915–1919 (Paris: Payot, 1932), pp. 300–317. Venizelos later told Margulies that the Greeks had participated in the intervention only upon French insistence. They got little credit for their assistance, he said, but an unfair share of the blame. See M. S. Margulies, op. cit., II, 10.

[89] Bolshevik accounts tend to exaggerate the role of their propaganda in forcing the evacuation. For a typical Communist interpretation of recent years see B. E. Shtein, Russkii vopros na Parizhskoi mirnoi konferensii (Moscow: Gosizdat, 1949), pp. 316–326. Gukovskii's earlier account, the best Soviet account, is much more objective. While he gives considerable attention to the advance of Red forces, to the work of the underground, and to the collapse of morale in the French forces, he finally concludes that the evacuation was a "self-willed" act expediently ordered before it became imperative. See Gukovskii, Frantsuzskaia interventsiia, pp. 188, 226. By contrast, Andre Marty, the French sailor who played an important but not exclusive role in the brief mutiny on French ships at Odessa, comes close to giving himself sole credit for the failure of the intervention. See André Marty, The Epic of the Black Sea Revolt (New York: Workers' Library Publishers, 1941), abridged translation of La révolte de la Mer Noire (Paris: Bureau d'Editions, 1932). In weighing the causes one must of course consider the division in French policy, the attitude of Franchet d'Esperey, and certainly the popular mood in France, where one Socialist deputy in the Assembly called the Black Sea mutiny "a true revolutionary movement in the highest and purest sense of the word" by the "sons of the great French Revolution." See Annales de la chambre des députés, Débats parlementaires, Tome II (1919), pp. 2341–2342, session of June 12. Cf. Deygas, op. cit., pp. 310–311.

⁹⁰ Cf. Sannikov, op. cit., pp. 23–27.

⁹¹ See Paul Mantoux, Les délibérations du Conseil des Quatre (Paris: Editions du Centre National de la Récherche Scientifique, 1955), Vol. I, pp. 22–23, 52, 56–57; and Paris Peace Conference, IV, 379–383. In a subsequent letter the British commander, Milne, wrote to Denikin that at French insistence "the question of the evacuation of Odessa was decided in Paris in the Council of Ten on the basis of the reports of General d'Anselme and Colonel Freidenberg on the catastrophic conditions of supply in Odessa." Denikin, Ocherki russkoi smuty, V, 69. The Hoover Relief Commission had been consulted on the food problem and had made efforts to get supplies in, but relief on the scale required was impossible. See U. S. National Archives, American Food Mission to Southern Europe, Near East, Constantinople Office of the Director of the Mission, FA 276A-A1, general correspondence, drawers Nos. 909 and 912. See also Deygas, op. cit., p. 309. Just before the evacuation, an Inter-Allied Supply Commission was being established, apparently to assume responsibility for supply of the whole area, but no immediate assistance for Odessa was forthcoming. See Documents of the Crimean Government, announcement of the establishment of the Commission by d'Anselme, March 17, 1919, File No. 5 (Hoover Library).

⁹² Xydias, op. cit., p. 302.

⁹³ See Lukomskii, Memoirs, p. 222; and Denikin, Ocherki russkoi smuty, V, 69. Three days later Franchet d'Esperey was reportedly in Bucharest organizing an international expedition to march into Hungary to suppress Bela Kun's soviet rebellion. When Clemenceau wired orders prohibiting him from further participation in this scheme, Franchet d'Esperey concluded that "Clemenceau has always been convinced that military men are imbeciles and knows nothing of employing their services." See Azan, op. cit., p. 251.

⁹⁴ Annales de la chambre des députés, Débats parlementaires, Tome I (1919), p. 1448, session of March 29, 1919. Further discussion by Pichon of the situation which was soon to lead to the evacuation may be found in ibid., Tome I, pp. 1276–1278, 1284–1285, 1302–1307; Tome II, p. 308. See also C. H. Sloves, La France et l'Union soviétique (Paris: Rieder, 1935), pp. 95–106. The British Cabinet had also decided to evacuate Arkhangelsk and Murmansk in March, although evacuation was in fact not carried out until later. See W. S. Churchill, The World Crisis: The Aftermath (London: Thornton Butterworth, 1929), p. 240.

⁹⁵ See "Ocherk' vzaimootnoshenii vooruzhennykh sil' Iuga Rossii i predstavitelei frantsuzskago komandovaniia," loc. cit., pp. 251–252. Cf. Xydias, op. cit., pp. 302–305.

⁹⁶ Xydias, op. cit., p. 306.

⁹⁷ Ibid., pp. 307–311, 324. See also Gukovskii, Frantsuzskaia interventsiia, pp. 221–222; and Deygas, op. cit., p. 309. Cf. M. S. Margulies, op. cit., II, 32. The Directorate's brief rule over the Ukraine was ended at this time also, of course, although it continued its struggle to regain power. The Ukrainian troops that retreated toward Odessa received French cooperation in obtaining permission from Rumania to pass through Bessarabia to Galicia. Meanwhile the Directorate itself virtually disintegrated. Vynnychenko continued his former effort to forge an alliance with the Bolsheviks, now suggesting a three-way alliance with Bela Kun's soviet Hungary, while Petliura joined his troops in Galicia, where he sought

support for a new offensive in the summer. Petliura's subsequent activities and his relations with Poland will be noted later. For further detail see Reshetar, *op. cit.*, p. 263 ff. It should be noted that the Allied squadron under Admiral Amet remained on the Black Sea and continued to control it despite the evacuation of land forces.

[98] Xydias, *op. cit.*, p. 318.

[99] Denikin, *Ocherki russkoi smuty*, V, 52–54. The funds in the possession of the Odessa authorities were carried to Constantinople, where a bitter feud then began between Shvarts' council and Volunteer representatives over their disposal. See Gurko, *op. cit.*, pp. 78–79.

[100] Quoted in "Ocherk' vzaimootnoshenii vooruzhennykh sil' Iuga Rossii i predstavitelei frantsuzskago komandovaniia," *loc. cit.*, p. 249. According to the acting head of the Volunteer Foreign Affairs Department, Neratov, the French mission at Volunteer headquarters had still not received any information concerning the evacuation even two weeks after it had been carried out. See Neratov to Sazonov, April 14, 1919, MA, Series B, Packet II, Dossier 8.

[101] "Ocherk' vzaimootnoshenii vooruzhennykh sil' Iuga Rossii i predstavitelei frantsuzskago komandovaniia," *loc. cit.*, pp. 250–251. Cf. Xydias, *op. cit.*, pp. 288–289.

[102] "Ocherk' vzaimootnoshenii vooruzhennykh sil' Iuga Rossii i predstavitelei frantsuzskago komandovaniia," *loc. cit.*, pp. 256, 260; Gukovskii, "Krymskoe kraevoe pravitel'stvo v 1918–1919 g.," *loc. cit.*, p. 96. The total number of troops both in Odessa earlier and now in the Crimea is difficult to establish, since the sources vary widely. In all probability a total of around 60,000 men were all that were ever available to the French Command in all areas of South Russia combined, and not all of these were fighting men or available at one time. See Gukovskii, *Frantsuzskaia interventsiia*, pp. 45–48.

[103] See the agreement between the Volunteer Army and the Crimean government putting all military forces under Denikin's command in return for the latter's guarantee not to intervene in the internal administration of the Crimea, Documents of the Crimean Government, File 9, Hoover Library. Further information on Volunteer-Crimean relations is also contained in Denikin, *Ocherki russkoi smuty*, V, 54 ff.; and in the journal of the meeting of the Crimean government on April 16, 1919, in Documents of the Crimean Government, File 12, which is also printed in *Arkhiv Russkoi Revoliutsii*, Vol. II (Berlin: Izdatel'stvo "Slovo," 1921), pp. 135–142. For a detailed record of events in the Crimea in this period see Gukovskii, "Krymskoe kraevoe pravitel'stvo v 1918–1919 g.," *loc. cit.*; and "Krym v 1918–1919 gg.," *loc. cit.*

[104] See Gukovskii, "Krym v 1918–1919 gg.," *loc. cit.*, XXVIII, 151–172.

[105] See regulations forwarded to Vinaver, from the French Command, dated March 29, 1919, Documents of the Crimean Government, File 5.

[106] A detailed history of events involving Sevastopol fortress, written by its chief of staff, may be found in F. P. Rerberg, "Istoricheskiia zagadki v revoliutsii v Rossii," Vol. II, "Krepost' Sevastopol pod vlastiu Germantsev, Anglichan, Frantsuzov i Dobrovol'tsev Gen. Denikina" (MS, Hoover Library).

[107] "Ocherk' vzaimootnoshenii vooruzhennykh sil' Iuga Rossii i predstavitelei frantsuzskago komandovaniia," *loc. cit.*, p. 257.

[108] *Ibid.*, pp. 257–258.

[109] This account is based upon the minutes of the Crimean cabinet meeting of April 16, which contain an account of events of the preceding two weeks. See Documents of the Crimean Government, File 12. See also Gukovskii, Frantsuzskaia interventsiia, pp. 214–215.

[110] For further details on these financial questions see also Documents of the Crimean Government, File 17. Cf. L. Poliarnyi, "Interventy v Krymu," in K desiatiletiiu interventsii: sbornik statei, pp. 146–150.

[111] This document may be found in Documents of the Crimean Government, File 5, "Act" dated April 12, 1919, and signed by Krym, Bart, Vinaver, and Nabokov. Cf. Shliapnikov, Les alliés contre la Russie, pp. 295–296.

[112] "Ocherk' vzaimootnoshenii vooruzhennykh sil' Iuga Rossii i predstavitelei frantsuzskago komandovaniia," loc. cit., pp. 260–261. According to one account Trousson threatened to turn naval guns on the Volunteers if they tried to retreat or to leave the Crimea. See Gukovskii, "Krym v 1918–1919 gg.," loc. cit., XXIX, 81. Denikin, however, states that the threat to use force was made by the French naval captain in charge of the squadron guarding the Kerch peninsula, Captain Benet. Denikin, Ocherki russkoi smuty, V, 66.

[113] "Ocherk' vzaimootnoshenii vooruzhennykh sil' Iuga Rossii i predstavitelei frantsuzskago komandovaniia," loc. cit., pp. 260–261.

[114] Shliapnikov, Les alliés contre la Russie, p. 254.

[115] See Deygas, op. cit., p. 313; and Gukovskii, Frantsuzskaia interventsiia, pp. 217–218. Related documents, including a report by Admiral Amet, may also be found in E. Moulis and E. Bergonier, eds., En marge du conflict mondial (Paris: Jehan, 1937), pp. 175–180.

[116] Denikin, The White Army, p. 249.

[117] Denikin, Ocherki russkoi smuty, V, 69.

[118] Ibid., IV, 239–241; V, 69. See also Paris Peace Conference, V, 545–548.

[119] See Churchill, op. cit., p. 177; Paris Peace Conference, IV, 14–15; Documents on British Policy, III, 367, 412.

[120] Quoted in Denikin, Ocherki russkoi smuty, V, 67–68; and in Lukomskii, Vospominaniia, II, 293–295. The protocol is also printed in French in Shliapnikov, Les alliés contre la Russie, Annex No. 6, pp. 290–291.

[121] See Denikin, Ocherki russkoi smuty, V, 169; and "Ocherk' vzaimootnoshenii vooruzhennykh sil' Iuga Rossii i predstavitelei frantsuzskago komandovaniia," loc. cit., p. 249. See also Serafimov (Constantinople) to Maklakov, May 21, 1919; and Ikskiul to Maklakov, May 22, 1919, MA, Series B, Packet II, Dossier 8; and telegram from Denikin to Franchet d'Esperey, April (?), 1919, Correspondence with the French Command, Denikin Archives.

[122] This question had come up informally before, and was raised on a number of other occasions. As Lukomskii has stated: "In connection with the question of external trade, the question of giving our allies various concessions was repeatedly raised. . . ." Lukomskii, "Iz vospominanii," Arkhiv Russkoi Revoliutsii, Vol. VI (Berlin: Izdatel'stvo "Slovo," 1922), p. 151.

[123] The French had a statement to this effect inserted in a report of the Financial Section of the Inter-Allied Council on War Purchases and Finance in February 1918. See Foreign Relations, 1918, Russia, III, 34.

[124] Quoted in Shliapnikov, Les alliés contre la Russie, p. 377. This statement is from a letter from the French representative in Arkhangelsk, Guillard, to the

Northern Government on April 9, 1919. In the letter it is further stated by Guillard: "Following the instructions which I have received, I have the honor of informing the government of the northern region of the point of view of the French government on this question; the governments of Omsk [Kolchak] and Ekaterinodar [Denikin] are being informed simultaneously." For further details on French investment in Russia and trade see Gukovskii, *Frantsuzskaia interventsiia*, pp. 28–36.

[125] See Denikin, *Ocherki russkoi smuty*, IV, 45–48; and statement quoted in P. N. Wrangel, *Always With Honor* (New York: Robert Speller and Sons, 1957), p. 120. General Wrangel, who sharply disagreed with Denikin on his policies, later blamed their financial difficulties on "General Denikin's obstinate refusal to use the enormous natural wealth of South Russia to attract foreign capital." *Ibid.*, p. 150. Denikin, notably, observed a significant contrast between French persistence in raising the question of repayment or compensation and the more diplomatic British approach, a contrast made all the more notable, he felt, by the fact that the British were giving considerably more material aid. See Denikin, *Ocherki russkoi smuty*, V, 170.

[126] Denikin, *Ocherki russkoi smuty*, V, 170. See also Shliapnikov, *Les alliés contre la Russie*, pp. 299–300.

[127] Shliapnikov, *Les alliés contre la Russie*, p. 300.

[128] Denikin, *Ocherki russkoi smuty*, V, 170. This question is taken up further below in Chapter VI.

[129] *Foreign Relations, 1919, Russia*, p. 760. See also General Riggs' comments in *ibid.*, pp. 751–752.

[130] General Grishin-Almazov, who had been carrying the letter to Kolchak when his ship was captured at Aleksandrovsk, committed suicide rather than surrender to the Bolsheviks. See Denikin, *Ocherki russkoi smuty*, V, 88–89. The text of the letter may also be found in Shliapnikov, *Kto dolzhnik*, pp. 409–410. For a detailed account of the capture of the letter, see N. N. Lishin, *Na Kaspiiskom more* (Prague: Izd. Mor. zhur., 1938), pp. 157–164. General Dragomirov, on a mission to establish better communications in Paris, wrote to Denikin that in referring to the letter Clemenceau had "abruptly tried to attack us as 'the enemies of France.'" Denikin, *Ocherki russkoi smuty*, V, 89, 168. The French Command claimed that France was bearing half of the cost of the aid being delivered by the British. Such an agreement had in fact been entered in September 1918, but this applied only to European Russia, and according to Curzon it was never put into practice because the planned financial body was never established. See *Foreign Relations, 1918, Russia*, III, 143; and *Documents on British Policy*, III, 367. British representatives told Denikin that France was not sharing in the aid, and faced with the question in the Council of Four on May 23, 1919, Clemenceau admitted that the French had given little aid to Denikin "mainly because Great Britain had to supply the shipping," and he later quipped that even that given "had gone to the Soviet through Denikin's army." See *Paris Peace Conference*, V, 901; and VII, 857. See also the account of Margulies' talk with a representative of the French Foreign Ministry on this question in M. S. Margulies, *op. cit.*, I, 330–331.

[131] The protocol was dated April 11 but was not transmitted to Denikin, along with the 1917 agreement, until June 9. This was the first notice to Denikin that

any such agreement existed. See Denikin, *Ocherki russkoi smuty*, V, 68, 88, 170–171; and Denikin, *The White Army*, p. 230. The British government had already decided to begin a withdrawal of its forces in the north and in Transcaspia and to concentrate aid on the Volunteers. A week before the evacuation of Odessa, Churchill wrote to Foch to defend the Volunteers against the "unfavorable opinion" held by the French Command and indicate that it had been decided to extend "all possible assistance" to Denikin. See Churchill's letter of March 28 in *Iz istorii grazhdanskoi voiny*, II, 35–36. Shortly after the evacuation Denikin was informed by the British commander, General Milne, that the British had "energetically protested against the proposal to evacuate Odessa quickly, but the French insisted on immediate evacuation. . . ." See Denikin, *Ocherki russkoi smuty*, V, 69. From June on, Denikin, whose relations with the British had always been better than with the French, got special attention from the former. See Churchill, *op. cit.*, p. 250; *Foreign Relations, 1919, Russia*, pp. 435–436; *Documents on British Policy*, III, 366, 390–391.

[132] Apparently a similar rivalry had also developed in Allied relations with Kolchak in the spring of 1919, at least to the extent that the British and French representatives at Kolchak's headquarters, Generals Knox and Janin, disagreed over what advice to give the Russian leader, and Janin complained that Knox was ignoring the fact that he, Janin, was supposed to be Allied supreme commander on the Siberian front. See the letter from Clemenceau of May 15, instructing the Foreign Ministry to bring this matter to the attention of the British government, in *Iz istorii grazhdanskoi voiny*, II, 45–46.

[133] See Krasnov, "Vsevelikoe voisko Donskoe," *loc. cit.*, pp. 308–309; Denikin, *Ocherki russkoi smuty*, IV, 75–76; and the letter from Krasnov to Denikin, January 21, 1919, Miliukov Personal Archives. Cf. Piontkovskii, *op. cit.*, p. 433; and E. E. Iakushkin, *Frantsuzskaia interventsiia na iuge, 1918–1919* (Moscow: Gosizdat, 1929), p. 24. Denikin and Krasnov both protested against Fouquet's action, and Fouquet was subsequently recalled, but Krasnov could not as easily dismiss the incident as Denikin, whose resentment against French behavior in general was at least partly assuaged in this case by the fact that Fouquet was supporting his claim to authority over Krasnov. Krasnov's position was indeed untenable after the arrival of Allied forces, and pressure on him to resign became increasingly great. In February, when his chief army commander, General Denisov, was attacked in the Krug, which passed a vote of no confidence against him, Krasnov took the weight of opinion in the Don parliament as tantamount to a vote of no confidence against himself and resigned. In his place was elected General A. P. Bogaevskii, who had both Allied and Volunteer backing. See Krasnov, *Kazach'ia "samostinost'*," p. 28; and Dobrynin, *op. cit.*, pp. 72–74. See also the Memorandum of the Don Republic Delegation to the Peace Conference, May 15, 1919, in the collection of delegation propaganda of the Hoover Library. It was printed at the time as *Memorandum delegatsii Donskoi respubliki na Konferentsii Mira* (Paris: Imp. Berezniak et fils, 1919).

[134] Denikin, *Ocherki russkoi smuty*, IV, 71; Lukomskii, *Memoirs*, pp. 203–204, 215. See also the account by the Don representative at Volunteer headquarters in A. A. Smagin, "Vospominaniia" (MS, Columbia University Russian Archive), pp. 27–32; and Krasnov, "Vsevelikoe voisko Donskoe," *loc. cit.*, pp. 277–278; "Discours du General Krasnov avec le General Pool" (MS, Hoover Library); and

Denikin to Poole, December 27/January 9, 1919, Correspondence with English representatives in South Russia, Denikin Archives.

[135] On these questions, see Denikin, *Ocherki russkoi smuty*, IV, 42, 215–216, 240–245; and V, 167–170; M. S. Margulies, *op. cit.*, II, 13–16; letter from Maklakov to S. V. Panin et al., May 16, 1919, WMA, File 151, pp. 256–279; and *Paris Peace Conference*, V, 725, 736.

[136] *Documents on British Policy*, III, 364–375.

[137] *Ibid.*, pp. 409–410.

[138] *Ibid.*, p. 469.

[139] *Ibid.*, p. 527.

CHAPTER V: BRITAIN AS A BUFFER

[1] For Denikin's review of developments in the North Caucasus and their significance, see A. I. Denikin, *Ocherki russkoi smuty*, Vol. IV (Berlin: "Slovo," 1924), p. 97 ff.

[2] *Ibid.*, III, 240.

[3] The National Guard was technically not part of the Georgian army but an arm of the soviets of Georgia. Its appearance marked an ominous turn in relations with the Volunteers, since it was generally regarded as a considerably more radical organization and somewhat autonomous as a military force.

[4] See Denikin, *Ocherki russkoi smuty*, III, 240–242. This was a very mixed area in terms of its population, a fact which made the question of jurisdiction exceedingly difficult. Georgia's ancient history enabled it to claim much through inheritance, but the northern border of the Georgian nation both before the revolution and today touches the Black Sea at a point just south of Adler, that is, well over 100 kilometers south of Sochi. Sukhum, however, was and is some 90 kilometers south of that border in Georgian territory. The border in question was also the southern border of the Kuban, which hoped to step into the disputed territory as a buffer between the Volunteers and the Georgians. The appeal for liberation was in part, however, a result of the deployment of German troops along the coast.

[5] The stenographic journal of the conference may be found in the Georgian publication, *Dokumenty i materialy po vneshnei politike Zakavkaz'ia i Gruzii* (Tiflis: Tip. Pravitel'stva Gruzinskoi Respubliki, 1919), pp. 391–414.

[6] *Ibid.*, pp. 391–392. See also Denikin's account of the conference and the issues involved in *Ocherki russkoi smuty*, III, 240–243. Alekseev had already authorized a credit of 250,000 rubles for the purchase of grain to be sent to Georgia, but he indicated the necessity for settling the border question, the issue of the treatment of Russians in Georgia, and the problem of relations with the Germans before further cooperation could be assured. Accounts by Russian officers in Transcaucasia, relating in some cases rather harsh treatment by the Georgians, may be found in General N. K. Khagondokov, "Vospominaniia," (MS, Columbia University Russian Archive), p. 934 ff.; and in General P. Shatilov, "Zapiski" (MS, Columbia University Russian Archive), Part I, Section B, pp. 558–584; and Section D, pp. 616–637.

[7] See Gegechkori's comments in *Dokumenty i materialy po vneshnei politike*

Zakavkaz'ia i Gruzii, pp. 394–396, 400–403, 409–410, 413.

[8] *Ibid.*, pp. 413–414. General Alekseev stated at the close of the conference: "We have reached a point beyond which our talks can advance only when it is made clear whether the representatives of Georgia want to remove these areas from Russia or not. Only then can we proceed, but I am sure that then all remaining questions can be decided easily and quickly. . . ."

[9] See Bych's remarks in *ibid.*, pp. 394, 403–404. At the conference Bych stated that he felt sure that Georgia would have no objection to the incorporation of the disputed territory into the Kuban. Bych's government had indeed had friendly dealings with Georgia and with other socialist governments in the South. Denikin, however, became convinced that there was more involved than appeared on the surface; he believed that Bych was negotiating with the Georgians and others behind the Volunteers' back. See Denikin, *Ocherki russkoi smuty*, III, 242. In September a council of the socialist parties in Sochi passed a resolution declaring that while close economic ties bound the area to the Kuban, continuation of the union with Georgia was preferable in the immediate future. See *Dokumenty i materialy po vneshnei politike Zakavkaz'ia i Gruzii*, pp. 388–389. A peasant conference in Sochi in December adopted a similar resolution calling for union with Georgia until Russia could be restored as a democratic federated republic. *Ibid.*, pp. 414–415. Georgia later put a claim before the Peace Conference in Paris and then before the League of Nations for borders including Sochi district. See the map in the Georgian publication, *Documents présentés par le gouvernement de la république de Géorgie à la première Assemblée de la Société des nations* (London: Williams, Lea and Co., 1920).

[10] For an opposite interpretation of Georgian-Volunteer relations, see I. M. Shafir, ed., *Secrets of Menshevik Georgia* (London: Communist Party of Great Britain, 1922), p. 6 ff. Here it is declared that the Georgian Menshevik government "went over openly to national chauvinism and treachery to the revolution" and adopted a policy of "staunch support of all the White Guards under the leadership of Alexeiev, Denikin, Wrangel, and many others who were determined to crush the Workers' and Peasants' Republic."

[11] See A. A. Takho-Godi, *Revoliutsiia i kontr-revoliutsiia v Dagestane* (Makhach-Kala: Dagestanskoe Gosizdat., 1927), p. 94.

[12] A British mission under a Major Goldsmith that had been sent to Vladikavkaz was arrested by the Bolsheviks and quickly taken to Astrakhan because of demands for its release made by local elements and even the local soviet. The report of the arrest first appeared in *Izvestiia*, November 15, 1918. See J. M. Meijer, ed., *The Trotsky Papers*, Vol. I (The Hague: Mouton, 1964), pp. 180–181.

[13] Takho-Godi, *op. cit.*, p. 96; W. E. Post et al., "A Resumé of Events in the Caucasus" (MS, Hoover Library), Chap. 6.

[14] Quoted in A. Raevskii, *Angliiskaia interventsiia i Musavatskoe pravitel'stvo* (Baku: Gostip. "Krasnyi Vostok," 1927), pp. 161–162. Cf. Denikin, *Ocherki russkoi smuty*, IV, 123–124.

[15] Denikin, *Ocherki russkoi smuty*, IV, 106 ff. An account of Volunteer operations and the political situation is also in P. Shatilov, *Zapiski* (MS, Columbia University Russian Archive), p. 667 ff.

[16] Denikin, *Ocherki russkoi smuty,* IV, 115 ff.

[17] Report on Mountain Republic delegation, Takho-Godi, *op. cit.,* p. 190.

[18] Although rebuffed by the Volunteer Command, the delegation received a warm reception by Kuban political leaders, who encouraged resistance against Volunteer demands on the Mountain government. See *ibid.,* pp. 194–195.

[19] *Ibid.,* pp. 196–197.

[20] *Ibid.,* p. 200.

[21] While nothing came of Denikin's negotiations with the Mountain government's representatives, he did at this time begin talks with the Chechens, which led to a separate truce, thus at least temporarily pacifying one more element of the Mountain Republic's constituency. See Denikin, *Ocherki russkoi smuty,* IV, 127.

[22] The Red squadron was prevented from rescuing the Bolsheviks in Dagestan by the Russian flotilla on the Caspian, about which more will be noted below. These events are related in Takho-Godi, *op. cit.,* p. 98 ff.

[23] *Ibid.,* pp. 105–106.

[24] Almost a year before, in July 1918, the pro-Turk element in the government had gone so far as to draw up a treaty to unite with Azerbaidzhan and put both under the religious leadership of the Sultan. Such a treaty was never entered, but the link with Azerbaidzhan was to be the basis of some of the subsequent activities of the refugee Mountain government. See *ibid.,* pp. 104–105; and the text of the proposed treaty, pp. 187–188.

[25] See telegrams to the British Command, December 1918, in Correspondence with English Representatives in South Russia, Denikin Archives (Columbia University Russian Archive). See also Denikin, *Ocherki russkoi smuty,* IV, 131–132.

[26] Intelligence reports Nos. 32 and 36, January 10 and 12, 1919, Wrangel Military Archives (Hoover Library), File 181.

[27] Denikin, *Ocherki russkoi smuty,* IV, 131.

[28] Pichon to Paul Cambon, March 3, 1919, MA, Series B, Packet II, Dossier 11. This dispatch quotes reports from Col. Chardigny for February 15 and 26.

[29] Denikin, *Ocherki russkoi smuty,* IV, 154–156. This apparently coincidental correlation between Armenian-Georgian hostilities and the Volunteer advance convinced the Georgians that the two were secretly acting together, and General Walker reportedly warned the Armenian government against any such collusion with Denikin. However, Armenians in the Sochi area and elsewhere along the coast continued to take a hostile attitude toward Georgia and appealed to the Volunteers for intervention on their behalf. See *ibid.,* p. 154.

[30] See the report by Erdeli in the Wrangel Military Archives, File 153, p. 148; and a letter from Erdeli to Denikin of January 18, 1919, Denikin Archives.

[31] Letter from the British military mission to Volunteer headquarters, April 7, 1919, Correspondence with English Representatives in South Russia, Denikin Archives.

[32] Lukomskii, *Vospominaniia,* II, 300–301.

[33] Erdeli report, Wrangel Military Archives, File 153, p. 148.

[34] For Georgian and Azerbaidzhan protests to the British over Volunteer movements, see Denikin, *Ocherki russkoi smuty,* IV, 125–126.

[35] *Ibid.,* p. 156.

[36] Later in talks with Georgian Prime Minister Zhordaniia, who claimed that Denikin had advanced his troops in direct violation of British instructions not to

do so, the British representative, General Beech, pointed out that while com-
munications had been sent earlier to Denikin, none had been received before the
Volunteer advance. In fact British policy was not actually clarified, according to
Beach, until the arrival of General Briggs at Volunteer headquarters in February.
See the transcript of a May 24, 1919, meeting in " 'Demokraticheskoe' pravitel'-
stvo Gruzii i angliiskoe komandovanie," *Krasnyi Arkhiv*, Vol. XXI (Moscow:
Gosizdat, 1927), p. 145.

[37] Denikin to Milne, January 14/27, 1919, Correspondence with English Representatives, Denikin Archives. See also Denikin, *Ocherki russkoi smuty*, IV, 156.

[38] Denikin to Thomson, January 24/February 6, 1919, Correspondence with
English Representatives, Denikin Archives.

[39] Denikin, *Ocherki russkoi smuty*, IV, 156.

[40] *Ibid.*, p. 157. See also Denikin to Walker, February 1/14, 1919, Correspondence with English Representatives, Denikin Archives.

[41] Denikin, *Ocherki russkoi smuty*, IV, 157.

[42] The British mission to Ekaterinodar was headed in turn by Poole (November
1918–February 1919), Briggs (February–June 1919), and finally General Holman
(June 1919–March 1920). According to Denikin, General Walker declared to a
Volunteer representative that he considered Poole obviously uninformed as to
British policy. Poole's departure for Constantinople was initially described as a
trip for consultation, but he did not return. Denikin adds to this his testimony
that Poole urged the support of Volunteer authority in Dagestan and personally
protested the policy directives coming through the Transcaucasian Command.
Ibid., pp. 131, 158.

[43] *Ibid.*, p. 131. See also C. E. Bechhofer-Roberts, *In Denikin's Russia and
the Caucasus 1919–1920* (London: Collin's Sons, 1921), pp. 18–20, 27–28.

[44] The transcript of this meeting is in " 'Demokraticheskoe' pravitel'stvo Gruzii
i angliiskoe komandovanie," *loc. cit.*, pp. 127–140.

[45] For a British observer's account which portrays Georgian duplicity toward
the British on several occasions and charges Georgia with being "a classic example
of an imperialist 'small nation' . . . [whose] chauvinism was beyond all bounds,"
see Bechhofer-Roberts, *op. cit.*, p. 14 ff.

[46] Since Briggs gave Denikin written assurance that these British troops would
prevent any Georgian action against the Volunteers, the latter thus received a
de facto recognition of the movement of the demarcation line southward from
Tuapse to the Bzyb. See Denikin, *Ocherki russkoi smuty*, IV, 160.

[47] *Ibid.*, pp. 159–160. Similarly, an Azerbaidzhani representative was accredited
to the Kuban government but not to the Volunteer Army. *Ibid.*, 170.

[48] This warning, from Milne, was in response to Denikin's note of January 27
noted above. See Milne to Denikin, February 11, 1919, Correspondence with
English Representatives, Denikin Archives.

[49] Cf. Denikin, *Ocherki russkoi smuty*, IV, 131.

[50] Dissatisfaction with Liakhov had apparently been building up for some time,
especially because of friction between him and his subordinates. See *ibid.*, p.
117; and Shatilov, *op. cit.*, p. 680 ff.

[51] Denikin, *Ocherki russkoi smuty*, IV, 131, 133. See also Briggs to Denikin,
February 22, 1919, Correspondence with English Representatives, Denikin
Archives.

⁵² Denikin, *Ocherki russkoi smuty*, IV, 133.

⁵³ Denikin to Briggs, February 22, 1919, Correspondence with English Representatives, Denikin Archives. It is interesting to note that the Russian chargé d'affaires in London, Nabokov, was at about this time wiring that the "War Ministry has assured me that supplies for the Volunteer Army will definitely continue and no orders have been given to stop them." Nabokov to Sazonov, February 20, 1919, Wrangel Military Archives, File 6. But in a telegram dated February 27, Nabokov informed Sazonov that the British *Foreign* Office wished it known that: "As concerns the Transcaucasian republics, the English Government believes that their final status will be subject to the decision of the Peace Conference. Until such a decision is taken it is desirable that no intervention be undertaken from the Russian side. It has already been indicated to General Denikin that in the opinion of the English Government his military action should be restricted to the area north of the line suggested to him and that the support and sympathy of the English Government will depend upon strict observance of this condition." Nabokov to Sazonov, February 27, 1919, Maklakov Archives, Series B, Packet IV, Dossier 11.

⁵⁴ Briggs to Denikin, February 21, 1919, Correspondence with English Representatives, Denikin Archives.

⁵⁵ Denikin, *Ocherki russkoi smuty*, IV, 132–133.

⁵⁶ *Ibid.*, p. 133.

⁵⁷ Takho-Godi, *op. cit.*, p. 107.

⁵⁸ Denikin, *Ocherki russkoi smuty*, IV, 134.

⁵⁹ *Ibid.*, p. 171.

⁶⁰ *Ibid.*, p. 134.

⁶¹ *Ibid.*, p. 135.

⁶² Transcripts of these meetings on May 16, 24, 27, 31, and June 6 are in " 'Demokraticheskoe' pravitel'stvo Gruzii i angliiskoe komandovanie," *loc. cit.*, p. 141 ff.

⁶³ Denikin, *Ocherki russkoi smuty*, IV, 161.

⁶⁴ The disorder referred to here was one of the first appearances of the Leftist movement of "Greens," whose activities were chiefly to involve rebellion against the Volunteers but whose position in the civil war generally was that of "neutrality." See *ibid.*

⁶⁵ *Ibid.*, p. 162.

⁶⁶ " 'Demokraticheskoe' pravitel'stvo Gruzii i angliiskoe komandovanie," *loc. cit.*, p. 144.

⁶⁷ *Ibid.*, p. 148.

⁶⁸ Denikin, *Ocherki russkoi smuty*, IV, 162–163.

⁶⁹ Denikin credits Briggs with beginning at this time a long personal campaign to win support for the Volunteer Army in Bucharest, in Warsaw, in the War Office, and in Parliament. Briggs' activities in this regard, Denikin claims, incurred "considerable opposition on the part of the Minister of Foreign affairs, Curzon." *Ibid.*, p. 163, footnote 1. For similar comment upon Holman's subsequent complaints about lack of support from London, see Bechhofer-Roberts, *op. cit.*, pp. 186–187.

⁷⁰ The text uses the term *miles* at one point and *versts* at another, making the exact distance unclear.

[71] Denikin, *Ocherki russkoi smuty*, IV, 135.

[72] *Documents on British Policy*, III, 451. (Italics added.)

[73] Denikin, *Ocherki russkoi smuty*, IV, 135. The opposition certainly resulted from something more than Bolshevik agitation, but it was true that the Bolshevik underground skillfully used Moslem leaders to generate hostility against the Volunteers, especially against the Cossacks. One such leader, Ali Khadzhi, wrote to Khalilov: "Whoever sympathizes with the Cossacks will be eternally damned" and will fall under the "rage of God." See Tkaho-Godi, *op. cit.*, pp. 110–111. According to Takho-Godi, the Georgian and Azerbaidzhani governments did not deal directly with the Bolsheviks in this work, but the Georgian National Guard secretly offered arms for any rebels recruited. *Ibid.*, p. 114. Cf. J. Loris-Melikof, *La révolution russe et les nouvelles républiques transcaucasiennes* (Paris: Alcan, 1920), pp. 149–150.

[74] Z. D. Avalov, *The Independence of Georgia* (London: Headley, 1940), pp. 189–190. By this time Azerbaidzhan had a fairly good army in being, thanks partly to the assistance of disguised Turkish officers. See F. J. F. French, *From Whitehall to the Caspian* (London: Odhams, 1920), p. 163.

[75] *Foreign Relations, 1919, Russia*, pp. 766–767.

[76] See Lt. Colonel Sir Alfred Rawlinson, *Adventures in the Near East, 1918–1922* (London: A. Melrose, 1923), pp. 157, 160. Cf. Avalov, *op. cit.*, pp. 148–149; and Denikin, *Ocherki russkoi smuty*, IV, 173. One observer attributes British coolness toward Armenia to policy makers in London who frustrated the efforts of more favorable British representatives on the scene. See Bechhofer-Roberts, *op. cit.*, p. 265 ff.

[77] Earlier, when German aid had been obtained, Georgia had taken over certain territory claimed by Armenia on grounds that it was necessary to keep it out of the hands of the Turks. When the Germans left, the Armenians moved back into Kars, Ardahan, and part of Aleksandropol district, coming into conflict with the Georgians. The British imposed a truce at this point before the Armenians could achieve their goals. For a detailed account of Georgian-Armenian conflicts, from the Armenian point of view, see M. Varandian, *Le conflict armeno-géorgien et la guerre du Caucase* (Paris: Imp. M. Flinikowski, 1919). Cf. Avalov, *op. cit.*; and Karl Kautsky, *Georgia, A Social-Democratic Peasant Republic* (London: International Bookshops, Ltd., 1921).

[78] Denikin, *Ocherki russkoi smuty*, IV, 173–174.

[79] Avalov, *op. cit.*, p. 190.

[80] Denikin, *Ocherki russkoi smuty*, IV, 172. Armenia had rejected an invitation to join the Azerbaidzhan-Georgian alliance. In September General Sul'kevich, Azerbaidzhan's chief of staff, referred to Armenia as the "natural and constant ally" of the Volunteers and warned of the necessity of being prepared on both fronts. See Sul'kevich's telegram of September 7, 1919, in the Dratsenko Documents, File No. 1.

[81] Denikin, *Ocherki russkoi smuty*, IV, 175, 177.

[82] *Ibid.*, p. 177.

[83] *Ibid.*, p. 176.

[84] *Ibid.*, pp. 137–138.

[85] One British officer described the hostility of the Georgians rather starkly: "In Georgia hatred against the Russians had reached such a pitch that assassina-

tion had become legalized, practically at least, if not formally." French, *op. cit.*, p. 210.

[86] Denikin, *Ocherki russkoi smuty*, IV, 139. General Lukomskii cites as the chief cause of trouble between the British and the Volunteers the impression among the latter that the former were supporting separatist tendencies in Georgia and Azerbaidzhan in order to create new buffer states between Russia and a British-dominated Persia. See Lukomskii, *Vospominaniia*, II, 304.

[87] Deniken, *Ocherki russkoi smuty*, IV, 128.

[88] *Ibid.*

[89] *Ibid.*, pp. 128–129. According to Denikin, Thomson intended for the Russian troops to move farther north than Petrovsk, but he (Denikin) ordered them to remain there. See also Raevskii, *op. cit.*, p. 95; and B. Baikov, "Vospominaniia o revoliutsii v Zakavkaz'i," *Arkhiv Russkoi Revoliutsii*, Vol. IX (Berlin: "Slovo," 1923), pp. 162–163.

[90] French, *op. cit.*, p. 171.

[91] The seizure did, however, involve a chase at sea during which British boats fired torpedoes at the Russian ships. The torpedoes missed, the British boats had engine trouble, and the Russian crews returned to harbor unscathed. For accounts see N. N. Lishin, *Na Kaspiiskom more* (Prague: Izd. Mor. zhur., 1938), p. 114 ff.; and French, *op. cit*, p. 143 ff. and p. 170 ff.

[92] Difficulty with the workers was not new for the British. A four-day general strike had forced police supervisor Col. Cockeril to release several agitators arrested in December. See French, *op. cit.*, pp. 156–157; Lishin, *op. cit.*, pp. 83–89. A brief strike of protest followed the seizure of the flotilla in March, and another strike was reported in May. See Lishin, *op. cit.*, pp. 134–135; and Raevskii, *op. cit.*, p. 163. The Baku proletariat, in so far as it was influenced by socialist and Bolshevik elements, was decidedly pro-Russian and against separatism, but between Azerbaidzhan and the Volunteers it tended to prefer the former because of its weakness and its anti-Volunteer stand.

[93] Denikin, *Ocherki russkoi smuty*, IV, 129–130. See also the report by the Volunteer representative in Baku, Lt. Bulashevich, dated June 17, 1919, in Shliapnikov, *Kto dolzhnik*, pp. 406–407. Bulashevich describes the flotilla as consisting of three imperial navy ships and four ships armed since the revolution. See also Lishin, *op. cit.*, p. 114 ff.

[94] Lt. Bulashevich in his report noted above states that British Commodore Norris had informed the Russians that the British naval command would assume all responsibility for naval operations against the Bolsheviks and for oversea supply on the Caspian. See Shliapnikov, *Kto dolzhnik*, p. 406. Sir Percy Sykes states in his account that "Norris . . . set to work to dominate the Caspian," and under his leadership "British supremacy on the Caspian was unchallenged and a brilliant page of British naval achievement was written." See Sir Percy Sykes, *A History of Persia*, Vol. II (London: Macmillan, 1951), pp. 497–498.

[95] See French, *op. cit.*, pp. 110, 181.

[96] Lishin, *op. cit.*, pp. 144–145.

[97] Neratov to Maklakov, November 23, 1919, Maklakov Archives, Series B, Packet II, Dossier 11.

[98] French, *op. cit.*, p. 137. Lt. Col. Browne of the British Inland Water Transport Section was made shipping controller in Baku. *Ibid.*, p. 133.

[99] *Ibid.*, p. 142. The major ships in the British flotilla were the *Kruger*, the *Venture*, the *Asia*, the *Emanuel Nobel*, the *Slava*, the *Zoroaster*, the *Bibi Eibat*, the *Windsor Castle*, and the *Volga*. Among the Russian flotilla ships associated with the British during the first months were the *Kars*, the *Ardahan*, the *Alla Verdi*, and the *Astrabad*. During the spring of 1919 six fast (40 knots) "coastal motor-boats" were added to the British force after movement by rail from Batum. *Ibid.*, p. 172. Also in the spring a Royal Air Force unit under Lt. Col. Bowen was attached to the naval squadron and stationed at Chechen Island northeast of Petrovsk. *Ibid.*, pp. 187–188.

[100] French, *op. cit.*, pp. 196–197; Lishin, *op. cit.*, p. 166.

[101] French, *op. cit.*, p. 207.

[102] *Ibid.*, p. 242.

[103] F. M. Bailey, *Mission to Tashkent* (London: Cape, 1946), pp. 82–83. A French Captain Capdeville was also in hiding in Tashkent. See *ibid.*, p. 170.

[104] *Ibid.*, pp. 96–97.

[105] A. H. Brun, *Troublous Times* (London: Constable, 1931), pp. 180–184.

[106] Bailey, *op. cit.*, pp. 130–131. Bailey's account of the January rebellion is in *ibid.*, p. 115 ff. Cf. S. A. Piontkovskii, ed., *Grazhdanskaia voina v Rossii* (Moscow: Izd. Kom. univ., 1925), p. 643 ff. According to Bailey, brothers of both Kerenskii and Kornilov had been involved in anti-Bolshevik activities in Turkestan and both had been killed. See Bailey, *op. cit.*, pp. 101, 121.

[107] Bailey, *op. cit.*, p. 212 ff.

[108] Cf. V. A. Gurko-Kriazhin, "Angliiskaia interventsiia," *Istorik Marksist*, No. 2 (Moscow, 1926), pp. 133–134.

[109] Bailey, *op. cit.*, p. 238 ff.

[110] C. H. Ellis, *The British "Intervention" in Transcaspia, 1918–1919* (Berkeley: University of California Press, 1963), p. 145.

[111] *Ibid.*, pp. 113, 128–129, 153.

[112] *Ibid.*, pp. 113, 141–143.

[113] *Ibid.*, p. 116.

[114] Z. I. Mirkin, "Interventsiia v Zakaspii," in *K desiatiletiiu interventsii: sbornik statei* (Moscow: Gosizdat, 1929), pp. 189–191. Cf. Gurko-Kraizhin, *op. cit.*, pp. 128–129.

[115] Ellis, British "Intervention," pp. 129–130.

[116] See Bailey, *op. cit.*, p. 51; and Ellis, British "Intervention," pp. 132–133.

[117] The British government had decided against further military action as early as November 1918, but no decision was made on evacuating Malleson's force until February. See Ellis, "Operations in Transcaspia," in D. Footman, ed., *Soviet Affairs*, No. 2 (New York: Praeger, 1959), pp. 148–149; and R. H. Ullman, *Anglo-Soviet Relations, 1917–1921*, Vol. I, *Intervention and the War* (Princeton: Princeton University Press, 1961), pp. 326–328.

[118] Ellis, British "Intervention," pp. 145–146.

[119] *Ibid.*, pp. 149–151.

[120] Denikin, *Ocherki russkoi smuty*, V, 240.

[121] *Ibid.*, p. 241.

[122] See the report of the Department of Finance, August 1918, in the Bernatskii Papers (MS, Columbia University Russian Archive); and Denikin, *Ocherki russkoi smuty*, V, 240.

[123] Ellis, British "Intervention," pp. 154, 159.

[124] Mirkin, op. cit., pp. 196–197.

[125] Krasnovodsk finally fell in February 1920. See ibid., p. 199.

[126] Denikin, Ocherki russkoi smuty, V, 242.

[127] Ibid., pp. 243–244. For further details on these events, including the question of Georgian, Azerbaidzhan, and Turkish aid, and the efforts of the Bolsheviks to use the situation to their own advantage, see Takho-Godi, op. cit., p. 115 ff.

[128] Documents on British Policy, III, 308–312. It was in this speech that Lloyd George committed that slip which revealed the state of Western knowledge of Russian affairs: he referred to "General Denikin, Admiral Kolchak, and General Kharkoff." The latter, of course, is a city.

[129] W. S. Churchill, The World Crisis: The Aftermath (London: Thornton Butterworth, 1929), p. 169.

[130] Cf. Curzon's remarks in Paris Peace Conference, IV, 688, and a collective note to the Allied governments from the representatives of Estonia, Latvia, Belorussia, the Ukraine, Northern Caucasus, Georgia, and Azerbaidzhan protesting against support for anyone claiming authority over former Russian territories now independent, in Raevskii, op. cit. pp. 53–54.

[131] Documents on British Policy, III, 409–410. Churchill also supported this view. As he added in a later memorandum: "Every effort should therefore be made to guide affairs into the channel which leads into a federalized Russia, without prejudice either to local autonomy or the principle of general unity." Churchill, op. cit., p. 252.

[132] Documents on British Policy, III, 412–415.

[133] Balfour to Curzon, July 10, 1919, ibid., pp. 424–425.

[134] Ibid., pp. 423–424.

[135] Curzon to Wardrop, July 22, 1919, ibid., pp. 451–452. Wardrop had been British consul-general in Moscow in 1917–1918.

[136] Ibid., pp. 474–476. For a statement by the Russian Council in Paris on this question, see A. D. Margolin, Ukraina i politika antanty (Berlin: Efron, 1921), pp. 377–380.

[137] See the transcript of the conference between General Beach and Zhordaniia on May 24, 1919, in " 'Demokraticheskoe' pravitel'stvo Gruzii i angliiskoe komandovanie," loc. cit., p. 143; and Raevskii, op. cit., p. 55.

[138] This view was encouraged by the description of the change-over as "purely military" by General Thomson in his notification to the Azerbaidzhani government on May 10. He undoubtedly wanted to soften the reaction by making it seem almost routine. See Raevskii, op. cit., p. 55.

[139] Curzon to Balfour, August 12, 1919, Documents on British Policy, III, 482–484.

[140] Foreign Relations, 1919, Russia, p. 750. For the original proposals, appropriation of funds, etc. see U. S. National Archives, Foreign Affairs Section, File 184.016 (Mission to Southern Russia, Colonel Riggs), Documents Nos. 3–25. General descriptions are presented in memoranda by J. C. Grew and P. Tyler in Documents Nos. 24 and 25.

[141] See Foreign Relations, 1919, Russia, p. 751 ff. For the mission's reports see U. S. National Archives, Foreign Affairs Section, Files 184.016 and 184.01602.

[142] U. S. National Archives, Foreign Affairs Section, Doc. No. 184.016/76.

[143] Ibid., File 184.016, Doc. Nos. 53, 55, 56 (Memorandum by C. A. Herter on Polish-Ukrainian negotiations), 66, 79, 80, 87. See also Foreign Relations, 1919, Russia, pp. 763, 769–770.

[144] U. S. National Archives, Foreign Affairs Section, Doc. No. 184.016/50–51.

[145] Ibid., Doc. Nos. 184.016/93 and 184.016/105.

[146] Ibid., Doc. Nos. 184.016/107 and 184.016/112.

[147] A. J. Toynbee, ed., Survey of International Affairs, 1920–1923 (London: Oxford University Press, 1927), p. 364.

[148] U. S. National Archives, Foreign Affairs Section, Doc. No. 184.016/50–51.

[149] D. E. Enukidze, Krakh imperialisticheskoi interventsii v Zakavkaz'i (Tiflis: Gosizdat G.S.S.R., 1954), pp. 180–181.

[150] The part of the mission under Prince de Savoy arrived in Baku on May 16 and was joined there on May 22 by Colonel Gabba, chief of the military mission. See Le 28 Mai, 1919, p. 20; and Foreign Relations, 1919, Russia, p. 763.

[151] See French, op. cit., pp. 200–202; " 'Demokraticheskoe' pravitel'stvo Gruzii i angliiskoe komandovanie," loc. cit., pp. 165–169 (conference between Wardrop and Gegechkori, September 4): and Raevskii, op. cit., pp. 55–56. Denikin also strongly opposed Italian occupation and, despite past difficulties, much preferred that the British stay. See Denikin, Ocherki russkoi smuty, IV, 178.

[152] " 'Demokraticheskoe' pravitel'stvo Gruzii i angliiskoe komandovanie," loc. cit., p. 168. It should be noted, however, that Batum was not yet considered a part of Georgia. Its significance for all of Transcaucasia was the basis for the idea (initially inserted in the Treaty of Sevres) of maintaining it as a free or international port. Turning it over to Georgia might have denied its use to Armenia in particular. British troops were, therefore, ordered to remain in Batum until this question could be settled.

[153] See Avalov, op. cit., p. 202 (citing F. Nitti, L'Europe sans Paix, pp. 186–188).

[154] Raevskii, op. cit., p. 57; Enukidze, op. cit., p. 179. It is notable that Georgian leaders were at this point speaking favorably of a future federation with Russia, probably because this was the view which Allied spokesmen presumably wanted to hear. Cf. Loris-Melicof, op. cit., pp. 180–182. Georgian leaders were, however, divided on the question of whether a mandate would be compatible with the claim to full independence already set forth. See Avalov, op. cit., pp. 188, 194–198.

[155] Documents on British Policy, III, 478–479.

[156] See Hoover's report in Foreign Relations, 1919, Russia, pp. 785–787.

[157] This statement and the following comments are based upon General Harbord's report to the secretary of state, October 16, 1919, to be found in Papers Relating to the Foreign Relations of the United States, 1919, Vol. II (Washington: Government Printing Office, 1934), p. 841 ff.; and in International Conciliation, No. 151 (June 1920), pp. 275–312. Other reports of the Harbord mission may be found in the U. S. National Archives, Foreign Affairs Section, File 184.02102, Doc. No. 18 of this series being a summary report after the mission's return to Paris. The mission consisted of eleven officers and one representative each of the Relief Administration, the Commission to Negotiate Peace, and the Department of Commerce, plus minor assistants.

[158] *Papers Relating to the Foreign Relations of the United States, 1920,* Vol. III (Washington: Government Printing Office, 1936), p. 784. See also *Documents on British Policy,* III, 481.

[159] The official Allied request that he do so was formulated at San Remo in April 1920. See *Foreign Relations, 1920,* III, 779, 783. For the President's generous proposals on the Armenian boundary, see *ibid.,* pp. 795–804, and a map appended at the end of the volume.

[160] *Foreign Relations, 1920,* III, 571–573. Admiral McCully's reports are in *ibid.,* p. 574 ff.

[161] Eliot to Curzon, August 13, 1919, *Documents on British Policy,* III, 485–486.

[162] Curzon to Balfour, August 21, 1919, *ibid.,* pp. 519–526.

[163] For a comment on Wardrop's pro-Georgian attitude see Bechhofer-Roberts, *op. cit.,* p. 48.

[164] Curzon to Wardrop, October 2, 1919, *Documents on British Policy,* III, 574–575.

[165] Curzon to Wardrop, October 4, 1919, *ibid.,* pp. 577-578. See also Wardrop's dispatches in *ibid.,* pp. 601–602, 603–604.

[166] Curzon to Cox, November 14, 1919, *ibid.,* p. 647.

[167] The efforts and experiences of this French envoy are recorded in Loris-Melicof, *op. cit.;* see especially pp. 170 ff. and his report to the Foreign Ministry, pp. 183–189.

[168] See Ellis, *British Intervention,"* pp. 154–155; and also Toynbee, *op. cit.,* pp. 377–382; and G. Lenczowski, *The Middle East in World Affairs,* 2nd ed. (Ithaca: Cornell University Press, 1956), pp. 209–210. It is interesting to note at this point that in August 1919 Trotskii, in a general survey of world revolutionary prospects, put particular emphasis upon the opportunities opening up in India and advocated "preparation of a military thrust against India to aid the Indian revolution." One "authoritative military official," he noted, had already prepared "a plan for creating a cavalry corps (30,000-40,000 riders) with the idea of launching it against India," and there was no reason why this plan should not be given favorable consideration, since the Bolsheviks "had never abandoned the idea of offensive revolutionary wars." Meijer, *The Trotsky Papers,* I, 622–625.

[169] See Curzon's comments on this treaty quoted in H. Nicolson, *Curzon: The Last Phase, 1919–1925* (New York: Harcourt, Brace and Co., 1939), p. 138.

CHAPTER 6: DENIKIN'S MILITARY AND POLITICAL STRATEGIES

[1] For an account of the military operations of the Armed Forces of South Russia during 1919, see A. I. Denikin, *Ocherki russkoi smuty,* Vol. V (Berlin: "Slovo," 1926), pp. 72–84, 104–137.

[2] The 150,000 men in the line were distributed roughly as follows: Mai-Maevskii's Volunteer corps, 40,000; the Don army, 45,000; the Crimean Volunteer corps, 15,000; the Caucasus army, 20,000; and Wrangel's army 30,000. However, the Red Army, with a maximum of around 180,000, continued to outnumber Denikin's forces.

[3] Denikin, Ocherki russkoi smuty, V, 117.

[4] On the dispute between Trotskii and Stalin, see J. M. Meijer, ed., The Trotsky Papers, Vol. I (The Hague: Mouton, 1964), pp. 135–136, 159–160, 165, 197, 241–245, 247–249; and I. Deutscher, The Prophet Armed (New York: Oxford University Press, 1954), p. 436 ff.

[5] See Denikin, Ocherki russkoi smuty, V, 85 ff.; and materials in Foreign Relations, 1919, Russia, pp. 341, 375–379; Documents on British Policy, III, 474–476; and Neratov to Sazanov, May 2, 1919, Maklakov Archives (MA), Series B, Packet III, Dossier 11 (Hoover Library).

[6] Denikin, Ocherki russkoi smuty, V, 95–98.

[7] On the Tsaritsyn campaign and the dispute over strategy between Denikin and Wrangel, see also (besides Denikin's account) P. N. Wrangel, Always with Honor (New York: Speller, 1957), pp. 70, 76–99; and P. Shatilov, "Zapiski" (MS, Columbia University Russian Archive), pp. 716–793.

[8] Wrangel, op. cit., p. 89; see also pp. 111–115.

[9] See Wrangel's account in ibid., p. 79 ff.; and his letter to Denikin making these charges in Denikin, Ocherki russkoi smuty, V, 114.

[10] This charge is made in a letter from one of Kolchak's "field atamans" to Denikin, July 23, 1919, Wrangel Military Archives (WMA), File 181 (Hoover Library).

[11] See the telegram from Clemenceau to Janin, April 17, 1919, and the memorandum of the Allied Military Command, May 17, 1919, in Iz istorii grazhdanskoi voiny v SSSR: sbornik dokumentov i materialov, Vol. II (Moscow: Institut Marksizma-Leninizma, 1961), pp. 40–41, 47–49. Cf. R. H. Ullman, Anglo-Soviet Relations, 1917–1921, Vol. I (Princeton: Princeton University Press, 1961), pp. 238, 263; and Peter Fleming, The Fate of Admiral Kolchak (London: Rupert Hart-Davis, 1963), pp. 155–156.

[12] See Churchill's memorandum of June 24, 1919, in Paris Peace Conference, VI, 684–686. Cf. J. F. N. Bradley, La legion tchecoslovaque en Russie (Paris: Centre National de la Recherche Scientifique, 1965), p. 113.

[13] See Bradley, op. cit., pp. 113–114.

[14] Denikin, Ocherki russkoi smuty, V, 92–93. Denikin states that he was informed that the British mission on the Siberian front supported Gajda's action, thus making it difficult for Kolchak to overrule him. The reason for this, of course, was that the British were hoping to unite the Siberian and Northern fronts and saw greater prospects at the time in this effort than in a similar effort to unite with the South. On Kolchak's relations with Gajda, see also Fleming, op. cit., pp. 102–103, 150, 158–195; and Bradley, op. cit., pp. 101–102.

[15] Denikin, Ocherki russkoi smuty, V, 89–90.

[16] Cf. N. N. Golovin, Rossiiskaia kontr-revoliutsiia v 1917–1918 gg. (Paris: "Illiustrirovannoi Rossii," 1937), Vol. V, Bk. 2, pp. 7–12, 17–20.

[17] Makhno's own memoirs provide the most intimate and dramatic account of his struggle in three volumes: Russkaia revoliutsiia na Ukraine, Pod udarami kontr-revoliutsii, and Ukrainskaia revoliutsiia (Paris: 1929, 1936, and 1937 respectively). See also P. Arshinov, Istoriia makhnovskogo dvizheniia, 1918–1921 gg. (Berlin: Gruppa russkikh anarkhistov v Germanii, 1923). A very useful and briefer account may be found in David Footman's essay on Makhno which is

both in Footman, *Soviet Affairs*, pp. 77–127, and in Footman, *Civil War in Russia*, pp. 245–302.

[18] See Footman, *Soviet Affairs*, p. 101 ff. Grigoriev, one of several local military leaders who served both the Bolsheviks and their own ambitions, had played a major role in Bolshevik efforts to drive the French out of Odessa, but he defected in the last stages of that campaign. When he then visited Makhno's headquarters to seek an alliance, Makhno had him killed on the spot, a deed which undoubtedly facilitated further cooperation with the Bolsheviks and for a time alleviated the latter's concern that he would follow Grigoriev's example.

[19] See Denikin, *Ocherki russkoi smuty*, V, 130–134.

[20] *Ibid.*, pp. 134–135. Later, when Wrangel himself took command from Denikin, he tried to attract Makhno's support and sent representatives to negotiate. All that resulted was the deaths of the emissaries on Makhno's orders. This event notably occurred after a complete break between Makhno and the Bolsheviks in January 1920. Makhno's subsequent battles with the Bolsheviks between January and October 1920 undoubtedly aided Wrangel, although not intentionally.

[21] While Petliura was making plans to continue the fight against the Bolsheviks, his former partner in the Directorate, Vynnychenko, was negotiating for an agreement with them. After the Hungarian revolution, Vynnychenko and Bela Kun reached agreement on a plan to form a coalition government in a Soviet Ukraine which would include Eastern Galicia and provide a bridge to Hungary, but both Moscow and the Ukrainian Bolsheviks rejected this plan to the chagrin of Kun, whose regime, without Russian aid, soon collapsed. See V. Vynnychenko, *Vidrodzhennia natsii* (Vienna: Dzvin, 1920), Vol. III, p. 321 ff.

[22] One of Petrushevich's first acts under a new law of June 9, giving him dictatorial powers to deal with the situation, was to appoint General Michael Grekov, who had negotiated with the French in Odessa on behalf of the Directorate, to command the Galician army. See J. S. Reshetar, *The Ukrainian Revolution* (Princeton: Princeton University Press, 1952), pp. 280–281.

[23] See A. Skrzynski, *Poland and Peace* (London: G. Allen and Unwin, 1923), p. 43, for a description of this policy and its rationale. See also the translator's note in J. Pilsudski, *The Memoirs of a Polish Revolutionary and Soldier*, translated and edited by D. R. Gillie (London: Faber and Faber, 1931), p. 364. Cf. Titus Komarnicki, *Rebirth of the Polish Republic* (London: W. Heineman, Ltd., 1957), pp. 419, 436–437, 450–456.

[24] See *Paris Peace Conference*, IV, 379 ff.

[25] *Ibid.*, V, 775 ff.

[26] *Ibid.*, VI, 194.

[27] *Ibid.*, IV, 828 ff.

[28] *Ibid.*, VI, 677, footnote 4.

[29] A. D. Margolin, *Ukraina i politika antanty* (Berlin: Efron, 1921), pp. 145–146; see also Appendix No. 2, pp. 372–374.

[30] The Russian ambassador in Rumania, Poklevskii-Kozel, wired Neratov on October 20 that French representatives in Bucharest had received instructions from Clemenceau "to do all possible to prevent an armed clash between General Denikin and the forces of Petliura." MA, Series B, Packet II, Dossier 4.

[31] Denikin, *Ocherki russkoi smuty*, V, 255.

[32] Margolin, op. cit., pp. 148–152. In September the French Foreign Ministry even offered its assistance if Margolin himself would go to see Denikin and try to reconcile the Ukrainian and Volunteer views. However, Margolin had at this time broken with the Ukrainian delegation, largely because of its opposition to his favorable views on federation and his willingness to accept mediation with the Volunteers, and he was thus not in a position to undertake the mission suggested. Ibid., p. 172.

[33] Denikin, Ocherki russkoi smuty, V, 255.

[34] Ibid., pp. 255–256.

[35] Ibid., p. 255. See also Churchill's review of the situation to the Cabinet on September 22, 1919, in W. S. Churchill, The World Crisis: The Aftermath (London: Thorton Butterworth, 1929), pp. 251–253.

[36] According to Margolin, his appeals to the United States delegation in Paris for aid to Petliura were also turned aside on grounds that Petliura could obtain support only in alliance with Denikin, since the United States refused to recognize the dismemberment of Russia. See Margolin, op. cit., p. 161. On United States policy see also Paris Peace Conference, XI, 253; and Foreign Relations, 1919, Russia, p. 783.

[37] Denikin, Ocherki russkoi smuty, V, 253.

[38] Ibid., p. 254.

[39] Ibid.

[40] Ibid., p. 255. United States sources reported from Sweden on October 10 that an "International Commission" had left for Odessa to seek a conciliation between Petliura and Denikin, but no other evidence has been found to confirm the establishment of such a mission to clarify this mention of it. See U. S. National Archives, Foreign Affairs Section, Doc. No. 861.00/5363.

[41] Margolin, who saw Petliura in the fall of 1919, indicates that Petliura believed that no agreement with Denikin was possible and that the only way out for the Ukrainians would be to turn to the Poles. See Margolin, op. cit., pp. 189–191. In a letter to M. Jean Pelissier on October 28, 1919, Petliura appealed to "French democracy" to support his movement, noting that "at present our most dangerous adversary is General Denikin, who, instead of fighting the Bolsheviks, has turned against us the artillery and rifles which he got from the Allies, and thus he weakens the anti-Bolshevik front." S. V. Petliura, "Un appel du president Petliura à la democratie française," in Ukrainian Delegation Propaganda, Hoover Library.

[42] Denikin, Ocherki russkoi smuty, V, 256–257. Kolchak agreed basically with Denikin's position and supported it, although he did suggest the expediency of some temporary arrangement with Petliura if it would keep the Allied Powers out of the question and if it could be made without prejudicing the principle of "One Russia." See Sukin (Kolchak) to Neratov (Denikin), September 1, 1919, MA, Series B, Packet II, Dossier 4.

[43] Denikin, Ocherki russkoi smuty, V, 257.

[44] See Maklakov to Omsk, March 29, 1919; Maklakov to Pichon, September 4, 1919; Maklakov to Neratov, September 9, 1919; and Pichon to Maklakov, November 19, 1919, in MA, Series B, Packet II, Dossier 4.

[45] See Curzon to Mackinder, December 2, 1919, in Documents on British Policy, III, 672–678. See also Denikin, Ocherki russkoi smuty, V, 179.

[46] Denikin, Ocherki russkoi smuty, V, 258. See also M. Lozynsky, Halichina v

rokakh 1918–1920 (Vienna, 1922), p. 198. The Polish attack in the spring, to be noted below, made the promise to recognize Petrushevich practically meaningless. In any case, Petrushevich had not approved Tarnovskii's agreement with the Volunteers and had taken refuge in Rumania, although his representatives in Paris had informed Maklakov that he favored federation with Russia and wished to negotiate with Denikin. See Maklakov to Neratov, Nevember 19, 1919, MA, Series B, Packet II, Dossier 4. According to Margolin, Petrushevich had proposed that the Directorate, on behalf of both Petliura's forces and the Galicians, seek agreement with Denikin, but he had opposed splitting their alliance by allowing only the Galician element to enter such a union with the Volunteers. See Margolin, *op. cit.*, p. 188.

[47] Denikin, *Ocherki russkoi smuty*, V, 175.

[48] See Report No. 2 and dispatch dated September 21, 1919, Cheriachukin Papers, File IV.

[49] Denikin, *Ocherki russkoi smuty*, V, 175.

[50] Report No. 2 and dispatch of July 3, 1919, Cheriachukin Papers, File IV.

[51] *Ibid.*, dispatches of July 28 and August 11, 1919.

[52] *Ibid.*, dispatch of September 21, 1919.

[53] See "Doklad o poezdke v Pol'shu i Belorussiiu c 1-go po 16 Noiabria 1919 goda," Von Lampe Archives, File No. 41. Cf. Volunteer bulletin No. 266-2, dated November 19, 1919, in WMA, File 158, pp. 60–61.

[54] Neratov (Denikin) to Maklakov (Sazonov), September 18, 1919, MA, Series B, Packet II, Dossier 4.

[55] Denikin, *Ocherki russkoi smuty*, V, 175.

[56] *Ibid.*, pp. 175–176.

[57] Conversations with Przezdziecki are reported in a confidential memorandum drawn up at the time. See Denikin Archives.

[58] Denikin, *Ocherki russkoi smuty*, V, 177. See also WMA, File 158, p. 35. American sources reported that Poland would specifically demand Eastern Galicia in return for aid. See Admiral Bristol (Constantinople) to Secretary of State, December 11, 1919, *Foreign Relations, 1919, Russia*, p. 777.

[59] Neratov wired Sazonov on December 18 that the negotiations with Poland had not thus far achieved an agreement because of the "tendency of the Poles to use their position to secure for themselves additional territory at our expense." The talks, he added, would "make no progress so long as the Poles hold to this position." Denikin, however, was "prepared to follow a most conciliatory policy toward Poland," and he hoped that the Allies would help by trying to moderate Poland's ambitions. See MA, Series B, Packet III, Dossier 1.

[60] Pilsudski's grand design for the dismemberment of Russia and creation of states more or less dependent upon Poland in the Ukraine and Belorussia was undoubtedly one of the important reasons for his negative attitude toward the Volunteers. Defeat of those who stood for restoration of Russia, even a liberal Russia, would be required for the realization of this idea. Pilsudski in fact began his approach to Petliura in this context with the establishment of arrangements to prevent clashes between their troops on September 1. See Piotr Wandycz, "Secret Soviet-Polish Peace Talks in 1919," *Slavic Review*, XXIV, No. 3 (September 1965), pp. 434, 443, 447. See also M. K. Dziewanowski, "Pilsudski's Federal Policy, 1919–1920," *Journal of Central European Affairs*, X, No. 2 (July 1950),

pp. 113–128; No. 3 (October 1950), pp. 271–287; and R. Machray, *The Poland of Pilsudski* (London: G. Allen and Unwin, 1936). On the border question, see M. M. Laserson, *The Curzon Line* (New York: Carnegie Endowment for International Peace, 1944).

[61] The text of this memorandum, dated October 12, 1919, is in the Denikin Archives. See also Denikin, *Ocherki russkoi smuty*, V, 173. In a speech given in August 1923 Pilsudski recalled that Allied representatives in Warsaw had urged him to cooperate with Denikin but that he refused to accept Denikin's proposal to introduce Russian administration in disputed territories "beyond the Bug." See Jozef Pilsudski, *Pisma zbiorowe*, Vol. VI (Warsaw, 1937), pp. 123–124.

[62] See, e.g., C. Mannerheim, *The Memoirs of Marshal Mannerheim* (London: Cassell and Co., 1953), pp. 236–237, where Pilsudski is quoted to this effect.

[63] Denikin, *Ocherki russkoi smuty*, V, 177.

[64] See Komarnicki, *op. cit.*, pp. 466–469. Cf. the evidence on this point, consisting chiefly of the memoirs of General Haller and a speech by General Kutrzeba on May 7, 1937, presented in Val', *Kak Pilsudski pogubil Denikina* (Tallin: Izdanie avtora, 1938); and Denikin, *Kto spas' sovetskuiu vlast' ot gibeli* (Paris: Izdanie Soiuz' Dobrovol'tsev, 1937).

[65] See Karnicki's comments in the Polish paper, *Torpeda*, October 4, 1936, cited in Komarnicki, *op. cit.*, pp. 468–469.

[66] See *Documents on British Policy*, I, Doc. Nos. 57 and 58; and Komarnicki, *op. cit.*, pp. 469–470. Cf. Wandycz, "Secret Soviet-Polish Peace Talks in 1919," *loc. cit.*, p. 433.

[67] An account of Polish talks with Soviet representatives in October and November, based upon Polish archives, may be found in Wandycz, "Secret Soviet-Polish Peace Talks in 1919," *loc. cit.*, pp. 425–449. See also *Dokumenty vneshnei politiki*, II, 235, 278–283; and notes Nos. 52 and 53 on p. 744. Cf. Deutscher, *op. cit.*, pp. 458–459; and the works of the chief Soviet negotiator, Iulian Markhlevskii, *Ocherki istorii Pol'shi* (Moscow: Gos. Sots.-Eko. Izdat, 1931) and *Voina i mir mezhdu burzhuaznoi Pol'shei i proletarskoi Rossiei* (Moscow: Gosizdat, 1921).

[68] The British representative, Rumbold, reported to Curzon on November 17 that Pilsudski equally disliked the Bolsheviks and Denikin, since he believed that the former would create a great Russia allied to Germany and the latter would create a great Russia which would revert to the old imperialism. See *Documents on British Policy*, III, 633–636. Soviet-Polish talks had begun secretly on October 11 after lengthy arrangements in progress from early August. Official negotiations were opened on October 27 and continued formally until December 15. Pilsudski's private talks with the Bolsheviks conducted through his representative, Capt. Ignacy Boerner, and the Soviet "Red Cross" representative, Iulian Markhlevskii (Marchlewski), continued from October 16 through November 23. In these talks Pilsudski specifically assured the Soviet government that he would not aid Denikin but would aid Petliura. He in turn received assurances that his territorial ambitions would be satisfied; the Bolsheviks, of course, expected to turn on Poland after defeating Denikin. See Wandycz, "Secret Soviet-Polish Peace Talks in 1919," *loc. cit.*, pp. 438–444.

[69] Karl Radek, *Vneshniaia politika sovetskoi Rossii* (Moscow: Gosizdat, 1923), p. 56. Cf. G. V. Chicherin, *Two Years of Foreign Policy* (New York: Russian

Soviet Government Bureau, 1920), p. 32; and Denikin Ocherki russkoi smuty, V, 180.

[70] This letter is quoted in Denikin, Ocherki russkoi smuty, V, 178–179.

[71] Documents on British Policy, II, 744–745; Paris Peace Conference, IX, 848.

[72] The text of this agreement is in Reshetar, op. cit., pp. 301–302.

[73] Political leaders associated with the Volunteer Army conferred with Mackinder and approved accepting the terms which he said Pilsudski would accept, viz., to take the Curzon line as the provisional border and hold plebiscites in territories to the east of that line. The condition to be put to Pilsudski was that the Poles begin military cooperation immediately in the form of an offensive against the Bolsheviks. Mackinder also stated at this time that he believed a similar plebiscite agreement could be reached with Rumania with regard to Bessarabia. Denikin accepted Mackinder's suggestions in general with the understanding that any border agreement would ultimately have to be determined by treaty between an all-Russian government and the other governments concerned. Mackinder left South Russia with assurances that he would arrange a meeting between Denikin and Pilsudski soon. See Denikin, Ocherki russkoi smuty, V, 305–306.

[74] Ibid., pp. 179–180.

[75] Churchill, op. cit., p. 255.

[76] Quoted by Denikin from a report to him by Colonel Keyes, the chief of staff of the British mission, in Ocherki russkoi smuty, V, 183. See also Rattigan to Curzon, October 8, 1919, Documents on British Policy, III, 585–586.

[77] Denikin, Ocherki russkoi smuty, V, 183. This Committee was not a Volunteer organization, but its self-styled liberation activities were designed to use the Volunteers to support them as much as possible. See the report on Bessarabia in WMA, File 180.

[78] Noting that the Galician and Bessarabian questions stood between Denikin and cooperation with Poland and Rumania, Curzon suggested leaving these issues to the Peace Conference as the best way to overcome the barrier they presented. Denikin, however, would also not consent to the idea of determination of such questions solely by the Peace Conference, especially without Russian participation, since any proposed settlement would still have to be approved by a reconstructed Russian authority later. See Curzon to Crowe, October 27, 1919, Documents on British Policy, III, 615–617.

[79] Denikin, Ocherki russkoi smuty, V, 183–184. Cf. Rattigan to Curzon, November 5, 1919, Documents on British Policy, III, 631.

[80] See Shcherbachev's report on the quantities and locations of the materials in Shcherbachev to Sazonov, July 10, 1919, Archives of the Director of the Foreign Supplies Board, materials on Russian military property in Rumania; and Hermonius to Beliaev, August 8, 1919, and letter to Marshal Foch, September 20, 1919, WMA, File 8. Cf. Paris Peace Conference, VII, 342–343.

[81] See Gerua to Director of the Foreign Supplies Board, June 1919, and Shcherbachev report, WMA, File 8.

[82] The arms given to Petliura apparently did not come from Russian stocks, but since the Rumanians armed their own troops with Russian equipment to compensate for the arms given away, the difference was small. See Denikin, Ocherki russkoi smuty, V, 183; and Rattigan to Curzon, October 8, 1919, Documents on

370   The Volunteer Army

British Policy, III, 585–586. See also reports on an investigation of this matter in WMA, File 8.

[83] French Foreign Ministry to Maklakov and Shcherbachev, August 4, 1919, and joint note of the representatives of France, Britain, Italy, and the United States to Russian Ambassador Poklevskii-Kozel, August 7, 1919, WMA, File 8.

[84] French Legation to Ministry of Foreign Affairs, August 24, 1920, ibid.

[85] See Paris Peace Conference, VII, 342–343.

[86] Sazonov and Maklakov were invited to attend the meetings of the conference of Ambassadors discussing the Bessarabian question, the only case where they participated directly in the work of the Peace Conference. They put the Russian case before these meetings, but they obtained nothing since even the plebiscite idea failed to be accepted. See S. D. Sazonov, Fateful Years, 1909–1916 (London: J. Cape, 1928), pp. 269–270. For materials on the Allies' handling of the Bessarabian question, including the Supreme Council's statement, see A. J. Toynbee, ed., Survey of International Affairs, 1920–1923 (London: Oxford University Press, 1927), pp. 276–277, 501–503; and Documents on British Policy, VII, 379–380; VIII, 189–190.

[87] Paris Peace Conference, VII, 784–785. See also Documents on British Policy, XII, 760, 773, 788.

[88] Denikin, Ocherki russkoi smuty, V, 182.

[89] Paris Peace Conference, VII, 784–785.

[90] These events are recorded in Val', K istorii belago dvizheniia, pp. 61, 66, 71 ff.

[91] Ibid., p. 73.

[92] Ibid., pp. 73–76.

[93] See telegram from Lukomskii to Mackinder, January 14, 1920, Documents on British Policy, III, 792–793.

[94] See Paris Peace Conference, VII, 425, 426. See also the proposal to organize a "Western Volunteer Army" of 200,000 men from Russian prisoners-of-war in Germany and Austria contained in a letter from General Hermonius to Mr. E. Dresel of the United States Commission to Negotiate Peace, February 24, 1919, WMA, File 66.

CHAPTER 7: RETREAT AND THE END OF ALLIED AID

[1] W. S. Churchill, The World Crisis: The Aftermath (London: Thornton Butterworth, 1929), pp. 256–259.

[2] See Denikin, Ocherki russkoi smuty, IV, 86; and Churchill, op. cit., p. 250. In November 1919 the War Office estimated in a report to Parliament that total aid to all parties during the previous year could be valued at 46,590,000 pounds in current prices. See Great Britain, 5 Parliamentary Debates, House of Commons, Vol. CXX (November 5, 1919), p. 1636. According to a later survey, British naval and military operations up to the spring of 1920 resulted in the extension of 2,457,000 pounds worth of marketable stores to Denikin alone. In addition, the maintenance of troops in Transcaucasia had cost 503,000 pounds, and over 3,000,000 pounds had been spent on naval operations in the Baltic and Black Seas combined. The total cost of all these operations connected with the intervention from November 1918 to March 1920 was estimated at 55,973,000

pounds. See Great Britain, *Parliamentary Papers*, 1920, Vol. XXVIII, Command Paper No. 772, "Statement of Expenditures on Naval and Military Operations in Russia from November 11, 1918, to March 31, 1920." These figures do not give a clear picture of aid to Denikin, however, since in part they include expenditures outside of South Russia, and in part they do not include all credits approved for Denikin. No exact statement of total aid in separate categories of uses and recipients is available.

[3] Early in November 1919 General Hermonius of the Russian Supplies Board in Paris stated in a note that France had contributed aid in the value of 50,000,-000 francs to Denikin, and the United States had provided around the same amount chiefly in medical supplies. However, this estimate probably did not represent the full contribution of either. See Hermonius (Germonius) to Votkin, November 7, 1919, Wrangel Military Archives (WMA), File 71.

[4] Maklakov to A. A., no date, WMA, File 71. The general rule insisted upon by the Ministry of Finance at this time was that no materials could be supplied to any foreign government except for immediate payment or in accordance with a prior financial arrangement approved by the Ministry. See circular dated August 4, 1919, *ibid.*

[5] Sinderskii to Shcherbachev, September 9, 1919, *ibid.*

[6] Memorandum to Maklakov, dated October 22, 1919, Maklakov Archives (MA), Series B, Packet II, Dossier 7. See also Maklakov to Denikin, no date, MA, Series B, Packet III, Dossier 10; and Maklakov to Denikin, September 29, 1919, WMA, File 71.

[7] Maklakov to A. A., no date, WMA, File 71.

[8] See Maklakov to Neratov, November 28, 1919, and Neratov to Maklakov, November 20/December 3, 1919, MA, Series B, Packet II, Dossier 7.

[9] The French in particular urged the use of trading companies as fronts for trade relations, while Lloyd George was persuaded of the value of dealing through the cooperatives with both the Bolsheviks and the anti-Bolsheviks in Russia. See letter to Maklakov from Raffalovich, November 25, 1919, *ibid.*

[10] See letter to Pindar from British Foreign Office, letter to Maklakov from A. Raffalovich, November 25, 1919, and Maklakov to Ministry of Foreign Affairs, Irkutsk, November 30, 1919, *ibid.* See also note of French Foreign Ministry, November 9, 1919, and Clemenceau's instructions to General Mangin on November 28, along with other correspondence on trade during September and October 1919, WMA, File 39 and File 71.

[11] As Maklakov noted, this meant that if exports now had to be exchanged for military supplies, this income would be cut off, with shattering effects for internal operations. Besides, South Russia had neither the apparatus necessary for large-scale trade nor enough exportable goods to compensate both Britain and France. See Maklakov to A. A., no date, WMA, File 71.

[12] Maklakov to Neratov, September 27, 1919, in *ibid.*

[13] See Memorandum to Maklakov from Department of Supply, AFSR, October 22/November 4, 1919; and "Aide-Memoire" on negotiations dated November 4, 1919, MA, Series B, Packet II, Dossier 7; and WMA, File 71.

[14] See letter to Major Pindar from Department of Supply, AFSR, October 5/18, 1919, *ibid.*

[15] See Memorandum to Maklakov from Department of Supply, AFSR, October

22/November 4, 1919; and note from Major Pindar to Maslov, Department of Supply, October 31/November 13, 1919, ibid.

[16] See Maklakov to Neratov, December 25, 1919; Raffalovich to Maklakov, November 25, 1919; and Maklakov to Ministry of Foreign Affairs, Irkutsk, November 30, 1919, MA, Series B, Packet II, Dossier 7; and Clemenceau's instructions to General Mangin regarding terms, November 28, 1919, WMA, File 71.

[17] The text of the "Projet de Contrat" and comment by Maklakov were transmitted by the latter to South Russia on December 25, 1919. See Maklakov to Neratov, December 25, 1919, MA, Series B, Packet II, Dossier 7. Included in the negotiations were Generals Shcherbachev, Hermonius, and Sviderskii; and Bazili and Maklakov from the Russian Embassy; and the French ministers of finance, foreign affairs, and war; and G. Eybert, secretary of the Inter-Ministerial Commission on Russian Financial Affairs.

[18] For an imposing list of Russian objections to the French terms already set forth earlier, see Hermonius to Senator Paul Doumer, November 4, 1919; and Aide Memoire dated December 4, 1919, WMA, File 71.

[19] See Prime Minister to Shcherbachev, October 24, 1919, and list of Russian materials in France, WMA, File 63; see also Prime Minister to General Sviderskii, WMA, File 71.

[20] See French Ministry of War to Shcherbachev, February 29, 1920, WMA, File 39.

[21] Informal negotiations with Soviet representative M. Litvinov were conducted in Stockholm during December. Soviet peace proposals and hints at trade prospects had been made on several occasions before this. See Foreign Relations, 1919, Russia, pp. 127–128, 131–132. For a general statement of Soviet policy by Chicherin see ibid., pp. 111–115.

[22] For an example of Kerenskii's vituperative public campaign against aid, see interviews in the Daily News, November 14, 1919, and the Sunday Chronicle, November 23, 1919. Cf. Nabokov to Maklakov, July 1, 1919, MA, Series B, Packet III, Dossier 10.

[23] See Foreign Relations, 1919, Russia, pp. 435–436, 442; and Great Britain, 5 Parliamentary Debates, House of Commons, Vol. CXX (1919), pp. 1635–1645.

[24] See Great Britain, 5 Parliamentary Debates, House of Commons, Vol. CXXI (1919), pp. 474, 721–724. The Guildhall speech of November 8 may be found in the London Times, November 10, 1919. See also Bechhofer-Roberts, In Denikin's Russia and the Caucasus (London: Collin's, 1921), p. 121.

[25] See Foreign Relations, 1919, Russia, p. 126, from Commission to Negotiate Peace to Lansing, November 29, 1919.

[26] Denikin, Ocherki russkoi smuty, V, 186.

[27] There was, however, some indication that Lloyd George's blunt remarks at this time shocked Clemenceau, at least in so far as they were regarded as premature. Clemenceau did not advocate any further aid to Denikin or to other Russian forces, but he feared that Lloyd George intended to wash his hands entirely of the effort to maintain a barrier against the Bolsheviks. What was at stake was the "cordon sanitaire" and particularly aid to Poland; it was not a question of differences over aiding the Volunteers. For Clemenceau's position, see Jean Mordacq, Le ministère Clemenceau (Paris: Plon, 1931), Vol. IV, pp. 144, 172–174.

²⁸ The United States had notably followed a consistent policy of refusing to recognize or deal with parts of Russia as independent states and continued to maintain this policy even after the Allied governments had changed toward recognition of the borderland governments. An unintended exception to this American policy occurred, however, when American personnel in France who were responsible for the disposal of surplus supplies entered an unauthorized agreement to sell over $11 million worth of such materials to the Ukraine (Petliura). When knowledge of this reached Lansing, rather late as it turned out, he immediately ordered the arrangement voided. About $8 million worth out of the total had already been delivered, but at least the question of policy was clarified. See *Foreign Relations, 1919 Russia*, pp. 780–790. Lansing also blocked the attempt by L. Martens to obtain recognition as the representative of Russia (on behalf of the Soviet government) and thus gain access to Russian funds in the United States. The Provisional government's representative, Bakhmetev, continued to be recognized as ambassador of Russia. See *Ibid.*, pp. 133–149.

²⁹ Late in 1918 Russian Ambassador Bakhmetev had been instrumental in making arrangements for establishing a $7 million credit in the United States for the purchase of supplies for Russia. Later special financial agents, S. A. Ughet and P. A. Morozov, in the United States entered numerous contracts with both government agencies and private companies on behalf of Kolchak, although the other anti-Bolshevik governments were also expected to benefit. Records show, for example, agreements for the purchase of 268,000 rifles and 17 million rounds of ammunition from the United States Army, 963 automatic machine guns and spare parts from the Marlin-Rockwell Corporation, and 100 million rounds of rifle ammunition from the Weston Cartridge Company. Other items contracted for included boots, locomotives, and rolling stock. For texts of such contracts and details as to the items involved, see records in WMA, Files 121 and 122. On the initial establishment of credit, see U. S. National Archives, Foreign Affairs Section, Doc. No. 861.24/121; and Denikin, *Ocherki russkoi smuty*, V, 185. On the shipments to Denikin, see WMA, File 121, pp. 107–108; and File 126, pp. 471–472, 499. The two shipments to Denikin in mid-1919 were recorded as follows:

ship	departed from New York	value of cargo
Irtysh	May 28, 1919	$ 853,815.42
Vladimir	July 31, 1919	5,301,078.05

The *Vladimir* reportedly brought a sizable cargo of raw materials from South Russia to New York, thus providing some funds for freight payments.

³⁰ On the conditions for an exchange which applied to Denikin, see the correspondence between Morozov and Ughet and the Shipping Board for August 20–21, 1919, WMA, File 121, pp. 109–113. Outgoing freight charges on the first shipment were to be prepaid, but those on all subsequent shipments and all incoming shipments could be postponed until sale of Russian raw materials in the United States had been made. Much of the material purchased by Ughet and Morozov had in fact been produced for Russia under World War I aid agreements but had then been held for Kolchak, who had priority over Denikin. Ultimately, however, Denikin got a good deal of that originally intended for

Kolchak. See WMA, File 128, p. 31; and a report on supplies sent to South
Russia from the United States in File 122, pp. 117–138.

[31] The four shipments after the August agreement were recorded as follows:

ship	date of departure from U. S.	value of cargo
Black Arrow	September 25, 1919	$2,127,914.66
Dochet	October 7, 1919	1,968,596.45
Sangaman	November 19, 1919	6,434,723.11
Cincinawa	November 27, 1919	236,810.72

The total value of the six shipments between May and December 1919 was over
$16 million, about 60 per cent of which Denikin received before the evacuation
of Novorossiisk. This was in addition to food and medical supplies distributed in
various parts of South Russia under the relief program. Freight charges were prepaid only for the Black Arrow. See WMA, File 121, pp. 66, 113. See also
Bernatskii Papers, where the value of the Sangaman's cargo is listed as 5,969,-
338.54 rubles.

[32] Later procurements for Wrangel will be noted below.

[33] See Morozov and Ughet correspondence with U. S. Shipping Board, March
31 and April 8, 1920, WMA, File 121, pp. 116–118.

[34] See agreements for scrapping in WMA, File 121, pp. 78–90. In November
Lansing put in a good word for sending clothing and the like to South Russia,
but the War Department replied that "insecure credits, uncontrolled profits, distribution, etc." made it inadvisable to do so. See Foreign Relations, 1919, Russia,
pp. 775–776. Denikin made a belated appeal to Kolchak's headquarters in December for gold, but in vain. See Denikin to Kolchak, November 28/December
11, 1919, MA, Series B, Packet II, Dossier 6. See also Foreign Relations, 1919,
Russia, pp. 214–215, 221, 233, 411, 445.

[35] For additional correspondence on Shcherbachev's efforts, see WMA, File 33.

[36] See Paris Peace Conference, VII, 85, 391–392, 524–525, 530–531. United
States Commissioner Frank Polk also pointed out that under Article 169 Germany could not be required to give up war materials until two months after the
signature of the treaty. Polk to Schilling, August 29, 1919, WMA, File 71.

[37] Paris Peace Conference, VII, 524–525.

[38] Maklakov letters to Neratov on January 12 and 21, 1920, Denikin Archives.
Columbia University Russian Archive.

[39] Documents on British Policy, III, 790–792.

[40] See Denikin, Ocherki russkoi smuty, IV, 201, 210; see also ibid., III, 262–
263.

[41] Ibid., IV, 215–216, footnote No. 2. This statement was sent to the Allied
governments on April 23, 1919.

[42] Rather than constituent assembly, Denikin preferred to use the term national
assembly. The only real difference involved here concerned whether the old assembly or a new one should be convoked. Denikin believed that a new one would be
necessary, while most of the socialists believed that the old one should be restored.
The Allied representatives also used the term national assembly, which they translated into Russian as "natsionalnoe sobranie," while Denikin's term was "narodnoe
sobranie" (which could equally well be translated into English as popular assembly). See ibid., p. 211.

[43] The land-policy statement is given in full in *ibid.*, p. 212, and a labor-policy statement issued at the same time is quoted on p. 214. For the interim orders see p. 223. The labor-policy statement called for preservation of private property but also for the protection of the interests of the working class by the establishment of an eight-hour day, workers' insurance, labor unions, health and safety inspection, programs to improve living conditions, measures to end unemployment, and institutions to arbitrate labor-management disputes. Legislation on these matters was introduced in July 1919 but was not adopted until November, and then only a partial bill was adopted owing to the difficulty of reconciling workers' interests with the views of the industrialists. See also S. A. Piontkovskii, ed., *Grazhdanskaia voina v Rossii* (Moscow: Izd. Kom. univ., 1925), pp. 507–509.

[44] See Denikin, *Ocherki russkoi smuty*, IV, 213–214, 222–224. Denikin notes that Kolchak supported his efforts to get a good agrarian reform law.

[45] See *ibid.*, V, 273–274; and P. N. Wrangel, *Always with Honor* (New York: Speller, 1957), pp. 87, 112. Cf. A. A. Smagin, "Vospominaniia" (MS, Columbia University Russian Archive), pp. 37–38; V. Dobrynin, *La lutte contre le bolchevisme* (Prague: "Melantrich," 1920), pp. 90–91; and G. N. Rakovskii, *V stane belykh* (Constantinople: "Pressa," 1920), pp. 1–13.

[46] Denikin, *Ocherki russkoi smuty*, IV, 218–219; see also V, 154. The British mission chief, General Holman, was notably among those urging Denikin to find more competent persons to staff the administration. Although Holman kept such advice strictly secret, Denikin expressed concern that it would become known and undercut his own authority. See Denikin's note to Holman, January 25, 1920, in the Denikin Archives, Correspondence with English Representatives.

[47] On the problem of governmental reorganization and relations with the Cossacks, especially the Kuban Cossacks, with whom a violent showdown occurred, see Denikin, *Ocherki russkoi smuty*, IV, 43, 49, 54; and V, 277–278; Wrangel, *op. cit.*, pp. 100–107; P. Shatilov, *Zapiski* (MS, Columbia University Russian Archive), pp. 794–831; "Spravka ob otnosheniiakh glavno-komandovaniia Dobrovol'cheskoi Armii k Kazakam," in the Gessen Archives (Hoover Library), Folder I, Redbox No. 1; V. Ivanis, *Stezhkami zhitta: spohadi*, Vol. III (Neu-Ulm: "Ukrainski Visti," 1959), p. 138 ff.; G. K. Pokrovskii, *Denikinshchina: god politiki i ekonomiki na Kubani* (Berlin: Izd. Grzhebina, 1923), pp. 240–247; and A. P. Filimonov, "Razgrom Kubanskoi rady," *Arkhiv Russkoi Revoliutsii*, Vol. V (Berlin: "Slovo," 1922), pp. 322–329, 358–360.

[48] Denikin, *Ocherki russkoi smuty*, V, 292–293, 307. See also Dobrynin, *op. cit.*, pp. 96–100.

[49] Denikin, *Ocherki russkoi smuty*, V, 103, 285–286, 310.

[50] The members of the government were N. M. Mel'nikov, chairman; Lt. General Kel'chevskii, minister of war and navy; General N. N. Baratov, minister of foreign affairs; V. F. Zeeler, minister of internal affairs; V. M. Krasnov, minister of justice; P. M. Ageev, minister of agriculture; M. V. Bernatskii, minister of finance; L. V. Zverev, minister of communications; F. S. Leontovich, minister of trade and industry; F. S. Sushkov, minister of education; N. S. Dolgopolov, minister of health; N. V. Chaikovskii (former head of the North Russian government at Arkhangelsk), minister of propaganda. General Kel'chevskii declined to join the government so as to continue as chief of staff of the Don army. For addi-

tional information on the formation of the new government and the problems connected with this reform see "Organizatsiia vlasti na iuge Rossii," *Arkhiv Russkoi Revoliutsii* Vol. IV (Berlin: Izdatel'stvo "Slovo," 1922), pp. 241–251; K. N. Sokolov, *Pravlenie Generala Denikina* (Sofia: Rossiisko-Bolgarskoe knigoizdatel'stvo, 1921), *passim*; and V. M. Krasnov, "Iz vospominanii o 1917–1920 gg.," *Arkhiv Russkoi Revoliutsii*, Vol. XI (Berlin: Izdatel'stvo "Slovo," 1923), p. 154 ff. For a British observer's interpretation of the reorganization as a Cossack victory, see Bechhofer-Roberts, *op. cit.*, p. 189. For the liberal proposal on the formation of a new government, made by Kadet members of the Volunteer Special Council, and used by Denikin as the model for his subsequent orders, see Denikin, *Ocherki russkoi smuty*, V, 282–284.

[51] Estimates put the number of dead from typhus and exposure during the period of the retreat as high as 200,000. See G. Stewart, *The White Armies of Russia* (New York: Macmillan, 1933), pp. 341–342. Bechhofer-Roberts observed: "No one who has seen the panic in a South Russian town before the Bolsheviks' coming is likely ever to forget the sensation. It teaches one more about what has happened in Russia during the last three years than a thousand books." Bechhofer-Roberts, *op. cit.*, p. 102.

[52] For the background and character of the Green movement, see N. Voronovich, ed., *Zelenaia kniga; sbornik materialov i dokumentov; istoriia krest'ianskago dvizheniia v Chernomorskoi gubernii* (Prague: Izdanie Chernomorskoi Krest'ianskoi Delegatsii, 1921). See also Denikin, *Ocherki russkoi smuty*, V, 248 ff. The text of the Green program is in Voronovich, *op. cit.*, pp. 46–48. See also the address to the Allied missions in Tiflis in December, *ibid.*, pp. 48–53; the appeal to Georgia for aid against "Great Russian imperialism," *ibid.*, pp. 54–55; and the address to the Bolsheviks and the Council of People's Commissars, *ibid.*, pp. 55–56. Cf. Piontkovskii, *op. cit.*, pp. 547–549.

[53] Denikin, *Ocherki russkoi smuty*, V, 251.

[54] Dobrynin, *op. cit.*, pp. 103–104.

[55] Voronovich, *op. cit.*, Doc. No. 33, pp. 71–73.

[56] *Ibid.*, Doc. No. 38, pp. 76–78. An acount of Keyes' efforts may also be found in Bechhofer-Roberts, *op. cit.*, p. 180 ff.

[57] Voronovich, *op. cit.*, Doc. No. 39, pp. 78–79.

[58] *Ibid.*, Doc. Nos. 47, 48, 55, 56, pp. 95–96, 110–113, 116–117.

[59] See Denikin, *Ocherki russkoi smuty*, V, 252. Denikin later accused Keyes (now British diplomatic representative) of sounding out leading persons about arrangements for the overthrow of Denikin himself and the establishment of a new authority at the same time that the military representative, Holman, was doing everything possible to support and protect Denikin and his authority. See *ibid.*, p. 340. Holman's remarkable loyalty to Denikin and his personal heroism during these last days is recounted in Bechhofer-Roberts, *op. cit.*, pp. 130, 186–187, 207–208.

[60] See Voronovich, *op. cit.*, pp. 123–125, 149 ff.

[61] This effort was notable, however, as another of the many efforts to head off hostilities between the Volunteers and opposing Kuban leaders, who were now backing the Greens. Denikin was particularly bitter about reports that some Kuban leaders were now advocating an agreement with the Soviet government to obtain recognition in return for neutrality. See Denikin, *Ocherki russkoi smuty*,

V, 313–314. According to a Soviet source, one Kuban leader, Timoshenko, went to Tiflis in April to negotiate with the Georgians and there declared that the Kuban would adopt neutrality in the war if the Soviet government would extend recognition and accept Kuban incorporation of the Black Sea province. See Shafir, *Secrets of Menshevik Georgia*, p. 67. On the Greens' relations with the Kuban see Voronovich, *op. cit.*, pp. 86–87, 116–117, 127–128.

[62] Voronovich, *op. cit.*, pp. 123–125.

[63] Denikin, *Ocherki russkoi smuty*, V, 246.

[64] See the materials on the meetings of the prime ministers and ministers of foreign Affairs in London and Paris, December 11 to January 21, especially the meetings of December 11 and 12, in *Documents on British Policy*, II, 736 ff.

[65] See text in *ibid.*, p. 782.

[66] See record of Council of Foreign Ministers, January 10, 1920, Inter-Allied Conference Documents (Hoover Library). Lloyd George had already on November 24 told the American representative, Polk, that he opposed Russian reunification and wanted to see the Transcaucasian states and others established as independent states. See *Foreign Relations, 1919, Russia*, p. 126. The British Cabinet had begun discussions on the possible recognition of the Transcaucasian states late in December. In these discussions it was suggested that such recognition should be conditioned upon their agreement to cooperate with the Volunteer Army for the duration of the war and to join in steps to form a Russian federation in the future. See *Documents on British Policy*, III, 700–702, 735. See also Wardrop to Gegechkori, January 12, 1920, in *Documents présentés par le gouvernement de la république de Géorgie à la première Assemblée de la Société des nations*, p. 37. Cf. Z. D. Avalov, *The Independence of Georgia* (London: Headley, 1940), p. 252.

[67] Council of Premiers, January 16, 1920, Inter-Allied Conference Documents; *Documents on British Policy*, II, 912. The British representative on the Allied Military Council had recommended on January 12 that a military force, including two Allied divisions, be placed along the Caucasus range as a barrier against Bolshevik attack and that meanwhile aid be continued to Denikin. In discussion of the latter point, however, it was noted that Denikin was virtually defeated already, and so the recommendation was changed to exclude further aid to Denikin and concentrate it all upon Transcaucasia, especially Georgia. To this the French representative added on February 19 a proposal that the suggested force be composed mainly of native troops under a joint Allied command and that it be posted at key points along the Vladikavkaz-Petrovsk railway, especially in Dagestan. Lloyd George may have considered such proposals but apparently rejected them. See American Embassy, Paris, E.S.H. Bulletins, Nos. 118 and 173, Hoover Library.

[68] See Council of Premiers, January 16, 1920, Inter-Allied Conference Documents; and *Documents on British Policy*, II, 912. On February 12 Britain also culminated several months of negotiations with Soviet representatives by signing a prisoner-exchange agreement. See *Dokumenty vneshnei politiki*, II, 364–367. On February 21 Curzon also conceded the loss of Arkhangelsk in a note to Chicherin, in *ibid.*, p. 385.

[69] Council of Premiers, January 19, 1920, Inter-Allied Conference Documents.

[70] *Ibid.* Cf. Avalov, *op. cit.*, p. 220 ff. It would appear that Churchill was

partially successful here, at least to the extent of having set aside the recommendation of the British representative on the Military Council on January 12 regarding
the suspension of all aid to Denikin.

[71] Council of Premiers, January 19, 1920, Inter-Allied Conference Documents.

[72] *Ibid.*, meeting of January 20 and Appendix A. See also *Documents on British Policy*, II, 797. The United States, in keeping with its policy of not recognizing any new governments in Russia at this time, declined to associate itself
with these decisions. Those who saw an oil magnates' conspiracy in Allied and
American policy called this divergence a result of Standard Oil's fear that recognition would enable the British to monopolize Transcaucasian oil. See L. Fischer,
Oil Imperialism, p. 33. Japan, on the other hand, did join in the recognition of
Georgia and Azerbaidzhan, reported on February 6, and then of Armenia, reported
on March 6. See Conference of Ambassadors, meetings of February 6 and March
6, Inter-Allied Conference Documents. See further *Documents on British Policy*,
XII, 557 ff.

[73] Before leaving London, Mackinder talked with Russian representatives there
and apparently convinced them that the British government had never had a
policy of opposing Russian interests in Transcaucasia. As one Russian representative
reported to Sazonov after seeing Mackinder, the poor relations between the Volunteers and the British in Transcaucasia in the past had been "largely the fault of
the policy of local military agents whose activities Mackinder was not constrained
to characterize as chaotic." See Sablin to Sazonov, November 22, 1919, MA,
Series B, Packet III, Dossier 1.

[74] See Mackinder's report in *Documents on British Policy*, III, 768–786.

[75] Denikin to Mackinder, January 14, 1920, *ibid.*, pp. 792–793.

[76] Denikin, *Ocherki russkoi smuty*, V, 245 ff.

[77] See the transcript of the telephone conversation, March 7, 1920, between
Den and Erdeli, who was relaying Baratov's instructions, in the Dratsenko Documents.

[78] There was apparently some exchange of grain for both coal and oil begun at
this time. See Shafir, *op. cit.*, pp. 53–57.

[79] Den did, however, complain of the presence of a delegation from the Cossack
Supreme Krug which was attempting to negotiate independently with Georgia
despite assurances given to him from headquarters that they had no authority to
do so. See conversations with Erdeli, February 27, 1920, Dratsenko Documents.

[80] Den to Baratov, March 12, 1920, Dratsenko Documents.

[81] See F. Kazemzadeh, *The Struggle for Transcaucasia* (New York: Philosophical Library, 1951), pp. 278–279; A. Raevskii, *Angliiskaia interventsiia i Musavatskoe pravitel'stvo* (Baku: "Krasnyi Vostok," 1927), p. 179; and D. E. Enukidze,
Krakh imperialisticheskoi interventsii v Zakavkaz'i (Tiflis: Gosizdat. G.S.S.R.,
1954), p. 194.

[82] *Documents on British Policy*, VII, 81 ff.; XII, 557, 561–562, 567–568, 572–
574, 580–583, 590–591, 595, 599, 610, 618, 643.

[83] *Documents on British Policy*, VII, 141–143, 216; XII, 558, 570–571, 642;
Raevskii, *op. cit.*, pp. 165–166, 181 ff.

[84] Actually, orders to evacuate Batum had been issued by General Milne early
in February pursuant to a Cabinet decision (made in Curzon's absence) to use
the Batum garrison to reinforce British troops in Constantinople. However, upon

his return to London, Curzon (supported by both Wardrop and Admiral de Robeck) had urged a reversal of this decision, since withdrawal at this time would have disastrous effects, and the Cabinet had decided to postpone the evacuation pending further discussion with the Allies. The addition of French and Italian troops was thus considered necessary to continue the occupation. See *Documents on British Policy*, VII, 254–255, 639 ff.; VIII, 98–101; XII, 558–572, 600, 603–608, 611, 615, 619–627, 631–632. See also Avalov, *op. cit.*, p. 233 ff.

85 See *Documents on British Policy*, II, 875, 898–899; and Avalov, *op. cit.*, p. 227. In April Curzon made it clear that aid did not mean military intervention; in a note to Wardrop on April 27 he warned against allowing a misunderstanding on this point and stated flatly that there was "no question of our giving Georgia and Azerbaijan active military support in case of an attack on them by Soviet forces." *Documents on British Policy*, XII, 599.

86 Raevskii, *op. cit.*, p. 185.

87 Kazemzadeh, *op. cit.*, pp. 280–281; Raevskii, *op. cit.*, p. 185; A. Popov, "Iz epokhi angliiskoi interventsii v Zakavkaz'i," *loc. cit.*, pp. 211–212. See also *Documents on British Policy*, XII, 569–571.

88 See Shafir, *op. cit.*, p. 44 ff.

89 See Den to Erdeli, March 15, 1920; telephone conversation with Erdeli, March 18, 1920; and Den to Baratov, no date, Dratsenko Documents.

90 Den to Baratov, March 22, 1920, Dratsenko Documents.

91 The Caspian flotilla was supposed to be allowed to continue to defend the coast under its own officers, but Azerbaidzhan soon repudiated this part of the agreement and tried to seize the ships. The flotilla's officers, however, chose to sail to Enzeli. There, contrary to previous assumptions, they were not greeted as allies but interned, in this case with British apologies, to protect Persia's neutrality. Subsequently Bolshevik troops landed at Enzeli, and both the British and the Russian crews fled to the south. See Den to the Allied Missions, March 18, 1920, Dratsenko Documents; and Denikin, *Ocherki russkoi smuty*, V, 351–352. For an account of the Enzeli incident, see also G. Lenczowski, *Russia and the West in Iran, 1918–1948; a Study in Big-Power Rivalry* (Ithaca: Cornell University Press, 1949), p. 52 ff. See also *Documents on British Policy*, XII, 581, 584, 586.

92 Den to Baratov, April 2, 1920, and Den to Allied Missions, April 7, 1920, Dratsenko Documents.

93 See Den's report of April 21, 1920, Dratsenko Documents. The evidence is not clear, but the Georgian government itself may not have been a party to this ruse. One account, while eager to indict Georgia, for example, admits that the Georgian minister of war permitted the evacuation of the prisoners only after obtaining written statements on each trip from the captain of the ship involved that the destination was Constantinople. See Shafir, *op. cit.*, pp. 96–98. Trotskii notes this same requirement of statements from the captains, but suggests that the Georgian government was thus merely covering up deliberate aid which not only enabled possibly some 30,000 men to go to the Crimea but also supplied them with fuel through "private" transactions. See L. Trotsky, *Between Red and White: a Study of Some Fundamental Questions of Revolution, with Particular Reference to Georgia* (London: Communist Party of Great Britain, 1922), pp. 55–57. For a subsequent Soviet protest charging the British with aiding in the

shipment of men and supplies from Batum to the Crimea, see Litvinov to Curzon, July 19, 1920, *Documents on British Policy*, XII, 751–752. Curzon denied the charges. *Ibid.*, p. 759.

[94] Raevskii, *op. cit.*, p. 190; Enukidze, *op. cit.*, pp. 199–200.

[95] See *Documents on British Policy*, XII, 600, 657, 670; Avalov, *op. cit.*, pp. 247–263. Cf. A. J. Toynbee, ed., *Survey of International Affairs, 1920–1923* (London: Oxford University Press, 1927), p. 365.

[96] The Polish attack which coincided with the Red Army's march into the Transcaucasian republics was probably the chief reason for not pressing the conquest into Georgia and Armenia immediately and instead making peace with Georgia.

[97] Avalov, *op. cit.*, pp. 261–262; Enukidze, *op. cit.*, pp. 202–205. For the text of the treaty, see *Traité conclu le 7 mai, 1920, entre la République democratique de Géorgie et la République Socialiste Federative Sovietiste Russe* (Paris: Imprimerie P. Dupont, 1922). Cf. Chicherin's remarks on Soviet relations with Georgia, *Dokumenty vneshnei politiki*, II, 657, 693–694.

[98] On the withdrawal and subsequent Allied policy toward Transcaucasia, see *Documents on British Policy*, VIII, 98–101, 138; XII, 603 ff. See also Avalov, *op. cit.*, pp. 271–275, 284. Cf. A. D. Margolin, *Ukraina i politika antanty* (Berlin: Efron, 1921), p. 256.

[99] Denikin, *Ocherki russkoi smuty*, V, 347–348.

[100] See Curzon to Mackinder, *Documents on British Policy*, III, 672–678.

[101] See the account by the then quartermaster general, General P. S. Makhrov, "V beloi armii generala Denikina" (MS, Columbia University Russian Archive), p. 659 ff.

[102] Quartermaster General Makhrov was named the new chief of staff. In his farewell to Romanovskii, Denikin declared: "History will brand with contempt those who for selfish motives have woven a web of base slander around his honorable and spotless name." Denikin, *Ocherki russkoi smuty*, V, 354. Makhrov points out that neither Denikin nor Romanovskii would take the steps necessary for their personal protection, despite constant rumors of assassination plots. It was Makhrov who, on the urging of the British representative, General Holman, had stationed a guard around the train serving as headquarters. See Makhrov, "V beloi armii generala Denikina," p. 633. The particularly great hostility toward General Romanovskii is sympathetically but vividly described in the memoirs of Protopresviter Georgii Shavel'skii, "Vospominaniia" (MS, Columbia University Russian Archive), pp. 422–434. He notes that one officers' group had threatened assassination if Romanovskii were not removed, himself describing both Denikin and Romanovskii as "democrats in the true sense of the word."

[103] Makhrov, "V beloi armii generala Denikina," pp. 677–678. See also "Organizatsiia vlasti na iuge Rossii," *loc. cit.*, pp. 249–251.

[104] The date chosen for the conference made it appear rather sudden, although Denikin had considered resigning for some time. The reason for selecting it, however, was apparently in part the information that the field commander in the Crimea, General Slashchev, who was now campaigning for his own advancement, planned to call a public conference on April 5 with the intention of demonstrating opposition to Denikin and calling upon him to resign. Denikin did not need

a public demonstration to know that strong opposition existed, and he also wished to resign in his own way. See Denikin, *Ocherki russkoi smuty*, V, 355–356; and Makhrov, "V beloi armii generala Denikina," pp. 685–686.

[105] The following account of the conference is based largely upon Makhrov, "V beloi armii generala Denikina," p. 688 ff.; and Denikin, *Ocherki russkoi smuty*, V, 358 ff. In the latter, pp. 362–363, Denikin also provides an account of a part of the conference by General Bogaevskii.

[106] The Volunteer corps commander, General Kutepov, was present, but he had not supported the strong position taken by the other Volunteer Corps officers either in their own caucus on this question or in the plenary session. General Slashchev also left the conference and returned only after the selection of Wrangel had been made. Then he ordered a parade as a greeting to the new chief to demonstrate his "complete agreement with what had occurred." He also denounced those who had spoken out for Denikin at the conference and suggested that they be removed from important posts. See Ia. A. Slashchev-Krymskii, *Trebuiu suda obshchestva i glasnosti: oborona i sdacha Kryma; memuary i dokumenty* (Constantinople: Knigoizdatel'stvo M. Shul'mana, 1921), pp. 10–12.

[107] General Bogaevskii, who had been one of Denikin's closest supporters, took the initiative in raising Wrangel's name at this meeting, since Wrangel seemed to be the only one who both wanted the command and could assure respect for it. In a letter several years later, however, Bogaevskii took the "blame" for recommending Wrangel and added: "Unfortunately I knew Wrangel too little." See letter from Bogaevskii to Shapron, November 8, 1924, Denikin Archives.

[108] See Denikin, *Ocherki russkoi smuty*, V, 110, 263, 289–292; Wrangel, *op. cit.*, pp. 118, 121–123; Shatilov, *op. cit.*, p. 826 ff.; and Rakovskii, *V stane belykh*, pp. 38–44.

[109] See especially the account by the new chief of staff, General Makhrov, "V beloi armii generala Denikina," p. 481 ff. Denikin points out that there had never been close relations between headquarters and the naval command. Admirals Neniukov and Bubnov, who had just been given their posts in the fall of 1919, were second choices made necessary by Kolchak's objection to Admiral Sablin, who had been designated by the Navy Department chief, Admiral Gerasimov, to command the fleet but was then removed. See Denikin, *Ocherki russkoi smuty*, V, 331–335. On the dispute with Wrangel which assumed major proportions after Wrangel had gone to the Crimea, see Shatilov, *op. cit.*, pp. 868–875. On the "Orlov affair," a revolt by a junior officer against Volunteer authorities in the Crimea which seriously complicated relations with Wrangel, see Ia. Shafir, "Orlovshchina," in *Antanta i Vrangel: sbornik statei* (Moscow: Gosizdat, 1923), pp. 125–137. Slashchev, who commanded the major forces in the Crimea, also gives an account of his own as well as others' conspiratorial activities at this time in Slashchev-Krymskii, *op. cit.*, p. 5 ff.

[110] The text of Wrangel's letter may be found in the Wrangel Personal Archives, Kotliarevskii Section, PW Files, Packet I, No. 2. It and Denikin's reply may also be found in the Miliukov Personal Archives, and in Makhrov, "V beloi armii generala Denikina," pp. 523–543. See also Denikin, *Ocherki russkoi smuty*, V, 338–339. For a translation into English of some excerpts of the Wrangel letter see G. Stewart, *op. cit.*, p. 345. According to Shatilov at his insistence the

language of the letter was somewhat toned down from Wrangel's original.

[111] Denikin, *Ocherki russkoi smuty*, V, 339.

[112] In addition to the more obvious reasons for British concern over the break between Denikin and Wrangel, there was also the reputations of their respective followings as pro-Allied and pro-German to be considered. According to one British observer the fear that this split threatened a revival of Germanophile tendencies was one reason why Mackinder made a point of questioning Wrangel on his differences with Denikin at some length. This observer also notes the hostile attitude of Lukomskii toward the British at this time. See Bechhofer-Roberts, *op. cit.*, pp. 110, 120, 165. As will be noted, Wrangel did not subsequently indicate any Germanophile inclinations, and, indeed, turned chiefly to France for support.

[113] Wrangel, *op. cit.*, p. 129.

[114] Shatilov, *op. cit.*, pp. 879–881.

[115] Denikin, *Ocherki russkoi smuty*, V, 338. General Holman's letter may also be found in the Wrangel Personal Archives, Baroness Olga Wrangel Section, File I, Section 2(f).

[116] Wrangel, *op. cit.*, pp. 130–131.

[117] See WA-DC, Case I, File 5. For an English translation, see Wrangel, *op. cit.*, pp. 131–132; and Stewart, *op. cit.*, pp. 356–357. See also Curzon's instructions to de Robeck on the note to be sent, March 31, 1920, in *Documents on British Policy*, XII, 691–692.

[118] Denikin, *Ocherki russkoi smuty*, V, 363, citing Bogaevskii's account. Denikin himself did not see these documents—the British note and Wrangel's statement—until his departure from Russia, but he had been informed earlier by General Bridges that the British government felt the situation hopeless and would propose its mediation to obtain a truce with the Bolsheviks. At that time Denikin categorically rejected the idea. See *ibid.*, p. 347. See also Wrangel Personal Archives, Baroness Olga Wrangel Section, File I, Section 2(a).

[119] Denikin, *Ocherki russkoi smuty*, V, 357–358.

[120] For reports on the subsequent investigation of this incident, see the record of the inquest in WMA, File 109.

CHAPTER VIII: THE CRIMEAN EPILOGUE

[1] P. N. Wrangel, *Always with Honor* (New York: Speller, 1957), p. 155. General Wrangel's memoirs, which provide the best general account of this last period of Volunteer history, may be found in Russian ("Zapiski") in A. A. von Lampe, ed., *Belo delo; letopis' beloi bor'by*, Vol. V, pp. 9–306; and Vol. VI, pp. 5–261. The original contains some material not included in the English translation that the reader may wish to consult. However, in the following notes the Wrangel Archives are used as the primary source for documentation from Wrangel's materials, with references to the English translation of the memoirs being used for nondocumentary material or to indicate a translation of the documentary evidence cited from the Archives or another source.

[2] Telegram to Admiral de Robeck at Constantinople, April 4, 1920, Wrangel Archives, Diplomatic Correspondence Section (hereafter WA-DC), Case I,

File 5; Wrangel, op. cit., pp. 147–148. See also Documents on British Policy, XII, 696–697, 701–702.

[3] Wrangel, op. cit., pp. 143, 150–153.

[4] Admiral Seymour to Wrangel, April 19, 1920, WA-DC, Case I, File 5. Curzon's note to Chicherin proposing an end to the struggle also took credit for the resignation of Denikin. Denikin himself vehemently denied this, however, and replied subsequently in the London Times that Curzon had no direct relations with him and exerted no influence on his decisions. See Denikin, Ocherki russkoi smuty, V, 347–348. The relevant part of Curzon's note to Chicherin on April 11, 1920, reads as follows: ". . . I have exerted my utmost influence with General Denikin to induce him to abandon the contest, and have promised him that if he did so, I would use my best efforts to make peace between his forces and yours, and to secure the safety of the rank and file of his followers, and the population of the Crimea in general. General Denikin finally decided to act upon this advice, and has left Russia, resigning his command to General Wrangel, who has stated his willingness to accept the mediation which I offered. I therefore communicate with you at once to request you, in the interests both of Russia and of humanity, to issue orders for the termination of hostilities, and to grant a general amnesty upon the disbandment of the Volunteer Army." Documents on British Policy, XII, 698–699. The Soviet reply of April 14 evaded the issue here by raising numerous other questions, such as the fate of members of Bela Kun's government being held in Austria. It offered only to begin negotiations on all such questions directly with the British government through Litvinov. Dokumenty vneshnei politiki, II, 453–454. In a note to Litvinov (in Copenhagen) on April 18, Chicherin revealed that this reply to Curzon had been delayed in transmission because of radio difficulties, and as a result the Soviet government had just received another note from Curzon expressing disappointment over the lack of an answer and warning that military operations on the Black Sea and in the Crimea would continue. Ibid., p. 459.

[5] Mangin to Struve, April 23, 1920, WA-DC, Case I, File 5. Cf. Wrangel, op. cit., p. 178.

[6] Shcherbatskoi to Sazonov, April 13, 1920, WA-DC, Case I, File 5. This opinion was based upon the belief that the weakness of Wrangel's position at this time would make it difficult to obtain any concessions from Moscow.

[7] See the letter to Curzon quoted in H. Nicolson, Curzon: The Last Phase (New York: Harcourt, Brace, 1939), footnote 1, pp. 143–144. The British Labour delegation which visited Russia during the spring of 1920, however, strongly condemned any continuation of aid or intervention and emphatically called for peace. See British Labour Delegation to Russia, 1920: Report (London: Labour Party, 1920).

[8] Documents on British Policy, XII, 710–711; General Percy to Wrangel, April 29, 1920, forwarding Curzon's note, WA-DC, Case I, File 5. In a note to Chicherin on April 24, 1920, Curzon indicated that he had received the Soviet reply to his appeal for an end to hostilities and found it unsatisfactory. He could not, he pointed out, see the connection between the Crimean question and the other questions raised by the Soviet note, or could he agree to accept Litvinov as representative of the Russian government in London for negotiation of these ques-

tions. He had hoped to see peace and economic relations restored, Curzon added, but saw no possibility as long as the Soviet government continued hostilities. *Documents on British Policy*, XII, 711; *Dokumenty vneshnei politiki*, II, 491–492. See also the exchange between Chicherin and Curzon, April 29, May 3 and 4, 1920, *Documents on British Policy*, XII, 713–715.

[9] Wrangel, *op. cit.*, p. 144. Makhrov quotes Wrangel as saying specifically that he would continue the war at the same time that the note to Britain was being drafted. See P. S. Makhrov, "General Vrangel i B. Savinkov" (MS, Columbia University Russian Archive), p. 8.

[10] Struve to Maklakov, April 13, 1920, WA-DC, Case I, File 5.

[11] Wrangel, *op. cit.*, pp. 153, 155.

[12] See *ibid.*, pp. 155, 159, 162–163, 167–168, 174–177, 182, 186–187. Admiral de Robeck provided some British ships to assist in the evacuation of Kuban troops to the Crimea after the Kuban government had fled to Georgia.

[13] Wrangel to General Percy, May 2, 1920, WA-DC, Case I, File 5: *Documents on British Policy*, XII, 716–717. Cf. Wrangel, *op. cit.*, pp. 180–181.

[14] Wrangel, *op. cit.*, p. 152.

[15] *Ibid.*, p. 185.

[16] *Ibid.*, p. 150.

[17] *Ibid.*, pp. 162–163.

[18] Wrangel himself gives a good example of his dealing with liberals, who as it happened had a predominant position in the city governments of the Crimea. On the orders of the regent (Wrangel) stringent civil controls were imposed upon these cities under military commanders. The exercise of these controls through a court martial "ruthless in its sentences" in Simferopol led to vigorous protests on the part of the local government and its mayor. When the mayor took his appeal directly to Wrangel, the latter sternly reminded him that the regent alone would decide what was best and would "stop at nothing" to see that his orders were carried out. This included hanging "anyone who tries to stop me," Wrangel declared, adding: "I would not hesitate to increase the number by one, and that one would be yourself." A few days later the mayor resigned because of "illness." *Ibid.*, pp. 168–169.

[19] *Ibid.*, p. 172.

[20] *Ibid.*, p. 162.

[21] Struve initially took up the duties of a foreign minister but subsequently became Wrangel's chief representative abroad, while Trubetskoi acted as foreign minister at home. For a self-appraisal of Struve's background as a "legal Marxist" and the evolution of his views see P. B. Struve, "My Contacts and Conflicts with Lenin," *Slavonic and East European Review*, Vol. XII (April 1934), pp. 573–595; and Vol. XIII (July 1934), pp. 66–84.

[22] Wrangel, *op. cit.*, p. 163. A convention defining the authority of the regent and the autonomy of the Cossack governments was signed on August 4. It gave authority over the armed forces, foreign relations, railways and telegraph lines, and common financial questions to Wrangel. *Ibid.*, pp. 243–244.

[23] *Ibid.*, p. 183. This position applied even more so to the Greens, whom Wrangel regarded as "the riff-raff of the population, deserters, common-law criminals, and Bolsheviks." It also applied to workers who disobeyed orders by strik-

ing. Wrangel promised better wages but also drafted strikers into the army and shipped them to the front. Such a policy, however, did not apply to potential allies or useful elements outside the Crimea, such as Makhno's forces for example.
[24] Wrangel's account of this incident is in *ibid.*, pp. 166–168. See also Rakovskii, V *stane belykh*, p. 45.
[25] Wrangel, *op. cit.*, pp. 175–176.
[26] *Ibid.*, p. 192.
[27] *Ibid.*, p. 194 ff. Cf. M. S. Margulies, *God interventsii* (Berlin: Grschebin, 1923), Vol. III, p. 233.
[28] Wrangel, *op. cit.*, p. 200.
[29] *Ibid.*, p. 286. Property ownership was the basis of electoral rights.
[30] *Ibid.*, p. 197.
[31] *Ibid.*, pp. 224–225; Struve to Millerand, June 20, 1920, WA-DC, Case I, File 5.
[32] Struve to Maklakov, April 13, 1920, WA-DC, Case I, File 5.
[33] Report of conferences on aid, WMA, File 122, pp. 209–210.
[34] See letter from Struve, June 17, 1920, Bernatskii Papers.
[35] See M. S. Margulies, *op. cit.*, III, 197, 207, 210.
[36] Bazili to Paléologue, April 24, 1920, MA, Series B, Packet V, Dossier 2; letter to Hermonius, July 19, 1920, Neratov to Struve, June 12, 1920, and Hermonius to French Ministry of War, June 24, 1920, WMA, Files 29 and 34.
[37] See *Documents on British Policy*, VII, 141–143, 149–151, 195–209, 216; VIII, 756.
[38] For the text of this treaty and comment, see J. S. Reshetar, *The Ukrainian Revolution* (Princeton: Princeton University Press, 1952), p. 300 ff.
[39] Maklakov to Struve, May 1, 1920, WA-DC, Case I, File 5. Cf. Wrangel, *op. cit.*, p. 179. The French government also subsequently (May 30) refused to participate in the negotiations with the Soviet economic delegation invited to London. See *Documents on British Policy*, XII, 723, 726–727, 730.
[40] Krivoshein to Paléologue, May 7, 1920, WA-DC, Case I, File 5.
[41] Paléologue to Krivoshein, May 8, 1920, *ibid.*
[42] Maklakov to Russian representative, Constantinople, May 26, 1920, *ibid.* See also Admiral de Robeck's report of suspected secret arrangements between the French and Wrangel, *Documents on British Policy*, XII, 722.
[43] Krivoshein to Paléologue, May 7, 1920, WA-DC, Case I, File 5. The possibility of collaboration with the Poles had in fact been broached as early as April 24 in Bazili's note to Paléologue. See MA, Series B, Packet V, Dossier 2.
[44] Trubetskoi outlines Mangin's inquiries in a letter to Struve, May 28, 1920, WA-DC, Case I, File 5, Hoover Library. In Paris Marshal Foch was simultaneously urging General Shcherbachev to convey to Wrangel a call for energetic military action as soon as possible. Shcherbachev, who believed that such action would help no one but Poland, advised against it and, when Wrangel proceeded anyhow, resigned from his post. See Val', *K istorii belago dvizheniia*, pp. 150–156.
[45] Trubetskoi to General Mangin, May 17, 1920, WA-DC, Case I, File 5.
[46] In his letter to Struve on May 28, in *ibid.*, Trubetskoi indicated that Wrangel would offer to stay to the east of the Dnepr so as to avoid a clash with either

the Poles or Ukrainians, since the restoration of the latter to power would apparently be confined largely to the western bank. He also was willing to negotiate with the Ukrainians in terms of autonomy in a union with Russia but not to accept the terms of the Polish-Ukrainian treaty. It was, therefore, better to avoid raising the question directly, at least until the French could sound out the prospects. Cf. P. S. Wandycz, *France and Her Eastern Allies* (Minneapolis: University of Minnesota Press, 1962), p. 142.

⁴⁷ Trubetskoi to Struve, May 14/27, 1920, WA-DC, Case I, File 5.

⁴⁸ Shcherbatskoi to Sazonov, April 13, 1920, *ibid*.

⁴⁹ Wrangel, *op. cit.*, p. 227. See also Trubetskoi's letter to Struve, May 28, 1920, where it is stated that Mangin was preparing a report to his government also advocating moral, material, and financial support for Wrangel, in WA-DC, Case I, File 5.

⁵⁰ Neratov relates Milne's visit in a note to Maklakov, May 23, 1920, WA-DC, Case I, File 5; see also *Documents on British Policy*, XII, 720.

⁵¹ See de Robeck to Lukomskii, May 31, 1920, and Neratov to Struve, June 1, 1920, WA-DC, Case I, File 5, and de Robeck to Curzon, June 7, 1920, in *Documents on British Policy*, XII, 732.

⁵² British Mission to Wrangel, May 29, 1920, WA-DC, Case I, File 5; *Documents on British Policy*, XII, 719–720. Cf. Wrangel, *op. cit.*, pp. 207–208.

⁵³ Rear Admiral G. Hope to Wrangel, June 3, 1920, WA-DC, Case I, File 5; *Documents on British Policy*, XII, 728.

⁵⁴ Admiral Hope (for de Robeck) to Wrangel, June 5, 1920, WA-DC, Case I, File 5. See also de Robeck's report to Curzon, June 3, *Documents on British Policy*, XII, 729–730.

⁵⁵ Trubetskoi to Struve, June 6, 1920, WA-DC, Case I, File 5. Cf. Wrangel, *op. cit.*, pp. 227–228. In his farewell remarks General Percy told Wrangel that he was still hoping that his government's policy would change, but that if it did not he would refuse further service and retire.

⁵⁶ Neratov to Trubetskoi, June 6, 1920, WA-DC, Case I, File 5. Neratov noted that the French high commissioner had not received such orders and was not subject to the British directive. Despite his government's order, moreover, Admiral de Robeck, according to a subsequent report by Russian Admiral Sablin, indicated that he would help the Russian naval command to obtain oil through unofficial channels. See Vice Admiral M. Sablin to Black Sea Fleet headquarters, secret, June 25, 1920, *ibid*. Curzon's instructions to de Robeck and material on the withdrawal of the British mission are in *Documents on British Policy*, XII, 728, 733, 746–747.

⁵⁷ Wrangel to Admiral de Robeck (for London), June 5, 1920, WA-DC, Case I, File 5; *Documents on British Policy*, XII, 730–731. Cf. Wrangel, *op. cit.*, p. 209.

⁵⁸ Wrangel, *op. cit.*, pp. 215, 216.

⁵⁹ Maklakov (for Struve) to Neratov (for Trubetskoi), June 8, 1920, WA-DC, Case I, File 5. When Curzon instructed the British Embassy in Paris to inquire into reports of negotiations between the French government and Wrangel's representatives, Sir G. Grahame replied on June 15 that Paléologue told him that there had been no negotiations "properly speaking," although the French gov-

ernment was more inclined than the British to consider Wrangel's requests for aid. The French Foreign Ministry, it was added, knew nothing regarding any negotiations between Wrangel and the Poles and Ukrainians. See Documents on British Policy, XII, 738.

[60] Trubetskoi to Struve, June 8/21, 1920, WA-DC, Case I, File 5.

[61] Trubetskoi to Constantinople, June 13, 1920, ibid.

[62] In a later note to Polish Foreign Minister Witos, United States Secretary of State Colby made a pointed reference to this fact. The Polish advance into Russia, he wrote, created "a National sentiment in that country, which ignored the tyranny and oppression from which the people suffered and afforded an undeserved support to the Bolshevik regime. . . ." Foreign Relations, 1920, III, 392.

[63] Struve to Trubetskoi (Maklakov to Neratov), June 11, 1920, WA-DC, Case I, File 5. For the text of such assurances to Chicherin, sent on July 2, see Documents on British Policy, XII, 746–747.

[64] Struve to Trubetskoi, June 27, 1920, WA-DC, Case I, File 5.

[65] Documents on British Policy, VIII, 502–506. See also Wandycz, op. cit., p. 153 ff.; and Nicolson, op. cit., p. 204.

[66] Documents on British Policy, VIII, 517, 530. For Curzon's note to the Soviet government, see Dokumenty vneshnei politiki, III, 54–55; and Great Britain, 5 Parliamentary Debates, House of Commons, CXXXI (1920), 2372–2374. Cf. Wandycz, op. cit., pp. 156–157.

[67] See notes from Curzon to the Soviet government, July 20, 26, and 29, 1920, Dokumenty vneshnei politiki, III, 62–64.

[68] Struve to Wrangel, July 17, 1920, WA-DC, Case I, File 5. The British proposals were read in the House of Commons on July 14. See Great Britain, 5 Parliamentary Debates, House of Commons, CXXXI (1920), 2372–2374. See also Documents on British Policy, VIII, 517.

[69] Letter from Trubetskoi to Struve, July 20, 1920, WA-DC, Case I, File 5.

[70] Struve to Trubetskoi, July 21, 1920, ibid. See also Struve to Wrangel, July 26, 1920, ibid.; London Times, July 26, 1920; I. V. Kliuchnikov and A. Sabanin, eds., Mezhdunarodnaia politika noveishego vremeni v dogovorakh, notakh i deklaratsiakh, 3 vols. (Moscow: Litizdat NKID, 1925–1928), Vol. III, Part I, pp. 34–38; Dokumenty vneshnei politiki, III, 47–53; Great Britain, 5 Parliamentary Debates, House of Commons, CXXXII (1920), 974–975; and Wandycz, op. cit., p. 157.

[71] Documents on British Policy, VIII, 649–650; and Dokumenty vneshnei politiki, III, 62–64. See also the comments by Millerand in Annales de la chambre des députés, Débats parlementaires, Tome II (1920), pp. 2622–2623, session of July 20; and Curzon's note, in Great Britain, 5 Parliamentary Debates, House of Commons, CXXXII (1920), 1635–1636.

[72] For a revealing study of Soviet actions with regard to Poland at this time, see Warren Lerner, "The Russian Plan to Sovietize Poland in 1920" (unpublished M.A. thesis and Russian Institute Essay, Columbia University, 1954). See also I. Deutscher, The Prophet Armed (New York: Oxford University Press, 1954), pp. 463–466.

[73] Nicolson, op. cit., p. 206; A. J. Toynbee, ed., Survey of International Affairs,

1920–1923 (London: Oxford University Press, 1927), p. 15.

[74] Struve to Wrangel, quoting Millerand's speech, July 22, 1920, WA-DC, Case I, File 5. See *Annales de la chambre des députés, Débats parlementaires,* Tome II, (1920), pp. 2622–2623, session of July 20.

[75] Struve to Wrangel, July 20, 1920, WA-DC, Case I, File 5. Cf. Wrangel, *op. cit.,* pp. 241–242.

[76] Trubetskoi to Struve, July 31, 1920, WA-DC, Case I, File 5. Cf. Wrangel, *op. cit.,* pp. 242–243. See also Bazili to Millerand, July 23, 1920, MA, Series B, Packet V, Dossier 2.

[77] *Documents on British Policy,* VIII, 653–656.

[78] Trubetskoi to Maklakov, July 20, 1920, WA-DC, Case I, File 5. See also Trubetskoi to Neratov, August 2, 1920, *ibid.* It is interesting to note, with regard to the French objection to mining the ports, that a prisoner-exchange agreement had been signed with the Soviet government on April 20 which obligated France to return all Russian soldiers and civilians who wished to do so to Soviet territory from France through Black Sea ports. It was anticipated in the agreement that some 22,000 Russians would be so returned. This, however, was April and not August. See R.S.F.S.R., *Vestnik narodnogo komissariata innostrannykh del,* No. 4–5, June 20, 1920, pp. 129–134; and *Dokumenty vneshnei politiki,* II, 463–467. At the same time France had pledged through its representatives in negotiations with Litvinov that it would "not intervene in the internal politics of Russia and would not support any aggressive measures against the Soviet Republics of Russia and the Ukraine." See *Dokumenty vneshnei politiki,* II, 462. The British, as noted, had also signed an exchange agreement with Litvinov in February, but it had not specified the return of Russians to Soviet Russia and had not indicated particular ports of entry. See *Vestnik narodnogo komissariata innostrannykh del,* No. 3, February 27, 1920, pp. 83–84; and *Dokumenty vneshnei politiki,* II. 364–367. The British fleet was also participating in the Black Sea blockade, but this was explained as intended to prevent contacts between the Bolsheviks and Kemal in Turkey. See Great Britain, 5 *Parliamentary Debates,* House of Commons, CXXXIV (1920), 845; and *Documents on British Policy,* XII, 744.

[79] For correspondence relating to this affair, see Report of the Military Agent in Turkey, May 11; Captain Shcherbachev to Fleet Commander, June 26 and June 31, 1920; Admiral de Robeck to Captain Nikanov, August 7, 1920; and Captain Le Grosdidier to Captain Shcherbachev, August 26, 1920, WA-DC. Case I, File 5. Wrangel mentions the official rejection of permission to operate the station but makes no reference to the information cited above in Wrangel, *op. cit.,* p. 293.

[80] See Poklevskii-Kozel to Paris Embassy, August 30, 1920, MA, Series B, Packet V, Dossier 2.

[81] Note of the Political and Commercial Affairs Section of the Foreign Ministry, July 19, 1920, WMA, File 29.

[82] French Legation, Bucharest, to Foreign Ministry, Paris, August 24, 1920, WMA, File 8.

[83] General Petin, Military Attaché in Rumania, to Ministry of War, August 31, 1920, *ibid.*

84 For a brief history of this question, with lists of materials sent and indications of the difficulties, see Captain Berger to Ministry of War (Paris), September 9, 1920, WMA, File 6. See also Marshal Foch to General Miller, August 26, 1920; Maklakov to Paléologue, September 14, 1920; Marshal Foch to Ministry of War (Paris), September 16, 1920; Gerua to Sevastopol, September 30, 1920; and Lukomskii to General Franchet d'Esperey, October 9, 1920, *ibid.*

85 The American Chargé d'Affaires reported on August 8 that Red forces were only thirty miles from Warsaw and the defense line had been overrun. See White to Secretary of State, August 8, 1920, *Foreign Relations, 1920*, III, 387. On Lloyd George's talks with Kamenev and Krasin, see *Documents on British Policy*, VIII, 669–708.

86 *Documents on British Policy*, VIII, 709–716, 725–741. See also Lloyd George's statement to the House of Commons on August 10, Great Britain, 5 *Parliamentary Debates*, House of Commons, CXXXII (1920), 261–262. With regard to Pilsudski it was agreed that he should be replaced as commander-in-chief but could remain as head of state.

87 *Documents on British Policy*, VIII, 745–747.

88 See Bazili to Struve, August 3, 1920, and to Constantinople, August 3/16, 1920, WA-DC, Case I, File 5. In a later note to the Soviet government Lloyd George indicated that he had accepted the suggestion that Wrangel be invited to London to discuss the fate of his forces "but not in the capacity of a member of the conference." See *Dokumenty vneshnei politiki*, III, 136. See also Lloyd George's proposals on a truce in *ibid.*, 97–98.

89 See *Foreign Relations, 1920*, III, 393–394, 395. See also the Soviet representatives' report on Lloyd George's warning to them on August 4 that this would be done in *Dokumenty vneshnei politiki*, III, 81.

90 See Great Britain, 5 *Parliamentary Debates*, House of Commons, CXXXII (1920), 351–353, session of August 20.

91 Struve to Wrangel, July 26, 1920, WA-DC, Case I, File 5.

92 Trubetskoi to Struve, July 26/August 8, 1920, *ibid.*

93 Secretary of State to Italian Ambassador, August 10, 1920, *Foreign Relations, 1920*, III, 463–468.

94 French Chargé d'Affaires to Secretary of State, August 14, 1920, *ibid.*, 469–470.

95 Girs to Struve, August 14, 1920, WA-DC, Case I, File 5.

96 Millerand to Bazili, August 10, 1920, *ibid.* For Wrangel's response, see Wrangel to Millerand, August 15, 1920, *ibid.* The United States, of course, did not extend such recognition. The Russian ambassador in Washington, Bakhmetev, cautioned again against expecting American aid because, as he put it, financial conditions were poor and besides the United States was "very conservative and slow." See Bakhmetev to Girs, August 26, 1920, *ibid.* For a comment on the negative British attitude toward French recognition of Wrangel, see the note dated August 12, 1920, in U. S. National Archives, Foreign Affairs Section, Doc. No. 861.01/228. Cf. Lloyd George's comments to the House of Commons on August 11 in Great Britain, 5 *Parliamentary Debates*, House of Commons, CXXXIII (1920), 496–498.

⁹⁷ Millerand to Marshal Foch, August 16, 1920, citing previous note of August 9, 1920, WMA, File 48.

⁹⁸ Foch to General Miller, August 19, 1920, ibid. See also Bazili to Struve, August 5/18, 1920, WA-DC, Case I, File 5.

⁹⁹ See Documents on British Policy, VIII, 786–791; and Dokumenty vneshnei politiki, III, 100–101. See also Kliuchnikov and Sabanin, op. cit., III, Part I, 47–49; and the London Times, August 24, 1920. When on August 15 the Soviet government protested to Lloyd George against French recognition of Wrangel and charged the British government with going back on its word, Lloyd George replied that the British government had not at all changed its policy toward Wrangel, had no intention of recognizing his government, and sought only to bring about an end to the hostilities in the South on terms which would assure the personal security of Wrangel's supporters. However, he added, this policy might have to be reconsidered if the Soviet government persisted in offering to Poland only such terms as would violate its sovereignty and independence. See Dokumenty vneshnei politiki, III, 131–136.

¹⁰⁰ See Russian Envoy, Bulgaria, to Sevastopol, August 7, 1920, WA-DC, Case I, File 5.

¹⁰¹ For an account of the Kuban campaign and the initiation of new efforts to keep the Poles in the struggle, see Wrangel, op. cit., p. 249 ff.

¹⁰² Struve to Maklakov, September 1, 1920, WA-DC, Case I, File 5. Cf. Wrangel, op. cit., pp. 261–262.

¹⁰³ Struve to Maklakov, September 8, 1920, WA-DC, Case I, File 5.

¹⁰⁴ Maklakov to Struve, September 12, 1920, ibid.

¹⁰⁵ See the Daily Herald, August 30, 1920. The text may also be found in Iakushkin, Frantsuzskaia interventsiia, p. 77; Gukovskii, Frantsuzskaia interventsiia, pp. 22–23; I. Al'f, Antanta i Vrangel, pp. 25–26; and in T. Tolokonnikov, Frantsuzskaia burzhuaziia i Iuda Vrangel; dogovor Frantsii s Vrangelem (Moscow: Gosizdat, 1920).

¹⁰⁶ A draft agreement looking toward the opening of credits for Wrangel is mentioned in letters from General Hermonius to the French Ministry of Commerce, August 14, 1920, and to Bazili, August 20, 1920, but no specific terms are noted. Terms are mentioned, however, in Neratov to Paris Embassy, October 24, 1920, and Maklakov to Neratov, October 15, 1920, MA, Series B, Packet V, Dossier 2. See also Russian Chargé d'Affaires, London, to Struve, September 26, 1920, Bernatskii Papers. A British Foreign Office memorandum of September 20 expressed concern that the French were "endeavouring to establish a complete monopoly" in economic relations with Wrangel and noted that some "Russian financiers" were prepared "to sell the whole economic future of South Russia to France." Documents on British Policy, XII, 784–785.

¹⁰⁷ Maklakov to Neratov, October 15, 1920, MA, Series B, Packet V, Dossier 2.

¹⁰⁸ A report by General Hermonius on November 5, 1920, stated that the total "value" of military supplies sent by France between July and October amounted to 11,209,516 francs. It would appear from a note dated December 1, 1920, from the Ministry of War to General Miller that almost all of that had been paid for, leaving a debt on these goods of only about 350,000 francs. See Liste des cessions, in a letter from General Hermonius to the French Ministry of War, November

5, and the Ministry of War to General Miller, December 1, 1920, WMA, File 47. Some purchases were made in the United States, especially coal, under Ughet's arrangements, but again the amounts were apparently inadequate. See U. S. National Archives, Foreign Affairs Section, Doc. No. 861.24/268a and 270. Likewise small funds were available in England under previous arrangements with Kolchak. See Lukomskii, Vospominaniia, II, 226; and Ispoved' Savinkova: protsess, p. 77.

[109] Wrangel, op. cit., pp. 283, 295–296. Cf. M. S. Margulies, op. cit., III, 241, 254.

[110] Wrangel, op. cit., p. 300; Struve to Tatishchev, October 22, 1920, WA-DC, Case I, File 5.

[111] Makhrov, "General Vrangel i B. Savinkov," pp. 186–208. Wrangel's diplomatic representative at this time was V. M. Gorlov. For a Soviet account of Wrangel's relations with Poland, see S. Budkevich, "Vrangel i Pol'sha," in Razgrom Vrangelia: sbornik statei (Moscow: Gosvoenizdat, Kommunisticheskaia Akademiia, 1930), pp. 41–54.

[112] There were some Cossack troops, but most of the others were apparently refugees from earlier campaigns in the northwestern theater. Forces under General Bulak-Balakhovich, for example, were chiefly partisan units but had previously served under Iudenich. Among the political delegations there was even a Kuban mission, which denounced Wrangel's policies toward the Cossacks and declared that Wrangel was just continuing Denikin's dictatorship and the restorationist effort. See note of the Kuban mission, October 7, 1920, in S. A. Piontkovskii, ed., Grazhdanskaia voina v Rossii, 1918–1921 gg. (Moscow: Izd. Kom. universiteta, 1925), pp. 486–495.

[113] On the Bredov corps' return, see Wrangel, op. cit., pp. 251, 275. See also Allied Supreme Council considerations of the transfer of the corps in U. S. Embassy, Paris, E.S.H. Bulletins, Nos. 428, 509, 536, 628, 635, and 784, Hoover Library. Makhrov's position was also somewhat awkward as a result of the fact that Poland had not recognized Wrangel's government. The Polish government continued in this policy, according to Makhrov, on the advice of the French, who feared upsetting the negotiations with the Soviet government. See Makhrov, "General Vrangel i B. Savinkov," p. 261. See also Documents on British Policy, XII, 715–716, 718, 744–745.

[114] Makhrov, "General Vrangel i B. Savinkov," pp. 213, 256. Savinkov was apparently also the only one with access to intelligence sources and with direct communication to Paris, including, according to Makhrov, even directly to Foch's staff. Ibid., p. 358. See also Ispoved' Savinkova: protsess, pp. 36, 96.

[115] An agreement signed by Savinkov with one of the Russian generals in Poland in August stated that Savinkov had a secret understanding with the Polish High Command that all Russian forces were to be under his political direction and maintained by funds recognized as a state debt of Russia. Any territory taken was, by this agreement, to be given land reform and democracy. See the agreement, dated August 27, 1920, in the Miliukov Personal Archives. Additional documents on Savinkov's position and his understandings with the Polish High Command and Russian troops in Poland (and Estonia and Latvia) may be found in the archives of the Jozef Pilsudski Institute of America (New York). It was

understood that all forces under Savinkov's "Political Center" would subscribe
to the slogans of the Center: (1) constituent assembly, (2) land for the people,
(3) democracy, and (4) federation.

116 Makhrov, "General Vrangel i B. Savinkov," pp. 218–219, 255. Makhrov
adds later, however, that political circles in Poland were sharply divided on policy, with resulting uncertainty as to the future. Ibid., pp. 262–270.

117 Ibid., pp. 220–223.

118 Ibid., p. 231. By the same token Pilsudski expressed doubts as to such
persons as Krivoshein and others in Wrangel's government and mentioned disturbing rumors of a pro-German orientation among Wrangel's associates, if not
in himself. The poles, Makhrov reported, were afraid that Wrangel's "democratic
principles" declared abroad might turn out to be "only tactical maneuvers." Ibid.,
pp. 343–344.

119 A statement issued on October 2 by Savinkov's Political Committee declared
its recognition of Wrangel's authority but added the understanding that the Committee's policy would continue to include close cooperation with Poland, recognition of the right of self-determination for the border states, and the future
restoration of Russia through the convocation of a constituent assembly on the
basis of universal, direct, equal, and secret suffrage. See Declaration of the Russian
Political Committee in Warsaw, October 2, 1920, in the Miliukov Personal
Archives.

120 Makhrov, "General Vrangel i B. Savinkov," pp. 242, 247.

121 Ibid., p. 257.

122 Ibid., pp. 258–269.

123 Ibid., p. 260.

124 Ibid., pp. 329–330; Wrangel, op. cit., pp. 275–276. It is interesting to note
that at his trial in 1924 Savinkov stated that the idea of forming a Russian army
in Poland had been Pilsudski's idea from the start. It was Pilsudski's proposal
to this effect which brought him to Warsaw in January, 1920, from Paris, Savinkov testified, and it was this assignment upon which he set to work in the
spring of 1920 at Pilsudski's request. See Ispoved' Savinkova: protsess, p. 82. Of
course, the troops involved were already there; what Pilsudski sought was a political leadership for them which would make their aims compatible with his own.
It was with this in mind that he contacted Savinkov. See correspondence between Savinkov and Pilsudski in the archives of the Jozef Pilsudski Institute of
America (New York). On the formation of the Third Army, see also correspondence in the General Miller Archives, File 6(m), Hoover Library.

125 Makhrov, "General Vrangel i B. Savinkov," pp. 328–329. General Count
Palen had accepted Savinkov's program and subordinated his forces to the Rus-
sian Political Center in political questions. See documents in the Jozef Pilsudski
Institute of America (New York).

126 Makhrov, "General Vrangel i B. Savinkov," p. 338.

127 Ibid., pp. 272–273.

128 Ibid., p. 292.

129 Wrangel, op. cit., p. 274.

130 Ibid., pp. 284–285.

131 See Piontkovskii, op. cit., p. 637.

[132] See the letter of the Ukrainian National Committee to Maklakov, July 18, 1921, MA, Series B, Packet II, Dossier 3.

[133] Wrangel, *op. cit.,* p. 285. Cf. M. S. Margulies, *op. cit.,* III, 247; and Makhrov, "General Vrangel i B. Savinkov," p. 346.

[134] General Slashchev, who was an outspoken advocate of such steps, describes several such projects in Ia. A. Slashchev-Krymskii, *Trebuiu suda obshchestva i glasnosti* (Constantinople: Knigoizdat. M. Shul'mana, 1921), pp. 57–59, 62–66.

[135] Makhrov, "General Vrangel i B. Savinkov," p. 345; Wrangel, *op. cit.,* p. 276. Wrangel had informed General Miller on September 18/October 1 of plans for the organization of troops in Poland and ordered him to do everything possible to get the Poles to draw out the truce negotiations so as to give more time. See WA-DC, Case I, File 5.

[136] Makhrov, "General Vrangel i B. Savinkov," pp. 346–347. Marshal Foch noted in a letter to General Miller on October 1 that the plans for the formation of Russian troops in Poland would be difficult to realize without an accord with the Ukrainian forces. Foch to Miller, October 1, 1920, WA-DC, Case I, File 5.

[137] Makhrov, "General Vrangel i B. Savinkov," p. 348. The text of the Polish-Soviet-Ukrainian agreement is in *Dokumenty vneshnei politiki,* III, 245–258. The exchange of ratifications putting the treaty into effect did not actually take place until November 2.

[138] Makhrov, "General Vrangel i B. Savinkov," p. 349. See also the statement on Bulak-Balakhovich's position in the paper entitled "Pro Memoria," Miliukov Personal Archives.

[139] Makhrov, "General Vrangel i B. Savinkov," pp. 351–352.

[140] *Ibid.,* p. 373. Makhrov at this time expressed doubts as to Savinkov's reliability and wished to handle the relations with the Ukrainians himself. Savinkov himself later testified that a representative of Wrangel in Poland had "secretly obstructed" his efforts and that he (Savinkov) had resisted Wrangel's attempt to gain control of the troops in Poland because this would have destroyed his own position. The French, he added, tried to force him to submit to Wrangel's leadership. See *Ispoved' Savinkova: protsess,* pp. 83–84.

[141] Makhrov, "General Vrangel i B. Savinkov," p. 382 ff.

[142] *Ibid.,* p. 385. In his confession to the Soviet court in 1924 Savinkov declared that he had helped arrange agreements with both Petliura and Wrangel to coordinate their operations. *Ispoved' Savinkova: protsess,* pp. 14, 86. He also stated this in a letter to Wrangel dated October 15, 1920. See "Letter from the representative of the Russian Political Committee in Poland to General Vrangel," MS, Hoover Library.

[143] *Velikaia Rossiia,* October 1/14, 1920, interview with Prince Liubomirski (this is V. V. Shul'gin's paper, formerly *Rossiia,* being published at this time in the Crimea; issues of May 31 to October 23, 1920, are in the Wrangel Archives, Hoover Library). See also Wrangel, *op. cit.,* pp. 292–293.

[144] Wrangel, *op. cit.,* pp. 292, 294. Millerand had become president of France in September, and Paléologue had decided to retire from his post in the Foreign Ministry, but Bazili wired from Paris that Millerand would retain control over foreign policy. The new government, it was reported, continued to adhere to

the policy of support for Wrangel. See Bazili to Struve, September 25, 1920, and Bazili to Struve, September 27, 1920, WA-DC, Case I, File 5.

¹⁴⁵ Captain Shcherbachev, Constantinople, to Fleet Commander, October 9, 1920, relaying Admiral de Bon's message, WA-DC, Case I, File 5. De Bon indicated in subsequent messages that this included continued efforts to obtain military supplies. See Vice Admiral de Bon to Captain de Vaissea, Attaché with the Russian fleet, October 14, 1920, ibid.

¹⁴⁶ Maklakov (Struve) to Tatishchev, October 22, 1920, ibid. See also Wrangel, op. cit., p. 292.

¹⁴⁷ Wrangel, op. cit., pp. 297–298; Velikaia Rossiia, October 8/21, 1920. See also the interview with Martel in Velikaia Rossiia, October 10/23, 1920, Wrangel Archives.

¹⁴⁸ Wrangel, op. cit., p. 311.

¹⁴⁹ Ibid., p. 317; Admiral Dumesnil to Wrangel, November 11, 1920, WA-DC, Case I, File 5.

¹⁵⁰ Wrangel, op. cit., p. 321; P. Shatilov, "Zapiski" (MS, Columbia University Russian Archive), p. 916; Wrangel to Martel, November 13, 1920, WA-DC, Case I, File 5.

¹⁵¹ Some British and American ships participated in the operation in a protective capacity, but Curzon had categorically rejected direct British participation and refused appeals to assist in the evacuation. See Documents on British Policy, XII, 802. On British relief activities in Constantinople after the evacuation, see ibid., pp. 817–820.

¹⁵² Wrangel, op. cit., pp. 324–327, 337. Those evacuated included 50,000 combat troops, 40,000 rear military personnel, 3,000 military school cadets, 6,000 wounded, and 50,000 civilians.

¹⁵³ In paying his respects to Wrangel after the ships were at sea, Admiral Dumesnil wrote: "I realized the anguish this step has cost you. But you must find some satisfaction in the knowledge that the evacuation has been conducted in an exemplary manner. The French Fleet rejoices to see the evacuation so brilliantly terminated." Ibid., pp. 326–327.

¹⁵⁴ See Foreign Relations, 1920, III, 721–723. For a summary of British relations with the Soviet government from April to September 12, 1920, see Documents on British Policy, XII, 778–782; from September 12 to December 12, 1920, VIII, 866–869.

¹⁵⁵ M. S. Margulies, op. cit., III, 260.

¹⁵⁶ Wrangel, op. cit., p. 339; French High Commissioner, Constantinople, to Neratov, December 7, 1920, Wrangel Personal Archives, Kotliarevskii Section, Case I. File 8.

¹⁵⁷ Statement to Martel, November 13, 1920, Wrangel Personal Archives, Kotliarevskii Section, Case I, File 8. See also Wrangel, op. cit., p. 321.

¹⁵⁸ Shatilov, op. cit., p. 926; Wrangel to Martel, November 14, 1920, WA-DC, Case I, File 5. Unsuccessful private negotiations were apparently also undertaken on the possibility of joining the Ukrainians in Poland or going to Georgia. See M. S. Margulies, op. cit., III, 257, 259–260. On these questions see also the British reports in Documents on British Policy, XII, 825–832.

¹⁵⁹ Wrangel, op. cit., p. 339.

[160] Greece declined to receive any because of its own refugee problems and the Allied governments overruled their movement into Hungary. See note from foreign minister of Greece, November 15, 1920, WA-DC, Case I, File 5; and Wrangel, op. cit., p. 342.

[161] Wrangel, op. cit., pp. 340–341.

[162] See French Ministry of War to General Hermonius, November 25, 1920, WMA, File 63. See also Shatilov, op. cit., p. 917.

[163] See statement of the Liquidation Commission, Neratov to French High Commissioner, December 12, 1920, and Struve to Prime Minister Leygues, December 6 and December 18, 1920, Wrangel Personal Archives, Kotliarevskii Section, Case I, File 8.

[164] See Document A, Wrangel Personal Archives, Kotliarevskii Section, File 2.

[165] The British also contributed sizable sums for this purpose. See Great Britain, 5 Parliamentary Debates, House of Commons, CXXXVI (1920), 1394.

[166] Makhrov, "General Vrangel i B. Savinkov," pp. 388–391. Savinkov himself survived this ordeal and continued to plot the downfall of the Soviet government until 1924, when he was tricked into returning to Soviet territory by a police ruse and the betrayal of one of his former associates. He was tried and convicted for treason. His death sentence, however, was commuted to ten years in prison on the recommendation of Soviet secret police chief Felix Dzerzhinskii, who turned out to be an old friend of his. Savinkov, the revolutionary and adventurer, however, could not bear to be confined, and it seems he ended his own life by a leap from the window of his special apartment in Dzerzhinskii's headquarters. For details on these events see the preface to Boris Savinkov, Memoirs of a Terrorist (New York: Albert and Charles Boni, 1931); and the record of his trial and confession in Ispoved' Savinkova: protsess.

[167] League of Nations Treaty Series, Vol. VI (1921), p. 131; Dokumenty vneshnei politiki, III, 618–658, with map.

[168] Wrangel, op. cit., pp. 344–348; Documents on British Policy, XII, 831-832.

[169] Wrangel, op. cit., pp. 346–348.

CHAPTER IX: POST-MORTEM

[1] This incident was related by A. Mikoyan in recalling Churchill's first visit to Moscow during World War II, in The New York Times, January 29, 1959, p. 1.

[2] See V. I. Lenin, Lenin o vneshnei politike sovetskogo gosudarstvo (Moscow: Gospolitizdat, 1960), pp. 226–228, 371. See also Vos'maia konferentsiia RKP(b), dekabr' 1919 goda: protokoly (Moscow: Gospolitizdat, 1961), p. 11 ff.

[3] See Lenin, Lenin o vneshnei politike, pp. 226, 338, 371.

[4] A good general review and critique of the anti-Bolshevik movements, especially the "Whites," is P. N. Miliukov, Russia Today and Tomorrow (New York: Macmillan, 1922), pp. 1–187. See also P. B. Struve, Razmyshleniia o russkoi revoliutsii (Sofia: Rossiisko-Bolgarskoe knigoizdatel'stvo, 1921), pp. 3–18.

[5] Cf. Struve, Razmyshleniia o russkoi revoliutsii, p. 6 ff.

[6] W. S. Churchill, The World Crisis: The Aftermath (London: Thornton Butterworth, 1929), p. 272.

[7] For a notable expression of this point of view, see F. L. Schuman, *Soviet Politics At Home and Abroad* (New York: Knopf, 1946).

[8] E. V. Gulick, *Europe's Classical Balance of Power*, (Ithaca: Cornell University Press, 1955), pp. 62–63.

[9] J. L. Brierly, *The Law of Nations*, 5th ed., (London: Oxford University Press, 1955), pp. 308–309.

[10] G. F. Kennan, *Russia and the West Under Lenin and Stalin* (Boston: Atlantic-Little, Brown and Co., 1960), pp. 190–191.

[11] Churchill, *op. cit.*, p. 175.

[12] *Ibid.*, pp. 233–234.

[13] *Ibid.*, p. 274.

[14] *Ibid.*, p. 177.

[15] *Ibid.*, p. 273.

[16] *Ibid.*, p. 273.

[17] Denikin, *Ocherki russkoi smuty*, II, 198–199.

[18] *Ibid.*, p. 199.

[19] P. N. Wrangel, *Always with Honor* (New York: Speller, 1957), p. 71.

[20] One example of this unfortunate situation was the treatment of Jews in the area controlled by the Volunteer Army. Denikin declared that the Jews were to be given the same cultural and religious freedom as everyone else, and he issued orders prohibiting discrimination against Jewish officers and censuring any use of violence against Jews. However, there was a good deal of antisemitism in South Russia, both among the population generally and within the Volunteer Army, and Denikin's orders had little effect toward curbing it. See Denikin, *Ocherki russkoi smuty*, V, 145–150. For a first-hand critique of Volunteer policy and behavior toward the Jews as well as the Ukrainians, see A. A. Gol'denveizer, "Iz Kievskikh vospominanii," *Arkhiv Russkoi Revoliutsii*, Vol. VI (Berlin: Izdatel'-stvo "Slovo," 1922), p. 258 ff.

[21] See Miliukov's note to the Allied governments, in the Miliukov Personal Archives, and in part in Miliukov, *Russia and England* (London: Russian Liberation Committee, 1920), p. 49.

[22] Denikin, *The White Army* (London: Cape, 1930), p. 300.

[23] Denikin, *World Events and the Russian Problem* (Paris: Imprimerie Rapide, 1939), p. 38.

[24] Commenting upon this situation, Ambassador Buchanan states in his memoirs his belief that if Allied actions alienated any Russians, it was not because of intervention per se but because of their fear that it was directed toward dismemberment of Russia. See Sir George Buchanan, *My Mission to Russia* (London: Cassell, 1923), Vol. II, p. 259. Cf. Denikin, *Ocherki russkoi smuty*, IV, 140–141. Louis Fischer quotes British spokesmen who favored dismemberment of Russia for Allied advantages in his *Oil Imperialism* (New York: International Publishers, 1926), pp. 30–31, attributing this point of view particularly to the chairman of the Bibi Ebat Oil Company, Herbert Allen, whose remarks were presented in the *Financial News*, December 24, 1918. Fischer concludes that British policy had "always been the dismemberment of Russia," a rather exaggerated view. For further examples, see F. L. Bertie, *The Diary of Lord Bertie of Thame* (London: Hodder and Stoughton, 1924), Vol. II, pp. 310–311; and L. I. Strakhovsky, "The

Franco-British Plot to Dismember Russia," *Current History*, Vol. XXXIII (March 1931), pp. 839–842. For British and French statements to the contrary, see Curzon to Wardrop, October 2 and 4, 1919, *Documents on British Policy*, III, 574–575, 577–578; and French Ministry of Foreign Affairs to M. Paul Cambon, March 3, 1919, and telegrams of Colonel Chardigny, in the Maklakov Archives, Series B, Packet II, Dossier 11 (Hoover Library).

[25] Denikin, *Ocherki russkoi smuty*, IV, 245.

[26] See C. E. Bechhofer-Roberts, *In Denikin's Russia and the Caucasus* (London: Collin's, 1921), p. 16.

[27] Churchill, *op. cit.*, p. 87.

[28] On the historical background of the nationalities problem, see V. A. Maklakov, *Vlast' i obshchestvennost' na zakate staroi Rossii; vospominaniia* (Paris: Prilozhenie k "Illiustrirovannoi Rossii," 1930), pp. 223–233. Cf. E. G. Val', *Kak Pilsudski pogubil Denikina* (Tallin: Izdanie avtora, 1938), pp. i-xxiii.

[29]Cf. Struve, *Razmyshleniia o russkoi revoliutsii*, p. 17; and Miliukov, *Russia Today and Tomorrow*, pp. 8–17.

[30] Miliukov, *Russia Today and Tomorrow*, p. 32.

[31] Churchill, *op. cit.*, p. 273.

BIBLIOGRAPHY

UNPUBLISHED MATERIALS AND ARCHIVES

Alekseev, M. V. "Account Book of the Volunteer Army." MS, Hoover Library.

American Commission to Negotiate Peace. S-H Bulletins. Paris, 1919. MSS (typed), Hoover Library.

American Embassy, Paris. E. S. H. Bulletins, Paris, 1919–1920. MSS (typed), Hoover Library.

Aprelev, Iu. P. "Zametki o sobytiiakh v Rossii, 1917–1918–1919 gg." MS (typed), Columbia University Russian Archive.

Bernatskii, M. V. Papers. MSS, Columbia University Russian Archive.

———. Papers on Russian Finance. MSS, Hoover Library.

Birkin, V. N. "Povesti minuvshikh let." Vol. VII: "Kornilovskii pokhod." MS (typed), Columbia University Russian Archive.

Bogaevskii, M. P. Papers. MSS, Columbia University Russian Archive.

Brofel'dt, B. M. "Vospominaniia," MS (typed), Columbia University Russian Archive.

Cheriachukin, A. V. Papers of the Don Envoy. MSS, Hoover Library.

Denikin, A. I. Papers. MSS, Columbia University Russian Archive.

Documents of the Crimean Government. MSS, Hoover Library.

Documents of the Terek Cossack Government. MSS, Hoover Library.

Dratsenko, D. P. Documents. MSS, Hoover Library.

Gessen, G. V. Archives. MSS, Hoover Library.

Golitsyn, A. D. (Prince). "Vospominaniia, 1917–1920." MS (handwritten and typed), Columbia University Russian Archive.

Herron, G. D. Papers. Vol. X: Russia. MSS, Hoover Library.

Interallied Conference Documents. Council of Ministers, Premiers, and Ambassadors, January 10, 1920–August 17, 1921. MSS (mimeograph), Hoover Library.

"Istoriia Markovskoi artilleriiskoi brigady." MS (mimeograph) in 2 vols. compiled by the history commission of the Markov Artillery Division. Paris: Izdanie IKMAD, 1931. Columbia University Russian Archive.

Kefeli, Ia. I. "S. Generalom A. V. Shvartsem v Odesse, osen' 1918–vesna 1919 gg.: vospominaniia." MS (typed), Columbia University Russian Archive.

Khagondokov, N. K. "Vospominaniia." MS (typed), Columbia University Russian Archive.

Kovalevskii, P. E., "Dnevniki, 1918–1921." MS (typed), Columbia University Russian Archive.

Krasnov, P. N. "Discours du Général Krasnov, Ataman du Don, le 13 Dec. 1918 lors de se rencontre avec le General Pool." MS, Hoover Library.

von Lampe, A. A. Archives. Files 1–57. MSS, Hoover Library.

Makhrov, P. S. "General Vrangel i B. Savinkov." MS (handwritten), Columbia University Russian Archive.

———. "V beloi armii generala Denikina." MS (handwritten), Columbia University Russian Archive.

Maklakov, V. A. Arkhiv Russkogo posol'stva v Parizhe, 1918–1923. MS, Hoover Library.

———. Archives, Series B. MS, Hoover Library. (Cited as MA in notes.)

Mandrajy (Mandrachi), Constantin. "Begin at the Beginning." Memoirs translated by Vera Mandrajy. MS (typed), Columbia University Russian Archive.

Maximova-Mulaev, A. A. "Account of the Occupation of Koslov by General Mamontov's Cossack Detachment, a Part of General Denikin's Troops, in August 1919." Interview given to Nadia Lavrova by the author in San Francisco, October 1932. MS, Hoover Library.

Miliukov, P. N. "Dnevnik." MS (typed), Columbia University Russian Archive.

———. Personal Archives. MSS, Columbia University Russian Archive.

Miller, E. K. Archives of the Military Representative in Paris. MSS, Hoover Library.

Nikolaev, K. N. "Vospominaniia, 1917–1918 gg." and Papers. MSS (typed), Columbia University Russian Archive.

Poliakov, I. A. "General Kornilov." MS (handwritten), Columbia University Russian Archive.

Post, W. E. et al. "A Resumé of Events in the Caucasus Since the Russian Revolution." MS (typed), Hoover Library.

"Prikazy i rasporiazheniia po Dobrovol'cheskoi i Donskoi armiiam, otnosiashchiesia k periodu grazhdanskoi voiny na Iuge Rossii, 1918–1919 gg." MSS, Hoover Library.

"Prikazy, mandaty, tsirkuliary, i t.d., otnosiashchiesia k periodu grazhdanskoi voiny na Iuge Rossii, 1918–1920 gg." (Bolshevik materials.) MSS, Hoover Library.

Rerberg, F. P. "Istoricheskiia zagadki o revoliutsii v Rossii." Vol. II: "Krepost' Sevastopol' pod vlast'iu Germantsev, Anglichan, Frantsuzov i Dobrovol'tsev Gen. Denikina: zapiski Nachal'nika Shtaba Sevastopol'skoi Kreposti." MS (typed), Hoover Library.

Sannikov, A. S. "Vospominaniia, 1918–1919." MS (typed), Columbia University Russian Archive.

Savinkov, B. V. "Letter from the Representative of the Russian Political Committee in Poland to General Vrangel, Commander-in-Chief of Russian Armed Forces in the South of Russia." Warsaw, October 15, 1920. MS, Hoover Library.

Shatilov, P. "Zapiski." MS (typed), Columbia University Russian Archive.

Shavel'skii, Protopresviter Georgii. "Vospominaniia." MS (typed), Columbia University Russian Archive.

Shcherbachev, D. G. Papers. MSS, Hoover Library.

Smagin, A. A. "Vospominaniia." MS (typed), Columbia University Russian Archive.

Svechin, M. A. "Dopolnenie k vospominaniiam." MS, Columbia University Russian Archive.

Tikhobrazov, D. "Vospominaniia." MS (handwritten), Columbia University Russian Archive.

United States National Archives, Foreign Affairs Section. Materials chiefly from Files 763.72 and 861.00, with additional items in Files 183.9, 184.016, 184.02102, 860 E, 861.01, 861.24, 861.48, 861.50, 861.51, 861.77, and in the materials of the American Food Mission for Southern Europe, FA 276 A–A1.

Vatatsi, M. P. "The White Movement, 1917–1920: Memoirs." MS, Hoover Library.

Vinaver, Rose G. "Vospominaniia." MS (typed), Hoover Library.

Wrangel, P. N. Archives. Diplomatic Correspondence Section. MSS, Hoover Library. (Cited as WA-DC in notes.)

———. Military Archives. MSS, Hoover Library. (Cited as WMA in notes.)

———. Personal Archives. Kotliarevskii Section. MSS, Hoover Library.

———. Personal Archives. Baroness Olga Wrangel Section. MSS, Hoover Library.

Zen'kovskii, A. V. "Vospominaniia, 1919–1920." MS (handwritten), Columbia University Russian Archive.

DISSERTATIONS AND THESES:

Benjamin, Alfred. "The Great Dilemma: The Foreign Policy of the Russian Provisional Government, March–May, 1917." Ph.D. dissertation, Columbia University, 1950.

Engel, D. H. "Soviet-Polish Relations, November 1918 to April 1920." Russian Institute Essay, Columbia University, 1949.

Fedyshyn, O. S. "German Plans for the Ukraine in 1918." Russian Institute Essay, Columbia University, 1955.

——. "German Plans and Policies in the Ukraine and the Crimea, 1917–1918." Ph.D. dissertation, Columbia University, 1962.

Godwin, Robert K. "Russian-Georgian Relations, 1917–1921." Russian Institute Essay, Columbia University, 1951.

Klein, David. "The Basmachi: A Case Study in Soviet Policy toward National Minorities." M. A. Thesis, Columbia University, 1952.

Lerner, Warren. "The Russian Plan to Sovietize Poland in 1920." Russian Institute Essay, Columbia University, 1954.

Marin, David P. "Failure in the South: An Account of André Marty, the French Mutiny and Withdrawal from Southern Russia (November, 1918–April, 1919)." Russian Institute Essay, Columbia University, 1950.

Park, Alexander G. "Soviet Nationality Policy, 1917–1927: A Study of Bolshevik Doctrine and Practice with Special Reference to Central Asia." Ph.D. dissertation, Columbia University, 1953.

Priest, L. W. "The Cordon Sanitaire, 1918–1922." Ph.D. dissertation, Stanford University, 1954.

——. "The French Intervention in South Russia, 1918–1919." M.A. thesis, Stanford University, 1947.

Raphael, Joan R. "Russia, America and the Armenian Problem, 1918–1921." Russian Institute Essay, Columbia University, 1948.

Rosenberg, William G. "A. I. Denikin and the Anti-Bolshevik Movement in South Russia." Amherst College Honors Thesis No. 7, 1961.

Sahlin, Margaret. "The Foreign Policy of the Provisional Government, May–November, 1917." Russian Institute Essay, Columbia University, 1958.

Spector, Sherman D. "Rumania at the Paris Peace Conference: A Study of the Diplomacy of Ioan I. C. Bratianu." Ph.D. dissertation, Columbia University, 1960.

Stearns, Muriel. "British Relations with Russia from the Armistice

to the Signing of the Trade Agreement." M.A. thesis, Stanford
University, 1931.
Thompson, John M. "The Russian Problem at the Paris Peace Con-
ference, 1919." Ph.D. dissertation, Columbia University, 1960.
———. "The Proposal for a Conference on the Prinkipo Islands,
1919." Russian Institute Essay, Columbia University, 1949.
Yenish, Joseph. "The Problem of Soviet Russia at the Paris Peace
Conference of 1919." Ph.D. dissertation, Pennsylvania Univer-
sity, 1952.

SELECTED BIBLIOGRAPHY OF PUBLISHED MATERIALS

DOCUMENTS:

The Armenian Question Before the Peace Conference. (Memorandum of the Armenian Delegation in Paris.) Paris: Imp. P. Dupont, 1919.
Azerbaidzhan, Ministry of Foreign Affairs. Le 28 Mai, 1919: Le jour
du premier anniversaire de l'indépendance de la République
d'Azerbaidjan. Baku, 1919. (Hoover Library.)
Bol'sheviki v bor'be za pobedu sotsialisticheskoi revoliutsii v Azerbaidzhane, 1917–1918. Baku: Gosizdat, A.S.S.R., 1957.
Bor'ba za pobedu sovetskoi vlasti v Gruzii: dokumenty i materialy,
1917–1921 gg. Tbilisi: Gosizdat G.S.S.R., 1958.
British Labour Delegation to Russia, 1920: Report. London: Labour
Party, 1920.
Browder, R. P., and Kerensky, A. F. (eds.). The Russian Provisional
Government 1917; Documents. 3 vols. Stanford: Stanford Uni-
versity Press, 1961.
Bunyan, J., and Fisher, H. H. (eds.). The Bolshevik Revolution,
1917–1918. Stanford: Stanford University Press, 1934.
Bunyan, J. (ed.). Intervention, Civil War and Communism in Rus-
sia, April–December, 1918: Documents and Materials. Balti-
more: Johns Hopkins Press, 1936.
Cumming, C. K., and Pettit, W. W. (eds.). Russian-American Rela-
tions, March 1917–March 1920: Documents and Papers. New
York: Harcourt, Brace and Howe, 1920.
Degras, Jane (ed.). Soviet Documents on Foreign Policy. Vol. I.
London: Oxford University Press, 1951.
" 'Demokraticheskoe' pravitel'stvo Gruzii i angliiskoe komandova-
nie," Krasnyi Arkhiv, Vol. XXI, pp. 122–173; Vol. XXV, pp.
96–110. Moscow: Gosizdat, 1927.
"Denezhnye dokumenty Generala Alekseeva," Arkhiv Russkoi Revo-
liutsii, Vol. V. pp. 345–357. Berlin: Izdatel'stvo "Slovo," 1922.

Dokumenty o geroicheskoi oborone Tsaritsyna v 1918 godu. Moscow: Institut Marksa-Engel'sa-Lenina, Gospolitizdat, 1942.

"Dokumenty po istorii chernomorskago flota v marte-iiune 1918 g.," Arkhiv Russkoi Revoliutsii, Vol. XIV, pp. 151–224. Berlin: Izdatel'stvo "Slovo," 1924.

Don Cossack Army, Upravlenie General-kvartirmeistera Donskoi Armii. Ocherk politicheskoi istorii Vsevelikago Voiska Donskogo. Novocherkassk: Obl. V. Voiska Donskogo Tip., 1919. (Hoover Library).

France, Assemblée Nationale. Annales de la chambre des députés, Débats parlementaires, 1917–1921.

France, Ministère de la Guerre, Etat-Major de l'Armée. Les Armées françaises dans la Grande Guerre. Tome VIII, Vol. III. Paris: Imprimerie Nationale, 1934.

Georgia (République de Géorgie). Documents présentés par le gouvernement de la République de Géorgie à la première Assemblée de la Société des nations. London: Williams, Lea and Co., Ltd., 1920.

Georgia, Ministerstvo Vneshnikh Del. Dokumenty i materialy po vneshnei politike Zakavkaz'ia i Gruzii. Tiflis: Tip. Pravitel'stva Gruzinskoi Respubliki, 1919.

Golder, F. A. (ed.). Documents of Russian History, 1914–1917. New York: Century, 1927.

Les gouvernements alliés contre les Soviets: quatre documents. Moscow: Gosizdat, 1918.

Great Britain, Foreign Office. Documents on British Foreign Policy, 1919–1939. First Series. Edited by E. L. Woodward, R. Butler, and J. P. T. Bury. Chiefly Vols. II, III, VII, VIII, XII. London: H. M. Stationery Office, 1949, 1958, 1962. (Cited as Documents on British Policy).

Great Britain. Parliamentary Debates, 5th Series. House of Commons, Vols. CX-CXXXIX.

Great Britain. Parliamentary Papers, 1919. Vol. LIII (Accounts and Papers, Vol. XXII). Cmd. Paper No. 8, "A Collection of Reports on Bolshevism in Russia." London: H. M. Stationery Office, 1919.

Great Britain. Parliamentary Papers, 1920. Vol. XXVIII (Accounts and Papers, Vol. II). Cmd. Paper No. 772, "Statement of Expenditures on Naval and Military Operations in Russia from the Date of the Armistice to the 31st March 1920." London: H. M. Stationery Office, 1920.

Great Britain. Parliamentary Papers, 1923. Vol. XXV (Accounts and Papers, Vol. XIII). Cmd. Paper No. 1846 (Russia No. 1),

"Correspondence Between H. M. Govt. and the Soviet Govt. Respecting the Murder of Mr. C. F. Davison in Jan. 1920." London: H. M. Stationery Office, 1923.

History of the Great War Based on Official Documents: The Campaign in Mesopotamia, 1914–1918. Vol. IV. Compiled by Brig. General F. J. Moberly under the direction of the Historical Section of the Committee of Imperial Defense. London: H. M. Stationery Office, 1927.

Ispoved' Savinkova: protsess Borisa Savinkova. Berlin: Izdanie zhurnala "Russkoe Ekho," 1924.

Iz istorii grazhdanskoi voiny v SSSR: sbornik dokumentov i materialov. 3 vols. Moscow: Institut Marksizma-Leninizma pri TsK KPSS, Izdatel'stvo "Sovetskaia Rossiia," 1960–1961.

Khrystiuk, Paul. *Zamitky i materialy do istorii Ukrains'koi revoliutsii, 1917–1920 gg.* 4 vols. in 2. Vienna: Ukrains'kii Sotsiol'ohichnii Instytut, Drukernia J. N. Vernay, 1921.

Kliuchnikov, I. V., and Sabanin, A. (eds.). *Mezhdunarodnaia politika noveishego vremeni v dogovorakh, notakh i deklaratsiiakh.* Vol. III. Moscow: Litizdat NKID, 1928.

Kroupensky, A. N. (ed.). *L'occupation roumaine en Bessarabie: documents.* Paris: Imp. Lahure, 1920.

Lozinski, N. (ed). *Décisions du Conseil suprème sûr la Galicie orientale; les plus importante documents.* Paris: Bureau Ukrainien, Imp. Robinet Houtain, 1919. (Hoover Library).

Meijer, Jan M. (ed.). *The Trotsky Papers, 1917–1922.* Vol. I. The Hague: Mouton and Co., 1964.

Mints, I. I., and Gorodetskii, E. N. (eds.). *Dokumenty o razgrome germanskikh okkupantov na Ukraine v 1918 godu.* Moscow: Gospolitizdat, 1942.

——. (eds.) *Dokumenty po istorii grazhdanskoi voiny v SSSR.* Vol. I. Moscow: Ogiz, Gospolitizdat, 1940.

——, and Eideman, R. (eds.). *Krakh germanskoi okkupatsii na Ukraine, po dokumentam okkupantov.* Moscow: Ogiz, Istoriia grazhdanskoi voiny, 1936.

——. (ed.). "Vneshniaia politika kontr-revoliutsionnykh 'pravitel'-stv' v nachale 1919 g. iz. dokumentov Parizhskogo posol'stva," *Krasnyi Arkhiv,* Vol. XXXVII, pp. 69–101. Moscow: Gosizdat, 1929.

Mirnye peregovory v Brest-Litovske: polnyi tekst stenogramm. Vol. I. Moscow: Izdatel'stvo NKID, 1920.

Moulis, E., and Bergonier E. (eds.). *En marge du conflict mondial; la guerre entre les alliés et la Russie, 1918–1920; documents.* Paris: Librairie generale de doit et de jurisprudence, Imp. H. Jehan, 1937.

"Organizatsiia vlasti na iuge Rossii v period grazhdanskoi voiny, 1918–1920 gg.: dokumenty," *Arkhiv Russkoi Revoliutsii*, Vol. IV, pp. 241–251. Berlin: Izdatel'stvo "Slovo," G. V. Gessen, 1922.

Partiia v period inostrannoi voennoi interventsii i grazhdanskoi voiny, 1918–1920 gody: dokumenty i materialy. Moscow: Gospolitizdat, 1962.

Petliura, Simon V. Un appel du president Petlioura à la démocratie française (letter to Jean Pelissier, October 22, 1919). (Hoover Library.)

Piontkovskii, S. A. (ed.). *Grazhdanskaia voina v Rossii, 1918–1921 gg: khrestomatiia.* Moscow: Izd. Kom. universiteta im. Ia. M. Sverdlova, 1925.

Pobeda velikoi Oktiabr'skoi sotsialisticheskoi revoliutsii v Turkestane. Tashkent: Gosizdat, USSR, 1947.

Protokoly tsentral'nogo komiteta RSDRP(b), Avgust 1917–Fevral' 1918. Moscow: Institut Marksizma-Leninizma pri TsK KPSS, Gospolitizdat, 1958.

R.S.F.S.R., Commissariat du peuple pour les affaires étrangères. *Correspondance diplomatique se rapportant aux relations entre la République russe et les puissances de l'Entente, 1918.* Moscow: Commissariat du peuple pour les affaires étrangère, 1919.

R.S.F.S.R., Commissariat du peuple pour les affaires étrangères. *Livre rouge: recueil des documents diplomatiques relatifs aux rélations entre la Russie et la Pologne, 1918–1920.* Moscow: Edition d'état, 1920.

R.S.F.S.R., Narodnyi komissariat inostrannykh del. *Sbornik sekretnykh dokumentov iz arkhiva byvshago Ministerstva inostrannykh del.* Petrograd: Gosizdat, 1917. (Hoover Library.)

R.S.F.S.R., Narodnyi komissariat inostrannykh del. *Vestnik*, 1917–1920.

Sed'moi ekstrennyi s"ezd RKP(b), mart 1918 goda; stenograficheskii otchet. Moscow: Institut Marksizma-Leninizma pri TsK KPSS, Gospolitizdat 1962.

Seymour, Charles (ed.). *The Intimate Papers of Colonel House.* Vols. III-IV. New York: Houghton, Mifflin Co., 1926–1928.

Shafir, I. M. (ed.). *Secrets of Menshevik Georgia; the Plot Against Soviet Russia Unmasked: Documents.* London: Communist Party of Great Britain, 1922.

Shliapnikov, A. G. (ed.). *Kto dolzhnik? sbornik dokumentirovannykh statei po voprosu ob otnosheniiakh mezhdu Rossiei, Frantsiei a drugimi derzhavami Antanty.* Moscow: Avioizdat, 1926.

———. (ed.). *Les alliés contre la Russie avant, pendant et après la guerre mondiale: faits et documents.* Paris: A. Delpeuch, 1926. (Essentially the same as *Kto dolzhnik?*)

Shlikhter, A. G. (ed.). Chernaia kniga: sbornik statei i materialov ob interventsii antanty na Ukraine v 1918–1919 gg. Kharkov: Gosizdat Ukrainy, 1925.

Subbotovskii, I. (ed.). Soiuzniki, Russkie reaktsionery i interventsiia; iskliuchitel'no po ofitsial'nym arkhivnym dokumentam Kolchakovskogo pravitel'stva. Leningrad: Vestnik Len. soveta, 1926.

Sumbatov, Prince. Mémoire soumis par le prince Soumbatoff, délégué du gouvernement géorgien, aux représentants des Puissances alliées à Berne au mois de novembre 1918. Paris, 1918. (Hoover Library.)

Tashleva, Sh. (ed.). Turkmenistan v period inostrannoi voennoi interventsii i grazhdanskoi voiny, 1918–1920 gg.: sbornik dokumentov. Ashkhabad: Gosizdat T.S.S.R., 1957.

Tolokonnikov, T. (ed.). Frantsuzskaia burzhuaziia i Iuda Vrangel' (dogovor Frantsii s Vrangelem). Moscow: Gosizdat, 1920.

United States, Department of State. Papers Relating to the Foreign Relations of the United States, 1918, Russia. 3 vols. Washington: Government Printing Office, 1931–1932.

United States, Department of State. Papers Relating to the Foreign Relations of the United States, 1919, Russia. Washington: Government Printing Office, 1937.

United States, Department of State. Papers Relating to the Foreign Relations of the United States, 1919. Vol. II. Washington: Government Printing Office, 1934.

United States, Department of State. Papers Relating to the Foreign Relations of the United States, 1920. Vol. III. Washington: Government Printing Office, 1936.

United States, Department of State. Papers Relating to the Foreign Relations of the United States: The Lansing Papers, 1914–1920. 2 vols. Washington: Government Printing Office, 1939–1940.

United States, Department of State. Papers Relating to the Foreign Relations of the United States: The Paris Peace Conference, 1919. 13 vols. Washington: Government Printing Office, 1942–1947.

United States, Department of State, Russian Series, No. 3. Documents Relating to the Organization and Purpose of the Anti-Bolshevik Forces in Russia. Washington: Government Printing Office, 1919.

U.S.S.R., Komissiia po izdaniiu diplomaticheskikh dokumentov pri MID SSSR. Dokumenty vneshnei politiki SSSR. Vols. I–III (November 1917–March 1921.) Moscow: Gospolitizdat, 1957–1959.

Varneck, Elena, and Fisher, H. H. (eds.). The Testimony of Kolchak and Other Siberian Materials. Stanford: Stanford University Press, 1935.

Velikaia Oktiabr'skaia sotsialisticheskaia revoliutsiia i pobeda Sovet-
skoi vlasti v Armenii. Erevan: Gosizdat ASSR, 1957.
Volunteer Army (Dobrovol'cheskaia Armiia). Kratkaia zapiska istorii
vzaimootnoshenii Dobrovol'cheskoi armii s Ukrainoi. Rostov-
on-Don: Tip. "Donskogo akts. o-va. pech. i izd. dela," 1919.
(Hoover Library.)
Volunteer Army, General Staff of the Armed Forces of South Russia.
Ocherk' vzaimootnoshenii vooruzhennykh sil' Iuga Rossii i predstavitelei frantsuzskago komandovaniia. (The "Orange Book.")
Ekaterinodar: Volunteer Army, 1919. (Columbia University Rus-
sian Archive.) Also published in Arkhiv Russkoi Revoliutsii, Vol.
XVI, pp. 233–262. Berlin: Izdatel'stvo "Slovo," G. V. Gessen,
1925.
Volunteer Army. Sobranie uzakonenii i rasporiazhenii previtel'stva.
2 vols. Rostov-on-Don: Osobym Soveshchaniem pri Glavnokom-
anduiushchem Vooruzhennymi Silami na Iuge Rossii, 1918–
1919. (Hoover Library.)
Volunteer Army. The Voluntary Army as a National Factor in the
Renaissance of Great Russia, One and Indivisible. Ekaterinodar:
Volunteer Army, 1919. (Hoover Library.)
Voronovich, N. (ed.). Zelenaia kniga: sbornik materialov i dokumen-
tov. Istoriia krest'ianskago dvizheniia v Chernomorskoi gubernii.
Prague: Izdanie Chernomorskoi Krest'ianskoi Delegatsii, 1921.
West Ukrainian People's Republic. The Book of Bloody Cruelties:
Returns Concerning the Invasion of the Poles into the Ukrainian
Territory of Galicia in 1918–1919. Vienna: H. Engel and Son,
1919. (Hoover Library.)
Zeman, Z. A. B. (ed.). Germany and the Revolution in Russia, 1915–
1918: Documents from the Archives of the German Foreign
Ministry. London: Oxford University Press, 1958.

BOOKS:

Adams, A. E. Bolsheviks in the Ukraine, The Second Campaign,
1918–1919. New Haven: Yale University Press, 1963.
Alekseev, S. A. (ed.). Denikin, Iudenich, Vrangel. Moscow: Gosizdat, 1927.
———. (ed.). Nachalo grazhdanskoi voiny. Moscow: Gosizdat, 1926.
———. (ed.). Revoliutsiia na Ukraine po memuaram belykh. Moscow: Gosizdat, 1930.
Aleksandrov, Ia. Belye dni. Berlin: Grad "Kitezh," 1922.
Aleskerov, Ia. Interventsiia i grazhdanskaia voina v srednei Azii. Tashkent: Gosizdat USSR, 1959.
Allen, W. E. D., and Muratoff, Paul. Caucasian Battlefields: A. His-

tory of the Wars on the Turco-Caucasian Border, 1828–1921. Cambridge: Cambridge University Press, 1953.

Allen, W. E. D. The Ukraine. Cambridge: Cambridge University Press, 1940.

Anishev, A. Ocherki istorii grazhdanskoi voiny, 1917–1920. Leningrad: Gosizdat, 1925.

Al'f I. (Seimovich, I.) et al. Antanta i Vrangel: sbornik statei. Moscow: Gosizdat, 1923.

Antonov-Ovseenko, V. A. Zapiski o grazhdanskoi voine. 4 vols. Moscow: Gosvoenizdat, 1924–1933.

Arkomed, S. T. Materialy po istorii otpadeniia Zakavkaz'ia ot Rossii. Tiflis: Krasnaia Kniga, 1923.

Arshinov, P. A. Istoriia Makhnovskogo dvizheniia, 1918–1921. Berlin: Gruppa russkikh anarkhistov v Germanii, 1923. (L'histoire du mouvement makhnoviste, 1918–1921. Paris: Éditions Anarchistes, Librairie Internationale, 1924.)

Atlas, M. L. Bor'ba za sovety: ocherki po istorii sovetov v Krymu v 1919 g. Simferopol: Krymgosizdat, 1933.

Avakian, V. L. Inostrannaia interventsiia v Zakavkaz'i v 1918. Erevan: Erevan University, 1954.

Avalov (Avalishvili), Z. D. The Independence of Georgia in International Politics, 1918–1921. London: Headley Bros., 1940.

Azan, Paul Jean Louis. Franchet d'Esperey. Paris: Flammarion, 1949.

Babakhodzhaev, A. Kh. Proval angliiskoi agressivnoi politiki v Srednei Azii, 1917–1920. Tashkent: Gosizdat USSR, 1955.

Bailey, F. M. Mission to Tashkent. London: J. Cape, 1946.

Balabanoff, Angelica. My Life as a Rebel. London: E. Hamilton, 1938.

Bammate, Haider, The Caucasus Problem: Questions Concerning Circassia and Daghestan. Berne: Staempfli et Cie., 1919.

———. Le Caucase et la révolution russe. Paris: Union Nationale des Emigrés de la République du Caucase du Nord, 1929.

Bazhanov, B. (ed.). Pokhishchenie generala A. P. Kutepova bol'shevikami. Paris: no pub., 1930.

Bechhofer-Roberts, C. E. In Denikin's Russia and the Caucasus, 1919–1920. London: W. Collin's Sons and Co., Ltd. 1921.

Belenky, S., and Manvelov, A. The 1917 Revolution in Azerbaidjan. Baku: Azerbaidjan Istpart, 1927.

Beliaevskii, V. A. Pravda o gen. Denikine: prichiny prekrashcheniia belogo dvizheniia na iuge Rossii v 1920 g. San Francisco: no pub., 1959.

Benegin, M. F. Revoliutsiia i grazhdanskaia voina v Krymu. Simferopol: Krymgosizdat, 1927.

Beneš, Edvard. *My War Memoirs*. Translated by Paul Selver. Boston: Houghton, 1928.

Bertie, F. L. *The Diary of Lord Bertie of Thame, 1914–1918.* 2 vols. Edited by Lady Algernon Gordon Lennox. London: Hodder and Stoughton, 1924.

Blacker, L. V. S. *On Secret Patrol in High Asia.* London: John Murray, 1922.

Blair, Dorian, and Dand, C. H. *Russian Hazard: The Adventures of a British Secret Service Agent in Russia.* London: Robert Hale, 1937.

Bochagov, A. K. *Milli Firka; natsionalnaia kontr-revoliutsiia v Krymu.* Simferopol: Krymgosizdat, 1930.

Borian, B. A. *Armenia, mezhdunarodnaia diplomatiia i SSSR.* 2 vols. Moscow: Gosizdat, 1928.

Borisenko, I. *Sovetskie respubliki na Severnom Kavkaze v 1918 godu.* 2 vols. Rostov-on-Don: Gosizdat, 1930.

Borshchak, Il'ko. *L'Ukraine à la conference de la paix, 1919–1923.* Paris: no pub., 1938.

Bradley, J. F. N. *La legion tchecoslovaque en Russie, 1914–1920.* Paris: Centre National de la Recherche Scientifique, 1965.

Brun, A. H. *Troublous Times: Experiences in Bolshevik Russia and Turkestan.* London: Constable and Co., Ltd., 1931.

Bubnov, A. S., Kamenev, S. S., and Eideman, R. P. (eds.). *Grazhdanskaia voina, 1918–1921.* 3 vols. Moscow: Gosizdat, "Voennyi Vestnik," 1928–1930.

Buchan, John (ed.). *The Baltic and Caucasian States.* Boston: Houghton, Mifflin Co., 1923.

Buchanan, Sir George. *My Mission to Russia and Other Diplomatic Memories.* 2 vols. London: Cassell and Co., Ltd., 1923.

Budennyi, S. M. *Proidennyi put'.* 2 vols. Moscow: Voennoe izdatel'stvo, 1965.

Buiskii, A. *Bor'ba za Krym i razgrom Vrangelia.* Moscow: Gosizdat, 1928.

Bullitt, W. C. *The Bullitt Mission to Russia.* New York: R. W. Heubach, 1919.

Bystrianskii, V. A. *Antanta, Rossiia i revoliutsiia.* Petrograd: Gosizdat, 1920.

———. *Iz istorii grazhdanskoi voiny v Rossii.* Petrograd: Gosizdat, 1921.

Cambon, Paul. *Correspondance, 1870–1924.* Vol. III (1912–1924). Paris: Editions Bernard Grasset, 1946.

Carr, E. H. *The Bolshevik Revolution, 1917–1923.* Vol. III. London: Macmillan Co., 1953.

Chaikin, V. *K istorii rossiiskoi revoliutsii: Kazan 26 Bakinskikh Komissarev.* Moscow: Z. Grzhebin, 1922.

Chamberlin, W. H. *The Russian Revolution.* 2 vols. New York: Macmillan Co., 1935.

―――. *The Ukraine: A Submerged Nation.* New York: Macmillan Co., 1944.

Chebaevskii, F. V. *Razgrom vtorogo pokhoda Antanty.* Moscow: Znanie, 1952.

Chernov, V. *The Great Russian Revolution.* Translated and abridged by P. E. Mosely. New Haven: Yale University Press, 1936.

Chicherin, G. V. *Stat'i i rechi po voprosam mezhdunarodnoi politiki.* Moscow: Izdatel'stvo sotsial'no-ekonomicheskoi literatury, 1961.

―――. *Two Years of Foreign Policy: The Relations of the Russian Socialist Federal Soviet Republic with Foreign Nations from November 7, 1917, to November 7, 1919.* New York: Russian Soviet Government Bureau, 1920.

Chikalenko, Eugene. *Spohadi.* Vols. II and III. Lvov: no pub., 1925–1926.

Churchill, W. S. *The World Crisis: The Aftermath.* London: Thornton Butterworth, Ltd., 1929.

Clemenceau, Georges. *Grandeurs et misères d'une victoire.* Paris: Librairie Plon, 1930.

Coates, W. P. and Zelda K. *Armed Intervention in Russia, 1918–1922.* London: V. Gollancz, Ltd., 1935.

Coates, W. P. and Zelda K. *A History of Anglo-Soviet Relations.* London: Lawrence and Wishart, The Pilot Press, 1944.

Coen, Antonio. *La vérité sûr l'affaire Sadoul.* Paris: Comité pour la défense de Jacques Sadoul, 1919.

Dan, F. *Dva goda skitanii, 1919–1921.* Berlin: no pub., 1922.

Davatts, V. K. *Gody: ocherki piatiletnei bor'by.* Belgrade: no pub., 1926.

Deborin, G. A. *Sovetskaia vneshniaia politika v pervye gody sushchestvovaniia sovetskogo gosudarstva, 1917–1920 gg.* Moscow: Izdatel'stvo Pravda, 1951.

Delert, D. *Don v ogne.* Rostov-on-Don: no pub., 1927.

Denikin, A. I. *Kto spas' sovetskuiu vlast' ot gibeli.* Paris: Izdanie Soiuz' Dobrovol'tsev, 1937.

―――. *Ocherki russkoi smuty.* 5 vols. Berlin: Russkoe Natsional'noe Knigoizdatel'stvo "Slovo"; and Paris: J. Povolozky et Cie., 1921–1926.

―――. *The Russian Turmoil.* London: Hutchinson and Co., 1922.

―――. *The White Army.* Translated by Catherine Zvegintzov. London: J. Cape and Co., 1930.

————. *World Events and the Russian Problem.* Paris: Imprimerie Rapide, 1939.

Denisov, S. V. (ed.). *Belaia Rossiia.* New York: Izdatel'stvo glavnago pravleniia zarubezhnago soiuza Russkikh voennikh invalidov, 1937.

————. *Zapiski: grazhdanskaia voina na iuge Rossii, 1918–1919 gg.* Constantinople: Izdanie avtora, 1921.

Deutscher, I. *The Prophet Armed: Trotsky: 1879–1921.* New York: Oxford University Press, 1954.

Devdariana, G. *Dni gospodstva men'shevikov v Gruzii: dokumenty i materialy.* Tiflis: Gosizdat Gruzii, 1931.

Deygas, F. J. *L'Armée d'Orient dans la guerre mondiale, 1915–1919.* Paris: Payot, 1932.

Dimanshtein, S. M. (ed.). *Revoliutsiia i natsional'nyi vopros.* Vol. III. Moscow: Gosizdat, 1930.

Dnistrianskii, S. *Ukraina and the Peace Conference.* Berlin: Ukrainian Delegation, 1919.

Dobrynin, V. *La lutte contre le bolchevisme dans la Russie meriodionale; participation des Cosaques du Don à la lutte, Mars 1917–Mars 1920.* Prague: Imprimerie "Melantrich," 1920. (Also in Russian: *Bor'ba s bol'shevizmom na iuge Rossii: uchastie v bor'be donskogo kazachestva.* Prague: Slavianskoe Izdatel'stvo, 1921.)

Dobrzhinskii, G. V. *Osvobozhdenie Kryma.* Moscow: Vsesoiuznoe obshchestvo politikatorzhan i ssyl'no-poselentsev, 1932.

Dolenga, S. *Skoropadshchyna.* Warsaw: M. Kunytskyi (Nakladom Modesta Kunits'kogo), 1934.

Dolgorukov, P. D. (Prince). *Natsional'naia politika i partiia narodnoi svobody.* Rostov-on-Don: Osvag, 1919.

Donohoe, M. H. *With the Persian Expedition.* London: Edward Arnold, 1919.

Doroshenko, D. *Istoriia Ukrainy, 1917–1923 gg.* 2 vols. Uzhgorod: Nakladom d-ra Osipa Tsiupki, 1930–1932.

————. *Moi spomyny pro nedavne-mynule, 1914–1918.* 4 vols. Lvov: Chervona Kolnya, 1923–1924.

Dotsenko, Oleksandr. *Litopys Ukrains'koi revoliutsii.* Vol. I. Kiev: Nakladom avtora, 1923.

Drabkina, E. *Gruzinskaia kontr-revoliutsiia.* Leningrad: Priboi, 1928.

Drozdovskii, M. G. *Dnevnik.* Berlin: Knigoizdatel'stvo Otto Kirkher, 1923.

Dubreuil, Charles. *Deux années en Ukraine, 1917–1919.* Paris: Paulin, 1919.

Dumbadze, V. D. *The Caucasian Republics.* New York: F. Hubner Co., 1925.

Dunsterville, L. C. *The Adventures of Dunsterforce.* London: Edward Arnold, 1920.

Efremoff, I. N. *The Cossacks of the Don.* Paris: Imp. L. Fournier, 1919.

Egorov, A. I. *Razgrom Denikina, 1919.* Moscow: Gosvoenizdat, 1931.

Eideman, R., and Kakurin, N. *Hromadians'ka Viina na Ukraine.* Kharkov: Derzhavne vidavnitstvo Ukraini, 1928.

Ellis, C. H. *The British "Intervention" in Transcaspia, 1918–1919.* Berkeley: University of California Press, 1963.

Enukidze, D. E. *Krakh imperialisticheskoi interventsii v Zakavkaz'i.* Tiflis: Gosizdat G.S.S.R., 1954.

Erde, D. *Godi buri i natiska.* Kharkov: Gosizdat Ukraini, 1923.

Etherton, P. T. *In the Heart of Asia.* London: Constable and Co., 1925.

Evain, Emmanuel. *La problème de l'indépendance de l'Ukraine et la France.* Paris: F. Alcan, 1931.

Filippov, N. *Ukrainskaia kontr-revoliutsiia na sluzhbe u Anglii, Frantsii i Pol'shi.* Moscow: Moskovskii Rabochii, 1927.

Fischer, Louis. *Oil Imperialism: the International Struggle for Petroleum.* New York: International Publishers, 1926.

———. *The Soviets in World Affairs.* 2 vols. Princeton: Princeton University Press, 1951.

Fleming, Peter. *The Fate of Admiral Kolchak.* New York: Harcourt, Brace and World, 1963.

Footman, David. *Civil War in Russia.* London: Faber and Faber, Ltd., 1961.

———. (ed.). *Soviet Affairs. Number Two.* St. Anthony's Papers, Number Six. New York: Praeger, 1959.

Franchet d'Esperey, L. F. M. F. *Histoire militaire et navale de la nation française: la grande guerre, 1914–1918.* Vol. VIII of *Histoire de la nation française,* edited by G. Hanotaux. Paris: Plon-Nourrit et Cie., 1927.

Francis, D. *Russia From the American Embassy.* New York: Scribner, 1921.

French, F. J. F. *From Whitehall to the Caspian.* London: Odhams Press, Ltd., 1920.

Galoian, G. A. *Proval kontr-revoliutsionnoi interventsii angliiskikh i amerikanskikh imperialistov v Armenii, 1917–1920.* Moscow: Gosizdat, 1955.

Ganetskii, Iakov S. *Angliiskii imperializm i SSSR.* Moscow: Gosizdat, 1927.

General Kutepov: sbornik statei. Paris: Izdanie komiteta imeni generala Kutepova, Imp. d'art france-russe, 1934.

Gleichen, E. (ed.). *The Baltic and Caucasian States*. Boston: Houghton-Mifflin Co., 1923.

Gollin, A. M. *Proconsul in Politics: A Study of Lord Milner in Opposition and in Power*. New York: Macmillan Co., 1964.

Golovin, N. N. *Rossiiskaia kontr-revoliutsiia v 1917–1918 gg*. 5 vols. Paris: Biblioteka "Illiustrirovannoi Rossii," 1937.

Golubev, A. (ed.). *Perekop i Chongar*. Moscow: Gosvoenizdat, 1933.

——. *Shturm Perekopa*. Moscow: Izdatel'stvo TsK VLKSM, Molodaia gvardiia, 1938.

——. *Vrangelevskie desanti na Kubani, Avgust-Sentiabr', 1920*. Moscow: Gosizdat, 1929.

Gooch, G. P., and Ward, A. W. (eds.). *The Cambridge History of British Foreign Policy, 1783–1919*. Vol. III. Cambridge: Cambridge University Press, 1923.

Goode, W. T. *Is Intervention in Russia a Myth?* London: Williams and Norgate, Ltd., 1931.

Gor'kii, A. M. (ed.). *Zhenshchina v grazhdanskoi voine: episody bor'by na Severnom Kavkaze v 1917–1920 gg*. Moscow: Gosizdat "Istoriia grazhdanskoi voiny," 1937.

Graubard, S. R. *British Labour and the Russian Revolution, 1917–1924*. Cambridge: Harvard University Press, 1956.

Grenard, F. *La révolution russe*. Paris: A. Colin, 1933.

Gukovskii, A. I. *Antanta i oktiabr'skaia revoliutsiia*. Moscow: Gosudarstvennoe sotsial'no-ekonomicheskoe izdatel'stvo, 1931.

——. *Frantsuzskaia interventsiia na iuge Rossii, 1918–1919*. Moscow: Gosudarstvennoe sotsial'no-ekonomicheskoe izdatel'stvo, 1928.

——. (ed.). *Lenin ob interventsii*. Moscow: Ogiz "Mosk. rabochii," Tip. "Krasnyi proletarii," 1931.

——. Malakhovskii, V., and Melikov, V., (eds.). *Razgrom Vrangelia, 1920: sbornik statei*. Moscow: Gosvoenizdat, 1930.

Gul, R. *Ledianoi pokhod*. Berlin: no pub., 1921.

Gusev-Orenburgskii, S. I. *Kniga o evreiskikh pogromakh na Ukraine v 1919*. Petrograd: Z. Grzhebin, n. d.

Haumant, Emile. *Le problème de l'unité russe*. Paris: Editions Bossard, 1922.

Hayit, Baymirza. *Turkestan im XX Jahrhundert*. Darmstadt: C. W. Leske Verlag, 1956.

Heifetz, Elias. *The Slaughter of the Jews in the Ukraine in 1919*. New York: Seltzer, 1921.

Hill, G. A. *Go Spy the Land: Being the Adventures of I. K. 8 of the British Secret Service*. London: Cassell, 1932.

Hippeau, E. G. *Les républiques du Caucase: Géorgie-Azerbaidjan.* Paris: Editions E. Leroux, 1920.

Hodgson, J. *With Denikin's Armies.* London: L. Williams Co., Ltd., 1932.

Hoffmann, M. *War Diaries and Other Papers.* 2 vols. London: Martin Secker, 1929.

Iakushkin, E. E., and Polunin, S. *Angliiskaia interventsiia v 1918–1920 gg.* Moscow: Gosizdat, 1928.

Iakushkin, E. E. *Frantsuzskaia interventsiia na iuge, 1918–1919.* Moscow: Gosizdat, 1929.

Ianchevskii, N. L., *Grazhdanskaia bor'ba na severnom Kavkaze.* Rostov-on-Don: Gosizdat, 1927.

Iaroslavskii, E., and Radek, K. *Delo Borisa Savinkova: ispoved', protsess, i sbornik statei.* Moscow: Gosizdat, (1924?).

Ignat'ev, V. *Nekotorye fakti i itogi chetirekh let grazhdanskoi voiny, 1917–1921.* Moscow: Gosizdat, 1922.

Ilovaiskii, V. *God puti: zhizn' Dobrovol'cheskoi armii.* Rostov-on-Don: Tip. "Obnovlenie," 1919.

Ioffe, Ia. *Organizatsiia interventsii i blokady Sovetskoi respubliki, 1918–1920.* Moscow: Gosizdat, Otdel voennoi literatury, 1930.

Ishkhanian, B. *Kontr-revoliutsiia v Zakavkaz'i.* Baku: Tip. "Truzhenik" Prikaspiiskogo soiuza "Kooperatsiia," 1919.

Ispoved' Savinkova: protsess Borisa Savinkova, Avgust 1924. Berlin: Izdanie zhurnala "Russkoe Ekho," 1924.

Ivanis, Vasil'. *Stezhkami zhittia: spohadi.* Vols. II and III. Neu-Ulm: "Ukrainski Visti," 1959.

Ivashin, I. F., and Zuev, F. G. *Mezhdunarodnye otnosheniia v period provedeniia velikoi Oktiabr'skoi sotsialisticheskoi revoliutsii: vneshniaia politika sovetskogo gosudarstva v gody inostrannoi voennoi interventsii i grazhdanskoi voiny.* Moscow: Vyshaia partiinaia shkola pri TsK KPSS, 1955.

Jeanneret, P. *En campagne contre les Bolcheviks.* Lausanne: Bibliothèque Universelle et Revue Suisse, 1919.

Kadishev, A. B. *Interventsiia i grazhdanskaia voina v Zakavkaz'i.* Moscow: Gosizdat, 1960.

Kakhovskaia, I. K. *Souvenirs d'une révolutionnaire.* Translated by M. Livane and J. Newman. Paris: F. Rieder et Cie., 1926.

Kakurin, N. *Kak srazhalas' revoliutsiia.* 2 vols. Moscow: Gosizdat, 1925.

Kalinin, I. M. *Pod znamenem Vrangelia.* Leningrad: Rabochee izdatel'stvo "Priboi," 1925.

———. *Russkaia vandeia.* Moscow: Gosizdat, 1926.

Kalvari, M. A. *Interventsiia v Krymu.* Simferopol: Krymgosizdat, 1930.

Kandidov, B. P. *Religioznaia kontr-revoliutsiia 1918–1920 gg. i inter-ventsiia: ocherki i materialy.* Moscow: Izdatel'stvo obshchestva "Bezbozhnik," 1930.

Kantorovich, V. A. *Frantsuzy v Odesse.* Petrograd: Biblioteka Izda-tel'stva "Byloe," 1922.

Kapustianskyi, M. *Pokhid ukrains'kykh armii na Kyiv-Odesu v 1919 rotsi.* 2 vols. Munich: "Khvil'ovogo," 1946.

Karibi. *Krasnaia kniga.* Tiflis: Gruz. tov. pechati, 1920.

Kashen (Cachin), M. *Frantsiia organizator interventsii.* Moscow: Ogiz "Mosk. rabochii" tip. izdatel'stvo "Der emes," 1931.

Kautsky, Karl. *Georgia, a Social-democratic Peasant Republic.* Trans-lated by H. J. Stenning. London: International Bookshops, Ltd., 1921.

Kazemadeh, F. *The Struggle for Transcaucasia, 1917–1921.* New York: Philosophical Library, 1951.

Kazimirski, K. M. *Bor'ba imperialisticheskoi Anglii s Respublikoi Sovetov.* Kharkov: "Proletarii," 1927.

K desiatiletiiu interventsii: sbornik statei. Moscow: Gosizdat, Obsh-chestvo sodeistviia zhertvam interventsii, 1929.

Kennan, G. F. *Russia and the West Under Lenin and Stalin.* Bos-ton: Atlantic-Little, Brown and Co., 1960.

———. *Soviet-American Relations, 1917–1920.* 2 vols. Vol. I: *Russia Leaves the War.* Princeton: Princeton University Press, 1956. Vol. II: *The Decision to Intervene.* Princeton: Princeton Uni-versity Press, 1958.

Kerenskii, A. F. *The Catastrophe: Kerensky's Own Story of the Rus-sian Revolution.* New York: D. Appleton, 1927.

———. *The Crucifixion of Liberty.* New York: John Day, 1934.

———. *The Prelude to Bolshevism: The Kornilov Rebellion.* London: T. Fisher Unwin, 1919.

Kerzhentzev, P. M. *Les alliés et la Russie.* Moscow: Edition du Groupe Communiste Française, 1919.

Khrystiuk, P. (ed.). *Zamitky i materialy do istorii urkrains'koi revoliut-sii.* 4 vols. in two. Vienna: Ukrains'kii-Sotsiol'ohichnii Instytut, Drukernia J. N. Vernay, 1920–21.

Khovanskaia, A. S. *Vosstanie frantsuzskogo flota na chernom more.* Moscow: Gosizdat, 1929.

Kin, D. *Denikinshchina.* Leningrad: "Priboi," 1927.

Kirimal, E. *Der Nationale Kampf der Krimtuerken, mit besonderer Beruecksichtigung der Jahre 1917–1918.* Emstetten: Verlag Lechte, 1952.

Kiritchesco, C. *La Roumanie dans la guerre mondiale, 1916–1919.* Translated by L. Barral. Paris: Payot, 1934.

Kluev, L. *Bor'ba za Tsartisyn.* Moscow: Gosizdat, 1928.

Knox, Sir Alfred W. F. *With the Russian Army, 1914–1917.* 2 vols. London: Hutchinson and Co., Ltd., 1921.

Komarnicki, Titus. *Rebirth of the Polish Republic.* London: W. Heinemann, 1957.

Konovalets, Eugene. *Prychynky do istorii ukrains'koi revoliutsii.* 2nd ed. N. p.: no pub., 1948.

Korff, S. A. *The Constitution of the Cossacks.* Paris: L. Fournier, 1919.

Korostovetz, V. *Seed and Harvest.* Translated and abridged by Dorothy Lumby. London: Faber and Faber, Ltd., 1931.

Korotkov, I. S. *Razgrom Vrangelia.* Moscow: Voennoe Izdatel'stvo Minsterstva vooruzhennykh sil, 1948.

Kouchnire (Kushnir), M. *L'Ukraine, l'Europe orientale et la conférence de la paix.* Paris: Bureau de presse Ukrainien, 1919.

Kovtiukh, E. *Ot Kubani do Volgi i obratno.* Moscow: Gosvoenizdat, 1926.

Krasnov, P. N. *Kazach'ia "samostiinost'."* Berlin: "Dvuglavyi Orel," 1921.

Kritskii, M. A. *Kornilovskii udarnyi polk'.* Paris: Imp. "Val," 1936.

Kroupensky, A. N. *The Rumanian Occupation in Bessarabia.* Paris: Imp. Lahure, 1920.

Kutiakov, I. *Razgrom Uralskoi beloi Kazachei armii.* Moscow: Gosvoenizdat, 1931.

La Chesnais, P. G. *The Defense of the Cossacks Against Bolshevism.* Paris: L. Fournier, 1919.

———. *Les peuples de la Transcaucasie pendant la guerre et devant la paix.* Paris: Editions Bossard, 1921.

Ladokh, G. *Ocherki grazhdanskoi voiny na Kubani.* Krasnodar: Burevestnik, 1923.

von Lampe, A. A. (ed.). *Beloe delo; letopis' beloi bor'by.* 7 vols. Berlin: Russkoe natsional'noe knigoizdatel'stvo, "Mednyi Vsadnik," 1926–1928.

———. (ed.). *Glavnokomanduiushchii russkoi armiei general baron P. N. Vrangel: sbornik statei.* Berlin: Knigoizdatel'stvo "Mednyi Vsadnik." 1938.

———. *Prichiny neudachi vooruzhennago vystupleniia belykh.* Berlin: Otdel'nvi ottish iz zhurnala "Russkii Kolokol'," 1929.

Laserson, Max. M. *The Curzon Line.* New York: Carnegie Endowment for International Peace, 1944.

Lenczowski, G. *The Middle East in World Affairs.* 2nd ed. Ithaca: Cornell University Press, 1956.

———. *Russia and the West in Iran, 1918–1948: A Study in Big-Power Rivalry.* Ithaca: Cornell University Press, 1949.

Lenin, V. I. *Lenin o vneshnei politike sovetskogo gosudarstva*. Moscow: Institut Marksizma-Leninizma pri TsK KPSS, Gospolitizdat, 1960.
———. *Ob inostrannoi voennoi interventsii i grazhdanskoi voine v SSSR, 1918–1920 gg*. Moscow: Gospolitizdat, 1956.
———. *Polnoe sobranie sochinenii*. 5th edition. 55 vols. Moscow: Institut Marksizma-Leninizma pri TsK KPSS, Gospolitizdat, 1960–1966.
———. *Vse na bor'bu s Denikinym*. Moscow: Partiinoe Izdat., 1935.
Levidov, M. *K istorii soiuznoi interventsii v Rossii*. Vol. I. Leningrad: Rabochee Izdatel'stvo "Priboi," 1925.
Lipatov, N. P. *1920 god na Chernom More; voenno-morskie sily v razgrome Vrangelia*. Moscow: Gosvoenizdat, 1958.
Lishin, N. N. *Na Kaspiiskom more: god beloi bor'by*. Prague: Izdanie Morskogo zhurnala, 1938.
Lisovoi, Ia. M. (ed.). *Belyi arkhiv: sborniki materialov po istorii i literature voiny, revoliutsii, bol'shevizma, belago dvizheniia i t. p.* 3 vols. Paris: no pub., 1926–1928.
Liubimov, N. N. *SSSR i Frantsiia*. Leningrad: Rabochee Izdatel'stvo "Priboi," 1926.
Lloyd George, D. *The Truth About the Peace Treaties*. Vol. I. London: V. Gollancz, Ltd., 1938.
———. *The War Memoirs of David Lloyd George*. Vols. III-VI. Boston: Little, Brown and Co., 1933–1934.
———. *Memoirs of the Peace Conference*. Vol. I. New Haven: Yale University Press, 1939.
Lobanov-Rostovskii, A. *The Grinding Mill: Reminiscences of War and Revolution in Russia, 1913–1920*. New York: Macmillan Co., 1935.
Lockhart, R. H. Bruce. *Jan Masaryk, a Personal Memoir*. New York: Philosophical Library, 1951.
———. *Memoirs of a British Agent*. London: Putnam, 1932.
Loginov, P. N. (ed.). *Interventsiia i vnutrenniaia kontr-revoliutsiia, 1917–1918*. Moscow: Fabrik "Diafoto," 1932.
Loris-Melikof, J. *La révolution russe et les nouvelles républiques transcaucasiennes*. Paris: F. Alcan, 1920.
Lotots'kii, A. I. *Simon Petliura*. Warsaw: Nakladom Komitetu dlia vshanuvannia X richnitsi smerti Simona Petliury, 1936.
———. *Storinki minuloho*. Vols. II-III. Warsaw: Pratsi Ukrains'kogo naukovogo institutu, 1933–1934.
Lozyns'kii, M. *Halichina v rokakh 1918–1920*. Vienna: no pub., 1922.
von Ludendorff, Erich. *Ludendorff's Own Story: August 1914–November 1918*. 2 vols. New York: Harper and Brothers, 1919.

Lukomskii, A. S. *Memoirs of the Russian Revolution*. Translated and abridged by Olga Vitali. London: T. F. Unwin, Ltd., 1922.
————. *Vospominaniia*. 2 vols. Berlin: Otto Kirchner, 1922.
L'vov, G. E. *A nos frères ainés!* Paris: Edition de l'Union, 1919.
Lykholat, A. V. *Razgrom natsionalisticheskoi kontrrevoliutsii na Ukraine, 1917–1922 gg.* Moscow: Gospolitizdat, 1954.
Machray, Robert. *The Poland of Pilsudski*. London: George Allen and Unwin, Ltd., 1936.
Maillard, M. *Le problème russe; le mensonge de l'Ukraine separatiste: notes d'un témoin*. Paris: Imp. Berger-Levrault, 1919.
Maiskii, I. M. *Demokraticheskaia kontr-revoliutsiia*. Moscow: Gosizdat, 1923.
————. *Vneshniaia politika RSFSR, 1917–1921*. Moscow: Gosizdat, 1923.
Makarov, P. V. *Ad"iutant General Mai-Maievskogo; iz vospominanii nachal'nika otriada krasnykh partizan v Krymu*. Leningrad: Rabochee Izdatel'stvo "Priboi," 1929.
Makharadze, F. *Sovety i bor'ba za sovetskuiu vlast' v Gruzii, 1917–1921*. Tiflis: Gosizdat SSRG, 1928.
Makhno, Nester I. *Pod udarami kontr-revoliutsii*. Paris: Izdanie komiteta N. Makhno, 1936.
————. *Russkaia revoliutsiia na Ukraine, ot marta 1917 po aprel 1918*. Paris: Izdanie komiteta N. Makhno, 1929.
————. *Ukrainskaia revoliutsiia*. Paris: Izdanie komiteta N. Makhno, 1937.
Makhrov, P. *Kto i pochemu mog' pokhitet' gen. Kutopova i gen. Millera?* Paris: no pub., 1937.
Maklakov, V. A. *Rechi, sudebniia, dumskiia i publichniia lektsii, 1904–1926*. Paris: Izdanie Iubileinago komiteta, 1949.
Makoshin, R. *Chto sdelala Dobrovol'cheskaia armiia*. Rostov-on-Don: Osvag, 1919.
Malchevskii, I. S. (ed.). *Vserossiiskoe uchreditel'noe sobranie*. Moscow: Gosizdat, 1930.
Mannerheim, Carl. *The Memoirs of Marshal Mannerheim*. Translated by Count Eric Lawenhaupt. London: Cassell and Co., Ltd., 1953.
Mantoux, Paul. *Les délibérations du Conseil des Quatre (24 Mars–28 Juin 1919)*. 2 vols. Paris: Editions du Centre National de la Recherche Scientifique, 1955.
————. *Paris Peace Conference, 1919*. Geneva: Droz, 1964.
Marchand, René. *Why I Support Bolshevism*. London: British Socialist Party, n.d.
Margolin, A. D. *From a Political Diary: Russia, the Ukraine and*

America, 1905–1945. New York: Columbia University Press, 1946.

———. Ukraina i politika antanty. Berlin: Izdatel'stvo S. Efron, 1921.

Margulies, M. S. God interventsii. 3 vols. Berlin: Izdatel'stvo Z. I. Grzhebina (Z. J. Grschebin Verlag), 1923.

Margulies, Vladimir. Ognennye gody: materialy i dokumenty po istorii grazhdanskoi voiny na iuge Rossii. Berlin: Izdatel'stvo "Manfred," 1923.

Markhlevskii, Iulian. Ocherki istorii Pol'shi. Moscow: Gosundarstvennoe Sotsial'no-Ekonomicheskoe Izdatel'stvo, 1931.

———. Voina i mir mezhdu burzhuaznoi Pol'shei i proletarskoi Rossiei. Moscow: Gosizdat, 1921.

Marty, André P. The Epic of the Black Sea Revolt. New York: Workers' Library Publishers, 1941. (La révolte de la mer noire. Paris: Bureau d'Éditions, 1932.)

Masaryk, Tomas G. The Making of a State, Memoirs and Observations, 1914–1918. London: G. Allen and Unwin, Ltd., 1927.

Maynard, C. C. M. The Murmansk Venture, 1918–1919. London: Hodder and Stoughton, Ltd., 1928.

Mekler, N. V denikinskom podpol'e. Moscow: Ogiz Molodaia gvardiia, 1932.

Mel'gunov, S. P. N. V. Chaikovskii v gody grazhdanskoi voiny: materialy dlia istorii Russkoi obshchestvennosti, 1917–1925 gg. Paris: Librairie "La Source," 1929.

Mel'kumov, A. Materialy revoliutsionnogo dvizheniia v Turkmenii. Tashkent: Ispart TsKKPT, 1924.

Michelson, A. M., Apostol, P. N., and Bernatzky, M. W. Russian Public Finance During the War. Cambridge: Yale University Press, 1928.

Migal'skii. V. Vospominaniia. Odessa: Gosizdat, 1921.

Miliukov, P. N. Beloe dvizhenie. Paris: Izdanie Respublikansko-demokraticheskogo ob'edineniia, Imprimerie d'Art Voltaire, 1929.

———. The Case for Bessarabia: A Collection of Documents on the Rumanian Occupation. London: Russian Liberation Committee Publication No. 8, 1919.

———. Istoriia vtoroi russkoi revoliutsii. 3 vols. Sofia: Rossiisko-Bolgarskoe Knigoizdatel'stvo, 1921–1924.

———. La politique exterieure des Soviets. Paris: Giard, 1934.

———. Russia and Its Critics. New York: Collier, 1962.

———. Respublika ili monarkhiia? Paris: Izdanie Respublikansko-demokraticheskogo ob'edineniia, 1929.

————. *Russia Today and Tomorrow*. New York: Macmillan Co., 1922.

————. *Russia and England*. London: Russian Liberation Committee Publication No. 13, 1920.

Miller, David Hunter. *My Diary at the Conference of Paris*. 21 vols. New York: priv. pub., 1924–1926.

Mints, I. I. (ed.). *Sovetskaia Rossiia i kapitalisticheskii mir v 1917–1923 gg*. Moscow: Akademiia nauk SSSR, Institut istorii, Gospolitizdat, 1957.

Mordacq, Jean J. H. *Le ministère Clemenceau, journal d'un témoin*. 4 vols. in two. Paris: Librairie Plon, 1931.

Nabokoff, C. *The Ordeal of a Diplomat*. London: Duckworth and Co., 1921.

Naida, S. F. et al. (eds.). *Istoriia grazhdanskoi voiny v SSSR, 1917–1922*. 3 vols. Moscow: Institut Marksizma-Leninizma pri TsK KPSS, Gospolitizdat, 1959.

————. (ed.). *Iz istorii bor'by sovetskogo naroda protiv inostrannoi voennoi interventsii i vnutrennei kontr-revoliutsii v 1918: sbornik statei*. Moscow: Gosizdat, 1956.

————., and Aleksashenko, A. N. *Kommunisticheskaia partiia v period inostrannoi voennoi interventsii i grazhdanskoi voiny*. Moscow: Gospolitizdat, 1959.

————. *O nekotorykh voprosakh istorii grazhdanskoi voiny v SSSR*. Moscow: Gospolitizdat, 1958.

————. (ed.). *Reshaiushchie pobedy sovetskogo naroda nad interventami i belogvardeitsami v 1919 g. Sbornik statei*. Moscow: Gospolitizdat, 1960.

Nansen, Fridtjof. *Russia and Peace*. London: Allen, 1923.

Naumenko, V. G. *Iz nedavniago proshlago Kubani*. Belgrade: no pub., 193?.

Nazaruk, Osyp. *Rik na Velykii Ukraini, spomyny z Ukrains'koi revoliutsii*. Vienna: Vidannia "Ukrains'koho praporu," 1920.

Nazhivin, I. F. *Zapiski o revoliutsii*. Vienna: Knigoizdatel'stvo "Rus'," 1921.

Nemirovich-Denchenko, G. *V Krymu pri Vrangele*. Berlin: Tip. P. Ol'denburg, 1922.

Nesterovich-Berg, M. A. *V bor'be s bol'shevikami: vospominaniia*. Paris: Imp. de Navarre, 1931.

Nicolson, H. *Curzon: The Last Phase, 1919–1925*. New York: Harcourt, Brace and Co., 1939.

Niessel, Henri. *Le triomphe des bolcheviks et la paix de Brest-Litovsk: souvenirs, 1917–1918*. Paris: Librairie Plon, 1940.

Nizhegorodtsev, A. *Pochemu Dobrovol'cheskaia armiia voiuets' pro-*

tiv kommunistov Lenina i Trotskago. Kharkov: no pub., 1919.
Noulens, Joseph. *Mon ambassade en Russie Sovietique, 1917–1919.*
2 vols. Paris: Librairie Plon, 1933.
Oberuchev, C. M. *Vospominaniia.* New York; no pub., 1930.
Obolenski, V. A. *Krym pri Vrangele: mamuary belogvardeitsa.* Moscow: Gosizdat, 1927. (Prague: Edition "Vataga," 1925.)
Oktiabr' na Kubani i Chernomore. Krasnodar: Istpart, Burevestnik, 1924.
Oktiabr'skaia revoliutsiia i grazhdanskaia voina v Voronezhskoi gubernii. Voronezh: Istpart, Voronezhskaia Kommuna, n.d.
Osvobozhdenie Kryma ot anglo-frantsuzskikh interventov 1918–1919. Simferopol: Krymgosizdat, 1940.
Paléologue, Maurice. *An Ambassador's Memoirs.* 3 vols. London: Hutchinson and Co., Ltd., 1923.
Park, A. G. *Bolshevism in Turkestan, 1917–1927.* New York: Columbia University Press, 1957.
Partiia Men'shevikov i Denikinshchina. Moscow: Krasnaia Nov', 1923.
Pasmanik, D. S. *Revoliutsionnye gody v Krymu.* Paris: Imp. de Navarre, 1926.
Pavlovich, M. P. *Sovetskaia Rossiia i kapitalisticheskaia Frantsiia.* 2 vols. Moscow: Gosizdat, 1922. (See also Vel'tman, M. L.)
———. (Vel'tman, M. L.). *Ukraina kak ob'ekt mezhdunarodnoi kontr-revoliutsii.* Moscow: Gosizdat, 1920.
Paz, Maurice. *Les révoltes de la mer Noire.* Paris: Librairie du Travail, 1921.
Petriv, Vsevolod. *Spomyny z Chasiv Ukrains'koi revoliutsii, 1917–1921.* 4 vols. Lvov: Nakladom vidavnichoi kooperativi "Chervona Kalina," 1927–1931.
Petrushevskii, I. P. (ed.). *Istorik i sovremennik: istoriko-literaturnyi sbornik.* Vol. II. Berlin: Olga Diakow Verlag, 1922.
Pilsudski, Jozef, *L'année 1920.* Translated by Chas. Jese and J. A. Teslar. Paris: La Renaissance du Livre, 1929.
———. *The Memoirs of a Polish Revolutionary and Soldier.* Translated and edited by D. R. Gillie. London: Faber and Faber, Ltd., 1931.
Pipes, Richard. *The Formation of the Soviet Union: Communism and Nationalism, 1917–1923.* Cambridge: Harvard University Press, 1954.
Pittard, Eugene. *La République du Caucase du Nord.* Paris: Bureau de Presse Nord-Caucasian, Fultons, 1919.
Pokrovskii, G. K. *Denikinshchina: god politiki i ekonomiki na Kubani, 1918–1919 gg.* Berlin: Izdatel'stvo Z. I. Grzhebina, 1923.

Pokrovskii, M. N. Kontr-revoliutsiia za 4 goda. Moscow: Gosizdat, 1922.

―――. Oktiabr'skaia revoliutsiia i Antanta. Moscow: Gosizdat, 1927.

―――. Vneshniaia politika Rossii v XX veke. Moscow: Gosizdat, 1926.

Polovtsov, L. V. Rytsary ternovago ventsa; vospominaniia o 1-om Kubanskom pokhode gen. M. V. Alekseeva, L. G. Kornilova i A. I. Denikina. Prague: Tip. Griunkhut, 1921.

Popov, K. S. Vospominaniia Kavkazskago grenadera, 1914–1920. Belgrade: Russkaia tipografiia, 1925.

Poslednie dni Kryma: vpechatleniia, fakty i dokumenty. Constantinople: Tip. "Pressa," 1920.

Potemkin, V. P. (ed.). Istoriia diplomatii. Vols. II-III. Moscow: Ogiz, Gospolitizdat, 1945.

Pozhidaev, V. P. Gortsy severnogo Kavkaza. Moscow: Gosizdat, 1926.

Pravosudie v voiskakh generala Vrangelia. Constantinople: no pub., 1921.

Price, M. P. My Reminiscences of the Russian Revolution. London: G. Allen and Unwin, Ltd., 1921.

―――. Russia, Red or White. London: S. Low, Marston, 1948.

―――. The Soviet, the Terror and Intervention. Brooklyn: Socialist Publication Society, 1918.

―――. The Truth About the Intervention of the Allies in Russia. Belp: Promachos Publishing House, 1918.

Pridham, Francis. Close of a Dynasty. London: Wingate, 1956.

Rabinovich, S. Istoriia grazhdanskoi voiny. Moscow: Gos. sots.-eko. izdatel'stvo, 1935.

Radek, Karl. Vneshniaia politika sovetskoi Rossii. Moscow: Gosizdat, 1923.

Radkey, Oliver H. The Election to the Russian Constituent Assembly of 1917. Cambridge: Harvard University Press, 1950.

―――. The Sickle Under the Hammer. New York: Columbia University Press, 1963.

Radziwill, S. A. Les Ukrainiens pendant la guerre. Paris: no pub., 1937.

Raevskii, A. Angliiskie 'druzia' i musavatskie 'patrioty.' Baku: Gostip. "Krasnyi Vostok," 1927.

―――. Angliiskaia interventsiia i Musavatskoe pravitel'stvo; iz istorii interventsii i kontr-revoliutsii v Zakavkaz'i. Baku: Gostip. "Krasnyi Vostok," 1927.

―――. Partiia Musavat i ee kontr-revoliutsionnaia rabota. Baku: Gostip. "Krasnyi Vostok," 1929.

Rafes, M. *Dva goda revoliutsii na Ukraine*. Moscow: Gosizdat, 1920.
Rakoviskii, C. *Bor'ba za osvobozhdenie derevni*. Kharkov: Political
Department of the Council of the Ukrainian Labor Army, 1920.
Rakovskii, G. N. *Konets belykh ot Dnepra do Bosfora*. Prague: Izd.
"Volia Rossii," 1921.
———. *V. stane belykh: grazhdanskaia voina na iuge Rossii*. Con-
stantinople: Izdat. "Pressa," 1920.
Ratgauzer, Ia. A. *Bor'ba za sovetskii Azerbaidzhan*. Baku: Tip. "3-i
Internatsional," 1928.
———. *Revoliutsiia i grazhdanskaia voina v Baku*. Vol. I. Baku:
Gostip. "Krasnyi Vostok," 1927.
Rawlinson, Sir Alfred. *Adventures in the Near East, 1918–1922*. Lon-
don: A. Melrose, 1923.
Razgrom Vrangelia, 1920: sbornik statei. Moscow: Gosvoenizdat,
1930.
Reilly, Sidney. *Britain's Master Spy*. London: Harper and Brothers,
1933.
La République Arménienne. Paris: Armenian Delegation in Paris,
Imp. "Veradzenout," 1920.
La République Arménienne et ses voisins. Paris: Armenian Delegation
in Paris, Imp. "Veradzenout," 1920.
Reshetar, John S. *The Ukrainian Revolution, 1917–1920*. Princeton:
Princeton University Press, 1952.
Revoliutsiia v Krymu. Simferopol: Istpart, Krymskoe Gosizdat, 1930.
Rosenberg, William G. *A. I. Denikin and the Anti-Bolshevik Move-
ment in South Russia*. Amherst: Amherst College Press, Amherst
College Honors Thesis No. 7, 1961.
*Rossiiskaia Sotsialisticheskaia Federativnaia Sovetskaia Respublika i
Gruzinskaia Demokraticheskaia Respublika, ikh vzaimootnoshe-
niia*. Moscow: Gosizdat, 1922.
Rostov, B. *Pochemu i kak sozdalas' Dobrovol'cheskaia armiia i za
chto ona boretsia*. Rostov-on-Don: Osvag, 1919.
Rybakov, M. V. *Protiv Denikina. Stranitsy istorii sovetskoi rodiny*.
Moscow: Gospolitizdat, 1962.
Sadoul, Jacques. *Notes sûr la révolution Bolchevique, Octobre 1917–
Janvier 1919*. Paris: Editions de la Sirène, 1919.
Samurskii (Efendiev), N. *Dagestan*. Moscow: Gosizdat, 1925.
Savchenko, E. *Les insurgés du Kouban*. Paris: Payot, 1929.
Savinkov, B. V. *Bor'ba s bol'shevikami*. Warsaw: Izdanie Russkago
Politicheskago Komiteta, 1920.
———. *Memoirs of a Terrorist*. Translated by Joseph Shaplen. New
York: Albert and Charles Boni, 1931.
———. *Za rodinu i svobodu: na puti k "tret'ei" Rossii: sbornik statei*.
Warsaw: Izdanie Russkago Politicheskago Komiteta, 1920.

Sazonov, S. D. *Fateful Years, 1909–1916*. London: J. Cape, 1928.

————. *Vospominaniia*. Paris: Knigoizdatel'stvo E. Siial'skoi, 1927.

Schuman, F. L. *American Policy Toward Russia Since 1917*. New York: International Publishers, 1928.

Sejdamet, D. *La Crimée: passé, présent*. Lausanne: G. Vaney-Burnier, 1921.

Serge, Victor. *Mémoires d'un révolutionnaire, 1901–1941*. Paris: Editions du seuil, 1951.

Sergeev, A. *Dinikinskaia armiia samo o sebe; po dokumentam sobrannym na boevykh liniiakh voennym korrespondentam "Rosta."* Moscow: Gosizdat, 1920.

Shafir, Ia. M. *Grazhdanskaia voina v Rossii i men'sheviskaia Gruziia*. Moscow: Tip. "Tsustran," 1921.

Shaumian, L. S. *Rasstrel 26 Bakinskikh komissarov angliiskimi interventami*. Moscow: "Znanie" (Vsesoiuznoe obshchestvo po rasprostraneniiu politicheskikh i nauchnykh znanii), 1949.

Shaumian. S. G. *Stat'i i rechi, 1908–1918*. Baku: Izdat. "Bakinskii Rabochii," 1924.

Shchegolev, P. E. (ed.). *Frantsuzy v Odesse; iz belykh memuarov Gen. A. I. Denikina, M. S. Margulies, M. V. Braikevicha*. Leningrad: Izdat. "Krasnaia gazeta," 1928.

Shekhtman, I. B. *Pogromy dobrovol'cheskoi armii na Ukraine, 1919–1920*. Berlin, Ostjudisches historisches archiv, 1932.

Shekun, O. (ed.). *Perekop; sbornik vospominanii*. Moscow: Gos. sotsial'no-ekonomicheskoe izdatel'stvo, 1941.

Shelukhin, Serhi. *Varshavski dohovir mizh Poliakami i S. Petliuroiu*. Prague: no pub., 1926.

Should America Accept a Mandate for Armenia? New York: Pressbureau, Armenian National Union of America, 1919.

Shteifon, B. A. *Krizis dobrovol'chestva*. Belgrade: Russkaia Tip., 1928.

Shtein, B. E. *"Russkii vopros" na Parizhskoi mirnoi konferentsii, 1919–1920 gg.* Moscow: Gospolitizdat, 1949.

————. *"Russkii vopros" v 1920–1921 gg.* Moscow: Gospolitizdat, 1958.

Shul'gin, Oleksandr (Alexander). *Bez territorii*. Paris: F. Alcan, 1934.

————. (Choulguine, A.). *L'Ukraine contre Moscow*. Paris: F. Alcan, 1935.

————. (Choulguine, A.). *L'Ukraine, la Russie et les Puissances de L'Entente*. Berne: Imp. Reunies S. A. Lausanne, 1918.

Shul'gin, V. V. *Dni*. Belgrade: Knigoizdatel'stvo M. A. Suverin i ko., "Novoe Vremia," 1925.

———. *1920 g.: ocherki*. Sofia. Rossiisko-Bolgarskoe Knigoizdatel'-stvo, 1921.

Simonov, B. *Razgrom Denikinshchini*. Moscow: Gosizdat, 1928.

Skrzynski, Count A. *Poland and Peace*. London: G. Allen and Unwin, 1923.

Slashchev, Ia. A. *Krym v 1920 g.* Moscow: Gosizdat, 1924.

———. (Slashchev-Krymskii, Ia. A.). *Trebuiu suda obshchestva i glasnosti; oborona i sdacha Kryma: memuary i dokumenty*. Constantinople: Knigoizdatel'stvo M. Shul'mana, 1921.

Sloves, C. H. *La France et l'Union sovietique*. Paris: Editions Rieder, 1935.

Smirnov, A. P. *Soldaty i matrosy Frantsii otkazalis' streliat'*. Leningrad: Ogiz, "Priboi," 1931.

Smith, C. Jay, Jr. *The Russian Struggle for Power, 1914–1917: A Study of Russian Foreign Policy During the First World War*. New York: Philosophical Library, 1956.

Smolenskii, S. *Krymskaia katastrofa*. Sofia: Rossiisko-Bolgarskoe Knigoizdatel'stvo, 1920.

Sokolov, K. N. *Pravlenie Generala Denikina*. Sofia: Rossiisko-Bolgarskoe Knigoizdatel'stvo, 1921.

Stalin, I. V. *Sochineniia*. Vol. IV. Moscow: Ogiz, Gospolitizdat, 1947.

Stefaniv, Z. *Ukrainski zbroini syly v 1917–1921 gg.* Kolomyia: Vydavnytstvo Nasha Slava, 1935.

Stewart, G. *The White Armies of Russia*. New York: Macmillan Co., 1933.

Strakhovsky, L. I. *The Origins of American Intervention in North Russia*. Princeton: Princeton University Press, 1937.

Struve, P. B. *Razmyshleniia o russkoi revoliutsii*. Sofia: Rossiisko-Bolgarskoe Knigoizdatel'stvo, 1921.

Sukhanov, N. N. *Zapiski o revoliutsii*. 7 vols. Berlin: Z. I. Grzhebin, 1922–1923.

Sukhov, A. A. *Inostrannaia interventsiia na Odeshchine v 1918–1919 gg.* Odessa: Izd. Istpart otdel Odesskogo Okrkoma KPBU, 1927.

Suliatits'kii, P. P. *Narisi z istorii revoliutsii na Kubani*. Prague: Ukrains'kii institut hromadoznavstva v Prazi, 1925.

The Supreme Ruler Admiral of the Russian Nation A. V. Kolchak. Tokyo: Russian Press Bureau magazine, No. 1, 1919.

Suvorin, A. *Pokhod Kornilova*. Rostov-on-Don: Knigoizdat. "Novyi Chelovek," 1919.

Suvorin, Boris. *Za rodinoi; geroicheskaia epokha dobrovol'cheskoi armii, 1917–1918 gg.* Paris: O. D. i ko., 1922.

Svechnikov, M. S. *Bor'ba Krasnoi armii na severnom Kavkaze, sen-*

tiabr' 1918–aprel' 1919. Moscow: Gosvoenizdat, 1926.

Sykes, Sir Percy. *A History of Persia.* 3rd edition with supplementary essays. Vol. II. London: Macmillan Co., Ltd., 1951.

Takho-Godi, A. A. *Revoliutsiia i kontr-revoliutsiia v Dagestane.* Makhach-Kala: Dagestanskii Nauch.-Issl. Institut, Dagestanskoe Gosizdat, 1927.

Temkin, Ia. G. *Bol'sheviki v bor'be za demokraticheskii mir, 1914–1918.* Moscow: Gospolitizdat, 1957.

Temperley, H. W. V. *A Brief Summary of Diplomatic Events From the German Armistice to Locarno.* London: The Historical Association, 1926.

―――. *England and the Near East.* Vol. I: *The Crimea.* London: Longmans, Green and Co., Ltd., 1936.

―――. *A History of the Peace Conference of Paris.* 6 vols. London: H. Frowde, and Hodder and Stoughton, 1920–1924.

Timoshenko, V. P. *Rélations economiques entre l'Ukraine et la France.* Paris: Bureau Ukrainien, Imp. Robinet-Houtain, 1919.

Todorskii, A. *Krasnaia armiia v gorakh.* Moscow: Voennyi Vestnik, 1924.

Toynbee, A. J. (ed.). *Survey of International Affairs, 1920–1923.* London: Oxford University Press, 1927.

Tragediia kazachestva. Prague: Biblioteka "Vol'nogo kazachestva-Vil'nogo kozatstvo," 1933.

Trotskii, L. D. (Trotsky, Leon). *Between Red and White: A Study of Some Fundamental Questions of Revolution, with Particular Reference to Georgia.* London: Communist Party of Great Britain, 1922.

―――. *The History of the Russian Revolution.* 3 vols. New York: Simon and Schuster, 1932.

―――. *Kak vooruzhalas' revoliutsiia.* 5 vols. Moscow: Vysshii voennyi redaktsionnyi sovet, 1923–1925.

―――. *My Life: An Attempt at an Autobiography.* New York: Charles Scribner's, 1930.

Trukhanovskii. V. G. *Istoriia mezhdunarodnykh otnoshenii i vneshnei politiki SSSR, 1917–1939 gg.* Vol. I. Moscow: Izdat. I.M.O., 1961.

Tseretelli, Irakly G. *Séparation de la Transcaucasie et de la Russie et l'indépendance de la Géorgie.* Paris: Imp. Chaix, 1919.

―――. *Vospominaniia o Fevral'skoi revoliutsii.* 2 vols. Paris: Mouton and Co., 1963.

Ullman, R. H. *Anglo-Soviet Relations, 1917–1921.* Vol. I: *Intervention and the War.* Princeton: Princeton University Press, 1961.

Val', E. G. (von Wahl, E. G.). *Kak Pilsudski pogubil Denikina.* Tallin: Izdanie avtora, 1938.

———. *K istorii belago dvizheniia: deiatel'nost' General-ad"iutanta Shcherbacheva*. Tallin: Izdanie avtora, 1935.

———. *Prichiny raspadeniia Rossiiskoi imperii i neudachi russkago natsional'nago dvizheniia*. 4 vols. in one. Tallin: Izdanie avtora, 1938.

———. *Rol' Ukrainy po opytu 1918–1920 gg.* Tallin: Izdanie avtora, n. d.

Valentinov, A. *87 dnei v poezde Gen. Vrangelia*. Berlin: no pub., 1922.

Varandian, M. *Le conflict armeno-géorgian et la guerre du Caucase*. Paris: Ukrainian Delegation, Imp. M. Plinikowski, 1919.

Vavrik, V. R. *Karpatorossy, v Kornilovskom pokhode i Dobrovol'cheskoi armii*. Lvov: Izd. Tip. Stavropgiiskago instituta, pod upravleniem A. I. Ias'kova, 1923.

Vel'tman, M. L. *The Foundations of Imperialist Policy*. London: Labour Publishing Co., Ltd., 1922.

———. *Frantsuzskii imperializm*. Moscow: Gosizdat, 1926.

———. *Sovetskaia Rossiia i kapitalisticheskaia Amerika*. Vol. III: *RSFSR v imperialisticheskom okruzhenii*. Moscow: Gosizdat, 1922.

———. *Sovetskaia Rossiia i kapitalisticheskaia Frantsiia*. 2 vols. Moscow: Gosizdat, 1922.

Vetlugin, A. *Tret'ia Rossiia*. Paris: Izdat. "Franko-russkaia pechat'," 1922.

Villiam, G. *Raspad "Dobrovol'tsev" ("pobezhdennye"); iz materialov belogvardeiskoi pechati*. Moscow: Gosizdat, 1923.

Vinaver, M. M. *Nashe pravitel'stvo: Krymskiia vospominaniia, 1918–1919 gg.* Paris: Izdanie posmertnoe, 1928.

Vishniak, M. V. *Chernyi god*. Paris: Izdat. "Franko-russkaia pechat'," 1922.

———. *Vserossiiskoe uchreditel'noe sobranie*. Paris: Izdat. "Sovremenniia zapiski," 1932.

Volin, V. *Don i dobrovol'cheskaia armiia*. Novocherkassk: no pub., 1919.

Volkonskii, Prince P. N. *The Volunteer Army of Alexeiev and Denikin*. London: Russian Liberation Committee Publication No. 7, The Avenue Press, 1919.

Volkov, F. D. *Krakh angliiskoi politiki interventsii i diplomaticheskoi izoliatsii Sovetskogo gosudarstva, 1917–1924*. Moscow: Gospolitizdat, 1954.

Vopicka, Charles. *Secrets of the Balkans*. New York: Rand-McNally, 1921.

Vozrozhdenie russkoi armii. Constantinople: Buro russkoi pechati, 1920.

Vratsian, Simon. *Armenia and the Armenian Question*. Boston: Hairenik Publishing Co., 1943.

Vulliamy, C. E. (ed.). *The Red Archives: Russian State Papers and Other Documents Relating to the Years 1915–1918*. Translated by A. L. Hynes. London: Godfrey Bles, 1929.

Vynnychenko, Volodymyr. *Vidrodzhennia natsii*. 3 vols. Vienna: Dzvin, 1920.

Vyshevich, K. *Ukrainski vopros, Rossiia i Antanta*. Helsinki: Central Publishing Co., 1918.

Vyslotsky, Ivan (ed.). *Hetman Skoropadsky v osvitlenni ochevydtsiv*. Toronto: Vydavnytstvo "Ukrainskoho Robitnyka," 1940.

Warth, R. D. *The Allies and the Russian Revolution, From the Fall of the Monarchy to the Peace of Brest-Litovsk*. Durham: Duke University Press, 1954.

Wandycz, Piotr S. *France and Her Eastern Allies, 1919–1925*. Minneapolis: University of Minnesota Press, 1962.

Wasilowski, Leon. *La paix avec l'Ukraine*. Geneva: no pub., 1918.

Wheeler-Bennett, J. W. *The Forgotten Peace: Brest Litovsk, March 1918*. London: Macmillan Co., 1938.

Woytinsky, W. S. *La démocratie géorgienne*. Paris: Alcan Levy, 1921.

Wrangel (Vrangel), Baron P. N. *Always with Honor*. New York: Robert Speller and Sons, 1957. (Published earlier as *The Memoirs of General Wrangel*. Translated by Sophie Goulston. New York: Duffield and Co., 1930).

———. "Zapiski." Memoirs and documents published in A. A. von Lampe, ed., *Belo delo; letopis' beloi bor'by*, Vol. V, pp. 9–306; Vol. VI, pp. 5–261 (Berlin: Russkoe natsional'noe knigoizdatel'stvo, 1926–1928).

Xydias, Jean. *L'intervention française en Russie, 1918–1919: souvenirs d'un témoin*. Paris: Editions de France, 1927.

Zaitsov, A. A. *1918 god: ocherki po istorii russkoi grazhdanskoi voiny*. Paris: no pub., 1934.

Zhukov, V. K. *Chernomorskii flot v revoliutsii 1917–1918 gg*. Moscow: Molodaia Gvardia, 1931.

Zolotarev, A. *Iz istorii tsentral'noi Ukrainskoi radi*. Kharkov: Gosizdat Ukraini, 1922.

ARTICLES:

Alekseenkov, P. "Natsional'naia politika Vremennogo Pravitel'stva v Turkestane v 1917 g.," *Proletarskaia Revoliutsiia*, No. 8 (79), (1928), pp. 104–132.

"Angliiskaia politika v Turkestane v epokhu grazhdanskoi voiny v

Rossii," *Voennaia Mysl'* (Organ revvoensoveta Turkfronta), No. 3 (1921).

Astrov, N. I. "Iasskoe soveshchanie," *Golos minuvshego na chuzhoi storone,* No. 3 (1926), pp. 41–85.

Baikov, B. "Vospominaniia o revoliutsii v Zakavkaz'i, 1917–1920 gg.," *Arkhiv Russkoi Revoliutsii,* Vol. IX (Berlin: Izdat. "Slovo," 1923), pp. 91–194.

Balkun, F. "Interventsiia v Odesse, 1918–1919 gg.," *Proletarskaia Revoliutsiia,* No. 6–7 (18–19), (1923), pp. 196–221.

Bradley, J. F. N. "The Allies and Russia in the Light of French Archives (7 November 1917–15 March 1918)," *Soviet Studies,* Vol. XVI, No. 2 (October 1964), pp. 166–185.

Cheriachukin, A. V. "Donskaia delegatsiia na Ukraine i v Berline v 1918–1919 gg.," *Donskaia Letopis',* Vol. III, pp. 163–231.

Chokaiev, M. "Turkestan and the Soviet Regime," *Journal of the Central Asian Society,* Vol. XVIII, Part 3 (1931), pp. 403–420.

Dobranitskii, M. "Zelenye partizany," *Proletarskaia Revoliutsiia,* No. 8–9 (31–32), (1924), pp. 72–98.

"Dokumenty k vospominaniiam Generala Filimonova," *Arkhiv Russkoi Revoliutsii,* Vol. V (1922), pp. 358–360.

"Dokumenty k vospominaniiam N. Voronovicha," *Arkhiv Russkoi Revoliutsii,* Vol. VII (1922), pp. 321–334.

Doroshenko, D. I. "Voina i revoliutsiia na Ukraine (iz vospominanii)," *Istorik i sovremennik: istoriko-literaturnyi sbornik.* Vols. I, II, IV, V (Berlin: Olga Diakow and Co. Verlag, 1922–1924).

Dushnyck, Walter. "The Russian Provisional Government and the Ukrainian Central Rada," *The Ukrainian Quarterly,* Autumn 1946, pp. 66-79.

Dziewanowski, M. K. "Pilsudski's Federal Policy, 1919–1920," *Journal of Central European Affairs,* Vol. X, No. 2 (July 1950), pp. 113–128; No. 3 (October 1950), pp. 271–287.

Ellis, C. H. "Operations in Transcaspia, 1918–1919, and the 26 Commissars Case," in D. Footman, ed., *Soviet Affairs,* No. 2 (St. Antony's Papers, No. 6), pp. 131–150. (New York: Praeger, 1959).

————. ("Correspondent"). "The Revolt in Transcaspia, 1918–1919," *Central Asian Review* (London), Vol. VII, No. 2 (1959), pp. 117–130.

Etherton, P. T. "Central Asia and its Rise as a Political and Economic Factor," *Journal of the Central Asian Society.* Vol. IX-X, (1922–1923).

Favitskii, V. "Zelenaia armiia i Chernomor'e," *Proletarskaia Revoliutsiia,* No. 8–9 (31–32), (1924), pp. 43–71.

Filimonov, A. P. (Ataman General). "Razgrom Kubanskoi rady," Arkhiv Russkoi Revoliutsii, Vol. V (1922), pp. 322–329.

Fournol, Etienne. "La Politique russe du gouvernement française depuis l'armistice," Revue de Geneve, Vol. I (1923), pp. 24–41.

Frants, G. "Evakuatsiia germanskimi voiskami Ukrainy," Istorik i sovremennik: istoriko-literaturnyi sbornik, Vol. II (1922), pp. 262–269.

"Germanskaia interventsiia i Donskoe pravitel'stvo v 1918 g.," Krasnyi Arkhiv, Vol. LXVII (Moscow: Gosizdat, Tsentral'nyi Arkhiv RSFSR, 1934), pp. 97–122.

Gol'denweizer, A. A. "Iz Kievskikh vospominanii," Arkhiv Russkoi Revoliutsii, Vol. VI (1922), pp. 161–303.

"Gorskaia kontr-revoliutsiia i interventy," Krasnyi Arkhiv, Vol. LXVIII (1935), pp. 125–153.

Goul, Roman. "Kievskaia epopeia," Arkhiv Russkoi Revoliutsii, Vol. II (1921), pp. 59–86.

Gukovskii, A. I. (ed.). "Krymskoe kraevoe pravitel'stvo v 1918–1919 g.," Krasnyi Arkhiv, Vol. XXII (1927), pp. 92–152.

———. "Krym v 1918–1919 gg.," Krasnyi Arkhiv, Vol. XXVIII (1928), pp. 142–181; Vol. XXIX (1928), pp. 55–85.

———. "Iz istorii frantsuzskoi interventsii v Odesse," Krasnyi Arkhiv, Vol. XLV (1931), pp. 53–80.

Gurko, V. I. "Iz Petrograda cherez Moskvu, Parizh, i London v Odessu," Arkhiv Russkoi Revoliutsii, Vol. XV (1924), pp. 5–84.

Gurko-Kriazhin, V. A. "Angliiskaia interventsiia v 1918 i 1919 gg. v Zakaspii i Zakavkaz'i," Istorik Marksist, No. 2 (1926), pp. 115–139.

Harbord, J. G. "American Military Mission to Armenia," International Conciliation, No. 151 (June 1920), pp. 275–312.

Ianov, G. P. "Don pod bol'shevikami vesnoi 1918 g. i vostanie stanits' na Donu," Donskaia Letopis', Vol. III, pp. 12–31.

———. "Osvobozhdenie Novocherkasska i 'Krug Spaseniia Dona'," Donskaia Letopis', Vol. III, pp. 32–62.

Kakliugin, K. P. "Donskoi Ataman P. N. Krasnov i ego vremia," Donskaia Letopis', Vol. III, pp. 68–162.

Kashkaev, B. O. "Bor'ba za Sovetskuiu vlast' v Dagestane, mart 1917–mart 1920," Voprosy Istorii, No. 1 (1960).

"K istorii Iasskogo soveshchaniia," Krasnyi Arkhiv, Vol. XVIII (1926), pp. 105–118.

Kin, D. (ed.). "K istorii frantsuzskoi interventsii na iuge Rossii," Krasnyi Arkhiv, Vol. XIX (1927), pp. 3–38.

Knollys, D. E. "Military Operations in Transcaspia, 1918–1919," Journal of the Central Asian Society, Vol. XIII, Part 2 (1926), pp. 89–110.

Krasnov, P. N. "Na vnutrennem fronte," Arkhiv Russkoi Revoliutsii, Vol. I (1921), pp. 97–190.

———. "Vsevelikoe voisko Donskoe," Arkhiv Russkoi Revoliutsii, Vol. V (1922), pp. 190–321.

Krasnov, V. M. "Iz vospominanii o 1917–1920 gg.," Arkhiv Russkoi Revoliutsii, Vol. VIII (1923), pp. 110–165; Vol. XI (1923), pp. 106–166.

"Kubanskaia demokratiia i Angliia: dokladnaia zapiska Kubanskikh demokratov angliiskim interventam," Proletarskaia Revoliutsiia, No. 8 (20), (1923), pp. 222–235.

Labry, R. "Notre politique en Russie, les methods, les hommes," Mercure de France, Vol. 138 (Paris, 1920), pp. 5–24.

———. "Un comité consultatif des affaires russes," Mercure de France, Vol. 139 (Paris, 1920), pp. 34–50.

Leichtenbergskii, Duke G. N. "Kak nachalas' 'Iuzhnaia Armiia'," Arkhiv Russkoi Revoliutsii, Vol. VIII (1923), pp. 166–182.

Lockhart, Sir Robert Bruce. "The Unanimous Revolution," Foreign Affairs, Vol. XXXV, No. 2 (January 1957), pp. 320–333.

Low, Alfred D. "The Soviet Hungarian Republic and the Paris Peace Conference," Transactions of the American Philosophical Society, Vol. 53, Part 10, December 1963.

Lukomskii, A. S. "Iz vospominanii," Arkhiv Russkoi Revoliutsii, Vol. II (1921), pp. 14–44; Vol. V (1922), pp. 101–189; Vol. VI (1922), pp. 81–160.

Macartney, Sir George. "Bolshevism as I Saw it at Tashkent in 1918," Journal of the Central Asian Society, Vol. VII, Parts 2–3 (1920), pp. 42–58.

Magidov, B. "Organizatsiia Donetsko-Krivorozhskoi respubliki i otstuplenie iz Khar'kova," in Piat' let (KPbU) (Khar'kov: Gosizdat, 1922), pp. 65–67.

Maiborodov, V. "S frantsuzami," Arkhiv Russkoi Revoliutsii, Vol. XVI (1925), pp. 100–161.

Maillard, M. "L'Armée Volontaire du General Denikine: notre alliée de toujours," Les archives de la grande guerre, Année I, Tome I-II, No. 4 (Paris: Editions et Librairie, 1919), pp. 545–572.

Maiskii, I. "Rossiia i Antanta," Vestnik N.K.I.D., No. 15 (November 7, 1922).

Maklakov, V. A. "Iz perepiski V. A. Maklakova s Natsional'nym tsentrom v 1919," Krasnyi Arkhiv, Vol. XXXVI (1929), pp. 3–30.

Malleson, Sir Wilfrid. "The British Military Mission to Turkestan, 1918–1920," Journal of the Central Asian Society, Vol. IX, Part 2 (1922), pp. 96–110.

————. "The Twenty Six Commissars," *Fortnightly Review,* March 1933.

Mal't, M. "Denikinshchina i krest'ianstvo," *Proletarskaia Revoliutsiia,* No. 1 (24), (1924), pp. 140–157.

McNeal, Robert H. "The Conference of Jassy: An Early Fiasco of the Anti-Bolshevik Movement," in J. S. Curtiss, ed., *Essays in Russian and Soviet History* (New York: Columbia University Press, 1963), pp. 221–236.

"Military Operations in Transcaspia, 1918–1919," *The Near East and India,* Vol. XXVIII, No. 763 (December 1925), p. 774.

Mirkin, Z. I. "Interventsiia v Zakaspii," in *K desiatiletiiu interventsii: sbornik statei* (Moscow: Gosizdat, 1929), pp. 164–200.

Mogilianskii, N. M. "Tragediia Ukraini," *Arkhiv Russkoi Revoliutsii,* Vol. XI (1923), pp. 74–105.

"Nachale Vrangelevshchiny," *Krasnyi Arkhiv,* Vol. XXI (1927), pp. 174–181.

Norris, David. "Caspian Naval Expedition, 1918–1919," *Journal of the Central Asian Society,* Vol. X, Part 3 (1923).

"Otchet o komandirovke iz Dobrovol'cheskoi armii v Sibir v 1918 godu," *Arkhiv Russkoi Revoliutsii,* Vol. IX (1923), pp. 243–304.

Padalkin, A. "Poezdka v Moskvu k Leninu s pis'mom Donskogo atamana P. N. Krasnova," *Donskaia Letopis',* Vol. III, pp. 261–267.

Pierre, Andre. "L'intervention français en Russie meridionale, 1918–1919," *Le Monde Slave,* No. 1 (Paris, January 1927), pp. 143–160.

Poliarnyi, L. "Interventy v Krymu," in *K desiatiletiiu interventsii: sbornik statei* (Moscow: Gosizdat, 1929), pp. 126–163.

Popov, A. "Iz epokhi angliiskoi interventsii v Zakavkaz'i: po materialam arkhiva b. Min. In. Del. Azerbaidzhanskoi Respubliki," *Proletarskaia Revoliutsii,* No. 6–7 (18–19), (1923), pp. 222–274; No. 8 (20), (1923), pp. 95–132; No. 9 (21), (1923), pp. 185–217.

————. "Iz istorii revoliutsii v vostochnom Zakavkaz'i, 1917–1918 gg.," *Proletarskaia Revoliutsiia,* serial in NN. 5 (28), 7 (30), 8–9 (31–32), 11 (34), (1924); especially No. 8–9 (31–32), pp. 99–116.

Rabinovich, E. "V plenu u anglichan," *Proletarskaia Revoliutsiia,* No. 11 (34), (1924).

Radek, Karl. "Soviet Russia," in J. Cambon et al., *The Foreign Policy of the Powers.* New York: Harper and Brothers for the Council on Foreign Relations, 1935.

Raskol'nikov, F. "Tragediia chernomorskogo flota, 1918 g.," *Proletarskaia Revoliutsiia,* No. 2 (37), (1925), pp. 170–185.

Samurskii, N. "Grazhdanskaia voina v Dagestane," Novyi Vostok, Vol. III (1923), pp. 230–240.

Sef, S. "Partiinye organizatsii Kryma v bor'be s Denikinym i Vrangelem," Proletarskaia Revoliutsiia, No. 10 (57), (1926), pp. 114–155.

Shul'gin, Alexander. "Ukraine and its Political Aspirations," The Slavonic Review, Vol. XIII (January 1935), pp. 350–362.

Skoropadskii, Paul. "Urivok z 'Spomyniv'," Khliborobska Ukraina, Vols. IV and V (1923–1925).

Strakhovsky, L. I. "The Franco-British Plot to Dismember Russia," Current History, Vol. XXXIII (March 1931), pp. 839–842.

Struve, P. B. "My Contacts and Conflicts with Lenin," Slavonic and East European Review, Vol. XII (April 1934), pp. 573–595; Vol. XIII (July 1934), pp. 66–84.

Thompson, John M. "Allied and American Intervention in Russia, 1918–1921," in Rewriting Russian History: Soviet Interpretations of Russia's Past. Edited by C. E. Black. (New York: F. A. Praeger for the Research Program on the USSR, 1956.)

———. "Lenin's Analysis of Intervention," American Slavic and East European Review, Vol. XVII, No. 2 (April 1958), pp. 151–160.

Tod, J. K. "The Malleson Mission to Transcaspia in 1918," Journal of the Central Asian Society, Vol. XXVII, Part I (1940), pp. 45–67.

Tonapetian, A. "Angliiskaia interventsiia v Zakavkaz'i," Istoricheskii Zhurnal, No. 2 (Moscow, 1940), pp. 47–53.

Trubetskoi, E. N. "Iz putevykh zametok bezhentsa," Arkhiv Russkoi Revoliutsii, Vol. XVIII (1926), pp. 137–207.

Voronovich, N. "Mezh dvukh ognei," Arkhiv Russkoi Revoliutsii, Vol. VII (1922), pp. 53–183.

"Vrangelevshchina (iz materialov Parizhskogo 'posol'stva' Vrem. pravitel'stva)," Krasnyi Arkhiv, Vol. XXXIX (1930), pp. 3–46; Vol. XL (1930), pp. 3–40.

Wandycz, Piotr S. "Secret Soviet-Polish Peace Talks in 1919," Slavic Review, Vol. XXIV, No. 3 (September 1965), pp. 425–449.

Zalesskii, P. "Iuzhnaia armiia," Donskaia Letopis', Vol. III, pp. 232–260.

NEWSPAPERS AND PERIODICALS:

WESTERN:

American Slavic and East European Review (New York)
Current History (New York)
The Daily Herald (London)
Journal of the Central Asian Society (London)
Le Monde Slave (Paris)
The New York Times (New York)
Le Petit Parisien (Paris)
La Revue de Geneve (Geneva)
Slavonic and East European Review (London)
The Slavonic Review (London)
Le Temps (Paris)
The Times (London)

SOVIET:

Istoricheskii Zhurnal (Moscow)
Istorik Marksist (Moscow)
Izvestiia (Petrograd and Moscow)
Krasnyi Arkhiv (Moscow)
Novyi Vostok (Moscow)
Pravda (Petrograd and Moscow)
Proletarskaia Revoliutsiia (Moscow)
Vestnik N.K.I.D. (Petrograd and Moscow)
Voennaia Mysl' (Tashkent)
Voprosy Istorii (Moscow)

ANTI-BOLSHEVIK:

Arkhiv Russkoi Revoliutsii (Berlin)
Beloe Delo (Berlin)
Bor'ba (Tiflis)
Donskaia Letopis' (Belgrade)
France et Ukraine (Paris)
Golos Minuvshego (Paris)
Istorik i Sovremennik (Berlin)
Khliborobska Ukraine (Vienna)

Krymskii Vestnik (Simferopol)
The New Russia (London)
Posledniia Novosti (Paris)
Priboi (Sevastopol)
Rossiia (Velikaia Rossiia) (Ekaterinodar, Odessa, Sevastopol)
La Russie démocratique (Paris)
Vidrodzhennia (Kiev)
Vozrozhdenie (Paris)

INDEX

A

Afghanistan, 173, 182
African troops in Russia, 132, 135, 347 (n. 88)
Ageev, P. M., 227, 298(n. 51), 375 (n. 50)
Alby (General), 112
Aleksandrovsk, 169
Alekseev, M. V. (General), 7, 8, 15–17, 22, 28, 29, 34, 43, 44, 51, 58, 59, 147, 298(n. 45)
Alexander (Prince), 212, 213
Ali Khadzhi, 174, 358(n. 73)
Allied Powers (see also France, Great Britain, Italy, Japan)
  aid, 29, 33, 75, 216–221, 302(nn. 89 and 90), 305(n. 114), 351(nn. 125 and 130), 370(n. 2), 371 (n. 3)
  Allied Councils, 53, 54, 104–112, 133, 158, 197, 206, 222, 228, 233, 255, 336(n. 125)
  Allied Council for Russian Affairs (proposed), 111
  conferences, 26, 28, 106–112, 139, 228, 229, 234, 255, 257, 259, 260
  and Czech Legion, 51–53
  differences, 103, 107–112, 142–145, 249, 254–262, 352(n. 132), 386 (n. 59), 389(n. 96)
  and Galician question, 196–198
  policies, 25–28, 34, 53–56, 73–77, 83, 139–145, 216–221, 277–279, 281–285
  relations with Bolsheviks, 30, 32–35, 228, 229, 233, 377(n. 68), 388 (n. 78)
  representatives in Russia, 7, 27, 29,

30, 32–35, 59, 66, 67, 84, 284, 291, 294(n. 14), 352(n. 132), 356 (n. 42)
  trade negotiations with Volunteers, 216–219, 248, 263–265, 270, 371 (n. 9)
  and Transcaucasia, 228–235, 377(n. 67)
  troops, 53, 55, 60, 61, 75, 77, 86, 88, 91, 132, 135, 175, 235, 317 (n. 71), 334(n. 95), 339(n. 4), 349 (n. 102), 377(n. 67)
  and Ukraine, 28, 29, 31, 78, 85–90, 113–131
  zone agreement, 28, 29, 76, 139, 142–145, 301(n. 87), 396(n. 24)
Amanullah (Emir), 173, 182
Amet (Rear Admiral), 137, 349(n. 97)
Andrievskii, Opanas, 114
Andro de Langeron, D. F., 127–129
Ardahan, 38, 179
Arkhangelsk, 53, 55, 56, 75
Armed Forces of South Russia (see Volunteer Army)
Armenia, 14, 28, 39, 153, 164–166, 178–181, 229, 235, 355(n. 29), 358(nn. 76 and 77)
Ashkhabad, 64–66, 91, 171–174, 322 (n. 114)
Astrakhan, 40, 56, 168, 186
Astrov, N. I., 59
Auritti, Giacinto, 81
Avalov (Avalishvili), Z. D., 39, 100, 229
Averescu, Alexandru (Premier), 258
Avksent'ev, N. P., 59
Azerbaidzhan, 14, 38, 39, 70, 92–98, 154, 160, 163–167, 176, 193, 228–234, 355(n. 24), 361(n. 130)

General), 88, 117, 119, 120, 124, 129, 131, 351(n. 130)
Groener, Wilhelm (General), 47
Guchkov, A. I., 128, 293(n. 7), 344(n. 61)
Gulkevich (Ambassador), 105
Gurko, V. I., 81, 328(n. 23), 329(n. 24)

H

Haase (General), 44, 45
Habibullah (Emir), 173
Hadji Murat, 323(n. 114)
Hamadan, 61
Harbord, J. G. (General), 178, 180
Haskell, W. N. (Colonel), 178, 180
Henno, Emile, 80, 83–91, 113, 126, 328(n. 20)
Herron, George D., 109
Hicks, Will L. (Captain), 56
Hintze, Paul von (Foreign Minister), 49
Holman, H. C. (Major General), 162, 238, 356(n. 42), 375(n. 46), 376(n. 59)
Hoover, Herbert C., 112, 180, 348(n. 91)
Hope, G. (Rear Admiral), 252
Hucher (Colonel), 27
Hythe conference, 259, 260

I

Indian Army, 60, 64, 171
Ioffe, A. A., 49
Italy, 177–180, 229, 230, 249, 362(n. 150)
Iudenich, N. N. (General), 191
Ivanis, V., 227
Ivanov, N. I. (General), 57
Iwanicki, 205
Izvolskii, Aleksandr P. (Foreign Minister), 105

J

Jadwin, Edgar, 200
Janin, Maurice (General), 59, 60, 192, 352(n. 132)
Japan, 36, 307(n. 127), 310(n. 17), 378(n. 72)
Jassy, 77, 78
Jassy Conference, 80–83, 86, 106, 116,

117, 328(n. 23), 329(n. 24)
Jews, 97, 342(n. 41), 396(n. 20)
Joffre, Joseph J. C. (Marshal), 258

K

Kadet (Constitutional Democratic) Party, 3, 20, 38, 41, 42, 116, 118, 130, 310(n. 20), 311(n. 30)
Kaiser (Wilhelm), 47
Kaledin, A. M. (General, Don Ataman), 12, 15, 16, 17, 20, 21, 27, 296(n. 33)
"Kalpashnikov affair," 302(n. 88)
Kamenev, Leo, 259, 262
Kaplanov, 150
Karnicki (General), 205–208
Kars, 38, 102, 165, 179
Kartsevadze, 99
Kashgar, 66, 67
Kel'chevskii (Lt. General), 246, 375(n. 50)
Kemal, Mustafa, 182, 235, 388(n. 78)
Kerch, 137
Kerenskii, Aleksandr F. (Prime Minister), 3, 5–7, 11, 12, 51, 220, 336(n. 111)
Keyes (Brig. General), 225–227, 376(n. 59)
Khalilov (General), 150, 151, 160
Khan-Khoiskii, Fathali (Prime Minister), 98, 233
Kharkov, 82, 186, 187, 190
Kharlamov, V. A., 13
Kherson, 114, 127, 133
Khomiakov, N. A., 329(n. 24)
Kiev, 42, 44, 46, 57, 80, 81, 82, 85, 87, 114, 116, 186, 196, 199, 200, 254
Kirei (General), 267
Knox, Sir Alfred W. F. (Major General), 5, 59, 192, 29(n. 14), 352(n. 132)
Kolchak, A. V. (Vice Admiral), 59, 60, 88, 105, 106, 109, 159, 172, 189–193, 198, 213, 220, 221, 224, 364(n. 14), 366(n. 42)
Kolesov, F. E., 64
Konavalov, A., 105
Koniev (General), 153, 155
Kornilov, Lavr G. (General), 3, 5, 6, 7, 16, 17, 22, 23, 27, 34, 293(n. 7), 294(n. 12), 298(n. 45)
Kotsev, Pshemakho, 148, 150
Krasin, L. B., 258, 272